Communications
in Computer and Information Science 110

João Eduardo Quintela Varajão
Maria Manuela Cruz-Cunha
Goran D. Putnik
António Trigo (Eds.)

ENTERprise Information Systems

International Conference, CENTERIS 2010
Viana do Castelo, Portugal, October 20-22, 2010
Proceedings, Part II

Springer

Volume Editors

João Eduardo Quintela Varajão
University of Trás-os-Montes e Alto Douro, Dept. de Engenharias
Quinta de Prados, Apartado 1013, 5001-801 Vila Real, Portugal
E-mail: jvarajao@utad.pt

Maria Manuela Cruz-Cunha
Polytechnic Institute of Cávado and Ave, Campus do IPCA
Lugar do Aldão, 4750-810 Vila Frescaínha - Barcelos, Portugal
E-mail: mcunha@ipca.pt

Goran D. Putnik
University of Minho
Campus de Azurém, 4800-058 Guimaraes, Portugal
E-mail: putnikgd@dps.uminho.pt

António Trigo
Polytechnic Institute of Coimbra
Quinta Agricola - Bencanta, 3040-316 Coimbra, Portugal
E-mail: aribeiro@iscac.pt

Library of Congress Control Number: 2010936186

CR Subject Classification (1998): H.3, H.4, H.2, J.1, D.2, K.4.4

ISSN	1865-0929
ISBN-10	3-642-16418-8 Springer Berlin Heidelberg New York
ISBN-13	978-3-642-16418-7 Springer Berlin Heidelberg New York

springer.com

Printed in Germany

Typesetting: Camera-ready by author, data conversion by Scientific Publishing Services, Chennai, India
Printed on acid-free paper SPIN: 06/3180 5 4 3 2 1 0

Proceedings of the CENTERIS 2010 — Conference on ENTERprise Information Systems

Preface

CENTERIS—Conference on ENTERprise Information Systems—is an international conference addressing the largely multidisciplinary field embraced by enterprise information systems (EIS) from its social, organizational and technological perspectives.

Focused on *aligning technology, organizations and people*, the CENTERIS 2010 edition, was held in Viana do Castelo, Portugal. This was the place where, from October 20 to 22, 2010, under the *leitmotiv* of Enterprise Information Systems, academics, scientists, information technologies/information systems professionals, managers and solution providers from all over the world had the opportunity to share experiences, bring new ideas, debate issues, and introduce the latest developments from the social, organizational and technological perspectives of this domain.

More than 150 manuscripts were submitted to CENTERIS 2010, coming from the five continents. There were 92 selected papers for presentation and inclusion in the conference proceedings, representing 221 authors from academia, research institutions and industry.

This book of proceedings is organized in eleven sections, distributed by two volumes. Volume I includes the following five sections: Knowledge Society; EIS Design, Implementation and Impact; EIS Adoption; EIS Applications and IT/IS Management. The second volume comprises six sections: EIS Architectures; Business Aspects; Collaboration, Networked and Virtual Organizations; Social Aspects; IS in Education and Technical Aspects and Emerging Technologies.

These proceedings are intended for use by academics and practitioners that want to be aware of what is currently in the EIS agenda, from research to everyday business practice. We believe that the high quality and interest of the contributions received in CENTERIS 2010 makes this an important publication in the EIS field.

It is expected that this conference proceedings will effectively transmit to the readers the enriching and exciting communication, exchange of views and debate promoted within this truly global group of recognized individuals, as experienced by all who attended CENTERIS 2010.

Finally, on behalf of the organization, we would like to express our gratitude to all the authors for their visions and excellent contributions to the conference, as well as to the scientific committee members, who acceded to share their insights, prompt collaboration and constructive comments in the review process. We are also grateful to all who acceded to contribute to CENTERIS, some of them with high-quality manuscripts that unfortunately, due to several constraints could not see their work accepted for presentation and publication.

Please enjoy your reading!

October 2010

João Varajão
Maria Manuela Cruz-Cunha
Goran D. Putnik
António Trigo

Organization

CENTERIS 2010 was organized by the University of Trás-os-Montes e Alto Douro and the Polytechnic Institute of Cávado and Ave, Portugal.

General Chairs

João Eduardo Quintela Varajão	University of Trás-os-Montes e Alto Douro, Portugal
Maria Manuela Cruz Cunha	Polytechnic Institute of Cávado and Ave, Portugal

Program Chair

Goran D. Putnik	University of Minho, Portugal

Organization Chair

António Trigo	Polytechnic Institute of Coimbra, Portugal

Organization Committee

António Cunha	University of Trás-os-Montes e Alto Douro, Portugal
António Tavares	Polytechnic Institute of Cavado and Ave, Portugal
António Trigo	Polytechnic Institute of Coimbra, Portugal
João Varajão	University of Trás-os-Montes e Alto Douro, Portugal
Maria Manuela Cruz-Cunha	Polytechnic Institute of Cávado and Ave, Portugal
Miguel Alves	Polytechnic Institute of Viana do Castelo, Portugal
Ricardo Colomo Palacios	University Carlos III of Madrid, Spain
Ricardo Martinho	Polytechnic Institute of Leiria, Portugal
Rui Gomes	Polytechnic Institute of Viana do Castelo, Portugal

Scientific Committee

Adamantios Koumpis	ALTEC S.A, Greece
Adrián Hernández López	Universidad Carlos III de Madrid, Spain
Ahmed Elragal	German University in Cairo, Egypt
Albert Boonstra	University of Groningen, The Netherlands
Alberto Arroyo	Orienta, Spain
Alexandra Klen	Universidade Federal de Santa Catarina, Brazil
Américo Azevedo	University of Porto, Portugal
Ana Maria Fermoso Garcia	Pontifical University of Salamanca, Spain
Anca Draghici	Polytechnic University of Timisoara, Romania
Andrew Targowski	Western Michigan University, USA
Angappa Gunasekaran	University of Massachusetts Dartmouth, USA
Arthur Tatnall	Victoria University, Australia
António Gonçalves	Polytechnic Institute of Setúbal, Portugal
Antonio José Balloni	CTI, Brazil
Bart H.M. Gerritsen	TNO, The Netherlands
Bernard Grabot	École Nationale d'Ingénieurs de Tarbes (ENIT), France
Carmen de Pablos	Rey Juan Carlos University, Spain
Carola Jones	Universidad Nacional de Córdoba, Argentina
Carrillo Verdún	Universidad Politécnica de Madrid, Spain
Diane Poulin	Université Laval, Canada
Dimitrios Koufopoulos	Brunel University, UK
Dirk Schaefer	Georgia Institute of Technology Savannah, USA
Dirk Werth	Institut für Wirtschaftsinformatik, Germany
Dulce Domingos	University of Lisbon, Portugal
Duminda Wijesekera	George Mason University, USA
Efrem Mallach	University of Massachusetts Dartmouth, USA
Emad Abu-Shanab	Yarmouk University, Jordan
Ercan Oztemel	Marmara University, Turkey
Esra Tekez	Sakarya University, Turkey
Ethel Mokotoff	Alcalá University, Spain
Fahd Alizai	Victoria University Australia, Australia
Fernando Moreira	Universidade Portucalense, Portugal
George Leal Jamil	FUMEC/BH, Brazil
George Ioannou	Athens Faculty of Economics and Business, Greece
Gerald Goh Guan Gan	Multimedia University, Malaysia
Gilliean Lee	Lander University, USA
Giorgio Bruno	Politecnico di Torino, Italy
Hans-Henrik Hvolby	Aalborg University, Denmark
Heiko Duin	BIBA Bremer Institut für Produktion und Logistik GmbH, Germany
Henrique O'Neill	ISCTE, Portugal
Hugo Paredes	University of Trás-os-Montes e Alto Douro, Portugal

Igor Perko	University of Maribor, Slovenia
Jaideep Motwani	Grand Valley State University, USA
Jens Eschenbächer	BIBA Bremer Institut für Produktion und Logistik, Germany
Jonatan Jelen	Parsons The New School for Design, USA
Jorge Marx Gómez	Oldenburg University, Germany
José L. Leiva Olivenca	University of Malaga, Spain
José Sousa	University of Porto, Portugal
Kam Hou Vat	University of Macau, Macau
Klara Antlova	Technical University of Liberec, Czech Republic
Laura Ripamonti	Universitè degli Studi di Milano, Italy
Liane Haak	Carl von Ossietzky Universität Oldenburg, Germany
Ljubo Vlacic	Griffith University, Australia
Lorna Uden	Staffordshire University, UK
Luis Amaral	University of Minho, Portugal
Mahesh S. Raisinghani	Texas Woman's University, USA
Malihe Tabatabaie	University of York, UK
Manuel Pérez Cota	Universidad de Vigo, Spain
Marco Khrmann	Brunel University, UK
Mário Caldeira	Technical University of Lisboa, Portugal
Masakazu Ohashi	Chuo University, Japan
Matjaz Mulej	University of Maribor, Slovenia
Mayumi Hori	Hakuoh University, Japan
Meira Levy	Ben-Gurion University of the Negev, Israel
Michal Žemlicka	Charles University, Czech Republic
Miguel Mira da Silva	Instituto Superior Técnico, Portugal
Narciso Cerpa	University of Talca, Chile
Nicolaos Protogeros	University of Macedonia, Greece
Nuno Rodrigues	Polytechnic Institute of Cávado and Ave, Portugal
Nuno Lopes	Polytechnic Institute of Cávado and Ave, Portugal
Özalp Vayvay	Marmara University, Turkey
Ozden Ustun	Dumlupinar University, Turkey
Paulo Garrido	University of Minho, Portugal
Patrícia Gonçalves	Polytechnic Institute of Cávado and Ave, Portugal
Paulo Tomé	Polytechnic Institute of Viseu, Portugal
Pedro Anunciação	Polytechnic Institute of Setúbal, Portugal
Pedro Castro	Instituto Politécnico de Viana do Castelo, Portugal
Philip Powell	University of Bath, UK
Pedro Campos	University of Porto, Portugal
Pedro Quelhas de Brito	University of Porto, Portugal
Pedro Soto Acosta	Universidad de Murcia, Spain
Ricardo Colomo Palacios	University Carlos III of Madrid, Spain

Ricardo Gonçalves	University Nova de Lisboa, Portugal
Ricardo Simões	Polytechnic Institute of Cávado and Ave, Portugal
Rinaldo Michelini	University of Genova, Italy
Roberto Razzoli	University of Genova, Italy
Rossi Setchi	Cardiff University, UK
Rui Gomes	Polytechnic Institute of Viana do Castelo, Portugal
Rui Rijo	Polytechnic Institute of Leiria, Portugal
Salvador Lima	Polytechnic Institute of Viana do Castelo, Portugal
Samo Bobek	University of Maribor, Slovenia
Sanja Vranes	The Mihajlo Pupin Institute, Serbia
Snezana Pantelic	The Mihajlo Pupin Institute, Serbia
Subhasish Dasgupta	George Washington University, USA
Tomasz Ochinowski	University of Warsaw, Poland
Thomas Schlegel	University of Stuttgart, Germany
Tor Guimaraes	Tennessee Tech University, USA
Valentina Janev	The Mihajlo Pupin Institute, Serbia
Vitor Basto Fernandes	Polytechnic Institute of Leiria, Portugal
Vladimír Modrák	Technical University of Kosice, Slovakia
Vojko Potocan	University of Maribor, Slovenia
Vitor Carvalho	Polytechnic Institute of Cávado and Ave, Portugal
Vitor Filipe	University of Trás-os-Montes and Alto Douro, Portugal
Wai Ming Cheung	Northumbria University, UK

Sponsoring Institutions

UTAD - University of Trás-os-Montes e Alto Douro
IPCA - Polytechnic Institute of Cávado and Ave
GESITI

Table of Contents – Part II

EIS Architectures

Business Aspects

Collaboration, Networked and Virtual Organizations

Social Aspects

IS in Education

Technical Aspects and Emerging Technologies

Table of Contents – Part I

Knowledge Society

EIS Design, Implementation and Impact

EIS Adoption

EIS Applications

IT/IS Management

Enterprise Tomography Driven Integration Lifecycle Management of Federated ERP in Green Clouds

Jan Aalmink, Jorge Marx Gómez, and André Schubert

Carl von Ossietzky Universität Oldenburg, Wirtschaftsinformatik I / VLBA,
Ammerländer Heerstr. 114-118, 26129 Oldenburg, Germany
jan.aalmink@sap.com, jorge.marx.gomez@uni-oldenburg.de,
andre.schubert@bertelsmann.de

Abstract. Cloud Computing is finding its way into the architecture of current IT landscapes. The present paper depicts the challenges of the required changes of Enterprise Data Centers from on-promise solutions towards on-demand systems. Cloud standardization in the context of the Open Cloud Manifesto is discussed as well as a reference model basing upon semantic composition and federation (Federated ERP Systems). It is described how Enterprise Tomography can support the governance process and Integration Lifecycle Management of an Enterprise Cloud by comparing different system states. Finally, an outlook on an approach involving environmental aspects (Green Clouds) is given.

Keywords: Enterprise Tomography, Cloud Computing, Federated ERP Systems, Green Clouds.

1 Introduction

Enterprise Cloud Computing becomes more and more prevalent in the IT and Business Application Industry. The quality of Integration, i.e. the extent of vertical and horizontal Business Process Integration and its efficient Management is to be seen as a key IT asset in Enterprise Data Centers. The scientific approach now is to overcome most of the disadvantages of legacy on-premise solutions. Therefore, existing different research streams, requirements and semantic perspectives need to be converted into one central ubiquitous, optimized and standardized architectural approach. The goal is to perform on-demand and cross-enterprise business processes in the context of Very Large Business Applications (VLBAs). Also in this context cloud standardization is one of the biggest challenges of the Open Cloud Manifesto. This paper discusses and outlines, how a semantic composition and federation based reference model (Federated ERP-System) can be established for Enterprise Cloud Computing and set up for business operation. Furthermore, it is debated, how enterprises can develop and maintain enterprise software solutions in the Cloud Community in an evolutionary, self-organized way complying Cloud Standards. In this context a metric driven Semantic Service Discovery and the Enterprise Tomograph can be seen as an entry-point to an organic, gradable marketplace of

J.E. Quintela Varajão et al. (Eds.): CENTERIS 2010, Part II, CCIS 110, pp. 1–9, 2010.

processes exposed by cloud based Service Grids and Data Grids in graded levels of granularity and semantic abstractions.

Regarding Enterprise Cloud Computing, conflictual requirements and design principles need to be resolved. A convergence of the polymorphic streams towards a shared, cloud-based platform can be observed. The main motivation in utilizing Enterprise Cloud Computing for a customer is the reduction of TCO in different aspects: Pooling of resources and services regarding consumption peaks or simplification of legacy infrastructure from on-premise solutions towards an on-demand solution. From the perspective of an Enterprise Cloud Provider virtualization with multi-tenancy functionality proves as suboptimal. There is a higher degree of sharing and reuse possible. This leads to federated service-based cloud software which can grow organically. The scientific challenge is to provide a controllable reference model which serves as a common standard, where standards overcome the typical vendor-lock-in phenomenon and are prerequisite for acceptance.

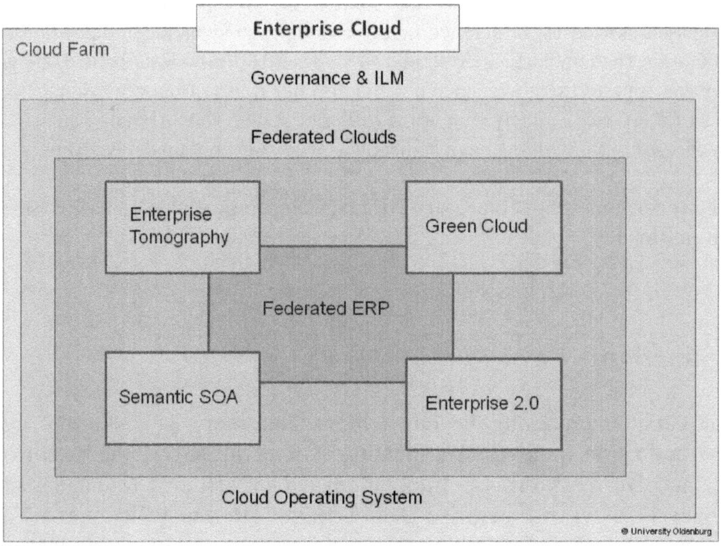

Fig. 1. Topology of an Enterprise Cloud Computing Farm based on FERP and Enterprise Tomography

In general, Federated ERP Systems (FERP Systems) based on web-services are heterogeneous software systems processing business data complying integration rules, so different customers have different views, i.e. access points to the FERP. Since the typical software ownership (provider-consumer) is transformed from 1:n to m:n ([4], [5]) and the complexity of such information eco-systems is increasing in the course of the life cycle, the superordinate target in the context of Enterprise Cloud Computing is to provide methodologies and mechanisms for streamlining and controlling the integration in federated ERP systems. The organic growth of interlinked Enterprise

Services Networks needs to follow compliance rules. Therefore semantic deviation-analysis of enterprise service consumption, Monitoring, Tracking becomes essential in distributed consumer-provider networks along the life cycle.

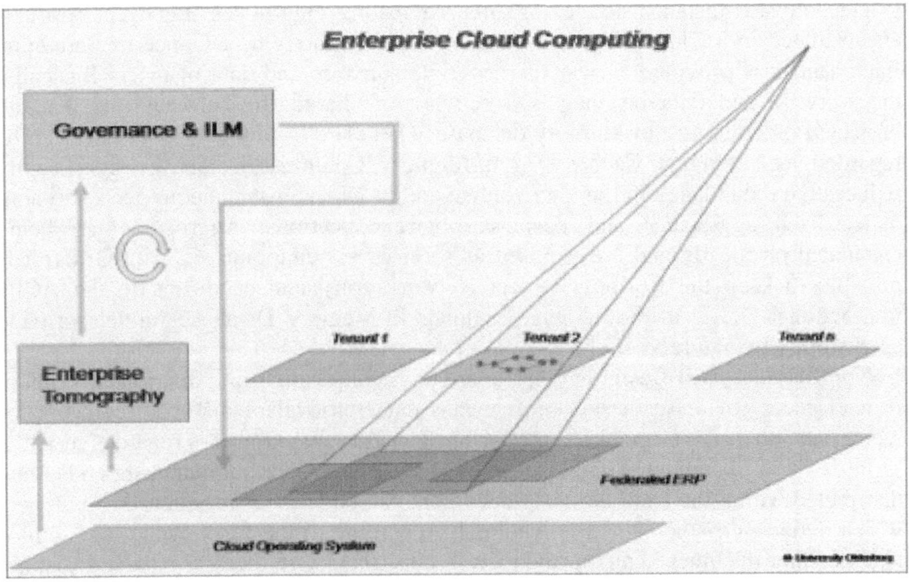

Fig. 2. Enterprise Tomography driven Governance of FERP in a Cloud Farm

The Enterprise Tomography approach enables the monitoring of the complete life cycle of a federated Enterprise Software. With Enterprise Tomography it is possible to make consumption patterns comparable. This comparison is based on a common interlingua represented as lightweight hierarchical ontologies and is achieved by applying the Delta Operator which determine the differences between system-status A and system-status B in a cloud. To be more precise, the comparison and evolution-tracking of integrated business process scenarios in a cloud represented as interlinked enterprise services ensembles is possible. The Enterprise Tomography approach provides the possibility to visualize differences with help of tomograms which aggregate indicators, metrics and serve as a decision basis in the governance process and Integration Lifecycle Management of an Enterprise Cloud [2].

Figure 1 illustrates an overview of the topology of a Cloud Farm. Different aspects and fundamental pillars of the FERP reference model are shown. The procedure, how Enterprise Cloud Evolution can be controlled is outlined in Figure 2.

2 Federated ERP in a Cloud

In reality, on-premise Standard Enterprise Software is widely used within the enterprise community. Standard means, there are common business process patterns which are highly configurable and extensible according to the business requirements.

Typically, this methodology results in similar composed, configured and enhanced Enterprise Software Systems deployed to many Enterprise Data Centers. Similarity means redundancy, which can be eliminated with the FERP approach.

According to Figure 2, in the cloud-based Federated ERP approach we have one single software instance active for all participating enterprises. Each enterprise is encapsulated in a Cloud Tenant according to the Separation of Concerns Paradigm. Each Tenant is provided a view on the single software and data instance. Basically, the software and data instance is a network of shared Business Objects that are projected on columnar In-Memory databases [12]. The In-Memory Databases can be regarded as intelligent Caches [9]. In-Memory Columnar Databases significantly reduces the redundancy in the data volume and provides instantaneous access to non-materialized aggregates and business object collections. Aggregates are being calculated on the fly and are exposed as services via endpoints of Data Grids. It is possible to keep the Business Object Network consistent according to the ACID transactional OLTP methodology. Columnar In-Memory Database Models provide extensibility by nature.

Non-frequent used Business Objects are physically stored in a distributed fashion. A read access of a Business Object means data retrieval of distinct fragments for reconstruction of the original Business Object. A Business Object is regarded as a tree serialized to a document. This document is fragmented. The fragments are coded and distributed within the Data Grids. A document can be seen as a sequence of numbers which defines a mathematical polynomial. According to the fundamental theorem of algebra, this document can be uniquely reconstructed, if there are only n distinct fragments (out of a redundant coded set) available. While retrieving, inconsistent fragments can be ignored and substituted by distinct consistent fragment retrieved from remote Data Grids [8].

In the FERP approach technical references to Business Objects are the payload of messages. E.g. if company A wants to send company B an invoice (Business Object) only the reference of the Invoice is sent as a payload. The invoice is in this case a shared and ubiquitous accessible Business Object. Company A has an individual view-based access to the Invoice via the reference only. The same applies to company B. Receiving the message, company B will change the status of the invoice to the value 'paid' as soon as the real payment is executed.

Columnar Databases are based on Inverted Indexing known in classical Information Retrieval. In (Plattner 2009) it is shown that this algorithmic approach is well-suited for parallel multi-core hardware. Systolic Arrays are in the position to accelerate string position/value matching even further with the rate of clock frequency speed [6].

View-based access via references to Business Objects has the big advantage, that no mapping and technical transformation of the Business Objects is required. Business Objects needs not to be moved within the memory. There is no need for asynchronous processing and updating anymore. This leads to tremendous scalability which is a prerequisite for cloud computing. Having instantaneous services in places, completely new quasi real-time applications will be possible in future.

In addition, the FERP reference model leads to a more data-consistent behavior. The cloud software can become much leaner in comparison to classical stacked on-premise enterprise software solutions are therefore less error-prone. A closed-loop feedback development process ensures a promptly iterative correction cycle. This leads to quality insurance.

3 Governance of Integration Lifecycle Management

The Federated ERP model can be regarded as a central shared and ubiquitous accessible network based approach. An error in the enterprise cloud software can lead to dramatic consequences and might have serious business impact.

An Enterprise client can extend its own business processes or even create and compose its individual business process schemas. The individual part of functionality can be shared with related tenants. So FERP leaves the classical Software Vendor / Software Client ownership model. In FERP approach each individual Tenant can be simultaneously in the role of a service consumer as well as a logical service provider. The services are exposed via a Semantic Service Discovery [9]. The essential point here is, that each service, composite service or business process is potentially provided with a set of alternatives distinguished by Quality of Service (QoS) and metrics.

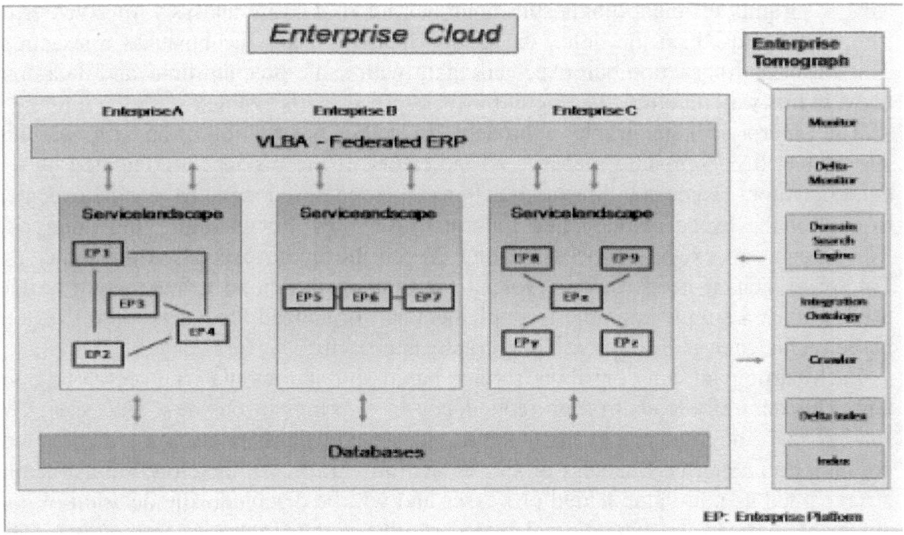

Fig. 3. Controlled Cross-Datacenter VLBA residing in an Enterprise Cloud

To be more general, the FERP approach can be seen as a definition of a governed service marketplace. Each individual participant can contribute materialized cloud content as shared services and shared (sub)-processes. Each participant can virtually compose his own ERP. In fact he gets a view on a service of an one software and data instance.

With Enterprise Tomography it is possible to make similar data contexts comparable. The comparison is based on a common Interlingua represented as lightweight ontologies. With a Delta Operator it is realizable to determine dynamically the differences between Service offering A and Service offering B. The Enterprise Tomograph provides the possibility to visualize semantic differences with help of tomograms. A comparison between two service offerings is possible as well as a comparison of a service offerings between two points in time. E.g. in a project a consulting team implements business processes and therefore changes Customizing or the alters the composition of an Enterprise Service Ensemble. This delta is of common interest, e.g. as an indicator for the quality of security evolvement in the last period of time. Another use-case is to determine the delta after a functional upgrade in the cloud. The delta is calculated between the previous reference version and the active version of Enterprise Service Ensemble. The delta in this case is the equivalent of new or changed functionality. This delta, represented as a hierarchical ontology tree, is a good basis for evaluation of new functionality. Test and training teams therefore can focus on new/changed functionality only. This results automatically in cost containment.

One more interesting use case for Enterprise Tomography is to calculate the data footprint of a selected business transaction or a business process in a cloud. Between two points in time the update on database is calculated with help of the Delta Operator. Based on the business data delta, the IT experts are in the position to assess the correctness of the behavior of the executed business transactions more efficiently. This is a highly efficient diagnostics approach for root cause analysis for given error symptoms. Based on the delta, the Undo Operator resets the business transaction. This business transaction can executed again with same preconditions and data contexts. In this way repetitive testing of business processes is enabled.

The Enterprise Tomography approach allows the construction of an early warning system based on semantic metrics and indicators. If the distance - computed by the delta operator - exceeds a threshold, actions (= cloud based services) can be executed to control the usage of dedicated Enterprise Services. For example, the Enterprise Tomograph can execute process mining. When the quota exceeds a threshold, the Enterprise Tenant needs to be invoiced for funding the cloud infrastructure he has used. This is a simple example to implement self-organized feedback control system based on the generic Enterprise Tomography approach.

Each participant can contribute service based software as materialized cloud content. This naturally leads to high redundancy in offerings of business processes. The Enterprise Tomograph can evaluate the services and business processes according real consumption patterns. Business processes with low traffic on the cloud infrastructure are regarded as non-value added processes and will be disabled. The decision of disablement is based on dynamic calculated results of the Enterprise Tomograph. The most useful services - or more general - the services with the highest Quality of Services will survive the market competition. This example illustrates how Enterprise Tomography approach can control the Integration Lifecycle Management of Enterprise Clouds and increase the overall quality in an Enterprise Cloud according to free definable metrics while fulfilling requirements in a prioritized manner.

In Figure 3 an advanced VLBA (FERP) across Data Centers of distinct owner (Enterprises) is displayed. The Enterprise Cloud encompasses federated clouds which exposes services and infrastructures. The lifecycle of the cross-federated VLBA is managed by the Enterprise Tomograph. Crawling of cloud entities, i.e. of business data, log files, data, metadata, operational data, master data, configuration data, service repositories and infrastructure content is executed on a permanent basis. Changes in ontologies can be calculated via delta determination of the Enterprise Tomograph. Deviation analysis and metric based rule infringement detection leads to immediate adaptive actions and events.

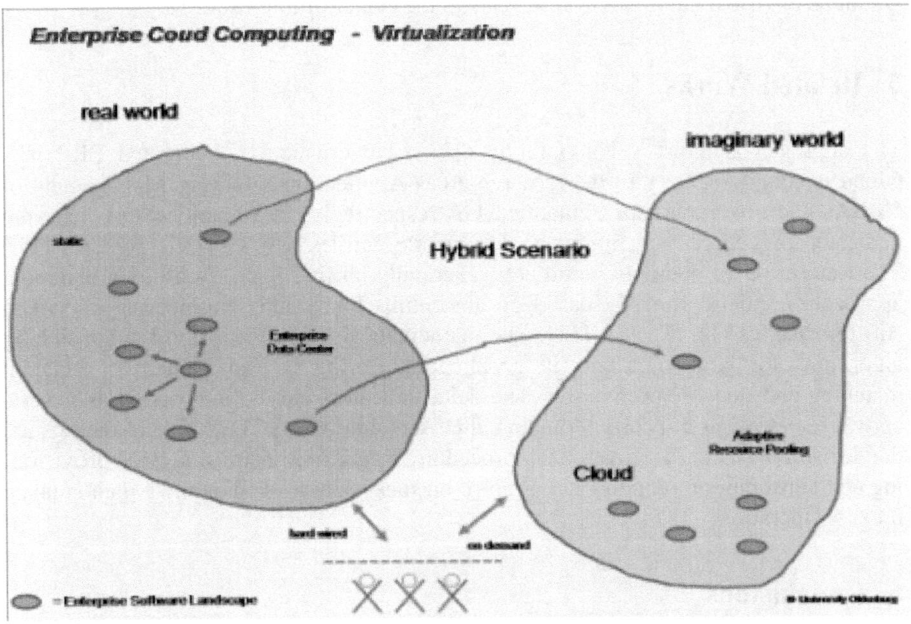

Fig. 4. Hybrid Scenarios regarding on-premise and on-demand solutions

The more business relevant partial architectural transformation from real world data centers to virtual data centers is shown in Figure 4. A subset of static infrastructures can be converted in virtual infrastructures. This allows a better sharing and assignment of resources. This enables an adaptive pooling of virtual resources. From user perspective, the transformation is non-transparent. Keeping Hybrid Scenarios in sync according to Business Process Integration requires definition of dedicated compliance rules which can be enforced with the Enterprise Tomography approach.

4 Green Clouds

Scientific purpose of the research field Green Clouds is analyzing enterprise software within cloud environments for the reduction of company-made environmental pollution. Solutions are worked out, to harmonize legal compliance, environmental compliance, cost indicators, complexity, and the degree of integrating environmental information systems. Centralized cloud solutions are used to avoid isolated views on enterprises. This can result in a federated ERP system enhanced by environmental aspects. The approach is showing similarities to an enhanced Balanced Scorecard model.

Enterprise Tomography approach can be advantageous to identify environmental indicators from ontology based network structures or reference models. A further domain of enterprise tomography is the integration management of environmental information systems (Integration Lifecycle Management). Integration of isolated solutions in virtual cloud environments is in the center of interest.

5 Related Works

The approach Enterprise Tomography driven Governance of Federated ERP in a Cloud is complementary to the research areas Application Lifecycle Management of VLBAs and governance of Semantic SOA respectively. In Semantic SOA there are dedicated procedures in alignment of semantic entities and semantic services [11]. The Enterprise Tomography approach generically unifies a set of ontology matching approaches and is primarily based on algorithms for genetic engineering known in Bio-Informatics [1], [3], [7], [13]. The mathematical model of a family of matching algorithms for large data sets in genetic engineering is transformed to semantic matching and delta determination. The delta indicators can be interpreted as generic software metrics in a specific domain called semantic view. The software metrics are the decision basis in the governance procedure. Regarding metrics, service provisioning and consumption (dependency graph), business data as well as meta-data is taken into consideration.

6 Conclusions

In previous chapters we have outlined the Federated EPR approach in the context of Enterprise Cloud Computing. It was discussed how FERP can increase scalability in a cloud. In addition we adumbrated the Integration Lifecycle Management of a Federated ERP network in a Cloud. With help of closed-loops the evolution of a shared Federated ERP system can be controlled according to cloud metrics, which are indicators calculated by the Enterprise Tomograph. The Enterprise Tomograph acts as a generic Delta-calculating search engine, which permanently crawls and observes the materialized cloud content. The search engine of the Enterprise Tomograph can be executed in delta mode as well as in full mode. With help of extractors for the Enterprise Tomograph we can have polymorphic search operator or delta operator which delivers the indicators as decision basis in the governance procedure.

References

1. Aalmink, J., Marx Gómez, J.: Enterprise Tomography - an efficient approach for semi-automatic localization of integration concepts in VLBAs. In: Cruz-Cunha, M.M. (ed.) Social, Managerial and Organizational Dimensions of Enterprise Information Systems (2009), ISBN: 978-1-60566-856-7
2. Aalmink, J., Marx Gómez, J.: Enterprise Tomography - an efficient Application Lifecycle Management approach supporting semiautomatic localization, delta-tracking and visualization of Integration Ontologies in VLBAs. In: Kumar, S., Bendoly, E., Esteves, J. (eds.) Frontiers of Research in Enterprise Systems, scheduled publication (2010)

3. Abels, S., Haak, L., Hahn, A.: Identification of common methods used for ontology integration tasks. Interoperability of Heterogeneous Information Systems. In: Proceedings of the First International Workshop on Interoperability of heterogeneous Information Systems, Bremen, Germany, pp. 75–78. ACM, New York (2005)
4. Brehm, N., Lübke, D., Marx Gómez, J.: Federated Enterprise Resource Planning (FERP) Systems. In: Saha, P. (Hrsg.) Handbook of Enterprise Systems Ar-chitecture in Practice, pp. 290–305. IGI Global, Hershey (2007)
5. Brehm, N., Marx Gómez, J., Rautenstrauch, C.: An ERP solution based on web services and peer-to-peer networks for small and medium enterprises. International Journal of Information Systems and Change Management (IJISCM) 1(1), 99–111 (2006)
6. Epstein, A.: Parallel hardware architectures for the life science. Doctoral thesis, Delft University Press (2004)
7. Haak, L., Brehm, N.: Ontologies supporting VLBAs; Semantic integration in the context of FERP. In: 3rd International Conference on Information and Communication Technologies: From Theory To Applications, ICTTA 2008, pp. 1–5 (2008)
8. Heuser, L., Alsdorf, C., Woods, D.: Enterprise 2.0 - The Service Grid – User-Driven Innovation - Business Model Transformation. In: International Research Forum 2007, Potsdam, SAP Research. Evolved Technologist Press (2007)
9. Heuser, L., Alsdorf, C., Woods, D.: The Web-Based Service Industry – Infrastructure for Enterprise SOA 2.0, Potential Killer Applications - Semantic Service Discovery. In: International Research Forum 2008, Potsdam, SAP Research. Evolved Technologist Press (2008)
10. Grünwald, C., Marx Gómez, J.: Conception of System Supported Generation of Sustainability Reports in a Large Scale Enterprise. In: Marx Gomez, J., Sonnenschein, M., Müller, M., Welsch, H., Rautenstrauch, C. (eds.) Information Technologies in Environmental Engineering. ITEE 2007 - Third International ICSC Symposium, pp. 60–68. Springer, Heidelberg (2007)
11. Panchenko, O.: Concept Location and Program Comprehension in Service-Oriented Software. In: Proceedings of the IEEE 23rd International Conference on Software Maintenance: Doctoral Symposium, ICSM, Paris, France, pp. 513–514 (2007)
12. Plattner, H.: A Common Database Approach for OLTP and OLAP using an In-Memory Column Database. International Conference on Management of Data. In: Proceedings of the 35th SIGMOD International Conference on Management of Data, Providence, Rhode Island, USA, pp. 1–2 (2009), ISBN: 978-1-60558-551-2
13. Tiun, S., Abdullah, R., Kong, T.E.: Automatic Topic Identification Using Ontology Hierarchy. In: Gelbukh, A. (ed.) CICLing 2001. LNCS, vol. 2004, pp. 444–453. Springer, Heidelberg (2001)

SOA Worlds

Jaroslav Král[1,2] and Michal Žemlička[1]

[1] Charles University, Faculty of Mathematics and Physics*
Malostranské nám. 25, 118 00 Praha 1, Czech Republic
kral@ksi.mff.cuni.cz, zemlicka@ksi.mff.cuni.cz
[2] Masaryk University, Faculty of Informatics,
Botanická 68a, 602 00 Brno, Czech Republic
kral@fi.muni.cz

Abstract. Service orientation and service-oriented architecture (SOA) are a successful philosophy, even the leading edge of current software development. Although many SOA systems have the same leading idea (they are composed as virtual peer to peer networks), practical implementations of SOA can be quite different. The implementation depends on several factors. The main factor is the logical size of the developed system measured by the number of services forming it and also by the relations between them. The technical properties of SOA and its capabilities depends substantially also on the way the SOA is designed and developed. It is whether the design and development are the top-down or the bottom-up ones. It, in turn, depends on the fact whether agility of implemented business processes and partly the agility of system development are required and how open the resulting system should be. The need for agile business processes induces the use of coarse-grained user-oriented messages and often excludes the application of OASIS SOA Reference Model. It is more or less a necessity, may be except SOA for large enterprises.

Keywords: SOA reference model, software confederations, agile processes.

1 Introduction

Service-oriented architecture (SOA) is for us any architecture constructing software systems as virtual peer-to peer systems of autonomous software components [1,2]. The components can behave like services in common sense. SOA is considered to be a mature technology, compare the hype curve published by Gartner Group in August 2009. A closer look shows, however, that the concept of SOA is still under development and that there are open questions.

For example the standard SOA Reference Model developed by OASIS group several years ago [3] is in many cases intended to be replaced by the standard

* This work has been supported by the grant of Czech Science Foundation No. 201/09/0983.

J.E. Quintela Varajão et al. (Eds.): CENTERIS 2010, Part II, CCIS 110, pp. 10–19, 2010.

Open Group Reference Architecture (OGRA, [4]). It should help in the governing of the development of SOA. OGRA supports features of the bottom-up development of SOA systems.

We can conclude that the basic ideas of SOA development are not fixed yet. It is to high degree the consequence of the fact, that the properties of SOA must the adjusted to the particular requirements on the properties of the resulting system. The requirements can imply many technical details like the granularity of the interfaces of services, user orientation of messages, integration of (batch) legacy subsystems, etc. Let us discuss the matter in details.

2 Business and Management Conditions of SOA

The properties of SOA depend heavily on the characteristics of its users and on the degree of the involvement of human beings in the processes supported by SOA.

If the users (project sponsors) have limited investments, the reuse (integration) of legacies could be a preferable, if not necessary, solution. A reason for it can be the retaining of the knowledge of employees or the simplifying of their training. It is often the case in small-to-medium enterprises (SME).

Limited investments available in SME almost exclude the expensive SOA development strategies like the ones proposed by OASIS not to speak about painful organizational changes required by them. It imposes furthermore limits on the use of the tools like ESB.

Limited resources (short terms, available people, training needs) further imply the necessity of gradual development (iterative – especially agile – development, or incremental development preferable in SOA). The big-bang development (all from scratch at once) or even the big-bang-like customization is then excluded.

If agile business processes are required or if the management of SME requires process owners to be responsible for their actions, it is highly desirable to have service interfaces coarse grained and to use message formats based on (related to) end-user knowledge domains. The bonuses are:

- Such a form of communication implies coarse-grained messages. It therefore reduces the burden of communication lines.
- It simplifies
  - the use of agile business processes,
  - outsourcing and insourcing,
  - the information hiding at a higher level that the one known from object-oriented methodologies as such an interface hides the whole internal structure of the software components implementing services[1].

[1] Coarse-grained module interfaces are also proposed by Microsoft – see Distributed System Patterns http://msdn.microsoft.com/en-us/library/ff648311.aspx. This paper, however, lists mainly the technical issues and advantages. It does not mention more sophisticated advantages discussed elsewhere in this paper. Examples are easier user involvement, flexibility, and scalability, advanced prototyping, and the integration of legacy systems.

A deeper discussion can be found in [5,6].

- log records can be easily used in
  - further testing (e.g. the generation of test cases),
  - in the analysis of business process and in the development of business intelligence (e.g. tuning of business processes,
  - effective variant of service prototyping, simulation and "hand control"; replacement of the services not existing yet, being temporarily inaccessible, or the failed ones [5],
  - as a data provider for service governance and service quality control.

Information hiding is a very important software design principle proposed by Parnas in his famous papers [7,8,9,10]. Similar idea can be found in the object-oriented world [11]. It is important that it is advantageous if the formats (syntax) and semantics of messages is similar to the syntax and semantics of user knowledge domain languages. It does not have the form of (remote) procedure call. XML can (but need not) be used here.

Note that the agility of business or development processes is especially needed if we are unable to define the process fully in advance. The agility is also necessary if the process must on-line respond to changing business conditions (failures, delays, urgent requirements, etc.).

Various SOA can be of a different size. The size (complexity) of SOA can be measured by the number of integrated services and by the number of various message formats. The SOA with many fine-grained messages and many small application services are obviously more complex than SOA with several services. It is observed that such systems are more difficult to develop and maintain.

Various variants of SOA have different impact on the interests and prospects of people. The adverse reactions of people can threaten the success of the development of SOA. In some cases the resistance of people can have even an institutional form.

3 Widely Used Variants for SOA Models and Their Implications

Let us now discuss some typical instances of SOA. There is a "continuum" of SOA variants. Let us talk about the most important or the most popular ones.

3.1 OASIS SOA Reference Model

The basic document, the standard "SOA Reference Model" [3], contains a very general and high level list of the topics that ought to be taken into account by developers. The model is very detailed. It consists of nine layers. The experience with it indicates that it is useful in the cases when the developed system is developed practically from scratch with the features of big-bang development. The resulting system consists of very many services and is quite expensive (see e.g. [12]). The model prefers rather the top-down development and it therefore does not support enough the integration of legacy and third-party systems (compare [13], where it is stated that SOA is not an integration).

The model requires skilled well-educated managers understanding user business needs as well as the technical aspects of the SOA.

The model requires many specialized experts. The development based on the model must be the task of a specialized (large) software firms (software vendors). It means that the model is not preferable for small or middle firms at user as well as at the developer side.

3.2 Open Group Reference Model (OGRM)

Open Group has introduced its SOA reference model [4] quite recently. It can be characterized as a layered model typically using Enterprise Service Bus (ESB, [14]) as communication mean between services. The architecture has nine layers like the OASIS model. The difference is that legacy and third-party systems as well as existing databases are allowed and expected to be integrated into the system. We can therefore expect that number of software artifacts necessary to build a system following the model need not be too high.

The use of ESB brings some restrictions to inter-service communication: The XML-based message formats are unified (different message formats must be converted to the canonical one). It is expected that WS-* standards (http://www.w3.org/standards/webofservices/) will be used.

It is expected that OGRM will be usable for small to medium enterprises and for multistep development process near to incremental development.

It is open whether OGRM is not too influenced by OASIS SOA Reference Model as it could be contraproductive for SME (the resulting system is too complex and implies the culture typical for large enterprises).

3.3 Software Confederations

Software Confederations [15,1,16] are inspired by soft real-time control systems and by structured design. The confederations are formed by a moderate number of large highly autonomous software services with coarse-grained interfaces. Structure of software confederation should mirror the structure of the organization or organizational unit that should be supported by the target system. It is, the organization is not forced to change its structure to be conformant with this type of SOA but SOA can be adapted to the structure. Moreover, the systems currently supporting activities of the organization (legacy systems) can be included into the new system.

Interfaces of individual services in the confederations should be inspired by the interfaces of their real-world counterparts. The reason for such inspiration is that the existing interfaces are typically used for a long time. We can expect that such interfaces fully cover the needs of users and are already optimized. If they are used for years or even decades without significant changes, then it is likely that they will not need change for further at least few years. The use of such interfaces may lead to the stable and simply maintainable resulting system.

It is moreover recommended that the language used in communication between the services is understandable to human users and it is advantageous if the syntax is simply understood by them. It is known that people concerning different problem domains use in their work different languages or language dialects. Hence it is likely to be desirable that different service interfaces use different dialects. This feature is disadvantageous for unification and standardization. This issue can be, however, well solved.

Software confederations can be formed by various number of services – it is possible to create a useful confederation having only a few services (what is good for small or medium enterprises), or can have tens or hundreds of services (it is required for large enterprises applying OASIS model. The services can, however, form hierarchical structure of unlimited depth.

The structure of the confederation can be seen as flat (each service can potentially communicate directly with any other). At the other hand the structure can be hierarchical – groups of services can use special architecture services described below to behave as composite services. The communication between services is restricted by the used message formats (only the services understanding the formats useful for given problem domain can efficiently communicate).

Other security and logical connectivity restrictions are derived from the use of other special architecture services (front-end gates) that equip other services with specialized interfaces available to dedicated groups of users. For communication within software confederations holds that the communication partners are known and they therefore can use agreed form of communication.

Another difference from the currently popular SOA types is that it is expected that the services can be provided or performed by human beings. It is the communication is asynchronous [16] to bridge different speed of individual services.

Another specific feature is the ability to combine efficiently interactive and batch services [17,16]. It simplifies development and maintenance costs as well as the chance for smooth integration of different legacy systems.

4 Simple SOA

We call the SOA consisting of not too great number (typically up to several tens) of services *simple SOA* or *lightweight SOA* for short. The criterion is that it is feasible that all the communication partners agree message formats ad hoc on everybody-with-everybody schema. The first systems using simple SOA were control (real time) systems. Real time systems are the systems fulfilling the requirement that their responses come within some time interval. There are two variants of the systems. Hard real time systems (HRT) must always respond within the given interval, soft real time system just answer in a limited mean time. The properties of HRT have typically hardware control system, e.g. machine tool control systems or avionics. Soft real-time systems are typical for the systems having the features of mass services, e.g. manufacturing control systems.

4.1 SOA in Hard Real-Time Systems

Complex technology control systems often have service-oriented architecture. The involvement of people in such control processes is very limited. The number of services is often not too high. The system need not (cannot) be changed substantially during system maintenance. Agility of processes is usually not needed. The inner message formats need not be legible for public (not experts). Fine-grained interfaces based on remote procedure call (RPC) can, and often should, be used. The message formats can be agreed ad hoc. Middleware can be specific for given system. The development has often the big-bang form. The most important is the fact that human involvement into processes is almost missing. It is clear that such SOA are simple in the above sense. It need not be the case of soft real time.

4.2 SOA in Soft Real-Time System and in Small-to-Medium Enterprises

First SOA in current common sense were used in soft real-time systems, for example in manufacturing systems like Flexible Manufacturing System [15] or some parts of computer integrated manufacturing (CIM [18,19]). It appeared, that such SOA is also used in ERP of small-to-medium enterprises (SME). They have the properties of soft real-time systems.

The business processes in such simple SOA cannot be as a rule completely defined in advance as there are not enough data and the complete process definition would be too expensive. The main snag, however, is that important business data are in principle missing as they, e.g., depend on actual market conditions. The conditions are changing and they cannot be fully predicted. As stated above, the user-oriented coarse-grained messages are under such conditions necessary and the agility of (business or manufacturing) processes is highly desirable. The messages used in SOA should be user oriented.

Some manufacturing systems are quite separated from the management of business processes. This can be also true for some parts of ERP of small enterprises as well.

There is a strong need of SME to reuse/integrate legacy systems and to enable outsourcing. The reorganizations of SME need not be desirable. The big-bang attitude is therefore rarely possible. OASIS model can hardly be used as it is too expensive, disables the use of legacy systems, and strongly prefers the top-down development in big-bang setting. There are technical solutions using organizational services acting as architecture building tools enabling an agile variant of integration process [20,6].

The simple SOA can, if developed carefully, provide systems that do not threaten the positions of employees, whose involvement is important for the process of developed system, and retains their experience. It may seem to be a simple task, it is, however, not. If the developers are not careful enough, they can push back people without whom the implementation of the system (definition of requirements inclusive) and loss important knowledge of leading employees (M. Chytil, private communication).

4.3 SOA in Large Enterprises

Large enterprises usually have enough resources to apply OASIS reference model. We can assume that the enterprise has resources to form necessary committees (centre of competence, service governance committee, etc.) to cover all the nine layers of the OASIS model.

The following challenges must be properly solved for OASIS model [13]:

- The complexity of the system.
- Big expenditures.
- Necessity of organizational changes.
- Changes of business processes.
- Application of SOA-related tools like ESB.
- Big-Bang top-down development.

The advantage is that the development process is well-tuned and that the OASIS standard [3] assumes the existence of a strong central authority able to effectively control the development process.

It is also important to apply some features proposed by the standards of the Open Group [21,4] especially the user-oriented coarse-grained interfaces of services and integration of legacy systems.

There are challenges specific for large enterprises. People can easily form informal groups to pursue their interests that need not be the optimal for the entire enterprise. Some barriers can be formed by internal regulations or can be related to enterprise culture. Note that the regulations can be pursued by the informal groups in order to enforce their "local" interests.

There are cases of the "application" of the antipattern "Standardization Paralysis" [22], i.e. improper application of (immature) standards. It is, many software standards are used without proper analysis whether the standards are adequate for intended purpose and mature enough.

4.4 SOA in e-Government, e-Health, and in Similar Systems

There are different variants of e-government-like systems: municipal systems, health-care systems (e-health), and so on. The common features of the systems are:

- From the outer look the systems integrate a moderate number of (complex) services being often information systems of individual offices/majorities. Such SOA systems are therefore almost simple SOA systems in the above sense.
- The services forming the systems tend to encapsulate (wrap) rather large and complex subsystems.
- Many aspects of the construction of the systems are regulated (hindered) by legislative or cultural barriers and prejudices. It is for example the case of strict bans on the use or even on the keeping sensitive data. It may be the consequence of particular interests of some groups in society, for example of some educational institutions [23] and medicament producers.

- The government and society in general are unaware of substantial losses and threats caused by the data use bans.
- The systems are used by citizens and organizations (by public) having occasionally contradictory interests.
- There is in fact almost no strong central authority with respect to the system design and development. It is due the political pressure and group interests excluding any unique will. It is one of the main reasons why the use of some tools like ESB is in this case difficult if not impossible.
- Benefits or losses related to the use of the systems are not clear.
- The processes in the systems should be controllable by citizens and supervised by trusted bodies but the access to some data and processes must be regulated. The rules of regulation are changing, often unclear and complex.

The requirement that the systems and their processes must be accessible by the public implies that the messages inside such systems should coarse-grained and user-oriented – in some sense similar to the messages in Simple SOA. It is important that the current practice forbidding the use of personal or sensitive data for the production of insensitive information [23] is very expensive as it bans the access to information necessary for the desirable social processes, epidemy prevention, and to information needed for governance and research.

Actual regulation leads to (virtual) shredding of large collections of important data. It is the reason why many people in good will want to evade the ban.

One can suspect that the missing forecast of current economical crisis is, at least partly, a consequence of this practice. This practice has some grotesque consequences. In Czech Republic a system hopefully making the production of narcotic at least harder was forbidden. The reason was that the system used but not disclosed sensitive data (release of medicaments).

Yet more pity is that the system could substantially reduce errors in medications having quite often fatal consequences. In Czech Republic it can reduce unnecessary health care expenses with savings equivalent to half billion USD a year. The return of investments would be less than 6 months.

5 Conclusions

We believe that there is too much tendency to consider all SOA to be almost equal. Another tendency is to assume that a system has SOA only if it complies with a very specific variant of SOA. It was probably the case of "SOA is death". In our treatment all virtual peer-to peer systems with asynchronous communication have SOA. But such systems can be very different. They have various structures, different capabilities, and different utilizations.

Some systems must integrate legacy systems and they must be therefore built in the bottom up manner. The bottom up development can be modified so that it admits agile integration of large services during the development of SOA [20].

The need for user involvement, outsourcing, and governance implies that the user-oriented coarse-grained messages must be almost always used. It follows that the top-down SOA development can be a good solution for SOA of large enterprises only. To be more specific, it can be a good solution for large organizations with strong central authority and somehow homogenous structure. Even in this case the elements of bottom-up development can be useful. It is typically the case of global decentralized enterprises. All these questions will be topic of a future study.

References

1. Král, J., Žemlička, M.: Software confederations – an architecture for global systems and global management. In: Kamel, S. (ed.) Managing Globally with Information Technology, pp. 57–81. Idea Group Publishing, Hershey (2003)
2. Erl, T.: Service-Oriented Architecture: Concepts, Technology, and Design. Prentice Hall PTR, Englewood Cliffs (2005)
3. MacKenzie, C.M., Laskey, K., McCabe, F., Brown, P.F., Metz, R.: Reference model for service-oriented architecture 1.0, commitee specification 1 (July 19, 2006), `http://www.oasis-open.org/committees/download.php/19361/soa-rm-cs.pdf`
4. Open Group: Draft technical standard SOA reference architecture (2009), `http://www.openinnovations.us/projects/soa-ref-arch/uploads/40/19713/soa-ra-public-050609.pdf`
5. Král, J., Žemlička, M.: Implementation of business processes in service-oriented systems. In: IEEE SCC, pp. 115–122. IEEE Computer Society, Los Alamitos (2005)
6. Král, J., Žemlička, M.: Implementation of business processes in service-oriented systems. International Journal of Business Process Integration and Management 3(3), 208–219 (2008)
7. Parnas, D.L.: Information distribution aspects of design methodology. Technical report, Department of Computer Science, Carnegie-Mellon University (1971)
8. Parnas, D.L.: A technique for software module specification with examples. Communications of the ACM 15(5), 330–336 (1972)
9. Parnas, D.L.: On the criteria to be used in decomposing systems into modules. Communications of the ACM 15(12), 1053–1058 (1972)
10. Parnas, D.L.: Designing software for ease of extension and contraction. IEEE Transactions on Software Engineering 5(2), 128–138 (1979)
11. Gamma, E., Helm, R., Johnson, R., Vlissides, J.: Design Patterns. In: Elements of Reusable Object-Orieneted Software. Addison-Wesley, Boston (1993)
12. Štumpf, J.: SOA a její implementace v Centrálním úložišti receptů (in Czech: SOA and its implementation in Central Repository of Recipes). In: Chlapek, D. (ed.) DATAKON 2009, Prague, Czech Republic, Vysoká škola ekonomická v Praze, Nakladatelství Oeconomica, pp. 83–93 (2009)
13. Kavis, M.: Top 10 reasons why people are making SOA fail (2008), `http://www.cio.com/article/438413/`
14. Chappell, D.A.: Enterprise Service Bus. O'Reilly, Sebastopol (2004)
15. Král, J., Demner, J.: Towards reliable real time software. In: Proceedings of IFIP Conference Construction of Quality Software, pp. 1–12. North Holland, Amsterdam (1979)
16. Král, J., Žemlička, M.: Software architecture for evolving environment. In: Kontogiannis, K., Zou, Y., Penta, M.D. (eds.) Software Technology and Engineering Practice, pp. 49–58. IEEE Computer Society, Los Alamitos (2006)

17. Král, J., Žemlička, M.: Architecture and modeling of service-oriented systems. In: Vojtáš, P., Bieliková, M., Charon-Bost, B., Sýkora, O. (eds.) SOFSEM 2005 Communications, Bratislava, Slovakia, Slovak Society for Computer Science, pp. 71–80 (2005)
18. Waldner, J.B.: Principles of Computer-Integrated Manufacturing. John Wiley & Sons, Chichester (1992)
19. Groover, M.P.: Automation, Production Systems and Computer-Integrated Manufacturing, 3rd edn. Prentice Hall, Englewood Cliffs (2007)
20. Král, J., Žemlička, M.: Agilní vývoj SOA zdola (in Czech: Agile bottom-up SOA development). In: Voříšek, J. (ed.) Systems Integration 2010, Vysoká škola ekonomická v Praze, Nakladatelství Oeconomica, pp. 206–213 (2010)
21. The Open Group: The Open Group service integration maturity model (OSIMM) (2009), Technical standard, `http://www.opengroup.org/pubs/catalog/c092.htm`
22. Brown, W.J., Malveau, R.C., McCormick III, H.W., Mowbray, T.J.: AntiPatterns: Refactoring Software, Architectures and Projects in Crisis. John Wiley & Sons, New York (1998)
23. Král, J., Žemlička, M.: Bottleneck of knowledge society. In: Lytras, M.D., Carroll, J.M., Damiani, E., Tennyson, R.D., Avison, D., Vossen, G., Pablos, P.O.D. (eds.) The Open Knowlege Society: A Computer Science and Information Systems Manifesto. Communications in Computer and Information Science, vol. 19, pp. 83–91. Springer, Heidelberg (2008)

An Architecture for a Web Service Based Product Configuration Information System

António Arrais de Castro*, Leonilde Varela, and S. Carmo-Silva

Dept. of Production and Systems, University of Minho, Campus de Gualtar, 4710- Braga, Portugal
arraiscastro@gmail.com, {leonilde,scarmo}@dps.uminho.pt

Abstract. Competition in the today's global economy is intensifying the use of the new paradigm of mass customization. Such a paradigm is characterized by the need to deal with a very large variety of products determined by a substantial increase in customer specific product requirements. Implementing this paradigm requires agility and effectiveness in the customer-producer interaction and also in the order-production-delivery cycle. Web-based product configurators can provide an opportunity for improved interaction between producer and customer, and for a more formal, agile and effective process of both product and customer orders specification. In this paper, we propose architecture and describe the functionalities of a web based system for interactive product and customer order configuration. The proposed system can be also of value for supporting product data management and the production and delivery functions.

Keywords: XML, Web Service, Mass Customization, Product Order Configurator.

1 Introduction

Industrial companies are nowadays faced with a continuous challenge for keeping up with growing competition and new requirements from customers. Globalization means a large number of business competitors and requires company's ability for maintaining customer satisfaction and competitiveness through wider product variety and good customer service market response which naturally requires production agility. Therefore, there is a need for improved processes in several dimensions. Production costs minimization is a requirement but is not enough in competition. Minimizing waste and increasing product variety and operations efficiency and agility is critical. Aiming at this, several methodologies and techniques focused on production processes and associated back-office systems have been adopted. These include Six Sigma [1], cellular and product oriented organization [2] and JIT techniques [3]. However the success achieved at the front-office side is much lower, particularly at the customer and partner interaction processes. Front-office activities, like sales and customer support, have not received the required attention by a vast

* Corresponding author.

J.E. Quintela Varajão et al. (Eds.): CENTERIS 2010, Part II, CCIS 110, pp. 20–31, 2010.

amount of companies. By improving front-office activities, these companies can achieve financial and operational benefits by providing information reliability and readiness, and reducing specification mistakes, waste and unnecessary manual activities, due to, for example:

- Incorrect or error-prone information
- Duplicated efforts
- Manual process handling
- Bureaucracy, paper based communication and
- Rigid processes

The transformation of prospect quotations into customer orders and these into work or production orders and production schedules are frequently associated with manual processes. Additionally, publishing information about company products and associated configurations is often outsourced to external companies responsible for the creation of catalogues and online publishing.

The challenges for process optimization are even higher for large companies. Multinational holdings integrating several small business units, as a result of merging operations, frequently have difficulties integrating front-office processes.

Besides optimizing the integration of front-office and back-office processes, the companies need to adopt a strategy of differentiation. The competitive market dictates that having the lowest prices is no longer enough. The companies have to adapt their products to the specific need of customers. Modern consumers are particularly exigent, demanding higher levels of quality, functionality and correspondence to their specific needs. Traditionally, the inclusion of product options and variants had more to do with charging "extras" and gaining financial profits than with offering the customer a richer buying experience.

Nowadays there is a growing demand for individualization, a tendency frequently called the "experience economy" [4]. The need to fulfil individual needs of customers while maintaining prices as low as possible is a permanent challenge for modern enterprises. Companies are forced to create product families with a growing number of variants, adopting a strategy of differentiation based on variety [5].

The concept of Mass Customization was defined as "producing goods and services to meet individual customers' needs with near mass production efficiency" [6]. Besides offering differentiation opportunities and cost optimization, mass customization allows for a richer interaction with customers, maximizing customer retention.

An effective and efficient mass customization strategy is based on the use of product modules, variants and options. Modular products are built from different combinations of the same component modules. This is a sound, economic and effective strategy for generating a large variety of products towards mass customization. This strategy can be combined with the product variant concept for increasing product variety. In this concept different products are generated using variants of product features, such as different engines or seats in the same basic car model. Additionally the adoption of product options can further enhance product variety and customized production response agility with minor production efforts and complexity. All these alternatives to product customization, together with others based on parameter specification, such as dimension, colour and materials, can easily be specified by customers through product configuration tools. These tools must provide agility in product specification and information processing and a high level of integration with existing information systems, particularly at product design, order engineering and production management levels. These requirements imply efficient management of information flows, from customer interaction to production.

Industrial companies can efficiently focus on customers only if they use information intensively [7]. As referred by Piller [5], in mass customization, the individual wishes and needs of each customer have to be transformed into the specification of unique products. The author considers that costs associated with product customization can be determined by quantifying the efforts associated with specifying customers' needs, individual product configuration, transfer of user preferences to the production stages, additional complexity at production management and interactions with suppliers and product distribution.

Companies adopting classical approaches, where products are mass-produced or manufactured to order, need to optimize their information processing strategies in order to evolve to a mass customization model.

Internet technologies offer privileged means for the implementation of interaction channels between client and producers on the mass customization scenario. The advantages can be summarized in two main categories:

a) Improved communication: the client interacts with the producer using a simple and efficient communication channel.
b) Expanded business models.

Using web-based interactive product configurators the customer is able to specify the product that closely matches his or her individual needs, thus enriching the producers' knowledge about market trends.

Outsourcing the time-consuming product configuration process to the customer enables the producer to sell products with reduced financial margins in a way that would be impossible using traditional channels with face-to-face interaction.

In this paper, we propose an architecture and describe the functionalities of a web service based system for interactive product and customer order configuration. The proposed system can be also of value for supporting product data management and the production and delivery functions.

After this introduction, in section 2 a brief literature review on product configuration techniques, strategies tools is presented. In section 3 the web based configurator features and manufacturing process environment are discussed. The system architecture is discussed and presented in section 4. In section 5 we present a conclusion and put forward further work intention.

2 Literature Review

Several product configuration techniques and methodologies have been proposed during recent years. Some of the techniques have been effectively implemented in information systems operating in industrial sectors.

One of the earliest product configuration systems proposed was XCON [8]. This system uses a rule-based engine that supports product configuration. The system was used by Digital Company to validate and guide the assembly of customer orders. XCON was responsible for the configuration of hardware components (processors, memory, cabinets, power supplies, hard disks, printers, etc.) and software, simultaneously checking marketing restrictions, prerequisites and technical validity.

XCON was fed with a vast set of rules that define how products were structured, their associated restrictions and assembly policies. With this knowledge XCON was able to support interactive selection of generic components, check their completeness, add required parts, if necessary, check software compatibility and prerequisites, check standard compliance, marketing or engineering restrictions and connect to a automate quotation system. It was considered a critical business tool for helping the company to face the continuous challenges imposed by the technological developments and growing technical product complexity.

The main problem with rule based configuration engines is the high cost associated with maintaining their knowledge base [9] and the inclusion of product structure, constraints and policies in a interweaved manner [10].

A natural evolution from rule-base systems are logic-based configurators. These systems use logical models to represent the knowledge needed to solve configuration problems. The PROSE system proposed by McGuinness [11] uses logical operations and semantic rules to represent and manage configuration information. It is based on the CLASSIC language.

An alternative system was proposed by Heinrich and Jungst [12], adopting a resource based paradigm. Components are represented as abstract modules. Starting from the desired functionality, components that partially fulfil its requirements are aggregated. The complete set of components will fulfil the required functionality completely.

Researchers Mittal and Falkenhainer [13] proposed representing a configuration problem using a constraint-based approach. Configurations are obtained from a set of variables, a domain of possible values for each variable and an associated constraint set. This model is known as a CSP – constraint satisfaction problem. Mailharro [14] proposes a CSP approach using an integrated object model, supporting classification methods, inheritance and algorithms to maintain configuration consistency.

Other authors propose alternative approaches. Mittal and Frayman [15] classify the configuration problem as a case based reasoning (CBR) problem. Basically, the technique consists on using the knowledge associated with previous cases, based on similarity criteria [16-18]. A "case" is just a set of existing configurations. When trying to solve a configuration problem, the system tries to find an identical case among the configurations that have been stored, adapting it to the new requirements. CBR configuration is mostly useful when the knowledge is incomplete [19]. Reusing product configuration knowledge and constraints is not supported. This can be a limiting factor when working with a vast and complex product catalog.

The OOKP - "one of a kind" is proposed by other authors as an interesting alternative to the previous methods [20]. Product variations and configuration parameters are modelled using AND-OR trees. Tree nodes contain the parameters associated with the rules. The configuration is built and optimized using a genetic algorithm that considered customer preferences and efficiency parameters. Zhou [21] performed identical work, incorporating configuration restrictions in the genetic algorithm (for example, inclusion and exclusion relations) trying to achieve a higher level of optimization. An identical strategy has been adopted by other researchers [22, 23].

Solving the configuration problem is one part of product configurator's requirements. Another important part is interacting with the customer, particularly when the customer has a reduced knowledge about the configuration details.

Luo [9] proposed the implementation of a matrix mapping technical customer requirements with technical product attributes, thus allowing for automatic selection of the most adequate configurations. Using this matrix the customer can delegate on the system the product selection and configuration process.

To help the customer choose the most adequate product configuration, recommendation systems are frequently used. There are several studies describing theses systems [24-26]. A vast number of internet portals available today help their customers while choosing or configuring their products using other customers' recommendations. These recommendations are frequently used for cross-selling (namely through Amazon.com and Pixmania.com sites).

A good recommendation system will help hiding technical details from the most inexperienced users, helping them configure their selections. The recommendation process can be implemented with an intelligent software agent that learns from customer product configuration processes and helps them choose the best options.

The majority of recommendation systems are hybrid and combine recommendations based on content (product parameters and customer relationship history) and collaborative methods (analyzing customer and product relations). Collaborative methods are popular since they allow using the knowledge captured during the interaction with other customers in distinct business contexts.

There are several recommendation techniques based on collaborative methods: graph theory [27], linear regression [28], semantic analysis [29] and case-based reasoning [30].

Although being very useful, recommendation techniques have several limitations, namely:

- Lack of knowledge about new products.
- Influenced by incorrect or manipulated recommendations published by other customers.

These problems suggest not using the collaboration techniques exclusively. Therefore, a better approach consists on complementing them with content-based recommendation methods.

3 Features of the Web Service Based System for Product Configuration

The implementation of a Web service based system for product configuration will allow creation of a central channel for the distribution of information about complex and simple products, supporting customers and business partners. This communication channel can be used to automatically feed distinct point of sale (POS) systems, including websites, interactive product configurators for physical points of sale, and promotional interactive media (DVDs, CDs, etc.).

Additionally, the system will connect these POS systems with management backends, including CRM and production management systems.

Several benefits can be realized in from customer to production, in several dimensions. In the customer dimension we identify the following ones: 1) interactive product selection and configuration; 2) better fulfilment of individual needs; 3) better product information, continuously updated and 4) better order support. At the reseller's side they are: 1) configuration opportunities for tailored products; 2) permanent access to updated product and pricing information; 3) no need to import product configuration information as it can be dynamically obtained from web services; 4) better support for electronic interaction, minimizing paper-based processes and 5) better B2B integration with producer. At the producer´s sales dimension the benefits are: 1) a wider range of products offered; 2) better understanding of customers' needs and preferences and 3) increased business opportunities, including support for niche markets. At order processing it is likely to be obtained: 1) a reduction in order specification mistakes and 2) delegation of the order configuration process to the system and customer. On product design and order engineering there are greater opportunities for design, based on modules, variants and options offered, as well as on the parameters specification based on controlled diversity of materials, product features and manufacturing agility.

The system will also help the implementation of agile production methods and approaches, like lean manufacturing. This approach is derived from TPS – Toyota production system, developed by Toyota after World War II. It aims to eliminate waste, targeting for eliminating any activities that do not create value for the end customer. The method has two pillar concepts: automation and JIT – just in time. JIT was introduced by Taiichi Ohno, chief engineer at Toyota in the 1950s, as a method for the fulfilment of customers' needs with a minimum of delays, while reducing in-process inventory. With JIT, inventory is seen as incurring cost and waste, instead of stored value. Nothing should be produced, transported or bought before the exact time. It all comes to having "the right material, at the right time, at the right place, and in the exact amount".

The make-to-order philosophy that JIT implies minimizes risks of having unsold products. Web based product configurators improve agility while capturing sales orders and converting them into production orders, thus helping to implement JIT.

Agile manufacturing was designed to make businesses more flexible, requiring a more dynamic process for production operations, setup and lead-time reduction and a greater efficiency while managing product information. An agile company needs to determine customer needs quickly and continuously repositioning itself against its competitors. This means that it also needs to design products quickly based on customers' individual needs.

The main component of the product configuration system is a web service layer that connects with the company's information systems (data import) and feeds external systems (data export). This layer will expose configuration engine functionality, facilitating the order capture process and its conversion to production orders. It will be a valuable tool to support the implementation of methodologies that require agile product and order information processing.

The web service based product configuration system will help capture customers' needs and preferences continuously, thus contributing to the agile processes.

4 System Architecture

The product configuration system (WBPC - Web Based Product Configurator) includes two main components:

- Integration module (responsible for integration with existing information systems), and.
- Service module (web service layer that interacts with external systems, client and server applications).

Integration will be built using connection modules called connectors. Several connectors will be available for reading and writing information from/ into external systems. Each read connector is responsible for reading the information available in a backend system and transform this information into XML. The write connectors receive XML data and convert it to a format that is adequate for the associated system. XML Schemas (XSD) will be used to help validate the information and check its completeness and integrity, as illustrated in Figure 1.

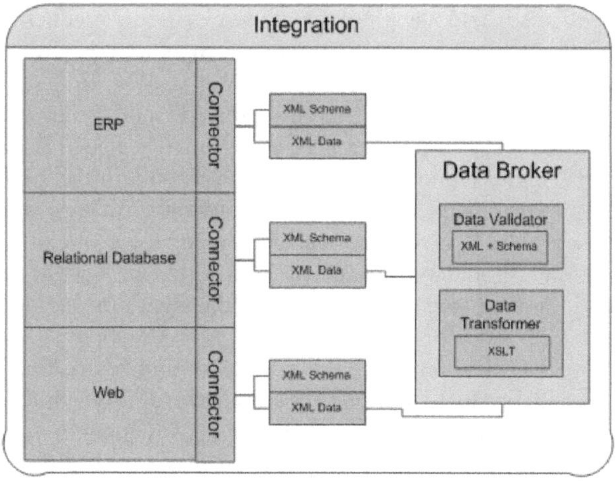

Fig. 1. Integration process

The data broker component is the central data processing module and controls how data import and export is managed. It includes two sub-components: data validator and data transformer. The data broker is isolated from the details of each external system, accepting only XML information. Data validator maps the information received by the broker to the corresponding XML Schema. Any validation errors cause the rejection of the underlying data.

The data transformer module is responsible for making the imported information compatible with the structure the service broker expects to receive. It uses XSLT Style Sheets (XSL Transformation), applying them to the previously validated XML data, and forwarding the transformation results to the web service layer.

The data broker component can be replaced by a third party middleware solution, like TIBCO (www.tibco.com) or BizTalk Server (www.microsoft.com/biztalk). These solutions will help modelling business rules at the integration level.

The web services layer is responsible for the implementation of functionalities that support product configuration and information publishing, including four main components, as shown in Figure 2.

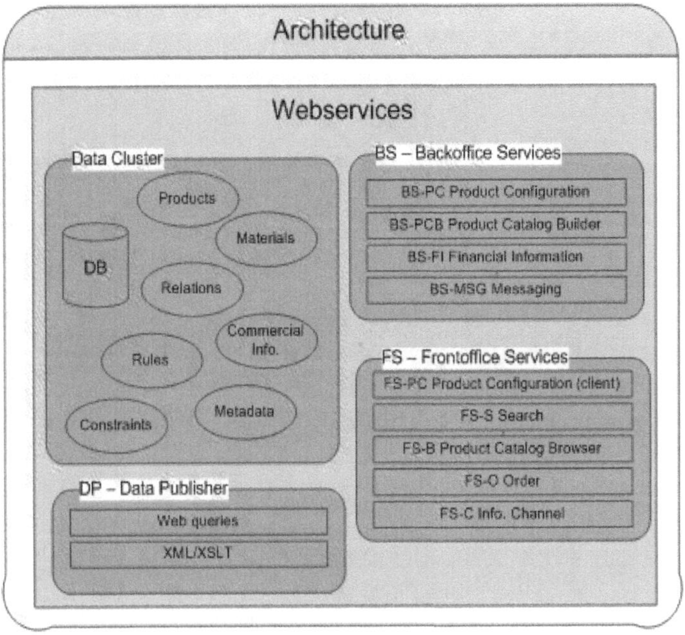

Fig. 2. System architecture

1. BS – Back-office services, including: BS-PC (product configuration services), BS-PCB (product catalog builder), BS-FI (financial information management) and BS-MSG (messaging engine for notifications and logging).
2. FS – Front-office services, including: FS-PC (product configuration services), FS-S (product search), FS-B (product catalog browser), FS-O (order processing) and FS-C (information channel publishing, i.e., information channels that aggregate one or more product categories).
3. DP – Data publisher, including: web queries (that allow external systems to import information and reporting data, and also scalar or tabular results are available), and XML/XSLT (web queries that return XML results, which supports result transformation using XSLT stylesheets to adequate information for external systems).
4. Data Cluster - Data storage (relational model, with redundancy).

Using XSD (XML Schemas), external systems can validate the data structure that they receive in XML format. This validation would be performed by integration connectors preferably. The following diagram represented in Figure 3 illustrates how an order would be validated before inserting it in the ERP external system.

During product planning the modules and product constraints are defined. The outputs control how products can be built, according to constraints and business policies.

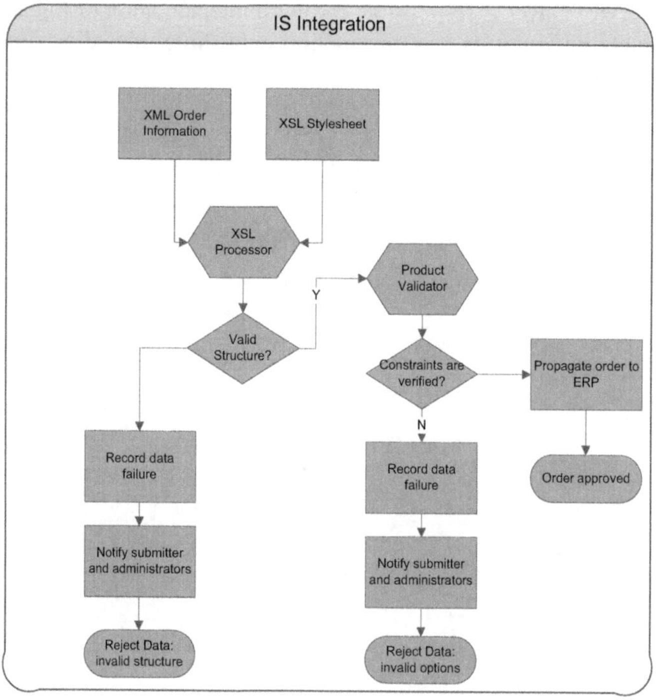

Fig. 3. Integration connectors

A set of pre-approved configurations can be published, although it is not mandatory. Later the list of configurations can be extended with configurations captured from user interaction.

Client applications' only requirement is the ability to call web methods using HTTP and SOAP, and process the returning data (XML formatted).

The diagram, in Figure 4, represents a business scenario where three external applications consume the services published by WBPC:

1. Client back-office application: windows forms application used to administer the system, performing typical activities, by using configuration engine (component management, properties management, constraint definition and management, and typical requirements management, also includes product configuration building and catalog building, configuration of data broker modules, security administration, business information management and reporting.
2. Client Front-office application: client application that the customer or business partner uses to interact with the system. Including, platforms: web, windows, Linux, mobile, etc. Several typical activities for product configuration, order submission, product catalog browse, and product search.
3. External Application: external information system, which uses data publisher to import data into local databases or other systems and typical activities include: import orders into ERP system, product data import into external applications, reporting and statistical processing.

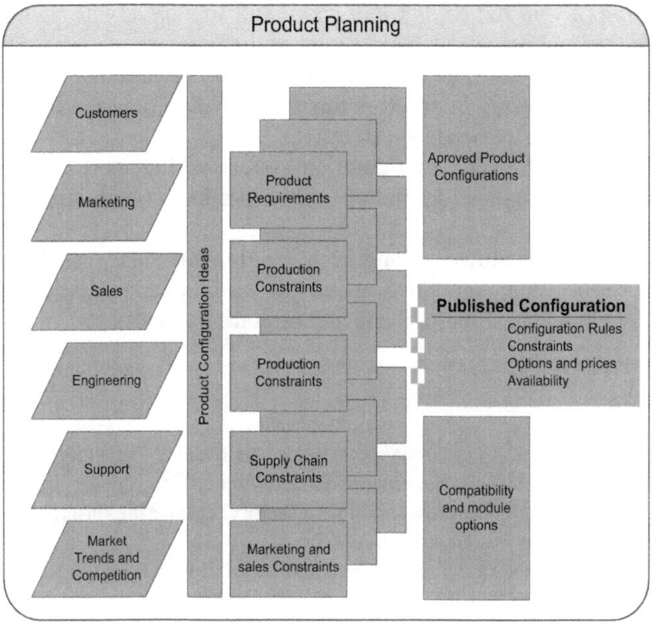

Fig. 4. Business scenario

5 Conclusion

It is our conviction that the proposed system will be a valuable tool to support the adoption of mass customization with minimum impact on existing information systems. The companies will obviously need to adopt agile production methods in order to quickly respond to customers' orders and configurations.

Promoting increased individualized interaction with customers and business partners will allow companies to obtain higher levels of customer retention.

Integrating web service based product configuration systems with their backend systems, including production and enterprise resource planning, will allow for greater cost savings and more agile processes. This level of integration will contribute to an efficient make-to-order strategy minimizing inventory costs. Adopting integration mechanisms, like a middleware layer, will support a richer level of integration with external information systems, minimizing information processing costs.

An effective mass customization strategy will only be possible if the company builds a successful information flow, covering the configuration process, product knowledge base, marketing and production restrictions and business rules and constraints.

Adopting recommendation techniques will help customers without significant knowledge about product details to express their needs and obtain a configuration that fulfils them. This way personalized interaction and individualization will not be exclusive for effective clients (who have sufficient knowledge about the products) and business partners, supporting new clients that know a lot about their needs and frequently know very little about product details and associated constraints.

The adoption of web standards widely used and supported will facilitate the evolution of the model and an easier implementation in different scenarios. The impact on existing information systems and IT environment will be minimal if the system architecture includes specialized connectors that exclusively know the details on how the information is stored in associated systems.

A modular approach to the configuration system will support the adoption of different configuration engines, depending on the product complexities and associated constraints.

Using adequate authentication and authorization mechanisms, the producer will support web service consumption from a wide range of heterogeneous clients, supporting the development of multi-channel configuration platforms.

References

1. Horman, P.: Business process change: a guide for business managers and BPM and six sigma professionals. Morgan Kaufmann, Burlington (2007)
2. Hyer, N., Wemmerlov, U.: Reorganizing the factory: competing through cellular manufacturing. Productivity Press, New York (2002)
3. Monden, Y.: Toyota Production System. Industrial Engineering and Management Press (1983), ISBN 0-89806-034-6
4. Pine, J., Gilmore, J.: The Experience Economy. Harvard Business School Press, Boston (1999)
5. Piller, F.: Customer interaction and digitizability - a structural approach to mass customization. In: Rautenstrauch, et al. (eds.) Moving Towards Mass Customization, pp. 119–138. Springer, Heidelberg (2002)
6. Jiao, J., Helander, M.G.: Development of an electronic configure-to-order platform for customized product development. Computers in Industry 57(3), 231–244 (2006)
7. Blattberg, R.C., Glazer, R.: Marketing in the Information Revolution. In: Blattberg, R.C., et al. (eds.) The Marketing Information Revolution, pp. 9–29. Harvard Business School Press, Boston (1994)
8. Barker, V.E., O'Connor, D.E.: Expert systems for configuration at Digital: XCON and beyond. Communications of the ACM 32(3), 298–318 (1989)
9. Luo, X., Tu, Y., Tang, J., Kwong, C.: Optimizing customer's selection for configurable product in B2C e-commerce application. Computers in Industry 59(8), 767–776 (2008)
10. Sabin, D., Weigel, R.: Product configuration frameworks — A survey. IEEE, Los Alamitos (1998)
11. McGuinness, D., Wright, J.: An industrial-strength description logic-based configurator platform. IEEE Intelligent Systems 13(4), 69–77 (1998)
12. Heinrich, M., Jungst, E.: A resource-based paradigm for the configuring of technical systems from modular components. In: Proceedings of Seventh IEEE Conference Artificial Intelligence Applications, Miami Beach, FL, USA (1991)
13. Mittal, S., Falkenhainer, B.: Dynamic constraint satisfaction problems. In: Proceedings of the Eighth National Conference on Artificial Intelligence, Boston, MA, USA (1991)
14. Mailharro, D.: A classification and constraint-based framework for configuration. Artificial Intelligence for Engineering Design, Analysis and Manufacturing 12(4), 383–395 (1998)
15. Mittal, S., Frayman, F.: Towards a generic model of configuration tasks. In: Proceedings of the 11th International Joint Conference on Artificial Intelligence (1989)

16. Tseng, M., Jiao, J.: Mass Customization. In: Handbook of Industrial Engineering, Technology and Operation Management, 3rd edn. (2001)
17. Lee, H.J., Lee, J.K.: An effective customization procedure with configurable standard models. Decision Support Systems 41(1), 262–278 (2005)
18. Hiramatsu, A., Naito, A., Ikkai, Y., Ohkawa, T., Komoda, N.: Case based function tree generator for client-server systems configuration design. In: Proceedings of the IEEE International Conference on Systems, Man and Cybernetics, Orlando, FL, USA (1997)
19. Yang, D., Dong, M., Miao, E.: Development of a product configuration system with an ontology-based approach. Computer-Aided Design 40(8) (Ago), 863–878 (2008)
20. Hong, G., Hu, L., Xue, D., Tu, Y., Xiong, Y.: Identification of the optimal product configuration and parameters based on individual customer requirements on performance and costs in one-of-a-kind production. International Journal of Production Research, 1–30 (2007)
21. Zhou, C., Lin, Z., Liu, C.: Customer-driven product configuration optimization for assemble-to-order manufacturing enterprises. The International Journal of Advanced Manufacturing Technology (2005)
22. Li, B., Chen, L., Huang, Z., Zhong, Y.: Product configuration optimization using a multiobjective genetic algorithm. The International Journal of Advanced Manufacturing Technology 30(1-2), 20–29 (2006)
23. Yeh, J., Wu, T., Chang, J.: Parallel genetic algorithms for product configuration management on PC cluster systems. The International Journal of Advanced Manufacturing Technology 31(11-12) (2007)
24. Hill, W., Stead, L., Rosenstein, M., Furnas, G.: Recommending and evaluating choices in a virtual community of use. In: Proceedings of the 1995 ACM Conference on Factors in Computing Systems, New York, USA (1995)
25. Shardanand, U., Maes, P.: Social information filtering: algorithms for automating word of mouth. In: Proceedings of the 1995 Conference on Human Factors in Computing Systems, Denver, CO, USA (1995)
26. Srivastava, J., Cooley, R., Deshpande, M., Tan, P.: Web usage mining: discovery and applications of usage patterns from Web data. SIGKDD Explorations 1(2), 1–12 (2000)
27. Aggarwal, C., Wolf, J., Wu, K., Yu, P.: Horting hatches an egg: a new graphtheoretic approach to collaborative filtering. In: Proceedings of the Fifth ACM SIGKDD International Conference, San Diego, CA (1999)
28. Sarwar, B., Karypis, G., Konstan, J., Riedl, J.: Item-based collaborative filtering recommendation algorithms. In: Proceedings of the 10th International Conference on World Wide Web, Hong Kong (2001)
29. Hofmann, T.: Latent semantic models for collaborative filtering. ACM Transactions on Information Systems 22(1), 89–115 (2004)
30. Tseng, H., Chang, C., Chang, S.: Applying case-based reasoning for product configuration in mass customization environments. Expert Systems with Applications 29, 913–925 (2005)

Applying Enterprise Architecture to the Design of the Integrated Forest Products Supply Chain Management System

A.F. Marques[1], J.G. Borges[1], P. Sousa[2], M. Fonseca[2], R. Garcia[2], and G. Batista[2]

[1] Centro de Estudos Florestais, ISA, Technical University of Lisbon, Tapada da Ajuda 1349-017 Lisbon (Portugal)
alexmarques@isa.utl.pt, joseborges@isa.utl.pt
[2] Link Consulting, Av Duque d'Ávila 23, 1000-138 Lisbon, Portugal
pedro.sousa@link.pt, manuel.fonseca@link.pt, ruben.garcia@link.pt, goncalo.batista@link.pt

Abstract. The forest products supply chains encompass a multitude of agents with independent business processes and information systems. The network of interrelationships and information flows among the agents is often neglected when designing information systems. Common procedures and automatic data exchanges can enhance collaboration as well as improve IT alignment with business needs across multiple organizations in the supply chain. This article proposes an Enterprise Architecture methodological approach for designing an integrated modular Forest Products Supply Chain Management System. Individual system requirements and data flows are driven from the Process Architecture Framework. Results of its application to the forest production, wood logistics and plant supply processes within Portuguese pulpwood, biomass and lumber-based supply chains are presented. Results show that this approach can effectively specify individual systems requirements driven from the processes representations built in collaboration with the agents. It further shows that a data service-oriented architecture can be derived, ensuring business information integrity and systems integration.

Keywords: enterprise architecture, processes, integration, forest management.

1 Introduction

The forest products supply chains (FPSC) can be seen as large networks of activities and agents throughout which the tree products are gradually transformed into consumer products. Forest owners and forest practitioners perform long-term forest operations planning in order to grow mature trees suitable for different utilizations. Yet they have also to either plan short-term harvesting and transportation operations, targeting specific transformation centers, or outsource these activities to entrepreneurs, sawmills or pulp and paper companies as part of forestland rental or harvesting agreements. The latter perform wood procurement medium-term planning in order to fulfill their monthly production plans. The subsequent stage involves a serious of

J.E. Quintela Varajão et al. (Eds.): CENTERIS 2010, Part II, CCIS 110 , pp. 32–40, 2010.

transformation activities (e.g. bucking, sawing, pressing, and drying) whose by-products are also exchanged among the transformation facilities and sold in intermediate markets. The consumer products are traded by merchants and distributed to specific markets. The distribution and transportation activities are usually conducted by independent service providers. The concurrent supply chain agents (involved in the same activities) usually do not interact, contrary to the frequent data exchanges and process triggering among different-staged agents. Recent integrated supply chain approaches did model the pulpwood flows and the information exchange (D'Amours, Ronnqvist et al. 2008)). Yet fragmented activity modeling approaches and information systems prevail (Ronnqvist, 2003). (Reynolds, Twery et al. 2007) presented an overview of Forest Management Decision Support Systems in use in North America, Europe, and Asia and underlined the importance of end-user involvement and integration for successful development of these systems. Often systems were tailored to meet single agents' business requirements or were developed in the context of research projects that did not need to take into account robustness and scalability for continuous use.

Enterprise Architecture (EA) methodology approaches have been successfully applied to design scalable information systems and integrated multi-activity forest-based systems. It is based on processes' modeling and information characterization (Schekkerman 2009) conducted in Process Architecture workshops with end-users (or supply chain agents). These workshops are instrumental for identifying system requirements to support business processes, ensuring the alignment between business requirements and the Information Technology (IT) function (Sousa and Pereira 2005). (Ribeiro, Borges et al. 2005) demonstrated the EA potential for specifying the Integrated Forest Management System strategic module for a major pulp and paper industry in Portugal (Grupo Portucel Soporcel). (Marques, Borges et al. 2009)) extended this approach to develop an information system for the entire pulpwood supply chain, also in the context of an integrated Portuguese pulp and paper company.

In this article we propose and test an extension of the EA methodology (Spewak and Hill 1992) to involve several agents in the specification of the information system needed to support each supply chain activity. The collaboration between supply chain agents that are involved in different chain segments enables the identification of data exchanges, interoperability and integration requirements of an integrated FPSC Management System. The first component of the proposed approach - Process Architecture (PA) focuses on forest production, logistics, and plant supply processes as well as on the business information of the Portuguese pulpwood, biomass and lumber-based supply chains. It further takes into account the SCOR - Supply Chain Operations Reference Model, proposed by the Supply Chain Council (The Supply Chain Council 2008), in order to develop Process Architecture Framework. Implementation guidelines, best practices and correspondent optimization models are identified for each process. The business information is structured into information entities in the course of the Information Architecture (IA). The third EA component, Application Architecture (AA) is built from previous EA artifacts (Marques, Borges et al. 2009). Namely, it identifies single supply chain activities sub-systems requirements, their data services and the overall interoperability and integration requirements. The fourth EA component, the Technological Architecture (TA) proposes the most adequate technologies to support each supply chain activity. The proposed approach extends the research conducted by (Ribeiro, Borges et al. 2005) and (Marques, Borges et al. 2009) as it simultaneously addresses the needs of several agents of the three major Portuguese forest products supply chains – pulpwood, biomass and lumber-based products. The common Process Architecture Framework and FPSC Management System requirements were validated by the agents involved in the case study.

2 Material and Methods

2.1 The Case Study

The pulp & paper and lumber & derivates production, with annual sales of $1623x10^3$€ and $1131x10^3$€ respectively, are key economic sub-sectors of the forest cluster and represent 14% of the GNP, 12% of exports and 9% of the industrial employment (INE, 2007).The seven existing operating units consume annually $5593x10^3m^3$ of pulpwood (mainly from *Eucalyptus globulus* Labill) to produce $1833{,}2x10^3m^3$ of eucalyptus pulp. Two of these units also consume about $731x10^3m^3$ of *Pinus pinaster*Ait. to produce $188{,}5\ x10^3m^3$ of pulp (CELPA, 2008). Most pulp production targets the European market, although about 45% is internally consumed in two integrated paper production units. These units also absorb the total recycled fiber pulp production ($327{,}9\ x10^3$ton). The industry is highly concentrated into two major economical groups, with self-owned forestland, thus controlling all the supply chain activities. Together, they are the major Portuguese private forest owners. The harvesting and transportation operations in self-owned of rented forestland are conducted by small-scale service providers. Alternatively, the industry relies on market wood delivery contracts established with local wood suppliers, who independently handle wood procurement, exploitation and transportation. International market supplies, usually carried by boat to the port nearest to the industrial units, allow the industry to overcome national wood shortages.

Contrary, there is a proliferation of traditional, small-scaled, disintegrated lumber transformation units, consisting of more than 250 sawmills and 12 panels production units, distributed mainly in the Center and North regions. These primary transformation units consume mainly *Pinus pinaster*, *Populus sp.*, *Eucalyptus sp.* and other residual softwoods, provided exclusively by local wood suppliers (entrepreneurs). These are crucial business intermediates as they establish multiple contracts with small-scaled private forest owners, conduct harvesting and transportation operations and deliver pre-defined monthly qualified amounts at the transformation units. There is little if any direct contact between the mills and the forest owners. These entrepreneurs also sustain the woodchips (sawmills by-products) supply to the panels units. Wood importation, negotiated directly by the individual transformation units, is gaining importance, especially from Spain, Brazil and USA. The lumber and panels support more than 4500 carpentry and furniture small-scale units, responsible for secondary transformation and consumer products commercialization (AIMMP, 2007).

The recent increase of the biomass sub-sector economical importance justifies its inclusion in this study. In fact, there are currently 6 biomass centrals operating in Portugal, and 4 new units planned until the end of 2010. The majority is located at pulp and paper facilities. Together they produce 133,6MW from about 1,4x10^6ton of forestry residues with origin in self-owned forestlands or internal market, usually chipped at the harvesting sites (Celpa, 2009). Up to now, the forest residues were managed independently in small-scale and trail operations conducted mainly by the pulp and paper industries. Its increasing demand fosters the systematic forest residues collection and chipping, preferably integrated with the traditional harvesting operations.

2.2 Methods

The EA approach aims at modeling the three main FPSC, namely their common forest production, logistics and plant supply processes. The nuclear EA team includes forest practitioners, logistic experts and IT technicians. They work in straight collaboration with a consultants committee, consisting of forest production experts and representants of each of FPSC and service providers. An average of 8 experts met in three half-day interactive process architecture workshops. The forest products procurement network was firstly characterized. It identified all product sources and destinations and possible product flows among them. Secondly, the hierarchical Process Architecture Framework was progressively defined, as the EA team and consultant experts designed to common, innovative processes. The process element was the elementary object. Similar to SCOR Supply Chain Operations Reference Model (The Supply Chain Council 2008), the first and second levels grouped the process elements into process types and categories, respectively. The FPSC overall model represented the process elements, their higher level types and categories and the main information flows among them. Each process element was divided into tasks (fourth level), whose input and output information were characterized. These are generic and referential tasks, upon which recommendations, guidelines and system requirements were driven. This level of detail does not allow a flowchart representation. It is suitable up to the fifth process level, were the task is detailed into organization-specific activities and sub-activities.

The process elements input and output information are instrumental for identifying the 22 information entities (IE) of the Information Architecture, in the course of EA team brainstorm meetings. Each IE should have a business responsible for its management and for performing operations such as acquisition, classification, quality control, presentation, distribution and assessment. It was characterized by a single identifier defined from a business perspective, description and a set of attributes (Marques, Borges et al. 2009).

Both process elements and IE were analyzed according to alignment rules (Sousa, Pereira et al. 2005) within a CRUD matrix (Create, Read, Update, Delete). The CRUD matrix manipulation enables FPSC management system modular components identification (sub-systems). Its functional requirements, data repositories, graphical user interfaces and data services were also described by the EA team in the Applications Architecture report. It further included the overall system integration requirements driven from the sub-systems data services and the supply chain agents' interoperability schemas. The FPSC management system technological requirements and development guidelines were discussed in the Technological Architecture report. All EA reports were validated by the consultants committee.

3 Results and Discussion

There are significant differences in production and logistics of eucalypt, pine logs and forest residues emerging from the forest products procurement network (Fig. 1). Both species can came from importation or national market. Currently, the self-owned forests are mainly for eucalypt supply and forest residues. All the products are transported by truck from the forest areas to the destinations. The forest residues transportation requires closed-trailer trucks. The eucalyptus logs railway transportation is frequent from the terminals to the pulp and paper production units.

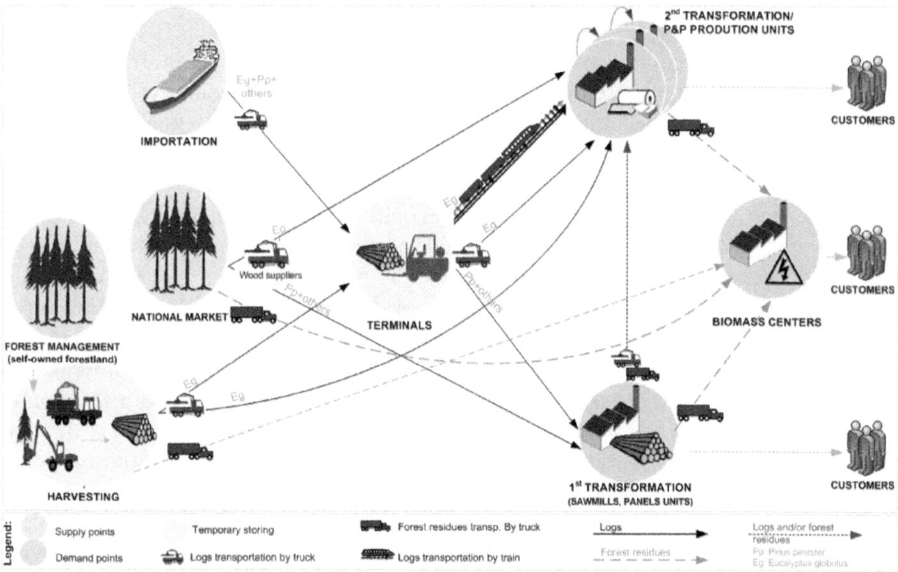

Fig. 1. The Forest products procurement network represents the supply, demand, temporary storing locations, and transportation flows for *Eucalyptus globulus*, *Pinus pinaster* logs and forest residues, considering the forest production, wood logistics and plant supply processes of the pulp & paper, lumber & derivates and biomass supply chains

The forest management (self-owned forestland) supply point is addressed by the process elements included in the Forest Production process type (FPSC Process Architecture Framework, Fig. 2). The forestland management category (1.1.) includes Forest properties registration (1.1.1.), forestland monitoring and protection against biotic and abiotic hazards (1.1.2.), forest inventory periodic inventory (1.1.3.) and new forestland properties acquisition or rental (1.1.4). The forest operations hierarchical planning process elements are included in Forest planning (1.2.). The operations follow-up and annual properties surveys by the forest owners or forest practitioners are grouped into the On-land operations management (1.3.). Specifically for integrated pulp and paper companies, this type includes the internal forest roads management (1.4.), which schedules the roads maintenance operations regarding foreseen harvest operations.

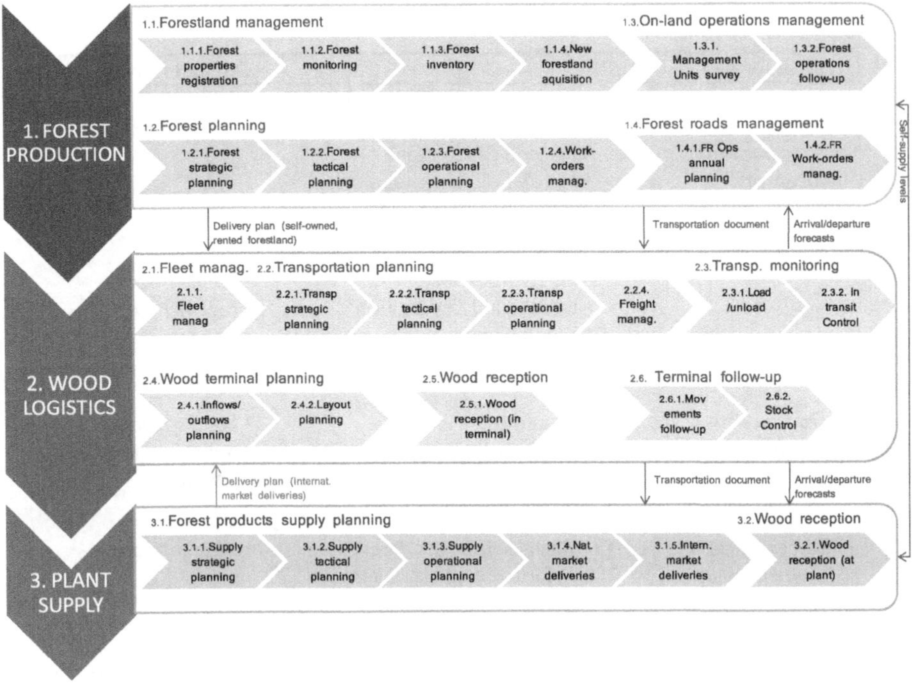

Fig. 2. The FPSC Process Architecture Framework groups the process elements into process categories, displayed into 3 main process types: 1. Forest production, 2. Wood logistics and 3. Plant Supply

The terminal temporary storing, truck and railway transportation flows correspond to the 2. Wood Logistics process type, mainly performed by the service providers, although the terminals usually belong to the transformation industries. Specifically, the fleet management (2.1.), transportation planning (2.2.) and transportation monitoring (2.3.) aim the transversal transportation management, while wood terminal planning (2.4.), wood reception (2.5.) and terminal follow-up (2.6.) control terminals functioning.

The product supply (logs, forest residues) at the transformation units and biomass centrals is commonly addressed by the third Process Type. Thus, the process category Forest products supply planning (3.1.) includes the overall supply hierarchical planning and the logs deliveries from the national (wood suppliers) and international markets. The plant wood reception (3.2.1.) presents similarities with the 2.5.1. process element. Its related tasks, identified in the process description (Table 1), perform trucks unloading and load evaluation based on the anticipation of the next incoming truck, estimated from the arrivals/departures forecasts available from the In-transit control (2.3.2.) process.

All the input and output information flows associated to the Forest Production process elements was grouped into 15 information entities (IEs), namely: Forest Property (E2), Management Unit (E1), Harvesting Unit (E3), Forest road (E15), Forest inventory (E20), Forest hazard (E19), Forest Operation (E4), Forest Plan (E21),

Table 1. Description of the Plant wood reception (3.2.1.) process element

Input information	Task	Output information
▪ *Arrival/departure estimates* ▪ *Transportation document*	3.2.1.1. Anticipate next incoming truck ▪ Estimate arrival date ▪ Provide destination ▪ Notify unloading team and equipment (if needed) ▪ If there is a delay,	▪ *Unloading notification*
	3.2.1.2. Verify truck load ▪ Load quality evaluation ▪ Wood weight	▪ *Load entrance registration*
	3.2.1.3. Truck unload	
▪ *Truck daily schedule*	3.2.1.4. Record truck exiting ▪ Truck exiting date ▪ Update next trip origin (if needed)	▪ *Load entrance registration update*
▪ *Trucks queue at plant entrance*	3.2.1.5. Manage truck queuing ▪ Prioritize and display truck entrance sequence	▪ *Next entering truck*

Work order (E12), Service Provider (E13), Equipment (E14), Crew (E16), Forest Product (E7) and Wood pile (E17). The Management Unit and Forest Operation are manipulated ("Read") by all of these processes. The first is managed ("Create", "Read", "Update", "Delete") by the Forest properties Registration process (1.1.1.) whenever a new property is acquired or a forest hazard, like a forest fire, obliges to new forestland segmentation. Each management unit, usually with a geographical representation, is homogeneous in terms of its characterization and foreseen and executed forest operations, although it can include many different forest properties. The forest operations are planned by management unit (within the forest plans), according to the silviculture models adopted. The on-land operations management processes (1.3.) "Create", "Update" and "Delete" the executed Forest Operations, and associate it to a Management Unit. Some of these IEs are also "Read" by the subsequent supply chain processes. Nevertheless, Logistics processes manage the Transportation Vehicle (E10), Logistic Plan (E22), Freight (E9), Terminal (E6) and Wood load (E18). The freight is the main IE of the transportation monitoring process (2.3.). It is "Created" at the origin (harvest unit or terminal), when a new transportation document is issued and "Deleted" (or sent to historic records) when the truck is unloaded. It includes the time estimates in each origin and destination, which can be periodically updated based on the vehicle real-time positioning. Finally, the Supply Plans (E8) and Wood Supplier (E11) are managed by Plant Supply processes. The Industrial Units are handled by these processes but its information is managed by external systems.

The confrontment between the process elements and EIs within the CRUD matrix and the application of IT alignment rules suggested FPSC management system partitioning into 12 modular components (Fig. 3). The Forest Patrimony Management (S2) and Forest Inventory (S4) sub-systems, adequate for forest owners and forest practitioners, foresee remote equipments for properties delimitation and on-land data collection. The vast area coverage of the Forest monitoring mobile devices (S3) and the required Operations Central justifies its adoption only by large-scale forest owners (such as the integrated pulp and paper companies) or forest-owners associations. These are also the main users of the Forest planning and operations management sub-systems (S1) and (S5). Forest plans can be integrated with supply plans (S12), in the case of integrated pulp and paper companies, although the simplified versions of the small-scaled forest owners usually do not account for market demands. The transportation planning sub-system (S6) includes the freights and service providers' selection and adjudication, conducted by the Pulp and Paper production units and individual wood providers, as well as the detailed truck scheduling performed by the service provider. The later manages a self-owned or associated vehicle fleet (S7). Similarly, the Transportation follow-up sub-system (S9) provide information on vehicle positioning, which is used for monitoring purposes by the service provider and for load reception anticipation in the terminals and production units. The wood stock control sub-system (S8), encompassing truck load/unload, wood reception and stock control at the terminals, assures wood flows quantitative control across the logistic network, according to integrated pulp and paper companies requirements. The transformation units, including sawmills and biomass centers, perform annual supply planning, based on the targeting production estimates (S12). This is the input for the Wood Supply management Sub-system (S11) responsible for all national and international wood market acquisition activities. The wood load verifications at the plant entrance are similar to terminal reception, which justifies a common module for both processes. Although the terminals, owned by integrated companies, are usually managed independently (S10).

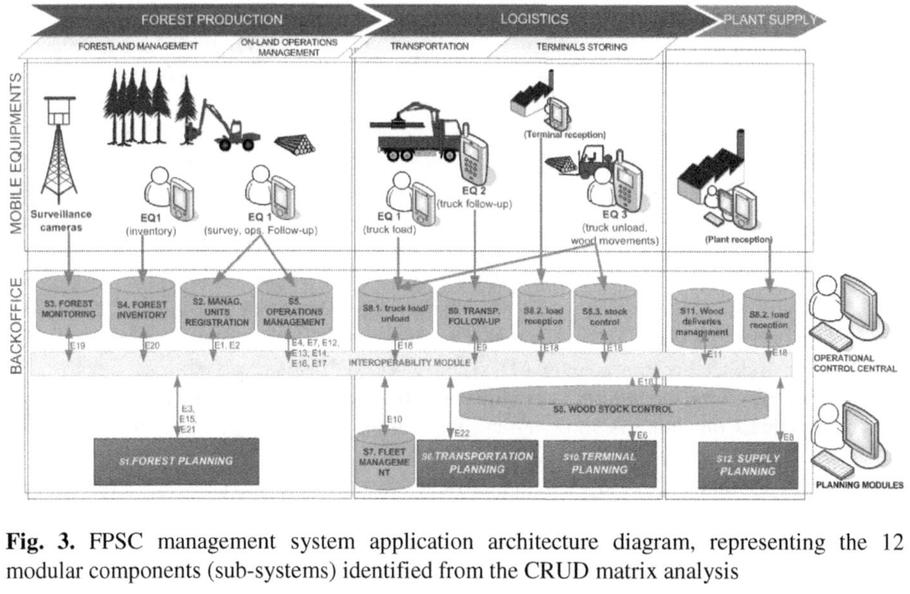

Fig. 3. FPSC management system application architecture diagram, representing the 12 modular components (sub-systems) identified from the CRUD matrix analysis

4 Final Remarks

The EA approach emphasized the overall FPSC management system integration requirements. Preliminary results show the possibility of normalizing macro-scale business processes for several FPSC agents. The proposed Process Architecture Framework constitutes a best-practices reference guide, leading to individual agent efficiency improvements and enhancing its collaboration with the other supply chain counterparts. It can be mapped into individual agent specific procedures. Data services provided by each sub-system were clearly identified. Detailed sub-system functional specifications have been produced and validated by the agents. This enables easier and contextualized system developments, thus reducing the overall IT costs.

Acknowledgements

This paper presents the preliminary results of the CAMTEC research project, conducted by Link Consulting with the support of Technical University of Lisbon and the QREN Governmental Program funding.

References

1. AIMMP (2007), Estatísticas sectoriais, http://www.aimmp.pt
2. Carlsson, D., D'Amours, S., Martel, A., Ronnqvist, M.: Supply Chain Management in the Pulp and Paper Industry, DT-2006-AM-3 (2006)
3. Celpa, Boletim estatístico (2008), http://www.celpa.pt
4. D'Amours, S., Ronnqvist, E.M., Weintraub, A.: Using Operational Research for Supply Chain Planning in the Forest Products Industry. Infor. 46, 265–281 (2008)
5. INE. Estatísticas Agrícolas (2007), http://www.ine.pt
6. Marques, A.F., Borges, J.G., Sousa, P., Pinho, A.M.: Pulpwood supply chain architecture. An application in Portugal. European Journal of Forest Research (2009) (submitted)
7. Reynolds, K.M., Twery, M., Lexer, M.J., Vacik, H., Ray, D., Shao, G., Borges, J.: Decision support systems in natural resource management. In: Burstein, F., Holsapple, C. (eds.) Handbook on Decision Support Systems. Springer Verlag International, Heidelberg (2007)
8. Ribeiro, R.P., Borges, J., Pereira, C., Sousa, P., Lé, J.: Designing an Integrated Forest Planning System for the forest industry: an application in Portugal. In: Bevers, M., Barrett, T.M. (eds.) Systems Analysis in Forest Resources. Proceedings of the 2003 Symposium, Stevenson, WA, USA, pp. 89–96 (2005)
9. Ronnqvist, M.: Optimization in forestry. Mathematical Programming 97, 267–284 (2003)
10. Schekkerman, J.: Enterprise Architecture Good Practices Guide: How to Manage the Enterprise Architecture Practice. IFEAD / TOGAF Open Standards (2009)
11. Sousa, P., Pereira, C.: Enterprise Architecture: Business and IT Alignment. In: Symposium on Applied Computing Archive, Proceedings of the 2005 ACM Symposium on Applied Computing, Santa Fe, New Mexico, pp. 1344–1345 (2005)
12. Sousa, P., Pereira, C., et al.: Enterprise Architecture Alignment Heuristics. Microsoft Architect Journal (2005)
13. Spewak, S., Hill, S.: Enterprise Architecture Planning: Developing a Blueprint for Data, Applications and Technology. Wiley-QED Publication (1992)
14. The Supply Chain Council, I. SCOR: The Supply Chain Reference Model (2008)

Enterprise Architecture to IT Governance: An Approach Based on Component Business Model and Performance Levels

Luis Fernando Ramos Molinaro, Karoll Haussler Carneiro Ramos, Tomas Roberto da Cotta Orlandi, and Humberto Abdalla Jr.

Campus Darcy Ribeiro, Universidade de Brasília, Dept. Engenharia Elétrica, Prédio SG-11 – 1° andar, Núcleo de Multimídia e Internet. Brasília - DF, Brazil
molinaro@nmi.unb.br, karoll.ramos@nmi.unb.br, tomasroberto@gmail.com, abdalla@ene.unb.br

Abstract. The aim of this paper is to present an approach for a model that supports IT governance and management through the alignment of business with Information Technology – IT using Enterprise Architecture concepts, considering efficiency, effectiveness and security. Firstly, a theoretical review will be done emphasizing the assumptions that support IBM`s Component Business Model, such as specialization, governance and strategy. Then, an approach is presented for the organization's decomposition, considering IT and business alignment. Moreover, the performance levels concept is introduced to the CBM®. Finally, a governance and management model for components to be applied in case study is presented.

Keywords: specialization, component business model, IT strategy, IT subsystems.

1 Introduction

There are many studies and reports that orient organizations to network as a way to face the current economic environment [1], [17]. Networks assume that organizations must focus on what they do best, learning therefore to specialize their services [1].

Service specialization brings with it supply chain unit cooperation and contributes at the same time to the organization's optimization. For the design of the organization from this new point of view, IBM has developed the Component Business Model (CBM®).

This model assumes that the organization's services can be arranged into business building blocks, self-controlled and self-managed. However, the decomposition strategy of building blocks, in addition to the governance and management mechanisms, are open to many approaches in this model [3].

This paper presents an approach to an organization's decomposition that applies the knowledge of CBM® and performance levels as a way to make enterprise architecture for achieving IT governance and management viable.

Justification for this paper comes from the current economic environment that is propitious for new models that favor service specialization in organizations. This

J.E. Quintela Varajão et al. (Eds.): CENTERIS 2010, Part II, CCIS 110, pp. 41–51, 2010.

approach collaborates so that the manager has a strategic view of the organization and learns how to control and manage it in a network environment.

2 Specialization Era

In 1911, [4] systematically compiled information about "how" to execute work. He generated a series of practical principles based on the separation of physical and mental work through task fragmentation. This fragmentation was determined through analysis of time and movements in factory activities [5] and [6].

Henry Ford, Taylor's contemporary, contributed to the mass production concept where the key-concept was in the simplicity of assembly. Ford totally assimilated Taylor's concepts and applied to them the mechanic production system [6] [7] [8].

In mechanic production systems, the machines and the worker are specialized in executing only one activity. This specialization reduced human exertion in assembly, increased productivity, diminished production costs and has increased product quality, directly contributing to mass consumption.

The current specialization context suggests that organizations focus on what they do best as a way of obtaining organizational performance [9], [1], [10]. This paper will developed around this specialization.

For [1], specialization promotes the strategic segmentation of suppliers and clients, aiming at supply-chain customization and increasing benefits to final-chain clients.

According to [11] specialization goes along two parallel paths: internal and external specializations.

Currently, many companies are devoting themselves to the external specialization phase, called *industry networked.* In this phase, companies focus on their specific specialization domains and begin to work as a part of one big "ecosystem" or flexible networks boosted/stimulated by collaboration, universal connectivity and standardization, i.e. iPod from Apple Computer [3].

Internal specialization proposes a new ideal optimization process that organizes the company as a cooperative business module network. In this phase, the organization works as a set of discrete building blocks or components that interact with all of the company's other elements as well as with other companies.

The building blocks are also a method for designing information systems [12]. The business building blocks and the information systems building blocks have a default structure that enables the integration of both, proportioning the creation of an enterprise architecture fundamental element.

IBM has developed a model to represent business building blocks called the Component Business Model – CBM®. It proposes a service specialization mechanism in specific business components [3].

As in specialization theory, components are characterized as internal and external. Internally, components aim at the optimization of the organization. Externally, components assist organizations to identify competences that they cannot create by themselves.

Components must be self-managed, self-controlled and at the same time they must work together so as to reach the business objectives.

Usually, this model has been introduced into organizations aiming to facilitate strategic planning. The benefits from the components map in those organizations mainly refer to the identification of: services with redundancy; critical services for business; non-existent services; and external components.

3 Governance and Strategy

It is worth recalling that CBM® components must be self-controlled and self-managed, however they should obey only one governance.

Governance is a system through which societies are controlled and monitored. The governance system allows the mission, the vision and the strategy to be transformed considering the desired goals and results.

Corporative governance encourages the release of great amounts of information by organizations [13]. This fact aids in the development of IT governance which aims to certify if the IT investments are aggregating value to the company's businesses. [14] affirms that IT governance to assure IT alignment with the organization.

IT alignment with business is what assures the organization that IT investments will be used to aggregate business value. This alignment may be obtained through business strategy and IT strategy communication in addition to IT's contribution to an organization's business unit strategic planning [15].

The strategy can be a business one or corporative. Business strategy defines the organization's main goals. Those goals are translated by corporative strategy that has the mission of implementing them. In this way, IT strategy emerges as a means for IT alignment with business. The next step defines the fundamentals that characterize the IT corporative strategy.

According to [14], IT strategy must be well defined in relation to its internal and external domains.

The way IT infra-structure must be configured and managed is defined in the internal domain, considering IT architecture components, processes and IT abilities. IT architecture guides the choice of service portfolios, hardware, software and communication configurations and data architecture that define technical infra-structure. IT processes determine the main IT infra-structure work processes and maintenance of support systems. IT abilities deliberate on acquisition, training and developing personal capabilities and knowledge required for effective IT infra-structure management and operation.

In external domains, it is necessary to define which position IT intends to establish, and this involves decisions regarding the scope of IT, as well as IT competences and governance. IT's scope deals with specific information technology, such as place and networks that support the organization's strategic initiatives. Competences establish IT strategy attributes like activity cost and the operation's flexibility level. Moreover, IT governance selects and uses strategic mechanisms for obtaining the required IT competence requirements obtaining.

[14] considers that internal and external domains have the same importance, although the traditional thought regarding IT strategy falls back on the internal domain. The internal domain features IT business that must work under a specific structure.

Some authors have defended that IT is functionally divided into Direct, Development and Delivery [16], [17], [18], [19], [20]. Those functionalities interact with each other and with the business, allowing IT alignment with business [18].

Direct, when implemented, brings IT closer to business. This happens through IT collaboration with strategic planning, with business units' projects and with management practices of business demands.

Development contributes to project portfolio organization through the use of best practices for project management. It also helps in project prioritization, keeps files on all projects and provides estimations for projects and project proposals.

Delivery intermediates Development actions that may have an affect service. In adapting Best practices, Delivery may be more agile in the construction of solutions/when constructing solutions.

Each functionality has distinct features that are aligned with models of management, processes, organizational structures, people, technology and knowledge.

4 Mapping IT and Business Components

Using the information presented previously, this section will develop a basic IT and business components map based on the following Component Business Model - CBM® assumptions: Performance Levels; IT Alignment with Business; and IT Subsystems.

According to [21], CBM® brings together models, methods and techniques that were created to organize, comprehend asses and finally transform an organization.

Each CBM® block can be decomposed into other blocks that are unique and integrated into a group of components [19]. One advantage of block decomposition is in gaining more detailed information regarding the service functionalities of an organization. So as to the construction of a basic IT components map, a map of the organization's basic components was initially proposed. This fact is justified by preference for a Top-Down view which analyzes the organization's context before analyzing the object of interest.

Initially, on the basic components map of the organization, only one essential macro competence was considered that would concentrate all of the organization's essential competences. At the same time, it would be represented by one component or block, called an organization component. One of this block's unique objectives was to embody in CBM® a basic structure that would assist in comprehending the organization as a whole and that could be applied to future components originating from this decomposition.

To facilitate an analysis of the organization's basic component, a structure called [22] performance levels was incorporated, more precisely the BTrends version, which is called the Performance Pyramid. This vision uses business processes as an integration link between the many elements that form the organization [23], [24], [25].

In BPTrends point of view , an organization is divided into Enterprise, Process and Implementation levels. Such an application is compatible with [11] proposed dimensions: business purpose, activities, resources, governance and business services. This compatibility is useful because it allows the use of dimensions through a more mature/developed approach.

Performance levels are also known as organizational integration models, once the organization reaches efficacy and efficiency when all performance levels are geared in the same direction. In order for this to happen, a network measurement is necessary, which detains the indicators, strategies and processes [22]. This characteristic of the model allows its use in IT governance and consequently in IT alignment with business.

4.1 IT Alignment and Business

The second step for creating a basic IT components map is the decomposition of the organizational component. Decomposing one block makes a new components map that has distinct competences, but separated from the previous competence.

To achieve this decomposition, models that propose IT alignment with business were researched in literature. So, the model selected was the IT strategic alignment model – SAM (Strategic Alignment Model) by [26].

SAM has as a premise dynamic IT planning that includes the organization's internal and external environments' evolution. So, SAM suggests that the organization should be divided into business and IT, considering the organization's basic functionalities or essential competences.

For each functionality, a component was established. So business functionalities acquired a business component and the IT functionalities acquired an IT component. It is worth saying that both IT and business components used a performance levels concept similar to the organization component.

When CBM® is used, the traditional chart is not relevant for rating components, once the interest is in internal (internal specialization) and external (external specialization) services offered/supplied by the organization.

Identifying these two components with distinct and segregated functions contributed to achieving new decompositions. The first decomposed component was the Business Component. For this decomposition it was necessary to know certain kind of business' functionalities.

From [27], a generic components map for manufacturing companies was also chosen. In this map, the essential business company competences are Manage, Project, Buy, Make and Sell.

4.2 IT Subsystems

For IT component decomposition, the essential IT components Direct, Develop and Delivery were chosen. These three IT subsystems interact amongst each other and with the whole organization, allowing IT alignment with business [16], [17], [18], [19].

In order to define IT essential competences, the main IT features that create IT value were extracted from [18]. They are planning and high level control (Direct); solution maker (Develop); operation and services maintenance (Delivery). IT component decomposition in three essential competences forms the first version of the IT Block Components Map.

The business and IT components' relationships form a network, having as a reference the set of offered and demanded services. In this way, the components relationship is established for offer and consumption relations.

The IT block basic components map has an array structure formed by columns that represents the essential IT competences and by lines that show accountability level. The accountability level classifies or reorganizes components in Direct, Control or Execution [11]. Notice that not only on the level of accountability but also in the IT subsystems the word Direct is utilized. For IT, Direct means a specific IT functionality, while Direct on the accountability levels represents planning or strategic plans for the higher hierarchy component.

4.3 Governance and Management Cycle`s Steps

After establishing the organization's basic components map and IT block basic components map, an analysis of which components aggregate more value to IT and business is done.

Next, architecture is designed from the Governance and Management Cycle (GMC) that is to be applied continuously at each component and in the component map as a whole. This cycle supports the governance and management dimension of each organization's components.

The GMC represents the governance and management aspects which involve assessment of the business results, strategy clarification and business model improvement through decision making procedures. This cycle must consider corporative governance necessities, business processes and information technology [20].

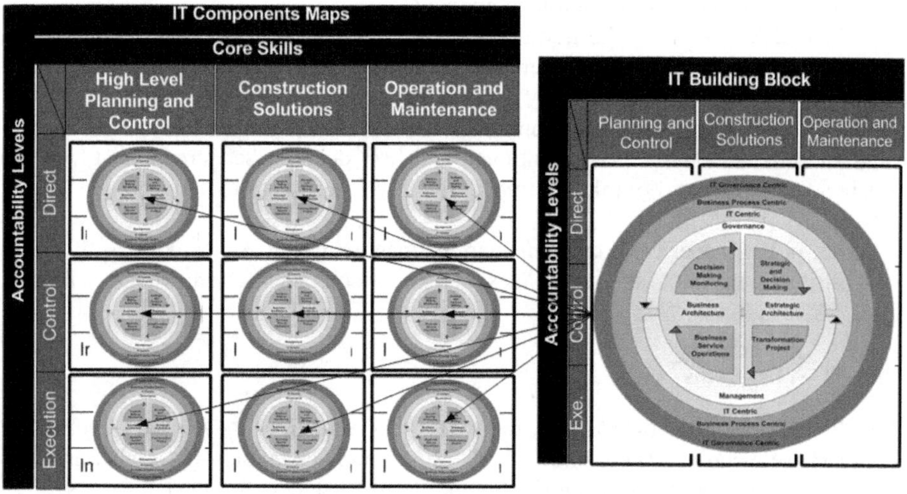

Fig. 1. Reflections of the Governance Management Cycle (GMC)

An important aspect is that each map component is self-controlled and self-managed, having its own Governance and Management Cycle, and at the same time is contained within a bigger cycle of its corresponding component map (Figure 1).

As GMC stresses, IT governance and management work simultaneously with strategic architecture and business architecture, both aimed at organizational alignment. In order to operationalize the GMC, eight main steps that explain how it works have been highlighted [28]: *i)* Stage 1 – Strategy; *ii)* Stage 2 – Guides and Management Best Practices and Environmental Management; *iii)* Stage 3 – Enterprise Architecture As Is (Control and Monitoring); *iv)* Stage 4 – Diagnosis; *v)* Stage 5 – Enterprise Architecture To Be; *vi)* Stage 6 – Migration Project; *vii)* Stage 7 – Project Implantation; *viii)* Stage 8 – Enterprise Architecture As Is (Execution) [28].

- **Stage 1** - *Strategy* - the strategy is formulated on an enterprise level, where the context is analyzed so as to find new opportunities, trends or a suitable solutions for a particular situation;
- **Stage 2** - *Guides and Management-* considers the guidelines and collections of good practices that may help with the strategy;
- **Stage 3** - *Enterprise Architecture As Is (control and monitoring)* – shows how business architecture, process architecture and IT architecture is working for the performance of the enterprise?. This work is evaluated by key performance indicators that could be shown in dashboards;
- **Stage 4** - *Diagnosis* - defines gaps in architectures (business, process and IT architecture) with *Strategy*;
- **Stage 5** - *Enterprise Architecture To Be* – designs the future enterprise architecture considering *Strategy* and *Diagnosis.*
- **Stage 6** - *Migration Project-* is the enterprise architecture's `s projects;
- **Stage 7** - *Project Implantation* - the project is implemented considering the enterprise`s context.
- **Stage 8** - *Enterprise Architecture As Is (execution)* - the new enterprise architecture starts operating.

4.4 GMC Implementation Scenery – Case Study

In order to understand better CGG's main steps, it will be introduced a corporative architecture project in a consultancy attached to University of Brasilia's Administration Department, *AD&M Consultoria Empresarial.* It is a relevant Project once through it there were the first practical results that helped on CGG eight steps' development. This consultancy works on Brazil's federal capital for 17 years and supports small and medium companies in areas as marketing, financial, business processes and human resources. The Project is presented considering CGG eight steps.

Stage 1 – In 2006 there was a strategic planning in which was presented a report showing that the services provided to clients did not solve the problems in a long term. From this finding it was decided the consultancy should aim the high performance of its projects.

So as to integrate those interests to organization's strategy, it was created the strategic goal "Services Improving" which has two performance markers: agreeing methodologies and methodologies improving.

Stage 2 – The first step of the "Services Improving" Project made an exploratory search to identify the Best consultancy practices. So non-structured interviews were made with a well reputed consultancy group in Brazil:

- The *IDS- SHEER Brazil* (process expertise) ex president and founder of *Symnetics Brazil* (strategy expertise);

- The president of *Grupo IDEA* (finances expertise);
- The president of IPTG – *Instituto de Pesquisa e Tecnologia Gerencial* (strategy, marketing research and processes expertise);
- The head-consulter of CDT/UnB – *Technologic Development Center of Universidade de Brasília* (technology expertise);
- The professor and consulter of *Fundação Dom Cabral* (strategic managing expertise).

Besides, clients and the consultancy board were interviewed.

Those interviews' results revealed that a high performance consultancy must: *i)* have investigation steps or survey information, problems identification or finding, study of viable alternatives, solutions propositions and, in some cases, the suggested solutions accompaniment and assistance; *ii*) clients expect to see their investment in a few months (three to five months for a large companies and twelve months for small ones); *iii)* negotiation is made through consultancy partners for having holistic view and business knowledge; *iv)* negotiation can be made by juniors only if the company has a consistent diagnosis methodology; *v)* since the negotiation process, it is accorded what would measure the project's performance.

Stage 3 – After the stage 2, the primary activities of value chain and the business processes were selected for reformulation because they were responsible for the problems. In Stage 3 has begun the current processes` description.

Stage 4 – Based on stage 3 and 4 information, a gap analysis was made, in which the main weak point were identified. They are:

- High non automated processes number, interfering on the customer service efficiency;
- High error numbers in the project time rating due to the lack of an efficient diagnosis;
- High modified scope number, again due to the lack of an efficient diagnosis;
- Difficulty of measuring the costumers services quality;

Stage 5 – To establish the new consultancy model, the Project chose for elaborating a framework that represents the new organization's competences and the new projects attached to them (Figure 2). This framework's support tool was Igrafx. In each framework's shape there are from activities flowchart to information technology interface.

Stage 6 and 7– The change for this architecture had two key concerns: the new processes` assessment and the change of workers' skills. For each process there was a prototype, even for the new processes or project methodologies. In this case a partnership was created between Consultancy and Clients, with no costs because it was an experimental project.

After the processes mapping, there was a gap analysis of consultancy collaborators' skills. The gap analysis allowed the capacity training to be developed. It is worth to say that the team which has developed the "Services Improving" Project was formed mainly by the collaborators of remade processes. These actions contribute for the non resistance of migration and implementation projects.

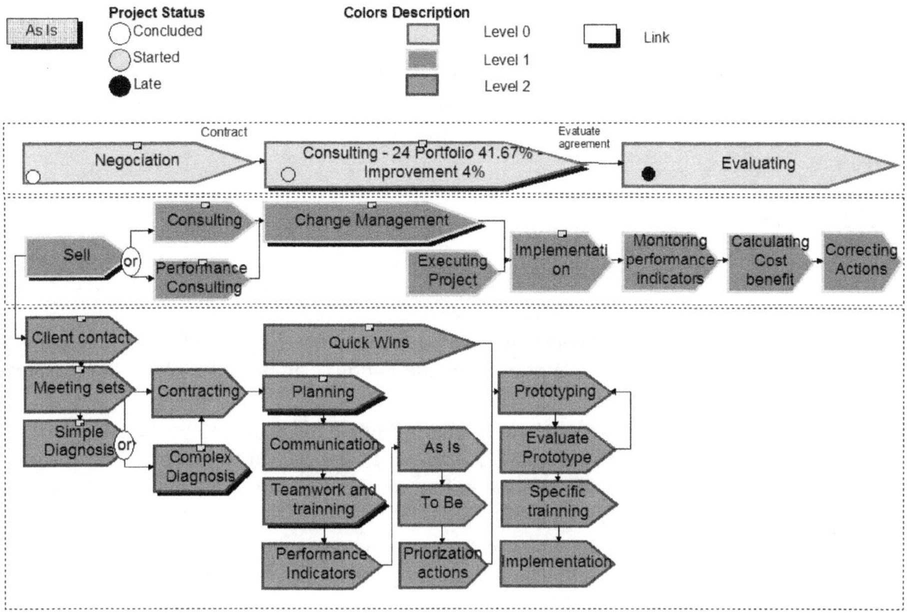

Fig. 2. High Performance Consultancy Projects' framework

Stage 8 - The framework implementation in consultancy has created a new function in consultancy, the architecture analysis. Today, the Board, the projects Office and the selling team take part of this competence and the framework's modification is authorized by performance and processes indicators.

5 Conclusion

This work emphasizes the importance of service specialization in organizations. From this consideration, the IBM model called Component Business Model (CBM®) was introduced. This model suggests that organizations can be decomposed into components that offer and demand services. Those components should be self-controlled and self-managed, although obeying central governance.

Governance's success depends on the quality of information from the organization. This fact has contributed to developing IT governance as a way of assuring that IT investments will generate value in the business.

IT strategy must be revised so as to fulfill this mission, taking into consideration the elements that allow IT alignment with business. As such, the main IT functionalities were introduced- Direct, Develop and Delivery.

From those considerations, the Component Business Model was revised, incorporating the performance levels concepts and establishing a criteria for IT alignment with business. Finally, an approach was introduced for the organization's decomposition that created an IT basic components map and a governance and management model, which was tested in a case study.

Finally, the GMC – Governance and Management Cycle was presented and introduced with a case study. The GMC represents the governance and management aspects, assessment of business results, strategy clarification and business model improvement through decision making procedures. The GMC cycle considers corporative governance necessities, business processes and information technology.

References

1. Bronzo, M.: Relacionamentos Colaborativos em Redes de Suprimentos. Revista de Administração de Empresas 44 (2004)
2. Kirkman, G.S., et al.: The Global Information Technology Report 2001-2002: Readiness for the Networked World. In: World Economic Forum: Commited to Improving the State of the World, Geneva (2002)
3. IBM: Component Business Modeling. IBM® Institute for Business Value (2004)
4. Taylor, F.W.: Scientific Management: Comprising Shop Management. In: The Principles of Scientific Management, Testimony before the Special House Committee. Harper & Brothers Publishers, New York (1947)
5. Woods Jr., T.: Fordismo, Toyotismo e Volvismo: os caminhos da indústria em busca do tempo perdido. Revista de Administração de Empresas 32(4), 6–18 (1992)
6. Cipolla, F.P.: Economia Política do Taylorismo, Fordismo e Teamwork. Revista de Economia Política 23(3) (2003)
7. Marochi, M.L.G.: Considerações Sobre os Modelos de Produção e a Psicologia do Trabalho. Revista FAE 5(1), 15–28 (2002)
8. Antunes, R., Alves, G.: As Mutações no Mundo do Trabalho na Era da Mundialização do Capital. Educ. Soc. 25(87), 335–351 (2004)
9. Celeste, J.L.: Especialização Flexível: uma alternativa promissora para o desenvolvimento econômico de regiões subdesenvolvidas. Revista de Administração de Empresas 33(6), 34–41 (1993)
10. Teixeira, F., Guerra, O.: Redes de Aprendizado em Sistemas Complexos de Produção. Revista de Administração de Empresas 42(4) (2002)
11. IBM: Component Business Models: Making Specialization Real. IBM® Institute for Business Value (2005)
12. The Open Group. TOGAFTM Version 9. Van Haren Publishing (2009), `http://www.opengroup.org/togaf`
13. Pelanda, M.L.: Modelos de Governança de Tecnologia da Informação adotados no Brasil: um estudo de casos múltiplos. 133 f. Dissertação de Mestrado em Administração, Universidade Metodista de São Paulo, São Bernardo do Campo (2006)
14. Van Grembergen, W.: Strategies for Information Technology Governance. Idea Group Publishing (2004)
15. Luftman, N.J.: Measure Your Business-IT Alignment. Optimize: Business execution for CIOs Magazine (2003)
16. Gibert, J.: The IT Management Status Quo and the 5 Year Challenge. IT Physician Heal Thyself (2003)
17. OGC (Office of Government Commerce). Business Perspective: The IS View on Delivering Services to the Business. The Stationary Office, United Kingdom (2004)
18. Betz, C.T.: Architecture and patterns for IT service management, resource planning and governance: making shoes for the Cobbler's children. Morgan Kaufman, USA (2007)

19. Ernest, M., Nisavic, J.M.: Adding value to the IT organization with components business model. International Business Machines Corporation, Estados Unidos (2007)
20. Molinaro, L.F.R., et al.: Governance and Management of Information Technology: Decomposing the Enterprise in Modular Building Blocks Based on Enterprise Architecture and Business Oriented Services. In: 11th Conference on Enterprise Information System, Portugal (2009)
21. Flaxer, D., Nigam, A., Vergo, J.: Using Component Business Modeling to Facilitate Business Enterprise Architecture and Business Services at the US Department of Defense. In: IEEE International Conference on e-Business Engineering, Beijing, pp. 755–760 (2005)
22. Rummler, G., Brache, A.P.: Melhores desempenhos das empresas. Makron Books, São Paulo (1994)
23. Berg, M.V.D., Steenbergen, M.V.: Building an enterprise architecture practice: Tools, Tips, Best Practices, Ready-to-Use Insights. Springer, Netherlands (2006)
24. Land, M.O., et al.: Enterprise architecture: creating value by informed governance. Springer, Berlin (2009)
25. Lankhorst, M., et al.: Enterprise architecture at work: modelling, communication and analysis. Springer, Berlin (2005)
26. Henderson, J.C., Venkatraman, N.: Strategic alignment: leveraging information technology for transforming organization. IBM Systems Journal 32 (1993)
27. Carter, S.: The new language of business. In: SOA & WEB 2.0. IBM Press, USA (2007)
28. Ramos, K.H.C., et al.: Enterprise Architecture Applied Towards Sustainable IT Governance. In: Teuteberg F; Gomez J.M. Corporate Environmental Management Information Systems: Advancements and Trends, IGI Global (2010)
29. AD&M Consultoria Empresarial. Modelo e Metodologia de Consultoria (2007), http://www.admconsultoria.com.br

Framework Based on Benefits Management and Enterprise Architecture

António Rodrigues and Henrique O'Neill

ISCTE-IUL
arodrigues.home@gmail.com,
henrique.oneill@iscte.pt

Abstract. The relationship between Information Technology and Business is something that has been growing over the years, materialized through investment increasing. IT investments typically have a negative connotation, as such companies have been seeking alternative models like Outsourcing, Managed Services or Cloud Computing. The aim of this paper is to inform a framework that aims to reconcile the benefits of IT Management Benefits who can give a different view of IT investments. On the other hand the advantage of having an Enterprise Architecture is to provide a guideline to the different projects.

Keywords: Investments, Benefits Management, Enterprise Architecture, Business, IT.

1 Introduction

Information Technology (IT) are today as an absolutely critical element for the economy and society in general. Is impossible ignores the dependence that businesses and anonymous user have towards IT. The heads of businesses when questioned no longer put into question the importance that IT has for the business, regardless of industry. In Accenture survey [3], result to the question: "Do you agree with these statements regarding IT's contribution to a high- performance business?". The result is positive in IT point of view, 82% of respondents think a high performance in the IT contributes directly to the business performance

This relationship was accentuated by virtue of globalization and increased competitiveness, IT must be able to respond to this new market dynamics. IT is also identified as a key element for economic recovery for many companies, as proved by a survey conducted by Accenture [1] "*72 per cent of business and IT executives have stated that their organizations now place more importance on the IT functions of their companies than they did before the financial crisis*"

1.1 Investment versus Productivity

All preponderance that IT has on business is reflected in a steadily increasing investment. A study made by Accenture [4] that projects planned investments in IT, from 2008 to 2012. It appears that despite the time restraint there is a growing investment. This concluded that managers in IT are an ally to recovery.

J.E. Quintela Varajão et al. (Eds.): CENTERIS 2010, Part II, CCIS 110, pp. 52–62, 2010.

When it is mentioned the term **IT investment** becomes almost impossible not to relate to productivity. The issue is not new, was first raised in the middle 80's, where investments have not yet assumed the proportions that they currently have. Robert Solow, Nobel Prize in Economics in 1987 said ironically: "*Can you see the computer age everywhere but not in the Productivity Statistics*", this statement came to be known as the **productivity paradox**. Despite the claim to have more than twenty years, the problem remains, and others authors continues to reflect on the theme, especially Diana Farrell and Michael Porter.

The interest of Diana Farrell [2] went so far to investigate whether the fact that the indicators productivity and IT investment had risen at the same time during the 90's, were actually structurally related or was it just a statistic coincidence. In this study it is concluded that the increase in productivity is due primarily to an increase in competitiveness, which forced managers to innovate in management methods used.

After all IT is important, but they are the primary source of competitiveness, then the essence of the new economy associated with higher productivity growth, is in the cycle: (Competition → Innovation → Productivity Growth) and not in IT itself only "*Firms Must Understand That it alone is almost never a true differentiator.*"

The thought that is not enough to invest in IT to increase productivity levels is also supported by Michael Porter [6], which reflect on the Strategies and the Internet, has highlight that companies must continue to invest in their traditional strengths as the stake in unique products with a strong knowledge of them, strong customer relationships. In this context the Internet has to be seen as a means and not the purpose of strengthening the advantages mentioned.

1.2 Benefits Management

IT investments continue to remain doubts as to the expected return, according to the authors quoted above it is concluded that IT must be seen as a means and not an end. It is known from the outset that there is no single formula and each case is unique. So John Ward identifies a model of benefits management where companies can inspire and adapt to its reality. According to the author *benefits management is a process of organization and management that allows the potential benefits arising from the use of information technology in organizations are achieved.*

Different assessments made by the author with a group of company's leads to the conclusion that the IT projects that were supposed to bring benefits to business, do not always meet expectations, some of the reasons are identified in Table 1.

Table 1. Survey of IS investment appraisal

	YES	NO
Is IT investment appraisal seen as important by business managers?	55%	45%
Do you have am effective investment appraisal process?	22%	78%
Are business managers adequately involved in IT investment appraisal?	30%	70%
Does the appraisal process consider the implications of business changes?	10%	90%
Do people making decisions understand the business cases?	25%	75%
What % of projects deliver the benefits that justified the investment	27%	73%

Becomes urgent to create a process for evaluating investments, which can address the interests of business managers and responsible for IT. Through a program undertaken by the Information System Research Center (ISRC) belonging to the Cranfield School Management, consolidated in the years 2004 and 2007. The model developed to John Ward and colleagues was implemented in organizations located in Europe, USA and China, which aims to reverse this trend.

2 Framework Based on Benefits Management and Enterprise Architecture

It is intended that this article has the added value of presenting a framework centered on the combination of components management benefits for investments in IT and Enterprise Architecture.

By combining these two components are the necessary conditions to achieve a strategy in the always difficult relationship between Information Technology and Business.

This method of managing such benefits will be developed in detail later in the article. The import retain for now is a new way materialized in the development of projects that are undertaken in the company if the management of benefits we seek to achieve greater alignment with business and higher rates of productivity, Enterprise Architecture is bring the thread needed to compile each project, ensuring that the technical solution of each is as defined policies by Enterprise Architecture.

As will be detailed in the component Enterprise Architecture, Information Systems business has changed, companies have sought new solutions to their technology architectures, while a very recent past is not predominant calls traditional architectures in which companies had teams IT, equipment, etc. Other trends have been gaining space in terms of market share to bet on alternative models such as Outsourcing, Managed Services and Cloud Computing each of his way intended to represent new ways of managing IT, having one common goal to reduce costs and increased levels of performance.

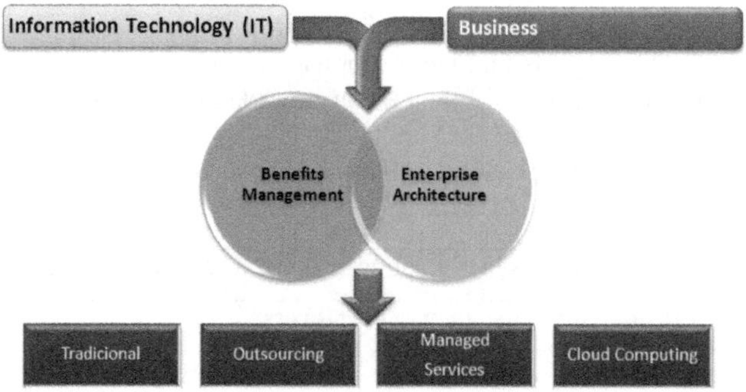

Fig. 1. The Framework should be interpreted by layer, first layer consists of two important components in each company as are the Business and IT, which aims to align through the combination of Enterprise Architecture and Benefits Management, which constitute the second layer, the third layer is made possible by the models to manage IT

The need to sometimes be combined in a single information system in various models, has been giving importance to the need that exists in creating an Enterprise Architecture that can unify models increasingly heterogeneous.

2.1 Benefits Management

The management component of benefits, aims to provide companies with techniques to help manage the projects of IT with the business. Trying to introduce a new mentality, leaving behind the idea that IT projects are managed differently and are always associated with expenditure without the expected benefit.

The model proposed here, although along the lines of John Ward, has its own particularities that give it its originality. The model is divided into two layers, the first dedicated to the management portfolio of projects and the latter more concerned with managing the projects themselves.

2.1.1 Projects Portfolio Management

In vision of Projects Portfolio Management the projects are split into two types according to its nature and motivations:

- **Innovation Based Projects:** These are projects aimed at innovation is the availability of a new product or new process aimed at achieving particular purpose, such as increased market share in a given segment;
- **Problem Based Projects:** Projects that aim to solve problems, increase levels of efficiency, provide systems with higher levels of security or compliance;

As illustrated in Fig. 2 the target component Projects Portfolio Management is to get an overview of all projects carried out, irrespective of their nature. This way its possible a correct relationship and priority of projects and get to combine the inputs and outputs of each project, as shown in figure there are projects that begin to depend on the finalization of others.

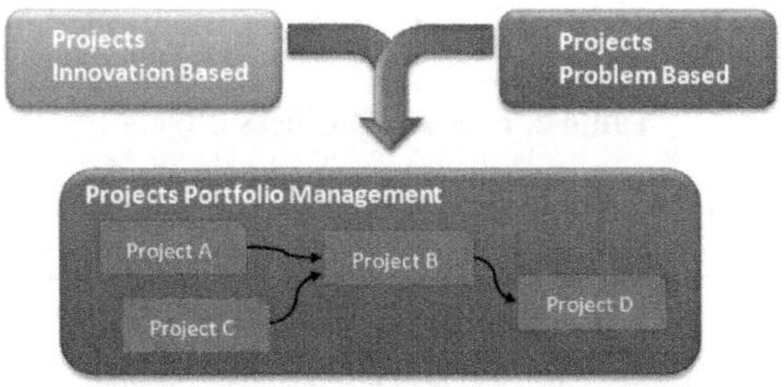

Fig. 2. The figure intends to illustrate the "activity" of the PPM, the projects profiled according to their nature and managed as a whole in order to achieve dynamic inputs and outputs of each project

2.1.2 Benefits Management Focused in Projects

The management of benefits when applied to projects is not intended to be a new way to manage projects, they should continue to be managed by following the methods that companies find it more convenient for its reality. The proposed Framework is intended as an aid to projects aimed at transmitting higher levels of frame with the business, aligning with the architecture, a new way to conduct business case, ending with an evaluation of results and future prospects.

All of the above advantages are organized by the six phases that constitute the framework and that will be detailed below (Fig. 3):

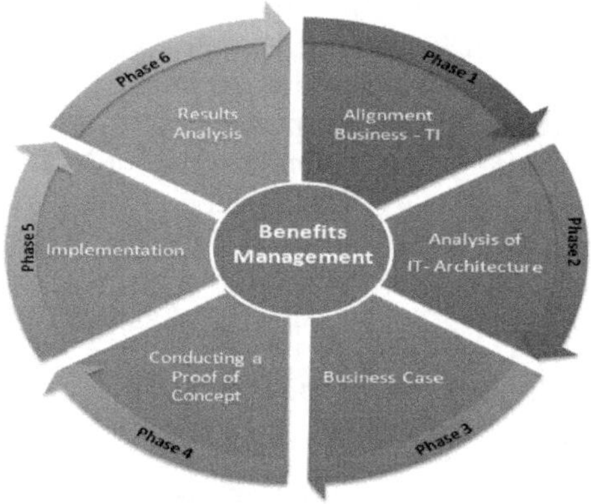

Fig. 3. The proposed management benefits applied to projects presented here, is divided into 6 distinct phases

Phase #1

As has been referred throughout the article, there is a constant concern about the investment necessary to realize a particular project. The investment term requires an positive return over the invested capital. The aim of the first phase, is making the alignment of the project against the business and its investment, is based on answering the questions:

- **Why?:** Why is being able to undertake the investment;
  With the answer to question **why**, the project is intended to define the business drivers, these can be based on various sources, as mentioned in Table 2.

Table 2. Kinds of business drivers

Infrastructure	Related developments in the field of IT, as an example a project to carry out an infrastructure that enables greater mobility for employees
Context	Projects aimed at providing the company works according to a directive magnet an oversight body, such as the Bank of Portugal for companies or organizations in the financial sector
Result-Oriented	Projects aimed at achieving specific purpose, such as cost reduction, integration of a set of features to make it possible to provide a new service

To complete the answer to **why**, there must be a clear and commonly agreed by all stakeholders in the process, which aims.

- **What?:** What are the benefits that the organization hopes to obtain;
  After defining the objectives, duly supported by an investment, it becomes possible to combine the benefits in terms of business to be achieved. It is understood by the benefit of business, an advantage the company as a whole, or a specific group, you

can withdraw after completion of the project [5]. Projects and investments are not consequential may deplete the standpoint of IT, they must represent an added value in terms of affirmation of the organization.

- **How?:** How do I change the combination of business and IT changes can achieve these benefits;
  After defining the business drivers and benefits from the standpoint of business, it is necessary to identify factors that facilitate change and the expected changes to the business.

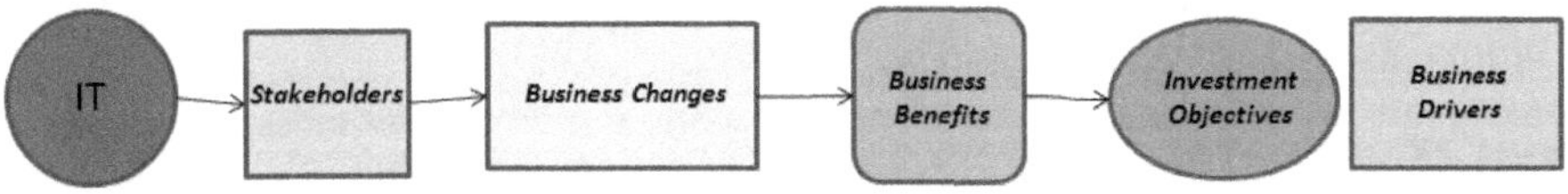

Fig. 4. Through the **Benefits and Dependence Network**, it becomes possible to visualize graphically the dependence between the various actors in the project

The net benefit has the power to achieve aggregate and relate to, not just those involved in the project but also the objectives to be achieved and the expected benefits, without losing sight of the business drivers that were in their origin. A document to be followed during project lifetime, assuming vital importance in the last phase, where it will be confronted with the results indeed obtained

Phase #2

The phase 2 is intended for alignment of necessity from the viewpoint of architecture-specific project, with the enterprise architecture principles adopted by the company. This stage is even more important when we choose to solutions where the internal information system, must interact with an external provider of a service.

Therefore it is suggested an integration architecture that suggests a set of principles to be followed.

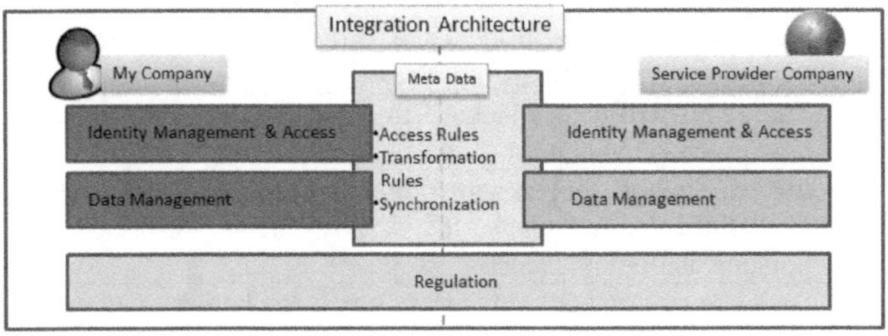

Fig. 5. Architectural Drawing Integration, where we see the integration of two information systems, (My Company) and enterprise service provider (Service Provider Company)

Then the key points of the integration architecture:

- **Identity and Access Management:** Implementation of mechanisms for authentication and authorization, to regulate who accesses the data and how is it that makes it. Always with one objective in mind, the fact that there is a need to access data that is external to the company geographically should be transparent to the business processes.

- **Data Management:** Why data management is defined as everything that is related to access to them. Data access should be preferred to use Web Services thus becomes transparent to the applications which the data repository to be used.
- **Regulation:** Ensuring all legal requirements are met, the measurement of service levels (SLA), providing audit preferably carried out by specialized companies to ensure the consistency of the system as a whole.
- **Meta-Data:** Dictates the rules of transformation and adaptation necessary for two different systems can communicate.

Phase #3

In order to reverse the trend and somehow prove that IT investments that bring in added value for companies and organizations. There has been a concern in measuring the success of investments. The most common form of carrying out the assessment of an IT Investment is by making a business case [7]. In most cases it is done around the calculation of ROI (**R**eturn **O**n **I**nvestment).

Calculating the ROI has a gap, which is the failure to include the time variable. Then came the need to introduce financial indicators, where the time variable is taken into account. Such as NPV (**N**et **P**resent **V**alue), by bringing together the different indicators it is possible to classify the projects in terms of financial and give it as a priority to implement them. As projects should not summarize the financial point of view, they intend to follow a method based on Table 3, which uses a matrix where all variables are important for proper evaluation of the project.

Companies that take decisions on projects based solely on financial variables, probably will chose only departmental projects instead of implementing projects or cross-sectional basis for the whole company, which may be critical to its future.

Table 3. "New" business case

	New things	Different ways	Stop doing old things
Financial	By applying a cost-price or a different financial formula, it becomes possible to build a financially benefit		
Quantifiable	There was sufficient evidence to make it possible to make a prediction of how much is the benefit of the changes		
Measurable	It is expected to apply a way of measuring performance. But it is not possible to estimate how much the improvements will be the end of the implementation of changes		
Observable	By having a large dose of subjectivity is the hardest. Agreed criteria are used by individuals or specific groups, which based on their experience, will decide to what extent the objective was achieved		

Phase #4

As mentioned in phase 2, when there is need to interact with external companies, other care must be taken. From the technical point of view cited in phase 2 through integration architecture, from the standpoint of quality of service, should be completed a proof of concept before full adoption of the solution.

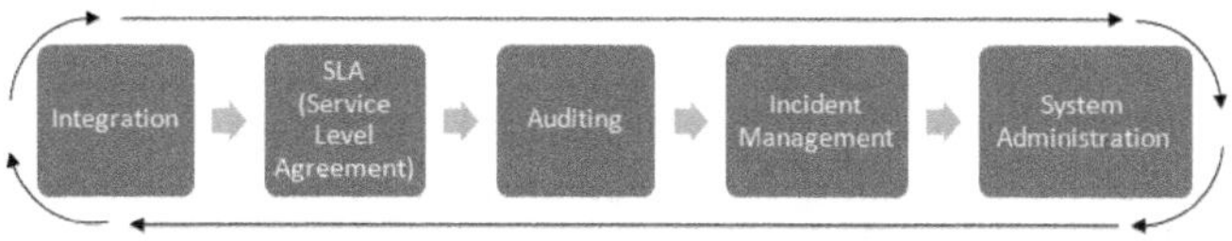

Fig. 6. Steps to be taken into account during the proof of concept

The Fig. 6 shows the cycle that must meet proof of concept, it should only be taken as completed when they are given all the answers to the points:

- **Integration:** Identify and test levels of integration with applications "residents" should be measured the level and ease of integration with the existing information system.
- **Lever Service Agreement:** An important component when there is a relationship between entities is the service levels agreed between them. Therefore mechanisms should be introduced to enable the entity client can assess to what extent they are not being met or agreed levels.
- **Auditing:** Evaluation of mechanisms for authentication and authorization agreed. Verify to what extent that those mechanisms are effective.
- **Incident Management:** It is understood by management of incidents, assess how the service provider manages incidents related to the application.
- **System Administration:** For management tasks, means a set of more specialized tasks in order to ascertain the capacity of the service provider had to meet this task.

Phase #5

In the implementation phase it is important that the applications and services are classified as to its importance and the company's strategy will consider whether or not the development of specific application to the prospect of cloud computing, according to the example of Fig. 7.

The above table is not eternal and there are variables that can change an application of quadrant, such as technological changes or changes in business.

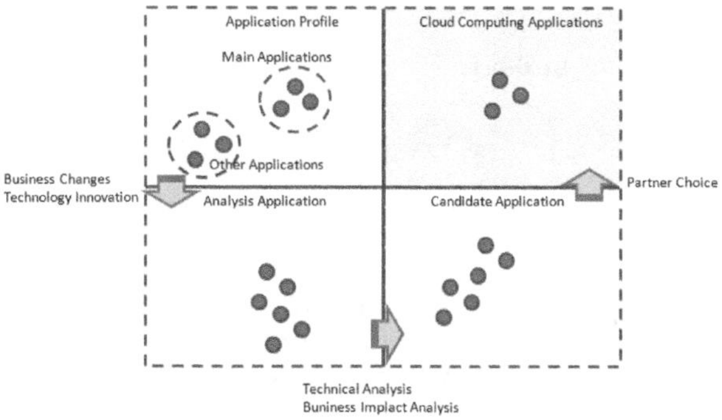

Fig. 7. Table of example classification and evolution of applications in the way "traditional" for the cloud computing concept

Phase #6

For stage 6 is reserved for analysis of results, the main objective of this phase is compiled the results coming from previous stages of the framework.

This phase has its importance, is through analysis of data collected is able to ascertain whether the model is to match the expectations.

2.2 Enterprise Architecture

The importance of enterprise architecture has gained importance due to the complexity and heterogeneity of information systems. Making the analogy with the construction of a garage where you can possibly think of will start build without having architecture. The construction of a building will be unthinkable not to have a well defined architecture. With information systems the process is identical. The aim of this paper is not to find alternatives to the Zachman Framework or others as TOGAF (**T**he **O**pen **G**roup **A**rchitecture **F**ramework). The concept followed in this article of Enterprise Architecture is the logical organization between business processes and technologies of information reflecting the requirements of integration and unification [8]. The way to materialize the concepts magnet Architecture business is through the IT architecture is a more detailed architecture that addresses four types of architecture:

- **Business Processes:** activities or tasks identified by the responsible business as the most important;
- **Data or information:** definitions standards so that data can be accessed by multi-applications
- **Applications:** development of common interfaces for communication between them to be facilitated
- **Technology:** common services infrastructure and development of standard technology

The architecture business despite being in a more conceptual level is largely influenced by the IT architecture, as shown in Fig. 9 where we conducted a historical overview of different architectures in the short history of IT. In each technological leap that happened, there were both opportunities for business processes.

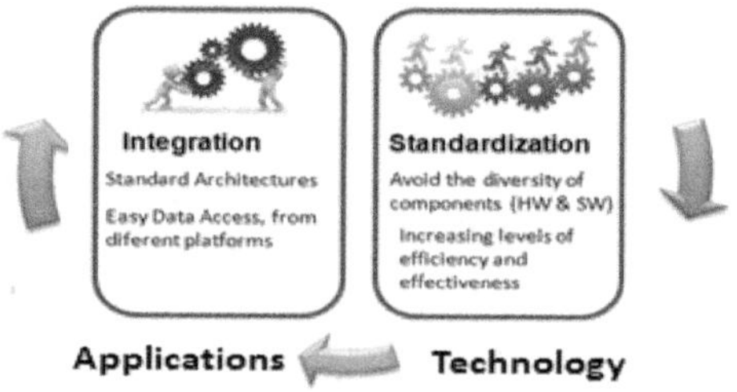

Fig. 8. The basis of the enterprise architecture concept followed here, is the pillar integration that enables the subsystems to communicate with each other, for such it is important that data can flow between the various levels of the company's decision. Another pillar is the Standardization trying to ensure the uniformity of SW and HW.

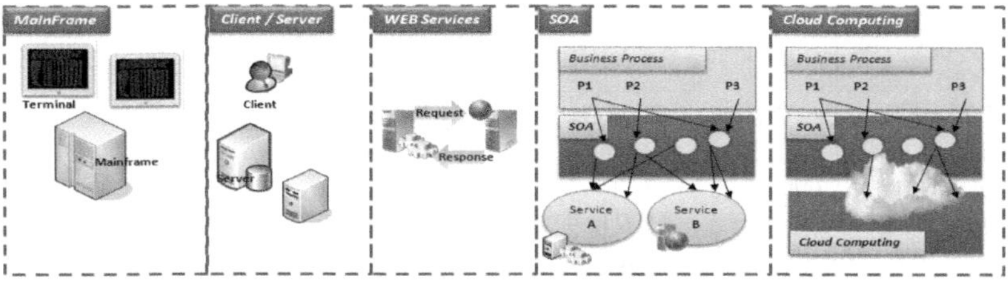

Fig. 9. The figure represents the evolution of IT architectures, from the mainframe, through Client / Server, Web Services, SOA (Service Oriented Architecture) and finally the adoption by Cloud Computing

Since the older systems based on a mainframe to the cloud just computing passed a few years, however, represents a shift in the thinking of those who manage information technology.

The importance of enterprise architecture is to provide companies with a strategy with regard to IT that prepare them to adapt the management model best suited to your reality. And most likely in the near future is that companies do not hold a single management model, is the traditional one, either the cloud or the other, the wager must be at hybrid models that we have an information system composed of several pieces software from various sources the benefit of enterprise architecture will homogenize them and more standard as possible.

3 Conclusion

In a troubled season so as we live it is important that the management of information technology will not walk drift, so the implementation of a framework such as that suggested seems appropriate.

As is suggested that a new way of managing benefits for IT investments that although inspired by the model of J. Ward, has unique features like Integration Component Architecture (Phase 2) for key projects that interact with elements in the cloud, innovate with respect to the test of concept (Phase 4) and creates a profile of the company with regards applications (Phase 5).

In relation to Enterprise Architecture, has to justify its existence, without falling into a defined model, identifies basic elements that must be guaranteed with the increasing.

The combination of these two concepts is essential if the benefits management teaches investing in order to bring added value to enterprise architecture brings the thread to the various projects.

References

1. Accenture Global Survey Foresees Rise in IT Investment, USA (March 2010), http://itechaudit.com/news/accenture-global-survey-foresees-rise-in-it-investments-in-2010.html

2. Farrell, D.: The Real New Economy. Harvard Business Review (October 2003)
3. In Pursuit of High Performance: A Multi-Sector Global Study of IT, Accenture 2006 (2006)
4. IT Cloud Services Forecast – 2008, 2012: A Key Driver of New Growth
5. Ward, J., Daniel, E.: Benefits Management – Delivering Value from IS& IT Investments. Wiley, England (May 2007)
6. Porter, M.E.: Strategy and the Internet. Harvard Business Review, USA (March 2001)
7. Ross, J.W., Beath, C.M.: Beyond the business case: New approaches to IT investment. MIT Sloan Management Review (2002)
8. Ross, W.J., Weill, P., Robertson, C.D.: Enterprise Architecture As A Strategy
9. Weill, P., Ross, W.: IT Savvy

Value Model for Enterprise and Process Architectures Alignment Verification

Carlos Páscoa[1, 2], Nuno Belo[1], and José Tribolet[2, 3]

[1] Department of University Education, Portuguese Air Force Academy, Sintra, Portugal
[2] Department of Information Systems and Computer Science,
Instituto Superior Técnico, Technical University of Lisbon, Portugal
[3] CODE - Center for Organizational Design & Engineering,
INOV, Rua Alves Redol 9, Lisbon, Portugal
cjpascoa@gmail.com, nunobelo7@gmail.com, jose.tribolet@inesc.pt

Abstract. The Portuguese Air Force is making an effort to looking at problems related to the inadequacy of information systems to help managers in attaining business objectives in rigid hierarchical structures.

To solve the problem the Air Force initiated, in 2009, the (still ongoing) identification of its business processes in order to determine the organizational "AS IS" state, essential to determining the "TO BE" state.

Simultaneously, the Air Force is studying concepts related to enterprise architecture whilst trying to deepen the relationship between enterprise architecture concepts, such as mission, vision, goals, objectives, strategy, tactics, policy rules, business rules and process architecture.

In this context, considering important to create and identify a way to validate the consistency between business objectives and business processes, one would propose the creation of a value matrix, representing objectives and processes, and associate a set of rules for its creation, update and validation.

Keywords: Enterprise Architecture, Process Architecture, Business Objectives, Business Processes, Value Matrix, Value Model, Management Objectives.

1 Introduction

Organizations have been subject to profound changes due to the growing competition that has been seen over the years. Factors such as market uncertainty, development of marketing strategy and the increase of supply urge companies to act quickly in order to survive. The traditional way in which organizations used to be viewed is therefore inappropriate in the evolving world we live in today.

Along with changes in organizational environment, one can observe on one hand, the development of theories of management and, on the other, the technological development of Information Technology (IT). Over the years, various methods, tools and standards that support the process of decision making have emerged, providing a new way of looking at organizations whilst taking into account the final product as well as customer satisfaction. The discipline of Organizational Engineering (OE)

J.E. Quintela Varajão et al. (Eds.): CENTERIS 2010, Part II, CCIS 110, pp. 63–72, 2010.

contains within it the knowledge of those methods, tools and standards. In the OE perspective, the desired result is not only the outcome of the sum of different parts, but the benefit of the efficient coordination of all the factors outlined before [1].

All these changes, inevitably, lead to the new direction that the Portuguese Air Force is taking. Access to information in real time as well as knowledge of the organization by its employees, are just one example of the objectives that companies today look to achieve. To attain it, IT, Business Objectives (BO) and Business Processes (BP) must be perfectly aligned.

One of the purposes of the existence of Information Systems Architecture (ISA) is that Information Systems (IS) meet the objectives for which they were created [2]. The IS must be perfectly aligned with BO and provide the information necessary to BP that occur in the organization. The alignment of architectures that constitute the ISA has been studied by OE. For this work the alignment between the Enterprise Architecture (EA), where BO stands, and Process Architecture (BA), where BP stands, is essential to determine the consistency between objectives and processes.

Creating effective, flexible and dynamic organizational methods to allowing the Air Force to adapt to its outside environment entails a set of activities, including the identification of BP. In an organization, a desired result is achieved more efficiently when activities and related resources are managed as a process [3]. In this context, it is considered that BP must be perfectly aligned with BO they are designed to achieve.

It is then desirable that, through a simple form, one may able to identify which business processes achieve the objectives for which they were created. We considered the possibility of creating a simple and intuitive matrix, allowing for this identification and subsequent validation.

Quivy & Campenhoudt [4] suggest a methodology for research, applied to social sciences, which supports the existence of several stages. At the first stage a starting question (SQ) must be set and auxiliary questions (AQ) with hypotheses (H) that may validate the answers. Accordingly, the starting question is: "SQ. How to create a value matrix that crosses business processes with the objectives for which they were created, making it an effective tool that supports decision making?"

The questions were divided as follows:

- AQ1. How to create the value matrix that crosses the business processes with the objectives for which they were created?
- AQ2. What is the best way to check the consistency between BO and BP?
- AQ3. What rules are needed to create and update the matrix?
- AQ4. Does the value matrix check the consistency between EA (BO) and PA?
- AQ5. Is the value matrix an effective tool for decision making support?

The assumptions built for verification of the questions are:

- AQ1-H1. In order to create the value matrix it is necessary to cross EA (related to BO) and PA (related to BP).
- AQ2-H2. The BO and BP must be related in the way that BP achieve the BO for which they were created. For this, a set of requirements and rules, that govern this relationship, will need to be defined.

- AQ3-H3. To create and update the value matrix a set of requirements and rules will be defined.
- AQ4-H4. The value matrix crosses EA and PA, therefore it is considered that it can be used to verify the consistency between these two architectures.
- AQ5-H5. It is considered that the matrix of value can be an effective tool for decision-making support.

2 Alignment of Architectures

The alignment of enterprise architecture with the process architecture assumes, as already mentioned, an essential dimension to the context of the problem. It is therefore essential to review and deepen the concepts of information systems architecture, business processes and their dimension.

2.1 Information Systems Architecture

IT has become inevitable in the dynamic and often turbulent environment in which organizations are inserted. While in the past, managers could delegate, ignore and avoid decisions based on IT, is now impossible in most sectors and industries [5].

The purpose of ISA is to create a map of IT and business processes and a set of governance principles that allow for the discussion of business strategy and how it can be expressed by the IT [6].

ISA must be constructed by observing the following four architectures [2]:

1. Enterprise Architecture (EA), at high level, where there is a defined strategy, goals and objectives.
2. Process Architecture (PA), which can be understood as structuring the processes in management lines and value chain setting the required levels.
3. Information Architecture (IA), which identifies where the important information to the business is and how to access it [6].
4. Application Architecture (AA), which is a map of the relations of different software applications of a company [6].

For the context of this work it is important to highlight EA and PA, as well as the relationship between them.

2.2 Definition of Business Processes

The Business Process can be understood as being a set of activities that are performed in coordination in organizational and technical environments. These activities together achieve a business objective [7]. It can be said that BP have the following characteristics:

- To meet a specific and well defined objective that can be translated into added value for a particular customer;
- Use and/or produce transversal artifacts, along the set of activities in accordance with a responsible stakeholder.

2.3 Dimensions of Business Processes

The multi-dimensional representations of EA were the target of Mario Maçarico's (2007) study where he concluded that: "*The association between dimensions allows us to represent architecture through the links of interest to a stakeholder*" [8].

According to this author, the conceptual layer of the Zachman framework makes it possible to relate the interrogatives of this framework with the dimensions of business processes. To this end, it is necessary to question the organization when setting business processes with the following:

- "What?", should indicate which informational entities are created or consumed by the process;
- "Where?" represents the dimension of the location of the process, such as organizational units or geographical locations;
- "How?" is the basis for the business process indicating how a certain activity is performed;
- "Who?" answers to which actors are involved in the process;
- "When?" indicates the frequency that the process occurs (once a day or three times a year);
- "Why?" explains the objective and the reason for the business process to exist.

The questions "Who?" and "Where?" are related to the way that actors should be assigned to work sites. The "Why" question is considered to be the most important for the scope of this work since it is related to business objectives.

2.4 Scope

To know clearly what business objectives are, it is important to understand how they arise. Chaplin (2003) identifies two stages before the business objectives: the business problem and business solution [9].

The business problem can be understood as a concern for the organization, for example: the organization is losing business because the competitors are cheaper; the customers are not buying the products because the customer support service is not good enough; the product of the organization is not as good as its competitors.

In order to respond to business problems business solutions arise. For example: to achieve greater market share, make customers more satisfied, reduce the cost of manufacturing, speed up order processing.

To achieve the business solutions business goals have to be defined. A single definition of a clear target that must be reached to satisfy a business solution and effectively resolve a business problem, exemplified by [9]: profit increase of 10% by next quarter, reducing the rate of employee's turnover by 15%, ensuring that at least 95% of orders are processed in less than 2 minutes.

Another approach made to the origin of the objectives is that of The Business Rules Group (BRG) [10], the Business Motivation Model (BMM) (2007). For the BRG, objectives and goals, despite being considered "desirable results" are different things. Goals, being related to strategy, are a declaration of a state or condition of the organization that must be achieved by appropriate means. Goals contribute to achieving the vision of an organization and must be quantified by objectives.

Objectives are a business target that should be measurable and defined in time through their achievement is reached goals. Tactics are defined towards the achieving of objectives. The understanding of objective according to the BRG is consistent with the criterion "SMART" popularly known in the industry: Specific, Measurable, Attainable, Relevant, and Time-based [10].

3 Model Construction

For the construction of the assumptions in which the model developed is based, we revisit the relationship between business objectives and business processes by presenting the context of the problem and the rules for establishing the value matrix.

3.1 Relation between Business Objectives and Business Process

In BMM it is believed that in an organization "Means", "Ends", "Influencers", "Assessment" and "Potential Impact" should be clearly identified. All must be aligned and should be taken into account when managers define the "Ends" and the "Means" to achieve them. In a simple way strategy, which is a mean to achieve the vision, can be translated into the path or direction that must be followed to achieve the goals, which, in turn, can be divided into objectives. It is considered that business objectives must be defined following the SMART rules.

The relationship between objectives and business processes has been the subject of discussion in the preceding paragraph. For the scope of this work, and to be used by the Air Force to validate the consistency between both, it is considered that the business processes must achieve business objectives for which they were created.

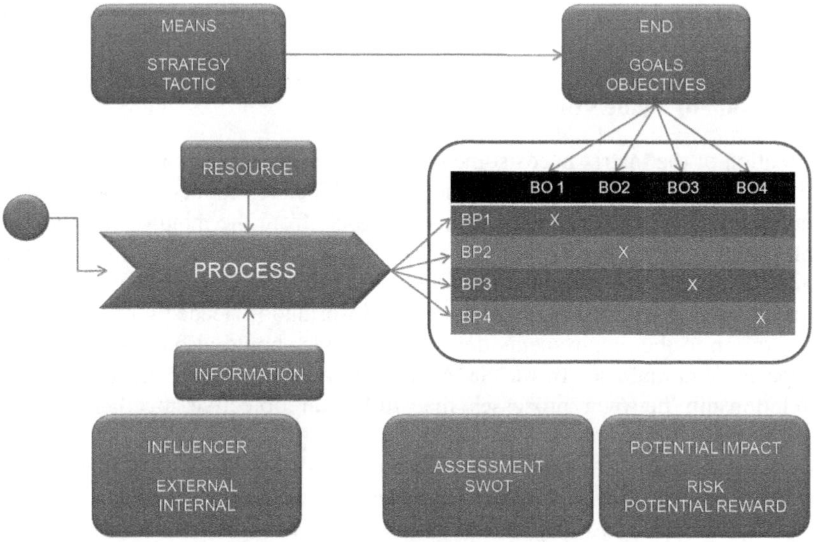

Fig. 1. Context of the study (source: [11])

The main aim of this study is the relationship between objectives and business processes and their treatment according to the form of a matrix. Figure 1 depicts in red the context in which the study is inserted.

Taking the organization as a whole, where all points are considered important, the matrix comes from the crossing of the business objectives with business processes, which, in a simpler form, means that the objectives belonging to enterprise architecture are to be crossed for consistency with processes that belong to process architecture.

Both architectures (EA and PA) crossed in this matrix, for the scope of this work, are components of Information Systems Architecture, previously discussed in Section 2. Although business objectives are only a small part of EA, we consider that all the remaining elements, like goals, strategy for example, are interrelated. In fact, business objectives are defined in function of the goals, which, in turn, come from vision.

Since the business process is used to attain business objectives, PA can be understood as structuring the processes in management lines and value chain defining the required levels. Therefore, it is essential to find if the business processes attain the corresponding business objectives.

It is considered that the processes used in the matrix must be defined in the PA and objectives should be set in EA, ensuring a closer alignment with the business. The two architectures must also be aligned with the EA model. The example of BMM that indicates how the objectives, goals, strategies and vision should relate has been given. The study of Mendes, et al. [12] is considered important for the creation of this document; this author looks at the issue of objectives modeling, especially in the requirements for the creation of the matrix discussed below.

It is also important to state that the method proposed here has not been to put to practice yet. However, it will be used, when the time arrives, to validate the consistency between the Air Force BO and BP.

For the master thesis validation [11] (2010), however, the higher level BO and higher level BP were used.

3.2 Creation of Value Matrix

The creation of the matrix needs some requirements in order to be considered a useful tool in the organization. The requirements for objectives modeling, identified as essential are [12]: i) to capture all the business goals from the mind of stakeholders, ii) to link business processes with business goals they achieve iii) to identify the metrics and indicators that provide means of controlling the degree of fulfillment of objectives iv) to identify processes that produce the information needed for the indicators.

In addition to the requirements defined above we should also consider the following aspects: i) compliance of the SMART criteria by objectives, ii) identification of the relationship between processes that fulfill an objective together; associating control points.

After checking the requirements for the creation of the matrix, it is then possible to move on to its instantiation. Companies have associated business processes and business goals. Given the growing need that today companies have to be agile, it is quite likely that business goals and business processes change with certain frequency. It is then important to discuss the concepts of the existing and the new.

For the purpose of this study existing objectives and processes, have been considered all running in the organization before the start of the verification of business objectives, if necessary. The new objectives are defined in the act of developing a new strategy, which is initially set on goals and then, on objectives as explained above. New business processes are needed to achieve new objectives. For the instantiation of the matrix a simple four steps solution has been defined:

1. Identify the business objectives that were previously defined by the stakeholders and transcribe them according to SMART criteria previously discussed;
2. Identify the existing business processes and business objectives they achieve, and new business processes necessary to achieve new goals;
3. Identify the relationship between new business objectives, existing business objectives, and new business processes and existing business processes;
4. Moving data to a matrix.

An example it is then given of what would be an initial matrix that crosses five Business Objectives (BO) with six Business Processes (BP). In order to allow for a better assessment of its content and therefore a global view of company business, we grouped the processes that achieve the same objectives by highlighting them, as shown in Figure 2.

	BO 1	BO 2	BO 3	BO 4	BO 5
BP 1	X				
BP 2	X				
BP 3		X			
BP 4			X		
BP 5				X	
BP 6					X

Fig. 2. Initial Value Matrix (source: [11])

3.3 Cases for Diagnosis

There are situations, called cases for diagnosis, which can occur when creating the matrix, that need to be verified.

Case 1 - A Process that achieves several Objectives
One of the cases that is important to diagnose is when a process achieves several objectives. In this case the following steps should be followed:

1. Check if there has been no lapse in completing the matrix, such as the accidental duplication of business objectives eliminating possible redundancies. If the situation is not resolved move on to the next step.
2. Verify that all business processes are inserted in to the matrix and if there is any other more appropriate to the objective. If the situation is not resolved move on the next step.
3. Since there are business processes that contribute to the achievement of various objectives it is necessary to analyze the interdependence and complementarity between them checking their derivables and the resources they consume.

Case 2 – A Process that does not achieve any Objective

In the case of a business process that does not achieve any business objective some aspects should be noted. This situation may occur during the construction of the initial matrix. In this situation we suggest the following steps:

1. Verify if, by mistake, has been left out some objective that the process achieves. If the answer is positive, point out the objective(s) in question. Otherwise go on to the next step;
2. Verify if, by mistake, some business goal has been forgotten. If it has been forgotten, insert the objective and verify its consistency with the process. If you have not forgotten any objective or the objective you introduced is not consistent with the process in question, go to the next step;
3. Eliminate business process.

Case 3 – The Objective is not achieved by means of any Process

When you set new goals in an enterprise it is possible that none of the existing processes achieve those objectives. In this situation we suggest the following steps:

1. Check if there was no error in filling in the matrix, it is possible that one of the processes that achieve the objective may not have been signed. If the problem is not resolved go to the next step;
2. Verify the importance of the objective. If this is not an important objective remove it from the matrix, otherwise proceed to next step;
3. Create processes that achieve the objective. Mechanisms that allow the objective to be accomplished should be established; because the objective was considered essential for the organization. One recommend a "to be" approach where are defined all business objectives and the creation of a new matrix starting the verification of changes that may occur with the introduction of a new business process.

Case 4 - Objective achieved by several Processes

Another situation to diagnose is when there is an objective that is accomplished by several processes. It is considered a frequent situation in a company, not being necessarily harmful. For the resolution of this case we suggest the following steps:

1. Check if there was some mistake in filling in the matrix, eliminating possible repeated processes if the problem is not resolved, go to the next step;
2. Carry out the division of the objectives so that each new objective is only achieved by a business process.

Naturally, it can be the case that one business objective is achieved by several business processes and it is even designed like that. In this situation, the business processes should be compared for precedence and complementarity.

4 Conclusion

In order to create a value matrix that allows the validation of consistency between objectives and business processes we developed an appropriate model that contains a set of rules and steps. The model was applied to the objectives and business processes of the Portuguese Air Force, and identified as a set of questions (Q) that would allow its validation (V).

1. Q1 - How to create the value matrix that crosses the business processes with the objectives for which they were created?
   V1 - By crossing Enterprise Architecture (related to objectives) and Process Architecture (related processes) it is possible to create the matrix that crosses objectives with the business processes that achieve them. This hypothesis is considered validated.
2. Q2 - How to check the consistency between objectives and business processes?
   V2 - For the value matrix to be considered useful it is necessary to know the exact way objectives and business processes relate. It is considered that the processes achieve the objectives for which they were created. It is also considered that the objectives should be divided into activities that can be accomplished by processes. Considering this a set of requirements for the objectives and business processes were defined so that they could be treated in a matrix. This hypothesis is considered validated.
3. Q3 - What rules are needed to create and update the matrix?
   V3 - To create the matrix a set of requirements and rules have been defined in paragraph 3. These requirements and rules permit the creation and updating of the value matrix. This hypothesis is considered validated
4. Q4 - Does the value matrix check the consistency between Enterprise Architecture and the Process Architecture?
   V4 - As the matrix of value crosses objectives (defined in Enterprise Architecture) and processes (as defined in Process Architecture), it is considered that this may be a tool for verifying the consistency between these two architectures. The hypothesis is considered validated.
5. Q5 - Is the value matrix an effective tool for decision making support?
   V5 - The value matrix deals with two fundamental aspects of any organization: business processes and objectives. Relating these two concepts in the form of a matrix gives an business overview, which can be considered useful for both managers and for the rest of the employees. This hypothesis is considered validated.

Once the hypothesis is validated, it is possible to answer the central question or questions of departure:

How to create a value matrix that crosses business processes with the objectives for which they were created, making it an effective tool that supports decision making?

The answer to the central issue is not direct and must take into account a number of factors. In order to be considered an effective tool that supports decision making it is necessary for the matrix to be an integral part of the organization. The objectives should then be defined by the EA and the processes by the PA, being necessary processes and objectives to have certain characteristics that enable its treatment by means of a matrix. When these assumptions are true, it is considered that the value matrix can be an effective tool in supporting decision-making.

References

1. Magalhães, R., Rito, A.: White Paper on Organizational and Design Engineering. In: Center for Organizational and Design Engineering, Lisboa (2009)
2. Sousa, P.: Notes from classes of Organizational Engineer 2008/09, Academia da Força Aérea, Sintra (2008)
3. Tribolet, J., Páscoa, C.: Notes from classes of Organizational Engineer 2008/09, Academia da Força Aérea, Sintra (2009)
4. Quivy & Campenhoudt: Manual of Investigation in Social Sciences (1998), http://www.fep.up.pt/docentes/joao/material/manualinvestig.pdf
5. Grembergen & Haes: Enterprise Governance of Information Technology, 1st edn. Springer, Heidelberg (2009)
6. Minoli, D.: Enterprise Architectures A to Z: Frameworks, Business Process Modeling, SOA, and Infrastructure Technology. Taylor & Francis Group, New York (2008)
7. Weske: Business Process Management: Concepts, Languages, Architectures, 1st edn. Springer, Heidelberg (2007)
8. Maçarico, M.: Representação Multi-Dimensional de Arquitecturas Empresariais. Master Thesis, Instituto Superior Técnico, Lisboa (2007)
9. Chaplin, D.: Making Projects Succeed: Part 1 - Measurable Business Goals (2003), http://www.byte-vision.com/BusinessGoalsArticle.aspx (accessed in 2009-11-09)
10. The Business Rules Group: The Business Motivation Model: Business Governance in a Volatile World 2007 (2007), http://www.BusinessRulesGroup.org
11. Belo, N.: Definição de um Modelo de Processos com Valor e Respectiva Decomposição. Master Thesis, Academia da Força Aérea, Departamento de Ensino Universitário, Sintra (2010)
12. Mendes, et al.: Understanding Strategy: a Goal Modeling Methodology. In: OOIS 2001, 7th International Conference on Object Oriented Information Systems, Calgary, Canada, pp. 27–29 (2001)

Business Intelligence and Contribution of Entrepreneurial Information Architecture

Sílvia Fernandes

CIEO – Research Center for Spatial and Organizational Dynamics, Faculty of Economics, Univeristy of Algarve, Campus de Gambelas, 8005-139 Faro, Portugal
Sfernan@ualg.pt

Abstract. We are witnessing the need for a quick and intelligent reaction from organizations to the level and speed of change in business processes. The arising problems can be: from wrong lasting information; systems not fully used or explored; slow reaction to change; etc. This requires two main confluent action methods: people to synchronize their visions, ideas and strategies in the whole organization; and, in that context, select the information that strictly answers to the performance factors at the right moment. The proposed methodology turns to the potential of approach to the entrepreneurial architecture as well as to the potential of the information system in order to integrate the data and resources needed for that performance. The modeling of an information architecture of the company and its business helps in the identification of critical information, the one which is according to the mission, prospects and business success factors.

Keywords: information systems, business process, critical information, business intelligence, entrepreneurial architecture.

1 Introduction

Since the transition from the industrial society to the information society, it has been necessary to organize and select data in enterprises. This organization gave rise to new values, equal to or more important than the traditional ones, such as information and knowledge. Technology has made so much difference that its association with human capital has made this emerge as a greater potential. The joint exploration of these two dimensions (technological and human) is actually the basis for organizational innovation. Emergent information technologies are the platform for the company's ability to develop information systems that meet the new requirements of management. For example, the increasing ability to control large volumes of information in huge databases, such as the *data warehouses* using advanced tools for debugging these data (*data mining*), responds to an even more dynamic and varied public.

The two central issues that significantly determine the success of a company are business processes and information systems. These issues are closely related as the main purpose of a corporate information system is to support the business process in an effective and efficient way. It is then necessary to rethink the ways how to present products or services and seek for different dissemination channels. Facing these

J.E. Quintela Varajão et al. (Eds.): CENTERIS 2010, Part II, CCIS 110, pp. 73–82, 2010.

challenges, companies should develop new solutions to maintain or enhance their competitive position in the market.

The roles that information society and knowledge management play are absolutely relevant and complementary in current business scenarios. Connectivity, mobility, real-time reaction and innovation are some of the keywords in today's vocabulary. The sustainable competitive advantage is found in a company's ability to channel the critical information to generate the business intelligence that enables it to constantly rethink its goals and methods to meet its needs in real time. An international consultant for innovation (Basadur, researcher and founder of the enterprise *Basadur Applied Creativity*) said that many companies have good ideas or initiatives, 'but not at the right time'. Given the pace of present change and business instability, companies have to deal well with real-time business events. This requires that organizations and professionals adopt new attitudes and ways of using their information systems for managing business intelligence to address numerous emerging events.

2 Tendencies in Information Systems

In Portugal, the companies (mostly small and medium-sized) invest little in information systems and technologies due to their limited financial and organizational capacity. Then, they rarely adopt new ways of managing the business intelligence to address the numerous emerging events. One form of innovation these companies should bet on, especially those with a culture of customer service, is the creation of a platform based on technological tools easy to use, such as CRM (Customer Relationship Management systems), CMS (Content Management Systems) and ERP (Enterprise Resource Planning systems). These tools, converging on well planned platforms, contribute to the implementation of new business ideas, design of new products and services, improvement of existing processes and creation of new ones. Given this enormous potential, which may lead to a total reconfiguration of an organization, entrepreneurs should not only be familiar with this type of infrastructures, but also get involved from the very beginning of their adoption covering everyone in the organization.

The ERP systems, for example, have followed the financial systems which automatically processed invoices and other reports from the balance such as income statements according to the legislation. Analyzing the process of decision support, it was found that managers make decisions based on many other documents and data to know what products they can offer, what amount, what is the best way of distribution, the best location for shopping, how to organize the transport, etc. And adding to this, the enormous amount of data that result from having a *website* which leads to use new tools for database management with advanced statistics, especially based on data and process integration. The ERP can do this work, allowing greater product information trace, from the moment of the order until knowing its stock level. Information flows become more rapid, complete and correct, contributing to a better inventory management and a greater consistency with the customer's order. Some companies have resisted the adoption of an ERP system due to the time of adaptation/conversion from existing systems to the ERP, which has become too extensive in some cases.

This explains why some companies do not want to adopt ERP systems as these can disrupt their normal activities (Vasilev and Georgiev, 2003). Currently, technology companies are committed to put into their ERP new modules tailored to the business reality of several sectors (industry, health, banking, commerce, etc.) to turn them more flexible and complementary. Unlike departmental systems, the ERP are multi-functional, covering different levels and functions in the organization. They are integrated systems, making the information flow easily between different areas and departments to be shared by different processes (Figure 1). The information is then accumulated in a single huge repository (*data warehouse*), which is available to all business units at all functional levels. Managers have all the information they need more accurately and in real-time (Laudon and Laudon, 2004).

For example, this type of system allows issues such as: immediately inform customer if the product he ordered is in stock; maintain customer informed of the whole processing course of his order; easy production communication with the financial area to know new production plans, etc. Departmental systems, in contrast, create much fragmentation of data which results in expensive and complex links that proliferate in companies as these systems function separately by departments. The ERP systems, by consolidating the available data, help to eliminate unnecessary or redundant links, having a positive impact on the efficiency of business performance.

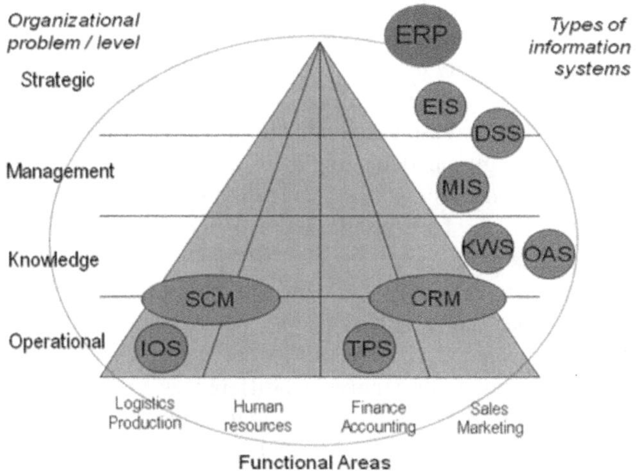

Fig. 1. ERP and their degree of integration compared to other enterprise information systems

Combining CRM tools, which consist of analytical functions to manage the relationships with clients, the ERP can consolidate information from different sources or channels of communication (phone, email, Web, *wireless* points) to answer questions such as: what is the value of a certain client for the company; who are the most loyal customers; who are the most profitable ones; etc. Companies can use the answers to those questions for acquiring new customers; improve their products and services; customize them according to customers' preferences; etc. The CRM techniques are used to select and combine key information, from different points of view, to help companies create unique services and successful innovations. CRM processes can, by means of advanced techniques like *data mining*, capture profiles and behaviors that were not perceived before. These tools have become effective in engaging a customer to the point of waiting for the goods or services that he previously outlined (Vasilev and Georgiev, 2003).

3 Business Intelligence Imperatives

The expansion of the internet platform and the exponential amount of customers and employees that it brought to companies in promoting and selling their products, has led to a need for tools that could help to cope with this trend. The major challenge is keeping the same patterns of relationship in interacting with more customers and stakeholders. The multiplying effect of this aspect, from a growing number of companies placed online, brings the need to compete more in real time. This justifies the increased adoption of the integrated information systems previously mentioned such as ERP, CRM, among others. Companies should consider the implementation of these tools from a strategic perspective, for fully exploration of their potential straightly in line with business needs for better business event monitoring.

As said before, the main purpose of a corporate information system is to support the business processes in an effective way. And within this overall problem, there are a number of important sub-problems whose solution contributes substantially towards the solution of the overall problem. In this context, there is a persistent problem in companies, related to an increasing amount of unnecessary information or misinformation that lasts for a long time, damaging their daily performance and their relationships with customers and employees. There are two main factors leading to this problem: - one refers to the fact that there are many new information systems and technologies in organizations (such as mobile ERP and electronic CRM, SCM) whose potential is far from being fully explored, either in themselves or integrated with other existing systems; - other factor is that people work differently, one from another, differing in terms of: training, willingness to work with technologies, willingness to cooperate with others, among other individual differences.

These factors raise the need for a work model in which people can synchronize their 'visions' throughout the organization and together, within the same mind-set targets, for answering instantaneously the information strictly needed. Therefore, this paper aims to propose a methodology to analyze this problem, which can be referred as an approach to critical information systems. It should be understood here as a 'critical information system', the platform of tools of business intelligence (relational databases, ERP, CRM, *data warehouse*, *data mining*, intranet, etc. - Figure 2) combined to filter only the data that match business success factors at the right time. It is not the system that is critical, such as systems supporting areas like medicine, security or others which deal with risk or critical time lags. In the approach under study, critical is the information obtained through data and processes that are event-oriented, giving executives the right answers to decide in real time. This should be the main objective to consider when structuring metadata in the company's databases. A *data warehouse* is the most appropriate 'data center' for this, because it normally contains data from all departments and functions in the organization. Separate databases get in trouble for lacking uniformity, being from different manufacturers, and lacking integration incurring in errors, delays, repeated data and more staff than it is necessary. The present approach to critical information systems requires an action to be taken at the level of information architecture in order to link the 'performance profile' (based on the performance indicators of the information system) with the 'competitive profile' (based on the performance indicators, or critical success factors, of the business).

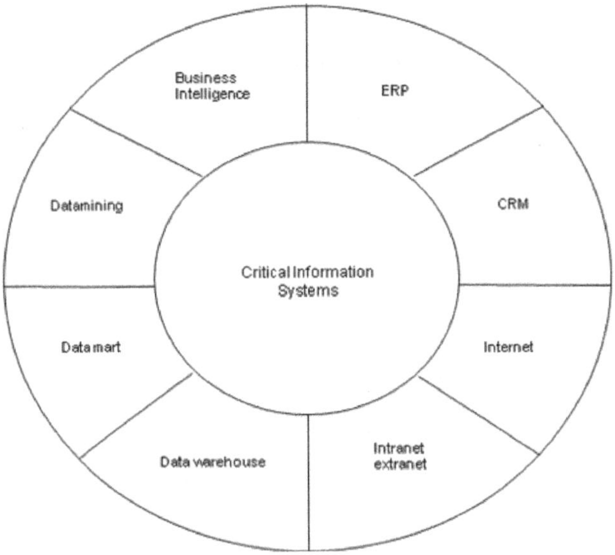

Fig. 2. Technologies and tools for real-time business intelligence

Legend: 'Business Intelligence' - this dimension in Figure 2 includes forecast analysis, performance analysis, production reporting, *benchmarking*, *text mining*, among other analytical tools.

The concept of critical information system considered here (center of Figure 2) is a platform of tools and methodologies for business intelligence, taking advantage of relational databases, ERP, CRM, *data warehouse*, *data mining* and intranets, managed or combined to select the data that match business success factors at the moment of decision. This is real time business intelligence, as the process of delivering the right information about business operations as they occur. In this context, real time means a too short time to answer after the business event occurred. While traditional business intelligence generally presents historical data for manual analysis, real time business intelligence compares current business events with historical patterns to automatically detect problems or opportunities. This automated analysis capability will enable corrective actions to be initiated or business rules to be adjusted to optimize business processes. An approach to event driven architectures is to increase the refresh cycle of an existing *data warehouse* to more frequently update the data. These real time data warehouse systems can achieve by real time update of data, where the data latency is typically in higher ranges of time. Facing the current market instability and its informational asymmetries, changing business models and processes, there is a growing need for immediate responses to which should contribute the ideas and competences from everyone in the organization. The entrepreneurial information architecture can play an important role in structuring the alignment between individuals and business process changes.

4 Entrepreneurial Information Architecture

Given the growing need for immediate responses to which should contribute the initiatives and information from whole organization, communication is desirable and necessary to transfer knowledge. One of the stages in the knowledge creation model of Nonaka and Takeuchi (1995) is 'socialization', which arises from tacit knowledge exchange between individuals. The shared experiences and their articulation consolidate knowledge, creating shared mental models and trust forms. Nonaka said that knowledge is created by individuals and the organization has a role in expanding the knowledge created by its individuals and "crystallize" it as a part of the organizational knowledge network.

Systems analysts and engineers are those that deal more with the need to synchronize views in dialoguing with the entities that request them for systems development. For this dialogue, they use models to represent the reality they need to appreciate, through a structured design (architecture) to quickly explore and find the solution. Accordingly, *ontologies* have been increasingly used as they are models that represent a set of concepts within a domain and the relationships between them, in order to make inference on the objects of the domain. *Ontologies* generally describe individuals, classes, attributes and relationships. They are used in artificial intelligence, web semantic, software engineering and information architecture as forms of representing knowledge about events. Given the speed of emergency and change in business processes, new computing paradigms should be increasingly addressed using entrepreneurial architecture approaches. Next section concerns the contribution that entrepreneurial information architecture can have to the under discussion methodology, in which the increasing need for modeling data and process flows is implicit. The aim is to better discern and act at the linkage between 'performance analysis' (indicators of corporate information systems performance) and 'competitive analysis' (indicators of company's performance which are its business success factors).

4.1 Assessment of Some Models

Entrepreneurial information architectures can contribute to the present methodology, in what Zachman's framework proposes (see Zachman International website): crossing the prospects of the company's management with the support given by information systems and processes (his approach has also served internal IS creation). The resulting matrix of this crossing exercise has the following structure (Figure 3):

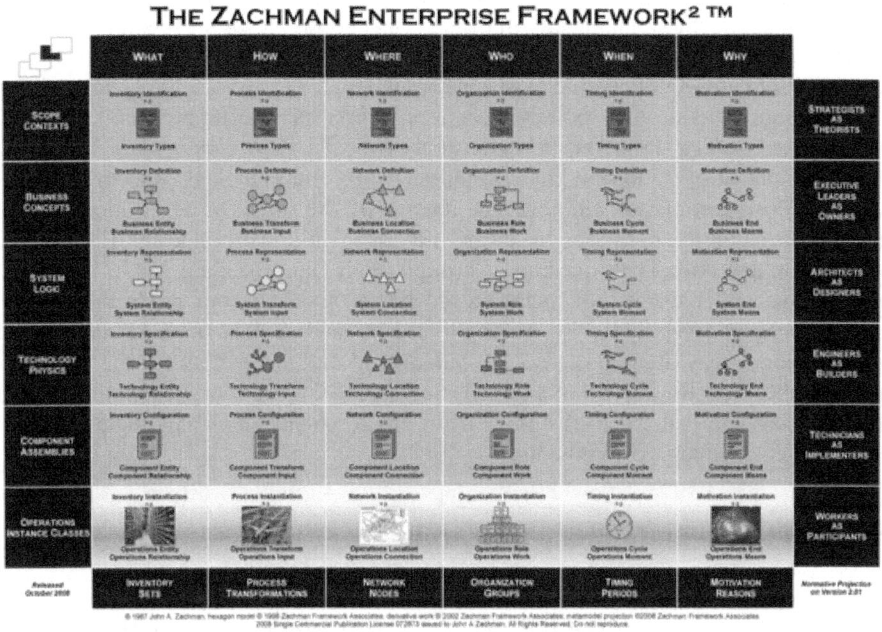

Fig. 3. The Zachman's entrepreneurial information architecture

Legend: *What?*: data and relationships between them;
How?: processes (functional description);
Where?: network (components location in the company);
Who?: who performs the job, leadership chain, participation level;
When ?: when events occur;
Why?: motivations, purposes, goals, strategies.

Another architecture is the EAP model (*Enterprise Architecture Planning*) by Spewak and Hill (1992) proposing the layers and components that answer to four key issues (Table 1):

Table 1. The approach of EAP's entrepreneurial architecture

Phase	Plan/method
1. Starting point	How is the work done now and what methodology is used
2. Where are we today?	Current knowledge base about the business and information used to manage it
3. Where do we want to be?	Data necessary to support sustainable business
4. How to get there?	Required implementation and migration plans

Another model is from the Center for Organizational Engineering (Caetano *et al.*, 2007) whose main objective is to model the definition of criteria to align business processes with the information and supporting IS/IT. The resulting model consists of a set of 5 layers or perspectives: *Technology*, *Application*, *Information*, *Business* and

Organization. This architecture is based on three concepts: entities, roles and activities. Entities are the components that make up the organization (people, machines, places, etc.). Roles are the observable behaviors of entities and the activities reflect how a set of entities collaborate to reach a result.

There are several other models of entrepreneurial architectures, such as the EUP (*Enterprise Unified Process*), an extension of the RUP (*Rational Unified Process*) from Ambler *et al.* (2005), doing a comprehensive and complete collection of these aspects. However, one should note that generically the nature of descriptions in these models focus on the questions raised by the Zachman's matrix and the EAP method of Spewak and Hill. Their questions, through an iterate procedure, could help assess the linkage under discussion: between the perspectives of company's management and the support given by the IS. Among the mentioned models, the EAP and the EUP methodologies pay attention to social, human and cultural factors for the success of their application. But all the mentioned models consider the 'organizational change' factor as an external force, resulting from environmental or technological changes which affect business requirements.

5 Conclusion and Future Research

The entrepreneurial information architecture of a company and its business, easy to understand and communicate, can help the identification of the critical information, consistent with the company's mission, objectives and business success factors. It is mainly modeled with objects such as: activities (functional and cross-functional, internal and external); resources (functional and cross-functional, internal and external) and products (internal and external). It then supports information systems management as it helps the identification of requirements for those systems according business needs. However, given the heterogeneity of those objects and data that characterize them, one of the most pressing problems has been the conversion between structured and unstructured data.

On this subject, the authors Carvalho and Ferreira (2001) carried out a survey for technological tools assessment, related with knowledge management and conversion between tacit and explicit knowledge, discussing their internalization or outsourcing. Some of these tools are: knowledge portals (corporate *intranets* and *extranets*); knowledge maps (lists of "who knows what": skills/profiles); EDM (Electronic Document Management: cataloging, indexing, etc.); OLAP (Online Analytical Processes for data normalization); *Data mining* (advanced techniques to explore large amounts of data looking for consistent patterns); qualitative analysis tools; among others. In this context, the *Web2* platform, a concept that means the second-generation of community-based web services involving social networks, may well provide models and methods on the subject of *ontologies* and enterprise information architectures. Although this term seems to be connoted with a new version for the Web, it does not refer to any technical specification update, but to a change in the way it is perceived by users and developers as an environment for interaction and sharing, which encompasses numerous visions and motivations today.

One of the trends in modern computing architectures is *SOA - Service Oriented Architecture*. This kind of architecture may have an important role in critical information architectures and systems, since it is designed to flexibly provide the right services, not just at the right time, but also at the right level of generality. The 'service' orientation relates to the objectives of: reducing the customer's effort to use the service and thus the impact of change; re-using the service without having to go through the source code and ensuring that the service is usable throughout the whole organization (and even re-designable together). Another current trend is *cloud computing*, an architecture in which a service is resolved or provided through several computers that may not function in the same place. Forming a "computing cloud" they share tools, services, software and information through the interconnection of different systems via internet, instead of having these resources locally (in internal servers). Thus, companies will not spend much time maintaining their systems, data, applications and information. Then they will have more time to focus on managing the connection intended to be better in organizations, between the perspectives of a company's business and the support given by its information system.

Future research on the approach covered in this paper will focus on analyzing the results from a survey application and the inclusion of new levels/issues in it, mostly related with the computing trends on socializing communication channels such as the *Web2*, *SOA* architectures and *cloud computing*. In order to test the proposed methodology, a survey should be implemented to collect the necessary data. The selected sample should focus on firms within the same sector, since there are several factors (external and internal) influencing different sectors, which lead to biased results and conclusions. Recalling the methodological issue under discussion - act on the connection between the 'performance analysis' (indicators of the information system performance) and 'competitive analysis' (indicators of a company's performance, or its business success factors) - the necessary data should focus particularly on knowing: what information systems and technologies those firms have; what are their critical success factors; if those systems and technologies are helping to meet them; if they use entrepreneurial information architecture approaches; if their systems are planned to obtain real time critical information; if some of their systems are not being fully explored and what functions are affected; and if they are using any *cloud services*.

Acknowledgments. This paper has been partially supported by the Portuguese Foundation for Science and Technology (FCT).

References

1. Ambler, S., Nalbone, J., VizVizde, M.: Enterprise Unified Process: Extending the Rational Unified Process. Prentice Hall, New Jersey (2005)
2. Caetano, A., Sousa, P., Vasconcelos, A., Pereira, C., Tribolet, J.: Enterprise architecture modeling with the UML 2.0. In: Rittgen, P. (ed.) Enterprise Modeling and Computing with UML. Idea Group Inc., Hershey (2007)
3. Carvalho, R., Ferreira, M.: Using Information Technology to Support Knowledge Conversion Processes. Information Research 7(1), 1–24 (2001)
4. Laudon, C., Laudon, J.: Management Information Systems: Managing the Digital Firm, 9th edn. Prentice Hall, New Jersey (2004)
5. Nonaka, I., Takeuchi, H.: The Knowledge-Creating Company. Oxford Press, New York (1995)

6. Spewak, S., Hill, S.: Enterprise Architecture Planning: Developing a Blueprint for Data, Apllications and Technology. John Wiley & Sons, New York (1992)
7. Vasilev, J., Georgiev, G.: Tendencies in the Development of ERP Systems. In: International Conference on Computer Systems and Technologies. Economical University of Varna, Bulgária (2003)
8. Zachman International, http://zachmaninternational.com/index.php/home-article/13#maincol

Stakeholder-Driven Enterprise Process Model for Complex Services Adaptation

Jay Ramanathan, Rajiv Ramnath, Joe Bolinger, and Praveen Nagarajan

CETI, Computer Science and Engineering, Ohio State University, Columbus, Ohio 43210, USA
ramanathan.2@osu.edu

Abstract. Service - oriented organizations often deal with incoming non-routine request types, each with significant variations in requirements consequently *driving* discovery of processing needs. At the same time such organizations are often challenged with sharing high-cost resources and executing *static* processes that do not lead to effective delivery. This requires an ontology designed for flexible adaptation to facilitate performance traceability and knowledge mining. Specifically we present a formal dynamic *service ontology* that 1) obtains tacit knowledge as explicit *in-the-micro* feedback from workers performing roles, 2) provides *in-the-small* evolutionary (dynamic) process instance structures and monitoring mechanisms, and 3) aggregates process instances metrics into a performance and decision-making facility to align to *in-the-large* goals of stakeholders. The multidimensional ontology for process flexibility and performance traceability was derived from industry case studies and is cognizant of stakeholder interests. We use *customer service request* data to validate the ontology through its use in adaptive decision-making applied to a large IT shared services organization.

Keywords: Enterprise Architecture and Services, Stakeholder based performance modeling, intelligence mining, organizational change, micr and macro modeling.

1 Non-routine Service Requests and Stakeholders

Our goal is to improve the performance of knowledge-intensive processes that arise in the context of *non-routine service requests* and requirements. The needs of such processes are not met by the static precedence-driven workflows of *production* processes designed for *routine requests.* At the same time the workflow provides the structure for traceability that is a great source of information for decision-making. Our experience in deploying numerous enterprise-integration-level workflows for processing non-routine service requests has led to a service ontology. This in turn 1) motivates the formal ontology for complex systems, 2) its applicability to performance traceability and adaptive decision making, and 3) ontology validation through illustrating the adaptation achievable using data from a services organization. The overall conceptual architecture is applicable to the operational systems such as cyber infrastructures that have collaborative front ends and federated backend systems.

J.E. Quintela Varajão et al. (Eds.): CENTERIS 2010, Part II, CCIS 110, pp. 83–96, 2010.

We start below with customer-originated *request events* (custom orders, help tickets, etc.) that allow an organization to 'sense' new needs and then 'respond'. To contrast traditional make-sell with sense-and-respond organizations, we begin with *routine requests* as a starting point for characterization and comparison between routine and *non-routine requests* respectively.

Characteristics of routine requirements and production workflows
Routine requests can be predicted thus, *in that predictable context* we can have pre-designed workflows, data flows, transition guards, role assignments, and the like based on the static characteristics of the process and the organization. Specifications and examples are documented by bodies like the W3C, Workflow Coalition and other initiatives. Such designed workflows also can optimize the assignment of resources to achieve cost effective quality on a repeatable basis. The rules in such definitions are often represented in a formal model such as a petri net and are the best practices and knowledge of the organization. The rules are extracted by process designers from what is known about the type of product, the individual process steps to produce it, the organization's culture, etc. making the process a valuable representation of organizational *knowledge at a point in time*.

Characteristics of non-routine requests and complex systems
Next focusing on *non-routine* service request events and context, we note that these involve *dynamic discovery and are knowledge-intensive* and thus not well-suited to static process specifications. Services in general require a significant amount of human expertise and flexibility largely because processing required depends on the challenges of the particular request and its knowledge requirements. We use the term *complex system* to emphasize the process decisions and flows of knowledge that are dynamic, distributed across organizations and systems.

COMPLEX SYSTEM AND DIMENSIONS: A good example of a complex system is the emergency admittance in a hospital. In this case the patient condition and requirements are not fully known. Hence the right questions must be asked by the 'triage' role to identify the right skill assignments (i.e. a cardiac specialist), and the services are delivered when the resources as knowledge resources become available. That is, during any *interaction* the need for other *sub-interactions* are often dynamically *discovered* in the context of the current task. This is also an example of the *micro-dimension* where each knowledge worker makes decisions about the *local workflow*. (Here we use the term '*dimension*' to refer to a *stakeholder group with similar interests and roles.*) At the same time the patient flow process *in-the-small-dimension* from the emergency room to the discharge also varies. Finally, at *a macro-dimension* all patients are attended by the same organizations in a predetermined manner to deliver effective health care services. At the highest dimension, the variations apparent at the lower dimensions are not visible due to lack of traceability. Thus, complex systems are creative in nature and challenging to manage because they fundamentally encourage participants to apply their own evolving personal expertise to *augment* shared and static organizational process knowledge. Since non-routine requests are not well-determined, it is difficult for a static workflow model to meet the needs of all variations. Thus, here we propose a multi-dimensional non-deterministic ontology.

RESOURCE SHARING AND KNOWLEDGE INTENSIVE PROCESSES: Another important aspect of knowledge intensive processes and instances is that they *share expensive resources*. In the emergency room example the cardiac specialists provide services to multiple patients in their particular *role*. The knowledge about the patients and emerging practice must also be shared. Another example, this time related to systems in an IT (information technology) organization, is expensive enterprise servers that are shared providing virtual machines to multiple applications and business processes. Here too there is emerging knowledge regarding sharing high-cost resources and the lowering of energy consumption. Also, these are just two examples of many different non-routine types that abound within any enterprise, making it complex. Thus any effective service-oriented ontology must consider resources that are shared and facilitate knowledge management. The approach here focuses on roles and resources and the recording of tacit individual knowledge and leveraging it for future work and adaptation by integrating this with performance information.

DISTRIBUTION OF PROCESS EXECUTION: In the typical enterprise there are many enterprise applications each with static workflows contained within them! It is also true that *customer service delivery* often requires responses that span multiple organizations and applications. Each of these has its own user interactions that are part of the end-to-end customer facing process. It is therefore not always practical to create a workflow engine that has tightly-coupled interfaces to multiple systems, especially as the service processes adapt to external circumstances. Thus we propose a process engine that can flexibly execute interactions 1) directly through an interface with the resource(s) (i.e. a user or an application service), 2) indirectly through the capture of the execution metrics that are a side-effect of one or more interactions completed in other systems, and 3) indirectly through the reporting of metrics and actions played out in the physical world.

MULTI-DIMENSIONAL ALIGNMENT OF STAKEHOLDERS' VALUE: We also take the engineering life-cycle stance where ultimately a process brings together resources to complete interactions that deliver value to specific *stakeholders - the customer, business, operations, and individual*. Thus the value to each of these stakeholders must be traced through the ontology and as the key benefit of process execution. As mentioned earlier, *traceability* is through the recording of dynamic objects, associations and metrics during execution. Thus, here we explicitly identify the stakeholder groups as *dimensions* and address *continuous improvement* or adaptation towards goals.

1.1 Introduction to a Complex Life-Cycle Management Case Study

The complex service system characteristics above are reflected by many non-routine organizations within any enterprise. In general, the end-to-end LCM (Life Cycle Management) type processes reflect service challenges that exist in many organizations such as the Software Systems and Engineering, Customer Service Center, Emergency, Repairs, Design Engineering, and Process Planning. We have selected *LCM* within a large internal *IT organization and its operational systems and software* for illustration of the adaptation solution.

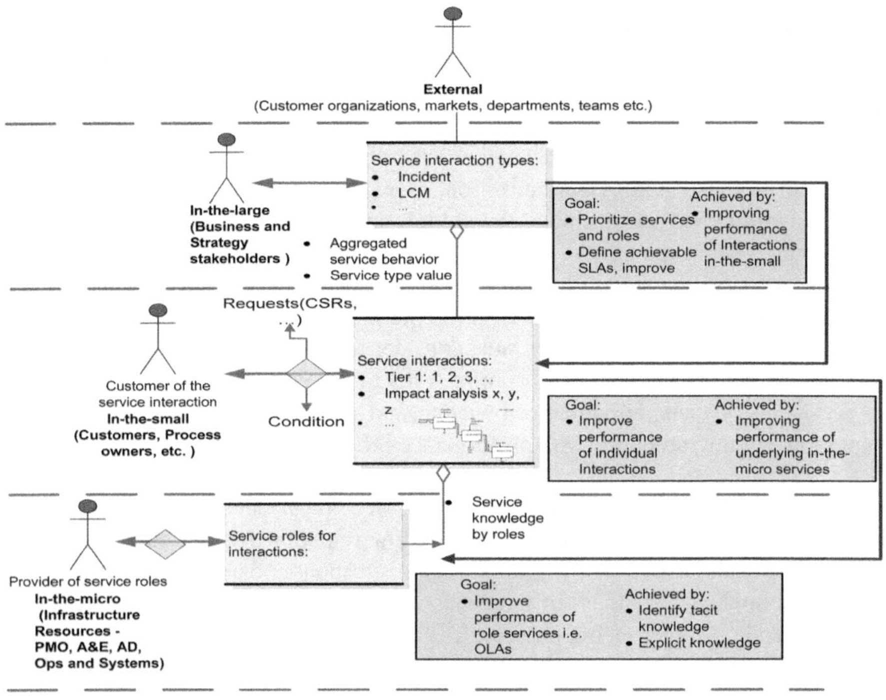

Fig. 1. Multi-dimensional concepts for adaptation (execution in blue arrows and feedback in red arrows)

A *Customer Service Request* (or CSR) to the internal IT organization starts a chain of events within multiple other organizations (like the Project Management Office (PMO), Architecture and Engineering (A&E), Application Development (AD), and Production Operations (PO), all staffed with skilled resources and specialists that address the particular lifecycle and changes to enterprise application systems. The CSRs are requirements that originate from multiple customer departments. As the impact of the CSR is understood, individuals with specific skills are then assigned to the roles of the process to perform activities that research, use, create, review, and deploy the artifacts for the system enhancements. The CSR typically starts a Life-Cycle Management (LCM) process to ensure that 1) functional and non-functional requirements of the change are identified, 2) implementation tasks are executed, and 3) deployment is assured with respect to the approved plans and monitored. Finally, the stakeholders must be satisfied that processes are effective and are providing value.

1.2 Related Work and Key Concepts for Adaptation

Related Research and Technologies

WORKFLOW ENVIRONMENTS: Considerable relevant work in different environments for processes and collaboration exists. Different ideas for flexible workflow and

CSCW systems, the focus of our work, have been motivated in several publications [1, 2, 3, 4, 5, 6]. There also has been a realization that we need tools which look beyond process automation to a more comprehensive notion of support for organizational processes [1]. This includes giving humans more insight into decision making activities for computer-supported organizational processes and allowing such processes to be flexible and adaptable. Research [2] also supports this idea of flexible workflow through a notion of *adhocracies*. Adhocracies are characterized as organizations facing a complex and dynamic environment, resulting in a chosen organizational form with extensive use of liaison devices, selective decentralization and coordination by mutual adjustment. This work also distinguishes between ridged enterprise workflow (we call *in-the-large*) and workgroup workflow in which autonomous workgroups must maintain some control over process definition (we call *in-the-small*). These ideas are the context for our ontology. Complex systems and processes fall into this dynamic adhocracy category by virtue of having process activities and participants dependent on the project requirements. The way to facilitate this dynamic relationship is to give project teams the ability to define and execute activities freely, within an overall structure.

Workflow Knowledge Mining: Related work also includes process and activity mining from various enterprise data stores and user contexts [5]. Activity centric workflow models have been generated through the mining and correlating of data from transactional systems .Additionally finer grain user workflow and tacit knowledge can be extracted (such as through the use of an interactive context tracking help bubble [5]). Other types deal with the development of organizational structure by mining data in a variety of different contexts. Finally work in recommender systems provides insights into ways in which user preference patterns can be used to make additional recommendations. While the context and application for each of the works above are quite different, they provide process background and insights for our work aligning in-the-large/small/micro. That is working in a collaborative enterprise setting provides process and organizational footprints by which we can extract valuable knowledge. By embedding interfaces for the generation and collection of workflow data into everyday tools, we allow for a more integrated and informative process and organizational footprints, thus facilitating traceability advantages of traditional workflows.

Architectures and Cyber Infrastructures: The motivation here was to explore how the value of a process can be identified and delivered to the stakeholders of a complex cyber infrastructure. The goal is the architecting of such a cyber infrastructure (with data federation and tools) within a public or private enterprise. This is also related to work on the management of enterprise architectures consolidated in TOGAF and the operational aspects in ISO20000 (ITIL). Here we build on sense-and-respond strategic planning, goal-directed change management and ontology-based concepts of a dynamic fractal architecture based on customer-provider transactions. We present and validate a process ontology that 1) implements an enterprise knowledge infrastructure that makes aspects of tacit knowledge more explicit, 2) supports the mining of knowledge to guide decision making, and 3) illustrates the use of knowledge to create a sense-respond organization.

1.3 Key Adaptation Concepts Addressed in This Paper

Here we take the approach that process stakeholders and traceability beneficiaries can be viewed in four dimensions

- external context of future non-routine requests in a sense and respond organization
- in-the-micro service provider
- in-the-small process composed of multiple provider roles complete a customer request
- in-the-large stakeholders that view business performance in aggregate

IN-THE-MICRO DIMENSION OF SERVICE PROVISIONING ROLES: 'In-themicro' refers to the service provisioning roles. While pre-defined process discipline can sequence the tasks (e.g. *produce architecture* must precede *review architecture*), tacit knowledge is used to identify, use, and create information on a fine-grain level with little guidance possible at the generic macro process. This results in ad-hoc collaborations and deviations, or what would be called exceptions in the production/formal workflow model. These collaborations are extremely valuable and can be leveraged to mine information, capture knowledge, and add additional guidance during the process. Knowledge workers are involved in sensing variation in non-routine requests and can indicate how their explicit responses deviate from the established processes. For example if during the execution of a *produce architecture* process results in successful delivery by one particular resource that often hands-off architecture information to a networking resource, then future executions of the workflow benefit from this hand-off under similar requirement conditions. Thus, the value is the capture of tacit knowledge and it availability for subsequent service delivery to improve customer perceived quality. Thus the complex system structure must provide a way for gathering the interesting user knowledge and provisioning metrics.

IN-THE-SMALL DIMENSION OF SERVICE CUSTOMER AND PROCESS INTERACTIONS: While the sensing of variation occurs locally by individual resources, the process interactions 'in-the-small' ensures that all the needed resources are applied in the right sequence. To enable this, the complex system structure must also enable process flows that are dynamically discovered. (We will not focus here on routine requests that are well handled in existing applications.)

IN-THE-LARGE DIMENSION OF STRATEGIC ADAPTATION ROLES: Information is also critical for adaptation - detecting global organization trends, prioritizing changes and alignment to business and strategy goals. The aggregated performance of process instances provides 'in-the-large' trends to align decision-making to customer/market and business goals. The traceability to in-the-micro provisioning and in-the-small process instances also allows more specific information to be relayed to local roles which can adapt to future non-routine requests and task executions.

VALIDATION ILLUSTRATING VERTICAL TRACEABILITY AND BENEFITS: Using 600 CSR records collected from a large organization presented earlier, we will show vertical traceability information across dimensions provided by the meta model given below has value to each stakeholder group as follows 1) collection of tacit information and its future availability in-the-micro, 2) performance capture within dynamically evolving processes, 3) in-the-large to in-the-micro traceability for decision making and alignment. This is also continuous improvement; however we call it 'adaption' because new behaviors are allowed to emerge dynamically.

We next introduce the specific ACE ontology that allows us to deliver these types of features.

2 Multi-dimensional Service Ontology

2.1 Adaptive Complex Enterprise (ACE) Service Ontology

A multi-dimensional ACE process has five building blocks - *Interactions, Roles, Artifacts, and Event-Condition-Interactions* - described below.

INTERACTIONS (I): Examples of service interactions or just interactions include 'Incident management', Emergency treatment, Book purchase at a .Com site. A *process* is a collection of related interactions. An Interaction completes a transaction between a customer and provider role (these can be either internal or external to the organization). Each interaction might also have many other roles. An interaction starts upon the arrival of an event *if its condition is met* and it has a definite end. At the end of an interaction artifacts (see below) are produced and the resources performing its roles are 'released'. An interaction can also have more specific sub-interactions associated and these can be initiated by a request. This is similar to other activity-centric models of collaboration that have been proposed in order to capture a handoff between roles.

SERVICE LEVEL (SL): An interaction provides the structure for customer-centered performance attributes like when started, where (e.g.GIS location) executed, why executed, how long in execution, when completed, wait time for sub interactions, what roles, and what resources were assigned to roles, etc. An interaction also has internal *states and priorities* discussed later. In particular many of these attributes help us synthesize the *service level* achieved from the customers' perspective.

ROLES (R): Roles are capabilities that the *provider* role makes available for the completion of the interaction and to create/enhance artifacts. Hence, roles define what resources and skills are needed to perform each Interaction. The actual assignments of resources to roles can be made just prior to interaction execution.

- A role is *executed by resources* that can include humans, systems, and physical resources and assets. For example the roles for the customer service desk might include a help desk operator and a customer relationship management system.
- A role may be a *composite*, meaning it is an aggregation of other roles.
- A role may use *shared* resources. A resource can thus be assigned to different interactions and their roles. Thus with each resource we have metrics attributes that include: Time a resource is applied in a role and interaction, Capacity of a resource that is available / allocated, Cost of a resource. Also resources in a role can provide important feedback as characterized later.

Operating level (OL): A basic role is itself an interaction that has associated operating metrics like capacity, availability, skill etc. It has a one-to-one relationship with a resource. That is, role interactions are shared. We will often use the term role to mean either role or its actual assigned shared resource.

Artifacts (A): An artifact is information (or a widget or asset) associated (i.e. used, produced) by an interaction. It may be some representation of the final service (or product) or some intermediate information that is shared from one interaction to another. Artifacts can contain other artifacts and even play a role in an interaction. Often artifacts from one interaction are required in order to start some other interaction (as in a data flow view). These result in dependencies as a given artifact may depend on a number of other artifacts and interactions that produce them. The interaction process is itself started off by a *request* for an artifact. Metrics attributes related to an artifact include quality, what interaction, location (possibly GIS), and so on. Every role has the ability to view the details of all the artifacts in the process instance that it is authorized to see. When assigned to an interaction to perform it may add dependencies to the artifacts indicating that additional information is needed in order to carry out the work. Roles may also add additional items to its artifacts, or define new ones, indicating information it would like to pass along to others or for recording purposes.

Event - condition – interaction (ECI): Examples of events are the arrival of an external request (an order, an incident, a patient etc.), the completion of an interaction, routinely scheduled timer-based, or an exception. An *event* causes interactions if certain *conditions* are met. As a result of an event(s), as the context, *conditions* are checked. If the condition is met, the interaction is executed with the associated roles. Thus, upon the arrival of an event, if its condition is met, the associated interaction type is instantiated and executed to *produce or modify* a set of artifacts *using* a set of roles as represented by: E_x: $I_x \rightarrow \{A_x\} \underline{\searrow} \{R_x\}$. This *traceability* between objects related to *execution* instance x is also illustrated graphically in Figure 2. Furthermore, these associations are the basis for mining knowledge as illustrated in the following validation section. Finally, there can be local constraints attached to any of the above objects.

2.2 ACE Execution Engine

At runtime, instances of interactions are executed (enacted interactively by the user if needed) according to the details given below.

Process execution and dynamic evolution in-the-small: A process has at least one main interaction. The main interaction originates with an event. For example, a specific CSR request starts its LCM interaction if the condition is true. In this case the condition is the assignment of resources that are available for that particular CSR. The following rules govern the process execution and evolution. Interactions can start sub-interactions. Interactions can also be sequenced. Also, if any interaction is started but has unmet dependencies on an artifact, the unmet interaction dependencies are also started. The typical engine rules for execution are based on priority.

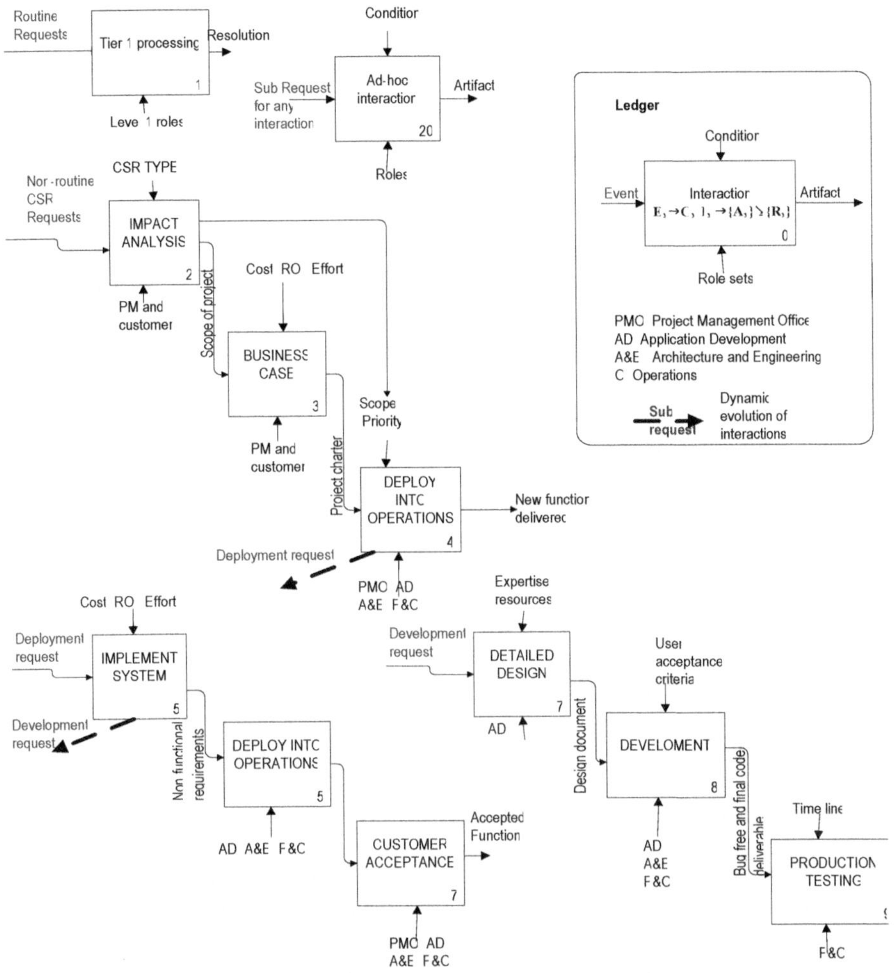

Fig. 2. LCM as an ACE System of interactions and dynamic sub interactions

At any time a set of interactions are ongoing and in different states. Interaction states include:

- Requirements - the event has happened and the condition is being checked
- Executing – the roles are assigned and producing artifacts
- Delivery – the artifacts are being provided to the customer(s) or to 'customer' interactions.
- Waiting – the interaction is waiting on a sub interaction stopped that has been initiated in one of the following ways. Interactions can initiate other request events and sub-interactions in a fire-and-forget/wait-to-complete/wait-to-execute modes.
- Completed – the interaction is finished and the roles are released.

Loosely Coupled Distributed execution: The execution of process interaction is itself loosely coupled to the ACE engine that determines what conditions are met and updates the states of active interactions. For example, a human or an automated system can pick up an interaction description, perform it in the physical world and report completion. Alternatively, the interactions can be executed by a production workflow contained in another enterprise application and the execution results imported to the ACE database (based on the ontology). In this case the ACE tools treat the data the same as if the ACE engine generated the data.

Non-deterministic: In a typical workflow system a transition is deterministic and moves the process from a source to a target step, terminating the source step. In our model above, transitions or interaction activations are dynamic (and even user initiated) and more non-deterministic. Conditions can examine the attributes of other interactions, artifacts and roles to allow for more flexibility. The process does not encode a particular routing, but rather detects dynamic conditions that require other interactions to be activated by a request event. Many interactions may enter a ready state due to conditions that are met. The execution itself is therefore non-deterministic.

3 Meta Model Application and Validation

Validation of ACE: Having presented the ACE ontology (derived from industry case studies as mentioned earlier), the question we next ask is what are we validating? It is clear that we are not validating our particular ontology implementation (The Mirror cyber infrastructure) as many workflow engines exist and their implementation specifications are now widely established by standards bodies.

Instead, our main thesis is this: *The flexibility of the ACE ontology better facilitates the traceability for collaborative stakeholder decisions within sense-and-respond non-routine service organizations.* The vertical synthesis of information (in blue) and the feedback to roles (in red) across stakeholders is also illustrated in Figure 1. That is, we address the validation question with two specific illustrative cases.

- *Case 1*: Without in-the-micro feedback, what is the limitation of in-the-small and aggregated in-the-large performance metrics captured by typical production workflow engines?
- *Case 2:* How does ACE's addition in-the-micro process traceability leverage vertical visibility to make better informed decisions?

Industry data: Our validation cases are based on a sample of industry interaction data for the CSR-LCM process (Figure 2). The data set collected is for 90 days and the sample size has 541 records. It is for the primary LCM interaction from the project management system capturing useful information like requests, interaction state changes, recording of the start and stop times of CSRs, modification of artifacts, resource assignments to roles, and so on. Also, separately to illustrate Case 2, associated each CSR interaction is the *in-the-micro role* feedback on the difficulty of the request and interaction (*easy, medium, hard*). With this we can now illustrate the value of a multi-dimensional performance model to decision-making in our internal IT organization introduced earlier. This includes the stakeholders roles such as business managers, project managers, architects, programmers and operational.

In summary, below we present two cases: *Case 1)* the *in-the-small* traceability here is used to understand the *approximate* behavior of roles (in this case software engineers and enterprise systems) in the CSR-LCM interaction, and *Case 2)* shows when there is *in-the-micro explicit* knowledge *feedback* from roles, the actual insights result in better decision making.

Goal (for Case 1 and 2): reduce response time.	
CASE 1: AGGREGATION OF PERFORMANCE DATA WITHOUT IN-THE-MICRO ROLE FEEDBACK (BLUE ASSOCIATIONS IN Figure 1)	
In-the-micro	No input from the knowledge workers in this case.
In-the-small Customer Service Request (CSR). This is an example non-routine request type.	CUSTOMER OFFICE: ABC CREATE_DATE: 1/15/2009 10:48 DOC_ID: CRISE_CSR_4530 PRIORITY_INITIATOR: HIGH STATUS: CLOSE BUSINESS SYSTEM: CRISE TYPE: code change ACTION_DATE: 1/31/2009 16:50 TITLE: Remove Obsolete COBOL Run Time Libraries From Procs SERVICE NEEDED: Remove dataset SDC.VS31.COB2LIB from the load library concatenations in procs.
In-the-large aggregation of interaction performance (using Starlight™ by Future Point Systems for data mining). • **Node is the CRISE role/ enterprise business system** • **Lowest layer - all the CSR requests pertaining to that system, including those that are finished;** • **Middle layer is the time to complete CSR.**	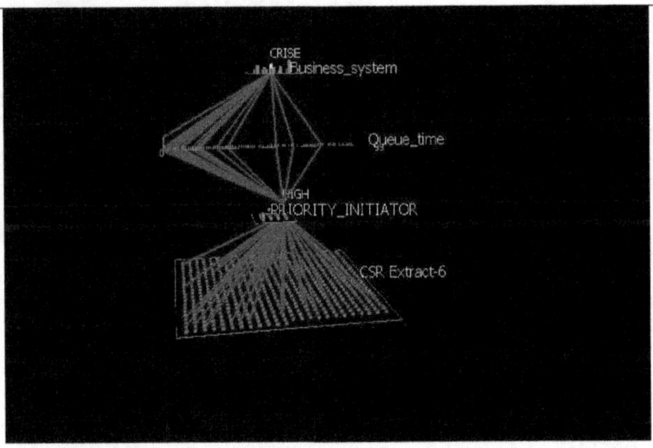
CASE 1: Decision making for improvement and feedback (red associations in Figure 1).	**Poor Traceability:** We do not have any insight into what can be done to improve performance. Cannot relate time taken (a symptom) to causes in-the-micro (eg. role knoweldge) in this view.
CASE 2: PERFORMANCE TRACEABILITY TO ROLE KNOWLEDGE FOR DECISION-MAKING (BLUE AND RED ASSOCIATIONS IN Figure 1)	
In-the-micro Interaction Assistant	Local Ad-hoc interactions (sticky note user interface, for example) dynamically introduced by roles to make their **knowledge explicit. In our example each of the 600 CSRs is further identified with role input as Easy/Medium/High difficulty.**
In-the-small Customer Service Request (CSR).	Same as above.

<table>
<tr>
<td>In-the-large aggregation of CSR instances presenting the different systems (e.g. CRISE) with the number of CSRs in each of its different interaction states. For example: Red represents 'open' CSRs, Yellow represents 'closed' CSRs, Blue represents those in 'impact analysis' and so on.
Note that CRISE has a large number of open and close CSRs. This is in contrast to its peer (SCOTI etc.) which has fewer open records. Note also that this view still does not give us insights into the 'cause'.</td>
<td>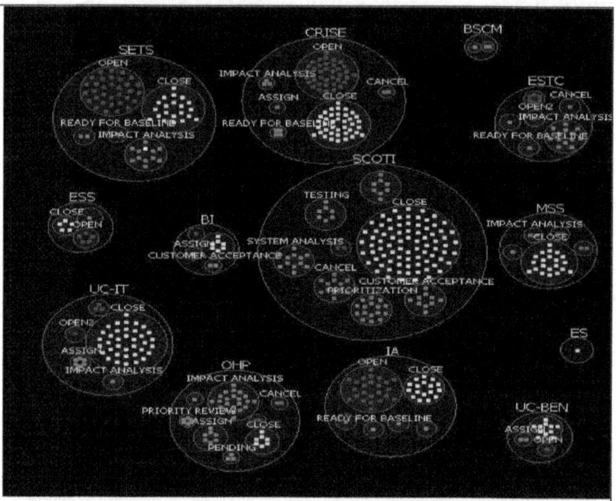
</td>
</tr>
<tr>
<td>Combining in-the-small and in-the-micro feedback from knowledge workers. We can now see the CSRs with the CRISE knowledge worker role input (easy, medium and hard). Colors are used as follows: blue - started but not completed, red-open/unclosed, yellow- closed. One can now see that many 'easy' tickets are not closed. Why?</td>
<td>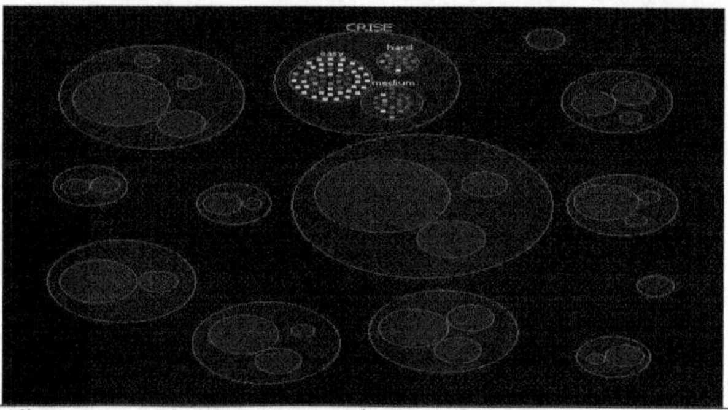
</td>
</tr>
<tr>
<td>CASE 2: Decision making for improvement and feedback (red associations in Figure 1)</td>
<td>Alignment to goal: We can now see the result of the 'difficulty' in-the-micro feedback from roles to determine that even 'easy' interactions are open for the same time period as the 'hard' ones. This points specifically to further options for improvement that need to be investigated: better documentation, better role assignments based on domain knowledge, etc. Finally, smarter triage rules based on this will allow more interactions to move in parallel, for a fixed number of resources.</td>
</tr>
</table>

Better decision making requires the traceability of in-the-micro knowledge to performance goals in the large, as the two cases illustrate. This is achieved better by Case 2 using the traceability between explicit in-the-micro role knowledge (difficulty) to in-the-small interaction performance (span time of the CSR-LCM process) to in-the-large aggregated performance goals (which system is high priority and poor performing).

3.1 Recommendations for Complex System Improvement

Generalizing from the above example, we can now claim in general that much of the decision-making for complex system improvement can be supported and automated by identifying underlying axioms and principles. For example, the next step in decision-making related to Case 2 is Case 3: Understand whether resource skills play a role in easy CSRs that are open for an unusually long time. This illustrates other in-the-micro information that becomes useful in the detection of interesting behavior:

> *No deviation from peers*: If any resource, *R*, assigned to role, *X*, produces part of an artifact with performance metrics that is significantly different than R's peers performing the same interaction, no deviation from peers is violated.

The related principle allows us to look for resource-related reasons for interesting data phenomenon, yet protect the individuals based on HIPAA [http://www.hipaa.org/].

This axiom actually applied twice earlier in the validation example above. First at the in-the-large dimension, by looking at the CSRs related to systems we conclude that CRISE has the highest number of open CSRs and is therefore deviating from its peers and interesting. Second, by tracing to the explicit 'difficulty' knowledge 'in-the-small' of the engineers and peers the somewhat counter-intuitive insight is that most of the CSRs are actually not that difficult. They are actually of easy or medium difficulty. This insight leads to better project management decisions to make process improvements. Thus, we claim that ACE type process models with execution traceability between stakeholder interests provide the basis for dashboard - type functionality to manage and improve complex systems. We have shown that in general deviation from peer allows us to look for target areas where the enterprise is misaligned.

4 Conclusions and Future Work

We have introduced 1) a dynamic approach to complex systems and processes that incorporates an event-based context sensing approach, 2) a dynamic framework for response based on process evolution and mechanisms for tacit knowledge capture, and 3) finally a multi-dimensional framework synthesizing top down performance knowledge (based on priorities and value) *and* bottom up knowledge flow. Further we illustrate the advantages of such traceability applied to decision -making by customer and provider stakeholders. In the future we envision *an intelligent ACE assistant* layer on the internet (using web services for data mediation and security) that synthesizes execution patterns and makes suggestions to stakeholders that manage sense-and-respond complex systems. Our goal is to develop and validate principles and axioms to consolidate interesting facts across instances and develop collaborative tools for knowledge and performance evolution. We are developing a Cyber Infrastructure for research based on the ACE meta model. Such infrastructures must federate many organizations and systems. Currently have a prototype of the architecture. In parallel we have validating the meta model through numerous projects on-going within our Industry University Collaborative Research Center.

Acknowledgements

This research has been conducted within the National Science Foundation funded Center for Experimental Research in Computer Science (CERCS) at Georgia Tech and The Ohio State University. We would like to thank industry sponsors and affiliates especially those at Ohio Department of Job & Family Services. We wish to thank Battelle and Future Point Systems for the support of Starlight. We also wish to thank the CETI team and in particular Kelly Yackovich and Shubhanan Deshpande for their inputs

References

1. Smith, T.F., Waterman, M.S.: Identification of Common Molecular Subsequences. J. Mol. Biol. 147, 195–197 (1981)
2. May, P., Ehrlich, H.C., Steinke, T.: ZIB Structure Prediction Pipeline: Composing a Complex Biological Workflow through Web Services. In: Nagel, W.E., Walter, W.V., Lehner, W. (eds.) Euro-Par 2006. LNCS, vol. 4128, pp. 1148–1158. Springer, Heidelberg (2006)
3. Foster, I., Kesselman, C.: The Grid: Blueprint for a New Computing Infrastructure. Morgan Kaufmann, San Francisco (1999)
4. Czajkowski, K., Fitzgerald, S., Foster, I., Kesselman, C.: Grid Information Services for Distributed Resource Sharing. In: 10th IEEE International Symposium on High Performance Distributed Computing, pp. 181–184. IEEE Press, New York (2001)
5. Foster, I., Kesselman, C., Nick, J., Tuecke, S.: The Physiology of the Grid: an Open Grid Services Architecture for Distributed Systems Integration. Technical report, Global Grid Forum (2002)
6. National Center for Biotechnology Information, http://www.ncbi.nlm.nih.gov

The Use of Experts Panels in ERP Cost Estimation Research

Ahmed Elragal[1] and Moutaz Haddara[2]

[1] German University in Cairo, New Cairo, Egypt
[2] University of Agder, Norway
ahmed.elragal@guc.edu.eg, moutaz.haddara@uia.no

Abstract. This paper is an effort towards illustrating the use of expert panel (EP) as a mean of eliciting knowledge from a group of enterprise resource planning (ERP) experts as an exploratory research. The development of a cost estimation model (CEM) for ERP adoptions is very crucial for research and practice, and that was the main reason behind the willingness of experts to participate in this research. The use of EP was very beneficial as it involved various data collection and visualisation techniques, as well as data validation and confirmation. Beside its advantages, one of the main motives for using a group technique is that it is difficult to find a representative sample for a casual survey method, as ERP experts and consultants are rare to find, especially in the scope of SMEs' ERP implementations. It is worth noting that the panel reached consensus regarding the results of the EP. The experts modified and enhanced the initial cost drivers (CD) list largely, as they added, modified, merged and split different costs drivers. In addition, the experts added CF (sub-factors) that could influence or affect each cost driver. Moreover, they ranked the CD according to their weight on total costs. All of this helped the authors to better understand relationships among various CF.

Keywords: ERP; cost estimation; expert panel.

1 Introduction

As they say, *"it's about the journey, not the destination"*, research techniques are very crucial for any research endeavour. They can lead researchers to the right path, or deviate them away from the desired destination. Moreover, the significance of any research results is determined by several measures, and the data collection and analysis techniques are on top of them.

In our proposed research phases, different data collection techniques are *used* and proposed. Some of those techniques are qualitative in nature, some are quantative, and some are mixed approaches. The variety of methods chosen should help in identifying the different costs and factors that influence costs in the Enterprise Resource Planning (ERP) systems adoption processes, in order to establish a cost estimation model (CEM). In addition, these techniques should provide a multi-perspective on costs through involving various key stakeholders from beneficiaries, independent consultants, and vendors that participate in ERP adoption projects.

J.E. Quintela Varajão et al. (Eds.): CENTERIS 2010, Part II, CCIS 110, pp. 97–108, 2010.

In particular, this paper discusses the Experts Panel (EP) approach that was used as a part of our "initial model development phase" *(see fig. 2)*. The paper is an effort on arguing why *group discussions and interviewing* techniques are proposed in our initial exploratory research phase, and why we preferred the term "Experts Panels" over Delphi and Focus Groups (FG).

The remainder of the paper is organized as follows: the next section presents the research overview, researchers' perspective of costs, followed by a description of the EP conducted. Moreover, a brief comparison between the EP and other related techniques followed by a conclusion.

2 Research Overview

In the next sections, scope, perspectives, and data collection are discussed.

2.1 Research Scope

As previously mentioned, this research focuses on identifying costs and the factors that influence costs within the adoption process in SME's in order to develop a CEM. *Adoption* in this research starts prior to phase 1, and ends at phase 5 *(see fig. 1)*. In other words, the focus starts with the cost drivers (CD) occurring during the feasibility study, consultant selection, vendor selection, contracting, etc till the Go-live phase. Post installation costs are often recurring within the ERP system lifetime. These costs are hard to take account of within this research. Thus, costs that occur after ERP installations are off boundaries of this research effort and maybe left for future research, yet the standard agreed-upon maintenance costs in contracts fall within this research's boundaries.

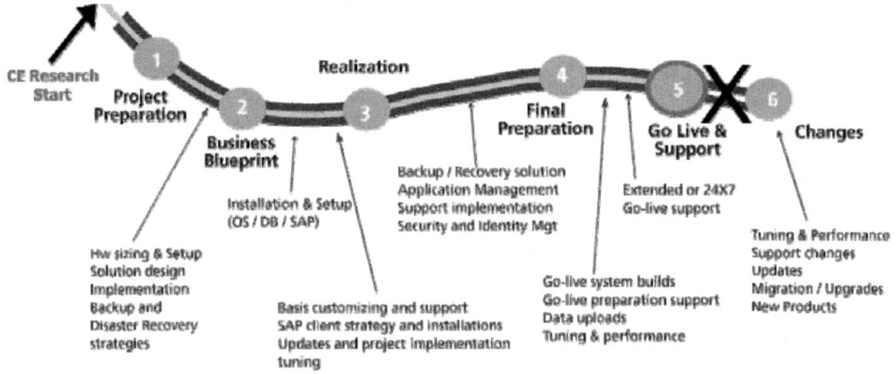

Fig. 1. SAP's accelerated methodology (ASAP) – Adapted from www.sap.com

2.2 Researchers' Perspective *(The Cost Lens)*

This research is not concerned with cost/benefit analysis; it is more focused on the relation (or difference) between estimated ERP adoption costs with actual adoption costs of completed projects. The cost lens proposed in this research is because sometimes benefits in relation to costs are not important or unattainable. For example, when an SME's budget is crossed, it does not matter how much benefits it will gain through dedicating more money to the project, as it might be out of the required resources already. In addition, benefits and their associated costs should be projected correctly from the beginning, as many companies implementing ERP systems filed for bankruptcy e.g. FoxMeyer Drug [1], [18], [21], and this was mainly due to a faulty ERP budget and schedule estimations [12], [13], [17]. Thus, in the previous example, the costs view is more crucial despite the potential benefits, as you can always gain more benefits when you pay more money, but it is all about your budget and your resources' availability. Moreover, the CEM should be used in order to project more realistic cost estimates, while benefits should be the motive for implementing an ERP in first place. Usually the expected benefits are the system requirements based on the requirements analysis included within the *request for proposal* (RFP) invitation.

2.3 Research Methods and Design

It is hard to predict the future without studying the past. Hence, this research will be based on data collected from EPs along with actual data from organisations that already completed their ERP adoption process. And this will be done through a multiple case study design, as it has more investigative recompense compared to single case study, as well as it provides a flexible approach for Information Systems research [3], [8], [32]. This research will apply a multi-method research technique, encompassing multiple case studies, empirical literature findings, EPs, documents analysis, interviews, as well as surveys. Furthermore, in order to build strong substantiation of constructs, data triangulation as a mixture of qualitative and quantitative data collection methods will be used [8].

To reach the goal of developing a CEM, this research project will tackle different research questions and aspects within the very domain of ERP cost estimation within SMEs. These aspects will require different perspectives, methods, and tools within its development cycle. After identifying relevant perspectives through inductive methods that can assist in identifying factors that influence costs and cost driver to be included in a priori CEM within phase one. Then phase two will start, and in this phase, an empirical test of the cost model will be conducted in order to identify the relative contribution of the different cost concepts in understanding the resulting costs of ERP adoption in SMEs. While phase one will be qualitative and inductive in nature, phase two will be deductive and quantitative.

This research will conduct multiple case studies. Fig 2 presents an initial map of the proposed research design. Within the initial model development, theory, literature review of empirical research and the researchers' experience will be used in order to develop an *a priori* CEM. In addition to that, several EPs with vendors, consultants, and beneficiaries are going to be held in order to direct the a priori CEM development into the right direction.

The theory to be used in this phase is the stakeholder theory (ST), which plays a role in identifying the stakeholders and cost associated with them in these ERP adoption process using its stakeholder identification instruments. Besides ST, the empirical findings and data collected will compliment ST in CD' identification. The a priori CEM will be used in the second stage as an initial guide for pilot interviews. Then an interview guide will be developed, and interviews will be conducted to the cases selected.

In the following stage, a mixture of qualitative and quantitative analysis will be undertaken. As the ST has a very good technique to identify stakeholders and respondents, still it lacks relevance to information and technological aspects. Thus, a complementary theory(ies) will be considered after this initial research step. The findings from the analysis are crucial, because they will be used in mapping candidate theories to these findings, in other words, an iterative theory relevance check will be conducted.

In case of not finding a relevant theory, a grounded approach will be an alternative for theory building from case study data as advised by [8]. After theory mapping or building, the research design will be modified to accommodate the chosen theory. Then a survey will be conducted followed by quantative analysis.

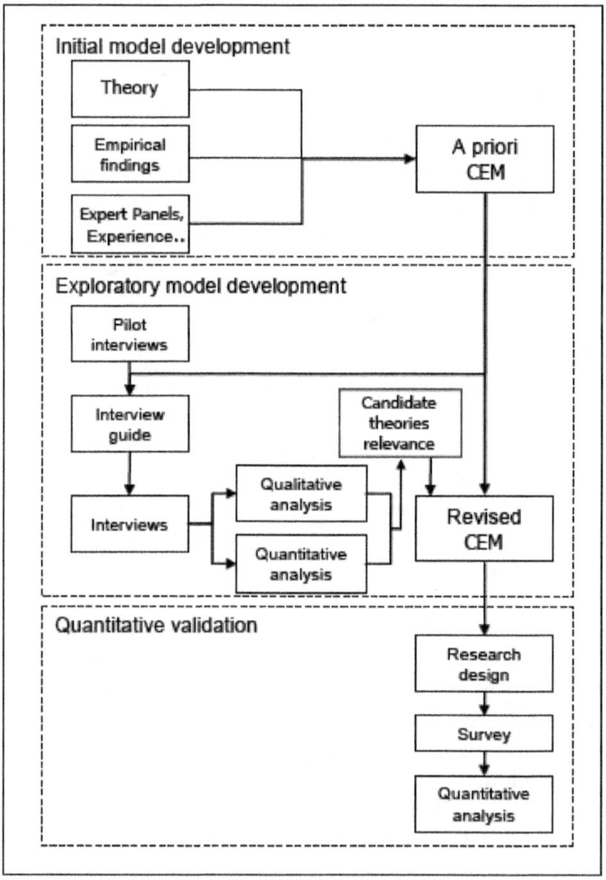

Fig. 2. Proposed research design: Adapted from [7]

2.4 Sources of Data and Data Collection Methods

In order to develop an effectual CEM, this research will collect actual data from the industry. The data required is as follows:

1. ***Data*** is based on finished projects.
2. ***Data Sources:*** Beneficiaries, consultants, vendors, and any stakeholder identified through the stakeholders analysis.
3. ***Type of data:*** Company size, industry type, cost factors (CF) and drivers (e.g. Business process reengineering, vendor selection costs, new hires, contracts, etc).

A further description of each data collection technique is as follows:

a) **EP:** incorporates different techniques and data collection methods. The panels includes various key experts in the ERP adoption field, including consultants, vendors, and key project representatives from beneficiaries.
b) **Interviews:** *semi-structured* interviews will be conducted with beneficiaries, consultants, and vendors, and guided by [19] 'recommendations for qualitative interviewing'. The interviews will be carried out with diverse employee positions within the organisations in accordance to 'triangulation of subjects' strategy proposed by [26], and based on the initial interviewee's sample plan identified by the stakeholder analysis.
c) **Document Analysis:** analysis of project documentations including feasibility studies, project plan, project schedule, cost estimations, actual project expenses, as well as any documents recommended by the people involved in the project.
d) **Surveys:** some are conducted as a part of EP in order to collect preliminary data about CF and CD within SMEs. Other proposed surveys will be conducted in order to get feedback on the adequacy of the *a priori* CEM developed.

3 The Experts Panel

Due to the implications of this research into practice, an EP has been conducted. The EP recommendations and insights would be very valuable to this research within its exploratory stage, as experts would provide more inputs that would help the researchers to understand the phenomena or the problem they are studying.

The EP serves as an initial research kick off, that will ensure the mapping of the researcher's ideas and research problems with practice. Moreover, the EP is used as a mean of eliciting knowledge from ERP experts.

The panel included key persons involved in ERP implementations in Egypt. The participants were from the elite ERP consultants, vendors' representatives and implementation project managers. The expertise of the participants represents "state-of-the-art" knowledge in a broad range of international companies and industrial sectors. Eight potential participants were contacted by phone and via e-mail, and eight experts responded and participated. The panel included vendor consultants from SAP, JD Edwards, Focus ERP, independent ERP consultants, and project champions and managers from different industrial beneficiaries. The variety of experts was to ensure that the researcher captures different views and perspectives on costs.

- *The Briefing*

Prior to the actual panel discussion, a research briefing was sent by email to participating experts. It contained information about the research, the panel setting, the research objectives, as well as the expected implications for practice.

- *The EP Discussion*

On the first panel meeting, an explanation (reminder) about the research objectives was provided. A set of presentations took place to explain the CEM, and what is needed from them in order to develop a model for estimating costs within the ERP adoption phase. Additionally, we illustrated the importance and need for such a model by beneficiaries, consultants, and vendors. Moreover, a less formal discussion was held at the beginning of the panel regarding their experiences with ERP projects in SMEs. Participants were asked predefined questions centred on the features of ERP adoption cost estimations within SMEs in Egypt, and its success rate of finishing projects at hand within budgets. Moreover, they were asked about the challenges facing implementers and costs' impact on ERP adoptions in SMEs. Some participants from major ERP vendors mentioned that they use CEMs to estimate budgets needed from beneficiaries to cover their part of costs, but they said that these models are not accurate, nor give a realistic view for beneficiaries about all the dimensions of costs needed for the whole ERP adoption project. One major note from several experts was that organisations regularly do not face cost problems in selection nor post-adoption phases, the majority of ERP problems and costs pop-up during the adoption phase, and that the research should focus and start with these costs.

- *The First Round*

In the first panel round, the participants were provided with an initial CD conceptual model (mind map). The initial mind map (fig. 3) was a visualisation of CF gathered through literature and researchers' own experience with previous ERP adoption projects. The visualising of CD and factors in a mind map (tree-like) format is believed to enhance the participants' insights and interpretations.

While the mind map was presented to the participants, group discussions took place and were managed by two moderators. One moderator's role was to ensure that the session advances smoothly, and the other's role was to ensure that all the topics are covered. Both of them were taking notes. The moderator had predefined list of questions for group interviewing, and these questions evoked the discussion and brainstorming among participants. The discussions were about which CD and factors should be merged or split, change their naming, CF' approximate weight on total costs, and their priority pertaining to SMEs, etc.

Although some debates on some specific CD' importance took place, the moderator reminded the group about the focus of discussion, and that they should adopt a *costs view* within an SME setting, and this minimised the level of debates between them. From our point of view, the discussion between participants was very fruitful, as it initially consolidated their views, and made the participants brainstorm together and start to provide valuable suggestions and remarks.

Further, each participant was provided with a questionnaire in a table (list) format that contained the compiled ERP costs. Their task was to verify if the listed CD were appropriate to build a CEM, and to ensure whether there are missing CD or existing ones that should be apart or combined, according to their relevance to the adoption process in SMEs. The questionnaire contained four main parts:

1) A list of CD;
2) A column to associate them with other CD that can influence these factors;
3) A column to CF according to impact on SMEs' ERP adoption projects;

4) A space to comment or add additional CD or factors that can influence these costs, which should be considered and were over looked.

The CD list was gathered through literature and the author's personal experience in the field. This was to ensure the relevance of the data collected through research and experience in the field with practice. The questionnaire was a combination of open and closed ended questions. The open-ended questions were to help the experts provide their insights, recommendations or suggestions about which additional CF to include, exclude, combine, or split. The costs factors column contained cost items compiled from literature and researchers' previous experience with ERP adoption projects. The cost items scale was from very high to very low in relevance to overall costs in an SME setting. The main initial CD were vendors, change management, business process reengineering, project management, hardware, software, human resources costs.

The participants' feedback helped in further developing CD, adding new factors, merging some factors, decomposing some factors to include important sub-factors, and identifying CD that can influence other CF. This brought us to a better understanding of CD that should affect an ERP adoption process.

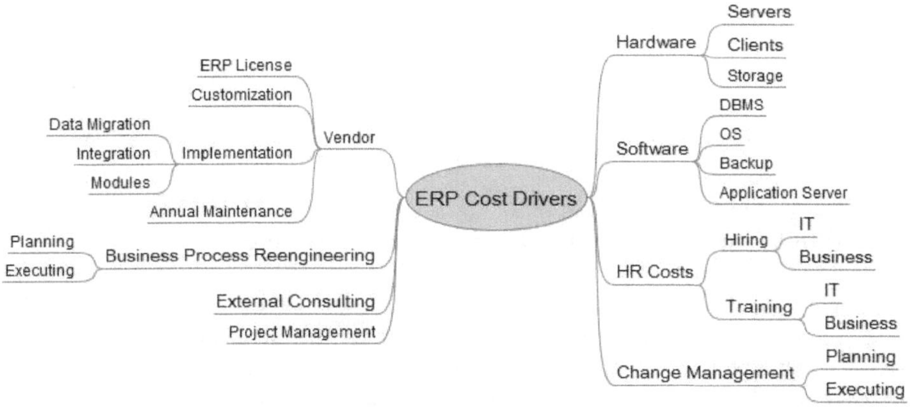

Fig. 3. Initial CD mind map

- *The Second Round*

In the second round, an updated list of CD was provided for participants. The list contained the new updated CF and drivers captured during the first round's questionnaire, interviews, and discussions. The updated list was presented in a table format as well as a mind map. The moderator initiated a discussion about the comprehensiveness of this list, and this stimulated group discussions and interactions. During this round, the participants have agreed upon some slight modifications to the CF' list, and the list was directly updated accordingly. At the end of this round, the participants were provided with the reviewed CF list and were asked to rank them *independently*. Their task was to re-rank the costs and to make sure that all the presented CF and our interpretations are complying with their suggestions and recommendations. The provided rankings of CD were: very high, high, medium, low, and very low. The participants were alerted that CD should be ranked to their importance to the adoption phase within SMEs and from a cost perspective.

The data was analysed and showed that the experts has reached consensus. Moreover, the updated and consolidated mind map was sent electronically to the participants in order to confirm the validity of the CD presented. The updated mind map is in fig 4.

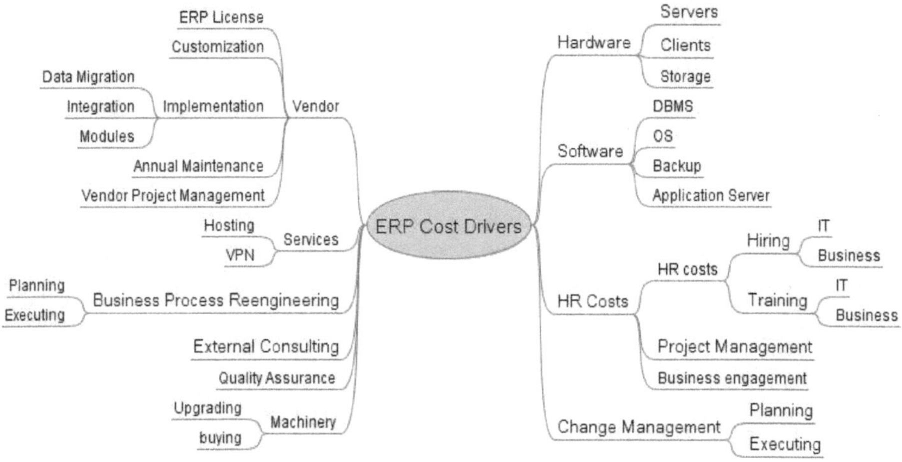

Fig. 4. Updated mind map

4 EP in Contrast with Delphi and FG Techniques

As researchers should choose the best method *they think* satisfies their research objectives, the method used and proposed in this research is a combination of several techniques. Although it is difficult to establish clear boundaries between the EP conducted in this research, and Delphi and FG, but WE will try in the following section to illustrate the main common similarities and differences between them. Part of this difficulty or confusion comes from literature itself, as the Delphi and FG studies have various variations which sometimes conflict with their own main principals, like incorporating fact-to-face group discussions in Delphi studies for example [5]. Moreover, while writing this paper, we have discussed it and consulted several colleagues in order to obtain their opinions about categorising the method used in this research. Some of them viewed it as a Delphi style research technique, and others viewed it more of FG research. These different views made me affirmative that the research technique used here is none of them; it is actually a combination of them whilst incorporating other techniques from other research methods as well.

As mentioned above, the next part will discuss the technical and conceptual differences between the EP in comparison with other "similar" techniques. In addition, we will provide arguments about why the technique used is more adequate than these techniques.

- **Similarities and Differences**

The EP technique used in this research shares similarities with Delphi, FG and NGT research methods. Although Delphi and FG techniques are considered data collection techniques through group interviewing or surveying, still they have basic differences.

- EP and Delphi
    - *Similarities*

In literature, the Delphi method has been used to acquire knowledge from single or multiple experts [25. The Delphi technique serves as a systematic method to collect ideas, opinions, and judgments on a particular topic at stake through the use of sequential questionnaires combined with feedback and summaries derived from previous responses [4]. The Delphi method is primarily used when the problem at stake does not suit itself with precise analytical techniques but can benefit from collective subjective judgments and opinions [16]. Moreover, one of the main goals of the Delphi technique is to reach consensus position from experts [4], [20]. Some Delphi studies use sound ranking measurement techniques (e.g. Kendall's W) through its iterations in order to measure the degree of consensus [2], [27].

- *Differences*

Although the above-mentioned characteristics and goals match with those of EP, yet there are basic differences between both techniques. The typical Delphi method is asynchronous and does not incorporate face-to-face interactions between participants or experts [28], as the anonymity of respondents is believed to give the method positive recompenses over face-to-face interactions [16].

In order to reach consensus, there have been rounds in the EP that are similar to those of Delphi; on the other hand, these rounds incorporated surveys, rankings, *plus* group discussions and interviews. Furthermore, the EP incorporated ideas and suggestions from the experts' group discussions, as group interaction and brainstorming would enhance the amount and quality of responses, and would initiate new ideas in contrast with individual brainstorming [22], [23] in [28]. Moreover, group interactions can be used to examine not only what individuals think, but also how they think and why they think that in a particular way [14]. In our point of view, face-to-face interactions are better when there is a group of experts that represents clients' side and vendors' side in order to decrease bias through objective discussions. In addition, group discussion would enable participants to exchange ideas and point-of-views, which would help in narrowing down and reaching consensus. Furthermore, Delphi presents data, key issues, and items in a *list* format to participants [2], [29]. On the other hand, during the EP rounds, lists and mind maps were used. Instead of presenting CF in lists only, mind maps were used to visualise information and to help participants grasp the full picture of the factors and the relationships among them. A mind map is an information construction tool represented as a graphical illustration of connections between concepts and ideas that are related to one core subject, and the process of constructing mind maps engages the participants with the content [31]. Mind maps are useful in situations where developing understanding, problem solving, brainstorming, delivering information, and evaluation of participants understanding are needed [31]. Moreover, mind maps are very similar to the notion of *cognitive maps,* which are used to record and graphically present qualitative data [6]. The mind map used was dynamic; as we modified the map instantaneously according to their recommendations and suggestions to enable the experts to view the changes and re-evaluate them.

- EP and FG
  - *Similarities*

FG is a qualitative data collection technique through conducting organised group discussions and interactions, moderated by one or more moderators. In addition, FG is a form of group interview that relies on communication between group participants in order to generate data [14]. The participants in this group are selected and assembled by researchers in order to discuss and reflect on, from their personal experiences, the topic of researchers' interest [24]. FG can be used at the initial or exploratory stages of a research [11], [15]. The chief purpose of FG research is to draw upon respondents' beliefs, experiences, and responses in a way in which would not be suitable using other techniques like one-to-one interviewing or questionnaires [10]. Moreover, several researchers have also indicated that group discussions can generate more significant comments than usual interviews [11], [30].

  - *Differences*

FG are usually conducted in one rounds and do not capture comprehensive reflections from participants [9], on the other hand the EP was conducted in two rounds in order to reach consensus. In FG, data collection relies on the group interaction, interviews, and discussions solely, while in EP, those techniques were incorporated with surveys, mind maps, and rankings in order to ensure data validity and reliability. One of the core differences between the EP and FG is that, FG research is not considered a consensus oriented technique, and it is typically conducted in social research in order to observe the behaviour, reactions, and interactions among the group [11], [14]. On the contrary, the primary goal of the EP, was to reach *consensus* about the ERP CF and CD within SMEs.

5 Conclusion

This paper is primarily an effort towards illustrating the use of EP technique as a mean of eliciting knowledge from a group of ERP experts as an exploratory research. The developing of a CEM for ERP adoptions is very crucial for research and practice, and that was the main reason behind the willingness of experts to participate in this research. In our point of view, the use of EP was very beneficial, as it involved various data collection and visualisation techniques, as well as data validation and confirmation. Beside its advantages, one of the main motives for using a group technique is that it is difficult to find a representative sample for a casual survey method, as ERP experts and consultants are rare to find, especially in the scope of SMEs' ERP implementations.

It is worth noting that the panel reached consensus regarding the results of the EP. The experts modified and enhanced the initial CD list largely, as they added, modified, merged and split different costs drivers. In addition, the experts added CF (subfactors) that could influence or affect each cost driver. Moreover, they ranked the CD according to their weight on total costs. All of this helped the authors to better understand relationships among various CF.

References

1. Al-Mashari, M.: Enterprise resource planning (ERP) systems: a research agenda. Industrial Management & Data Systems 102(3), 165–170 (2002)
2. Brancheau, J.C., Wetherbe, J.C.: Key Issues in Information Systems Management. MIS Quarterly 11(1), 23–45 (1987)
3. Cavaye, A.L.M.: Case study research: a multi-faceted research approach for IS. Information Systems Journal 6(3), 227–242 (1996)
4. Delbecq, A., Van de Ven, A., Gustafson, D.: Group techniques for programme planning: a guide to nominal group and Delphi processes. Scott, Foresman & Company, Glenview (1975)
5. Dick, B.: Delphi face to face (2000), `http://www.scu.edu.au/schools/gcm/ar/arp/delphi.html` (retrieved December 4, 2009)
6. Eden, C., Ackermann, F.: Cognitive mapping expert views for policy analysis in the public sector. European Journal of Operational Research 152(3), 615–630 (2004)
7. Eikebrokk, T.R., Iden, J., Olsen, D.H., Opdahl, A.L.: Validating the Process-Modelling Practice Model. EMISA 3(2), 3–17 (2008)
8. Eisenhardt, K.M.: Building theories from case study research. Academy of Management Review (AMR) 14(4), 532–550 (1989)
9. Frankfort-Nachmais, C., Nachmais, D.: Research methods in the Social Science, 7th edn. Worth Publishers, New York (2008)
10. Gibbs, A.: Focus groups. Social Research Update, Department of Sociology, vol. 19 (1997), `http://www.soc.surrey.ac.uk/sru/sru19.html`
11. Hines, T.: A Evaluation of Two Qualitative Methods (Focus Group Interviews and Cognitive Maps) for Conducting Research into Entrepreneurial Decision Making. International Journal of Qualitative Market Research 3(1), 7–16 (2000)
12. Holland, C.R., Light, B.: A critical success factors model for ERP implementation. IEEE Software 16(3), 30–36 (1999)
13. Jones, C.: Estimating software costs Bringing realism to estimating, 2nd edn. McGraw-Hill Companies, New York (2007)
14. Kitzinger, J.: Qualitative Research: Introducing focus groups. BMJ 311(7000), 299–302 (1995)
15. Kreuger, R.: Focus groups: a practical guide for applied research. Sage, London (1988)
16. Linstone, H., Turoff, M.: The Delphi Method: Techniques and Applications. Addison-Wesley, London (1975)
17. Martin, M.H.: An ERP Strategy. Fortune, pp. 95–97 (February 2, 1998)
18. Moon, Y.: Enterprise Resource Planning (ERP): A review of the literature. International Journal of Management and Enterprise Development 4(3), 200 (2007)
19. Myers, M.D., Newman, M.: The qualitative interview in IS research: Examining the craft. Inf. Organ. 17(1), 2–26 (2007)
20. Nevo, D., Chan, Y.E.: A Delphi study of knowledge management systems: Scope and requirements. Information & Management 44(6), 583–597 (2007)
21. Newman, M., Zhao, Y.: The process of enterprise resource planning implementation and business process re-engineering: tales from two chinese small and medium-sized enterprises. Information Systems Journal 18(4), 405–426 (2008)
22. Osborn, A.F.: Applied Imagination, revised ed. Scribners, New York (1957)
23. Parnes, J., Meadow, A.: Effects of Brain-Storming Instruction on Creative Problem-Solving by Trained and Untrained Subjects. Journal of Educational Psychology 50 (1959)

24. Powell, R., Single, H.: Focus groups. International Journal of Quality in Health Care 8(5), 499–504 (1996)
25. Roth, R.M., William, C., Wood, I.: A Delphi approach to acquiring knowledge from single and multiple experts. Paper Presented at the Proceedings of the 1990 ACM SIGBDP Conference on Trends and Directions in Expert Systems (1990)
26. Rubin, H.J., Rubin, I.S.: Qualitative interviewing: The art of hearing data, 2nd edn. Sage, Thousand Oaks (2005)
27. Schmidt, R.C.: Managing Delphi Surveys Using Nonparametric Statistical Techniques. Decision Sciences 28(3), 763–774 (1997)
28. Van de Ven, A., Delbeco, A.: Nominal versus Interacting Group Processes for Committee Decision-Making Effectiveness. The Academy of Management Journal 14(2), 203–212 (1971)
29. Van de Ven, A., Delbecq, A.: The Effectiveness of Nominal, Delphi, and Interacting Group Decision Making Processes. The Academy of Management Journal 17(4), 605–621 (1974)
30. Watts, M., Ebbutt, D.: More than the sum of the parts: research methods in group interviewing. British Educational Research Journal 13, 25–34 (1987)
31. Willis, C.L., Miertschin, S.L.: Mind maps as active learning tool. J. Comput. Small Coll. 21(4), 266–272 (2006)
32. Yin, R.K.: Case study research: Design and methods, 3rd edn., vol. 5. Sage, Thousand Oaks (2003)

Military Medical Department Research Centers

Joseph Wood[1], Mary M. Klote[2], Hui-Lien Tung[3], Max E. Stachura[4], Elena V. Astapova[5], Donald A. Sofge[6], James Grayson[7], and W.F. Lawless[8, *]

[1] Dwight D. Eisenhower Army Medical, Chief, Department of Clinical Investigation, Ft. Gordon, GA 30905
Joseph.C.Wood@us.army.mil
[2] US Army Medical Research and Materiel Command, Director, Clinical Investigation Regulatory Office, 504 Scott Street, Bldg 1452, Fort Detrick, MD 21702
Mary.Klote@us.army.mil
[3] Department of Management, 401 Lowder Business Building, 415 West Magnolia Avenue, Auburn, AL 36849-5241
hzt0007@auburn.edu
[4] Director, Center for Telehealth, Medical College of Georgia, 1120 15th Street, EA-100, Augusta GA 30912-1655
maxs@mcg.edu
[5] Associate Director, Center for Telehealth, Medical College of Georgia 1120 15th Street, EA-100, Augusta GA 30912-1655
eastapova@mail.mcg.edu
[6] Navy Center for Applied Research in Artificial Intelligence Naval Research Laboratory, Washington, DC
donald.sofge@nrl.navy.mil
[7] Associate Professor of Business, Augusta State University, 2500 Walton Way, Augusta, GA 30904
jgrayson@aug.edu
[8] Paine College, 1235 15th Street, Augusta, GA 30901-3182
wlawless@paine.edu

Abstract. We review our research with military Medical Department Research Centers (MDRC; a pseudonym). In 2006, we first proposed an electronic data system with metrics to better measure performance for the MDRCs. The data management system evolved into an electronic system for an Institutional Review Board (e-IRB) at one site. We foresaw that an e-IRB could provide the metrics to better monitor MDRC practices. Now that the eIRB is operational, metrics can measure how well the present mission of the MDRCs is being met across its system (improved patient care, increased scientific knowledge, and improved graduate student education); and, how well its vision is achieved (transforming the present mission of MDRCs to prepare for future missions).

Keywords: Organizational uncertainty, metrics, interdependence.

* Corresponding author.

J.E. Quintela Varajão et al. (Eds.): CENTERIS 2010, Part II, CCIS 110, pp. 109–118, 2010.

1 Introduction

We review our work-in-progress by discussing the status of MDRC's eIRB; its metrics; and its process of transformation. The Concept of Operations Plan, outlining the current status of how the eIRB approval of protocols works and how the system will enhance operations, has been completed and submitted to the Army Medical Command for approval. The Office of the Undersecretary of Defense (OUSD) Health Affairs Personnel and Readiness (P&R) has approved funding to pay for sites performing Defense Health Program research to join the eIRB. A contract modification has been approved at OUSD(P&R) to allow E-MDRC's server to be "moved" to the P&R servers (E-MDRC is one of 7 sites, all pseudonyms). The date of transfer of server responsibility is FY2010. All military services and the Uniformed Services University have been invited to join.

2 Background

2.1 Review of Prior Research

In our first studies the of MDRC system [10],[12], we noted that traditional models of organizations did not work, encumbering rational management. In contrast, we have made substantial progress with an interdependent uncertainty model of organizations, begun with a case study.

We generalized uncertainty for organizations into a bistable model. Mindful of forthcoming machine-based real-time metrics afforded by the semantic web, our model predicted tradeoffs that could be managed better with metrics.

Models should be at least as complex as the system modeled. We addressed organizational growth and mergers or, conversely, organizational fragmentation and collapse. Our research implied tradeoffs between uncertain resources (ΔE) and the time (Δt) to execute a plan with expenditures, $\Delta t \Delta E \geq c$; if c is known, ΔE, could be derived to determine, say, the number, N, needed to control a market.

There were other advantages to uncertainty and tradeoffs: our model succeeds where game theory has not by accounting for differences between an aggregate and a group constituted of the same individuals; and it explains why traditional models based on individual perspectives of rationality fail (e.g., self-reports of self-esteem do not correlate with academic or work performance [2]).

We drew two other broad conclusions. First, while cooperation is critical to organizational effectiveness, it requires enforcement [6]. And, second, however, to solve ill-defined problems in the production of knowledge, K, and to change organizations, cooperation marginalizes incommensurable data.

Scientists, too, fall into the trap of believing that cooperation alone increases social welfare, i.e., that self-interests must be overcome to promote common causes [5], without the turmoil of capitalism and democracy. But as concluded above, in countries with forced cooperation, science was significantly less innovative than in more competitive societies; e.g., under enforced cooperation in Venezuela, frequent electricity shortages have occurred [11], reflecting misallocation; in contrast, the open market that exists today for cell phones has not experienced shortages. While organizations require command decision-making, across a system command or central decision-making can reduce social welfare by reducing innovation e.g., Muslim repression produces poor health, poverty, and corruption [1].

In our third study [21], we contrasted the organizational performance of MDRC against its assigned mission: improving patient care in the field; reducing the costs of care; and increasing the impact of research products. We found no clear link between research products and the mission; no measure of publication impacts; and no direct way to measure organizational productivity against its peers (reduced or negligible states of interdependence). In general, the organizations in the MDRC network were fragmented, with each pursuing its own path to mission success. No overarching measure of system performance existed for the MDRCs that the separate organizations could follow to guide their collective behavior. As a consequence, long-term work practices and cultural differences predominated. We noted, however, that the approval to adopt an eIRB had set the stage to turn around the lack of organizational and system-wide knowledge of performance outcomes.

Monte Carlo Simulations. For a study of tradeoffs and interaction rates, we devised a mathematical model of social interaction sufficient for machine learning and recombination operators [10]. We adapted this model for our research on organizations, e.g., training MDRC physicians with the experimental method. In the latter case, the model becomes, $\Gamma = N_1 N_2 v_{12} \sigma_{12} exp(-\Delta A/<A>)$, where Γ is the physician-as-trainee publication rate; N_1 represents those in the physician population who have not yet learned how to publish scientific papers; N_2 represents the population of those who have learned (viz., mentors); v_{12} represents the velocity of knowledge passed between them, with the minimum effect occurring under censorship; σ_{12} represents how well the two groups match their beliefs, with the maximum effect occurring under social agreement (interdependence, reflecting social resonance); and $exp(-\Delta A/<A>)$ represents the probability of knowledge exchanges, where ΔA represents the energy or effort required for the knowledge to be acquired, and $<A>$ represents the average amount of effort being expended by the members of an MDRC, its mentors, support staff, and physician students. Rearranging, if χ represents the knowledge required before a physician trainee can become published, then $\Gamma = \partial\chi/\partial t \approx \Delta\chi/\Delta t$, and $\Delta\chi = \Delta t * \Gamma = \Delta t * N_1 N_2 v_{12} \sigma_{12} exp(-\Delta A/<A>)$. Given an average time to learn experimental and publication methods at an MDRC, various tradeoffs exist for an MDRC to improve the probability that its physician trainees will publish ($\Delta\chi$) a paper (article, book chapter, etc.). Increasing the numbers of those who actively support the trainees increases the occurrence of mentor-(N_1)-to-trainee (N_2) speech acts. Increasing the velocity (v_{12}) of knowledge passed between the two groups improves the acquisition of knowledge. Increasing the match (σ_{12}) between mentors and physician trainees can dramatically increase the knowledge gained (e.g., study groups; trainee focus groups; mentor-trainee focus groups). But also the probability of publishing can be increased by reducing the barriers that students face ($-\Delta A$; e.g., choosing better qualified entrants or skills enhancements for weaker entrants). Finally, by increasing the overall average effort or excitement by an MDRC directed toward learning and publishing ($<A>$), an MDRC can strongly improve the odds that its students will become published. Inversely, these factors can also decrease or adversely impact learning outcomes.

From Monte Carlo simulations, we concluded that an MDRC can improve Γ by lowering ΔA (raising the skill levels of trainee candidates to achieve the publishing standards for physician trainees) or by raising $<A>$ (increasing the average motivation of trainees, raising the overall number of demands by mentors of their trainees, or placing trainees in more "high-energy" and skilled mentoring groups).

Ideally we would like to improve both ΔA (improved physician trainee skills) and $<A>$ (increased overall excitement of the trainees or their mentors) to obtain a higher value for Γ; however, if management could only do one thing it would be to improve systems so trainees become more productive (less energy required per scientific product) by adopting an electronic system to help them to do more on average. Increasing matching between mentors and trainees also has the potential to be a significant contributor to productivity as a state of social resonance occurs between them (low reactance), but only if mentors have a high level of skills.

In the next two papers [18],[19], we discussed organizational attention and decision-making, which we found could range in from fragmented to well-focused. At that time, the US spent more on healthcare than any other industrialized nation but continued to have a significant underserved population along with rising health costs. Home health and hospice care faced the challenge of monitoring vital signs and other physiological parameters of geospatially scattered patients. With remote data collection, we expected that technology could solve this problem, reduce healthcare costs and extend healthcare services.

We reviewed Telemedicine and eHealth from an organizational perspective over three years. Theory of the conservation of information (COI) provides the means to study effectiveness from the tradeoffs across space and over time as Telemedicine and eHealth management make operational decisions for virtual communities users of eHealth acroos the State of Georgia.

Over the time studied, the regional network in Georgia had become self-sustainable, increasingly paying for itself through new services and savings in travel expenses and time, Telehealth also reduced nursing staff turnover.

The eHealth network conducted another year-long study of hospitalization rate changes and telemedicine. Hospitalization rates without telemonitoring held nearly steady while rates with telemonitoring fell. As a consequence of its success, the eHealth network experienced a significant increase in the number of referring physicians, and its care managers had more than doubled the number of patients that they could handle. While other healthcare industries experience increased costs along with technological advances, telemonitoring in home health represents a health care industry in which improving quality simultaneously decreased costs.

In the next study [23], self-reported data collected at six of the MDRCs from IRB committee members and researchers were analyzed. First, from the correlation matrix with only IRB committee members, those committee members who felt positive about IRB meeting documents also felt positive about the timeliness of the reviews that were conducted, and that they had clear responsibilities. They tended to report protocol completeness, positive communications and helpful interactions with researchers that required little follow-up, and to report that IRB meeting minutes were accurate. Overall, these committee members were satisfied with the current manual system, and reported no need to switch to a web-based system. But, a second perspective indicated that not all committee members held a positive outlook for the current IRB system. Those committee members who reported the need to communicate with protocol coordinators also felt that the IRB committee meetings were not well-organized nor easy to follow nor was there sufficient time to review the protocols. They also felt that their responsibilities were not clear nor were protocol packets complete nor the minutes accurate and that interactions with researchers were not helpful. The perspective of these IRB committee members indicated that they were not satisfied with the current system and they felt that a shift to a web-based system would be beneficial.

Second, those researchers who reported to be satisfied with the current manual protocols still felt burdened by regulations and a lack of timely reviews. Yet, they were satisfied with the current system. In their view, the need for and quality of communication with committee members as well as the need for a web-based system was marginal. But, researchers who reported the need to communicate with committee members also reported that they did not like the current protocol system, and felt that the required protocol documents were not well-defined. Overall, they were dissatisfied with the current protocol process, felt communication with committee members was poor, and a web-based system would be beneficial.

To be able to look more closely at these two very different sets of interpretations and oscillations between committee members and researchers regarding the present manual IRB system of protocols and the soon to be operational web-based system, additional analyses were performed over the five questions that both committee members and researchers answered. First, we had found that committee members believed significantly that communications with researchers were helpful. Second, researchers felt the need to communicate with protocol coordinators significantly more than did committee members. Third, committee members reported getting significantly more out of their interactions with researchers. Fourth, committee members were significantly more satisfied than researchers with the present protocol system. And finally, researchers believed significantly more than committee members that a web-based system would be a beneficial improvement to the current manual system. Possibly, committee members may have felt more in control of the manual IRB process, whereas researchers felt that it was a burden that may be lessened with the new web-based system. We will further study how these self-reports change by site and over time after the new system becomes operational.

2.2 Summary of Prior Studies

We had begun to study the MDRC system in 2006 [10]. At the time of our last review of the MDRC project [21], the military had funded a secure web-based system at one of its MDRCs (viz., E-MDRC) for research protocols submitted to its Institutional Review Board (IRB) for review and approval. To modify data gathering to improve IRB processes and to increase the timeliness of management analytics, the data collection and analysis system morphed into a real-time web-based system to manage the protocols. The eIRB was funded at the end of FY 2008.

But well before the installation of the eIRB in 2009 and before data collection could begin and analyzed to determine the operational results at E-MDRC, the Department of Defense (DoD) liked the concept so much that it considered mandating its implementation across DoD for all IRBs.

In late 2009, the eIRB at E-MDRC was operational. Two other MDRCs (of seven total) joined (WR-MDRC and B-MDRC; to protect confidentiality, these acronyms are fictitious). More importantly, after its review of the system's parameters and based on its initial performance, DoD implemented the eIRB system DoD-wide through its division of Health Affairs in the Office of the Under Secretary of Defense (Force Management Policy) for Personnel & Readiness (awaiting a continuing resolution from Congress).

Under the Concept of Operations Plan, OUSD's Health Affairs Personnel and Readiness (P&R) has approved funding to pay for sites performing Defense Health Program research to join the eIRB. A contract modification has been approved at OUSD(P&R) to allow E-MDRC server to be "moved" to P&R's servers. The anticipated date of transfer of server responsibility is 2010. All military services and the Uniformed Services University have invited to join the network.

One of the major operational concerns with metrics for an eIRB system is that the separate data sets from the different MDRCs need to be fused into a single data mart to be able to provide uniform metrics across the MDRCs (A data mart is a *tactical* subset of an organization's *strategic* data warehouse, oriented to a specific purpose; analytical data subsets; and often derived from a data warehouse, itself derived from the union of an organization's data marts). A key integration problem for a single data mart is to require that all of the data meet the standard of conformed facts and dimensions (e.g., with a Universal Data Architecture, or UDA; a simple example of a UDA would be a uniform rating scale for a single and universally adopted survey item, instead of using non-uniform scales for different items at different sites). Conformed data structures promote an integrated culture, while data bases with a lack of conformity promote different work practices, procedures and cultures, one of the problems we encountered when we first analyzed the data at E-MDRC (i.e., the evidence indicated the existence of multiple or "fractured" cultures across the MDRC complex; in [10]).

3 Theory

We theorized that system fragmentation is characterized by multiple work cultures and practices. For an organization, fragmentation impedes the execution of a business model [10]. In the case of the MDRC system, we found that fragmentation increased the difficulty of gaining a knowledge of the effectiveness of the system with a desired degree of confidence. Uncertainty existed in the knowledge about MDRC's publication rates, publication quality (scientific impacts), and scientific peer status (comparative quality of its scientists). Adopting a system to reduce this uncertainty led to the eIRB at E-MDRC.

Collecting information from well-defined networks for social network analysis (SNA) is relatively straightforward. But even when the information is readily available, the signals collected from social networks have not led to valid predictions about their actions or stability [14]. This failure with SNAs, game theory, and organizations in general [15] has led to a wide request for new social theory to better understand the effects of interdependence [15].

Traditional social and game theories, known collectively as methodological individualism, have been used to study interdependence for decades. Game theory was one of the first to model interdependence to solve it in the laboratory for two sets of non-cooperative opponents. These "toy" problem solutions are known as Nash Equilibria, which Luce and Raiffa [13] believed resulted in unfair distributions of a game's resources among its participants. However, outside of the laboratory, game theory has not been validated [16] nor produced satisfactory solutions [17].

With our new theory, Nash equilibria become a valuable asset to a society. A Nash equilibrium is usually defined as a stable state where participants cannot improve their self-interests based on the choices made by other participants; e.g., when two market firms compete directly, "aggressive moves … trigger ruinous price wars" [12]. We reinterpret an NE as a set of opposed positions defended by self-interests. More importantly, those who occupy an NE drive their relatively stable views into a stable opposition with the ultimate goal of obtaining widespread support for their self-interests. From our perspective, with reality being not easy to access or capture), an NE plus feedback provide sufficient information and knowledge to solve ill-posed problems [11].

Nash equilibria act as points of conflict that drive a public's attention back and forth as a conflict is driven across time by self-interests, generating a model of a social-psychological harmonic oscillator (SPHO; e.g., market traders neutral to who wins in a market but not neutral to the information that leads them to making a winning bet). Based on the literature, SPHO (moderated competition) situations serve to improve learning [4], political processes [3], and decision-making in the courtroom [11]. But, the absence of SPHO oscillators indicates a consensus-driven minority rule such as a dictatorship, which significantly reduces social welfare.

Oscillations from an SPHO generate fluctuations form information characteristic of an stability response and the conservation of information (COI). In general [11], all else being equal, COI predicts that organizations with unified commands are more stable than those under dual or shared commands; that larger organizations are more stable than smaller ones; and that the best run organizations have a clear mission under a central chain of command but with minimum bureaucracy.

Specific to the military MDRCs, top-down (minority) hierarchy is desired to optimize the control and operation of an organization by fulfilling the mission in the field. However, minority control encumbers the practice of science, which depends on Nash equilibria (e.g., challenges to prevailing scientific theories). In organizations, reducing the existence of internal centers of conflict (Nash equilibria), is the goal of management. But removing Nash equilibria makes the practice of science inefficient or ineffective, a paradox. Thus, for optimal performance, scientists conducting research within an MDRC should be governed by its chain of command (e.g., achieving the mission, abiding by IRB standards, gaining protocol approvals), but in their practice of science, to be able to produce and publish top-notch scientific research, MDRC scientists must be governed by challenging and being challenged by military medical colleagues as well as scientists external to the MDRC system. But since the MDRCs have the specific military medical mission of being knowledge generators, this paradox should not be resolved. Instead, construing the paradox as a source of tension helps to conceptualize the dual role of MDRC scientists, where the tension can be exploited to both power mission performance and to change its vision in a way that revitalizes the organization and the system over time.

4 Data Analysis/Discussion of Organizational Impacts

The size of organizations has a physical limit that technology can remove [11]. Organizational and individual behavioral responses to the introduction of innovative technology could be studied with the end users of the MDRC' system's eIRB. We predict the eIRB will improve organizational efficiency by reducing staffing needs.

As an indication of an organizational value already derived from the new eIRB system, the time to process publication clearances at WR-MDRC has decreased from an average of 30 days to 4 days [20]. Thus, a significant reduction in wasted time and greater organizational efficiency has already been achieved.

Despite the savings in time and costs, encouraging DoD to adopt the eIRB system DoD-wide, is the strategic planning that the eIRB should provide with more accurate and reliable metrics. Metrics will permit an MDRC to see how it is performing compared to its peers. Further, scientists as well as the managers and IRB committee members within an MDRC will be able to evaluate whether the protocols within their command meet MDRC's mission and how an individual scientist's practice of science contributes to changing its vision.

Other benefits may accrue from the eIRB system [20]. E-MDRC's eIRB offers unique opportunities to perform strategic planning for management; opportunities to participate in research shared between residential staff, interns and physician trainees; and opportunities to produce better research products (presentations, publications, case studies on patient care, etc.). Overall, the ability to market research opportunities internally to military medical residents and trainees and externally to outside commercial pharmaceutical firms should increase E-MDRC's competitiveness, influence and power in the medical market to hire better quality staff, residents and physician trainees as well as to widen its range and depth of medical skills to engage a greater variety of patient problems at a greater level of complexity to the credit of the hospital and its clinics.

For example, medical informatics from mining clinical data at E-MDRC could rank order its top diagnoses along with all of its other diagnoses; clinical successes; and unsolved clinical cases. These analytical results along with de-identified raw data could be marketed to entities interested in research (e.g., Pfizer, etc.). Pharmaceutical firms like Pfizer often pitch potential research topics to E-MDRC's staff to search through its database, which remains mostly untapped because the data is either uncollected, non-aggregated, or inaccessible to digital searches. Responding to these opportunities in the past has largely been neglected because of the time and effort it would take to assemble the data by hand into a digital format. The eIRB system reverses that situation by providing an aggregated, comprehensive, and digitized database. Expanding on this opportunity, multi-clinical trials involving multiple sites or the entirety of the military medical system participating with the eIRB is also mostly untapped. This system contains the largest medical database in the world [20].

Information Technology (IT) impacts. The potential of IT to transform organizations rather than to simply automate or improve their business processes underlies the continuing value of studying IT and its organizational consequences at multiple levels of social analysis [8].

With IT, we expect to uncover the existence of bottlenecks [20]. But, knowledge may also be lost as well as the potential prestige of the researcher(s) and the organization involved. Per Klote [9] on organizational waste, if a protocol is initiated but fails to be completed, it amounts to about $130,000 in wasted effort.

Organizational and individual behavioral responses to the introduction of innovative technology could be studied with the end users of the eIRB. In discussions with the eIRB commercial system provider, based on anecdotal evidence, we have learned that WR-MDRC, the largest unit in the system, was initially very unhappy as an organization when its researchers were first required to use the eIRB technology, but its overall satisfaction has improved dramatically since their system became operational [20].

Based on an initial interview of MDRC's management [20], we have learned that "... [it] would be interesting to study ... [with] de-identified [participants, the following]: Comparison of military and civilian IRB behavior as well as protocol coordinator behavior upon implementation of the eIRB system and examine organizational behavior where the implementation of the eIRB system was driven top down or bottom up. I suspect there is a different adoption behavior if it is top down versus bottom up and I suspect government employee behavior will be different than civilian but who knows. Lastly, how does behavior change when members/staff are showed the de-identified statistics of several MEDCENS as we (E-MDRC) re-address what the IRB members/staff are expected to do in terms of reviewing documents. Of course, this should all be done in the spirit of improving our performance rather than a punitive approach! I would expect to see improved behavior after sharing stats ... I think that it is a very worthy thing to study and learn about our behavior. The data and technology gives us unparalleled visibility and potential to change/drive organizational behavior that w have never had before."

5 Future Work

From the commercial provider of the eIRB system, the expectations are that there will be more resistance to change from the military users than from non-military users (e.g., university). The reason is that in their experience, organizational behavior where the implementation of eIRB system is driven top-down (military) creates more resistance that those driven from the bottom-up (university). We plan to pay particular attention to whether this holds true for the MDRCs. Comparisons of military and civilian IRB behavior should include researchers, protocol coordinators, and IRB panel member behaviors and satisfaction before and after implementation of the eIRB system.

In addition, the operational eIRB has already caused management to think about its current office policies. It is the beginning of what has been termed "tele-commuting" or a "virtual office" (also known variously as e-work, telework, e-commuting, or working from home; E-MDRC is preparing a cost-benefit analysis of using the eIRB as a virtual office). Tentatively, informal data collected with the eIRB system has already provided evidence that work assignments were not being carried out effectively at E-MDRC (not all of the required documents were disseminated by IRB coordinators to all of the reviewers; and many of the reviewers logged into the eIRB system only about a day before the Board met to review protocols; however, no data has yet been collected on the eIRB's impact on operational effectiveness). This information amounts to "business intelligence". Overall, however, data already collected on the behavior of IRB members and coordinators at E-MDRC suggests that BI could lead to major policy changes regarding the improvement of current work practices.

6 Summary

As a work-in-progress, we have continued to build on theory and to extend it in the field to an application with MDRCs. From an applied perspective, we have produced several reports of the justification for an eIRB system [10], its development and its installation. With this study, we have begun to report on the operational effectiveness of the eIRB system.

Acknowledgements. This material is based upon work supported by, or in part by, the U. S. Army Research Laboratory and the U. S. Army Research Office under contract/grant number W911NF-10-1-0252.

References

1. AHDR, Arab Human Development Report, UN (2002), `http://www.undp.org/rbas/ahdr/`
2. Baumeister, R.F., Campbell, J.D., Krueger, J.I., Vohs, K.D.: Exploding the self-esteem myth. Scientific American (January 2005)
3. Coleman, J.J.: Benefits of campaign financing. CATO Institute Briefings, DC (2003)
4. Dietz, T., Ostrom, E., Stern, P.C.: Science 302, 1907 (2003)
5. Ehrlich, P., Kennedy, D.: Science 309, 562–563 (2005)
6. Gürek, O., Irlenbusch, B., Rockenbach, B.: Science 312(5770), 108–111 (2006)
7. Jasny, B.R., Zahn, L.M., Marshall, E.: Science 325, 405 (2009)
8. Klein, K.J., Danereau, F., Hall, R.J.: Academy of Mgt. Rev. 19(2), 195–229 (1994)
9. Klote, M.: Informal comments (2010)
10. Lawless, W.F., Bergman, M., Louçã, J., Kriegel, N.N., Feltovich, N.: Computational & Mathematical Organizational Theory 13, 241–281 (2007)
11. Lawless, W.F., Angjellari-Dajci, F., Sofge, D.: EU Economic Integration, Federal Reserve Bank of Dallas (March 18, 2010)
12. Lindstädt, H., Müller, J.: McKinsey Quarterly. McKinsey & Co. (January 2010)
13. Luce, R.D., Raiffa, H.: Games and decision. Wiley, New York (1967)
14. NRC, Applications of Social Network Analysis for building community disaster resilience, Magsino, S.L. Rapporteur. National Academy Press (2009)
15. Pfeffer, J., Fong, C.T.: Organizatonal Science 16(4), 372–388 (2005)
16. Sanfey, A.G.: Science 318, 598–602 (2007)
17. Schweitzer, F., Fagiolo, G., Sornette, D., Vega-Redondo, F., Vespignani, A., White, D.R.: Economic networks: The new challenges. Science 325, 422–425 (2009)
18. Stachura, M.E., Astapova, E.V., Tung, H.L., Sofge, D.A., Grayson, J., Bergman, M., Wood, J., Lawless, W.F.: Handbook of Research on Developments in e-Health and Telemedicine. In: Manuela Cunha, M., Tavares, A., Simoes, R. (eds.). IGI, Hershey (2009)
19. Stachura, M.E., Astapova, E.V., Wood, J., Tung, H.L., Sofge, D.A., Grayson, J., Lawless, W.F.: Telemedicine in Georgia. In: Cunha, M.M. (ed.). IGI (forthcoming 2010)
20. Wood, J.: Personal communication (February 17, 2010)
21. Wood, J., Tung, H.-L., Marshall-Bradley, T., Sofge, D.A., Grayson, J., Lawless, W.F., Manuela Cunha, M., Oliveira, E., Tavares, A., Ferreira, L. (eds.) Hndbk Research Social Dimensions Semantic Technologies Web Services. IGI (2009)
22. Wood, J., Klote, M., Tung, H.L., Sofge, D., Grayson, J., Lawless, W.F.: Representing organizational conservation of information. Journal of Information and Communication Technologies for Advanced Enterprises (forthcoming 2010)

Data Warehouse Based Knowledge Management Controlling

Jorge Marx Gómez and Peter Cissek

Carl von Ossietzky Universität Oldenburg
Department für Informatik, Abt. Wirtschaftsinformatik I
26129 Oldenburg, Germany
jorge.marx.gomez@uni-oldenburg.de, cissek@wi-ol.de

Abstract. In the past there were many efforts to combine data stored in a data warehouse, and knowledge, which can be accessed through a knowledge management system, in order to enhance key figure based reporting. But there is also a need for loading meta data about the knowledge base into a data warehouse. In this paper we will point out the demand for integrating a knowledge management system and a data warehouse in order to make knowledge management controlling with business intelligence possible. We will give reasons why a data warehouse should be loaded with meta data extracted from a knowledge management system and put emphasis on the interface for extracting and loading the data. Especially the challenges in extracting data will be dealt with. As a practical suggestion we want to present a way for an implementation with SAP Portal KM and SAP BW.

Keywords: knowledge management system, knowledge management controlling, data warehouse, integration.

1 Introduction

In 2010 there was an interesting contribution at the German trade fair CeBIT in the track "Knowledge Management", presented by the Community for Knowledge Management (Gesellschaft für Wissensmanagement (GfWM)) [1]. The track was about the future trends in knowledge management (KM) and one item on the agenda was KM controlling. It has been emphasized already many times in literature how important it is to estimate the value knowledge has to a company's value added [2, 3, and 4]. To fulfil this requirement a KM controlling should be established in the KM department. Like any other key figure based analysis and evaluation KM controlling needs data and a reporting-software to generate significant reports for the executive staff. As modern controlling departments usually are supported by business intelligence (BI), in this context especially by the data warehouse (DWH), the use of a DWH for KM controlling suggests itself.

2 Knowledge Management Controlling

When KM projects are launched, the necessity of reviewing what has been achieved by paying attention to a company's knowledge base and knowledge processes is

J.E. Quintela Varajão et al. (Eds.): CENTERIS 2010, Part II, CCIS 110, pp. 119–127, 2010.

always as present as difficult to turn into reality. Moreover many companies try to share information about their intangible assets with the stakeholders, so that the value of a company is presented in a more comprehensive way [5].

In most cases the value of knowledge cannot be quantified directly, although it is clear that the knowledge base is build up of knowledge the company uses in value added and which secures the company's future existence. Not only Probst made clear that the benefit of KM has to be estimated or calculated unconditionally, if possible. To cope with that issue there have been proposed many approaches in literature to overcome the difficulties in knowledge valuation. These approaches can be grouped into deductive-summarizing and inductive-analytical approaches. Table 1. A selection of approaches to estimate the value of knowledge enlists some popular approaches to reckon the value of knowledge [5, 6, and 7].

Table 1. A selection of approaches to estimate the value of knowledge

deductive-summarizing approaches	inductive-analytical approaches
Knowledge Value Added Method	Intangible Assets Monitor
Market to book value	Knowledge balance (Wissensbilanz)
Tobin's q	Balanced Scorecard
Calculated Intangible Value	Skandia Navigator

There is little problem in quantifying values for deductive-summarizing approaches, but the reliability and precision of these values is in question. Inductive-analytical approaches hence need key performance indicators to prove the value of knowledge or of an action designed to improve a company's the knowledge base or knowledge processes. In the following we will focus on supporting inductive-analytical approaches and give two examples for KM controlling with a DWH in the role of the information system for reporting and a representative for BI.

The first business case is about improving the quality of knowledge that is represented by documents. These documents are stored in a knowledge management system (KMS). They can be searched for and edited by the members of staff, who are working on a business process which demands knowledge. In this business case the business process is constantly becoming worse in its quality. Finally the employees who are involved in the business process complain that the knowledge they can access is neither sufficient in quantity nor of good quality. In detail the company's information system SAP BW needs to be maintained by the IT department, but there is a lack of basic knowledge about the customizations that have been implemented by an external consulting company last year. Now the KM department has to take measures so that the situation gets better. One action can be changing the guidelines for creating documents in the scope of SAP BW and establishing a process for quality assurance. Now to point out the effect of the improvements the KMS standard function to rate a document's quality by the users shall be used for controlling aims. It would be possible to estimate the employees' rating of documents, which contain knowledge that is used in the knowledge domain of the business process "SAP BW maintenance". If this data could be collected and loaded into the DWH, the KM department would be able to point out how severe the actual situation is and what difference in the rating has been caused by the implementation of measures for improving the situation. In a summary KM controlling needs master data about the knowledge domain and the rating of the documents in this domain.

The second scenario deals with the development of the knowledge base. A company decides to introduce data mining techniques in the financial department for pattern recognition. KM controlling has been consigned to tell whether there is any knowledge in data mining techniques in the company and if it has grown over the past year or not. KM controlling will analyse now the amount of documents which deal primarily with data mining. A time line analysis will reveal if the company's knowledge base has developed over the last months proved by an increase of documents in the knowledge domain "data mining".

To estimate the effect of the actions for improving the knowledge base, KM controlling needs to establish a reporting on the master data to make changes in knowledge quality and quantity noticeable to executive staff.

3 The Interface between KMS and DWH

In the past there has been a strong demand to combine the data stored in a DWH and knowledge stored in a KMS to make key figure values more transparent and comprehensible by offering context information [8]. The reason for that can be easily understood. Only if somebody who looks at a key figure definitively knows what its value presented in a report means, he will be able to interpret this information correctly in order to make well-founded decisions. Anyone who has ever dealt with reports from financial department is able to relate to it.

Now the integration of KMS and DWH often has been analyzed regarding the integration of data stored in the DWH and knowledge, which is present in the KMS. The main task was to combine the data and knowledge stored in documents or possessed by employees in order to make better suggestions or decisions than without this knowledge. With this in mind there have been various approaches to establish a connection between the two information systems in this scenario, KMS and DWH.

- KMS is leading, DWH is the source system for data only
- DWH is leading, turning itself into a KMS
- DWH deals with knowledge used for key figure context information and serves as a specialized KMS connected to a more general KMS

The first approach prefers the KMS to store knowledge in it and wants the DWH to serve only as a data source for business data. The DWH is accessed by the KMS through an OLAP request to return data, which becomes valuable information through the knowledge the KMS provides. In a large scale the KMS turns even to an Artificial Knowledge Manager, which integrates all data and knowledge that is available in an information system landscape [9].

The second approach has been proposed as the concept of a document warehouse, which also is called knowledge warehouse. It has been proposed by Bange and is based on the concept of the DWH. Documents stored in a document warehouse are semantically enhanced by further indexing, segmentation, classification and composition. According to the DWH concept meta data which characterizes a document is stored in a star scheme, too, and can be accessed by OLAP techniques [10].

"A document warehouse is an integrated, subject-oriented, time-variant and non-volatile collection of documents in support of management's decision-making process" [10].

The third approach appears in cases when an integration of the two information systems is difficult to implement. The KM infrastructure of SAP Portal KM and the document handling functionality in SAP BW is a vivid example for this solution. Documents stored in the SAP BW can be accessed by the SAP Portal KM, but the link between the data in the SAP BW and the documents cannot be maintained. So the SAP BW deals only with the documents which are connected to data, while the SAP Portal KM deals with all other documents including those in the SAP BW [11].

For KM controlling an approach like the document warehouse must be pursued. But instead of turning the DWH into a KMS, it has to serve as a data source for KM controlling. Here the aspect of data acquisition is of highest concern. All the master data about knowledge that is available in the information systems must be extracted to minimize restrictions in the reporting due to a lack of data. Creating a document warehouse for this aim is an option, but sumptuous. Nevertheless the knowledge domains have to be extracted, so that an integration of data can be achieved using a common interpretation of domains. Only if a knowledge domain can be determined for a document, the KM controlling is able to make statements about the knowledge basis.

In the first place it is vital to define the interface between the KMS and the DWH. In any way the DWH determines the interface's structure. Fortunately common DHW solutions offer a wide scope of interfaces for loading data. The SAP BW, for instance, accepts flat files as well as SQL-databases, other DWH, web services, 3rd party interfaces and SAP systems. This means that the data that is extracted from the KMS must fit into one of the available interface types. The next task is to identify the relevant data and where it is stored in the KMS. Like in any other BI project, the source system of a DWH must be analyzed before one can build a data model. In the case of KMS the following questions must be answered.

- How many KMS are used?
- What kind of technology do these systems refer to?
- How much of the knowledge used in the company is covered by these systems?
- What master data can be expected?
- How is a knowledge domain defined by the data?
- Where is the master data stored in?
- Can the master data be integrated with master data from business processes?
- Are there any interfaces already specified in the KMS?

The integration of the knowledge domains is a crucial point. It must be assured that domains can be extracted from the KMS in order to classify documents. Only in this case the meta data can be used to evaluate the state the knowledge base is in. If a data warehouse supports hierarchies on master data, taxonomy extraction could be implemented, too.

If the KMS can be used as a source system for the DWH, the data model can be designed in the next step. One major task is to pay attention to the classification criterion, which is needed to determine the knowledge domain. Next, the document and its attributes must be modelled. Due to the respect of time-dependency in master data most of the data must be stored in the data cubes, instead of storing it in the master data tables. This ensures a higher usability in reporting.

4 Possible Scope of Application

A practical example with SAP is given by preparing the loading of data from the KM module of SAP Portal into the DWH SAP BW, where reports for KM controlling are created. The strategy for extracting data is as follows. The SAP BW should use the file-interface to load data. This makes the whole ETL-process more transparent and easier to verify, because there is a clear step between extracting the data from the KMS and loading it into the DWH. In addition more data can also be added from other sources, like individual software for meta data extraction from documents.

As mentioned in the chapter before extracting the data from the KMS is very demanding. And it is even more if SAP Portal KM is concerned. The SAP Portal software is written in the programming language Java, whereas the SAP BW runs on the SAP ABAP application server. The communication between the Java- and the ABAP-stack is defined by RFC and not easy to implement. An interface between these two systems can be created with different techniques [11]. The more sophisticated the interface is, the more complex the programming becomes.

- Export to file from SAP Portal, load into SAP BW by ETL
- Web service in SAP Portal to pass data to SAP BW by ETL
- Data preparation in SAP Portal, RFC to SAP BW

To make the implementation less complex, the data has to be exported from SAP Portal KM into a file first. For this purpose the SAP Portal offers some classes and web services (see Table 2. Overview of helpful content management API-classes in SAP Portal). These web services can be used by Microsoft Excel [12]. With this software the received data can be saved as a CSV-file. Among the meta data in particular the created-date and the modified-date are important, because from this data the time dependency is derived in the ETL-process.

Table 2. Overview of helpful content management API-classes in SAP Portal

class	short text
com.sapportals.wcm.service.indexmanagement.retrieval.classification	Provides functions for taxonomies and classification
com.sapportals.wcm.repository.service.feedback	Provides a service for managing feedback on resources
com.sapportals.wcm.repository.service.rating	Provides a service for evaluating resources.

Besides Microsoft provides a library called “dsofile.dll”. It is very helpful to extract further meta data out of Microsoft Office documents, like the title. These properties are of great value for KM, because they make the content and the context of a document more transparent to the controller. Unfortunately a separate program must be written in .Net to create an additional import file [13].

Extracting the taxonomies is far more complex. As already described the taxonomy is needed to classify documents as parts of the knowledge base. First, one has to figure out where in the KMS the taxonomy is saved and how the relationship between a document and taxonomy is defined, if such a relation exists at all.

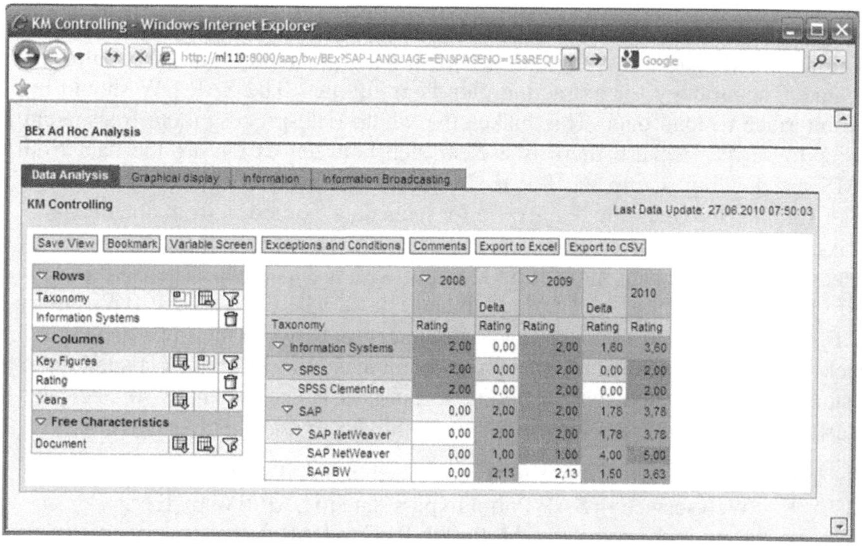

Fig. 1. KM controlling report no. 1

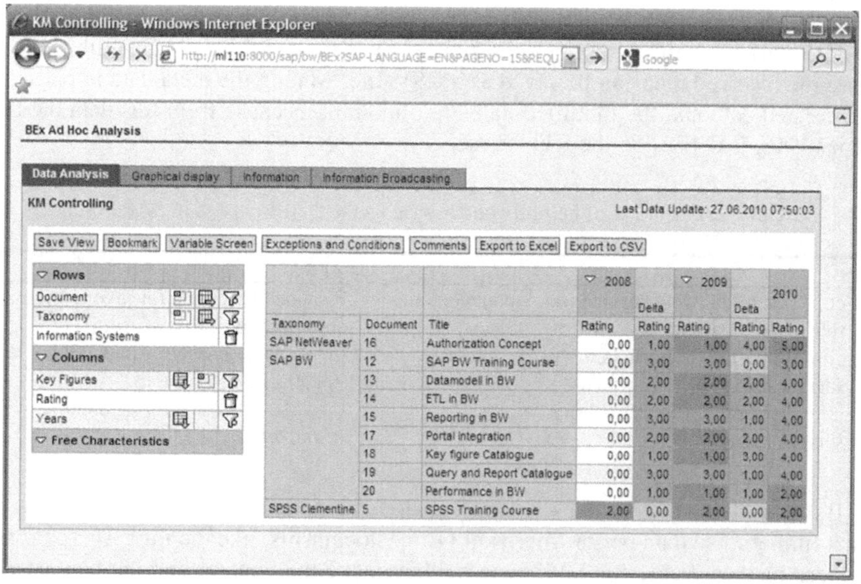

Fig. 2. KM controlling report no. 1 in detail

If all the data has been collected, the final CSV-files can be imported into the SAP BW. As the SAP BW distinguishes between master data texts, master data attributes and transactional data there have to be created some more files. In this example a file with texts for each attribute and one for the relation between documents and attributes are used. It must be emphasized, that in a more complex scenario master data management will become vital.

What the result could be like is illustrated in the following figures. As described in the first business case, there is a lack of quality in the documents SAP BW developers can access. Now Fig. 1. KM controlling report no. 1 shows what a report could look like in order to prove the deficit in document quality. The KM controller can see, that in the taxonomy "Information Systems" in the year 2009 there are documents available, which have a poor rating. The rating scale ranges from 1 to 5 where 5 is best. Most of the documents are rated 2 or less. After KM decided to improve the quality of the documents, the rating values raised. As shown in Fig. 2. KM controlling report no. 1 in detail the KM controller is even able to determine, which document has been rated better in 2010 than in the year before.

Scenario 2 was focused on the quantity of documents available in the topic "Data Mining". The company decided to expand the knowledge base for data mining in financials department. In 2009 first measures were taken to improve the situation. The report in Fig. 3. KM controlling report no. 2 shows clearly where in the knowledge base further documents have been created. Link-nodes in the hierarchy combine even two taxonomies, the "Business Topics" and "Data Mining". The report demonstrates that as intended by KM the company improves its knowledge base especially in the section of "Business Topics". And the controller can easily prove that there has been effort to create more knowledge about data mining in financials. What is more, Fig. 4. KM controlling report no. 2 in detail shows, which documents are new.

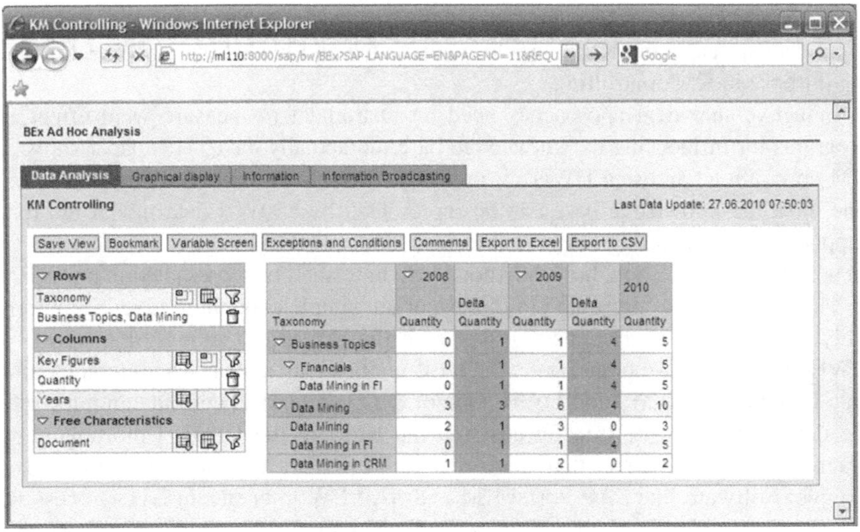

	2008	Delta	2009	Delta	2010
Taxonomy	Quantity	Quantity	Quantity	Quantity	Quantity
Business Topics	0	1	1	4	5
Financials	0	1	1	4	5
Data Mining in FI	0	1	1	4	5
Data Mining	3	3	6	4	10
Data Mining	2	1	3	0	3
Data Mining in FI	0	1	1	4	5
Data Mining in CRM	1	1	2	0	2

Fig. 3. KM controlling report no. 2

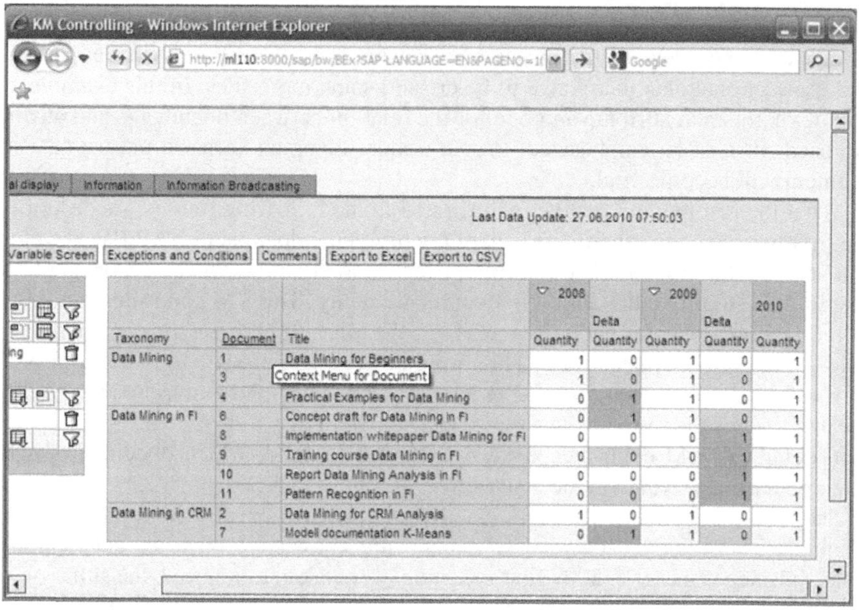

Fig. 4. KM controlling report no. 2 in detail

5 Conclusions

Nowadays most departments in a company take advantage of the intensive support BI offers them. KM should also benefit from BI. In this context there are many publications which focus on KMS and business data stored in databases. Yet the integration between KMS and DWH is not only a KM oriented, it has a reversed image, too. Meta data stored in the KMS should be extracted and loaded into a DWH for reporting purpose in KM controlling.

Inductive-analytical approaches need an instrument to measure what effect KM-programs for influencing the knowledge base did actually have. This paper shows that KM controlling can use a DWH for creating reports very well. The key idea is to define, how the knowledge base can be represented by a DWH data model in order to support controlling tasks. The main conceptual idea that has to be elaborated first gives an answer to the question, how the knowledge base shall be represented in a DWH.

The two scenarios presented in this paper are simple enough, to reveal comprehensibly the potential of a connection between the two information systems KMS and DWH. The paper also points out, which difficulties may appear when implementing a data flow between KMS and DWH. One of the main tasks is defining an interface for the data that has to be transferred from the KMS to the DWH. Unfortunately this practical example reveals that there are not sufficient standards implemented in a complex software like SAP Portal KM and SAP BW to create an ETL-process without expert knowledge on the software implementation. Especially the export of taxonomies is still problematic. In addition to that there are also difficulties in extracting advanced meta data from the documents like the title. Therefore future design and enhancements of KMS should emphasize on offering also an interface for a wide-spread meta data extraction.

This paper focuses on documents as a part of the knowledge base. But there are a lot more elements which should also be regarded to gain a complete view of the knowledge base, like contact persons and their skills or the processes of KM. Integrating them into the DWH for controlling reasons in KM should also be considered.

References

1. Gesellschaft für Wissensmanagemenet, http://www.wissensmanagement-gesellschaft.de/node/848
2. Probst, G., Raub, S., Romhardt, K.: Wissen Managen, pp. 211–229. Gabler Verlag, Wiesbaden (1997)
3. Davenport, T., Prusak, L.: Working Knowledge, pp. 113–118. Mcgraw-Hill Professional, New York (2000)
4. Stewart, T.A.: Intellectual Capital. Broadway Business (1998)
5. Peters, S., Reinhardt, K., Seidel, H.: Wissen verlagern, pp. 134–151. Gabler Verlag, Wiesbaden (2006)
6. Housel, T.J., Bell, A.H.: Measuring and Managing Knowledge (2001)
7. Bundesministerium für Wirtschaft und Arbeit: Wissensbilanz – Made in Germany. Dokumentation 536 (2005)
8. Dittmar, C.: Knowledge Warehouse. Gabler Verlag, Wiesbaden (2004)
9. Firestone, J.M.: Knowledge Base Management Systems and The Knowledge Warehouse, http://www.dkms.com/papers/kbmskwbak.pdf
10. Bange, C.: Business Intelligence aus Kennzahlen und Dokumenten. Verlag Dr. Kovac, Hamburg (2004)
11. SAPOnlineHelp, http://help.sap.com/saphelp_nw70/helpdata/en/e1/8e51341a06084de10000009b38f83b/frameset.htm
12. Knowledge Managment Property Maintenance Using Excel, https://www.sdn.sap.com/irj/servlet/prt/portal/prtroot/docs/library/uuid/9bfc45ba-0b01-0010-4890-da85753f0f58
13. Microsoft Support, http://support.microsoft.com/kb/224351/de

Business Intelligence Standardization and Corporate Strategy: A Paradox

José António Porfírio, Marc Jacquinet, and Tiago Carrilho

CIEO and Universidade Aberta, Lisbon, Portugal

Abstract. Market evidence suggests the increased investment of companies in BI systems to feed their strategy processes. The change in the strategy fundamentals increases substantially the value of information for both strategies' implementation and control. One domain neglected is the use of BI systems for strategy conception. And this is something increasingly important in today's constantly changing world of business, where new information in a knowledge economy is usually synonymous of more added value and competitiveness. However, together with this tendency, we experience a general trend for BI systems standardization, a dominant movement for BI solutions providers to standardize processes in order to take advantage of learning curves and processes, and economies of scale and scope. Considering that each strategy should be unique, and departing from the principle that BI systems are closely related with corporate strategy, it seems that there is a double paradox in BI markets that companies should solve as soon as possible, in order to take the most out of the momentum of BI markets.

Keywords: Business intelligence, corporate strategy, information, knowledge, information systems.

1 Introduction

Business Intelligence (BI) market stands for around US$ 9.3 billion in 2009, which represents a 4.2 per cent increase over 2008, where it grew about 22 per cent from the 2007 level [1]. Forecasts for the market consider that BI will be one of the fastest growing software markets despite the economic downturn [2].

A quick view on Information and Communication Technology (ICT) markets suggest that, in spite of the huge market investments being made, BI systems are still in its early stage of adoption cycle, since, side-by-side with business analytics, there is growing evidence regarding the competitive value of BI solutions for almost all every businesses.

Although the concept of BI is not new, being attributed to computer scientist H. P. Luhn, who published his seminal paper in the October issue of 1958 of the *IBM Journal* [3], only from the last decade of the twentieth century on, this concept gained wide acceptance in management and business community. Much of its success is related to the exponential growth of data and information produced everyday and the ubiquity of software systems in corporate life. Nowadays, BI systems are being used mainly to support corporate strategy's execution and implementation.

J.E. Quintela Varajão et al. (Eds.): CENTERIS 2010, Part II, CCIS 110, pp. 128–137, 2010.

Taking this into consideration, the aim of this paper is to analyze what is the relation between business intelligence (BI) and corporate strategy (CS) and if this relation could be considered satisfactory in the current period of crisis and restructuring where one assists to a change in the own fundamentals of corporate strategy.

To clarify briefly a central concept used in this paper and avoid any misunderstanding, it is important to define what we mean by corporate strategy.

CS must be considered broadly as referring to either the plans made or the actions taken, in an effort to help an organization fulfill its intended purposes [4]. CS "defines the scope of the firm in terms of the industries and markets in which it competes. CS decisions usually include investments in diversification, vertical integration, acquisitions, and/or new ventures" [5].

Before coming back to the notion of strategy in the next section, we will dedicate some time to the overall setting of the issue tackle here.

The context of our analysis could be defined by the central notion of complexity. As Rescher put it, our time is characterized by complex environment, "plagued with vast management problems and risks of mishaps" [6]. Social systems are of increasing complexity with problems growing faster than solutions and this confronts us "with major management and decision problems" [7]. Departing from this principles, in this paper we will start by presenting the main concepts of strategy and BI. We begin by characterizing the current stage of competition and the main issues associated with it, evolving to the presentation of the concepts of strategy and business intelligence linking them to the current use of BI for strategy purposes.

In the third section of this paper we will try to devise what are the issues and what is the real challenge posed to BI systems coming from the forecasted changes in corporate strategies showing, in the fourth section, an apparent double paradox that is coming from the tendency to standardize BI software and systems, which we consider to be a tendency that could be dangerous for the strategic goals of most companies.

We will conclude our analysis presenting a possible way out for this paradox and some research perspectives associated with this field of knowledge.

2 Business Intelligence: Concepts and Strategy

The large number of definitions for BI is a clear indication of the problems surrounding the capacity to operate with this subject from a theoretical point of view.

For Luhn [1], a BI system is "an automatic system that is developed to disseminate information to the various sections of any industrial, scientific or government organization (...) that utilize data-processing machines for auto-abstracting and auto-encoding of documents and for creating interest profiles for each of the "action points" in an organization". According to Luhn, this system operates on the basis of the incoming and internally generated documents and it must be able to identify who needs to know what, and to disseminate it efficiently either in abstract form or as a complete document.

In this definition, as well as in the mostly used definitions, a BI system is considered as a process that "may be defined as a set of mathematical models and analysis methodologies that systematically exploit the available data to retrieve information and knowledge useful in supporting complex decision-making processes." [8]. In most of the references made to BI on internet, it is considered as "a broad category of applications and technologies for gathering, storing, analyzing and providing access to data to help enterprise users make better decisions, here included the activities of decision support systems, query and reporting, online analytical processing (OLAP), statistical analysis, forecasting and data-mining" [9].

In general, this view of BI systems is preoccupied with the process underlying the search, capture and treatment of data and the production of information, ending in the production of reports for some managers in an organization. The production of dashboards or reports is another view of BI that considers it as a stage, that is, the production of certain pre-defined outputs that arises as a consequence of the underlying processes seen before.

Both views, however, could be considered more static than the view that one may have if we consider BI from a manager's perspective, since they represent views of BI more as an auxiliary to the strategy's implementation rather than an auxiliary to a strategy's definition and control, an approach more adequate to recent times.

From a strategist's point of view, a BI system should be conceived to work also as a lead – not just as a lag – input for the corporate strategy. That is to say that, more than just providing information about the execution of a pre-determined strategy, BI systems should be able to anticipate trends, providing the adequate information for managers to evaluate, to decide and to correct the path of a pre-defined strategy. To do this, it should take into consideration the recent information inputs that could arise permanently from the use of the most varied sources of information constantly scanned by the BI system. These sources could be usually found both within and outside a company and are mainly indicated by managers that are the first to know where to find the right data for their strategic needs.

To understand more clearly this issue, we should stick to the concept of strategy and to be able to devise the new foundations of this crucial management issue.

Strategy means the capacity of a company to conceive and implement a comprehensive master plan in order to achieve pre-determined objectives, by following a peculiar path of development. Strategy should pave the way to obtain, to strengthen, or just to maintain competitive advantages that will allow the company to operate in a certain market obtaining better performance than their competitors.

Every strategy must consider the environment where the company operates and where the business develops.

ICT development and the increased use of Internet changed radically the way most business agents interact and do business and, at the same time, changed the way companies work internally. These changes are still happening in the present, creating new business models, shifting competition in many industries and changing radically the value chain of the industries involved.

This is affecting radically the way competitive advantages are developed, maintained or lost. As pointed out by Alfred Chandler, in high technology industries, organizational strengths are mainly derived from learning capabilities [10] which turns knowledge into becoming a key issue for business and a real source of competitive advantage for companies.

By its turn, knowledge is increasingly scattered around the world and not just based in one placed as it happened before. Moreover, ICT development makes the costs of distance falling rapidly for commodities that are mobile, like capital, goods and information and which made them accessible to all [11].

Learning organizations are skilled at four main activities: solving problems systematically; experimenting with new approaches; learning from their own experiences and past history, as well as the experience of others; and transferring knowledge on an efficient and quick way throughout the organization [10].

This makes that competitive advantage is not just a question of cutting unnecessary costs or improving quality. Management is becoming the most important factor of competitiveness once responsiveness became a must in today's strategy. This increased management's role should translate into the capacity of a company to be smarter, more agile and more strategy focused than their main competitors, giving customers a greater variety of products and services, at lower costs and in less time than their most direct competitors [12, 13]. To do this, managers need to show the capacity to create, manage and share more information. While for the information technologist, information is an output from a certain data – a kind of fluid asset or a data stream – for the manager, information is an input, that should provide noble knowledge for his business and that should fundament their decisions, being fuzzy and taking many forms like knowing their customer's needs or providing information for where the market is heading. In the organization of the future, operating in a constantly changing environment, managers should be able to act as ancient manufacturers worked in a Taylor-like industrial production line. Everything can be summarized into the capacity to obtain and process information that will guide the actions. The capacity to collapse these time-cycles will be determinant, even for the success of the organizations of today [13].

BI systems have nowadays a double challenge, since they do not just need to provide the adequate information for the company's managers to act, but they should, at the same time, provide this information faster than the ability of its competitors to obtain it.

3 Standardization of Business strategy

3.1 Business Intelligence as a Process

We argue that BI is not just a "state" such as a report containing knowledge and structure information, nor even just a "process", understood narrowly, in the literature of information management, as a software system or solution that "permits converting data into knowledge" [14]. BI should serve entirely the strategy process of a company. From the strategic management's point of view, strategy must be treated as a shared process of all corporate employees and not just a responsibility of its top management, So, BI should be seen as a process, including all of the above, and the human organization of the firm that is responsible for collecting, creating, structuring, disseminating, presenting and selecting information and knowledge.

This broad BI view may be called the "organizational business intelligence", a process that represents the integration of the organizational process of knowledge management with some central notions of strategy as highlighted in the preceding conceptual section. Knowledge, by its turns, must be distinguished here from information and data. Information is data structured by knowledge and should increase existent knowledge. Therefore, it must be clear that knowledge is at a different – and higher level – than information. Knowledge is also much closer to the decision process; we could say that it is an important part of it. Whereas data or unstructured information can exist anywhere in the firm, knowledge is selected and structured information to foster the decision process in a specific organizational and strategic context. The problem, often, is that knowledge is incomplete and based on deficient information, i. e., a lack of research (knowledge) on what the relevant information is with regard to the decision to make.

The real value of a BI system could be calculated from its capacity to influence manager's actions and this is done through its capacity to feed knowledge in the company. Knowledge coming from adequate BI systems will only be crucial for a company if it is in the origin of its manager's adequate actions, those that ultimately will translate into added value for the company, which is the ultimate goal of every strategy.

Having this in mind, it is important to notice that by its nature, a strategy is unique for each company. Like in nature, when there are limited and scarce resources, if we have two competitors, only the strongest will have a real chance to survive. Translating this into the business field, in the same market, with limited and dully informed customers looking for the best opportunities it will not be easy for a company to succeed if another competitor put in place the same and exact strategy. At the end, the conditions to succeed will rest in the capacity to break with business-as-usual which implies having the adequate knowledge to do that. And that is more and more based on the capacity to put in place an effective BI system.

3.2 Tendencies to Standardization: Why and How? The First Paradox

In the early and even recent development of business intelligence software, there is a clear tendency for the standardization of products and solutions offered to users and customers.

The tendency toward standardization has to do with several factors. One is learning and its learning curves. Firms in software industry create knowledge in its core business and each learn in its own way but try to simplify business processes as stylized models that can be adapted to their own features.

Another reason for standardization from the part of software companies is the increasing costs of building a flexible and adaptive software and information system. This runs against economies of scale and scope. The wider the scope of features a program must deal with the larger are their costs. The more standardized or repeated is the solution the lesser the costs of developing and testing the product to be launched.

From the point of view of customer's exact needs, this is almost contrary to what any student of marketing has learned. Software customers with a knowledge base build their routines and tradition on the basis of their learning, sometimes in interaction with customers, but, most often than not, their products are following the industry and in-house standards, be them explicit or implicit. This means that the software solution adopted for BI purposes – or any other purposes – should be customized to be adapted to each and different client (customized is the exact and revealing word that is used in this specific trade).

The main question here is that usually, technologies are developed by software engineers that have only a partial view of what are the ultimate customer needs or what are their concrete or practical problems. Explicit and implicit "standards" defined and spread into the industry (such as data exchange protocols, structuring and relational data bases, etc.) do not reflect the variety of situations and use of information management. Thus, BI systems could be prepared to bring information to companies that adopt them but their capacity to bring knowledge management will be limited.

The need for a genuine and comprehensive notion of the entire process is reinforced if we look carefully at the components of business intelligence as described in the literature [6, 14], namely the human resources, the publications and databases and the tools, including software. The development, and above all the integration of these three elements, means organization and implementation of procedures and other norms that define the management processes put in practice in customer companies.

Without this complete view, and the capacity to adapt BI systems to the particular needs of the customers, we will risk to have some sterile BI systems that will not translate the real advantage of a company's adoption of BI software and this will present a paradox for BI companies since their products will probably lose value with regard to customers needs and preferences.

4 Competition and Cooperation in Knowledge-Intensive Firms: The (other) Paradox

Strategy cannot be associated to standardization as human needs imply unique goals and methods to satisfy them. A corporate strategy is build up upon opportunities recognized or created to develop and exploit a truly distinctive product or service. Firms carry on different paths due to market competition. In this way enterprises have to answer questions like 'which customers do we serve and will we serve in the future?', 'through what channels do we reach customers today and will we reach in the future?' or 'what skills or capabilities make us unique today and will make us unique in the future?'.

Corporate strategy implies managerial culture, team-work, a capacity to change and a willingness to share resources and to think long term. The real sources of long term advantages are in management's ability to consolidate corporate-wide technologies and production skills into competencies that empower individual businesses to adapt quickly to changing opportunities. Real opportunities can be also obtained by exploiting differences between countries in terms of culture, administrative and institutional context, geography and specific economic factors.

These last factors "... include differences in the cost of labour and capital, as well as variations in more industry-specific inputs such as knowledge or the availability of complementary products, technologies or infrastructures."[15] Strategy is an essential tool to communicate with customers because it reveals the broad direction without giving away every step of the firm's dynamics.

Each firm has its own specific 'nature' in terms of conception and implementation of strategy. Present products or services should reveal if capabilities have or have not been fully exploited, and this requires an audit of capabilities employed in production. In current markets, if existing products or services do not meet certain objectives enterprises can generate new ideas so as to create new products or services. Resource availability must be estimated in every instance. On entering in new markets firms apply different capabilities and skills: "in capitalizing on such an opportunity (the firm) must utilize a set of resources which differ substantially from those with which it is most familiar. (…) True diversification of major proportions will most likely carry the firm into areas beyond the realm of its recognized operating competences." [16]

For strategists, some challenging questions need to be considered: 'What new core competences will we need to build?', 'how can we be able to anticipate changing customer needs?', 'what nascent development programs should we project?', 'what alliances or networks will we need to form?'. Corporate strategy also implies flexibility and adaptation: "strategy must be responsive to changes both inside and outside the firm. If a major misjudgment has been made, if the organizational structure proves unequal to the prime task, if a major facet of the environment has changed, then there must be flexibility to permit new personnel, new structure, and new allocations, or it must permit reformulation to the corporation's strategy" [17].

Knowledge-intensive firms can implement strategy by solving their client's problems on the basis of direct application of knowledge and client's needs. The best experts and the best projects can be obtained through competition with rivals. But knowledge-intensive firms can also cooperate with their rivals: they "… routinely refer projects to rival firms better suited to solving the problem or they may even cooperate by sharing work on larger projects. (…) Knowledge-intensive firms may also cooperate to advance the professional or industry association through conferences, common training programs, or setting common standards." [18]

To study cooperation dynamics among firms we must consider network and partnership concepts.

A network constitutes an articulation of nodes through a certain number of connections. These nodes are a priori heterogeneous in time and space. This property is the basis of the need for network connections. By principle, "… the distance (or intensity or frequency of interaction) between two points (or social positions) is less (or more frequent or more intense) if the two points are nodes of a network than if they aren´t." [19] Networks imply a multitude of connections and alternative 'pathways' in order to reinforce the 'connection power'. Networks also imply rules and individual or collective actors to assure structure functioning on the basis of information and knowledge sources, human, financial and logistic resources, and specific conditions (technical, economic, social, political and environmental). The expansion of network penetrability in economic structure has the new information technology paradigm as its material basis. The dynamic of each network is related to flux power or 'connection power' so as to develop the "… capacity of gender knowledge and process information in an efficient way." [20] Considering also that networks constitute "… open structures capable of expanding themselves in an unlimited way, and integrating new nodes as long as they communicate inside the network, mainly if they share the same communication codes (for instance, values or performance objectives)." [21]. Networks also reflect hierarchic relations, 'exclusions', and dependencies, strong and weak connections. The network nodes do not have the same position in terms of 'connection power' because some of the nodes assume privileged roles while others assume secondary positions.

Partnership processes permit the development of local-regional based networks. A partnership concept can complement a network concept because it focuses on key-assumptions in actors' relations which are reflected on local-regional dynamics inherent to a certain set of activities. Network approach develops analysis focusing on actors' interrelations background and practical elements of interventions. We consider that a systematised analytical separation between components of the partnership concept would be necessary: a more intangible component and its corresponding practical component. The study of partnership allows us to analyse the connections between these two components. We consider that partnership dynamic implies the existence of key assumptions in actors' interrelations, namely agent diversity, activities focus, predisposition to 'negotiate' and to act in a changing context. These key assumptions correspond to key elements in the relations between actors which engender the coordination of different motivations and interests in order to define and implement objectives, activities, results and evaluation processes.

Partnership dynamic corresponds to the practical dimension of the key assumptions. Due to evaluation processes, objectives and activities are subject to changes and adaptations. Organizational changes can result in different activities and tasks that are habitually developed in origin institutions. Agents carry on relations to intervene on the basis of objectives and respective actions results. Actors' interrelations, linked to the key assumptions referred above, are reflected in key elements of the intervention. This dynamic consists of activities to reach objectives on the basis of available resources (financial, human, and logistic), results and process evaluation.

In order to be effective, BI systems should be able to respond to this new customer's competitive needs, adapting to the new competition rules and fundamentals. A BI system should show the capacity not just to deal with internally generated data but, at the same time, to look for data both within the surrounding partners of a company as well as data arising from the most varied sources. These other sources could be in the environment of a company's operations but, most times, one should consider that the most disruptive innovations – the ones that give competitive advantages to a company – arrive from domains that most people did not think before that could affect the business-as-usual of firms and industrial sectors.

This tailor-made BI's perspective it is also not compatible with its standardization.

5 Conclusions

In this paper, we showed the increased importance that BI systems have for the development of corporate strategic management capabilities.

Taking into consideration the rapid change in strategy fundamentals presented in this paper, and in order to justify the attention that most companies are directing to BI procedures, companies offering BI systems should reinforce its capabilities, not just to ensure an adequate corporate strategy implementation, but also to become important drivers of strategies' conception.

The tendency of BI systems for standardization, which is something that could be understood if we think that companies that provide BI systems will show a normal tendency to take advantage of their learning curves and to obtain efficiencies in their main processes, from the exploitation of economies of scale and scope, could be a shadow in the apparently promising future of BI systems.

Companies will only continue to invest in BI systems only if they are able to see real advantages coming up from their investments. Advantages should translate in added value for the company's strategy which is something that will only happen if manager's actions, guided by adequate information coming up from BI systems, really represent an increased capacity to provide faster and more efficiently products or services to their customers than their competitors.

One should say that the true pragmatic way out for this apparent double paradox – between BI standardization and the strategic needs of companies and, at the same time, between the need for BI companies to standardize and the capacity to provide better and more adequate BI systems to their customers – consists on service capacity. In order to solve this apparently difficult problem, BI companies must be able to provide a better service to their customers, selling BI systems at a lower price but showing the capacity to customize these systems to their customers' needs, by having a personalized service that must be able to translate the customer's strategy into responsiveness of their managers. Responsiveness should be understood by the capacity, not just to provide cheaper and better quality products or services but, mainly, to devise future strategies – or to adequate present strategy – faster than their competitors, making possible to obtain what in strategy is known as first movers advantage more often than before.

6 Future Work

Intelligence means the capacity to acquire and apply knowledge [22], which is something more than just transforming data into information. In management terms, this could be translated into a complex process that remains far away from the "simple" engineering perspective many times associated with BI systems capacity to transform data into information. At the same time, this breaks with the tendency for BI standardization and could explain the market tendencies for the interesting duel between the so-called BI pure-play vendors and the mega vendors.

Any BI systems' implementation must be looked as a true symbiotic process between management and the ICT resources of an organization. This symbiosis might originate a change in own fundamentals of management, especially concerning strategic management. Usually, any "strategy process usually involves changes within the overall culture, structure, and/or management system of the entire organization" [23] so as it must also happen with any BI system's implementation.

Business flexibility must also translate into knowledge increase. To measure the real benefits arising from the adoption of any BI system, we must be able to break with traditional knowledge regarding strategic management and to devise new strategic management fundamentals. And this might be the biggest challenge nowadays to the development of BI systems itself. Solving this puzzle might well pass through the development of an integrated theoretical work between managers and information technologists. Just by doing this it will be possible to assist to the real hype of BI systems.

References

1. Gartner: Market Report on Business Intelligence, in Inside SAP, Australia & New Zealand, vol. (9) (May/June 2010), http://www.insidesap.com.au/mayredirect/ (June 15, 2010)
2. Gartner: Market Report on Business Intelligence, in Inside SAP, Australia & New Zealand, vol. (9) (May/June 2010), http://www.insidesap.com.au/mayredirect/ (June 15, 2010)
3. Luhn, H.P.: A business intelligence system. IBM J. Res. Dev. 2(4), 314–319 (1958)
4. Miller, A., Dess, G.G.: Strategic Management, 2nd edn., International Edition. The McGraw-Hill Companies, Inc., New York (1996)
5. Grant, R.: Contemporary Strategic Analysis, 6th edn., p. 19. Blackwell Publishing, Malden (2008)
6. Rescher, N.: Complexity. A Philosophical Overview, p. 6. Transactions Publishers, New Brunswick (1998)
7. Rescher, N.: Complexity. A Philosophical Overview, p. 7. Transactions Publishers, New Brunswick (1998)
8. Vercellis, C.: Business Intelligence: Data Mining and Optimization for Decision Making, p. xiv. John Wiley & Sons Inc., New York (2009)
9. See, for instance, http://searchdatamanagement.techtarget.com/ (last access on February 26, 2010)
10. Wheelen, T.L., Hunger, J.D.: Strategic Management and Business Policy. Eleventh Edition, Pearson International Edition, Pearson Prentice Hall (2008)
11. Doz, Y., Santos, J., Williamson, P.: From global to Metanational: How Companies win in the knowledge economy. Harvard Business School Press, Boston (2001)
12. Oestreich, T., Buytendijk, F.: Introducing Management Excellence. Journal of Management Excellence 1, 5–11 (2008)
13. George Jr., S., Hout, T.M.: Competing against time: how time-based competition is reshaping global markets, p. 1. The Free Press/ Macmillan, Inc., New York (1990)
14. Michalewicz, Z., Schmidt, M., Michalewicz, M.: Adaptative Business Intelligence, p. vii. Springer, Heidelberg (2007)
15. Ghemawat, P.: The forgotten strategy. Harvard Business Review, 1–10 (2003)
16. Mason, R.H., et al.: Corporate strategy: a point of view. California Management Review XIII(3), 5–12 (1971)
17. Mason, R.H., et al.: Corporate strategy: a point of view. California Management Review XIII(3), 5–12 (1971)
18. Sheehan, N.T.: Why old tools won't work in the "new" knowledge economy. Journal of Business Strategy 26(4), 53–60 (2005)
19. Castells, M.: A Sociedade em Rede, Lisboa, Fundação Calouste Gulbenkian, p. 606 (2002)
20. Castells, M.: A sociedade em rede in Cardoso, G, et al. A Sociedade em Rede em Portugal, Porto, Campo das Letras, 19-29, pp. 21–22 (2005)
21. Castells, M.: A Sociedade em Rede, Lisboa, Fundação Calouste Gulbenkian, p. 607 (2002)
22. The American Heritage® Dictionary of the English Language, Fourth Edition copyright ©2000 by Houghton Mifflin Company (Updated in 2009) http://www.thefreedictionary.com/intelligence (June 15, 2010)
23. Wheelen, T.L., Hunger, J.D.: Strategic Management and Business Policy, 11th edn., p. 13. Pearson International Edition, Pearson Prentice Hall (2008)

A Business Model for the Portuguese Air Force

Carlos Páscoa[1,2], Pedro Leal[1], and José Tribolet[2,3]

[1] Department of University Education, Portuguese Air Force Academy, Sintra, Portugal
[2] Department of Information Systems and Computer Science, Instituto Superior Técnico, Technical University of Lisbon, Portugal
[3] CODE - Center for Organizational Design & Engineering, INOV, Rua Alves Redol 9, Lisbon, Portugal
cjpascoa@gmail.com, pmbleal@gmail.com, jose.tribolet@inesc.pt

Abstract. Organizations not only play an increasingly active role in today's society but also begin to address the everyday necessities and concerns of individuals. To achieve competitive advantage, it is becoming more and more necessary that organizations perform efficiently in order to survive.

As organizations can be defined as a group of people who work together to obtain one or more common results, it is imperative that all its constituents represent themselves as part of the whole. Important issues such as: who is the organization, what it does, for whom it operates and what its core values are can be answered using the business model. It is also important to characterize, in this context, the business model and artifacts like the Business Motivation Model which help to specify the enterprise business architecture and can be complementary.

This paper, using business model concepts as a basis, proposes a business model for the Portuguese Air Force that answers to the previous questions and can be instantied to any particular area, like one of the Air Force Air Units.

Keywords: Organizational Engineering; Business Model; Business Strategy; Enterprise Architecture; Organization Values; Business Motivation Model.

1 Introduction

Organizations appear as a response to the needs that society presents. Since their appearance, their business practice, irrespective of their activity, should produce something in order to receive value in return.

In order to identify the feasibility of a particular business, concepts such as "Mission", "Overview", Objectives and Strategy "[1], should be clearly presented and should also identify the final state seeking to be achieved and how to obtain it.

All organizations are situated in dynamic and flexible environments. It is important that both internal and external participants clearly understand the information about the substance of "Being" [2].

A Business Model responds to a number of important questions about the organization, such as: "who we are", "what we do"," how we behave", "what are our values".

J.E. Quintela Varajão et al. (Eds.): CENTERIS 2010, Part II, CCIS 110, pp. 138–147, 2010.

From the combination of Enterprise Architecture (EA) with the Business Model arises, not only the definition of the executable internal business [2], but also the presentation of substantial information about the organization allowing its classification, internally and externally. In fact, by way of example, it is worth mentioning that the presentation of the EA of a complete and well structured organization, together with a Business Model can answer questions about identity, regarding: i) an understanding of the contribution of each of the internal actors to achieve the objectives, ii) an understanding of the flight plan of the organization, iii) an understanding of identity, resources and values.

Accordingly, this paper presents the concepts necessary for the definition of EA in an organization, taking as reference the Business Motivation Model (BMM) [1] and also the concepts that underpin the creation of a business model. In addition, an Business Model for the Portuguese Air Force and a specification to an Air Unit are proposed.

The document is divided into four paragraphs. The second paragraph presents relevant literature on the mentioned concepts. The third focuses on the creation of the proposed business model for the Air Force, as well as a comparison of existing EA, with the BMM. The final paragraph is a brief conclusion of all the work.

2 Enterprise Architecture and Business Model

In this paragraph brief references will be made to the concepts used by Organizational Engineering, applied by the Center for Organizational Design and Engineering (CODE) and the BMM like: Business Model, Business Strategy, Values and Nonprofit Organizations.

2.1 Organizational Engineering

An organization can be defined as a group of people working together to achieve a common goal. This, too, can be seen as an aggregate of two or more people who carry out joint activities individually or coordinated and controlled within a certain environment in order to achieve a common result.

All organizations, knowing the environment in which they are inserted, must have their fundamental principles and objectives coordinating the human and material resources needed to carry out its business. Organizations should also seek excellence through efficiency and effectiveness in pursuit of quality in the services they provide, because only in this way they can continue their existence.

2.2 The Business Motivation Model (BMM)

The Business Motivation Model (BMM) is a framework to develop the architecture of the Business in an organized way. The BMM has five major distinct areas: “Ends”, “Means”, “Influencers”, “SWOT” and “Potential Impact”. "Ends", which states what the organization wants to achieve, are composed by "Vision", "Goals" and "Objectives"; "Means", the way the organization uses to achieve its "Ends" includes the "Course of Action " and within this, are the "Strategy" and "Tactics", and also the "Business Policies " and "Business Rules"; Internal and external "Influencers" perform actions that could significantly impact both the "Ends" and the "Means". The "Strenght, Weakness, Opportunities and Threats (SWOT) Analysis" lets one know what impact these influencers have in the "Means" and in the "Ends"; "Potential Impact" can limit or jeopardize the activities of the organization.

Although it is a model revealing the behavior of the organization pursuing what it wants to be achieved, and how it will be accomplished, the BMM is a model that has, as a main idea: to motivate the components of the organization. Through this model the elements understand the desired outcomes of the organization and how they are achieved, so there is a greater motivation on the part of its constituents.

Mission indicates the main activities of the organization, while the Vision indicates the state that is sought and amplified by Goals and Objectives.

Course of Action include both the Strategy and Tactics. The Strategy means the right approach to achieve the Goals; Tactics, in turn, in relation to Strategy, tend to fill in a shorter period of time, and have a more narrow perspective. Tactics are the tool for the achievement of defined Objectives.

Directives, in any organization, serve to rule the Course of Action. Business Policies are, in comparison with the Business Rules, less structured, less discrete and not so small. On the other hand, Business Rules are highly structured, very thorough, presenting the standard vocabulary of the business, authorizing, restricting or guiding the work of the organization in specific areas.

The external influences are those that stand outside the organization and create an impact on the application of Means or achievement of Ends. The internal influences come from within the organization and have an impact on employment of Means and in the achievement of Ends.

A SWOT analysis, according to the BMM, is a judgment on an Influencer, which affects the organization in its work to implement its Means or achieve its Ends, that is, an analysis of strengths and weaknesses, opportunities and threats.

With the development of the SWOT analysis the potential impact can be anticipated, that is, to anticipate what impact the Influencers will have on Means or Ends, positively or negatively. While negative influencers present a high Risk to the activity of the organization, positive influencers could, in turn, be used as a way to Potential Reward.

Risk arises from negative impacts indicating the probability of loss; obviously, without an analysis on the influencers, one cannot know the risk associated. The Potential Reward comes from positive results, indicating the winning probability. Like in the Risk, the absence of an analysis on Influencers, the organization will not know what good could draw from them.

2.3 The Business Model

The term Business Model can be defined as a logical summary of the value creation of an organization or a network of companies, including assumptions about their partners, competitors and customers. It is a very complex term that appeared on the Internet in the 90s, which advocates, in its beginnings, that the organization not only needs a strategy, a special competence and customer needs, but also a Business Model that promises big gains for the organization in its future.

The concept Business Model is used in many areas, including traditional theories, strategies, general management, innovation and management literature information. As a result, the concept of Business Model has different ideas, different assumptions and values. Some have a central vision of the organization, others are focused on the value of ends, a focus on Strategy, other on operational aspects; some are looking for innovation, others to technology aspects [3].

The Business Model serves as a competitive advantage when facing competition. If the organization clearly knows what its goal is, it responds to external and internal organization issues such as: "Who is?", "What does?", "To whom?" and "What values does it practice?".

Business Model and Business Strategy are different concepts and can be easily confused. The Business model shows the organization's system and how its elements come together and interact. However it does not take into account components that can influence the organization [4].

2.4 Business Strategy

Nowadays, due to dynamic markets and changing technologies, Strategy cannot be static. According to the new paradigm, the rivals can quickly steal any market position, and the apparent advantage is purely temporary [5].

In order to formulate a Strategy, the organization needs to find or create a structure in which the Strategy can be organized, determining what information is needed to apply it, identifying, then, how to capture the information and, ultimately, decide how this information should be processed within the structure to create, evaluate and optimize the Strategy or solution [6].

"*The strategy should be the main focus of cooperation, overlap the growth is a mistake that many organizations keep on committing.*" [5].

Thus, it may be that the organization's Strategy is very important and, so it should remain constant over time, as it is fundamental to achieve its "Ends".

In the organization, the existence of a Business Strategy is a plus, as it answers questions such as "Where is it done?", "How is it done?" and "When is it done?". Therefore, Business Strategy development is essential to obtain results since it allows identifying, during execution, failures or missed opportunities [4].

2.5 Strategic Management of Nonprofit Organizations

Non-profit organization exists primarily to bring about changes in individuals and in society, and there is not the figure of "profit". Typically, these organizations exist to perform righteous or moral acts or causes to serve. However, like in profitable organizations, they should optimize their resources in order to add efficiency and effectiveness to their processes.

Strategy implementation in this type of organization differs from the others. While the Strategy of the organization that seeks to profit leads to produce the maximum profit as a result of its operation, Strategy in the nonprofit organization is merely a means of maximizing resources.

2.6 Values of an Organization

The core values of an organization should reflect the deep values people embrace and must be totally independent from industry standards or management topics [7].

Values reflect the way of being of the organization and the people who work in it, determining how they operate and behave towards the business. The value statements come from the people and values of their chiefs [8].

3 Development of Business Model for the Air Force

Based on the model described above, this paragraph proposes and develops the Business Model that is thought to be the most appropriate for the Portuguese Air Force in general, instantiating it, then, to one of the Air Units.

3.1 Analysis of Interviews

During the development of the Business Model, several Air Force officers were interviewed. The questions received several responses that denote some dispute at the judgment across this theme. It should be noted, though, that the concept of "business" engaged in a military organization generates discomfort. However, all the interviewed agreed that, since financial resources are needed to the operation of the Air Force on a daily bases, it is also a business but in a non-profit way.

Moreover, there is still the opinion of some of the interviewed who affirm that there is an implicit business model in what the organization performs. However, there is a group that agrees that a Business Model would certainly influence the Strategy and further improve the organization, whose current output is already of high quality.

3.2 Comparison of EA of the Air Force with BMM

In order not only to identify parallels, but also to be able to find new ways to improve the Air Force's EA, a comparison was made between the current institutional artifacts that compose the Air Force's EA and the BMM concepts.

In this sense, there were found some substantial common points between the BMM and the Air Force in the areas of Ends and Means, and it was concluded that a direct application of the BMM could improve the mainstream of concepts used by the organization, grouping them by relating and aligning them with a derived view from the "Mission", published by the Government and the Vision of the Chief of General Staff: *"In the multi-faceted coverage of the mission, I envision an Air Force with a highly deployable nature, while maintaining a high degree of interoperability with other national and multinational forces, supported by the use of equipment that incorporate new technologies, served by a deployable command and control that enables operation in different environments, and a streamlined logistics, based on a modular structure, that eases expedited activation process.* "[9].

Down in detail, from the various concepts compared, it can be concluded that the process of studying external and internal influencers, and its relation to the SWOT analysis could be improved by adding effectiveness to the overall organization's EA.

Other of the conclusions stood on the need of introducing the organization and characterizing it in and out, answering questions such as: "Who are we?", "What do we do?", "What are our values?".

Since the Business Model answers questions such as those identified in the previous paragraph, it became important to complement the Business Architecture and add information about the organization itself, seeking to develop a Business Model appropriate to the Air Force, being identified the following development requirements: i) to appeal to patriotism, given the highly patriotic nature of armed forces; ii) be made into an easy and readable picture (symbol); iii) to represent the strategic level of the Organization; iv) to represent the Organizational Structure; v) to show the corporate values and mission; vi) to reflect areas (local) of employment; vii) to be capable of specification in the representation of entities from different levels (tactical and operational) of the organization.

3.3 Development of Business Model for the Air Force

While developing the Business Model for the Air Force, there were included the necessary articles to meet the above requirements: the description of the operational means, actions, values, organizational structure and the sites where it operates. The detail is described below. Additionally, it was necessary to produce an image easy to understand that would easily gather all the elements and explain the Business Model.

The Portuguese Air Force is a branch of the Armed Forces that, in the operational area, operates different weapon systems that can be characterized by high specialization, such as, for example, speed, mobility, range and flexibility of employment in any type of theater. Integrating the system of national forces, the Air Force's Mission, among others, cooperates in an integrated way, in defense of the Republic, through execution of air operations and air defense of the national space.

The structure of the Organization consists of the following: at the top of the hierarchy is the Chief of General Staff (CEMFA), which is supported by the General Staff (EMFA), the Inspector-General of the Air Force (IGFA), the Directorate of Finance (DFFA), by the Culture Organs (ONC) and by the Council Organs. These are followed by four functional commands, the Logistics Command (CLAFA), the Air Command (CA), the Personnel Command of the Air Force (CPESFA) and the Education and Training Command (CIFFA).

In its normal activity Air Force relates to the various entities including: the Portuguese Government, a regulatory element that ensures also a financial component, other state organs, such as the Presidency and the various Ministries and the Regional Governments, the military, for example, the General Staff of the Armed Forces, Army, Navy, Portuguese Official Language's African Countries (PALOP), and International Organizations such as the European Union and NATO, the Universities, the Media, Hospitals and cultural entities.

As part of its Mission, the Organization provides a range of services to entities described above, being the most relevant: the defense of national airspace, air transport operations, patrol, search and rescue, maritime surveillance and medical evacuation, formation, university and professional, research and development, health, courses of command and leadership and uses of the wind tunnel.

The Air Force is a military institution that practices noble values, such as the following: "Do well to well serve", "Ethics of Rigor", "Responsibility", "Demand", "Culture of Merit", "Integrity", "Dedication", "Competence", "Justice", "Permanent availability", "Honesty", "Leadership" and "Discipline"[9].

In carrying out its specific mission, the Organization operates around the Globe specially Portugal, Main Land and Islands, the area of influence of NATO, the European Union and the Western European Union and also within the Community of Portuguese Speaking Countries, having recently participated in several national and international operations of which stands out Afghanistan.

In Figure 1 the concepts presented above are illustrated in the representation of the Business Model for the Portuguese Air Force.

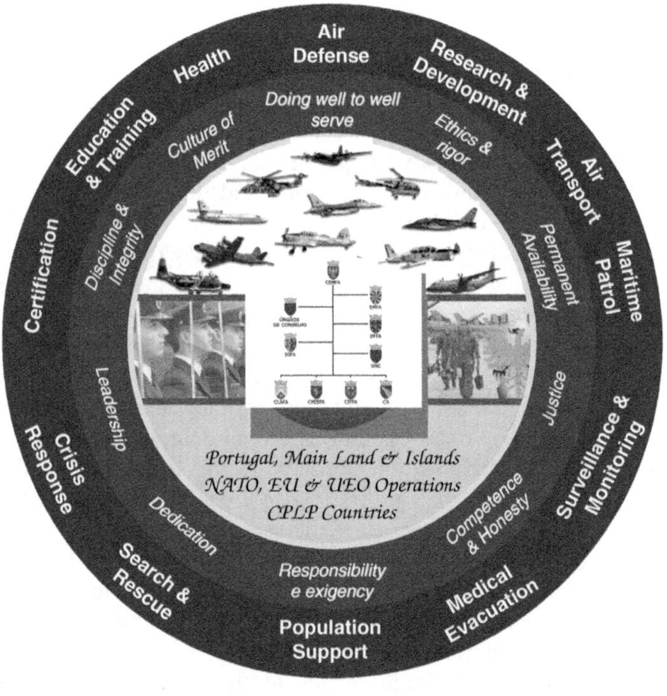

Fig. 1. Graphic representation of the Business Model for the Portuguese Air Force [10]

In a clear reference to patriotism and the highest values of the Nation, the colors of the National Flag can be observed in the two outer circles and in the small inner circle.

In the center there is the organizational structure of the Air Force and various images. On left there are shown the students of the Air Force Academy, representing the essential training for any organization and on the right the F-16 fighter aircraft personnel, representing the operational field.

Also in the center at the bottom there are the local activities of that organization, at the top are the operational means of the Air Force, in a setting that enhances the Air Force flies in all ways and directions.

In the green circle are observed values of all the Portuguese Air Force and in the red circle there are the various actions that the Air Force plays in civil and military components, in strict compliance with its mission.

On the overall, the picture combines all the attributes needed to represent the Business Model of achieving the purpose for which it is intended, namely the easy understanding of who you are, what you do, to whom you do it and what values are practiced, fulfilling all the requirements. The ability of specification of the model is measured by the development of the Business Model of the Air Units. In this case, for example (see Figure 2) it is shown the Business Model for Squadron 504, which operates the FALCON 50.

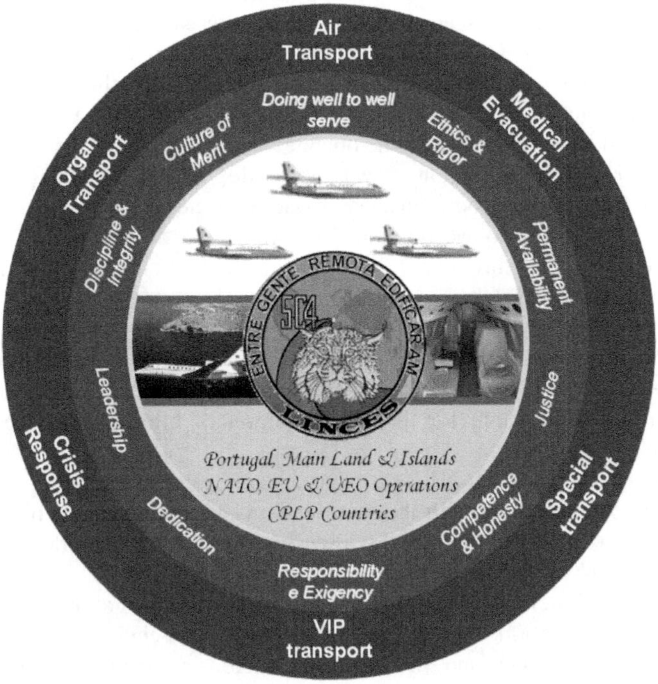

Fig. 2. Graphic Representation of the Business Model for Squadron 504 [10]

The Model of the Fleet 504 shows in the center, above, the image of three FALCON 50 aircraft; still at the center, there are images of the aircraft in flight and an aspect of its interior; instead of the organizational structure of the Air Force there is the patch of the Air Unit: the "Linces" and, finally, in the center there are referred the places of action (in this case, the same as the Air Force).

In the green circle remain the "Values" of the Organization while the outer circle describes the tasks that the Fleet 504 can do, such as: air transport, medical evacuation, special transportation, crisis response, VIP transport and organs transport.

The example shows that the model can be instantied to any organization at any level while informing the stakeholders what the organization is, what it does, to whom it does and what values it uses.

4 Conclusion

The Business Model complements the enterprise architecture of the organization, allowing the characterization and understanding not only of its business but also its identity and values, resulting in a better understanding by stakeholders, both internal and external.

In the process of understanding of what would be the best Business Model for the Air Force, it has been studied the formulation of its EA, compared with the BMM [1]. It was concluded that, considering that there is always room for improvement, implementation of the BMM, and SWOT analysis of influencers could add effectiveness to the activities related to the achievement of the mission.

One also sought to understand what the various internal stakeholders thought about the "Business Model" and its suitability to the organization. Several interviews were conducted that showed that most human resources think this model would be appropriate provided that it showed immediate gains in understanding the organization and how it relates with the outside.

After a thorough investigation, it was concluded that the Business model most suited to Air Force, would be a business model that clearly answered the questions "Who are we?", "What do we do" and "To whom we do it?" and "What are our values?", recognizable throughout the organization, being identified a set of requirements that the development should conform.

In addition to clearly explain what the organization does and how, the Business Model proposed for the Air Force (see Figure 1), reflects the its values, the air assets operated, what its top-level structure, in which areas of the globe it acts and provides services, having some room for the representation of high patriotic values as the colors of the National Flag.

The proposed Business Model is also specific and can be adapted to represent any unit inside the Air Force through the modification of some elements of its structure. An example was done designing the Business Model for Squadron 504, which operates the FALCON 50 aircraft (see Figure 2).

The Business Model, providing information to stakeholders about the identity and values of the organization, complements the enterprise architecture that defines the Mission, Vision, Objectives and Strategy. Thus, there is a complementary relationship between them.

The structure of the Business Model, shown in the image, is also suitable for the purpose intended, since it allows understanding of the relationship of a set of concepts in an immediate and easy way.

Future studies will be able to better identify the complementarities of the architecture of business and the Business Model, designing and proposing new artifacts that allow their composition.

References

1. The Business Rules Group (2007): The Business Motivation Model: Business Governance in a Volatile World, `http://www.businessrulesgroup.org/bmm.shtml` (consulted October 2009)

2. Tribolet, J., Páscoa, C.: Organizational Engineering I – Class presentations and notes, Portuguese Air Force Academy (2008)
3. Jägers, H., Jansen, W., Steenbakkers, W.: New Business Models for the Knowledge Economy. Gower Publishing Limited, Hampshire (2007)
4. Ramos, R.: Conhecimento de TI – Modelo de Negócio e Estratégia. Você tem? (2009), http://www.conhecimentoeti.com/2009/09/modelo-de-negocio-e-estrategia-voce-tem.html (consulted October 2009)
5. Porter, M.E.: What is Strategy? Harvard Business School Publishing Corporation (1996)
6. Ulwick, A.W.: Business Strategy Formulation: Theory, Process, and the Intellectual Revolution. Quorum Books, Westport (1999)
7. Marr, B.: Strategic Performance Management, 1st edn. Elsevier Ltd., Oxford (2006)
8. Person, R.: Balanced Scorecards and Operational Dashboards with Microsoft Excel. Wiley Publishing, Inc., Indianapolis (2009)
9. Araújo, L.: Speech of the Portuguese Air Force Chief-of-Staff (2008)
10. Leal, P.: Definição do Modelo de Negócio da Força Aérea, Master Thesis, Academia da Força Aérea, Departamento de Ensino Universitário, Sintra (2010)

The Role of Business Knowledge in Improving Information Quality Provided by Business Intelligence Systems

Pedro Simões Coelho[1,2], Aleš Popovič[2], and Jurij Jaklič[1,2]

[1] Instituto Superior de Estatística e Gestão de Informação, University NOVA
Campus de Campolide, 1070-312 Lisboa, Portugal
[2] Faculty of Economics, University of Ljubljana
Kardeljeva pl. 17
1000 Ljubljana, Slovenia
psc@isegi.unl.pt, ales.popovic@ef.uni-lj.si,
jurij.jaklic@ef.uni-lj.si

Abstract. The foremost purpose of implementing business intelligence systems is to increase the level of information quality provided to knowledge workers at various levels of an organization. However, at least at its present level of development business intelligence systems maturity affects information access quality more than content quality, while the biggest problems of providing quality information for knowledge-intensive activities relate to information content quality, not information access quality. The quantitative analysis carried out on data relating to 181 Slovenian medium and large organizations further shows that business knowledge positively moderates the relationship between business intelligence system maturity and information content quality. This has important implications: achieving higher levels of business knowledge for business intelligence initiatives results in narrowing the gap between the quality information provided by business intelligence systems and the information quality needs of knowledge workers when using information.

Keywords: Business intelligence, Business intelligence system maturity, Business knowledge, Content Quality, Information Quality, Information Access Quality, Structural equation modeling.

1 Introduction

In a decision-support context, business intelligence systems emerged as a promising technological solution with a wide range of analytical capabilities to provide stakeholders at various organizational levels with valuable information for their decision-making. When properly used, business intelligence systems assist management in developing a data-based decision-making environment that provides more consistent results compared to non-business intelligence methods. Although, business value of business intelligence systems can only result from changes and innovations in ways of working [1], they can be achieved indirecty through the use of improved information

J.E. Quintela Varajão et al. (Eds.): CENTERIS 2010, Part II, CCIS 110, pp. 148–157, 2010.

quality. Therefore, it is crucial to understand the means of business intelligence systems to improve the information quality and the factors that affect the ability to increase the success of business intelligence systems projects in terms of information quality improvement.

Several researchers [2; 3; 4] agree that the biggest problems of providing quality information for knowledge-intensive activities relate to information content quality, not information access quality. It was previously shown [5] that at the current level of development, business intelligence systems implementation projects do not adequately address the information content quality problems. Thus, there still exists a gap between the quality information provided by business intelligence systems and the information quality needs of knowledge workers when using information. Clearly, in order to improve the information content quality organizations need to primarily identify as accurately as possible knowledge workers' needs. This is a difficult task due to the non-routine and creative nature of knowledge workers' activities and requires an in-depth understanding of managerial business processes, knowledge of contemporary managerial concepts and capabilities of business intelligence technologies to improve the managerial an operational business processes.

With this research we aim to address the question of how can business knowledge for business intelligence initiatives contribute to narrow the above mentioned information quality gap [5]. The purpose of the paper is therefore to explore the role of business knowledge on the quality of information provided by business intelligence systems.

The outline of the paper is as follows: In Section 2 introduces the fields of business intelligence systems maturity, information quality, and the role of business knowledge in development of business intelligence systems. Section 3 aims to present the methodological framework for the study, while Section 4 deals with the testing of the proposed research model and hypotheses. Section 5 concludes with a summary and a discussion of the main findings.

2 Business Intelligence System Maturity, Information Quality, and the Role of Business Knowledge

According to The Data Warehousing Institute ('TDWI') in the field of business intelligence systems a maturity model illustrates how business intelligence systems evolve from low-value, cost-center tools to high-value, strategic utilities that drive performance [6]. Based on the reviewed business intelligence system maturity models we found no evidence of an agreement on the business intelligence system maturity concept. A deeper study of these models [5] suggests that none of them addresses maturity in a holistic way, but is more focused on the aspects it covers. In line with the purpose of this research we can derive two main emphasizes from the reviewed models. First, there is an awareness of the importance of integrating large amounts of data from disparate sources [7] and an awareness of the need to cleanse the data extracted from the sources [8]. Second, organizations are focusing on technologies (e.g. querying, online analytical processing, reporting, data mining) for the analysis of business data integrated from heterogeneous source systems [9]. On this basis, we propose the first hypothesis:

H1: Business intelligence system maturity is determined by data integration and analytics.

There is no unanimous agreement on how business intelligence systems provide value for organizations [10]. According to [11], the business value of business intelligence systems means getting the right information to the right user at the right time. In the view of [12], organizations that have successfully implemented business intelligence systems have better and timelier access to customer activities, marketplace trends, supply chain issues and other key performance indicators that cannot be easily measured in a non-business intelligence environment. Although this is a relatively limited view of the potential value that the implementation of these systems brings to organizations [13], improved information quality is certainly the most tangible benefit [14] and thus the most appropriate to be analyzed. All other outcomes, such as better decisions, improved processes, and increased market share are based on improved information quality. Therefore, the foremost purpose of implementing business intelligence systems is to increase the level of information quality provided to knowledge workers at various levels of an organization.

In the information systems literature, information quality is one of the major dimensions for evaluating the success of information systems [15]. To evaluate information quality we adopted *Eppler's* [16] *information quality framework* since it provides one of the broadest and most thorough analyses of the information quality evaluation criteria. The Eppler's framework separates views on information quality into two parts: content (relevance and soundness) quality relates to the actual information itself, while media quality (referenced herein as information access quality) relates to the management of that information and whether the delivery process and infrastructure are of adequate quality.

Koronios & Lin [17] identified some business intelligence technologies and activities, namely data cleansing, data integration, data tools and data storage architecture, as key factors influencing information quality. Nevertheless, Eppler [16] argues that technology mainly influences information access quality and has limited possibilities of influencing content quality, and Gurbaxani & Whang [18] similarly affirm that "modern information technology can reduce the costs of communicating information by improving the quality and speed of information processing". We can thus presume the maturity of business intelligence systems affects both dimensions of information quality, each in its own way. In this context, hypotheses 2a, 2b and 2c are put forward:

H2a: Business intelligence system maturity has a positive impact on content quality.
H2b: Business intelligence system maturity has a positive impact on information access quality.
H2c: Business intelligence system maturity has a different positive impact on content quality and information access quality.

To understand how the implementation of business intelligence systems actually contributes to solving issues of information quality in knowledge-intensive activities it is important to be familiar with the problems that may arise. Lesca & Lesca [2], for example, emphasize the limited usefulness of information due to an overload of information, ambiguity due to a lack of precision or accuracy leading to differing or wrong interpretations, incompleteness, inconsistency, information that is not reliable or trustworthy, inadequate presentation and inaccessible information. Similarly, Strong et al. [3] note problems such as too much information, subjective production and changing task needs.

The limited influence of technology on information content quality can be attributed to the fact that for information content the most important activity is to adequately specify knowledge workers' needs and requirements, which is a business issue rather than technological one. A clearer definition of their needs would ensure the comprehensiveness and conciseness of information. This emphasizes the need for the simultaneous implementation of contemporary managerial concepts that better define information needs in managerial processes by connecting business strategies with business process management. The latter includes setting organizational goals, measuring them, monitoring and taking corrective actions, and goes further to cascade organizational goals and monitoring performance down to levels of individual business activities. For example, a more extensive examination of critical success factors and related information needs might provide a better understanding of the information needs [19].

Tesch, et al. [20] recognize information systems development as a knowledge intensive process requiring integration across disciplines with domain knowledge as essential for successful systems design and implementation. However, data analysis as a business intelligence system development phase is different from a system analysis phase in a traditional information system development methodology [21]. It is a business-focused activity, not a system focused activity. In the context of business intelligence systems development it is therefore reasonable to assume that appropriate business knowledge will increase the chance of success in terms of improved information (mostly content) quality.

In information systems development two areas of knowledge are needed: knowledge on business processes and knowledge on information technology, which is to support the processes [22]. While Milovanović [22] asserts that users possess the former type of knowledge and information specialists possess the later one, it is worth to note that in the case of business intelligence systems development a knowledge gap often occurs.

On one side, business processes supported by business intelligence systems are usually less structured, less defined and even not clearly understood by the users due to non-routine nature of managerial activities. Contemporary managerial concepts, such as business performance management, put in place more structured approaches for managerial processes, which in consequence enable better understanding of information needs. Similarly, Brohman et al. [23] recognize the importance of a better understanding of the data analysis process.

On the other side, it is important that business users possess knowledge on information technology used in business intelligence systems, at least to some extent. This type of knowledge enables them to understand the possibilities for changing the current managerial practices. This knowledge therefore becomes the base for new spiral of knowledge creation in information system development context [22].

Therefore, we expect that employing business knowledge for business intelligence initiatives will improve the impact of business intelligence systems maturity on information quality, mostly on the content dimension of it. We thus upgrade previously studied conceptual model [5] by putting forward the following two hypotheses:

H3a: *The relationship between business intelligence system maturity and information content quality is stronger the higher the level of business knowledge for business intelligence initiatives.*

H3b: *The relationship between business intelligence system maturity and information access quality is stronger the higher the level of business knowledge for business intelligence initiatives.*

3 Methodology

This study used a survey to obtain data measuring business intelligence systems maturity, participants' perceptions of information quality, and perception about the required business knowledge. The questionnaire was developed by building on the previous theoretical basis in order to ensure content validity. Pre-testing was conducted using a focus group involving 3 academics interested in the field and 7 semi-structured interviews with selected CIOs who were not interviewed later. This was also used to assure face validity. We used a structured questionnaire with a combination of 7-point Likert scales and 7-point semantic differentials.

Based on the reviewed business intelligence and business intelligence systems' maturity models we modeled the business intelligence system maturity concept as a second-order construct formed by two first-order factors: data integration and analytics. The data integration construct is supported by the findings of [24]. Within the analytics construct we look at the different types of analyses the business intelligence system enables. We selected those indicators most used in previous works: paper reports [6], ad-hoc reports [25], online analytical processing ('OLAP') [9], data mining [6], dashboards, key performance indicators ('KPIs') and alerts [9].

To measure information quality we adopted previously researched and validated indicators provided by Eppler [16]. We included 11 of the information quality criteria from Eppler's framework in the research instrument (Table 1).

In order to assess the impact of business knowledge on the relationship between business intelligence system maturity and information content quality we included a question about the availability of such knowledge for business intelligence initiatives. The importance of business knowledge for business intelligence initiatives has been established in previous works [21; 26]. The moderating nature of business knowledge over the business intelligence systems maturity-information quality relationships was modeled through the use of an interaction term. This term was implemented creating a new construct, having as indicators the products of the standardized indicators relative to the underlying constructs involved in the interaction, following the approach of [27].

The target population for this study were Slovenian medium and large size organizations (1,329). Empirical data for this research were collected by means of paper and Web-based survey. Questionnaires were addressed to CIOs and senior managers estimated as having adequate knowledge of business intelligence systems, the quality of available information for decision-making and the use of information in business processes. The final response rate was 13.6%.

Table 1. Indicators for the constructs

Construct	Label	Indicator (description)
		(1 = Statement A best represents the current situation 7 = Statement B best represents the current situation)
Data integration	DI1	Data are scattered everywhere – on the mainframe, in databases, in spreadsheets, in flat files, in Enterprise Resource Planning ('ERP') applications. – Statement A Data are completely integrated, enabling real-time reporting and analysis. – Statement B
	DI2	Data in the sources are mutually inconsistent. – Statement A Data in the sources are mutually consistent. – Statement B
		(1 = Not Existent … 7 = Very much present)
Analytics	A1	Paper Reports
	A2	Interactive Reports (Ad-hoc)
	A3	On-Line Analytical Processing ('OLAP')
	A4	Analytical Applications, including Trend analysis, 'What-if' scenarios
	A5	Data Mining
	A6	Dashboards, including Metrics, Key Performance Indicators ('KPIs'), Alerts
		(1 = Strongly Disagree … 7 = Strongly Agree)
Content Quality	CQ1	The scope of information is adequate (neither too much nor too little).
	CQ2	The information is not precise enough and not close enough to reality.
	CQ3	The information is easily understandable by the target group.
	CQ4	The information is to the point, without unnecessary elements.
	CQ5	The information is contradictory.
	CQ6	The information is free of distortion, bias or error.
	CQ7	The information is up-to-date and not obsolete.
Information Access Quality	MQ1	The information provision corresponds to the user's needs and habits.
	MQ2	The information is processed and delivered rapidly without delay.
	MQ3	The background of the information is not visible (author, date etc.).
	MQ4	Information consumers cannot interactively access the information.
Business Knowledge	BK1	We possess appropriate professional business knowledge for business intelligence initiatives

4 Results

Data analysis was carried out using a form of structural equation modeling ('SEM'). For the estimation of the model we employed SEM-PLS (Structural Equation Models by Partial Least Squares) [28], also known as PLS Path Modelling ('PLS').

We first examined the reliability and validity measures for the model constructs. In the initial model not all reliability and convergent validity measures were satisfactory. Once all the items that did not load satisfactorily had been removed, the model was rerun. Figure 1 shows the results of testing the measurement model in the final run. In the final model all Cronbach's Alphas exceed the 0.70 threshold and were very marginal to 0.80. Without exception, latent variable composite reliabilities are higher than

0.80, and in general near 0.90, showing a high internal consistency of indicators measuring each construct and thus confirming construct reliability. The average variance extracted ('AVE') is higher than 0.50 (mostly around or higher than 0.60), except for Business intelligence system maturity construct (marginal to 0.50), indicating that the variance captured by each latent variable is significantly larger than variance due to measurement error, and thus demonstrating a convergent validity of the constructs. Reliability and convergent validity of the measurement model was also confirmed by computing standardized loadings for indicators and bootstrap *t*-statistics for their significance. All standardized loadings exceed (or were very marginal to) the 0.70 threshold and they were found, without exception, significant at 0.1% significance level, thus confirming a high convergent validity of the measurement model.

To assess discriminant validity, the following two procedures were used: 1) a comparison of item cross loadings to construct correlations, and 2) determining whether each latent variable shares more variance with its own measurement variables or with other constructs. The first procedure for testing discriminant validity was to assess the indicator loadings on their corresponding construct. All the item loadings met the requirements of the first procedure in the assessment of discriminant validity. For the second procedure we compared the square root of the AVE for each construct with the correlations with all other constructs in the model. All the constructs show evidence for acceptable validity.

A bootstrapping with 500 samples has been conducted to test the hypothesized relationships between the constructs. As shown in Figure 1, the standardized path coefficients range from 0.251 to 0.675 while the R^2 is moderate, i.e. between 0.284 and 0.326, for all endogenous constructs. We can see that about 33% of the variance in information access quality is explained by the influence of business intelligence system maturity, while about 28% of the variance in content quality is explained by the influence of business intelligence system maturity and business knowledge.

As indicated by the path loadings, business intelligence system maturity has significant direct and different positive influences on content quality ($\hat{\beta}$ = 0.363, p< 0.001) and information access quality ($\hat{\beta}$ = 0.524, p < 0.001). The *t*-statistic for the difference of the two impacts is 2.9 with p = 0.004 hence confirming that the two hypothesized impacts are indeed different. These results thus confirm our theoretical expectation and provide support for *H2a*, *H2b*, and *H2c*. To derive additional relevant information, sub-dimensions of the second-order construct (business intelligence system maturity) were also examined. As evident from the path loadings of data integration and analytics, each of these two dimensions of business intelligence system maturity is significant (p < 0.001) and of moderate to high magnitude ($\hat{\beta}$ = 0.488 and $\hat{\beta}$ = 0.675), supporting *H1* as conceptualization of the dependent construct as a second-order structure.

Moreover, the impact of business knowledge on information content quality is found to be significant and positive ($\hat{\beta}$ = .251, p<.001) while the impact of business knowledge on information access quality is positive ($\hat{\beta}$ =.066) but not significant. The interaction effect of business knowledge on the relationship between business intelligence system maturity and content quality is found to be significant and positive

($\hat{\beta}$ =.174, p<.01) thus supporting hypothesis *H3a*. On the other hand, the interaction effect of business knowledge on the relationship between business intelligence maturity and information access quality is positive ($\hat{\beta}$ =.141) but not significant and thus not supporting hypothesis *H3b*.

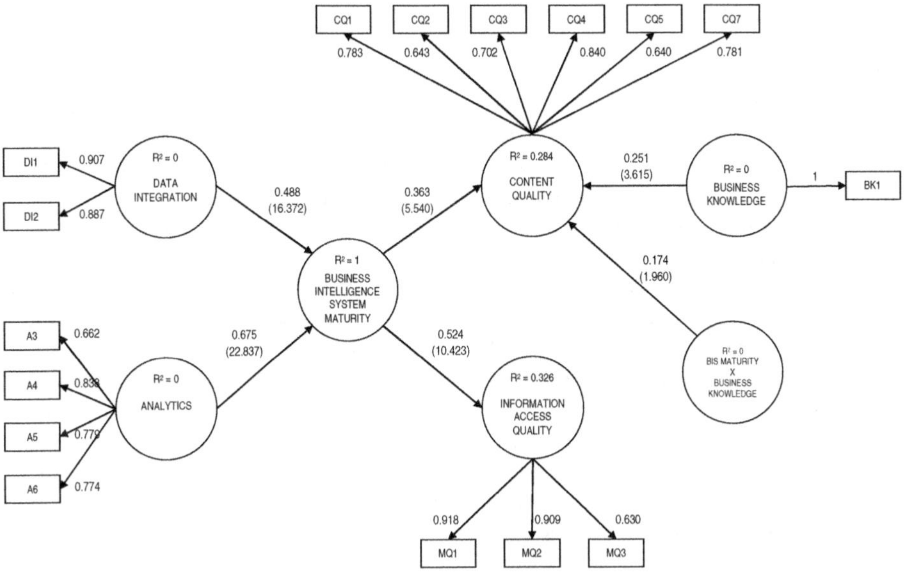

Fig. 1. Final model of business intelligence system maturity impact on information quality with the interaction effect of business knowledge

5 Conclusions

Even if both information quality segments are evidently well addressed with the implementation of business intelligence systems, one may expect that projects dealing with implementation of business intelligence systems are focused more on issues related to the main information quality issues in knowledge-intensive activities, i.e. content quality issues. This means that the implementation of such systems should contribute more to content quality than to information access quality. The results show that the implementation of business intelligence systems indeed differently impacts the two dimensions of information quality: higher levels of business intelligence system maturity affect information access quality more than content quality. It appears as organizations implementing business intelligence systems give less emphasis to the quality of information content and rather call attention to the information access quality.

To better address content quality issues through the implementation of business intelligence systems it is crucial to accurately define knowledge workers' needs – an usually difficult task considering the nature of knowledge workers' activities. While the development of business intelligence systems is supposed to be mainly a business-focused activity, we could expect that appropriate business knowledge will increase the odds of success in terms of improved information (content) quality. The results show that the impact of business knowledge on the relationship between business intelligence system maturity and information content quality is positive; it reinforces the direct impact of business intelligence system maturity on content quality. Note that the impact of intelligence system maturity on content quality can exceed the impact over information access quality for companies with business knowledge significantly higher than average. On the other hand for companies with very low business knowledge, the effect of intelligence system maturity on content quality can be almost nonexistent. This implies that higher levels of business intelligence system maturity will have a stronger effect on information content quality in organizations with better business knowledge related to business intelligence initiatives.

These findings have important implications for management: achieving higher levels of business knowledge for business intelligence initiatives results in a stronger impact of business intelligence maturity on information content quality. The targeted business knowledge includes the ability to understand and define as accurately as possible knowledge workers' needs which would improve the comprehensiveness and conciseness of information. Such business knowledge would ideally include knowledge about contemporary managerial concepts and proper metadata management that could improve the clarity of information. This further indicates that business intelligence implementation projects need to be business-focused and business-led, since this would result in improved potential value of business intelligence systems and easier justification of investments into these systems.

References

1. Peppard, J., Ward, J., Daniel, E.: Managing the Realization of Business Benefits from IT Investments. MIS Quarterly Executive 6, 1–11 (2007)
2. Lesca, H., Lesca, E.: Gestion de l'information, qualité de l'information et performances de l'entreprise, Litec, Paris (1995)
3. Strong, D.M., Lee, Y.W., Wang, R.Y.: Data quality in context. Communications of the ACM 40, 103–110 (1997)
4. Davenport, T.H., Jarvenpaa, S.L., Beers, M.C.: Improving knowledge work processes. Sloan Management Review 37, 53–66 (1996)
5. Popovič, A., Coelho, P.S., Jaklič, J.: The impact of business intelligence system maturity on information quality. Information Research 14 (2009)
6. TDWI. 2005 TDWI Poster: Business Intelligence Maturity Model (2005), `http://tdwi.org/Publications/display.aspx?ID=7288` (retrieved November 10, 2009)
7. Elbashir, M.Z., Collier, P.A., Davern, M.J.: Measuring the effects of business intelligence systems: The relationship between business process and organizational performance. International Journal of Accounting Information Systems 9, 135–153 (2008)
8. Bouzeghoub, M., Lenzerini, M.: Introduction to: data extraction, cleaning, and reconciliation a special issue of Information Systems. An International Journal. Information Systems 26, 535–536 (2001)

9. Davenport, T.H., Harris, J.G.: Competing on analytics: the new science of winning. Harvard Business School Press, Boston (2007)
10. Petter, S., DeLone, W.H., McLean, E.R.: Measuring information systems success: models, dimensions, measures and interrelationships. European Journal of Information Systems 17, 236–263 (2008)
11. De Voe, L., Neal, K.: When Business Intelligence Equals Business Value. Business Intelligence Journal 10, 57–63 (2005)
12. Thierauf, R.J.: Effective Business Intelligence Systems. Quorum Books (2001)
13. Popovic, A., Turk, T., Jaklic, J.: Analysis of business intelligence system improvement impact on improved business performance. WSEAS Transactions on Business and Economics 2, 173–179 (2005)
14. Watson, H.J., Goodhue, D.L., Wixom, B.H.: The benefits of data warehousing: why some organizations realize exceptional payoffs. Information & Management 39, 491–502 (2002)
15. DeLone, W.H., McLean, E.R.: Information Systems Success: The Quest for the Dependent Variable. Information Systems Research 3, 60–95 (1992)
16. Eppler, M.J.: Managing Information Quality: Increasing the Value of Information in Knowledge-Intensive Products and Processes. Springer, Heidelberg (2006)
17. Koronios, A., Lin, S.: Information Quality in Engineering Asset Management Information Quality Management: Theory and Applications. Idea Group Pub. (2007)
18. Gurbaxani, V., Whang, S.: The impact of information systems on organizations and markets. Communications of ACM 34, 59–73 (1991)
19. Huotari, M.-L., Wilson, T.D.: Determining organizational information needs: the Critical Success Factors approach. Information Research 6 (2001)
20. Tesch, D., Sobol, M.G., Klein, G., Jiang, J.J.: User and developer common knowledge: Effect on the success of information system development projects. International Journal of Project Management 27, 657–664 (2009)
21. Moss, L.T., Atre, S.: Business Intelligence Roadmap: The Complete Project Lifecycle for Decision-Support Applications. Addison-Wesley Professional, Reading (2003)
22. Milovanović: Knowledge sharing between users and information specialists: role of trust. Facta Universitatis, Series: Economics and Organization 3, 51–58 (2006)
23. Brohman, M.K., Parent, M., Pearce, M.R., Wade, M.: The Business Intelligence Value Chain: Data-Driven Decision Support in a Data Warehouse Environment: An Exploratory Study. In: 33rd Hawaii International Conference on System Sciences, Hawaii (2000)
24. Lenzerini, M.: Data integration: a theoretical perspective. In: Popa, L., Abiteboul, S., Kolaitis, P.G. (eds.) Proceedings of the 21st ACM SIGMOD-SIGACT-SIGART Symposium on Principles of Database Systems, pp. 233–246. ACM, New York (2002)
25. Claraview. Business Intelligence Maturity Model (2005), `http://www.claraview.com` (retrieved January 20, 2007)
26. Williams, S., Williams, N.: The Profit Impact of Business Intelligence. Morgan Kaufmann, San Francisco (2007)
27. Chin, W.W., Marcolin, B.L., Newsted, P.R.: A Partial Least Squares Latent Variable Modeling Approach for Measuring Interaction Effects: Results From a Monte Carlo Simulation Study and an Electronic-Mail Emotion/Adoption Study. Information Systems Research 14, 189–217 (2003)
28. Ringle, C.M., Wende, S., Will, A.: SmartPLS 2.0 M3. University of Hamburg (2007)

Business Process Model Dynamic Updating

Nuno Castela[1,2], Marielba Zacarias[1,3,4], and José Tribolet[1,5]

[1] Center for Organizational Design and Engineering, INESC INOVAÇÃO
[2] Superior School of Technology, Polytechnic Institute of Castelo Branco
[3] Research Center for Spatial and Organizational Dynamics
[4] Algarve University
[5] Dep. of Information Systems and Computer Science, Instituto Superior Técnico, Technical University of Lisbon
ncastela@ipcb.pt, mzacaria@ualg.pt, jose.tribolet@inesc.pt

Abstract. Enterprise representations can be used to improve the organizational self-awareness, allowing the communication of knowledge about these concerns among different organizational actors. In order to achieve this goal, the model must provide an updated, trustworthy and reliable representation. However, the typical usage of the enterprise model is restricted to support some organizational activities for limited time intervals. The recognized difficulty in maintaining it updated and aligned with the reality has prevented the usage of enterprise models as a repository of the organizational knowledge relevant for the daily activities execution. The present work proposes a process for continuously update the enterprise model trough the annotation mechanism. Annotations enable interaction contexts that allow actors to make explicit their knowledge about their activities through graphic representations. In this process, actors act as active updaters of the as-is model, through the comparison between the modeled activities and the ongoing real executed activities. This process is modeled by DEMO methodology in order to depict the essential transactions between actors of operational and model updating processes.

Keywords: Enterprise Engineering, Organizational Knowledge, Enterprise Modeling, Enterprise Ontology, Model Annotation.

1 Introduction

Enterprise engineering [1] puts together concepts, methods and technologies which allows to understand, model, develop and analyze different business concerns such as strategy, processes and supporting information systems, as well as the inter-relationships and inter-dependencies among them. In this context, business process models [2] allow to communicate, document and understand the operation of organizations. The model that represents business processes in present time, is called the *as-is* business process model, in contrast to the *to-be* model, which reflects future changes to processes resulting from business process analysis and improvement processes addressed by Business Process Management (BPM), Total Quality Management (TQM), Business Process Reengineering (BPR) among others.

J.E. Quintela Varajão et al. (Eds.): CENTERIS 2010, Part II, CCIS 110, pp. 158–167, 2010.

Building the as-is model has the following goals: redesign or improve the organization [3], [4], [5], [6]; improve enterprise integration [7], [8], [9]; act as a starting point to information systems architecture and to requirements gathering in information systems development [10], [11]; control the running processes [3], [6]; and act as knowledge repository of the organization.

The latter goal can be valuable enhancing the ability of organizations to become learning organizations [12], [13]. Organizational knowledge, regarding its operations, can be made explicit through the business process model, with the contribution of the individual knowledge possessed by all members of the organizations [14]. Achieving this goal entails supporting the interaction contexts shared among the different organizational actors, where knowledge about organizational processes, as well as their goals, activities, and resources are discussed [15].

The business process model needs to accommodate different points of view of organizational actors, while at the same time, needs also to assure the consistency of the model as a whole. Defining methods and tools to support this capability is an essential requirement to achieve organizational self-awareness [16], which refers to the capability of answering questions regarding any organizational concern at any given moment in time. The process model, integrated in the enterprise architecture, has a key role in enhancing organizational self-awareness, as it can be used in discussing current knowledge about operations, incorporating more knowledge in an iterative and incremental manner. Organizational actors are the individuals and groups involved in both the execution of operational business processes and the discussion of activity and process representations and eventual updating. It is important to notice that the execution of business processes and the discussions related to updating their representations define different interaction contexts where different conversations are developed.

Nonetheless, despite being recognized as an important organizational asset, the as-is business process model is not updated often, because the maintenance of this representation is not a trivial question and also because it tends to be constructed to be used and then "sit on the shelf" [17]. If the as-is process model could be continuously updated, it would provide an ideal knowledge repository in supporting organizational self-awareness. In this context, the present research has the following goals: to discover the process of updating the as-is business process; to build a tool supporting such process in order to improve the alignment of the model with the operational reality; to enable all organizational actors as the key agents in reducing the gap between the organization and its representation trough the definition a misalignment detection mechanism. This annotation mechanism should be also the key in establishing a conversation and negotiation channel among the individual actors (the parts) and between the individual actors and the organization (the whole), where the organization refers to all its members that previously shared and agreed upon model representations. In other words, the work presented in this paper aims to establish a process to automate and streamline the management and updating of the business process model in order to align it with the running processes and activities, using the annotation mechanism.

The remaining of this paper is structured as follows. Section 2 describes the related work about annotations. In section 3, the as-is enterprise model dynamic updating process (PROASIS) is defined. Section 4 presents the case study developed. The conclusions and future work are presented in section 5.

2 Annotations

In general, the annotations are an addition of information on a particular section of a document or other informational entity. Annotations have specific uses in distinct areas: in biology for genome annotation [18], in law science for annotated versions of legislation books, in language science for linguistic annotations, in programming languages like Java [19], in modeling languages like UML [20], in Web pages for analysis of documentation [21] and for adding comments, explanations or other external reference [22], in hypertext for establishing new connections, interpret materials and promote the creation of structure or content, increasing the body of inter-related material [23].

The use of the annotation concept in the course of this research is based on the work of Becker-Kornstaedt and Reinert [24] who applied this mechanism to capture the reasons for the changes that are normally made in software projects, caused by the implicit knowledge of development teams. The annotations should capture the activities, resources (entities) and the context involved (flows). The continuous improvement of processes requires that the experience is captured to be continuously incorporated into business processes and portrayed in the as-is model. The systematic capture and storage in the context where the experience was captured has three major benefits [24]: the experience can become explicit; the experience may be incorporated in the description of the process; the analysis of the experience can be reused in other processes for process improving.

3 As-Is Business Process Model Dynamic Updating Process

The idea to explore in defining the AS-IS business process model dynamic updating PROcess (PROASIS) is based on the analysis of misalignments between the shared model and ongoing executed processes. This misalignment analysis uses the annotations as a mechanism to collect the updates proposed by organizational actors. The language used to represent the business processes is the business process modeling notation (BPMN) due to its simplicity and widespread use [25]. The PROASIS is supported by a groupware prototype tool that distributes the business process model to the organizational actors, and supports the gathering of annotations as well as the underlying negotiation for refining and approving the annotations [26].

3.1 PROASIS Key Ideas

The update process is executed by the organizational actors that perform the activities composing the organizational processes. The annotations allow making proposals for correcting the model (corrective maintenance), capture changes in action or interaction contexts (adaptive maintenance), make free comments that could anticipate problems (preventive maintenance) and promote process continuous improvement (perfective maintenance) [24]. This process uses the revisions and evaluation of the annotations to establish the necessary negotiation among all the organizational actors involved in an update context.

In order to define a model updating process with widespread use, several granularity levels of the business process models were considered: process, activity and action levels (figure 1), as well as the organizational unit level [27].

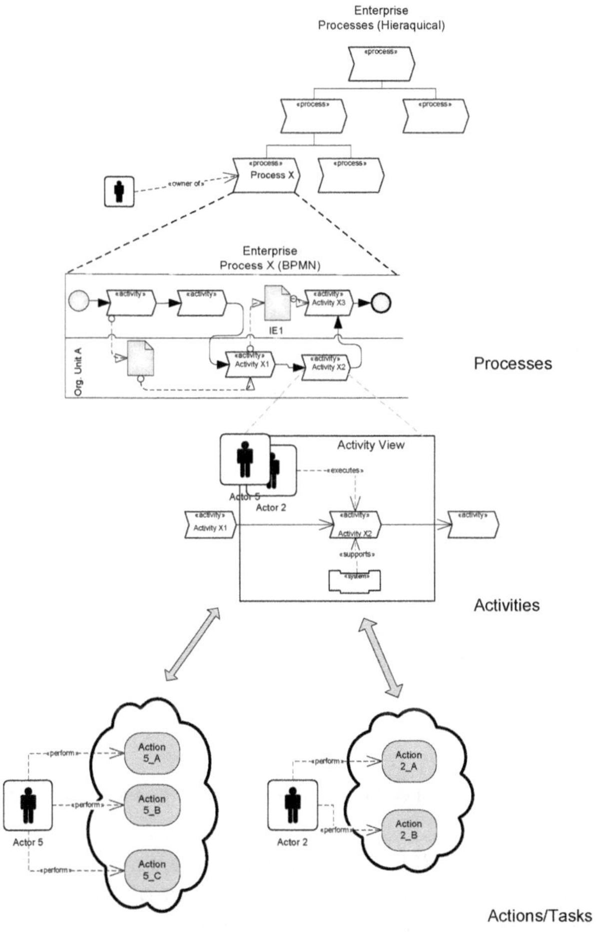

Fig. 1. Business Process Model Granularity Levels

The action level of detail, though considered in this work, is not subject of annotations to update the model, mainly because its representation depends on the personal and individual view of each organizational actor. However, this level of detail is important because it may therefore contain the motive that leads each of the actors to propose changes and updates to the shared common process model (activities, processes, organizational units). The levels of detail that are considered for updating the as-is model are the levels of detail that the business process model distributed in organizations have (process and activity, mainly).

The modeling elements considered in the BPMN models that can be updated (by allowing the actors to make annotations to them) are shown in the figure 2.

Depending on the modeling element in each level of detail, several actors that play different roles in the operational model can play different roles in PROASIS as annotators of the model, and reviewers or evaluators of the annotations made.

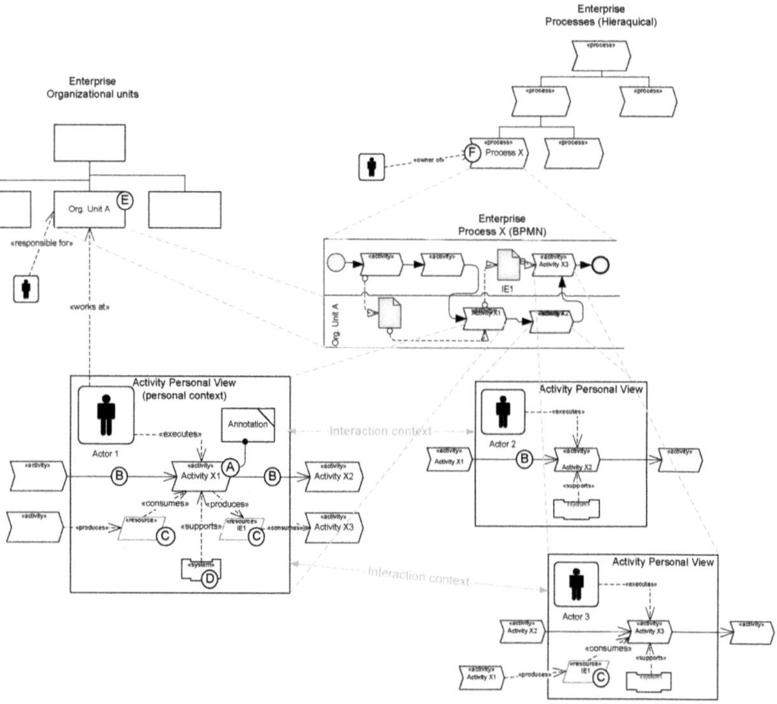

Fig. 2. Actors and contexts participating in the model dynamic updating

The update context (PROASIS) dynamically captures a set of actor roles of the operational context. This set is made up of a subset of the operational context actors, which will be the individuals who participate in the updating process (as annotators, reviewers and evaluators).

At the activity level of detail, an executor actor can make annotations to several modeling elements that are related to the activities that he or she executes (see tags from A to D in figure 2). The organizational actors that could make revisions to the annotations made in this level of detail are the same actors that according to the as-is business process model share the annotated modeling element. If the annotated element is the activity, the reviewers are all the actors that execute the activity. If the annotated element is a flow between activities, the reviewers are the actors whose activity is the starting point or the arriving point of the flow. If the annotated element is an informational entity, the reviewers are the actors who are performing activities that consume or produce informational entity. Finally, if the annotated element is the supporting information system, the reviewers are the actors who use the same information systems to support their activities. These revisions are made by the reviewers to express agreement or disagreement with the annotation made. The evaluation of the annotations will be performed by actors who possess operational responsibility to the annotated element and hierarchical responsibility on the annotator in the operational context, so whatever the element annotated in the activity level of detail, the annotation will be jointly evaluated by the respective process owner and by the responsible of the organizational unit. The result of this evaluation must be the joint approval for the update proposal expressed in the original annotation made means in order to be incorporated in the new version of the model by the modeler.

At the process level of detail, the standard annotator is the process owner. The process owner can make an annotation to the process which he owns as a whole, and this annotation is reviewed by the actors who are responsible for the organizational units where the activities that comprise the process are executed. The evaluation of the process annotation is made jointly by those involved in the review process (process owner and responsible for the organizational units involved).

At the organizational unit level of detail, the organizational unit responsible is the standard annotator. The review process of the organizational annotation involves the organizational unit responsible that originated the annotation and the process owners that have activities performed under the responsibility of the organizational unit annotated. The subsequent evaluation process involves the same actors that participate in the annotation review, where they have to make a joint approval to validate the annotation allowing the modeler to create a new version of the model.

One of the goals in defining the PROASIS was to approach as much as possible the collaborative process used to update models with the problem domain of business process modeling. To achieve this goal some actions were taken: the annotations made to the model are connected to the modeling elements; the annotations could be textual and/or graphic; the annotations are categorized as corrections, increase of detail or adaptation; the reviews are categorized as agreement or disagreement complemented with text and/or graphics; the evaluations are categorized as approval or disapproval complemented with text and/or graphics.

3.2 Modeling PROASIS with DEMO Methodology

The DEMO (Design and Engineering Methodology for Organizations) meta-ontology [28], [29] is used to develop business process models to in order to clearly distinguish between the world (states and events) and the causes of change in this world (actors and acts). The notion of ontology has as objective to understand the essence of the construction and operation of an organizational system. The following text expresses the essence of PROASIS:

"The "client" of PROASIS (corresponding role of the operational model that detects misalignment between the model and "reality") wants to update the model, so it makes an annotation (update request). This update request is received by the modeler (which is who actually update the model if the annotation is approved) and by the reviewers. When reviewers receive the annotation, they can begin the revision of the annotation (which is optional). The approval of the annotation is made based on the analysis of the annotation (update request) and reviews. If the annotation (request update) is approved, the model will be updated and delivered to the "client"".

In the text above, an independent transaction (T1) is identifiable, that corresponds to the delivery of a final product to the environment, which is in this case, the delivery of a updated enterprise business process model. The production fact of this transaction is the delivery of a particular update of the model. The following transaction result table shows the transaction T1 and the dependent transactions T2 and T3.

Table 1. Transaction Result Table of PROASIS

Transaction	Result
T1 – Model Update	R1 – The model M is updated with the annotation A
T2 - Revision	R2 – The Revision R of the annotation A was created
T3 - Approval	R3 – The Evaluation E of the annotation A was created

The process structure diagram shows the structure of PROASIS (figure 3): After an actor of the operational model has made an update request, we can see that to deal with the promise of T1 (T1/pm), the modeler performs two acts: the coordination act T3/rq (which means that he promises to update the model based on the annotation made only if there is an approval of the evaluator) and the execution act of T1 (which will only be executed if the evaluator approves the annotation). At the same time, when the actor of the operational processes requires an amendment to the model (T1/rq), this same actor "transposes to" to PROASIS as an annotator, and T1/rq leads to T2/rq, since it requires the revision of the annotation that he did. The transactions T2 and T3 both imply negotiation processes. The new instance of the model produced in T1, reflects the changes expressed in the annotation, and the set formed by annotation/reviews/approvals became part of it.

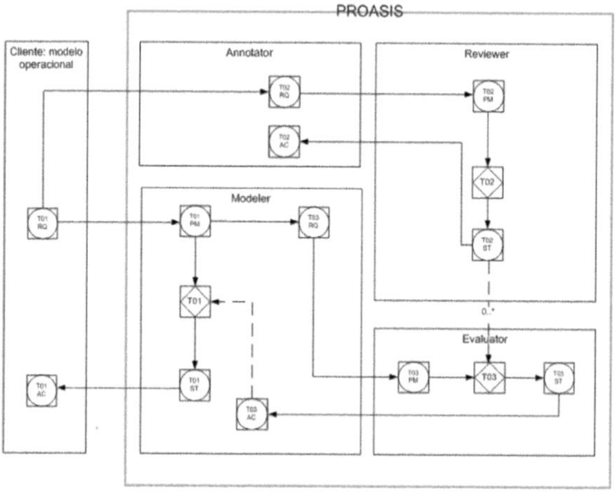

Fig. 3. Process structure diagram shows the structure of PROASIS

Figure 4 shows the association between the two models, the operational (the one that is being updated) and the PROASIS (one that is used to update the operational model, represented with the DEMO actor transaction diagram). This association is expressed by the dynamic relationship among the roles of each model. The initiation of the transaction T1(in PROASIS) is made by the operational actor role that makes an annotation, which could by any of the roles defined in the operational model, depending of the annotation context). Consequently, the reviewers and evaluators roles are dynamically assigned because they depend of the associations among the modeling elements of the operational model.

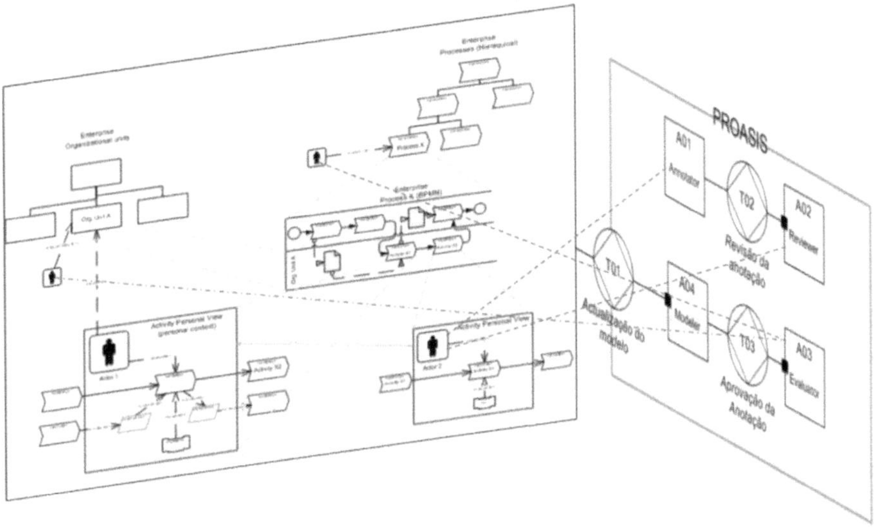

Fig. 4. Relationship between operational model and PROASIS

The PROASIS modeling with DEMO shows and emphasizes: The essential elements of PROASIS; the organizational roles involved (annotator, reviewer, approver and modeler) and the transactions of PROASIS (annotation, review, approval and modeling), and their relationship with the roles of the operational processes, which act as initiators of the transactions on PROASIS.

4 Case Study

A tool developed to support PROASIS is currently being used in a governmental organization in Portugal. The available results shows that initially the actors mostly made annotations as corrections to the shared model, allowing the involvement of all actors connected directly (executers) or indirectly (process owners and organizational units responsible) in validating and updating the enterprise model, aligning it with the reality in an interactive and shared way. So, the annotations and their extensions (reviews and evaluations) fit the requirement of being a suited mechanism in putting the actors talking about their activities and proposing changes to the enterprise model. Figure 5 shows a screenshot of the tool developed used in the case study.

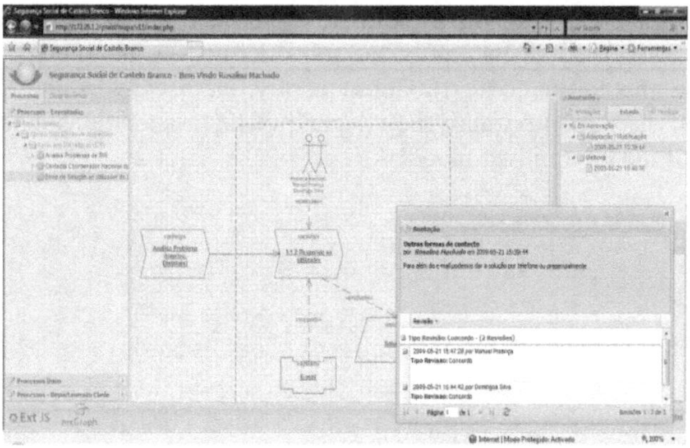

Fig. 5. Screenshot of the MAPA tool

5 Conclusions and Future Work

The introduction of the PROASIS in a real organization revealed that it could have an important role, not only in gathering the information needed to update the model, but also allowing the opening of communication channels to share and gather knowledge about the organizational activities.

DEMO reveal that is a well suited methodology to model the essential aspects of PROASIS and the negotiation implied in building and updating process models, due to the communications theoretic perspectives underlying it.

In an attempt to fit the PROASIS with the organizational practices, we can highlight the role of PROASIS in the scope of Business Process Management (BPM) initiatives. The activity of process redesign, included in the BPM lifecycle, is based on interviews and meetings, and is triggered by management needs. The philosophical basis of the PROASIS is different because it is activated by the detection of gaps and opportunities for improvement seen by those directly involved in the activities execution. It is not only a step of the BPM lifecycle driven by conscious and/or specific improvement/optimization felt by managers. PROASIS can run continuously in the background, and is triggered asynchronously by the actors in the organization at various levels, reducing the efforts of model redesign in BPM initiatives.

The future work, in operational terms, will focus on the consolidation of the case study in progress. In theoretical terms, it will focus on exploring the DEMO to represent meta-processes and negotiation patterns in the scope of PROASIS.

References

1. Tribolet, J., Winter, R., Caetano, A.: Editorial Message: Special Track on Organizational Engineering. In: ACM SAC, Santa Fe, New Mexico (2005)
2. Caetano, A., Silva, A., Tribolet, J.: Object-Oriented Business Process Modeling with Roles. In: 7th ISIM, Czech Republic (2004)
3. Bernus, P.: Enterprise models for enterprise architecture and ISO9000:2000. Annual Reviews in Control 27, 211–220 (2003)

4. Davenport, T.H.: Process Innovation: Reengineering Work through Information Technology. Harvard Business School Press, Boston (1993)
5. Hammer, M., Champy, J.: Reengineering the Corporation: A Manifesto for Business Revolution, HarperBusiness (1993)
6. Vinturella, J.: Management Briefing Business Process Management (BPM): Must Have? (April 30, 2005), `http://management-briefings.jbv.com`
7. Goul, M., Corral, K.: Enterprise model management and next generation decision support. Decision Support Systems 43, 915–932 (2007)
8. Kim, H.M., Fox, M.S.: Using Enterprise Reference Models for Automated ISO 9000 Compliance Evaluation. In: Proceedings of the 35th HICSS (2002)
9. Chapurlat, V., Kamsu-Foguema, B., Prunet, F.: Enterprise model verification and validation: an approach. Annual Reviews in Control 27, 185–197 (2003)
10. Sousa, P., Caetano, A., Vasconcelos, A., Pereira, A., Tribolet, J.: Enterprise Architecture Modeling with Unified Modeling Language. IRM Press (2005)
11. Loucopoulos, P., Kavakli, E.: Enterprise Modelling and the Teleological Approach to Requirements Engineering. International Journal of Intelligent and Cooperative Information Systems (1995)
12. Boudreau, M.-C., Robey, D.: Coping with contradictions in business process reengineering. Information Technology & People 9(4), 40–57 (1996)
13. Magalhães, R.: Fundamentos da Gestão do Conhecimento Organizacional, Sílabo (2005)
14. Zacarias, M., Pinto, S., Tribolet, J.: Redes de conhecimento em engenharia organizacional: o imperativo dos contextos de acção. Cadernos BAD 1, 6–23 (2004)
15. Zacarias, M., Pinto, H.S., Magalhães, R., Tribolet, J.: A 'context-aware' and agent-centric perspective for the alignment between individuals and organizations. Information Systems 35(3), 271–374 (2010) (in Press)
16. Magalhães, R., Sousa, P., Tribolet, J.: The Role of Business Processes and Enterprise Architectures in the Development of Organizational Self-Awareness. Polytechnical Studies Review, VI(9) (2008), ISSN: 1645-9911
17. Castela, N., Tribolet, J.: Representação As-Is em Engenharia Organizacional, 5ª CAPSI, Lisboa, Portugal (Novembro 3-5, 2004), ISBN: 972-99387-1-7
18. Stein, L.: Genome annotation: from sequence to biology. Nat. Rev. Genet. 2, 493–503 (2001)
19. Flanagan, D.: Java in a Nutshell. O'Reilly, Sebastopol (2005)
20. UML ISO IEC - UML Specification, Version 1.4.2, formal/05-04-01 (2005)
21. Oinas-Kukkonen, H.: Towards evaluating knowledge management through the 7C Model. In: ECITE 2005, Turku, Finland, September 29-30 (2005)
22. Yang, S.J.H., Chen, I.Y.L., Shao, N.W.Y.: Ontology Enabled Annotation and Knowledge Management for Collaborative Learning in Virtual Learning Community. Educational Technology & Society 7(4), 70–81 (2004)
23. Marshall, C.C.: Toward an ecology of hypertext annotation. In: Proceedings of ACM Hypertext 1998, Pittsburgh, PA, pp. 40–49. Engelbart Best Paper Award (1998)
24. Becker-Kornstaedt, U., Roman, R.: A Concept to Support Process Model Maintenance through Systematic Experience Capture. In: SEKE 2002, Ischia, Italy, July 15-19 (2002)
25. White, S., Miers, D.: BPMN Modeling and Reference Guide. Ed. Future Strategies (2008)
26. Dias, P., Castela, N., Fidalgo, F., Penedo, J., Tribolet, J.: MAPA: Ferramenta de Monitorização e Actualização de Processos e Actividades, 9ª, CAPSI, Viseu, Portugal (2009)
27. Zacarias, M.: Conceptual Framework based on Agents and Contexts for the Alignment between Individuals and Organizations, IST (2008)
28. Dietz, J.L.G., Habing, N.: A Meta Ontology for Organizations. In: OTM Workshops 2004, pp. 533–543 (2004)
29. Dietz, J.L.G.: Enterprise Ontology: Theory and Methodology. Springer, Heidelberg (2006)

Professional Risk Assessment Using Virtual Enterprise Network Support for Knowledge Bases Development

George Dragoi[1], Anca Draghici[2], Sebastian Marius Rosu[3], Alexandru Radovici[1], and Costel Emil Cotet[1]

[1] "Politehnica" University of Bucharest, Faculty of Engineering in Foreign Languages, PREMINV Research Center, Splaiul Independentei 313, sector 6, 060042 Bucharest, Romania
[2] "Politehnica" University of Timisoara, Management Faculty, 14 Remus str., 300191 Timisoara, Romania
[3] Special Telecommunication Service, IT Department, Bucharest, Romania
gdragoi@mix.mmi.pub.ro, adraghici@eng.upt.ro, sebastianrosu@sts.ro, msg4alex@gmail.com, costel@mix.mmi.pub.ro

Abstract. The paper presents some recent researches results based on the concept of collaborative infrastructure, in order to unify existing standards for supply chain management and to provide the support in various decision making process in manufacturing supply networks. Intended to facilitate and enhance the required knowledge management processes the proposed collaborative infrastructure, based on a virtual enterprise network, is expected to promote the development of the business services sector using a new product lifecycle paradigm according with the greater need for software tools for risk estimation. We focus on the professional risk assessment (PRA) as part of risk management process (RMP) and how the risk level can be established in collaborative infrastructures depending on probability and severity of consequences. A case study is presented to show PRA at the SMEs level.

Keywords: Virtual Enterprise Network, Knowledge Management, Knowledge Bases Applications, Professional Risk Assessment, Intranet, Internet, Extranet.

1 Introduction

Virtual enterprise network (VEN), conceived in the beginning of this century as a European response to the needs of manufacturing facing the knowledge economy, contributes with a high level strategy that provides the reference model for industrial transformation. The Research Innovation Value Chain, as an action line, represents the operational place where stakeholders can network to respond to the multi-objectives of modern enterprise in the new era of knowledge society [1]. In the 21st century, all enterprises continue to implement ICT strategies to improve manufacture, research, products quality, sales, services and to costs control. Today, new enterprise model architecture uses the Intranet/Internet/Extranet technologies.

As a general requirement for an infrastructure support is than the enterprises must be able to inter-operate and exchange information's and knowledge in real time so

J.E. Quintela Varajão et al. (Eds.): CENTERIS 2010, Part II, CCIS 110, pp. 168–177, 2010.

that they can work as a single integrated unit, although keeping their independence/autonomy. For the future, e-services and e-business, as were defined, require the enterprise re-thinking and re-modeling, with the system and applications design for an efficient use of new network technologies. Building the e-economy is a complex challenge and its main requirements are presented in Figure 1 [1].

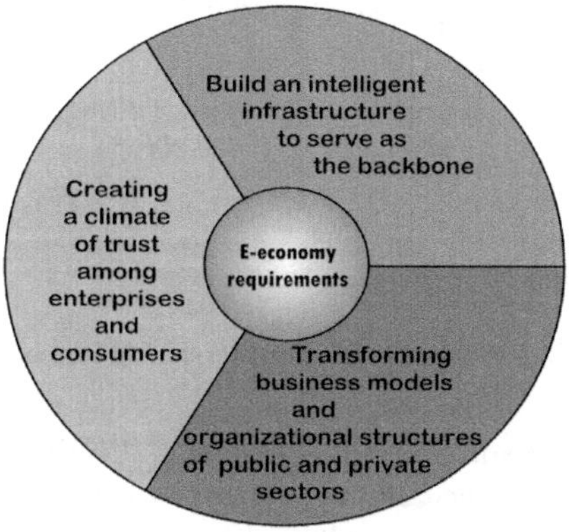

Fig. 1. The new digital economy (e-economy) requirements

Developing and implementing these strategies will require partnership and collaboration among the private, public and academic sectors as well as other agencies and organizations that strive to link these together. It will require the active involvement of consumers and citizens. The collaboration infrastructure, implemented in the PREMINV e-platform (from the "Politehnica" University in Bucharest), is intended to facilitate and enhance the required knowledge management processes. In the European countries more then 95% of the companies are small and medium-sized enterprises (SMEs) and majority of the European Union employees work in these companies. The proposed collaboration infrastructure, based on a VEN, is expected to reduce involvement of individual SMEs in networking efforts, enable better and faster decisions and promote the development of the business services sector. As a result of a new product development paradigm, there is a greater need for software tools to risk estimation. In addition, we describe a method to knowledge bases (KBs) built and used the professional risk assessment (PRA) as part of risk management process (RMP) and how can be establish the risk level depending on probability and severity of consequences.

2 Virtual Enterprise Network Solution in the PREMINV Platform

Today, companies feel the need to focus on their core competence and join together in virtual industrial groups, dispersed geographically to meet requirements of new products/services required in the market [2]. Hereby, the concept of virtual enterprise (VE) appears. Choosing partners to partnership creation (Figure 2) is very important when seeking to increase the competitiveness of the enterprise in a VE system [8] and represent a step in the process of VE forming (Figure 2).

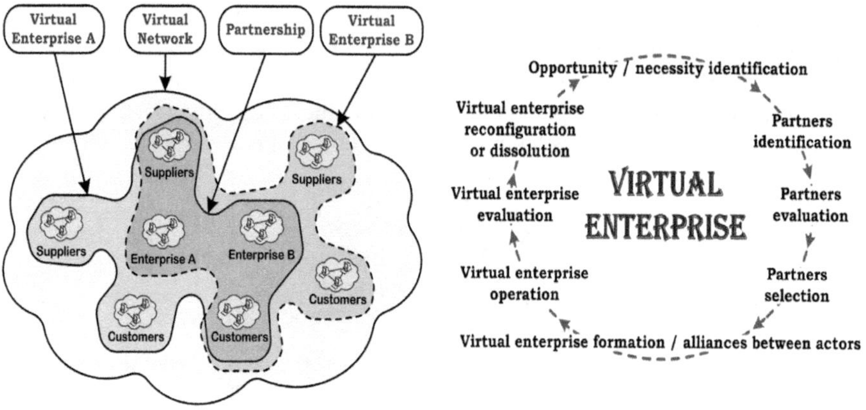

Fig. 2. Virtual enterprise partnership and framework

The basic idea of a *virtual enterprise network* (VEN) is meant to establish a dynamic organization by the synergetic combination of dissimilar companies with different core competencies, thereby forming a *best of everything* consortium to perform a given business project to achieve maximum degree of customer satisfaction. In this emerging business model of VEN, the decision support functionality, which addresses the issues such as selection of business partners, coordination in the distribution of production processes and the prediction of production problems, is an important domain to be studied [2].

A virtual enterprise network needs its own Private Member Collaboration System to communicate and develop its projects and bids. The term *virtual team* is used to cover a wide range of activities and forms of technology-supported working [3]. Virtual team is a group of people and sub-teams who interact through interdependent tasks guided by common purpose and work across links strengthened by information, communication and transport technologies [2]. With rare exceptions [4] all organizational teams are virtually to some extent. This era is growing popularity for virtual team structures in organizations [2]. The virtual teams are the teams whose members use technology to varying degrees in working across location, temporal, and relational boundaries to accomplish an interdependent task.

Enterprise virtual team's members are located in more than one physical location. This team trait has fostered extensive use of a variety of forms of computer-mediated communication that enable geographically dispersed members to coordinate their individual efforts and inputs [1]. Enterprise virtual teams work across boundaries of time and space by utilizing modern computer-driven technologies. Although virtual teamwork is a current topic in the literature on global organizations, it has been problematic to define what virtual means across multiple institutional contexts. Virtual teams are groups of individuals collaborating in the execution of a specific project while geographically and often temporally distributed, possibly anywhere within (and beyond) their parent organization [4]. The organizational context of a virtual team is a conglomeration of pieces related to the life worlds, organizational structures and work practices of the local organizational contexts (local sites), the distributed organizational context (global company) and the professional context (software process improvement).

Virtual teams can be defined as groups of workers geographically, organizationally and/or time dispersed brought together by information technologies to accomplish one or more organization tasks. The degree of geographic dispersion within a virtual team can vary widely from having one member located in a different location than the rest of the team to having each member located in a different country. The availability of a flexible and configurable base infrastructure is one of the main benefits (Figure 3) of virtual teams.

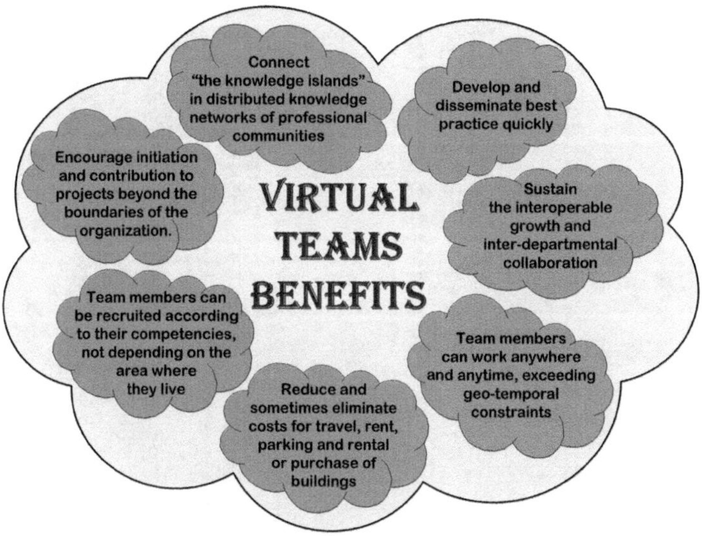

Fig. 3. The virtual team's advantages in a VEN system

Traditional infrastructures type Internet/Intranet/Extranet have now a fast dynamic, marking the transition to new generation networks to provide higher speeds to the user (end to end), for different types of transactions and a reduction in the number of servers by passing information between two nodes.

We propose in the PREMINV platform (Figure 4) a general architecture using Internet technologies or a provider network for a large enterprise or an industrial holding (with headquarters and branches), geographically dispersed (at the "Politehnica" University in Bucharest).

A VEN is necessary to combine a group of users regardless of their geographical position but such a manner that it flows together and to provide the best performance. The second advantage of a virtual network consists [1] of administrative solutions which accompany the products, allowing users moving from one group to another through a simple reconfiguration of the equipment.

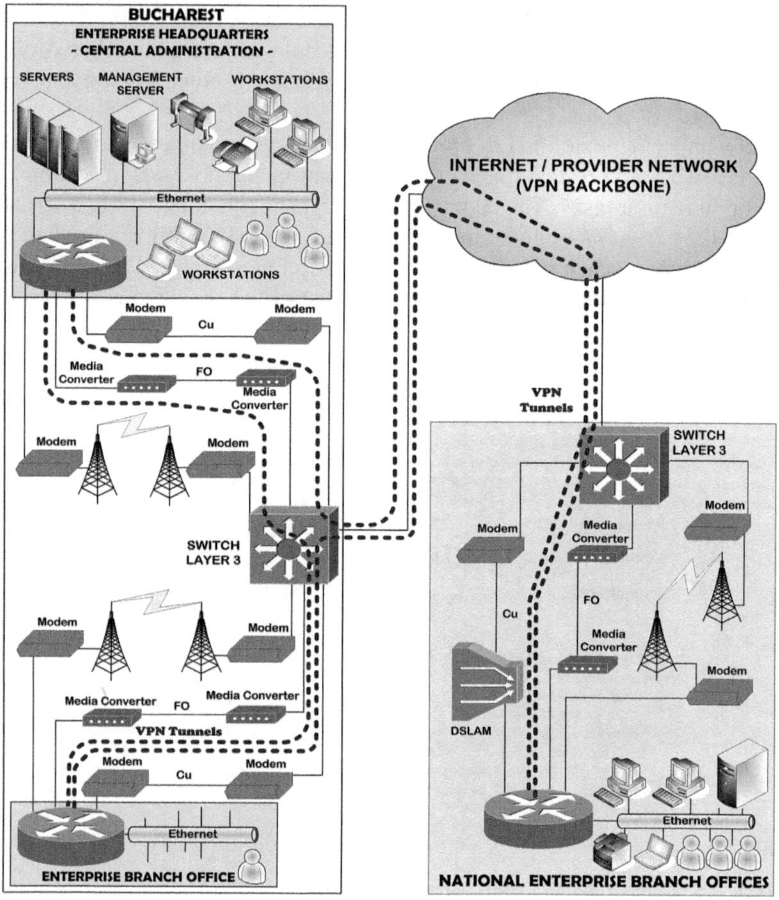

Fig. 4. A network general architecture for a large enterprise geographically dispersed

A virtual local network (VLAN) is a logical grouping of local network components without regard to their physical grouping. Clear trend is now evolving to intranets and extranets defined logic, which will lead to the reintegration of the various networks in single logical subdivisions with no physical. Structures that allow the approximation of this goal are virtual private networks.

Newer, VPNs can be used in different ways to support business processes, is the ideal solution if it is not efficient in terms of construction costs of a particular network for a firm with a workforce highly mobile, or for small firms that cannot justify the cost of their telecommunications network. VPNs can be purchased from a telecommunications company and as an alternative they can create by using existing network infrastructure as the Internet or public switched telephone network, and software through the tunnel crossing. The VPNs will be done according to enterprise network territorial expansion: local, metropolitan, national or international.

3 Risk Management Process: A KB Model to PRA in SMES

Commonly, the risk management process (RMP) includes three phases: risk identification, risk analyses and risk feedback. RMP is an important component of a successful project development process with informational system support [1]. Risk management is the process of identifying risk, assessing risk, and taking steps to reduce risk to an acceptable level [5]. The RMP should not be treated primarily as a technical function carried out by the IT experts who operate and manage the IT system, but as an essential management function of the organization. A hazard is anything that has the potential to cause harm. Hazards can affect people, property, processes; they can cause accidents and ill-heath, loss of output, damage to machinery, etc. workplace accidents and professional illnesses mustn't be perceived only as fatality, as it is more lucrative to consider them as a malfunction of the processes taking places at the SMEs level [6].

Occupational risk refers to the likelihood and the severity of an injury or an illness occurring as a result of exposure to a hazard. The main aim of occupational risk assessment is to protect workers health and safety. Risk assessment helps to minimize the possibility of the workers or the environment being harmed due to work-related activities. It also helps to keep your business competitive and effective. But, why is professional safety and health an essential part of good SMEs business?

Professional safety and health [7]: (1) helps demonstrate that a business is socially responsible; Protects and enhances brand image and brand value; (2) helps maximize the productivity of workers; (3) enhances employees' commitment to the business; Builds a more competent, healthier workforce; (4) reduces business costs and disruption; (5) enables enterprises to meet customers' OSH expectations; (6) encourages the workforce to stay longer in active life.

Under health and safety laws, all employers must carry out regular risk assessment [5]. To assess professional risk at the workplace we need to know: Where the workplace and/or the jobs performed are located and who works there: pay particular attention to those for whom occupational hazard may be more severe than usual, such as pregnant women, young workers or workers with disabilities; remember also, about part-time workers, subcontractors and visitors, and employees who work off-site (including drivers, those visiting clients' or customers' homes, etc.); what work equipment, materials, and processes are used; what tasks are performed; what the potential consequences of existing hazards are; what protective measures are used; what accidents, occupational diseases and other occurrences of ill health have been reported; what legal and other requirements are related to the workplace etc.

To identify hazards at the workplace there have been designed a *General Hazard Checklist* presented in Table 1 [5].

Table 1. The General Hazard Checklist

No.	Hazard	Yes	No
Does the hazard exist at the workplace produced by:			
1	Uneven or slippery surfaces (which can cause slips, trips, falls, etc.)?	x	
2	Moving vehicles and machines?	x	
3	Moving parts of machines?	x	
4	Objects and pieces with dangerous surfaces (sharp, rough, etc.)?	x	
5	Hot materials or surfaces?	x	
6	High workplaces or other climbing points (which can cause falls from a height)?	x	
7	Electrical installations and equipments?	x	
8	Noise?		x
9	Hand-arm vibrations?		x
10	Whole body vibrations?		x
11	Hot or cold temperatures?	x	
12	Work involving poor posture?	x	
13	Lifting and carrying loads?	x	
14	Chemical substances (including powders) in the air?		x
15	Fire?		x
	Others?	x	
Answer sum:			

The General Hazard Checklist can be extended (or adapted) according to a specific economic sector, such as: office work, construction, cars repair, woodworking, agriculture etc. By analyzing all the factors from the checklist, there have been designed an expert system that have been then implemented in the VP-Expert which effectuates workplace risk assessment. Production rules form the knowledge representation model used in this work. In the *PRA.KBS* knowledge base (KB) there are *if-then* structure rules (excluding the rules for inference engine operations), such as:

```
RULE 8     IF    risk>20      AND
                 risk<=22
THENprob=HIGHLY_IMPROBABLE
                 conseq=MEDIUM_HARMFUL
                 riskprof=SMALL
... ... ... ... ...
RULE 10-0 IF    surf=YES
THENrp1=0;
RULE 10-1 IF    surf=NO
THENrp1=1;
RULE 11-0 IF    vehicles=YES
THENrp2=0;
RULE 11-1 IF    vehicles=NO
THENrp2=1;
```

Direction of application of the rules is back chaining return (Figure 5).

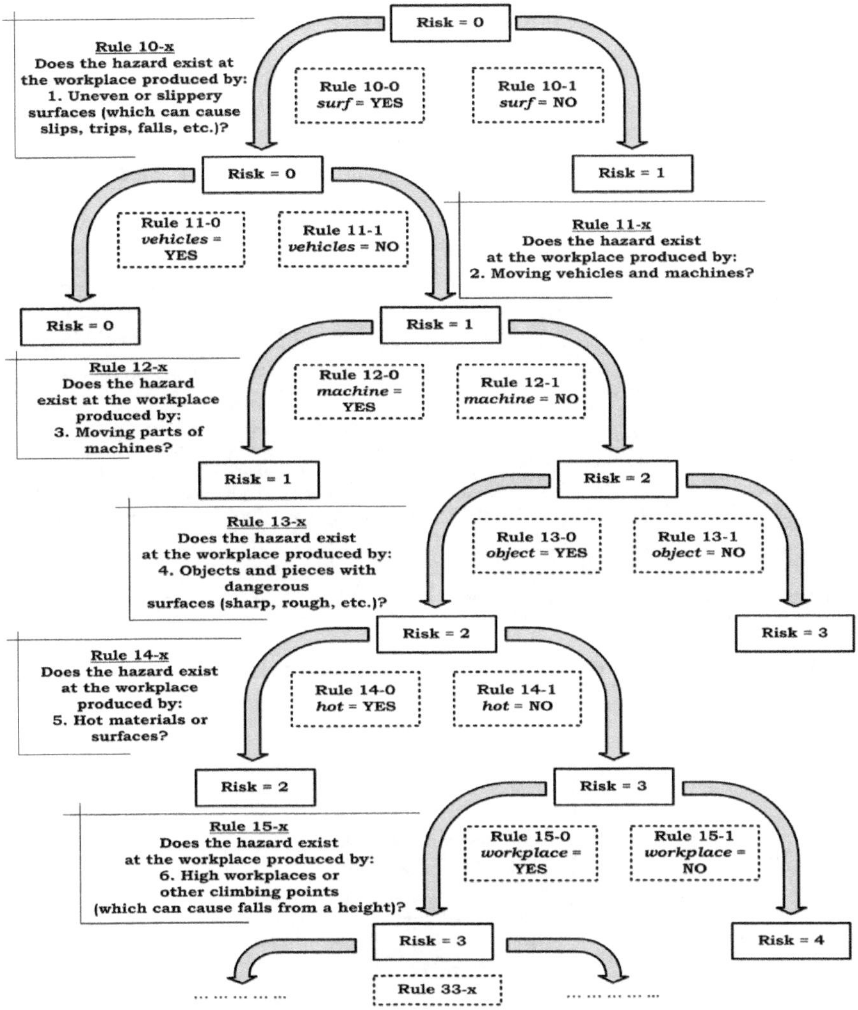

Fig. 5. Tree Production Rules

Before make the knowledge base, we establish the code variables: surf, vehicles, machine, object, hot, workplace, tools, pressure, etc. The knowledge base rules are following: rules for awarding point's variables, rules for calculation of the partial scores and total score and rules for assessment of probability and severity of consequences, and risk arising from hazards in accordance with the total score obtained. For all variables, we assign a value - 0 if the hazard exist (the answer from general checklist is YES) or 1 if hazard does not exist (the answer from general checklist is NO). Each value has an importance expressed by a factor with predetermined values (0 or 1). For all variables, the pondered factors must be introduced from keyboard during to knowledge base interrogation process (Figure 6). After querying the knowledge base will be displayed to evaluate the outcome of risk assessment conclusion and explanations on the likelihood and severity of injury in terms of consequences (Figure 6). Depending on the total score obtained and taking into account the probability and severity of consequences risk arising from hazards are evaluated – it may be *small*, *medium* or *high*. There have been considered the risk level depending on probability and severity of consequences as follows: small risk, medium risk and high risk and high risk are *unacceptabl*e and small and medium risks are *acceptable* (Figure 7).

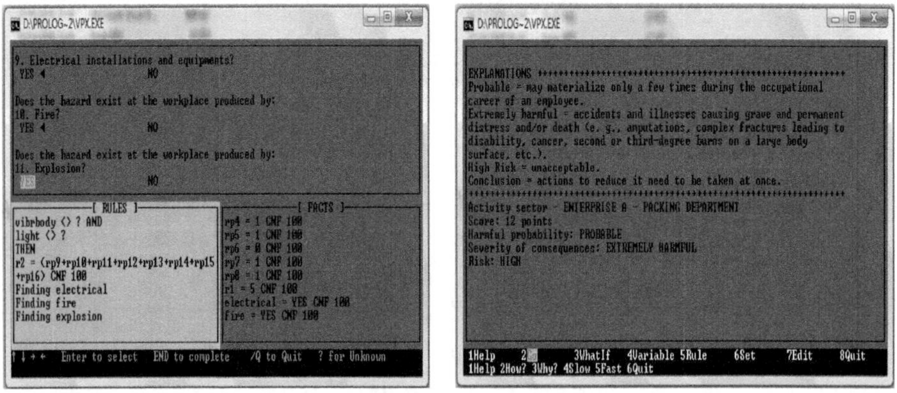

Fig. 6. The PRA.KBS interrogation and the PRA .for a department – shows results

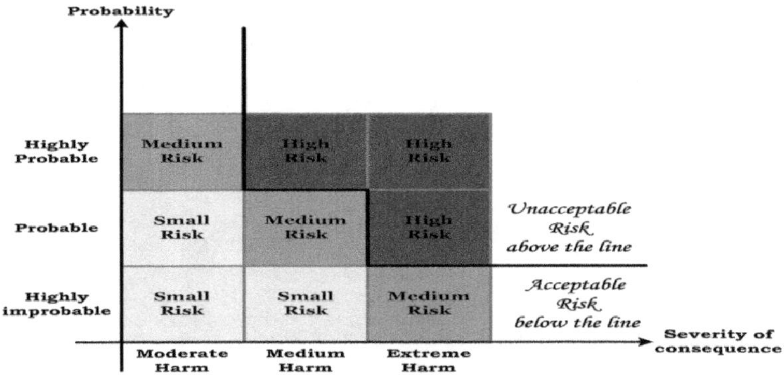

Fig. 7. The risk evaluation based on probability and severity of consequence

If the risk is assessed as unacceptable (height) reduction actions must be taken immediately. If risk is assessed as acceptable (average) is recommended plan of action to reduce or necessary to ensure that it will remain at the same level (in case of risk assessed as small). Measures of prevention and protection to be implemented in the organization are to eliminate or reduce to a minimum the danger by organizational measures, or use of collective protection equipment suitable for individual protection. We suggest a reassessment of activity sector after the implementation of these measures and to compare this result with that obtained at first evaluation in order to verify the effectiveness of measures for prevention and protection implemented.

4 Conclusions

The paper presents a solution for the risk management assessment by considering the support of a virtual enterprise network. This approach better leverage the knowledge bases development. The validation of the presented PRA solution meant to establish the risk level in collaborative infrastructures and is related to knowledge bases used at the SMEs level (work done in PROGPROC research project, CNMP 11014/2007). The project was meant to integrate the knowledge management processes from university to industrial partners for a proposed collaborative infrastructure, based on a virtual enterprise network. Using consistent, integrated data sets and tools that support the collaboration we have presented that a virtual team is formed with members geographically distributed using the e-platform in order to develop the business services sector using a new product lifecycle paradigm according with the greater need for software tools to risk estimation. This e-platform is a support system for resources planning and programming activities according to manufacturing processes management in virtual organizations. We intend that our future work in this area includes building other knowledge bases to evaluate eventually other SMEs activities who involve risks in the context of the new project: "Interdisciplinary research for the occupational risk evaluation platform development with impact upon the safety culture in organization" (ID 1022) financed by CNCSIS in Romania.

References

1. Roşu, S.M., Drăgoi, G., Guran, M.: A Knowledge Management Scenario to Support Knowledge Applications Development in Small and Medium Enterprises. Advances in Electrical and Computer Engineering 9(1), 8–15 (2009)
2. Dragoi, G., Draghici, A., Rosu, S.M., Cotet, C.E.: Virtual Enterprise Network Solutions for Virtual Product Development in SMEs. In: Proceedings of the CENTERIS 2009 – Conference on ENTERprise Information Systems, Ofir, Portugal, pp. 613–628 (2009)
3. Anderson, A.H., McEwan, R., Bal, J., Carletta, J.: Virtual team meetings: An analysis of communication and context. Computers in Human Behavior 23(5), 2558–2580 (2007)
4. Walvoord, A.A.G., Redden, E.R., Elliott, L.R., Coovert, M.D.: Empowering followers in virtual teams: Guiding principles from theory and practice. Computers in Human Behavior 24(5), 1884–1906 (2008)
5. European Agency for Safety and Health at Work, Risk Assessment Essentials, Printed in Nurnberg, Germany (2007)
6. Baetens, K.: Risk assessment in small and medium-sized enterprises (SMEs): UEAPME's point of view. Magazine of the European Agency for Safety and Health at Work 11, 3–5 (2008)
7. Yule, S., Flin, R., Murdy, A.: The Role of Management & Safety Climate in Preventing Risk-Taking at Work. International Journal of Risk Assessment and Management 7, 137–151 (2007)

An Approach to Cooperation-Oriented Business Processes

Giorgio Bruno

Politecnico di Torino, Torino, Italy
giorgio.bruno@polito.it

Abstract. This paper stresses the cooperative nature of business processes (BPs) and proposes an outside-in approach (called BPcoach) to their development. BPs are seen as the central players in collective actions carried out with a number of other participants including (human) users and automated services. BPs are assumed to act as the mediators among the various parties and, for this reason, binary collaboration models are first defined, which establish the interactions between the other participants (subdivided in roles) and the intended BP. The initial models of the BP and the associated information system can be automatically derived from such collaboration models, and then they are enriched until the requirements are completely met. The approach is exemplified with a case study.

Keywords: business processes; collaboration models; information models.

1 Introduction

Business processes (BPs) address complex ontological issues and therefore they can be considered from different viewpoints [1]. In particular, the work described in this paper starts from three of them, i.e. the orchestration-oriented viewpoint, the case-handling viewpoint and the conversational one.

The orchestration-oriented perspective emphasizes the activities to be carried out by the various participants and the control flow issues; BPMN [2] is a well-known representative of this category. The case-handling approach [3] stresses the integration with the business entities in the context of Process-Aware Information Systems, or PAISs [4]; the process evolution is driven by the state of the business entities rather than by the completion of the activities [5]. In the conversational viewpoint [6], the basic building blocks are the conversations between pairs of participants.

This paper stresses the cooperative nature of BPs because their raison d'être is to enable various participants to work together for the accomplishment of a common purpose. Participants may be (human) users, automated services or other BPs (either intra-organizational or inter-organizational). Participants are usually denoted by their roles, e.g. Buyer, Supervisor.

Two major aspects are focused on in this paper: how the various participations are organized in the process and how the development of the process can take advantage of such participations.

J.E. Quintela Varajão et al. (Eds.): CENTERIS 2010, Part II, CCIS 110, pp. 178–187, 2010.

In notations like BPMN, roles are given distinct swim lanes, each swim lane encompassing the activities pertaining to one role. The major drawback is the existence of one global control flow which may make it difficult to isolate the control flow for a particular role.

In the RAD approach [7], instead, roles are separate components of BPs and, therefore, they have their own control flow equipped with send/receive operations for the interactions with the other role components.

The conversational viewpoint proposes a standard interaction pattern between two parties based on the notion of conversation for action (CfA) [8]. In the Action Workflow approach [9], a typical conversation takes place between a requester and a performer and is made up of four major phases (request, commitment, performance and evaluation) forming the so-called workflow loop.

This paper proposes an approach named BPcoach (BP Cooperation-Oriented approACH) which stresses the conversational viewpoint and extends it in two directions: conversation models (called collaboration models) are not limited to the CfA pattern, and the interactions are interpreted in terms of events related to the business entities, thus providing a strong connection with the information model (which describes the entities of the underlying information system).

In addition, BPcoach proposes an outside-in approach to the design of BPs. This approach consists of three steps. First, the parties involved in the BP are indicated in the cooperation context of the BP: this context sets the environment of the BP. Then, the initial models of the BP and of the associated information system are automatically derived from the cooperation context. Third, both models are enriched with new elements (transitions and internal states for the BP, classes and relationships for the information model) until the requirements are completely met.

This paper is organized as follows. Section 2 illustrates collaboration models and presents an example to be used in the subsequent sections. Section 3 explains the outside-in approach to the design of BPs and introduces the notion of BP cooperation context. Section 4 gives an example of the initial models obtained from a cooperation context, while section 5 addresses the completion of the initial models. Section 6 presents the conclusion and the future work.

2 Collaboration Models

A collaboration model (CM) is a pattern of interactions between two parties, referred to as initiator (the one who starts the collaboration) and follower. The purpose of an interaction is to communicate an intention of its originator to its recipient. Examples of generic intentions are making a request, accepting a request, and providing a reply.

In the context of PAISs [4], interactions are to be strongly connected with the underlying information system. For this reason, in BPcoach, interactions are interpreted as business events: a business event notifies a change in the information system (usually the introduction of a new entity or a modification to an existing one) and is accompanied by the entity involved. An event is caused by an action of its originator and triggers the reaction of its recipient.

As an example, the following collaboration model (BS_C) between a buyer and a seller is illustrated in this section and will be used in the next ones. The requirements for BS_C are as follows.

Collaboration BS_C is started by a buyer when they issue a request for quote (rfq in short) for a given product type (Type): the rfq includes the number (n) of units required and two deadlines, d1 and d2. Types are global entities known to both parties; therefore an rfq does not include all the attributes of the product type needed but only a reference to it (i.e. a global identifier). If the seller intends to provide a quote, they must do so before d1 expires (as a matter of fact the quote is optional). A quote includes a price. If the buyer accepts the quote, they must issue an order including delivery information before d2 expires (the order is optional as well).

A CM is meant to describe the events that may take place and their precedence constraints in a single collaboration occurrence.

In BPcoach, collaborations are described by means of state models. State models are also used in Conversations for Action [8]), while in the domain of choreographies several approaches have been proposed, e.g. UML activity diagrams in BPSS [10] and extended Petri nets in interaction Petri nets [11].

A state model describing collaboration BS_C is shown in Fig.1.a. The states represent the events: the label in a state icon shows the originator of the event (I = initiator, F = follower), the event name and the name of the class of the business entity affected by the event. An event is always related to one business entity because it notifies the generation of the business entity or a modification to it.

Collaboration BS_C is based on three events: rs (request submitted), qp (quote provided) and os (order submitted).

Transitions establish the precedence constraints between the events. Event rs is the initial one because it has an input transition with no source associated (referred to as the initial transition). The names of the transitions are chosen to indicate their effects.

A CM needs a complementary information model showing the entity classes involved along with their attributes and relationships (Fig.1.b).

An rfq is linked to one global type: this requirement is represented by the relationship connecting class Rfq and class Type. The "g" stereotype associated with class Type means that (product) types are not conveyed in the BS_C interactions but can be referred to by the entities conveyed in these interactions.

The relationship between class Quote and class Rfq shows the cause-effect link between an rfq and a quote: a quote is always connected to the rfq it is a reply to, while an rfq might be connected to no quote as the quote is optional. Similar considerations apply to the relationship between class Quote and class Order.

For the sake of simplicity, cardinalities are omitted from the information model.

The initial transition starts a new instance of collaboration BS_C by generating the initial event. In general, the purpose of each transition must be defined so that users, when looking at collaboration models, can understand what they are expected to do. Annotations may be introduced to express constraints in the event flow and to describe the intended effects. In order to keep models as simple as possible, standard conventions may be adopted.

A standard convention with initial transitions is to assume that they generate a new instance of the class associated with the event produced. Hence, event rs is assumed to be related to a newly generated rfq with its three attributes set and with the link to the required type established. The stereotypes on the relationships in the information model show which transitions are responsible for generating the corresponding associations.

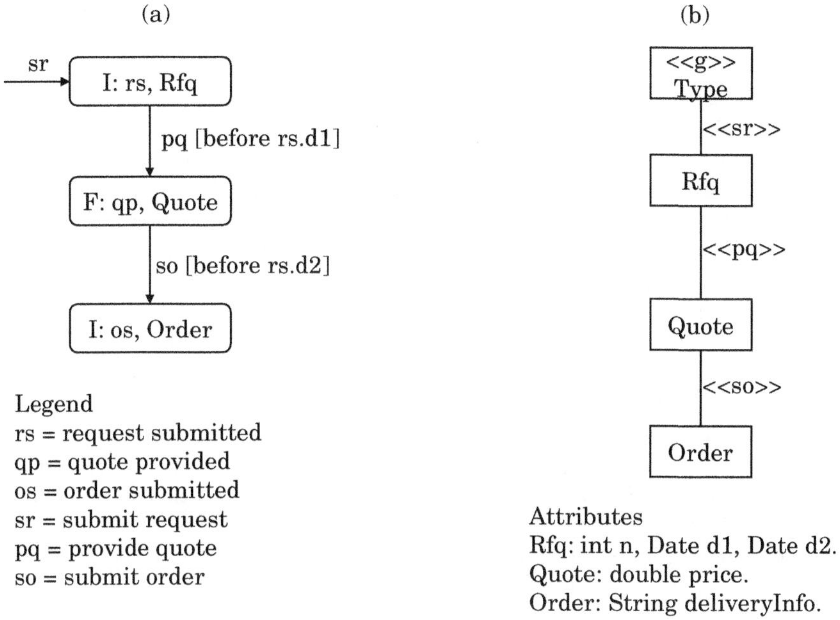

Fig. 1. Collaboration model BS_C: state model (a), information model (b)

When the entity classes associated with the input event and the output one of a given transition are different, it is assumed that the effect of the transition is to produce a new entity whose type is the one related to the output event: this entity has its attributes set and, what is more, it is linked to the entity related to the input event.

Transitions pq and so draw on this convention and this is the reason why a quote gets linked to an rfq and an order to a quote. These transitions are conditional and their conditions (written between []) depend on attributes d1 and d2 of the rfq. The rfq is the business entity conveyed by the initial event and can be referred to with the event name (i.e. rs).

All the events are final ones, because transitions pq and so are optional.

3 The Outside-In Approach to the Design of Cooperative BP

Since the BP is the mediator among all the other parties involved, first the interactions between the other parties and the BP must be worked out and defined in suitable collaboration models. The other parties are subdivided into roles and hence a collaboration model (CM) is needed for each role involved in the collective action being considered.

When all the CMs have been worked out, the design of the BP is carried out through an outside-in approach. First, the other parties involved are indicated in the cooperation context (to be illustrated later on in this section) of the BP, then the initial models of the BP and of the associated information system are automatically derived from the cooperation context.

The proposed approach is illustrated in this paper with the help of an example related to a distribution company (referred to as the distributor). The distributor is assumed to handle requests for quotes and purchase orders coming from buyers with a BP called SellingBP. The collaboration agreed upon by the distributor and the buyers is defined in collaboration model BS_C shown in Fig.1.

When a request for quote (rfq) is received, the process may ignore the rfq, or it may reply with a quote. The quote is immediately generated by the process, if the distributor is able to directly provide the goods involved. Otherwise a reselling initiative is started. There are three ways of handling an incoming rfq, but the details on how the decision is to be made are not given in this phase: it is only required to identify the actions corresponding to the three alternatives.

If reselling is needed, the goods requested by the buyer need to be first bought from a supplier and then sold to the buyer; therefore the process contacts a number of suppliers in order to get quotes from them. Then it selects the best quote and, if there is any, it builds a quote for the buyer on the basis of the supplier quote selected. The same collaboration model BS_C is assumed to be adopted by the distributor and its suppliers. If the distributor receives an order from the buyer, it sends an order to the corresponding supplier.

The cooperation context of SellingBP defines the collaborations to be handled in terms of collaboration descriptors as shown in Fig.2.

Collaboration b (case, name = rfq): model = BS_C, role = follower, partner = Buyer, mapping = {Rfq(B_Rfq), Quote(B_Quote), Order(B_Order)}.

Collaboration s*: model = BS_C, role = initiator, partner = Supplier, mapping = {Rfq(S_Rfq), Quote(S_Quote), Order(S_Order)}.

Fig. 2. The cooperation context of SellingBP

A collaboration descriptor includes the name of the collaboration (b denotes the collaborations with the buyers and s those with the suppliers), the collaboration model to be used, the role played by the process (follower of b collaborations and initiator of s ones).

A collaboration occurrence takes place through a number of events as discussed in the previous section. Any event defined in a collaboration model may be an input event or an output one depending on the role played by the party being considered. The events encompassed by collaboration b are: b.rs, b.order and b.quote. The first two are input events for SellingBP, and the third is an output event. The events in collaboration s are: s.rs, s.order and s.quote (the first two are output events, the third is an input event). The event names are prefixed with the collaboration name so that the events handled by a process are all distinct (as are the names of the collaborations in a cooperation context).

A collaboration descriptor also provides the links between the entity classes defined in the collaboration model and those to appear in the information model associated with the BP.

Collaboration model BS_C is based on a number of classes, i.e. Rfq, Quote, Order and Type. These names do not need to be the names of the actual classes in the information model, and then a mapping rule may be used. The mapping rules shown in Fig.2 indicate that the requests for quotes coming from buyers are represented by class B_Rfq and those sent to suppliers by class S_Rfq; different classes are also established for the quotes and the orders.

In addition, in the information system the partners of the collaborations must be represented by classes; one of the purposes of these classes is to indicate the originators of the business entities that the BP does not generate but receives through the collaborations. For example, an rfq coming from a certain buyer through collaboration b is an object of class B_Rfq associated with an object of class Buyer (this object representing the originator of the rfq). The partner class is indicated in the partner attribute of collaboration descriptors.

The meanings of the case attribute and the * multiplicity in Fig.2 will be explained in the next section.

4 The Initial Models of SellingBP and of the Information System

SellingBP participates in collaborations b and s defined in Fig.2, as it is meant to handle collaborations with buyers and suppliers.

However, since a BP is the description of a behavior to be put in practice in a number of process instances, the question arises on how those collaborations are to be distributed to the various instances. A thorough investigation is beyond the scope of this paper, and therefore only one solution is presented.

SellingBP is stimulated by b collaborations which do not interfere with each other; in addition, it may start several collaborations s to serve one collaboration b. These considerations lead to the conclusion that each collaboration b can be handled by a distinct instance of SellingBP and that, in addition, this instance may handle several collaborations s. What is more, the occurrence of collaboration b triggers the activation of a SellingBP instance. In analogy with case-handling processes, SellingBP can be thought of as a collaboration-handling process and the business entity conveyed by the initial event of collaboration b is the case of the process. The "case" term denotes the business entity associated with the process instance from the beginning; given this strong connection, the case can be referred to from any action included in the process with a pre-determined name. In Fig.2, collaboration b is marked as a case for the process and the case name is defined to be "rfq".

The multiplicity of collaboration s is also defined in Fig.2: the *operator means many or none (i.e. an instance of SellingBP may be involved in several collaborations s or in none).

The initial models of SellingBP and of the information system, which can be automatically obtained from the cooperation context presented in Fig.2, are shown in Fig.3.

The six boxes appearing in Fig.3.a are to be interpreted as process states associated with the collaboration events. Inside the states, two labels are shown: the name of the event associated with the state and the class of the business entity conveyed by the event.

If the state is an input state, the labels are preceded by the "?" qualifier; in the output states, the qualifier is "!", while the initial state has no qualifier. A small black dot marks the state as a possible final state.

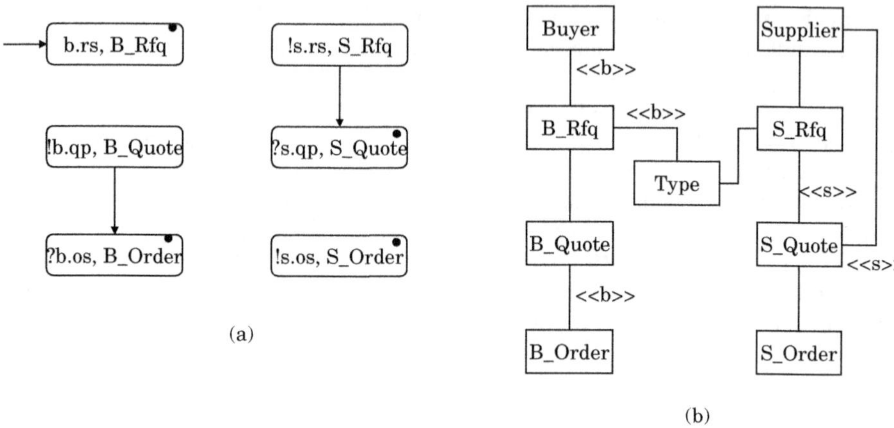

Fig. 3. The initial models of SellingBP: process model (a) and information model (b)

The initial state corresponds to the initial event of the case collaboration. When the process (instance) is in an input state, it is waiting for some events. The name of these events is indicated in the state, but their exact number and the time limit of the wait are given when the diagram is refined in the subsequent phases of development.

An output state means that the process has produced some events (their names match the event name in the state). When the process is in state b.qp, it has provided a quote to the buyer. What happens next depends on the buyer; the process then goes to state b.os in which it waits for the order. Since the order is optional, after the deadline expires, the process declares this state as final.

In addition to the states, the initial diagram includes a number of transitions inherited from the collaboration models; they are the transitions the partners are in charge of. For the process, such transitions are simply links from an output state to the input states where it can receive the input events caused by the output event(s) it has issued.

The initial model (Fig.3.b) of the information system associated with SellingBP includes the classes indicated in the mapping rules shown in Fig.2.

The portion on the left refers to the collaborations with the buyers (the b collaborations). The relationships marked with stereotype <<b>> are assumed to be instantiated by the b collaborations: as a matter of fact, when a SellingBP instance receives event b.rs, the associated entity is already linked to the type required and to the buyer entity representing the buyer that originated the request.

The relationship between B_Rfq and B_Quote comes from the fact that a quote event is a reply (actually, an optional reply) to an rfq event: it is a cause-effect relationship to be established by SellingBP (and hence there is no stereotype associated with it, in the initial model). The relationship between B_Quote and B_Order is another cause-effect relationship in charge of b collaborations. When an order is issued, it is issued in reply to a previous quote. No relationship between Buyer and B_Order is needed, as the originator of an order can be obtained through the path B_Order, B_Quote, B_Rfq, Buyer.

The relationships marked with stereotype <<s>> are assumed to be instantiated by the s collaborations.

5 Completing the Initial Models

The initial models are then improved with the addition of new elements (transitions and internal states for the process model, classes and relationships for the information model) until the requirements are completely met.

For the purpose of this paper, the process model has to show the cause-effect relationships between the events and also how the business entities are affected by the process actions. The result is a functional description of what the process is meant to do, while the details (i.e. "how it is done") are left to a subsequent phase. The final models are shown in Fig.4.

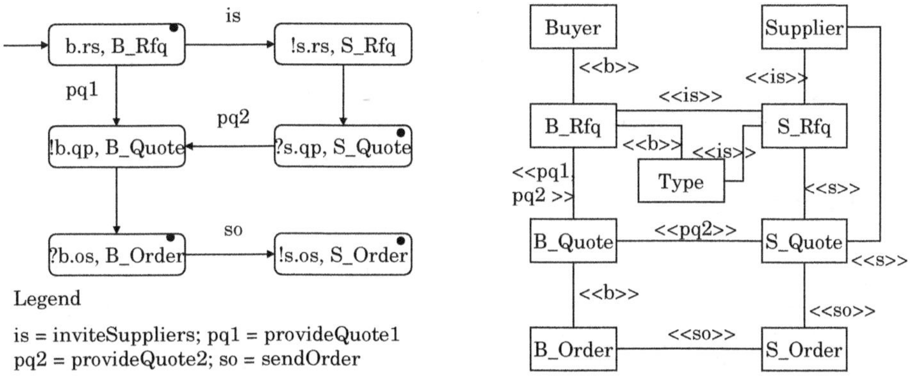

(a) (b)

Fig. 4. The final models of SellingBP: process model (a) and information model (b)

In the initial state, the process has received a request for quote from a buyer. It may ignore it, or provide a quote directly, or ask a number of suppliers to provide their quotes. The first case amounts to declaring the state final, the second to taking transition pq1, the third to taking transition is.

A transition may be given a pre-condition and a post-condition expressing the state of the information system before its firing and after it, respectively. As the requirements do not specify how the selection of the path to follow is to be made, the transitions above have no pre-conditions. In general, pre-conditions and post-conditions can be expressed with a formal language such as OCL [12].

However, a number of conventions can be used and when they suit the needs, formal expressions can be avoided.

One of such conventions (called data flow convention) can be applied when a transition connects two states with different entity classes; the assumption is that the transition generates one output entity (or possibly more than one) associated with the input entity. This convention applies to transitions "pq1" and "is"; the effect of the former is to produce one instance of B_Quote and that of the latter to produce a number of instances of S_Rfq.

In the final information model there are additional relationships and the process transitions responsible for their introduction are indicated as stereotypes. For example, transition "is" generates several instances of class S_Rfq (by virtue of the data flow convention) and connects each of them to the incoming B_Rfq instance, to a Type instance and to a Supplier instance. This description is too simplistic and is valid only for a quick functional sketch. In reality, the S_Rfq instances must be associated with the same Type instance as the input B_Rfq and the suppliers ought to be chosen on the basis of some criteria: these constraints should be expressed with post-conditions.

The data flow convention cannot be applied to transition pq2. When the process is in state s.qp, it waits until all the quotes expected have arrived or the deadline written in attribute d1 of the S_Rfq has elapsed: in the first case, it selects the best quote, while in the second case, it gives up (making the state final) if no quotes have been received or else it selects the best quote among those received.

After submitting a quote, the process goes into state b.os where it waits for a buyer order until the deadline written in attribute d2 of the case expires or the order arrives. In the second case, if a supplier has been involved, it sends it an order (whose class is S_Order) with transition so.

6 Conclusion

This paper has emphasized the central role played by business processes (BPs) in orchestrating the collaborations with various parties, which may be (human) users, automated services or other BPs (either intra-organizational or inter-organizational).

A proof-of concept approach (named BPcoach) to the design of BPs has been presented. It starts from the definition of the collaboration models (CMs) between each participating role and the BP being considered. The importance of CMs is twofold, for the users and for the process. The users can understand what their involvement is in terms of input events and output events, without being obliged to find it out from an aggregated process description with one global control flow. From the process perspective, the CMs are the starting point from which an initial version of the BP can be automatically obtained.

There are several directions of future work: one is concerned with the definition of a suitable workspace (an evolution of todo lists) in which participants can perform their actions on the basis of the collaborations they are involved in. Another direction is to extend collaborations to more flexible structures, such as wikis.

Acknowledgment

The work presented in this paper has been partly supported by MIUR under the PRIN 2008 project "Documentation and processes".

References

1. van der Aalst, W.M.P., Weske, M., Wirtz, G.: Advanced topics in workflow management: issues, requirements and solutions. Journal of Integrated Design and Process Science 7(3), 49–77 (2003)

2. Business Process Modeling Notation, http://www.bpmn.org
3. van der Aalst, W.M.P., Weske, M., Grünbauer, D.: Case handling: a new paradigm for business process support. Data & Knowledge Engineering 53(2), 129–162 (2005)
4. Dumas, M., van der Aalst, W.M.P., ter Hofstede, A.H.M.: Process-Aware Information Systems: Bridging People and Software through Process Technology. Wiley, Chichester (2005)
5. Künzle, V., Reichert, M.: Towards object-aware process management systems: issues, challenges, benefits. LNBIP, vol. 29, pp. 197–210. Springer, Heidelberg (2009)
6. Weigand, H.: Two decades of the Language-Action Perspective: introduction. Communications of the ACM 49(5), 44–46 (2006)
7. Ould, M.: Business Process Management: a rigorous approach. The British Computer Society (2005)
8. Winograd, T.: A Language/Action Perspective on the design of cooperative work. Human-Computer Interaction 3, 3–30 (1987-1988)
9. Medina-Mora, R., Winograd, T., Flores, R., Flores, F.: The Action Workflow approach to workflow management technology. In: Turner, J., Kraut, R. (eds.) 4th Conference on Computer Supported Cooperative Work. ACM, New York (1992)
10. Hofreiter, B., Huemer, C., Winiwarter, W.: Business collaboration models and their business context-dependent web choreography in BPSS. International Journal of Web Information Systems 1(1), 33–42 (2005)
11. Decker, G., Weske, M.: Local enforceability in Interaction Petri Nets. In: Alonso, G., Dadam, P., Rosemann, M. (eds.) BPM 2007. LNCS, vol. 4714, pp. 305–319. Springer, Heidelberg (2007)
12. UML 2.0 OCL Specification, http://www.omg.org/technology/documents/formal/ocl.htm

The Inter-organizational Business Case in ES Implementations: Exploring the Impact of Coordination Structures and Their Properties

Silja Eckartz[1], Christiaan Katsma[2], and Maya Daneva[1]

[1] Information Systems Group,
[2] Information Systems and Change Management Group
University Twente, Enschede, The Netherlands
{S.M.Eckartz,C.P.Katsma,M.Daneva}@Utwente.nl

Abstract. Developing the business case (BC) for an inter-organizational network is a major challenge. Factors like competition and differences in semantics between actors influence the stakeholders' willingness to share information necessary for the BC development. In this paper we develop an exploratory framework showing the effect that coordination structure and project scope have on the development of a shared BC. We defined several coordination properties, such as competition, decision making location and decision power that mitigate this effect. We applied the framework in a case study where a BC is developed for an inter-organizational network. Our findings show that current BC development methods need to be re-stated and complemented by extra tools and interventions to support stakeholders in the inter-organizational specific setting.

Keywords: Inter-organizational coordination, Business Case, Information sharing, Decision making

1 Introduction

Enterprise systems (ES) can be defined as commercial software packages that enable the seamless integration of information and information-based processes within and across functional areas in an organization [1]. Today ES do not only enable the integration and coordination of transaction-oriented data and business processes within one organization, but also go one step further and support the connection and management of information flows across several organizations. Such inter-organizational coordination is necessary in interactions between profit-and-loss responsible business units, or between independent companies, connected by IT that work together to jointly accomplish a task for a specific period of time [2].

This crossing of organizational boundaries not only increases the complexity of the ES but also creates substantial differences in semantics, processes, information and goals between the different actors [3]. Thus, the multiple actors that collaboratively work in inter-organizational coordination to reach a common goal often encounter problems when they need to share information in order to make a joint decision. In

J.E. Quintela Varajão et al. (Eds.): CENTERIS 2010, Part II, CCIS 110, pp. 188–197, 2010.

our research, we focus specifically on the process of how multiple actors arrive at a joint decision about whether or not to invest in an ES. Therefore, we will analyze the process of shared business case development (BCD).

The purpose of developing a business case (BC) is to describe the main rationale behind the ES implementation process. A BC enables participants to estimate the expected costs and benefits of an ES for the adopting organization [4-6]. In the field of Information Systems (IS) research, scholars take different perspectives upon this relatively young research sub-field [7-8]. Kishore et al. [9] take an IS design perspective and include coordination theory to exemplify the extra complexity due to the involved actors. Our research logically continues the line of reasoning of the prior contributions and uses this knowledge to apply it in the BC context. In this paper, we focus on the impact of the project scope and coordination structure among the involved actors during the early stages of inter-organizational ES implementations, when the BC is initiated.

Typical coordination properties, such as, decision power, competition and decision making location depend on the project scope and coordination structure among the organizations and are expected to influence the BC. These project realities require an adapted BCD approach that pays attention to the specific situation of the inter-organizational setting. In this paper we derive an exploratory framework that contains the identifying coordination properties for the BC during such ES implementations.

Based on this line of reasoning, we set out to answer the following research question: *What are the effects of project scope and coordination structure during the development of an inter-organizational business case?*

2 Research Method

This paper presents results that are part of a running research project on the implementation of inter-organizational IS and ES in particular. We build upon a rich inventory of ES implementation experiences and case study research. *This* paper investigates the deployment of BCD during the implementation process and focuses on the increased complexity due to inter-organizational coordination structure. Fig.1 shows our research model. It indicates the sections of the paper that discuss the key elements of the research model.

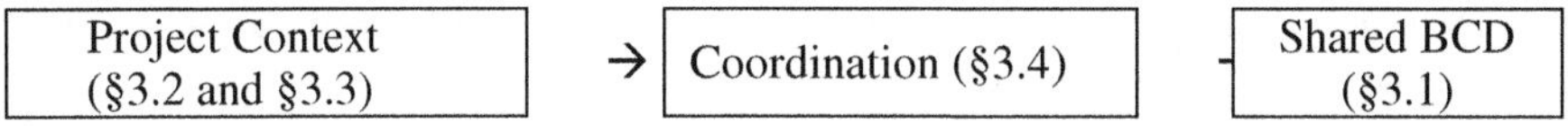

Fig. 1. Research model

We deployed the following research approach that also gives a short overview of the sections in our paper:

We first conducted an extensive literature review [10] covering scientific publications in the areas of BCD [6, 11], coordination mechanisms [9, 12-13], and inter-organizational ES implementation. Based upon this review we conclude relevant findings on the deployment of the BC during ES implementations in §3.1. In sections §3.2-3.4, we evaluate these findings from the perspective of the coordination structures in inter-organizational collaborations in particular and derive our exploratory framework. The objective of our framework is to make the increased complexity of the inter-organizational BCD during the early stages of the inter-organizational ES implementation process explicit. We explain the deployment of our framework in a case study in §4. The source of our empirical material is a large business network in the transportation sector in the Netherlands. It is formed by barge and terminal operators in the Rotterdam Harbor. Two researchers, within a period of 6 months, deployed participative observation techniques in workshops, conducted interviews, observed negotiation between actors, and, in a few occasions, guided the attempt to develop a shared BC for the network. We used a diary approach to record incidents. We reflected on the relevant events with different interviewees in informal unstructured interviews. In hindsight we participated in the following sessions:

- 6 individual interview meetings with different actors to get an understanding of the situation at hand and of the important concerns of each actor. These meetings concern unstructured interviews using mostly qualitative data.
- 5 meetings with different stakeholders (several barge operators the Transportation ministry, and the official from the Harbor of Rotterdam).
- 3 collaborative workshops with most stakeholders present except for the terminal operators.

We coded and clustered the information that was collected by means of our interviews and the other empirical materials using our conceptual framework in section §3.4.

3 Development of an Exploratory Framework

This section elaborates on our research model (Fig. 1 from §2).

Coordination structure & Project Scope (§3.2 and §3.3)	→	Coordination properties (§3.4)	→	Shared BCD (§3.1)

First, we specify the issues of shared BCD (§3.1), then we proceed from the left, and specify *coordination structure* and *project scope* as the two main identifying determinants (§3.2 and §3.3). We continue our line of reasoning by further zooming in on these two identifying determinants and specify what we call coordination properties, and then, we complete our exploratory framework in §3.4.

3.1 Introduction to Shared BCD

Our literature review and empirical studies indicate a variety in terminology and ambiguity in used terms. While this in itself is not unique for the IS field, for clarification purposes and to position our line of reasoning we start with a definition of what we mean by the concept of "Business Case". A BC as an artifact (a document possibly accompanied by designs or models) that specifies the main rationale and expected value for the ES-adopting organization. The BC evaluates and presents different implementation options, based on the expected costs, benefits and risks of each option during the entire implementation process. It is the result from a BCD process that is deployed between consultants and stakeholders from the ES-adopting organization. A BC however, should contain more than just a financial analysis of an action to take. The (non-)financial benefits, alignment, costs and risks, should be complemented with information on the methods and rationale that were used to quantify the benefits and costs [14]. The BCD is an iterative, tool-supported process that relies on stakeholders from different parts of the organization with different business knowledge.

An important aspect of BCD in inter-organizational settings is its linkage to the model that describes how the business network creates value for its clients and how the network distributes the value among the partner companies. This model, also called value model [15], serves two different, but related purposes: (i) it helps each partner company do a profitability assessment for themselves based on the information provided in the partner company's individual BC, and (ii) it helps assess if the entire network of cooperating organizations is profitable. If the network partners want to e.g. implement a shared ES, which is used by all partners, they need to make a shared investment decision, based on a joint BC for the entire network.

As the introduction indicated, BCs often cross boundaries, e.g. organizational, functional, and budgetary. Thus, for a network to build a BC, diverse input from all involved entities is required which add up to complex BCD [14]. This is because - despite partners' awareness of the need to share information, they might lack a shared understanding of the terminology used, might hesitate to release sensitive information (e.g cost data) due to competition or might disagree on how costs and benefits are distributed in a network.

3.2 Coordination Structures

Inter-organizational relations can be classified based on the type of relationship between partners and their coordination structure. A distinction can be made between markets and non-markets [16]. Markets are characterized by discrete interactions and limited personal involvement [17], while non-market interactions are usually based on some form of relationship between the partners. The latter can be classified as being either hierarchical or of a network nature. Hierarchical partnership structures, e.g. franchise or outsourcing contracts, rest on unilateral interaction and an authority relationship. Inter-organizational relations organized in a market structure, have often a short term focus and are mainly based on the price mechanisms. They fall into centralized and decentralized market structures. The first involve an intermediary or broker, and are characterized by high competitiveness and opportunistic behavior [18]. The network as a coordination structure is characterized by cooperation, collaboration, and the sharing of information [19]. Thus, it is different from a pure market structure; in fact, it is a hybrid of hierarchy and market based on bilateral, often long term interaction between partners. Partners are "free" to choose their counterparts (as in a market structure) and members are operationally dependant on each other (comparable with a hierarchy [20]). Such networks between partners are often referred to as collaborations.

3.3 Project Scope

To define the project scope, we make a distinction between single and multiple actors. For the purpose of this paper, an actor is defined as a decision making entity. When referring to a single actor, we mean in most cases one organization that may consist of several individuals but they do not have separate decision making power. Because we analyze the context of inter-organizational coordination, for the rest of the paper we will focus on the case of multiple actors only. If the project involves multiple actors, the majority of actors can either be in the same business sector, e.g. a payment system supporting a network of banks (Fig.2, column a) or in different business sectors, e.g. a typical retail supply chain integration network (column b). Moreover, the inter-organizational network can consist of actors from both the same as well as different sectors (column c). The project complexity increases from column (a) to (c).

Project Scope		
a) Multiple actors same sector	b) Multiple actors, different sectors	c) Multiple actors from both the same and different sectors

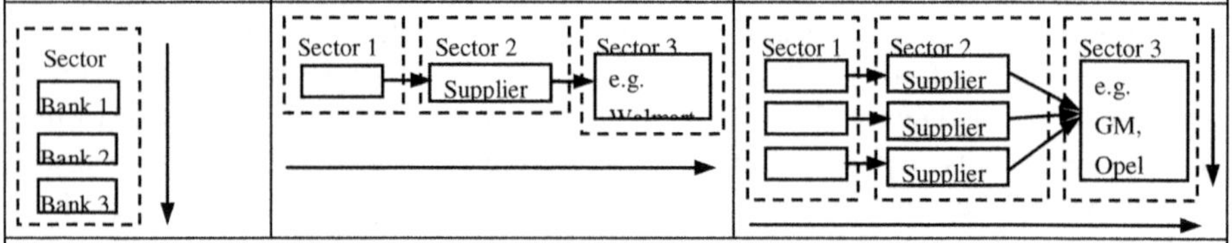

Factors influenced by project scope (competition, semantics and objectives)		
Competition: direct, between actors → do not share information easily Semantics: similar Objectives: similar	Competition: not direct → might share information Semantics: different Objectives: different	Competition: direct, between actors → do not share information easily Semantics: different Objectives: different

Fig. 2. Influence of project scope

3.4 Conceptual Framework and Coordination Properties

There is relevant research into the detailed properties and influences of coordination structure [3, 20-21]. Based on these sources, we find that coordination structure and project scope are expected to influence the following six coordination properties:

- Decision-making location (coordination authority/ level of control),
- Competition (resource sharing structure, risk/ reward sharing) [22]
- Decision Power [23]
- Semantics (use of similar language and sharing of similar mental models)
- Information sharing,
- Goals and objectives [3].

Fig. 3 shows our exploratory framework including the relationships between the different determinants and exemplary values (depicted in the boxed elements). We will explain how the coordination properties influence the shared BCD process (dashed numbered lines 1 to 5).

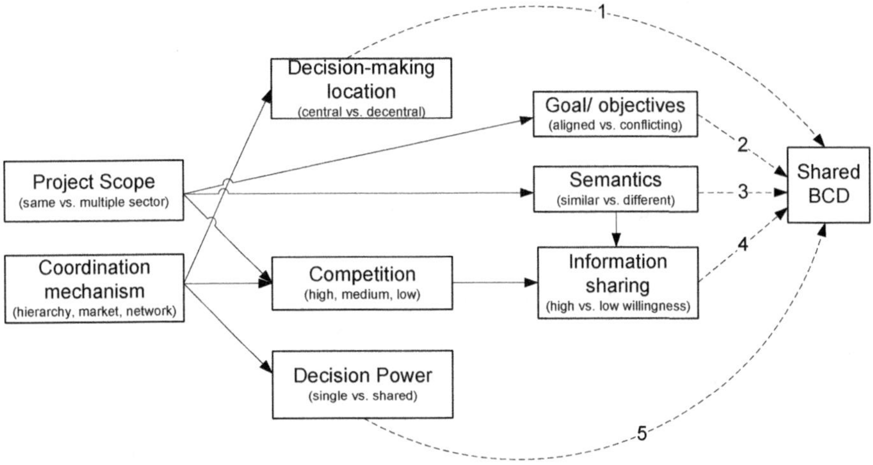

Fig. 3. Exploratory coordination - BCD framework

Decision-making location describes whether decisions in an inter-organizational network are made in centralized or decentralized manner. In the first case, only one BC is needed to evaluate an IT investment decision. In the case of decentralized decision-making, several BCs need to be prepared (Fig. 3. arrow 1), one for each decision-making unit. Decision-making also depends on the coordination structure, as e.g. in a network actors might need to develop, in addition to their own BC, a shared BC with the other actors in the network. Such a joint model is based on input from each actor's individual BC.

As some actors might be competitors depending on the coordination structure), they might not want to reveal sensitive cost and benefit information to the other network partners. The competition between actors is expected to be higher when (i) the different actors are operating in the same sector or (ii) the inter-organizational relation is organized with a market structure.

The coordination structures are also found to influence the power dependency between the actors. Power dependency describes whether the decision power rests with a single actor or is shared among multiple actors. When multiple actors share the decision power they need to agree on the final BC (arrow 5).

However, this might not be that easy, as they might not only have different goals (and thus have difficulties to agree on a BC, arrow 2) but also might speak a different language (and, consequently, would not agree on the terms used in the BC, arrow 3). This is especially true for actors from multiple sectors.

Information sharing is one of the most important aspects as it determines the willingness of actors to share their sensitive information, and their ability to actually put numbers in the BC (arrow 4). Information sharing is easier when actors speak the same language and is more difficult in case of competing actors.

4 Application of the Exploratory Framework in a Case Study

Below we describe and analyze the case in our research determinants: coordination structure, project scope and coordination properties by following the order used in §3. We also explain the impact on the shared BCD by applying our exploratory framework to the case situation.

4.1 Case Background (Coordination Structure and Project Scope)

The coordination structure shown in Fig. 4 presents the relations between the actors in our case setting. Barges are used to transport containers from the port of Rotterdam to the hinterland and vice versa. Whenever a barge visits the port, it has to call on several terminals to load and unload containers. To guarantee short sojourn times in the port, the barge operator (BO) schedules convenient arrival times at the concerning terminals. The terminal operators (TO) on the other hand want to operate efficiently and have to decide when a barge can be processed, taking into account all kinds of restrictions, e.g. specific times at which containers need to be at the terminal.

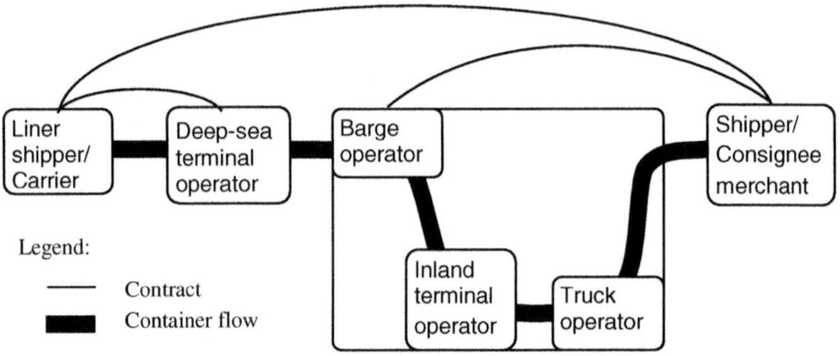

Fig. 4. Coordination structure of the case study setting

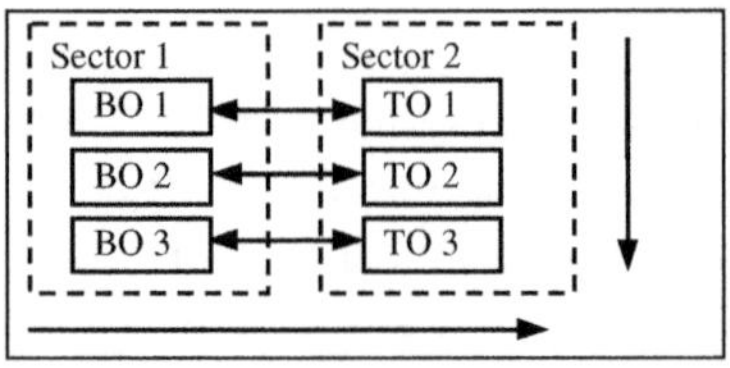

Fig. 5. Project scope case study

The Project scope, that we introduced in §3.3, is described for the case at hand in Fig. 5. There one can see that the network involves both actors from the same sector, e.g. several BO's and several TO's, and actors from different sectors. These business characteristics complicate the project scope, e.g., parties want to stay autonomous, have no contractual relationships, and are reluctant to share information that possibly undermines their competitive position.

Douma [24] shows that an integrated ES, enhanced by multi agent algorithms and controls, can support the alignment of barge rotations and terminal quay capacity, taking into account the business characteristics. We were involved in the BCD process to evaluate if an investment into such an integrated ES would be profitable.

4.2 Impact of Coordination Properties on the Shared BC

The application of BC guidelines developed earlier [25], turned out to be hardly possible as participating actors did not share sensitive cost and benefit information. To analyze the case study, we applied our conceptual framework introduced in §3.4 to our case and show the results in Fig.6.

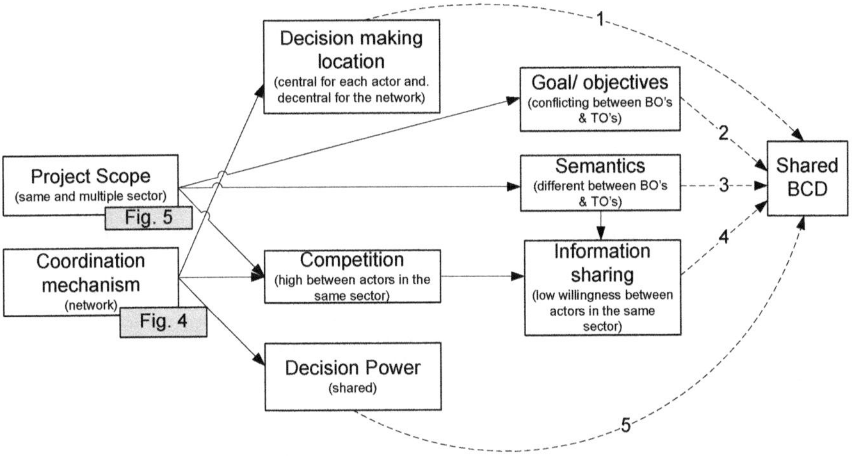

Fig. 6. Conceptual framework applied to the case study

Starting from the left, one can see that the harbor case involves several actors from both the same as well as different sectors, as it is illustrated in Fig. 5. The actors interact with each other in a network coordination structure, as it is shown in Fig. 4. Following from the network structure, the BCD process involved one individual BC for each actor (which was decided centrally by each actor) and a shared BC (Fig. 6. arrow 1). This was developed and decided on jointly by all actors in the network as they had shared decision power (arrow 5).

The proposition that actors from the same sector experience increased competition than actors from different sectors is supported by our case study where we observed high completion especially between the different BOs. This directly impacts the willingness to share sensitive cost and benefit information, which is needed for a shared BC (arrow 4). We found it particularly hard to quantify the expected benefits and costs mentioned vaguely by the different actors. However, without concrete numbers it is very difficult to arrive at a trusted BC, no matter which guidelines one uses. The willingness to share information was further negatively impacted as actors from different sectors did not speak the same language and had different mental models (semantics). This rendered the discussions ineffective as actors had to spend much time on clarifying the meanings of the different terms used in the BC to describe the costs and benefits (arrow 3). E.g. actors had different understandings of what it means to achieve cost reduction or an improvement in planning.

Analyzing the goals of the actors from different sectors in our case study, we found that they were conflicting. The main goal of the BOs is to keep sojourn times short in the port and thus waiting times short at the terminal. However, the main goal of the TOs is to have long waiting lines in front of their terminals, so that they always have work for their employees to do. As Fig. 4 indicates, in the current situation, there is no contractual relationship between the BOs and TOs; so, no fines will be paid when barges arrive too late at the terminal or when terminals do not handle barges in the agreed upon time slot. This makes it very difficult to get agreement between BOs and TOs on how a solution could look like. It also makes the BCD very challenging as the actors did not agree on the costs and benefits (arrow 2). The TOs actually did not recognize the problem as urgent, as they currently achieve their goal of having long waiting lines, and therefore also had no incentives in investing into an improved planning system.

5 Conclusion

This paper reported on the first result in investigating the effects of project scope and coordination structure during the development of a shared BC for ES in inter-organizational settings. Our contribution is an exploratory framework that explains how three coordination properties - competition, decision-making location and decision power, may help or impede the BCD process. This framework fills a gap in the current ES literature, which lacks comprehensive studies on BC decision-making in inter-organizational settings.

Our framework is a first proposal only. Our first application demonstrated that it made sense and was useful. To gain a deeper insight into the effects of coordination structure on the BCD process, we intend to use the framework as structure for further empirical investigations about shared BC in ES implementations.

The implications of our work are twofold: for practicing project managers, we think that if they are aware of these coordination aspects, they could devise strategies to mitigate their impact on the BCD process. For researchers, our framework could serve as an explanation vehicle that can be used in case study research. As we indicated earlier, we are interested in accumulating experiences which could evaluate the relationships between the concepts in our framework.

References

1. Kumar, K., van Hillegersberg, J.: Enterprise Resource Planning: Introduction. Communications of the ACM 43, 22–26 (2000)
2. Bakos, J.: A strategic analysis of electronic marketplaces. MIS Quarterly, 295–310 (1991)
3. Daneva, M., Wieringa, R.J.: A Requirements Engineering Framework for Cross-organizational ERP systems. Requirements Engineering 11, 194–204 (2006)
4. Schubert, P., William, S.: An Extended Framework for Comparing Expectations and Realized Benefits of Enterprise Systems Implementations. In: Americas Conference on Information Systems (AMCIS), San Francisco, California (2009)

5. Shang, S., Seddon, P.B.: Assessing and Managing the Benefits of Enterprise Systems: the Business Manager's Perspective. Information Systems Journal 12, 271–299 (2002)
6. Ward, J., Daniel, E.: Benefits Management: Delivering Value from IS& IT Investments. John Wiley & Sons, Chichester (2006)
7. Klein, R., Kupsch, F., Scheer, A.: Modellierung interorganisationaler Prozesse mit Ereignisgesteuerten Prozessketten. Saarland University, Saarbruecken (2004)
8. Schulz, K., Orlowska, M.: Facilitating cross-organisational workflows with a workflow view approach. Data & Knowledge Engineering 51, 109–147 (2004)
9. Kishore, R., Zhang, H., Rameshc, R.: Enterprise integration using the agent paradigm: foundations of multi-agent-based integrative business information systems. Decision Support Systems 42, 48–78 (2004)
10. Webster, J., Watson, R.T.: Analyzing the Past to Prepare For the Future: Writing a Literature Review. MIS Quarterly 26, xiii–xxiii (2002)
11. Ward, J., Daniel, E., Peppard, J.: Building Better Business Cases for IT Investments. MIS Quarterly Executive 7, 1–15 (2008)
12. Crowston, K.: A coordination theory approach to organizational process design. Organization Science 8, 157–175 (1997)
13. Malone, T.W., Crowston, K.: The interdisciplinary study of coordination. ACM Computing Surveys 26, 87–119 (1994)
14. Schmidt, M.J.: What's a Business Case? And Other Frequently Asked Questions, Solution Matrix (2003)
15. Gordijn, J.: Value-Based Requirements Engineering: Exploring Innovatie E-commerce Ideas. Vrije Universiteit Amsterdam, Amsterdam (2002)
16. Heide, J.B.: Interorganizational governance in marketing channels. The Journal of Marketing 58, 71–85 (1994)
17. Powel, W.W.: Neither market nor hierarchy: Network forms of organization. Research in Organizational Behavior 12, 295–336 (1990)
18. Ouchi, W.G.: Markets, Bureaucracies, and Clans. Administrative Science Quarterly 25, 129–141 (1980)
19. Jaffee, D.: Organization Theory: Tension and Change. McGraw-Hill, New York (2001)
20. Park, S.H.: Managing an Interorganizational Network: A Framework of the Institutional Mechanism for Network Control. Organization Studies 17, 795–824 (1996)
21. Xu, L., Beamon, B.M.: Supply chain coordination and cooperation mechanisms: an attribute-based approach. Journal of Supply Chain Management 42, 4–12 (2006)
22. Thorelli, H.B.: Networks: Between Markets and Hierarchies. Strategic Management Journal 7, 37–51 (1986)
23. Cook, K.: Exchange and power in networks of interorganizational relations. The Sociological Quarterly, 62–82 (1977)
24. Douma, A.M.: Aligning the Operations of Barges and Terminals through Distributed Planning, Universiteit Twente Enschede (2008)
25. Eckartz, S., Daneva, M., Wieringa, R.J., Hillegersberg van, J.: Cross-organizational ERP Management: How to Create a Successful Business Case. In: 24th Annual ACM Symposium on Applied Computing, SAC 2009, Honolulu, Hawaii, USA (2009)

A Model for Cooperation Networks: Promoting Information Share

Vítor José Domingues Mendonça[1], João Eduardo Quintela Alves Sousa Varajão[2], and Paula Cristina Ribeiro Coutinho Oliveira[3]

[1] Departamento de Informática e Comunicações, Instituto Politécnico de Bragança, 5370-326 Mirandela, Portugal,
mendonca@ipb.pt
[2] Centro ALGORITMI, Universidade de Trás-os-Montes e Alto Douro, 5001-801 Vila Real, Portugal,
jvarajao@utad.pt
[3] Departamento de Engenharias, Universidade de Trás-os-Montes e Alto Douro, 5001-801 Vila Real, Portugal,
poliver@utad.pt

Abstract. Cooperation networks are a promising model for companies. There are currently several models for the creation of this kind of networks. This paper presents a conceptual model for the development of cooperation networks, which aims at promoting the information sharing about business opportunities between members of a specific network. The proposed model is based on a Web Information System, and it is useful in the context of building and managing inter-organizational and/or intra-organizational networks.

Keywords: Cooperation Networks; Information Sharing; Business Opportunities; Information Systems.

1 Introduction

Organizations, over time, have faced many challenges, such as: industrialization; economic crises; globalization; and the emergence of a society based on information and knowledge.

The globalization, the emergence of large retail chains, whether nationwide or international, the increasing volume of information, the speed with which changes occur in the environment, are only few examples of some factors that have a significant impact in everyday life of the organizations, especially the Small and Medium Enterprises (SMEs).

According to Laudon and Laudon [1], some of the main factors that have changed the businesses environment are: the growth of the Internet and the convergence of technology; the transformation of organizations; the globalization; the rise of the information economy; and the emergence of digital firms.

In such a dynamic context, it is critical that organizations are always aware of the changes that constantly occur in their environment. Their competitiveness is directly

J.E. Quintela Varajão et al. (Eds.): CENTERIS 2010, Part II, CCIS 110, pp. 198–207, 2010.

related to how they perceive those changes, as well as the time it takes to act accordingly to the new market requirements.

Manuel Castells [2] notes that the traditional models that persist in many organizations do not fit the characteristics of the current market. He goes even further, stating that the traditional model of organization, based on vertical integration and functional management hierarchy, is in crisis.

The current market challenges are demanding: On the one hand, large companies aren't versatile to respond to requirements on time. On the other hand, SMEs do not reach the scale necessary to be innovative and truly competitive.

It is therefore crucial that companies adopt new organizational models, which should ensure more versatility to adapt to new market conditions. These models should enable organizations to gain sufficient scale to act globally, and simultaneously allowing them the necessary flexibility to adapt quickly to the market. Cooperation networks models appear as interesting solutions in this new reality [2, 3].

In this paper we propose a new model that promotes the information sharing about business opportunities between entities that are part of a cooperative network. The generic model could be applied to inter-organizational and/or intra-organizational networks.

Next sections, we will firstly introduce several concepts about cooperation networks and briefly describe the different types of cooperation networks. Then, we will present a conceptual model for developing an Information System (IS) for promoting the expansion of cooperation networks.

2 Cooperation Networks

The hierarchical bureaucratic form of structure that has prevailed in organizations during many years has become obsolete in the face of the current realities of the markets. So, organizations must adopt new organizational models, for instance, network configurations. Information Technology (IT) assumes in this context a leading role, so that the network integration could be a key of organizational versatility and all business activity [2].

The configuration of networked organizations should extend outside the organizational boundaries, providing the partners of organizations with complementary skills, allowing them to be more capable to respond [4].

The inter-organizational partnerships could be assumed as strategic. More recently the vocabulary used at the level of strategic management has been enriched by the inclusion of new words and expressions such as "networks", "collective strategy", "joint ventures", "strategic alliances" and "strategic outsourcing" [5].

The literature is consensual to recognize that a strategic alliance in networking form occurs when two or more organizations decide to join their efforts to follow a common strategic objective [6]. If two or more organizations are linked through a network of relationships, they thus constitute an inter-organizational network [7]. The networks between companies are a way of consortium intended to encourage the activity of each of them without necessarily being legally tied among themselves.

The concept of network is behind a vast number of forms of relationships between organizations. Joint ventures, strategic alliances, relations of outsourcing and subcontracting, industrial districts, consortiums, social networks, networks of cooperation between SMEs, among others, can be listed as an illustration of different forms of relationships between organizations.

The Cooperation networks between organizations should be considered as strategic: Cooperating organizations develop joint strategies that enable them to obtain and sustain competitive advantages that differentiate them from their competitors [8]. Thus, a cooperation network establishes itself as a center for bringing together the competencies of the cooperating organizations.

Networks act as gatekeepers. If within the networks new opportunities are constantly being created, outside the networks survival is increasingly difficult [2].

The purpose of cooperative relationships is to obtain the synergy effect on the outcome of the relationship which represents, more than the sum of its parts [4].

The cooperation among companies is encouraged by the growing recognition of the fact that an organization has not all the capabilities (resources and activities) necessary to meet market needs, which are increasingly demanding as far as response times are concerned, quality and the required diversity of products and services.

As a result of the challenges that business and the scientific world face, nowadays, a wide variety of cooperation networks have emerged [3]. The networks are now fundamental aspects of successful organizations, since there are means to expand business throughout the global economy. Furthermore, network integration has become the key to flexibility and organizational activity [2].

Therefore, inter-organizational alliances, or inter-organizational networks, are a model that fits the new requirements that currently the market demands [8].

Therefore, we can say that the cooperation networks represent an interesting model in the current context of organizations.

3 Cooperation Networks Typologies

In literature [9, 10, 11, 12, 13, 14, 15] we can find that the cooperation networks may take different forms.

Those forms may vary depending on several factors, such as [15, 4]: domain; number of partners; level of cooperation; extent of cooperation; degree of cooperation; and the legal form of cooperation.

Next, we highlight some of the typologies suggested by the literature review so to enframe of the model presented in Section 4.

The authors Miles and Snow [16] propose three types of structures for inter-organizational networks:

- Internal network: this structure characterizes the arrangements between different units or subsidiaries of a company, which act independently, for example networks of large multinationals, composed of geographically dispersed units, each with separate responsibilities;
- Stable network: these arrangements arise when multiple organizations are organized around a central organization, which has a core competency. Generally, these network structures tend to assume the vertical alignment, in which volunteer organizations act as subcontractors of the central organization;

- Dynamic network: the cooperating agents are organized around a broker agent. The broker assumes control of all relationships in the network.

IAPMEI[1], in the Program for the dynamization of inter-business cooperation [17], identifies other types of networks.

- Suppliers Club: This kind of network is organized around a common client. For this, the participants of the cooperative network are structured according to a linear activity, activity that is responsible for meeting customer needs. The participants in the cooperation network are organized according to their individual skills, so that the sum of powers is able to meet the demands of large activity, i.e., organized around the complementarities of skills; This kind of networks differs from others by the complementarities existing between the activities developed by contributors. In the development of a co-operative activity, which will produce an end product aimed at a specific customer, the participants establish links between them as complementary. Their interrelationship is a necessary condition throughout the value chain;
- Central Network: Networks with this kind of configuration are structured around a central agent, i.e., it is a centralized model for planning and developing activities. This model does not require mandatory establishment of relations between participants. The several actors relate only to the central agent;
- Cellular Network: Such networks are usually associated with needs and activities common among some participants in the Network, promoting different interactions among the various agents, aiming at the rationalization of resources to optimize the activity subject of cooperation;
- Multipolar Network: Multipolar networks present themselves as networks composed. The participants are organized in clusters, and there are intervenient members that establish relationships between different clusters of the network.

Irandoust and Benaskeur [18] identify and describe six types of multi-organizational structures arrangements, which are:

- Network - The inter-organizational networks are an arrangement in which several organizations, having a common interest, share information in order to obtain mutual benefits;
- Tacit Agreement - In this type of arrangement, generally, the parties carry out their activities independently, though the members of the arrangement have an implicit agreement on the achievement of a punctual goal;
- Coalition - A coalition is a temporary partnering of individuals, groups, organizations, or nations in order to achieve an explicit goal;
- Coordinating Unit - A coordination unit is an arrangement in which several organizations coordinates some of their activities with a shared drive that makes the coordination of activities of members;

---

[1] Instituto de Apoio às Pequenas e Médias Empresas e à Inovação (Institute of Support to Small and Medium Enterprises and Innovation) - www.iapmei.pt

- Alliance - An alliance is an agreement in which several organizations with similar goals intentionally synchronize their activities, and sometimes they can also share their resources;
- Union - The union between organizations is an extreme form of collaboration and there is when two or more entities unite. A Union is a fusion of organizations, often irreversible and permanent for the organizations.

Camarinha-Matos et al. [19] systematizes various categories of forms of collaboration, which resulted from many discussions and interactions with a large community of researchers in various international projects. These categories are: Collaborative network; Supply chains; Virtual government; Virtual enterprise; Virtual organization; Extended enterprise; Virtual team; Virtual organization breeding environment; Virtual laboratory networks; Disaster rescue networks; and Professional virtual community.

4 Conceptual Model

In this section it is presented a conceptual model that aims at assisting the establishment of cooperation networks, allowing agents that are part of a network to share information about their customers, as well as information about potential business that their clients can represent to other network members.

The proposed conceptual model also seeks to be a guideline for the development of a Web Information System (WIS) that empowers the creation of cooperation networks among agents who act in a certain economic value chain, with intention to share information about business opportunities.

Considering as example the sector of construction industry, the different economic agents (architect, construction builder, building materials sales companies, electrician, plumber, house painter, among others) may share information about their customers and the business opportunities that customers represent. For example, when a client contacts the architect to draw up an architectural project, the architect registers the client and the project in the system to inform the network cooperators about that business opportunity. Automatically, and based on default values, the system schedules phases of the project (architectural design, foundations, building, exterior finishes, exterior frames, electrical installation, installation of water network, interior finishes, painting, wiping, among others) conferring each phase the products and services needs (labor, architectural design, sand, cement, brick, tile, point of light, water tap, door, window, among others). These default values may be adjusted by any cooperator, whenever there are deviations. Thus, the cooperating agents can follow up the needs on time, making promotional offers to the customer according to each moment's needs.

Thus, the main objective is to strengthen customer loyalty in the cooperation network. The model application can also create a web of economic agents with complementary capabilities to meet the diverse needs of customers.

So, it aims at establishing a guideline for the formation of cooperative networks oriented to maximize customer loyalty in the networks, giving the cooperators the opportunity to promote and enhance business opportunities with them. The proposed conceptual model is illustrated in Figure 1.

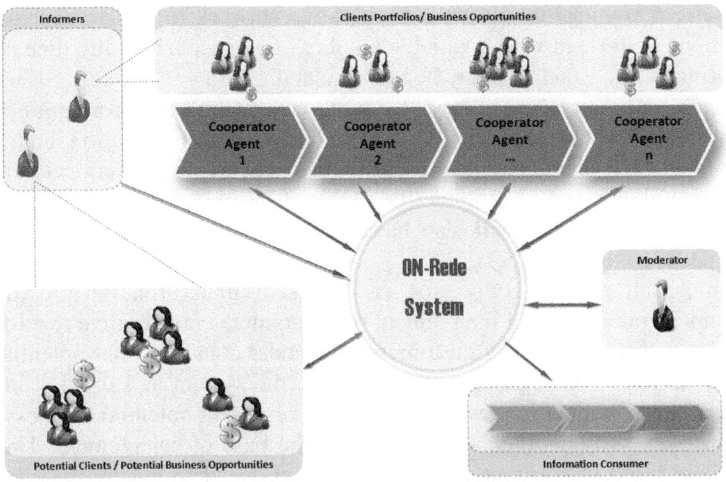

Fig. 1. Conceptual Model of ON-Rede system for sharing information in Cooperation Networks

The cooperative network is supported by a WIS (ON-Rede System - Business Opportunities into Network), which is responsible for supporting the sharing of information among network members. This system is also the main interface between the participants in the network.

The proposed model has three primary types of actors, which represent the basic elements in the network:

- Moderator - is responsible for managing participants of each network (moderator of the network, cooperators and informers), as well as managing the configuration of value chains on which the network will work;
- Cooperators - are agents that are part of the cooperative arrangement, and are responsible for enriching the system with information about their customers and the potential business opportunities that each client may represent to the network. This type of actor can make use of the information provided by the system, i.e., by other cooperators, informers and clients;
- Potential Customers - a potential customer is someone who, autonomously, can register himself in the system and register his projects so to get offers from companies operating in the system.

The model also allows incorporation of other actors, such as:

- Informers – they are agents in the cooperation network especially engaged to observe the market and inform the system about potential business interest to the network;
- Information Consumer - is a particular case of cooperators, whose differentiation lies in the fact that information consumers only take advantage of information of business opportunities shared on the network and do not contribute with relevant information to other cooperators.

In the center of the model is a WIS (ON-Rede) that enables and simplifies the interaction between the various actors of the model.

The system architecture allows a cooperative network to evolve over time. Thus, networks can be formed with a variable number of agents, and at any time new agents (either primary or secondary) may be incorporated.

It is each economic agent's duty to supply the system with information about customers whom it has business relationships with as well as information on the potential business that each client may represent to the network. Thus, cooperators have to engage more clients and to promote the potential business interest to the cooperative network. The cooperators will also have to follow and record the progress of the meeting needs of the customers.

In compensation, each cooperator has access to all information provided by the system and introduced by all intervenient members in the cooperative relationship.

To create a broader base of customers, the model considers that potential customers of the network can register themselves into the system and provide information about their needs, which, in view of the network represent potential business.

Informers embody another way to broaden the base of engagement. These agents are specially hired to constantly observe the market and to inform the system about potential customers and business. Informers may also follow the changing needs of customers and update the WIS.

The Information Consumers represent economic agents who by their nature do not have the profile required to cooperate, i.e., the information that could be provided is not relevant to the network. However, such agents are interested in the information which exists in cooperation network so they can promote their own business.

The model can be also applied to economic sectors of cyclical demand. In this case, customer loyalty in a cooperative network is even more advantageous, considering that customer needs have a cyclical nature, the model will enable retro-alimentation (feedback) of information about customer needs.

The application of the model in such sectors allows a better balance in regards to information feedback that the various cooperating agents obtain from the system. One should take into account that the information provided by an end of business cycle may correspond to an opportunity to relaunch the client into a new business round.

The characteristics of ON-Rede system are [20]:

- Manage multiple networks of cooperation, each network can be configured to support one or more value chains;
- Promote the sharing of information about customer and business opportunities, among members of cooperative networks;
- Leverage the basis for acquiring new customers of each cooperating organization, may be done cooperatively by all members of each cooperative network, by informants or independently by customers themselves;
- Maximize responsiveness to diverse needs of customers, fostered by the complementarily of cooperators agents;
- Promote customer loyalty within the networks of cooperation;
- Helping organizations to promote the sale along of customers in a timely manner, resorting to such scheduling of alerts depending on the timing of the phases of each business opportunity, and focused, considering the needs of every business opportunity.

The proposed model was developed to enable the establishment of inter-organizational networks, but its application can also be interesting at the creation of intra-organizational networks, whether between employees of the same organization, or among a group of sub-delegations business.

4.1 Inter-organizational Network

If we consider that an organization itself often lacks the ability to meet all customer needs, the application of the model will allow creating cooperation networks between organizations with complementary capabilities, and therefore this can maximize the responsiveness to customer needs.

Still considering the principles of the marketing relationship, in which it highlights the importance of customer loyalty [21], we can say that, combining the strategy of customer loyalty with an inter-organizational cooperation strategy, significant gains could be obtained. The acquisition and loyalty can be done at the network level, given that the customers will represent the sum of the clients of organizations belonging to the cooperation network.

In this context, the sharing of customer information and business opportunities that each customer represents, proposed by the conceptual model, allows cooperating enterprises to have a more comprehensive knowledge of the market, permitting the enterprises to promote efficiently their products and services to clients with whom they do not have business relationships. Thus, it is possible to generate business opportunities, providing the members of the network with rich information, so that they can be proactive in terms of sales.

The establishment of inter-organizational networks based on the model previously presented allows cooperating organizations to obtain several competitive advantages, which highlight:

- The increase in the base to attract new customers, which can be done by cooperating organizations, by the informers agents or autonomously by the customers;
- The reduction of the cost of acquiring new customers, being costs shared by members of the network
- The anticipation of customer needs and, consequently, the gain of the capacity to make promotional offers oriented to the needs of each client;
- The increased power of response to customer needs, i.e., the creation of co-operative arrangements among agents with complementary capabilities allows greater capacity to response to customer needs.

4.2 Intra-organizational Network

The proposed model also allows establishing networks between agents of the same organization, that is, provides intra-organizational networks. In this case, networking among employees of an organization or between organizational organic units can be promoted:

- Intra-organizational networks among collaborators: in this kind of networks, each collaborator of the organization takes the role of cooperator agent in the network. Such networks may be useful in organizations structured around the products/services, in this case, the cooperating agents could be the product managers of the organization;

- Intra-organizational networks among organic units: the units, affiliates or sub-delegations of a business group share information in the network to create synergies and maximize business opportunities within the group.

The creation of intra-organizational networks within the proposed model acquires greater interest when organizational agents (employees and units) represent complementary capabilities, as is the case of a business group whose different subsidiaries sell products or services, different but complementary.

The main competitive advantages come principally from synergies created by the complementary skills of cooperating agents, engaging clients at group level and loyalty within the group.

Note that an agent may participate in various cooperation networks, whether inter-organizational or intra-organizational. The cooperating agents that are part of several networks are links between the different networks allowing constitute multipolar network types.

5 Conclusion

Cooperation networks appear as a model enhancer of major competitive advantages, among which stands out organizational flexibility.

Taking into account that the information and knowledge are crucial elements in economic growth and the evolution of technology largely determined the productive capacity of society [2], IT could certainly take a decisive role in the development of cooperation networks.

In this context, the model proposed in this article contributes to the development of a WIS to promote cooperation through the sharing of information of business opportunities. The proposed model can be applied both in the formation of inter-organizational cooperation networks and to provide intra-organizational networks. Whereas the objective of the model is information sharing, the IS "ON-Rede" appears to be the key element of the model which will be subject of further work.

References

1. Laudon, K.C., Laudon, J.P.: Management Information Systems: Managing the Digital Firm. Prentice Hall, New Jersey (2006)
2. Castells, M.: The Rise of the Network Society: The Information Age: Economy, Society and Culture. Blackwell Publishers Inc., USA (2010)
3. Camarinha-Matos, L., Afsarmanesh, H.: Collaborative Networks: Reference Modeling. Springer Science, USA (2008)
4. Mendonça, V., Varajão, J., Oliveira, P.: Potenciar a Cooperação Interorganizacional: uma perspectiva baseada nas Tecnologias de Informação. In: ADM 2007 - Congresso Internacional de Administração, Ponta Grossa, Brasil (2007)

5. Mintzberg, H., Ahlstrand, B., Lampel, J.: Strategy Safari: Your Complete Guide through the Wilds of Strategic Management, 2nd edn. Pearson Education Limites, United Kiggdom (2009)
6. Aaker, D.A.: Strategic Market Management, 9th edn. John Wiley & Sons, Inc., USA (2009)
7. Ebers, M.: Formation of Inter-Organizational Networks. Oxford University Press, USA (1999)
8. Mendonça, V., Varajão, J., Oliveira, P.: Potenciar Oportunidades de Negócios em Rede: Modelo Conceptual para Redes de Cooperação Inter-Organizacionais. In: CISTI 2010 - 5ª Conferência Ibérica de Sistemas e Tecnologias de Informação, Santiago de Compostela, Espanha (2010)
9. Casarotto, F.N., Pires, L.H.: Redes de pequenas e médias empresas e desenvolvimento local, Atlas, São Paulo (1998)
10. Locke, R.M.: The Composite Economy: Local Politics and Industrial Change in Contemporary Italy, Massachusetts Institute of Technology (1994), `http://dspace.mit.edu/bitstream/1721.1/2540/1/SWP-3748-33502355.pdf`
11. Ernst, D.: Inter-firm networks and market structure: driving forces, barriers and patterns of control. University of California, Los Angeles (1994)
12. União Europeia: Guidelines on horizontal cooperation agreements, `http://europa.eu/scadplus/leg/pt/lvb/l26062.htm`
13. Grandori, A., Soda, G.: Inter-firm networks: Antecedents, mechanisms and forms, Organization Studies, Athens, Greece 16(2), 183–214 (1995)
14. Marcon, M., Moinet, N.: La Stratégie-Réseau, Éditions Zéro Heure, Paris (2000)
15. Pümpin, C.: Manual de Gestão para as Pequenas e Médias Empresas, Monitor – Projectos e Edições Lda, Lisboa (2003)
16. Miles, R.E., Snow, C.C.: Causes of failure in networks organizations. California Management Review 33(4), 53–72 (1992)
17. IAMPEI - Instituto de Apoio às Pequenas e Médias Empresas e ao Investimento: Manual do Agente Promotor / Facilitador, Programa de Dinamização da Cooperação Inter Empresarial, PEDIP II, Lisboa (2000)
18. Irandoust, H., Benaskeur, A.: Multi-Organizational Structures, Association for the Advancement of Artificial Intelligence, Technical Report WS-08-03, USA (2008)
19. Camarinha-Matos, L., Afsarmanesh, H., Galeano, N., Molina, A.: Collaborative networked organizations – Concepts and practice in manufacturing enterprises. Computers & Industrial Engineering 57(1), 46–60 (2009)
20. Mendonça, V., Varajão, J., Oliveira, P.: Proposal of a Web Information System to Support Cooperation Networks: a functional architecture to share business opportunities. In: IBIMA 2010 – 14th IBIMA Conference on Global Business Transformation through Innovation and Knowledge Management, Istanbul, Turkey (2010)
21. Kotler, P., Armstrong, G., Wong, V., Saunders, J.: Principles of marketing. Pearson Education Limited, United Kiggdom (2008)

Distributed Informal Information Systems for Innovation: An Empirical Study of the Role of Social Networks

Vasco Vasconcelos[1] and Pedro Campos[1,2]

[1] EGP-University of Porto Business School, Rua de Salazares, 842
4149-002 Porto – Portugal
[2] FEP and LIAAD INESC-Porto, LA

Abstract. Web 2.0 and Enterprise 2.0 concepts offer a whole new set of collaborative tools that allow new approaches to market research, in order to explore continuously and ever fast-growing social and media environments. Simultaneously, the exponential growth of online social networks, along with a combination of computer-based tools, is contributing to the construction of new kinds of research communities, in which respondents interact with researchers as well as with each other. Furthermore, by studying the networks, researchers are able to manage multiple data sources - user-generated contents. The main purpose of this paper is to propose a new concept of Distributed Informal Information Systems for Innovation that arises from the interaction of the accumulated stock of knowledge emerging at the individual (micro) level. A descriptive study is to unveil and report when and how market research professionals use social networks for their work, creating, therefore, distributed information systems for innovation.

Keywords: Distributed Informal Information Systems for Innovation, market research, social media, social networks.

1 Introduction

Innovation is essential to competitiveness and represents the way in which to anticipate, live with, or react to change [16]. Innovation capabilities and technological advance have been enhanced by strategic alliances and collaboration networks that have proliferated in recent years, particularly in information technology sectors [10]. Information and Communication Technologies are frequently seen as an important enabler for such networks and a key factor in Economy. With the fast diffusion of technologies, companies and individuals unable to face the challenge can rapidly become uncompetitive [17]. If they are not able to preserve their advantage on the long term, technological cooperation may be a possible course of action. Hakansson [11] suggests a new perspective that sees innovation (and technological development in general) as a product of exchange among different agents (firms, individuals, in the network). The former view treated innovation either as an individual fact (like a Nobel Prize) or as a secret process in a firm. Innovation systems include the interaction

J.E. Quintela Varajão et al. (Eds.): CENTERIS 2010, Part II, CCIS 110, pp. 208–217, 2010.

between the individual (or actors) who are needed in order to turn an idea into a process, product or service on the market [8].

Most of the information technologies that are used for communicating and spreading innovation fall into two categories: (i) direct channels (person-to-person communication by email or instant messaging), having low share and low commonality of information for the other agents involved and (ii) platforms, like intranets, corporate Web Sites and corporate portals [15]. Knowledge management systems have tried to elicit tacit knowledge, best practices and relevant experience from people throughout a company and put this information available to other in databases.

Nowadays, Enterprise 2.0[1] provides business managers with access to the right information at the right time through a web of inter-connected applications, services and devices. By providing such a wide quantity of resources to firms and individuals, Enterprise 2.0 makes the collective intelligence of many accessible, translating into a huge competitive advantage in the form of increased innovation, productivity and agility [18]. Within the concept of Enterprise 2.0, information systems are emergent. One of the most challenging examples of such an emergent information system is Wikipedia (www.wikipedia.org). Articles in this online encyclopaedia are assembled by ad hoc virtual teams. The social engineering of the wiki model is aimed at creating a cooperative and networked culture ([9], cf [15]).

In this paper, we study the use of social networks by individuals with the aim of creating innovation. Knowledge capture through the interaction of individuals is therefore accumulated in social networks. Informal structures of knowledge that is shared by firms or individuals (or both) can be seen as Distributed Informal Information Systems for Innovation. Our main research hypothesis is that social networks are used as Distributed Informal Information Systems for Innovations by market research professionals.

In order to capture the use of social networks, a survey was made in which a set of market research professionals (our target population) was analyzed, taking in consideration four social networks: Linkedin, Hi5, The Star Tracker and Twitter. To capture the innovation capabilities inherent to market research professionals, we gather information about eight main concepts: Finding Business Partners, Academic, New Business, Benchmarking, Find Human resources, Costumer experience, Concept testing and Product development. According to previous research conducted by [3] and [7], these concepts define the most common goals for the use of social networks by our target population. These are the main components for the creation of an Information System for Innovation.

The rest of the paper is structured as follows: in Section 2 the main concepts are presented. Section 3 contains the study design and the results and, finally, in Section 4 the concluding remarks are presented.

---

[1] According to [18], the premise of Enterprise 2.0 *is that the more easily people can communicate – with other workers, team members, customers, vendors, clients – the less information will be siloed. When information is free, people can get more feedback and input (collaborate), react more quickly (agility), and make better decisions. This is the opportunity inherent in Enterprise 2.0: a more efficient, productive and intelligent workforce through the use of participative means such as social networks, blogs, open source software, etc..*

2 Information Systems for Innovation and Web 2.0: A Market Research

2.1 Networks and the Accumulation of the Stock of Knowledge

In Economics, an inter-firm network is a set of firms (nodes) that interact through inter-firm relations (connections or links). These links are contracts or correspond to informal exchange of information in order to produce innovation. In a previous work, [2] proposed an Agent-Based approach to analyze the dynamics of network formation resulting from the collaboration between firms. Firms (the agents) contain cognitive attributes that help them build their own decisions. Four collaboration strategies have been compared and it was concluded that profit is associated with stock of knowledge and with small diameter of the networks. In addition, it has been proved that concentration strategies are more profitable and more efficient in transmitting knowledge through the network, and that the stock of knowledge is determinant for the growth of networks.

Networks play an important role in economics. Firms set up connections with other firms in order to establish production relationships, cooperation, etc. Therefore, firms expect to increase their profits and survival.

2.2 Distributed Informal Information Systems for Innovation (DIISI) and the Concepts of Innovation

A Distributed Information System consists of multiple autonomous entities (individuals, organizations, computers, etc.) that communicate through various means, usually computer networks. The way individuals communicate, nowadays, is distributed. The Internet and the Web evolved to a platform for collaboration, sharing, innovation and user-created content—the so-called Web 2.0 environment. This environment includes social and business networks, and it is influencing what people do on the Web and intranets, individually and in groups. One of the main advantages of the Web 2.0 is the ability to tap into the collective intelligence of users. It is known that the more users contribute the more popular and valuable a Web 2.0 site becomes. Enterprise 2.0 is a direct consequence of what Web 2.0 has introduced in firms: the socialization of business applications – moving from data - centric models to people - driven applications. Exploiting the analysis from the use of on line information services, Lamb and Kling developed an institutionalist concept of a social actor whose everyday interactions are infused with ICT use [13]. The authors changed the concept of the user to the concept of social actor in Information Systems, taking into consideration the complexity and multiplicity of the roles that people fulfill while adopting, adapting, and using information systems.

These "Distributed Informal Information Systems for Innovation" (DIISI), are "distributed" because the stock of knowledge is created through the interaction of the distributed agents at the micro-level (individuals) and spread at the macro level, with feedback to all agents in the network. They are also informal because, in many situations, there is no intention a priori of creating a formal information system. Furthermore, and taking in consideration the concept of Enterprise 2.0, information systems are emergent, and therefore this micro-macro mechanism promotes the creation of

DIISI. Affiliations comprise networks of relationships that link organizations and individuals within and across industries. Within this network of relationships, the use of online databases by organization members is best explained from a perspective that understands these ICTs as interaction technologies. Organization members, like attorneys, commercial real estate brokers or members of biotechnology companies, use online services to exchange information and interact with affiliated organizations, such as clients or regulators, in ways that are considered legitimate within the industry. When ICTs are used as part of those interactions—to package, present, and exchange information—they also construct identities for firms and their members [13].

2.2.1 Market Research and Innovation

Traditional market research has been accused of not being able to satisfyingly deliver answers for the client's needs and are, in an ever more complex society, challenged to embrace new mental models, based on different principles [3]. The corporate use of social media is quickly changing from an adoption stage – where companies use it as a channel to promote and manage brand awareness, products and services – to a paradigm focused on the comprehension of how people and institutions take advantage of it [14].

[3] and [7] define the concepts associated with the most common goals for the use of social networks for market research purposes: Finding Business Partners, Academic, New Business, Benchmarking, Find Human resources, Costumer experience, Concept testing and Product development. According to previous research by those authors, these concepts define the most common goals for the use of social networks by our target population, and enabled by new "arenas" opened up by these communities, backed-up by the Web 2.0 concept of collaboration and user-generated content. These are the main components for the creation of a DIISI.

3 Study Design

3.1 Research Problem, Information Sources and Sample Characterization

In this study, the research problem is specified by the question: how are social networks being used by market research professionals for innovation purposes. The components of this question are: (a) professionals and businesses that use social network for market research, (b) frequency of use of this type of tool, (c) objectives of use (d) social networks most used for market research, (e) relevance of social networks as information sources and (f) main advantages and disadvantages of using this type of market research tool. A non-documental indirect observation methodology was chosen through the form of an online survey, which was created using an online survey tool[2]. The questions were designed considering the objectives of the descriptive study and supported by information gathered through scientific literature review. The survey includes independent and dependent (both qualitative) variables, the latter being filter-origined. Which social networks are the most used and with which objectives constitute the dependent variables of the study. The sample was designed using a

[2] The survey tool used in this study is eSurveyspro, from Outside Software Inc. (2009), available in www.esurveyspro.com

convenience-based sampling methodology [6], following two steps: (1) selection of four social networks: Linkedin (www.linkedin.com), Hi5 (www.hi5.com), Thestartracker (www.thestartracker.com) and Twitter (www.twitter.com) and (2) selecting individuals within these networks. The dimension of the sample is, therefore, difficult to determine a priori, as the number of members of the discussion groups and blogs grows on a daily basis. A great difficulty that contributed for the sample's size non-determination is the fact that the URL posted on Twitter has been "retwitted" by the authors' followers. All the contacted individuals are somehow related or interested in market research and are members of social networks, whose habits of use of social networks for market research are intended to be studied, having been obtained 63 answers to the survey. Considering this is a convenience-designed sample, no inferences were drawn to the whole market researchers' population, or to the social networks studied. The restricted number of answers is a limitation of our study, but taking into account that this convenience-designed sampling was applied to a study that is based on professional networks (not completely opened to a wide audience), the dimension of the sample is to be considered as adequate. The respondents were contacted either by direct messaging through the chosen social network platforms and by posting the survey on discussion groups and forums available in the very same networks. This way of contact allowed the sample to overcome geographical boundaries as well as faster distribution of the survey and data collection. The survey was designed and formatted so that each respondent could answer only once, in order to better control the answers and narrowing chances of multiple responses per respondent, enabling more reliable results. The data were gathered between November 17 and December 30, 2009 and then exported to the SPSS© Statistics Software for statistical analysis. In the sample, 74,60% of the individuals are Portuguese. From a total of nine different nationalities, the second most represented country is the United States of America, with 9,52% of the respondents, followed by Argentina (4,76%) and Australia (3,20%). Several industries (15) are present in the sample: Information Technologies (IT) is the most represented (26,98%). Marketing and Information Management is the second, with 14,29% of the answers. In the bottom end stand Pharmaceutical Industry, Food and Beverages, Non-profit Organizations (NPO's), Publishers and Energy (1,59%). More than 58% of the respondents have a University Degree and almost 32% possess a MSc or PhD degree. From a total of 20 different professional headlines, 17,34% of the sample is composed by Marketers and 11,29% CEO's. Business Managers represent 9,68% and Market Researchers 8,06%.

3.2 Social Network Use

The analysis of the gathered data allows us to verify that, on what concerns social networks for market research, 22,22% of the respondents claim never to use it, whereas only 11,11% use social networks for such a purpose either frequently or all the time (the remaining professionals fitting in the other classes). The Pharmaceutical Industry and the NPO's never used social networks in this context. 50% of the Building Materials Industry claim not to use social networks; 42,86% of the Consulting and 40% of the Consumer Goods Industry get the same score. On the other hand, Web Development claims a continuous/permanent use (100%). 60% of the respondents of the Education Industry use social networks all the time, while the remaining 40% use them frequently. The consumer Services industry also uses social networks frequently (66,67%). Only 11,11% of Marketing and Information Management professionals never use social networks, whereas the other respondents in this Industry reveal diverse use rates: seldom (22,22%), sometimes (44,44%) and frequently (22,22%) (Fig. 2). All of these results are consistent with the 2009 Business Social Media Benchmarking Study (Business.com, 2009).

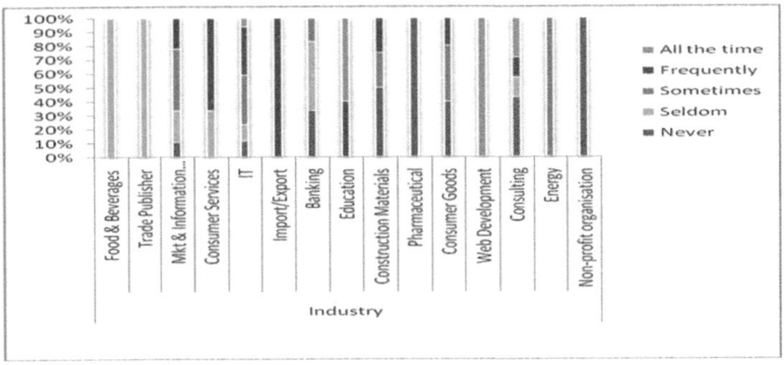

Fig. 1. Use of Social networks for market research

3.3 Most Frequently Used Social Networks in Market Research

Linkedin is the most commonly used social network for market research in the sample (58,73% of the respondents), being the only one used in the Building Materials Industry. A possible explanation for this is that Linkedin is the only professional network in the study. In fact, according to the "2009 Business Social Media Benchmarking Study", [1], 38% of the professionals have an active profile in this network. However, it is never used by 16,66% of the industries in the sample that use social networks as a market research tool. According to our data, the distribution of the social networks by the type of industry is as follows: Food and Beverages (Facebook (50%) and Hi5 (50%)), Trade Publishing (Facebook (50%) and Secondlife (50%)), Import/Export (Facebook (50%) and Twitter (50%)). Overall, Facebook is used by 46,03% of the professionals in the sample and, Twitter, by 31,75%. The Star Tracker (20%) and

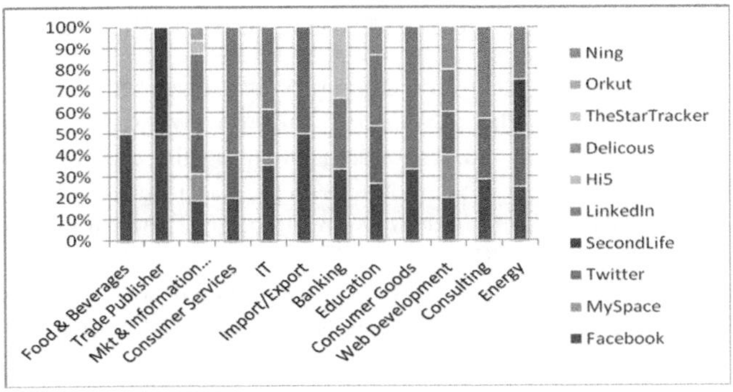

Fig. 2. Social networks used by Industry

Linkedin (37,50%) are the most commonly used social networks by the Marketing and Information Management Industry, being this the industry with the largest number of users of different social networks. Education professionals mainly use Twitter (26,67%) and Linkedin (33,33%). Overall, 46,03% of the respondents use Facebook.

3.4 Goals of Using Social Networks for Market Research

The main goals appointed by the sample in the use of Linkedin are: Idea Generation (27,78%), Concept Testing (13,39%), Product Development (13,39%) and Test Methodology (2,78%) being actually the only social network used to find human resources and new business partners. All of the respondents that use Hi5 claim to use it with the goal of Generating Ideas. The goals of using Facebook concern specially Idea Generation and Consumer Experience (33,33% each). Among the respondents that use Twitter as a market research tool, 30% do it for Idea Generation, whereas 33% has Consumer Experience in mind, 14,81% Concept Testing and 11,11% for Product Development purposes. The only social network exclusive to Portuguese users (Thestartracker) is used for Generating Ideas, Product Development and Consumer Experience (33,33% each). Within the sample, the concept of Benchmarking is explored through Myspace (25%), Twitter (5%), Delicous (100%) and Facebook (3,70%).[3] Overall, the goals Finding New Business Partners (4,76%) and New Business Opportunities (1,5%) are poorly mentioned.

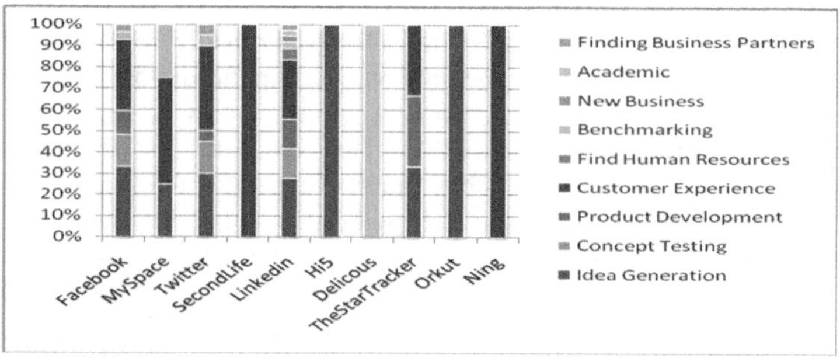

Fig. 3. Goals of using social networks for market research by social network

3.5 Perceived Advantages of the Use of Social Networks for Market Research

The main advantage perceived by the sample of this research study is the fact that the" information is *pulled* by the consumers", followed by "Rich Consumer Insights" (26,98%). More than 14% of the respondents mention the possibility of seeing the consumers as "part of a tribe". We can then perceive the influence of networks around friendship relations or common interests as an important factor in individual's life, as it was previously defended by [5].

The ability of social networks to identify weak signals from the market is mentioned by 12,70% of the sample. These signals are traditionally difficult to identify by more "mainstream" research methods (idem).

[3] Relative percents of goals of use given to each social network.

3.6 Perceived Disadvantages of the Use of Social Networks for Market Research

About 31,75% of the respondents point out the inability to cover all relevant types of individuals as the main disadvange of social networks, on what market research is concerned. The reason behind this answer is the fact that not all consumers – at least not all considered relevant for any given research – are members of social networks. The same percentage of our sample refers to poor control of the respondents as the main disadvantage. Another great disadvantage of this type of open and collaborative tool is the array of data one can collect from it. However, and by definition, this whole mechanism is out of the control of any entity, researchers included, thereby endangering the usual control procedures [3]. Simultaneously, this very same array of data, implies "fuzzy data" (idem), pointed out as the biggest disadvantage by 15,87% of the respondents of our research.

4 Concluding Remarks

In conclusion, one can verify that the social network phenomenon is seen by market research professionals in the most diverse industries and businesses as a new market research tool. The Web 2.0 and its collaborative tools bring new approaches and ways of seeing the professionals as social actors. This mechanism promotes the creation of Distributed Informal Information Systems for Innovation. For the studied sample, one can conclude that: (i) nearly 80% of the respondents use one or more social networks for market research purposes. These numbers indicate the importance and dimension of this phenomenon in which social networks are seen as a new market research tools, even though its use is not always consistent; (ii) several social networks are used, with clear tendency towards professional networks, namely Linkedin, the most commonly used by Marketing and Information Management professionals; (iii) the professional network Linkedin presents the broadest scope of different uses and it is the most commonly used for Finding Human Resources, which can be easily explained by its own definition. The main goals pointed out by the professionals in the sample concerning the use of Linkedin are: Idea Generation (27,78%), Concept Testing (13,39%), Product Development (13,39%) and Test Methodology (2,78%); (iv) social networks, while market research tools pass up some gaps or weaknesses found in more "traditional" research methodologies. According to the sample, social networks allow for a vision of the consumer as a dynamic entity, inserted in mutually influential groups, providing richer information on the consumers, mainly due to the fact that all data and contents are created by the consumers themselves, rather than by the researchers. On the other hand, there is poor control of the respondents, making the "traditional" control methods completely ineffective translating into fuzzy and not so clear data, making its analysis difficult. The fact that social networks do not include all types of relevant audiences is one of the most mentioned disadvantages by the professionals in the sample of this research study. Therefore, this sample is restricted to the groups of consumers that have access to the Internet, detain some computer skills and are registered in social networks; (v) as mentioned above, the restricted number of answers is a limitation of our study, but taking into account that this convenience-based sampling method was applied to a study that is based on professional networks (not completely opened to a wide audience), the dimension of the sample is to be considered as reasonable. The use of social networks (and social media) allows professionals to create and develop relationships and networks from which they can extract, mash-up and analyze data from several relevant sources, and maintain contact with those sources for long-term useful information for their business, in the same way intranets do inside companies and, therefore, working as DIISI: "(…) the people I follow provide me with more relevant links and information than any other tool." [1]. Bearing in mind the objectives defined for this study, as well as the results and analysis reported, and considering that the sample has been designed using a convenience methodology, it does not allow us to make any inferences or to take any conclusions for the whole population of market researchers, nor to the social networks studied. Anyway, we consider that the goals set were achieved, since it was possible to analyze how social networks are being used by our target population for innovation purposes. Within this community of users, and due to the interaction of the accumulated stock of knowledge emerging at the individual (micro) level, a new DIISI was observed in the sample. In this case, the scope of the DIISI was limited to the sample of market research professionals that use social networks for innovation purposes such as the ones stated by [3] and [7].

References

1. Business.com: Business Social Media Benchmarking Study (2009)
2. Campos, P., Brazdil, P., Brito, P.: Organizational survival in cooperation networks: the case of automobile manufacturing. In: Camarinha-Matos, L., Afsarmanesh, H., Ol-lus, M. (eds.) Network-Centric Collaboration and Supporting Frameworks, pp. 77–84. Springer, Heidelberg (2006)
3. Chadwick, S.: Client-driven change: The impact of Changes in Client Needs on the Research Industry. International Journal of Market Research 48, 391–414 (2006)
4. Charron, C., Favier, J., Li, C.: Social Computing, Forrester Research (2006)
5. Cooke, M., Buckley, N.: Web 2.0, Social Networks and the Future of Market Research. International Journal of Market Research 50(2) (2008)
6. Cochran, W.G.: Sampling Techniques, 3rd edn. Wiley, Chichester (1977), ISBN 0-471-16240-X
7. Day, G.S., Schoemaker, P.J.H.: Peripheral Vision: Detecting the Weak Signals that will Break or Make your Company. Harvard Business School Press, Cambridge (2006)
8. Freeman, J.: Organizational Life Cycles and Natural Selection Processes. In: Staw, B., Cummings, L. (eds.) Research in Organizational Behaviorm, ch. 4, pp. 1–32. JAI Press Inc., Greenwich (1982)
9. Giles, J.: Internet Encyclopedias Go Head to Head. Nature (December 2005)
10. Gordon, R.: Innovation, Industrial Networks and High-technology Regions. In: Camagni, R. (ed.) Innovation Networks: Spatial Perspectives, pp. 174–195. Belhaven Press, London (1991)
11. Hakansson, H.: Industrial Technological Development: a Network Approach. Croom Helm, London (1987)
12. Komninos, N.: Intelligent Cities and Globalization of Innovation Networks (2002)
13. Lamb, R., Kling, R.: Reconceptualizing Users as Social Actors in Information Systems Research. MIS Quartely 27(2), 197–235 (2003)

14. Lenhart, A.: The Democratization of Online Social Networks, Pew Internet &American Life Project, October 8 (2009)
15. McAfee, A.: MIT Sloan Management Review, Enterprise 2.0: The Dawn of Emergent Collaboration 47(3) (Spring 2006)
16. Ratti, R.: Small and Medium-Size Enterprises, Local. Synergies, and Spatial Cycles of Innovation. In: Camagni, R. (ed.) Innovation Networks: Spatial Perspectives, pp. 71–88. Belhaven Press, London (1991)
17. Solé, F., Valls, J.: Networks of Technological Cooperation between SMEs: Strategic and Spatial Aspects. In: Camagni (ed.) Innovation Networks: Spatial Perspectives, pp. 174–195. Belhaven Press, London (1991)
18. Wylie, S.: Enterprise 2.0: What, Why and How, White paper for the Enterprise 2.0 Conference, Boston (2009), http://www.e2conf.com/whitepaper

Vector Consensus: Decision Making for Collaborative Innovation Communities

Josep Monguet[1], Marco Ferruzca[1,2], Alfredo Gutiérrez[1,3,4], Yadira Alatriste[1], Claudia Martínez[1], Carlos Cordoba[1], Joaquín Fernández[1], Teresa Sanguino[1], and Josep Aguilà[1]

[1] Barcelona Tech, School of Engineers, Diagonal 647, 08028 Barcelona, Spain
[2] Metropolitan Autonomus University, Sn Pablo 180, 02200, México City, México
[3] University of Guadalajara, Marcelino García 1421, 44430, Guadalajara, México
[4] Secretariat of Education of Jalisco, Prol. Alcalde 1351, 44280, Guadalajara, México
{monguet.upc,marco.ferruzca,alfredogtzh,yadira.alatriste, eveun5,cordobacely,jfernandezupclam,tere.sanguino}@gmail.com

Abstract. To achieve a general agreement in relation to a specific proposal, members of a community must participate in the formal consensus process. This paper describes a web-based system (the Vector Consensus system) for supporting an ad hoc consensus process. The system was implemented in a collaborative innovation community with the aim to discuss how this organization understands some drivers affecting collaboration practices. The results have shown that Vector Consensus system enhance ultimate consensus and canalize personal contributions to the organization. Furthermore, the possibility to compare the one's personal opinion with respect to the rest of the community, given as a real-time feedback, appeared to have a positive impact on the group, augmenting the context knowledge awareness.

Keywords: Consensus, Awareness, Decision, Discussion, GDSS.

1 Introduction

To scan the context in order to take better decisions is an important task for any kind of organization [1]. It is a "must-do". Decisions are normally about trying to achieve some advantage for an organization. Including all the members in the organization and all the stakeholders is imperative in achieving environmental change [2]. The decision-making process can improve and obtain a realistic perspective if the following aspects are considered [3]: First, include soft and hard information. While soft information is tied to an individual person and can be subjective (tacit knowledge), hard information is explicit and can be easily quantified and processed. The first one is important because individuals can provide guidance, advice and encouragement[1]. Second, decision-makers should rely on information received on a solicited and unsolicited basis. Third, it is recommended to utilize the organization's internal and external resources to obtain information.

[1] Gould et al. [4] also suggests decision-making involves two key elements for a person: immersion in a decision-making situation and a reflective self-conscious element.

J.E. Quintela Varajão et al. (Eds.): CENTERIS 2010, Part II, CCIS 110, pp. 218–227, 2010.

Consensus is an idea associated with the decision-making process and the common-agreement building among most of the participants of an organization. In simple words, this concept is thus concerned with decision-making procedures.

In Collaborative Innovation Communities (CIC) as research groups, Living Labs Spaces or multinational organizations, it is ever more difficult to maintain competitive advantage on the basis of the traditional knowledge and economic models. Those who can stimulate and support open collaboration to leverage their local and dispersed resources should have more chances to succeed [5].

Nowadays, there are many current studies that highlight various factors affecting collaboration effectiveness and efficiency [6][7][8][9]. Some of the main collaboration barriers have to do with: a lack of clear leadership, a lack of mutual trust, a lack of motivation, unbalanced intellectual property rights and a lack of common knowledge and meaning. These factors create different types of barriers among collaborating people working in CIC's.

Although, there are a lot of strategies and tools oriented to solve collaboration practices, more efforts are needed to help CIC's ability to sustain competitive and to build cognition and consensus in developing their core capabilities [10]. These problems can be solved by implementing web-decision-making systems[2] which are rarely explored [11].

The present study deals with these issues by describing a web-based system expected to enhance consensus in a collaborative-innovation community. We are particularly interested in knowledge intensive domains like research groups where distributed individuals in several countries interact with each other in order to achieve personal and collective goals. However, this experience should be also useful for other kind of innovative communities.

Taking all of this into account, we developed a web-based system – the Vector Consensus[3] system – aimed at improving ultimate consensus in a research community involved with the development of Internet-based innovative projects. Vector Consensus addresses simultaneously: gathering information about a collective thought, promoting sharing knowledge and diminishing collaborative barriers. This system innovates by implementing in a web environment an ad hoc conceptual model for consensus, originally thought for enterprises, allowing distributed individuals discuss and subjectively measure some barriers affecting collaboration in the community. Furthermore, it innovates because it offers to each individual the possibility to compare his personal opinion with respect to rest of the community, given as a real-time feedback.

The purpose of this paper is to present and describe the first implementation of Vector Consensus system in a real world environment. It also intends to analyze its effects on users' perception. Specifically, in order to achieve these goals, data collected during its first trial as well as a survey applied to users are analyzed and further discussed.

---

[2] Sometimes also denominated as Group Decision Support System (GDSS).

[3] The name "Vector Consensus" was selected as an analogy to Euclidian vector in physics, and more specifically in a vector space, where each single member in an organization would be represented by a single vector, and a vector space would be the collectiveness. So as a vector space has a vector addition, an organization will have results based on the addition of multiple personal efforts. If individual vectors align then addition increases.

2 Overview of the Vector Consensus System

Vector Consensus is web-based system for supporting an ad hoc consensus process that depends on the collective participation of users. The proposed system is based in the conceptual model for consensus proposed by Aguilà and Monguet [11] where individuals has different personal opinions in relation to the main drivers that support and encourage organizations.

The conceptual model for consensus is composed of two main stages: one for achieving a diagnosis and consensus in relation to the current behavior of some drivers in the organization, and the second one for discussing the desirable level of performance of each one of those drivers in the organization. The priority to address the drivers is also ranked and discussed in this second stage. Table 1 summarizes these stages.

Table 1. Conceptual model stages for consensus

Main Stages	Second Level Stages	Purpose	Result
Current Scenario	Assessment	- To apply a test (survey) for individual diagnosis about the meaning of each driver. - To share personal knowledge.	Everybody shares the same meaning for each driver. The first response to the test establishes the actual collective though about the evaluated drivers. This behavior is represented in a graphic with the average and the dispersion level of the answers.
	Discussion	- To apply a test for consensus about the current level of the drivers. - On the basis of a discussion strategy to build a common agreement. The aim is try to converge as much as possible.	A first consensus process about the current level of the drivers in the organization is achieved. Graphical feedback is presented. All different opinions by individuals are shared.
Desirable Scenario	Ideal Situation and Ranking	- To apply a test for consensus about the desired future level, for example 1 year, of the drivers and their prioritization. Again a discussion strategy is required for individuals to try to converge as much as possible.	An ultimate consensus agreement about the desirable level of the drivers. Graphical feedback is presented Major awareness and understanding about the knowledge and priorities in the organization.
	Action Plan	-To analyze the whole consensus process and develop an action plan.	Strategies and tools.

In simple words, collective knowledge and consensus implies the reduction in dispersion between the first unconnected personal opinion (first stage) and the consensus collective awareness in second and third stages.

The group's consensus around the actual and desirable situation in the organization is promoted by using, during the whole process, a discussion strategy about each driver and comparing personal opinions every time. Fig. 1 represents the conceptual model for consensus proposed.

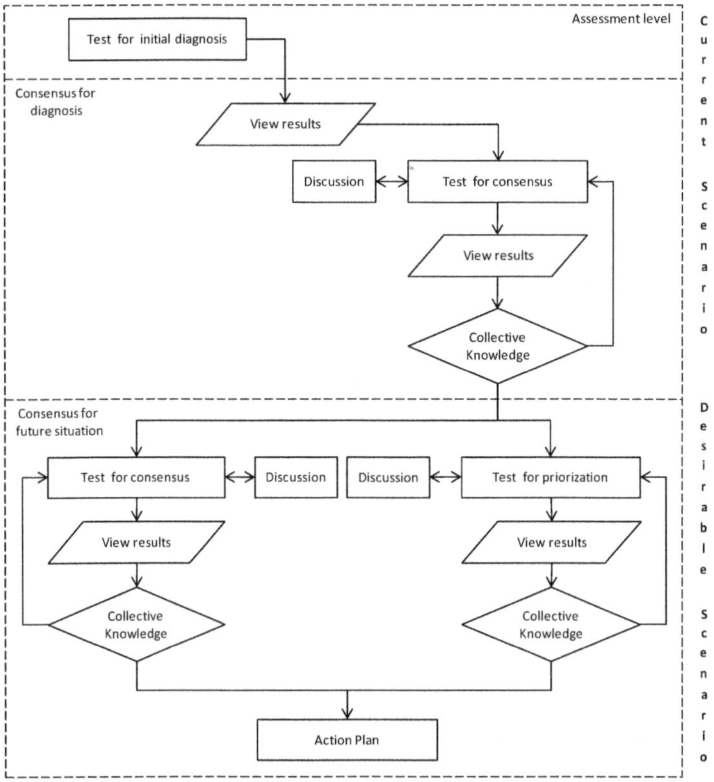

Fig. 1. Consensus conceptual model diagram

2.1 Design of the Vector Consensus System

Vector Consensus system provides users with gathering tools for registering their opinion: Semantic Differential Scale (SDS) questionnaire and forums (See Fig. 2). In relation with questionnaires, obtained data are analyzed and presented as graphic based-real time feedback (See Fig. 3). The visualization process consists in calculate for each driver at every stage the following variables: the mean value from personal user answers, the mean value from the whole group answers and the standard deviation. Results are then showed to users with a graphic using a simplified color code: red for the mean value which represents the personal opinion: green for the mean value representing the group's collective opinion, and gray to (± 1) standard deviation from the group's mean value to represent the statistical dispersion (Fig. 4).

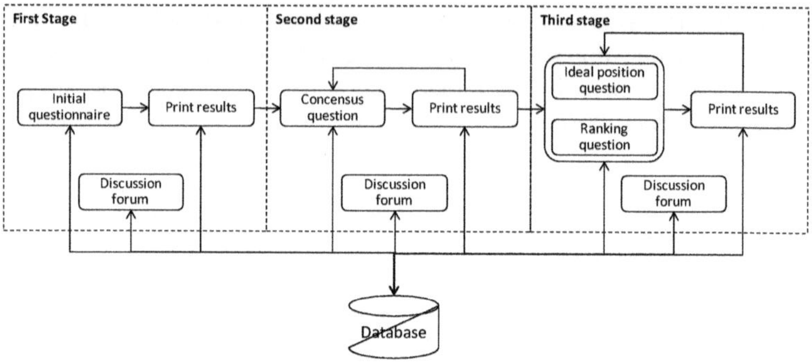

Fig. 2. VECTOR System flow scheme

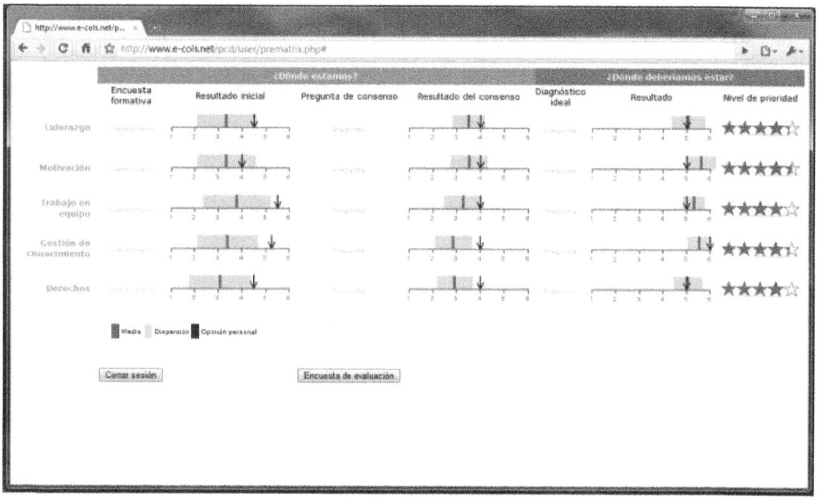

Fig. 3. Screenshot of the real-time feedback interface in the VECTOR System

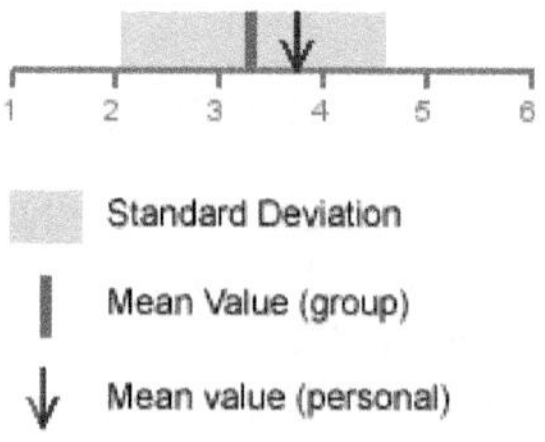

Fig. 4. Graphic representing unified driver´s statistical data

In synthesis, Vector Consensus is based on five user-interfaces (Fig. 5): one for each stage in the model, one to be queried by the user when more information is needed and the main one as a user's central panel working as start point to the others and as a feedback center, already presented in Fig. 3. The stages interfaces include an integrated discussion forum as well as a question or group of questions to be answered while the users can post any message (Fig. 6). This can be displayed in real-time to other users obtaining a between users knowledge flow and a better basis to get a well set of answers that will represent the collective awareness.

Vector Consensus system has the ability to log every user's activity, including every initial value or change to an answer, as well as adding a new post at the discussion forums. All of them aimed to be capable of make future depth analysis work in order to understand the user's behavior during the group consensus process, and to explore the consensus mechanisms in collaborative organizations.

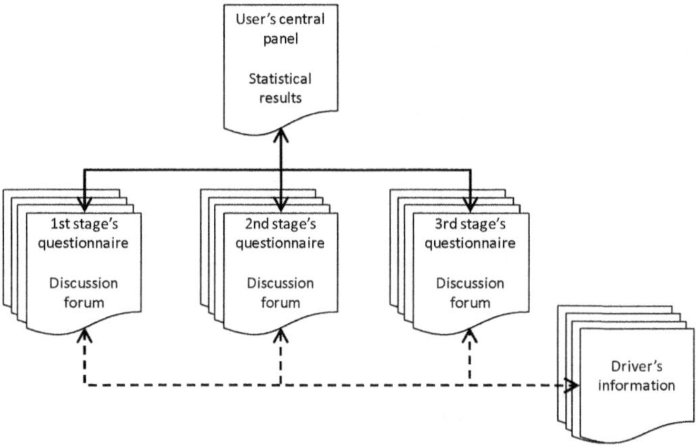

Fig. 5. Vector system interface diagram

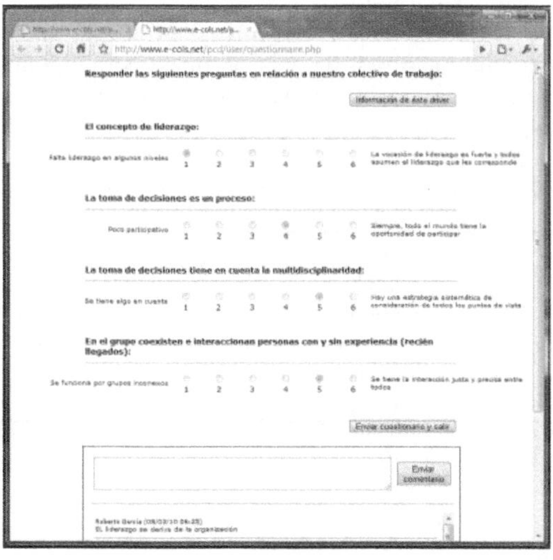

Fig. 6. An example of the interface for SDS questionnaire and forum

3 Method

3.1 Participants

This study was developed within a collaborative innovation community dedicated to the development of e-health services. In this group, innovation process relies upon multidisciplinary teams that bring together different expert knowledge domains (engineers, designers, mathematicians, anthropologists, psychologists, health professionals). Members of this group are distributed in several countries such as Venezuela, Mexico, Portugal, and USA. However, the main unit is located in Barcelona, Spain.

The community uses a web platform for sharing information and establishing face-to-face encounters.

30 members were invited to participate in this consensus strategy to discuss about some drivers capable of affecting collaboration in the organization. Specifically, the discussed drivers were leadership, motivation, collaborative work, intellectual propriety rights, and knowledge management.

3.2 Procedures

It was necessary to explain to users the purpose of the three stages that compose the consensus strategy, and also to give them complementary information about each driver in order to have a reference framework.

In this case, every stage had duration of three days. In each of them users had to answer a SDS questionnaire and interchange opinions through a forum. The questionnaire applied in the first stage had 20 items (4 per driver). The second stage included one item per driver and the last one had 8 items (2 per driver).

Every item was made as a 6-point SDS in order to assess five drivers based on *Barriers Affecting Collaboration Effectiveness and Efficiency* [6] see (table 2). Participants was asked to rate each item.

After using Vector for nine days, users were requested to fill out an on-line survey focused on users' perceptions about the effects of the strategy and the tool usability. This survey had six items. Five of them were dichotomous questions and the last one was for gathering free opinion.

Table 2. Drivers and main adjectives used in SDS questionnaires

Driver	Negative = 1	Positive = 6
1. Leadership	Lack	Have
2. Motivation	Unmotivating environment	Motivating environment
3. Collaborative Work	Unintegrative environment	Integrative environment
4. Knowledge Management	Inappropriate	Appropriate
5. Intellectual Property Rights	Disrespected	Respected

4 Results

4.1 Statistical Data

We used system logs (answers to the questionnaires) to describe the consensus process behavior and the building of common knowledge. As we have mentioned before, for each driver at every stage the following variables were calculated: the mean value from personal user answers, the mean value from the whole group answers and the standard deviation.

The trend to consensus can be observed in this study with a diminished dispersion in group perception with ranges from 9.5% to 31.4% This affirmation can be concluded after comparing the two level of dispersion obtained in the "Current scenario" stage (see Table 3).

Table 3. Statistical summary

Driver	Current				Desirable			
	Personal		Consensus		Personal		Consensus	
	Mean	Disp.	Mean	Disp.	Mean	Disp.	Mean	Disp.
Driver 1	3.42	0.87	3.38	0.60	4.80	0.93	4.20	0.75
Driver 2	3.34	0.87	3.56	0.79	5.50	0.74	4.50	0.59
Driver 3	3.80	1.06	3.19	0.73	5.20	0.60	4.15	0.73
Driver 4	3.39	0.86	2.88	0.78	5.37	0.67	4.32	0.65
Driver 5	3.09	0.95	2.94	0.75	5.00	0.71	3.90	0.77

In the "Current scenario" stage, diminutions on dispersion levels during consensus have a stronger meaning since there also were changes in the mean group's perception at each driver going from 1.2% to 16.2% obtaining mainly lower levels, based on these changes we can conclude it was a change in most of the personal opinions due to the consensus and discussion process in the model (See Fig. 6 and Fig. 7).

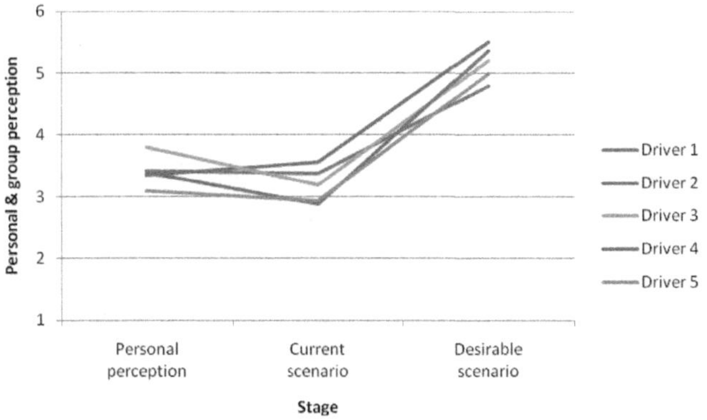

Fig. 7. Group's mean for each driver across the three stages

Based on the same statistical results, it is even possible to see a higher group's ability to obtain a relatively better level of consensus due to the mostly low dispersion levels in "Desirable scenario" stage compared to the first dispersion levels.

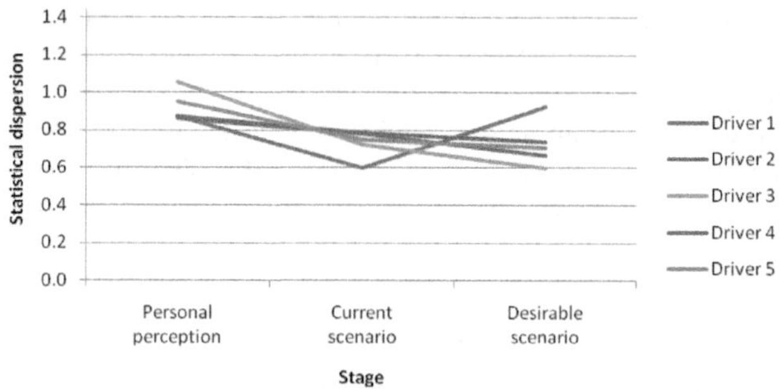

Fig. 8. Statistical dispersion for each driver across the three stages

4.2 Survey

Once applied the final user's perception survey as mentioned in section 3.2 the group's perception about the model and the system resulted as follows:

85.7% considers this consensus strategy helps to enhance group's collective goals and objectives.

57.1% thinks this consensus strategy contributes to increasing commitment in a personal level in relation to collective goals.

100.0% thinks this consensus strategy affords to elevate the knowledge members have about the group.

85.7% thinks this consensus strategy is useful to canalize personal contributions to the group.

Only 50% considers the system works well in sharing knowledge between collective's members.

5 Conclusions

This paper has presented Vector Consensus as a web-based system for supporting an ad hoc consensus process and its application to one real collaborative innovation community.

Results have shown that Vector Consensus allows users to augment their context knowledge awareness. Users considered that even when Vector Consensus system facilitates sharing personal ideas; more efforts are needed to share knowledge through this strategy.

Finally, the main conclusion of this work is that tools like Vector Consensus may be considered a good approach to achieve consensus and support decision-making, helping align the different individuals' opinion in an organization. Moreover, a better knowing on others' opinions has beneficial effects in the social capital of the organization.

Next experiences will focus in other domains of organizations, both in general aspects as well as in very specific questions. Vector Consensus will be tested for the consensus about the vision and mission of the organization, and will be implemented also as a tool for the decision-making process about the way innovative projects have to be managed or oriented.

References

1. Choo, C.W.: The knowing organization: How organizations use information to construct meaning, create knowledge and make decisions. International Journal of Information Management 16, 329–340 (1996)
2. Lozada, H.R., Calantone, R.J.: Scanning behavior and environmental variation in the formulation of strategic responses to change. Journal of Business & Industrial Marketing 11, 17–41 (1996)
3. Frishammar, J.: Information use in strategic decision making. Management Decision 41, 318–326 (2003)
4. Gould, S.J., Kramer, T.: "What's it Worth to Me?" Three interpretive studies of the relative roles of task-oriented and reflexive processes in separate versus joint value construction. Journal of Economic Psychology 30, 840–858 (2009)
5. Hansen, M.T., Nohria, N.: How To Build Collaborative Advantage. MIT Sloan Management Review 46, 22–30 (2004)
6. AMI@Work: ECOSPACE Newsletter No 11 (2009), `http://www.ami-communities.eu/wiki/ECOSPACE_Newsletter_No_11`
7. Riege, A.: Three-dozen knowledge-sharing barriers managers must consider. Journal of Knowledge Management 9, 18–35 (2005)
8. Fawcett, S.E., Magnan, G.M., McCarter, M.W.: Benefits, barriers, and bridges to effective supply chain management. Supply Chain Management: An International Journal 13, 35–48 (2008)
9. Cramton, C.D.: The Mutual Knowledge Problem and Its Consequences for Dispersed Collaboration. Organization Science 12, 346–371 (2001)
10. Lin, C., Hsu, M.: A GDSS for ranking a firm's core capability strategies. Journal of Computer Information Systems 47, 111–130 (2007)
11. Lin, C., Liu, A.C., Hsu, M., Wu, J.: Pursuing excellence in firm core knowledge through intelligent group decision support system. Industrial Management & Data Systems 108, 277–296 (2008)
12. Aguilà, J., Monguet, J.M.: Evoluciò de l'oferta en el quinari: nous models de negoci. ACC1Ó, Catalunya (2009)

Mashup Enabled Dynamic Capabilities in the Fuzzy Front-End of Innovation

Luís C.S. Barradas[1] and J.J. Pinto Ferreira[2]

[1] ESGTS-IPSantarem, Complexo Andaluz, Apartado 295, 2001-904, Santarém, Portugal
claudio.barradas@esg.ipsantarem.pt
[2] FEUP –DEIG / INESC Porto-UITT, Rua Dr. Roberto Frias s/n, 4200-465 Porto, Portugal
jjpf@fe.up.pt

Abstract. Innovation is today a widely used buzzword in the enterprises environments, because it is seen today as the support for long-term surviving and a lever for the creation of new and differentiated products or services. The Fuzzy Front-End of Innovation (FFE) is often experimental, involving strong interaction with the end-users. This enables the knowledge transfer from users, communities or Collaborative Innovation Networks to organizations. Enterprises may master a set of Dynamic Capabilities in order to manage, learn and integrate that shared knowledge. Today, using Web 2.0 applications, users are able to easily join together, share ideas, catalog information, spread and share their knowledge in a variety of ways. This paper presents a model to enable those Dynamic Capabilities using a Web 2.0 Mashup in the FFE of innovation.

Keywords: Innovation, Knowledge Management, Dynamic Capabilities, Web 2.0, Mashups.

1 Introduction

Today, innovation is a key point and a hot issue in business environments. The innovation processes have become increasingly important within companies, since innovation is seen today as a support base for their long-term survival in an increasingly volatile and demanding market, and a lever to the development of new and differentiated products and services.

The innovation processes include methods and techniques that differ on their approach and required competences [1]. They can be classified as «hard» - quantitative, empiric or numeric; or «soft» - qualitative, based on experience or reflecting tacit knowledge. Another classification consists on the assessment of such methods and techniques that tend to be normative – starting the process with a clear perception of the future needs; or exploratory – starting the process through the extrapolation of the present technological capacity. Given that innovation depends on information and knowledge, it is necessary to consider that an organization may not be autonomous in the innovation process, because the sources of ideas, information and knowledge can be internal or external [2]. Thus, this process is interactive and results from the

J.E. Quintela Varajão et al. (Eds.): CENTERIS 2010, Part II, CCIS 110, pp. 228–237, 2010.

contributions of many economic and social agents (users, customers, business partners, etc), owners of different type of information and knowledge. The combination and management of several sources of ideas, information and knowledge is an important challenge for companies in order to innovate and build capacity to cope with changes, since most of the problems (especially technological problems) involve the use of knowledge at various levels.

2 User Involvement in the Innovation Process

According the Product Development and Management Association (PDMA), the innovation process is divided in three areas [3]: the Fuzzy Front End of innovation (FFE), the New Product Development (NPD) and the Commercialization phase. The FFE also known as "Phase 0" or "Stage 0" [3], [4], designates the initial period of the New Product Development. The FFE includes all the initial phases from the formulation and selection of the initial ideas to the final concept definition, and must be considered as an essential part on the NPD. Although doesn't usually have high costs associated with it, it may consume 50% of the development time [3]. The FFE is often a non structured process, chaotic, from experimental nature, and involving a huge interaction between the NPD team and the user/customer. The PDMA has introduced the concept of New Concept Development in order to structure the activities developed at the FFE, which includes, among others, five key elements: (1) Idea Generation and Enrichment; (2) Idea Selection; (3) Opportunity Identification; (4) Opportunity Analysis; and (5) Concept Definition. The Concept Definition element is the unique gate to the NPD stage.

2.1 Listen the Voice of Customer

Innovation aims to create new and differentiated products and services that will help to create added value for end-users. Especially in industries where the innovation is driven by technology push (*e.g.* Information and Communication Technology), there

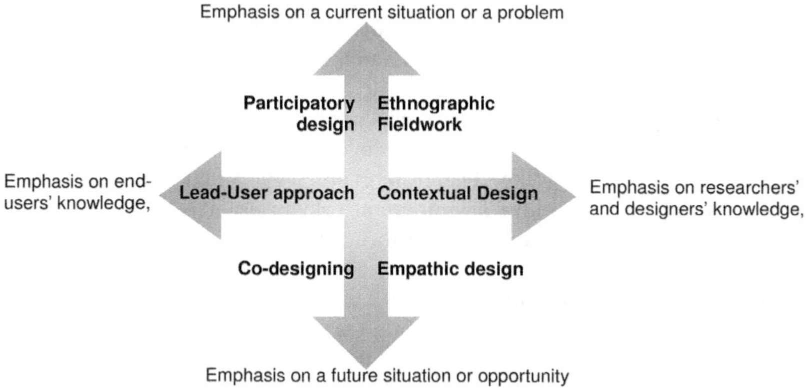

Fig. 1. Different human-centered design methods and practices [5]

is a risk that the innovation team creates any product or service that will fulfill the needs or expectancies of few customers/users. Thus, listening the Voice of Customer [3], [5], [6] in the innovation processes is extremely important, in order to identify unarticulated customer needs.

In [5] the authors proposed the Human-centered-design approach (HCD) in order to describe and classify the different ways used by the NPD team, to interact directly and constructively with users in their innovation projects. Fig.1 illustrates the six moves on HCD identified by [5]. Even thought stereotyped, in practice they can be combined. All these moves aim to obtain and apply end-users knowledge. However, there are differences between them in whose knowledge is leading the development and how knowledge is being transferred.

3 Knowledge Sharing and Dynamic Capabilities

The concepts presented on the previous sections show that the early stage of the innovation process can be described as an interactive process of knowledge transfer between users and the NPD team. By definition, knowledge is defined as expertise and skills acquired by a person through experience or education [7]. Knowledge acquisition involves complex cognitive processes: perception, learning, communication, association and reasoning. In organizations, knowledge can be divided in both **tacit** knowledge - which involves senses, skills and intuition; and **explicit** knowledge - which is formulated and captured, existing thus in the form of books and manuals [8]. From an epistemological approach, the tacit/explicit knowledge definitions follow the ones from the knowledge management literature [9]. The tacit side of knowledge is the aspect of knowledge that is omnipresent, taken for granted, and affecting our understanding without us being aware of it. Ontology-wise, tacit and explicit knowledge is considered as existing on various levels: individual, group, organizational and inter-organizational [10].

The terms "knowledge" and "information" are often used interchangeably [11]. Information is tangible and appears in the form of items or objects outside the human mind, and can be defined also as knowledge that can be transmitted without loss of integrity [12]. Knowledge, on the other hand, is a much less definable entity. Information per se contains no knowledge, and both data and information require knowledge to be interpretable, in order to create new knowledge [10]. Knowledge and Information are not understood by all equally. Their absorption depends on cultural, vocabulary or own assumptions (tacit) and new understanding comes from reflection [13]. Reflection, in its whole modalities (action, dialog, etc.), can transform tacit understanding in explicit understanding. Therefore enables us to understand how to learn. In this context, information plays an important role as a catalyst for reflection that may, by reaching its consumer, expand or relocate his knowledge state.

3.1 Sharing Knowledge for Innovation

The knowledge creation process involves five steps: (1) sharing tacit knowledge, (2) creating concepts, (3) justifying concepts, (4) building a prototype and (5) cross-leveling knowledge [8]. Users have knowledge about some practices as well as the NPD team. They share their knowledge in order to make design decisions, refine ideas and to create new knowledge. In Human Centered Design [5] there are two main questions related with the knowledge shared: whose and which knowledge should be privileged. The first question is related with who initiates a project. If end-users initiate a project, their knowledge is leading and their knowledge is moved towards to NPD team [5], [14]. The second question is related with what kind of knowledge should be taken as a starting point of a new innovation project, or taken as a seed for the development of new ideas.

3.2 Distributed Shared Knowledge: Collective Intelligence and Swarm Creativity

Many innovations have emerged not from an individual inventor, or even from a large corporate research laboratory, but from the effort of collaborative thinking and competition of many individuals. This phenomenon is described in [15] and [16] as Collective Intelligence - a combination of individual intelligence [17], [18]. However as a complex adaptative system that is, it's more than the addition of individual intelligence. The Collective Intelligence emerges gradually as the adaptative actors act individually or mutually. In this context, also emerges the concept of the Wisdom of Crowds [19] that states that the aggregation of information in groups, results in solutions, that are often better than could have been made by any single member of the group.

With the advent of Internet and Information Technologies (ICT), and specially the Web 2.0, Collective Intelligence and the Wisdom of Crowds concepts, have their own characteristics emerging on virtual environments, as blogs, social networks, wikis, etc. People are aggregating, sharing, selecting, modifying and tagging information, information flows and knowledge. This originates a mass of shared knowledge. In this context emerge the Collaborative Innovations Networks (COINs) – cyberteams of self motivated people with a collective vision, enabled by Internet and ICT to collaborate in creating a cool trend (an innovation) by sharing ideas, information, knowledge and work [20], [21], [22]. COINs are powered by swarm creativity [20] - the creativity unleashed by groups of humans, which swarm together in the same creative and innovative direction to produce the trends that are most interesting. Detect COINs inside or outside the boundaries of an enterprise is a complex task. In [22], the author states that future successful companies will be those that have skills of **Coolhunting** - the ability of searching and finding COINs which self-organize among intrinsically motivated people around creative ideas; and **Coolfarming** - the ability to getting involved in the actual creation of new trends by seeding, nurturing and cultivating new ideas. This practice of distributed innovation is described in [23] as Communities of Creation, that are grounded in the concept of "*ba*" [24]. It is suggested by the authors, that the diverseness of knowledge required to compete, specially in technology markets, is increasing. Simultaneously, firms are increasingly reducing their knowledge base in an effort to specialize and focus. In those environments firms may become unable to produce knowledge autonomously, so they must co-operate with their business partners and customers to create new knowledge. Knowledge co-creation, and especially knowledge co-creation with customers, is at the heart of knowledge-based NPD [25], [26]. To achieve an efficient co-operation in these turbulent environments, firms must develop and master a set of dynamic capabilities [23], [27], [28].

3.3 Knowledge Management and Dynamic Capabilities

In [26], the authors define dynamic capabilities as the firm's ability to integrate, build, and reconfigure internal and external competences to address rapidly changing environments. This reflects the organization's ability to achieve new and innovative forms of competitive advantage that depends on a set of enabling processes: Learning; Coordination and Integration [28].

Referring to customer knowledge co-creation, in [29] are stated the following set of dynamic capabilities:

- **Absorptive capacity**, *i.e.*, the aptitude to learn from customers;
- **Organizational Sharing capacity**, *i.e.*, the ability to integrate the customers knowledge, and reproduce it internally;
- and **Deployment capacity**, *i.e.*, how a firm acts upon the customer knowledge.

For customers, there are some requirements to fulfill in order to enable their participation in knowledge co-creation [29]:

- They **must speak the same language of the firm** in order to contribute with their knowledge;
- They **must deeply trust in the firm**, *i.e.*, any information they share, may not be used against their own interests;
- They **must be motivated** to take part in the knowledge creation process.

Regarding the co-creation through inter-firm partnerships, in [30] is proposed a model with a set of corresponding capabilities:

- **Absorptive capacity**, *i.e.*, the aptitude to learn from partners;
- **Coordination capacity**, which reflects the ability to sync tasks and resources;
- and **Collective mind,** the integration of contributions, representations and subordination into a collective system.

The concept underlying the dynamic capabilities clearly depends on the learning process and the supporting learning functions. Learning is indeed a critical process, because it has an impact in the ability to acquire new knowledge.

4 Enabling Dynamic Capabilities

Today's technologies, as Web 2.0, enable the realization of the eight essential learning functions that the learning process depends on [31]:

- **Ubiquity**, that provides independent temporal and spatial access to information (*e.g.*: Instant Messaging, Web Mail);
- **Deep Learning**, that fosters high order thinking, takes place when people are stimulated to analyze primary sources and digitalizes artifacts, which evolves navigation, sort, organize, analyze and make graphical representations (*e.g.*: tagging, Web 2.0 mind maps, etc.);

- **Making things Visible and Discussable**, that provides sharing ideas and conceptualization (*e.g.*: digital maps, multimedia elements, etc);
- **Expressing Ourselves**, **Sharing Ideas**, **Building Community**, that provides a social media (*e.g.*: Blogs, wikis and virtual worlds, tagging information and sharing tags);
- **Collaboration**, that helps people to learn and teach together, find experts and plan virtual meets (*e.g.*: wikis, Google docs, podcasts, webinars, VoIP, survey tools);
- **Research**, that can improve information quality and organization (*e.g.*: social bookmarking and tagging tools, citation engines, tag clouds);
- **Project Management**, which helps planning activities, time and resource management (*e.g.*: calendars, to-do lists, etc.);
- and finally **Reflection** and **Iteration**, that occur when someone examines his ideas from all sides and from others viewpoints, especially when supported by tools that support reflection and iterative development (*e.g.*: Blogs and wikis).

An important and classic feature of the Web 2.0 is the openness of their Application Programming Interfaces, which fosters the development of a large number of applications based on those exposed interfaces. A Mashup is a Web application that combines data and services from one or more sources into a single and integrated tool. Users can create mashups themselves, which make mashups as user-driven or user-centered micro-orchestrated [32]. Thus, within a mashup environment, users are provided with the tools to assemble the necessary data and services from various sources and to combine them according to their own ideas. In this context, they gather information and they combine it as needed, having as unique requirement the fulfillment of their own needs, the availability of the required data or service [32]. In fact, users, better than anyone, know what information they need, as well what services are needed and in which configuration. This virtual construction generates knowledge that can be shared with other users, and extended by these, starting thus a process of **collective learning** and **collective intelligence**.

4.1 A Mashup Based Conceptual Model to Enable Dynamic Capabilities

By their characteristics mashups can be used as a Knowledge Management Systems in security uncritical scenarios [32]. Based on the previously presented facts, we can assume that mashup platforms are useful to enable the user involvement in the innovation process. They are user-centered and enable the dynamic capabilities required on co-innovation processes. In this context, we propose a mashup based conceptual model, in order to support co-innovation processes, involving both customers/users and inter-firm partnerships, as illustrates Fig 2. Our concept proposes that Mashups can take place as shared spaces where users can collaborate and express their ideas around a "cool" trend or share their experience. Users can develop communities of interest around innovative ideas, and generate Collaborative Innovation Networks (COINs) powered by swarming creativity and collective intelligence. These shared spaces can be closed or open. If closed, they are strict to the enterprise environment - only opened to enterprise employees' participation. If open, they allow the participation of customers, in the case of customer co-innovation processes, or allow the participation of employees of partner enterprises, in the case of inter-firm partnerships.

As stated before, speaking the same language is a critical factor [29]. To overcome or fulfill this requirement, the proposed model comprises two types of glossaries. On the enterprise side, the internal glossary [33] defines terms and states how concepts are developed and structured internally (see Fig. 2).

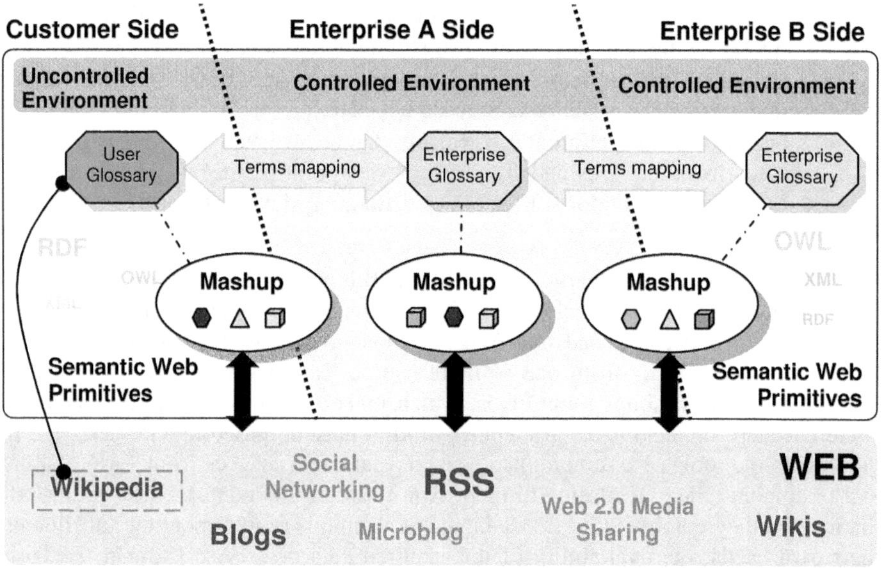

Fig. 2. A mashup based conceptual model to enable dynamic capabilities

This enterprise glossary is extremely controlled, organization specific, and designed through a collaborative approach [34] by the members of the organization. On the user side, the model comprises a shared glossary supported by web dictionaries and encyclopedias of terms (*e.g.* Wikipedia, Wikinary, etc.). Developed interactively by users, aims to ensure a consistent usage of concepts in the description of the shared ideas in the Mashup. Whenever needed, the enterprise internal glossary may be mapped with the user glossary. This map will not change the user's view of the external public glossary, but will offer the NPD team the tools to enable an easier discussion of the concepts being discussed in the public Mashup, by building the bridge between non-technical user language and the enterprise internal technical jargon. The same applies to inter-firm partnerships, where partners are provided with the means to map their own terms into each other.

4.2 Illustrating a New Concept Development Using Mashups

As illustrates Fig. 3, two possible scenarios can happen in the co-innovation processes: the enterprise may foresee a market opportunity and seed a COIN with an idea;

or the users/costumers start themselves the process in order to get some benefit and solve some problem/pain of their own.

Foreseeing a market opportunity, the enterprise NPD team develops a Mashup structure, combining several web resources such as feeds from twitter, blogs, flicker, etc, and shares it with the community of users seeding it with the core idea, starting thus a *coolfarming* process. Users swarm together around the seeded idea, in fact launched across several social networking platforms, sharing their experiences and ideas by combining, re-combining, annotating and integrating different services, information and media sources (videos, RSS feeds, Blogs, Mind Maps, etc.) in the seeded Mashup. During this iterative process users grow the Mashup with their contributions, supported by a tool that uses Wikipedia (for example) as a shared glossary, to ensure a shared meaning for all items and their relationships in the Mashup. This way we enable a semantic connection between all developed concepts (items) in the mashup. The new concepts are developed through an iterative process. In the second scenario, the process is similar, but users start themselves the process. Organizations use the infrastructure for *coolhunting* in order to acquire new product concepts. In both scenarios knowledge transfer and new knowledge creation is made by reflection on the shared information.

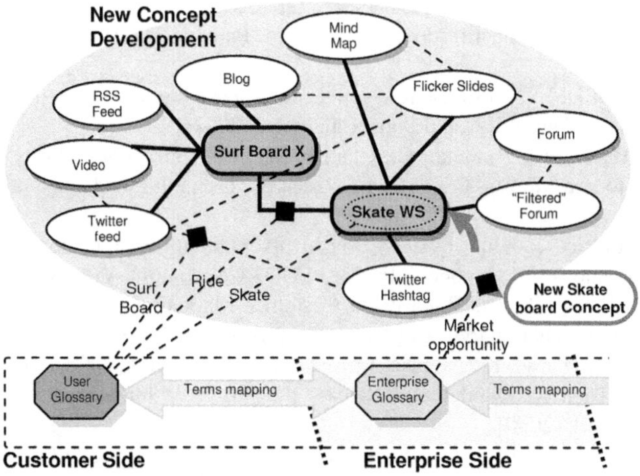

Fig. 3. Example of a new concept development using Mashups

5 Conclusion

In today's globalized world, the markets are increasingly competitive and volatile. In order to respond to market demands, enterprises are looking at innovation as the answer to the development of innovative products/service, and involving users in the innovation processes. The first stage of the innovation process is characterized by strong interactivity and knowledge transfer between users and organizations. To acquire and apply new knowledge (in all its forms), enterprises must master a set of dynamic capabilities, which ones hugely depend on learning ability. The wide and heterogeneous set of the available Web 2.0 based applications enables the realization of the essential learning functions, and the openness of their Application Programming Interfaces, allows that different applications can be extended or mashed up into a single and new application. A major advantage of Mashups is their user-centric characteristic, enabling users to assemble and combine the necessary data and services from various sources, according to their own needs. The conceptual model presented in this paper proposes the use of mashups to enable the referred dynamic capabilities, which ones, seem to be an effective platform to:

- Enable the realization required learning functions and reflection;
- Enable interactivity;
- Promote collective learning and collective intelligence concepts.

The user glossary assures the establishment of a common language between users/customers, and the underlying enterprise glossaries between users/customers and the organization and between inter-firm partners.

References

1. Terraforum, http://inove.terraforum.com
2. Lemos, C.: Inovação na Era do Conhecimento. Parcerias Estratégicas. 8ª edição. CGEE (2000)
3. PDMA: The PDMA Toolbook for New Product Development: effective methods, tools, and techniques. John Wiley and Sons, Chichester (2002)
4. Koen, P., Burkat, R., Ajamian, G., Clamen, A., et al.: Providing Clarity and a Common Language to the "Fuzzy Front End". Research Technology Management 44(2), 46–55 (2001)
5. Steen, M., Lottie, K., Klok, J.: Early user involvement in research and design projects – A review of methods and practices". In: 23rd EGOS Colloquium, Vienna (2007)
6. Griffin, A., Hauser, J.: The Voice of the Customer. Marketing Science 12 (1993)
7. Compact Oxford Dictionary, http://www.askoxford.com
8. Von Krogh, G., Ichijo, K., Nonaka, I.: Enabling Knowledge Creation: How to Unlock the Mystery of Tacit Knowledge and Release the Power of Innovation. Oxford University Press, New York (2000)
9. Elbanna, M.R.: Tacit-Explicit Knowledge: Is It Possible to Separate One from the Other? In: Knowledge about Knowledge, Rutgers - The State University of New Jersey (2008)
10. Nonaka, I., Takeuchi, H.: The knowledge-creating company. Oxford University Press, New York (1995)
11. Stenmark, D.: Leverage tacit organizational knowledge. Journal of Management Information Systems 17, 9–24 (2001)
12. Kogut, B., Zander, U.: Knowledge of the firm. Combinative capabilities and the replication of technology. Organization Science 3, 383–397 (1992)
13. Schön, D.: The reflective practitioner, p. 267. Basic Books, New York (1983)
14. Von Hippel, E.: Democratizing Innovation. MIT Press, Cambridge (2005)
15. Pór, G.: The Quest for Collective Intelligence. In: Gozdz, K. (ed.) Community Building: Renewing Spirit and Learning in Business. New Leaders Press (1995)
16. Nguyen, N.: Inconsistency of Knowledge and Collective Intelligence. Cybernetics and Systems 39, 542–562 (2008)

17. Lévy, P., Bonono, R.: Collective intelligence: Mankind's emerging world in cyberspace. Perseus Books, USA (1999)
18. Russell, P.: The global brain awakens: Our next evolutionary leap. Global Brain Inc., USA (1995)
19. Surowiecki, J.: The wisdom of crowds. Random House, USA (2004)
20. Gloor, P.: Collaborative Innovation Networks – How to Mint Your COINs? In: International Symposium on Collaborative Technologies and Systems Orlando. IEEE, USA (2007)
21. Gloor, P.: Swarm Creativity: Competitive Advantage through Collaborative Innovation Networks. Oxford University Press, USA (2006)
22. Gloor, P., Cooper, S.: Coolhunting: Chasing Down the Next Big Thing. AMACOM (2007)
23. Sawhney, M., Prandelli, E.: Communities of creation: Managing distributed innovation in turbulent markets. California Management Review 42 (2000)
24. Nonaka, I., Konno, N.: The Concept of '*Ba*': Building a Foundation for Knowledge Creation. Management Review 40, 40–54 (1998)
25. Sawhney, M.: Don't just relate – collaborate. MIT Sloan Management Review 43 (2002)
26. Kohlbacher, F.: Knowledge-based New Product Development: fostering innovation through knowledge co-creation. International Journal of Technology Intelligence and Planning (2008)
27. Teece, D., Pisano, G., Shuen, A.: Dynamic Capabilities and Strategic Management. Strategic Management Journal 18(7), 509–553 (1997)
28. Ettlie, J., Pavlou, P.: Technology-Based New Product Development Partnerships. Decision Sciences (2006)
29. Sawhney, M., Prandelli, E.: Beyond Customer Knowledge Management: Customers as Knowledge Co-Creators. In: Malhotra, Y. (ed.) Knowledge Management and Virtual Organizations. Idea Group Publishing, Hershey (2000)
30. Nelson, R., Winter, S.: An evolutionary theory of economic change. Belknap Press of Harvard University Press, Cambridge (1982)
31. Boss, S., Krauss, J.: Power of the Mashup - Combining Essential Learning with New Technology Tools. Learning & Leading with Technology 35(1), 12–17 (2007)
32. Bitzer, S., Ramroth, S., Schumann, M.: Mashups as an Architecture for Knowledge Management Systems. In: Proc. of 42nd Hawaii International Conference on System Sciences. IEEE, Los Alamitos (2009)
33. McGuinness, D.: Ontologies Come of Age. In: Fensel, D. (ed.) in Spinning the Semantic Web: Bringing the World Wide Web to Its Full Potential, pp. 171–191. MIT Press, Cambridge (2002)
34. Holsapple, C., Joshi, K.D.: A Collaborative Approach to Ontology Design. Communications of the ACM 45(2) (2002)

An Analysis of How Enterprise Information Systems Challenge Vested Interests

Albert Boonstra

University of Groningen,
Faculty of Economics and Businees
PO Box 800
9700 AV Groningen, The Netherlands
Albert Boonstra
albert.boonstra@rug.nl

Abstract. The purpose of this paper is to develop and validate a model that demonstrates the influence of ERP implementation on the power and interests of actors in a manufacturing environment. An empirical in-depth longitudinal case study examines how a medium-sized company in the graphics industry implemented an ERP system and how this has affected the interests and power distribution between the manufacturing and sales departments. The case study reveals that the power division among key players at the production-sales interface has been affected by the ERP implementation. These changes influence their attitudes and behaviours as well as the usage of the ERP system. The findings imply that those implementing ERP systems in such environments should, from the outset of the project, identify potential changes in the division of power and seek to reconcile stakeholder interests..

Keywords: Enterprise Resource Planning, implementation, power, interests.

1 Introduction

Enterprise Resource Planning (ERP) systems are software packages designed to integrate, standardise and automate processes within organisations and throughout their value chains. This is achieved by a collection of modules linked through one central database, from which all modules draw, manipulate and update data. The promises of ERP systems are clear and convincing: managers can make better-informed decisions, communication costs are reduced and firms become more integrated and coherent [1] [2] . ERP implementations are, however, also complicated processes because they affect many different stakeholders and social structures within an organisation [3]. This study focuses on how ERP implementations may influence the established relationships among actors within the production and sales units of a business organisation, with a particular focus on power distribution and actor interests. The purpose of this paper, therefore, is to present an empirical in-depth case study that illustrates how a medium-sized graphics company has implemented an ERP system and how this has

J.E. Quintela Varajão et al. (Eds.): CENTERIS 2010, Part II, CCIS 110, pp. 238–248, 2010.

affected the interests and power distribution between the manufacturing and sales departments.

In this paper, case data is analysed by developing and applying a model that focuses on the interdependency between ERP implementation and the power and interests of key actors at the production-sales interface. As will be illustrated in our case study, these actors use their varying amounts of power to influence the implementation process and the way the system will be configured. Additionally, the way the ERP software is ultimately used is also affected by existing power and interest relationships. The shaping of production-sales interfaces through ERP systems is, therefore, in many cases, not only a technical process but also a socially constructed one. In this paper, we aim to unravel some of the underlying mechanisms of this process. In so doing, a gap in the literature, on how ERP influences stakeholder power positions in production-sales networks, is addressed and explored. Hopefully, the resulting more-thorough understanding of the interests and power of these actors will also enable promoters to adopt more effective implementation approaches that will meet expectations and encourage acceptance.

2 Theoretical Perspectives

Over the last fifteen years, many organisations have made significant investments in ERP systems. One of the underlying reasons for implementing integrated information systems is rooted in the belief that the production-sales interface can benefit significantly from such systems. Recent studies indicate that improved communications, an accurate and timely exchange of information as well as stronger inter-functional coordination can be accomplished through ERP systems [4], [5]. Within the vast amount of literature on ERP implementations [6], [7], [8], there is a generally accepted view that a successful ERP implementation requires a careful launch strategy and mutual adaptation among the organisation, the technology and the business processes [9]. This proposition effectively argues that significant new technologies often require adjustments within the organisational structures and day-to-day business processes. The implementation of ERP systems, therefore, is not just a technical process aimed at adopting an information system but also encompasses an organisational change process [10], [11], [12].

This change process can strongly influence social structures and organisational relationships within an organisation [13], [14]. From studies in the field of information systems, there are clear indications that the social and organisational context of the production-sales interface plays a central role in understanding the acceptance of an ERP system [15]. Identifying the stakeholders involved in this process and addressing their perspectives on the ERP system can provide a more thorough understanding of the barriers and enablers regarding the implementation process. In addition, a stakeholder analysis of the production-sales interface can deepen our understanding of the underlying mechanisms that determine the way ERP systems are used.

In this paper, a power and interest perspective is adopted when assessing the influences of production and sales on the implementation and usage of ERP systems. From the literature, it is well known that interests can vary among the stakeholders involved at the production-sales interface [16]. Moreover, in practice, the performance of the production-sales interface is often highly affected by the distribution of power among the stakeholders involved. The implementation of ERP systems can potentially disturb the existing power and interest balance significantly. Enabling sales to gather information on the available production capacities through an integrated information system, for instance, clearly undermines one power source of production stakeholders.

The level of the various stakeholders' individual interests in the ERP system can vary from low to high. A low interest indicates that the individual stakeholders do not believe they have much to gain from the ERP system. This low interest can be caused by increased operational costs, being no longer able to meet the requirements of the business processes one is accountable for, or the system not meeting the individual goals of the stakeholder [3]. The increased transparency of information due to the implementation of an ERP system can, for instance, be a potential threat to certain stakeholders. Further, especially where a certain amount of slack is considered important in order to be able to make appropriate decisions, the attitudes of various stakeholders towards the ERP system can easily conflict. A high degree of interest in the ERP system, on the other hand, reflects situations where the ERP system supports the goals of the stakeholder, or a group of stakeholders. Improved decision-making, being better informed and being supported in the business processes one is responsible for are examples of situations where implementing an ERP system leads to high stakeholder interests [17]. In this study, we define interest as 'perceived interest', indicating that a stakeholder believes they will benefit from using an ERP system, and that this will outweigh the costs.

The attitude and behaviour of stakeholders towards an ERP system not only depends on their interests, but also on the power they possess to influence the implementation and usage of the system. Many definitions exist of power and, in this paper,

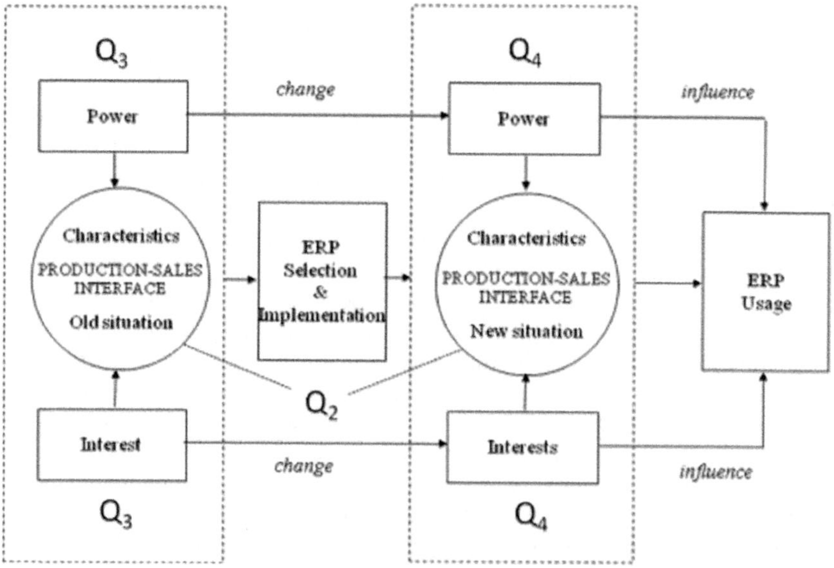

Fig. 1. Model of ERP implementation in a production-sales environment (Q2-Q4 refer to the research questions addressed)

we will define power as the capacity to exert one's will over others in order to realise desired benefits [18]. By taking this perspective in our analyses, power is viewed as a relational construct [19], which means that stakeholders may have a great deal, or very little, power in relation to other relevant stakeholders. Clearly, stakeholders can have different sources of power with which to urge others to implement and use an ERP system in a certain way. Various researchers have, for instance, pointed towards the role of knowledge, the authority and legitimacy of a person and to the available financial or other resources as important sources of power that enable stakeholders to exert their will over others [23]. Some studies in the field of information systems indicate that stakeholders also tend to use these sources to promote their own interests during the process of implementing new technologies [19], and there seems every reason to assume that this also be the case with ERP implementations.

Using the elements and theoretical concepts addressed above, Figure 1 summarises the preceding discussion in a model that depicts, on an aggregated level, the potential influence of the power and interests of stakeholders engaged at the production-sales interface in ERP implementations.

3 Methodology

In our research, we used a qualitative method, with a single case being studied, as this was appropriate for the issues under discussion [20], [21]. The research questions were exploratory in nature, intended to identify the interests and power of actors in terms of the ERP system. Further, the central issues of our research were rather unclear, and needed to be studied in their natural setting if one was to understand the nature and complexity of the subject and its context [22]. In our study, the unit of analysis is the ERP implementation process and its effects on the power and interest positions of actors at the production-sales interface. To ensure construct validity, several sources of evidence were used including semi-structured interviews, surveys, written reports, letters, observations and minutes from committee meetings. We sought internal validity by looking for patterns, dominant themes and explanations in the material, and tried to avoid bias by asking respondents to comment on our interpretations. External validity was sought by interviewing people from various departments.

Initial access to the company was negotiated in 2006, after which we interviewed 11 stakeholders who were close to the production-sales interface over three rounds. This resulted in 36 interviews, each of two hours. Three rounds (in some cases four rounds) were necessary to assess changes in the division of power and interests. All of the interviewees had the opportunity to react to transcripts of their interviews and confirmed that the facts were accurately documented. We also asked the interviewees to complete a survey that was directed at assessing the power and interests of themselves and others before, during and after implementation. The respondents were asked to express their assessments using a five-point Likert scale. These surveys were completed in the presence of the researcher in order to promote a high response rate and to enable questions to be answered.

4 Case Description

The empirical part of the research was conducted in a medium-sized company operating in a niche market for specialised graphical products. The enterprise consists of a publishing unit (approx. 30 employees) and a printing unit (approx. 70 employees). The printing unit specialises in the printing and completion of tailor-made books, brochures and other graphical products. Every year, about 300 customer- specific printing and publishing projects, with an average run of 10,000 units, are completed. Given the nature of customer-specific orders, almost no inventory is held. In recent years, the company has experienced strong growth, resulting in a doubling of the net profits over five years. To manage this growth, the company was forced to reorganise many of its procedures and business processes during the period 2005-2007.

In 2006-2007, the management team, consisting of a director, two business unit managers and a controller, decided to implement an ERP system. This system had to replace a legacy system that supported information provision in various functional departments. The strong growth of the company and the restructuring of the company into two business units were the main reasons for wanting to improve management information and decision-making. Management believed that an ERP system would help the company to make its business processes more formalised and cost-effective. Further, there was a strong conviction that a corporate-wide IT solution would strengthen information provision and planning. The ERP system would include business processes and information exchange at the production-sales interface.

This section addresses the first and second research questions, which are directed at identifying key players, the planning and information exchange both before and after ERP implementation.

Question 1 Who were the active players at the production-sales interface?
At the production-sales interface, various parties play a role in the acceptance and processing of customers' orders. Elven employees were identified as core figures in this interface, spread among the Board of Directors (2) and the Sales (4), Printing (3) and Finance departments (2).

The *director* identified is responsible for the Sales Unit, calculating offers, and represents the company to important customers and at sales events. *Sales representatives* maintain active contacts with customers. The customer network can be easily overseen due to the company's relatively small niche market. The Sales Unit also employs a junior to calculate offers. In recent years, this employee had developed a new product configurator and, for this reason, he was made a member of the ERP project group. The *Printing Unit* is responsible for producing and delivering the customer orders. Within this unit, the production manager is responsible for all the operations necessary to fulfil order requirements. Finally, the *Finance Department* also has a major role in the process of implementing the ERP system. The Finance Department employs four people but since the controller was a very experienced individual, who had previously been responsible for ERP implementations in other companies, he was generally considered to be the most influential.

Question 2 How was planning and information organised before and after ERP?
Before the ERP implementation, Sales Unit specialists discussed specifications with customers and then made a calculation resulting in an offer. To make these offers, the

company used two stand-alone systems; a Customer Relationship Management (CRM) application and a Calculation Management System. Given the variation in and the specific requirements of customer orders, the making of offers was a complicated activity. In particular, the in-house developed Calculation Management System was difficult to understand and fairly opaque. Further, it was impossible to derive lists of material requirements from this system. Once a project number had been attached to a project, the production manager looked for a comparable project from the past and modified this to fit the new project. From these project data, purchase and production orders were derived. However, much of this historical data included errors that were never corrected. Data on delivery times were also not recorded or used in planning new projects. This meant that critical paths could not be accurately calculated and, instead, had to be roughly estimated by the production manager. In many cases, these estimations led to delays in large and complicated projects. The managing directors also lacked information on available production volumes and likely delivery times. They hoped that the new ERP system would provide them with this information, enabling them to become more customer-focused and cost-effective.

After the ERP implementation, the system included almost all the popular business functions and these were complemented with some tailor-made modules. The Production Unit makes use of the Customer, Supplier, Inventory management, Production and Shop Floor Control modules. On top of this, parts of the Finance and HRM modules are used within the organisation. However, the CRM module of the new ERP system is not yet applied by the Production Unit, and the Sales Unit still uses the stand-alone CRM system. Sales claim that they lack the time to organise, become conversant with and implement this module. Additionally, it was concluded that the inclusion of the Product Configurator would be a very complicated process due to the huge variation in potential products. After several meetings, it was decided that the ERP system's Product Configurator would only be used by Sales in a limited mode, and only for transferring the project specifications of new orders to the ERP system. The fully integrated use of this module was seen as not feasible. Consequently, the original spreadsheets for order calculation are still in use and, today, two order calculation systems coexist. The Production Unit refused to implement the Material and Capacity Planning modules which makes it impossible to use the ERP system to calculate delivery times or to take current purchasing, production orders and planned capacities into account. Delivery times provided by Sales to customers are still based on rough and subjective estimates. In the new situation, the Production Unit has become fully dependent on product specifications generated by the Product Configurator. Serious operational problems have arisen because this configurator is not fully aligned with the new ERP system.

5 Case Analysis

In this section, we address the third, fourth and fifth questions, which are directed at the relative power and interest positions of the Production and Sales Units before and after implementation, and on how these were affected by the implementation and use of the ERP system.

Question 3 What were power and interest positions before and after the ERP implementation?

Power positions surrounding the production-sales interface are summarised in Table 1. In this table, the division of power is looked at from two perspectives: firstly in terms of the hierarchical power of stakeholders, and secondly in terms of their functional role. The table shows the assessment of where the power lies both before and after ERP implementation. In addition to the overall averages and standard deviations, the assessments made by the various subgroups of where the power lies are shown.

If we compare the results from before and after the ERP implementation, we observe that the relative power of the Directors have remained the same (3.6), while the power of the management team has slightly decreased from 4.5 to 4.4. The relative power of the other stakeholders increased from 2.2 to 2.8. Interview data reveal that the increase for these scores are probably attributable to the high degree of involvement of this group of stakeholders during the selection and implementation of the ERP system. During the interviews some of the respondents noticed that this has led to greater expertise with the new ERP system and appreciation for their efforts. Research findings also show that the power of the Sales Department has increased from 2.0 to 2.7. It is also striking that the Directors questioned think that 'other stakeholders' have gained much more power (2.7 → 3.7) through the ERP system. A more extensive analysis of the interview data shows that this increase is mainly due to a large change in the evaluation of the assistant controller's power. The Managing Director also assessed the power of the Sales Department to have increased from 2.0 to 3.5.

Table 1. Assessment of power-positions, before and after the ERP implementation

					Assessment made by					
Hierarchical classification	**average**		**deviation**		**Directors**		**MT**		**Others**	
	before	after	before	after	before	after	before	after	before	after
Directors	**3.6**	**3.6**	0.92	1.03	2.0	2.0	3.7	3.3	3.9	4.0
Management Team	**4.5**	**4.4**	0.62	0.41	4.0	4.3	5.0	4.3	4.3	4.4
Others	**2.2**	**2.8**	0.49	0.46	2.1	3.3	1.9	2.3	2.4	2.9

					Assessment made by							
Functional classification	**average**		**deviation**		**Sales**		**Production**		**Directors**		**Others**	
	before	after	before	after	before	after	before	after	before	after	before	na
Sales	**2.0**	**2.7**	0.74	0.72	2.8	3.3	1.2	1.8	2.0	3.5	1.8	2.4
Production	**3.2**	**3.4**	0.52	0.42	3.4	3.5	3.2	3.4	3.7	3.7	2.9	3.1
Directors	**3.6**	**3.6**	0.92	1.03	4.5	4.8	3.0	3.0	2.0	2.0	3.7	3.3
Others	**3.7**	**3.9**	0.59	0.42	3.9	4.3	3.7	4.0	2.7	3.7	3.9	3.4

Table 2 shows that the perceived interests of the Directors have hardly changed, with the average score slipping only slightly from 3.6 to 3.5, although the various stakeholders did have distinct assessments. The directors' representative thought that their strong interest in the ERP had increased further during the implementation (from 4.0 to 5.0), whereas the other subgroups had a different view on this, and thought that the interest of the directors had decreased. The average assessment of the interest of the management team with respect to the ERP system saw a sharp increase, from 3.9 to 4.6, with all three subgroups agreeing on an increase. This group of stakeholders felt that there was no alternative to the new ERP, which explains their strong interest in the proper functioning of the system. Similarly, all three subgroups thought the interest of the "other stakeholders" had increased (on average from 2.4 to 3.0).

Table 2. Assessment of interest positions, before and after the ER implementation

						Assessment made by					
	Hierarchical classification	average		deviation		Directors		MT		others	
		before	after	before	after	before	after	before	after	before	after
of	Directors	**3.6**	**3.5**	1.03	1.04	4.0	5.0	3.0	2.7	3.9	3.7
	Management Team	**3.9**	**4.6**	0.47	0.53	3.3	5.0	4.2	4.8	3.9	4.5
	Others	**2.4**	**3.0**	0.47	0.48	2.3	2.9	1.9	3.0	2.6	3.1

						Assessment made by							
	Functional classification	average		deviation		Sales		Production		Directors		others	
		before	after	before	after	before	after	before	after	before	after	before	after
of	Sales	**1.9**	**2.4**	0.60	0.57	2.0	2.1	2.0	3.0	2.0	2.3	1.7	2.4
	Production	**2.5**	**4.0**	0.40	0.60	2.9	4.1	2.6	4.4	2.0	3.7	2.2	3.7
	Directors	**3.6**	**3.5**	1.03	1.04	3.8	4.0	3.7	3.0	4.0	5.0	3.3	3.0
	Others	**4.3**	**4.5**	0.60	0.65	4.4	4.6	4.0	4.4	4.0	5.0	4.1	4.1

Turning to the assessment by function, before implementation, production had a slightly higher interest in the new system (2.5) than sales (1.9) although, clearly, neither unit was viewed as having a great interest in the ERP system. Interview data show that the Production Department's low interest in the system before its implementation can be explained by their appreciation of the existing information systems: they did not foresee many advantages with the new system. Production also enjoyed the power of expertise in the old system, which would become worthless under the ERP system. Their dependency on the new system after the implementation process explains their increased interest in it (2.5 → 4.0 on average). It is notable that the Sales Department's own estimate of their interest in the ERP system post-implementation is the lowest (2.1) of all the subgroups. Interview data reveal that this low interest is related to the fact that they still use their old stand-alone CRM applications and calculation spreadsheets.

Question 4 How did the ERP implementation affect the power and interests of the stakeholders?

The low involvement and commitment of the Sales Department is remarkable. The implementation of the new CRM module effectively failed to take off because this application belonged to the sales domain, and the sales personnel were unwilling to give up their old system and make their working procedures visible to others. The sales director had decided that the Sales Department would be represented in the ERP project team by two young employees with little expertise and power. A close analysis of the project documents as well the interview data show that this contributed strongly to the under achievement in terms of implementation objectives. Moreover, the sales personnel did not believe that the new system would give them any advantages over the existing set of systems (CRM and the project calculation system). They also tended to think that the new ERP system would threaten their traditional power basis. Production, on the other hand, felt that it was in their interests to realise a full implementation of the ERP system. Their interest increased further when their old system was no longer available. Production became highly dependent on the new system and on the data from the new product configurator. The old system had taken production data from previous projects and modified these to produce a new project. This often error-strewn procedure had been replaced by a new ERP module. Production had always been relatively powerful, and its power increased through the implementation of the ERP system. This power could be appropriated to force the Sales Department to use the new product configurator module. However, since Sales also maintain their old system, they now duplicate some activities.

Both the directors and the sales people had desired greater insight into delivery times and production capacities. For this to be achieved, the material planning and capacity modules needed to be implemented. Due to the low interest of the Production Department at the start of the project, their employees adopted a withholding attitude towards this idea. With the resulting slow implementation of these modules, the insertion of production parameters into the new system was also slow, and this resulted in insufficient time to properly design the material planning and capacity modules. The project group consequently decided to postpone the implementation of both modules. It is clear that the Production Department sees little value in greater transparency of available production capacity because they perceive this as a threat to their power.

The power and interest positions of the other stakeholders involved in the process (controller, assistant controller and business unit manager) have hardly changed. The late implementation of the working-hours registration module increased the workload of the Finance Department in calculating and paying salaries. The late implementation of the product configurator meant it was necessary to enter project data manually, and this led to errors that had to be corrected at a later stage.

6 Discussion and Conclusions

This paper confirms the value of taking account of stakeholders' power, interests and expectations in the context of ERP implementation at the production-sales interface. The study demonstrates that ERP implementations tend to challenge vested interests and often lead to the explicit display of the opposing views held by the various players. ERP systems are designed to integrate functions and to standardise business processes which were previously dispersed and diverse. This affects the power and interest positions of people at production–sales interfaces, and this has repercussions for the implementation and use of the system. The study shows that actors assess the implementation process on a continuous basis based on the extent to which the system is promoting their interests. This assessment affects attitudes and behaviours towards the system. Full use, partial use, non-use and outright resistance are all potential behaviours that are determined by the power and interest attributes of the various actors. If those who oppose the ERP system apply whatever power they have, this will make the implementation process more difficult and complex to manage. As such, ERP implementations are not only technically sophisticated projects; they are also socially constructed change processes.

This conclusion is clearly illustrated by our case data. On close examination of the implementation process, it was clear that stakeholders with a low interest in the new ERP system demonstrated resistive behaviours. In our case, the Sales Department had little interest and a low level of power, and this led to hidden resistance and very few initiatives to support the implementation process. Powerful players with a low interest in the system, such as the Production Department, were able to restrain the implementation process. Only once a definite decision to implement the ERP system and abandon the old systems had been taken, did the interest of production increase and priorities with regard to the configuration of the ERP system set. These observations also illustrate that a dependence on the performance of a new ERP system increases the interest of the parties involved. As long as alternative systems are in place, powerful parties with little interest in the new system can obstruct and continue to use alternative systems. Consequently, implementers and project managers should consider carefully the transition process to a new ERP system.

References

1. Paré, G., Sikotte, C.: Information technology sophistication in health care: an instrument validation study among Canadian hospitals. International Journal of Medical Informatics 63(2), 205–223 (2001)
2. Fowler, M., Gilfillan, R.: A Framework for Stakeholder Integration in Higher Education Information Systems Projects. Technology Analysis & Strategic Management 15(4), 467–489 (2003)
3. Boonstra, A., de Vries, J.: Analyzing inter-organizational information systems from a power and interest perspective. International Journal of Information Management 25(6), 485–501 (2005)
4. Dezdar, S., Sulaiman, A.: Successful enterprise resource planning implementation: taxonomy of critical factors. Industrial Management+Data Systems 109(8), 1037–1052 (2009)
5. Klaus, H., Rosemann, M., Gable, G.G.: What is ERP. Information Systems Frontiers 2(2), 141–162 (2000)
6. Shepherd, C., Clegg, C., Stride, C.: Opening the black box: A multi-method analysis of an enterprise resource planning implementation. Journal of Information Technology 24(1), 81–102 (2009)
7. Markus, M.L., Axline, S., Petrie, D., Tanis, C.: Learning from adopters experiences with ERP: problems encountered and success achieved. Journal of Information Technology 15(4), 245–265 (2000a)
8. Jacobs, F.R., Bendoly, E.: Enterprise resource planning: developments and directions for operations management research. European Journal of Operational Research 146(2), 233–240 (2003)
9. Bozarth, C.: ERP implementation efforts at three firms: Integrating lessons from the SISP and IT-enabled change literature. International Journal of Operations & Production Management 26(11), 1223–1239 (2006)
10. Palanisamy, R.: Organizational culture and knowledge management in ERP implementation: An empirical study. Journal of Computer Information Systems 48(2), 100–120 (2008)
11. Boonstra, A., Govers, M.: Understanding ERP system implementation in a hospital by analysing stakeholders. New Technology Work & Employment 24(2), 177–193 (2009)

12. Dery, K., Hall, R., Wailes, N.: ERPs as technologies-in-practice: social construction, materiality and the role of organisational factors. New Technology, Work & Employment 21(3), 229–241 (2006)
13. Davenport, T.H.: Putting the Enterprise into the Enterprise System. Harvard Business Review 76(4), 121–132 (1998)
14. Markus, M.L., Tanis, C.: Multisite ERP implementations. Communications of the ACM 43(4), 42–26 (2000b)
15. Pan, G.S.C., Flynn, D.: Information systems project abandonment: a case of political influence by the stakeholders. Technology Analysis and Strategic Management 15(4), 457–466 (2003)
16. Konijnendijk, P.A.: Coordination of Production and Sales. Maklu, Antwerpen (1992)
17. Bendoly, E., Soni, A., Venkataramanan, M.A.: Value chain resource planning: adding value with systems beyond the enterprise. Business Horizons 47(2), 79–86 (2004)
18. Buchanan, D., Badham, R.: Power Politics and Organizational Change, Winning the Turf Game. Sage, London (2004)
19. French, J., Raven, B.: The bases of social power. In: Cartwright, D. (ed.) Studies in Social Power, Ann Arbor, MI, Institute for Social Research (1958)
20. Yin, R.K.: Case study research. Applied Social Research Methods Series Sage Publications, Thousand Oaks, CA (1994)
21. Dubé, L., Paré, G.: Rigor in information systems positivist case research current practicies, trends and recommendations. MIS Quarterly 27(4), 536–597 (2003)
22. Benbasat, I., Goldstein, D.K., Mead, M.: The case research strategy in studies of information systems. MIS Quarterly 11(3), 369–386 (1987)
23. Bingi, P., Sharma, M.K., Godla, J.K.: Critical issues affecting an ERP implementation. Information Systems Management 16(3), 7–14 (1999)

Qualification and Certification of Research-Entrepreneur Skills Using the ECQA Platform

Anca Draghici[1], George Draghici[1], Monica Izvercianu[1], Andreas Riel[2], Serge Tichkiewitch[3], and Richard Messnarz[4]

[1] "Politehnica" University of Timisoara, Management Faculty,14 Remus str., 300191 Timisoara, Romania
[2] G-SCOP Laboratory, Grenoble University of Technology, 46 Avenue Felix Viallet, 38031 Grenoble, France
[3] EMIRAcle, 62 Rue du Trone, B-1050 Brussels, Belgium
[4] ISCN Ltd., Coordination Office, Florence House, Bray, Co, Wicklow, Ireland
{adraghici,gdraghici}@eng.upt.ro, monica.izvercianu@mpt.upt.ro, {andreas.riel,serge.tichkiewitch}@inpg.fr, rmess@iscn.com

Abstract. The paper presents a specific approach for defining a new job role so call Research-Entrepreneur that have to be trained and certified at the European level. These processes are supported by an e-learning platform developed by the European Certification and Qualification Association in the last ten years. After a brief description of the Research-Entrepreneur skill card definition there are presented the skills acquisition within the platform, the methodology of the skill sets provision and the qualification and certification procedures. Also, the link with a national e-learning platform in the same field is described.

Keywords: Entrepreneurship, Skill Card, Competencies, e-Learning, Platform.

1 Introduction

The European Commission (EC) defines "Entrepreneurship" as 'the mind set and process (needed) to create and develop economic activity by blending risk-taking, creativity and/or innovation with sound management, within a new or an existing organization [5]. Analyzing the world map of high-expectations entrepreneurship there is still an American dream in USA – the rate of high-expectation entrepreneurship in the general population is very high in North America, 15 in every 1,000 US adults; there is a new ambition capital of the world for China – there are more high-expectation entrepreneurs that any other country, with 17 in every 1,000 adults rate; Europe has limited levels of high-expectation entrepreneurship – just 4 in every 1,000 European adults are entrepreneurs with high-growth expectation – the lowest proportion of all world regions [13], [1]. The EC recognized the problem and made entrepreneurship one of the main objectives of the Lisbon agenda in 2000. Responding to this, EC launched a series of initiatives aimed at fostering support for small businesses in Europe. In January 2003, it adopted a "Green Paper on Entrepreneurship in Europe" to stimulate the debate amongst policy makers, businesses, representative organizations and experts on how entrepreneurship can be better promoted in Europe.

J.E. Quintela Varajão et al. (Eds.): CENTERIS 2010, Part II, CCIS 110, pp. 249–258, 2010.

This document set out to find answers to two fundamental issues: 'How to produce more entrepreneurs?' and 'How to get more firms to grow?' [3], [9].

On the other hand the EC report in 2008, regarding entrepreneurship teaching was that it is not yet sufficiently integrated in higher education institutions' curricula. Available data show that the majority of entrepreneurship courses are offered in business and economic studies. The diffusion of entrepreneurship is particularly weak in some of the Member States that joined the European Union (EU) in and after 2004. However, it is questionable whether business schools are the most appropriate place to teach entrepreneurship: innovative and viable business ideas are more likely to arise from technical, scientific and creative studies. In this context, the challenge is to build inter-disciplinary approaches, making entrepreneurship education accessible to all students specialization curricula, creating teams for the development and exploitation of business ideas, mixing students from economic and business studies with students from other faculties and with different backgrounds(by interdisciplinary training modules or courses) [4].

In the context of this paper, human resources training regarding their entrepreneurship competencies development have to be amplifying in the high education period and it has to continue with training during all professional life (as vocational training) with the support of the dedicated lifelong learning programs [7]. At higher education level, the primary purpose of entrepreneurship education should be to develop entrepreneurial capacities and mindsets. The entrepreneurship education programs can have different objectives, such as: (1) developing entrepreneurial drive among students (raising awareness and motivation); (2) training students in the skills they need to set-up a business and manage its growth; (3) developing the entrepreneurial ability to identify and exploit opportunities [2], [6], [12].

The paper debates: (a) the research-entrepreneur skill card as a basis of the training program development; (b) the qualification and certification system based on the European Certification and Qualification Association's (ECQA) IT platform and, (c) a case study given by a designed IT platform for entrepreneurship education at Politehnica University of Timisoara Romania and its link to ECQA platform.

2 Research-Entrepreneur Skills

The research motivation belongs to the ResEUr project development [10]. The proposed project aims at delivering to innovative researchers the qualification to determine if their work and/or their ideas have a market potential, as well as to be able to create a commercial interest for what they are doing. The results envisaged are a skill set which clearly describes the skills required for a researcher to turn his ideas into marketable products, and thus to be able to create and develop a sustainable enterprise. For all the skill elements training material will be provided in several languages and in an e-learning environment. A pool of test questions will be defined, which provides the basis for the certification of students. All these elements will be verified with a number of students in the context of initial trainings and certifications.

The qualification and certification of Research-Entrepreneur addresses itself at experienced researchers (young researchers, PhD students), master students who want to complement and/or certify their advanced entrepreneurial skills. The target group students typically have availability and abilities for develop an entrepreneurship behavior (creativity, innovative initiatives etc.). The certificate, however, is supposed to certify the target group of student's capabilities as future entrepreneurs and/or to develop their entrepreneurial behavior. One of the biggest challenges is to conceive a training program that covers the complete skills set that better satisfy the target group specific needs. As a preliminary research, each partner involved in the ResEUr project, has identify his target group and its specific needs (a number of unstructured interview were developed with potential students and also, with other companies and organizations that deliver training programs for entrepreneurs; preliminary observation of the local market specificity). Based on the collected information, during some virtual project meeting there have been established the working procedure and then it has been implemented for the development of the skill card.

Figure 1 shows a knowledge map of the skill set which provides the basis of our research and development activities. It is the result of an initial consolidation of our experiences in research, education, as well as in collaboration with industrial partners, and other business organizations (e.g. Chamber of Commerce, students' organizations, clusters in the business environment etc.). Although we consider this skill set already stable, it is supposed to evolve in the implementation stage of the project as we involve experts from different research sectors, and get the feedback from partners in industry (from employees of the research and development departments) and academia and from students of initial training seminars. The skill card is represented by a map (using the MindManager software) with the main branches consists of the skill units and the second branches that are the correspondent skill elements. Under each skill unit and element there are indicated: the specific code, the partner acronym that will develop the correspondent training material, and the estimated duration of the training. The third braches are allocated to the performance criteria of each element (that are in direct relation with the questions that shall be settled for the examination process related to the certification of the job role). This skill card representation allowed an optimal visualization of the whole developed work and also, the harmonization and integration of the partners for attending the project objectives. The skill set map was a good tool of communication between the partners and the IT specialists involved in the project, too. Each skill unit is described in the following: (1) **understanding entrepreneurship** unit provides highly condensed and concise information about key issues of entrepreneurship, which are typically taught in seminars which are currently offered by various institutions. The unit, however, does not want to replace such seminars and courses, but it rather seeks to give the student a convenient means of reflexion on whether she/he needs formation in the respective competence areas, and where she/he can find complementary courses; (2) **shaping ideas** unit deals with key skills that are required to leverage brilliant ideas, starting from creating an innovative mindset in students' heads, passing via methods for structuring ideas, and ending by discussing methods and best practices for presenting ideas; (3) **innovation transfer** focuses on issues concerned with the transfer of innovation from the academic environment to the competitive market. These issues are known to represent key success factors of entrepreneurship in the academic domain; (4) **knowledge networking** is considered the core competence area for entrepreneurs. Networking knowledge from several different domains and sectors can create the decisive competitive advantage of modern and future-oriented enterprises; (5) **empowerment by**

learning organization environments puts the concept of the Learning Organization in the middle of the successful enterprise creation and of an entrepreneurial behavior; (6) **general subjects** unit is dedicated to some specific subjects (skill elements definition) as: use of Web 2.0; open innovation; risk consideration and mitigation.

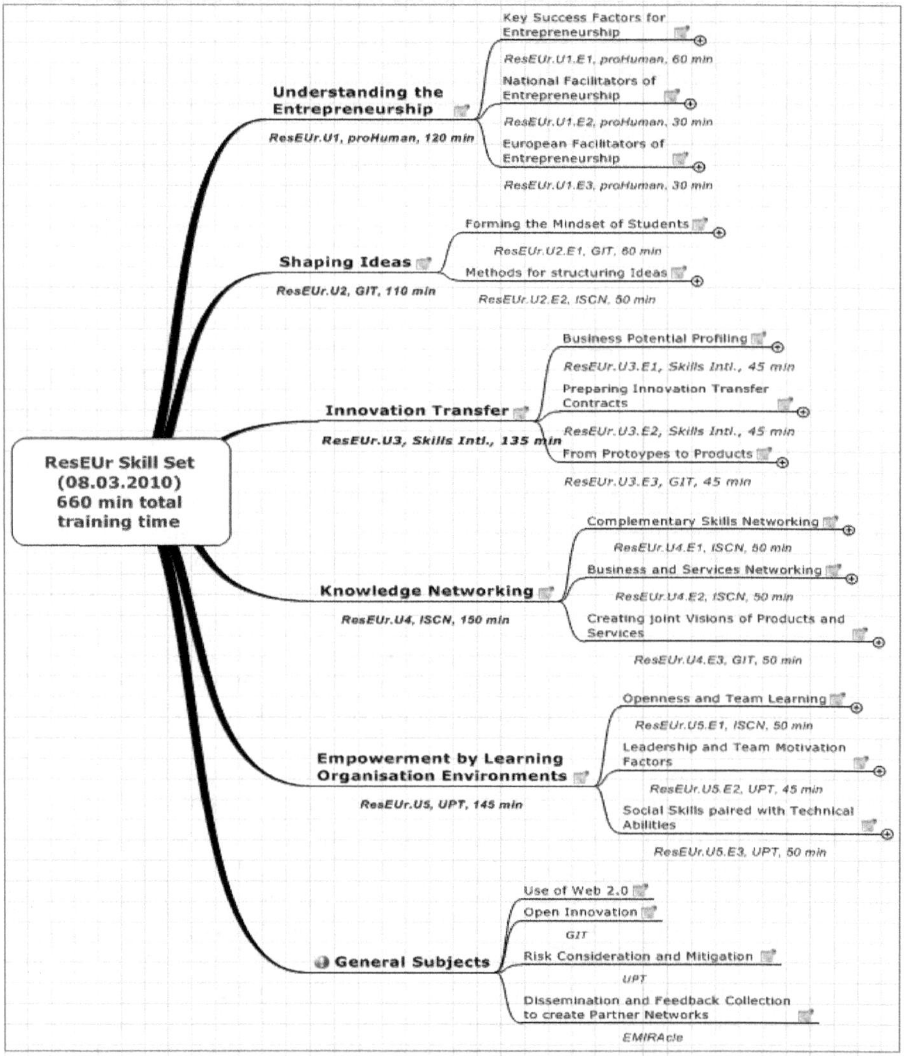

Fig. 1. The ResEUr Skill Set Map

With this brief overview about the skills units and the correspondent skill elements we have define the training materials domains. Also, the performance criteria associated with each skill element shows the content of the training materials. Taking into consideration the suggested structure of the skill card it is easy to imagine the structure of the e-learning platform. The aim of or following approach is to explain the qualification and certification IT system.

3 Qualification and Certification System with the Support of the ECQA Platform

This chapter gives an overview of the system and the platform proposed and implemented by the ECQA [7]. One of the major aims of this research is to show that both their system and their platform are very well suited to specify, implement and roll out the qualification and certification of modern and very required (on the market) job roles in Research-Entrepreneur.

3.1 Skills Acquisition with the ECQA Platform: Skill Sets Provision

The ECQA has set up a partnership of experienced partners in 18 European countries to create a pool of knowledge for specific professions. This pool can be extended to further professions. All the professions that have been configured in this system up to now, are based in the information and communication technology (ICT) area, and are thus closely related to Software Development. As integrated product development processes are increasingly related and/or linked to software development, new job roles from the entrepreneurial domain will profit from this sound basis [8].

Figure 2 gives an overview of the uncomplicated but efficient skill acquisition process supported by the ECQA platform: If there is a need, a person can attend a course for a specific job role online through an advanced learning infrastructure as described in the following. The student starts with a self assessment against the skills. Then she/he can sign into an online course. Here she/he is guided by a tutor and does a homework which is corrected by the tutor. Finally, the homework and the real work done in her/his project are sufficient to demonstrate the skills.

The learning platform is based on the web based public domain learning management system Moodle (www.moodle.com). The assessment process is supported by the so-called Capability Adviser, which is a web based assessment portal system with a defined database interface to connect the systems. Network Quality Assurance NQA is a web based team working tool which was developed in the previous project EU IST 2000 28162. So far many professions have been configuring in the platform (see www.eu-certificates.org).

The ECQA platform of knowledge is enhanced on an annual basis. Existing skills sets are being reworked and new skills sets are added. Joint knowledge is being configured in form of a job role with standard content structures like skills set, syllabus, learning materials and online configuration, as well as sets of test questions.

So-called Job Role Committees decide upon the content for a specific skills set. These committees are composed of academics and industrialists. The job role committee for the Innovation Manager, for instance, created a skills set of an innovation manager together with a set of online courses etc. People can register from their work places [7], [8].

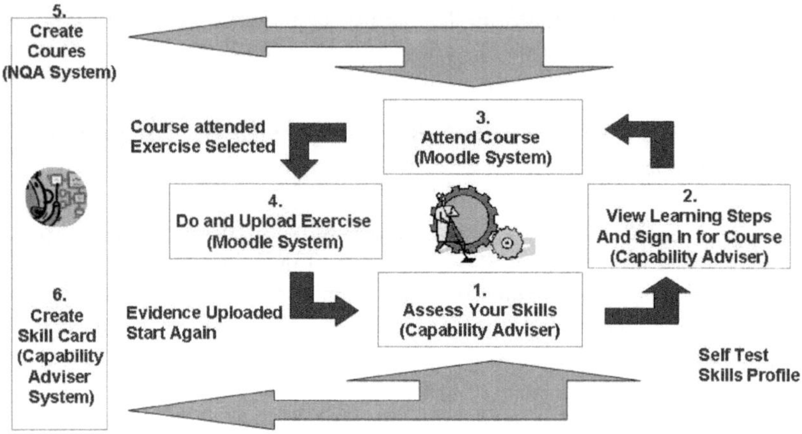

Fig. 2. Integrated European Skills Acquisition System

3.2 The Qualification and Certification Procedure

Nowadays and according to the Bologna Process, it is very important that training courses are internationally recognized and those successful course attendees receive certificates that are valid for all European countries. The EU supported the establishment of the European Qualification Network (EQN), from which the ECQA has evolved, with exactly this target in mind. This has resulted in a pool of professions in which a high level of European comparability has been achieved by a Europe wide agreed syllabus and skills set, a European test questions pool and European exam (computer automated by portals) systems, a common set of certificate levels and a common process to issue certificates [7], [8], [11].

Quality criteria to accept new job roles in the ECQA, to accredit training organizations and certify trainers, as well as to certify attendees have been developed. The existing skills assessment portals (already used by more than 5000 students in different learning initiatives) are extended to cover the new requirements of the ISO 17024 (General Requirements for Bodies operating Certification of Persons) standard. Among the international certification organizations that provide ECQA - compliant certification is the ISQI (International Software Quality Institute, www.isqi.org).

3.3 The Case of a National Platform for Entrepreneurship e-Learning

Considering the ECQA platform structure and development, and its specific use for European certification, the Romanian researchers (from Politehnica University of Timisoara) have planed to develop a dedicated e-learning platform for long life learning in the field of entrepreneurship based on the financial support of some programs based on structural found available. The main idea was to define an extended architecture that can cover various needs of the market in the field of entrepreneurship and that include the training program developed under the define job role for Research-Entrepreneurs. For attending this objective, a partnership with SIVECO Romania Company (www.siveco.ro) was established with the main purpose of having professional assistance for building an e-learning platform in the Management Faculty. Learning nowadays is a continuous and active process performed with a specified goal and applied to real life situations in relation with the economic and industrial environment needs, evolution/dynamics. The real education market, governed by rules identical to any other services market, has evolved. Because of this, many Romanian high prestigious academic institutions are prone to loosing some of their students in favour of other distance–located institutions, but better anchored in the education market. Also, the need for continuous learning processes has became a reality for many employees and this represent an attractive source of extra-financed the education processes of the public universities.

This were the main arguments of the academic staff of the Management Faculty to take the challenge and applies new learning techniques, with the aid of an integrated e–learning platform in the field of entrepreneurship competencies development. It represents an impressive development of the High School Educational Assistant – AEL (www.advancedelearning.com), the e–learning platform that is planed to be developed by SIVECO Romania S.A., running in over 1000 schools in Romania. Already familiar with AEL from their high school days, most students are able to take rapidly full advantage of ITC assisted education. The common structure of AEL and e-learning platform, as well as the reasonable costs involved in adapting and running such a platform, played an important part in starting this joint project and avoiding purchasing a commercial product.

The base knowledge in the system is supported by most common content types: html, pdf, rtf, Flash, ActiveX, Java applets, images, movies, sound, and MS Office documents. General content creation and editing for html files, math formula, and graphics are straightforward achieved by specific built-in editors. Moreover, powerful tests (single and multiple choice answers, items association or ordering, true/false expressions, variant evaluation, intermediate variants) can be created and managed. Import/export functions allow content packages with miscellaneous media files, archives/folders of resources to be easily redistributed.

The e-learning platform is designed according to the basic Sharable Content Object Reference Model (SCORM) requirements. SCORM is a collection of standards and specifications for web-based e-learning. It defines communications between client side content and a host system called the run-time environment (commonly a function of a learning management system). SCORM also, defines how content may be packaged into a transferable ZIP file. SCORM compliant renderer and editor allows creation of completely new courses or personalized courses from existing components. The system has other facilities according to SCORM: content annotation (with access privileges), hierarchical navigation (tree-navigation or breadcrumb-navigation), filtering and searching, full-text search in text, html, flash animations, pdf documents etc.

The main features of the system are:

Interactivity: this is one of the most important characteristics, ensuring efficient usage of the ITC resources by taking advantages of the system specific functions. Interactivity is assured by the content delivery-broadcast server which allows content and tests to be displayed simultaneously on all stations in the virtual classroom or to individual students. The user-system interface, including the menus and the design, is adapted to user role, according to profile and access privileges.

Management of educational process: this feature allows the e–learning system to include various technological and pedagogical functions (Figure 3): Web links, search engines, synchronous and asynchronous communication, course announcement areas, learner posting areas, learner records and interactions tracking or course management. They help administrating the learning process by bringing in automation, and offer a new flexible way of handling data to trainees, similar to how it helps learners handle their learning activity. The system enables asynchronous (self-paced) study with courses supervised by a tutor, discussion forums associated with courses, evaluation and self-evaluation tests and automatic, scheduled notifications. The tutor can track offline learning progress by means of reports and statistics. The testing and evaluation module electronically delivers the tests and offers automatic, semi-automatic or manual grading methods. The testing and evaluation module integrates the history of each student's courses, test, grades, and evolution. This evaluation process will be used only for internal purposes and for students outside the university (employees and unemployed) during some long life learning programs. For the European certification of the students, there will be used the examination section (but also, the training section) of the ECQA platform (described in the sections 3.1 and 3.2).

Availability as learners need to access easily data and administrators need the opportunity to use the administration feature remotely, from their home computer or an Internet Club. This function also helps promoting the system, thus helping the faculty gain access on the e–learning market.

The platform is organised as a flexible multi-tier system as follows: (1st level) thin, web-browser client; (2nd level) Web– and application server independent and (3rd

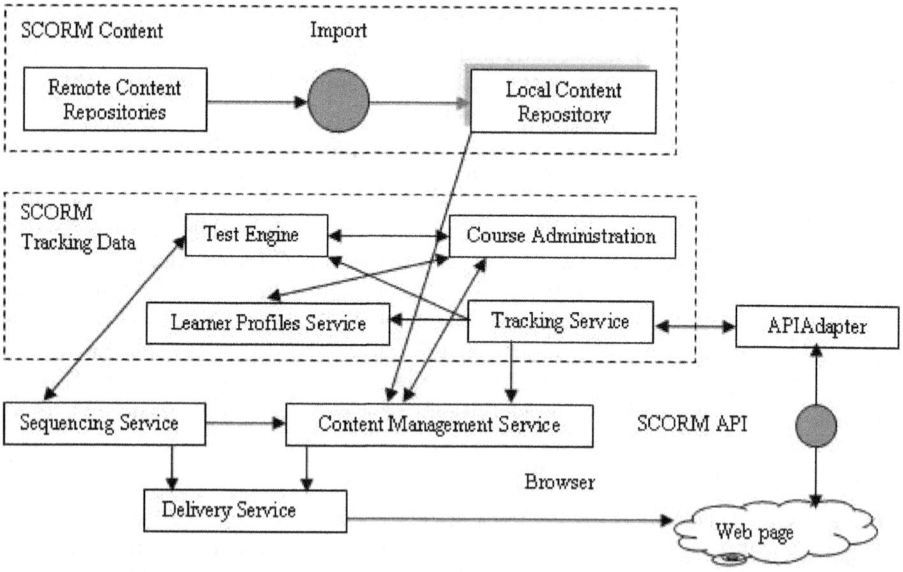

Fig. 3. The Proposed Architecture of the Entrepreneurship e-Learning Platform (Generalized Learning Management)

level): Java based web and application server; employs Enterprise Java Beans, JDBC, Java Servlets, JSPs, XML; tested on Oracle 9iAS, Orion, JBoss; database-independent, currently runs on Oracle 9i and PostgreSql DBMSs.

This three level architecture has the advantage of optimal hardware and software resource use by dividing functionality between the two servers: the application server, the logical–functional structure of the system, and the database server that stores information and provides data request management. The system is accessed by a web browser and needs no other application to be installed on client machines. The system has an open architecture, to enable modification according to future technology development. The network can be the Internet, a local or an extended network. A wide range of technologies and environments are used: distribution, audio, video, data environments, and interactive tools.

The content of the e-learning platform will be developed in a modular manner and it will include: assisted courses and seminars modules (exercises and case studies), a virtual library and an evaluation type module.

4 Conclusion and Perspective

The paper presents some important aspects regarding the entrepreneurship skills development (qualification) and certification and a possible, feasible solution for this problem at the European level. In the introduction there have been underlined the importance and the need of the entrepreneurship training in Europe, using relevant references. In the second chapter, there have been described the preliminary researches (in the context of a long life learning program) for the Research-Entrepreneur skill card definition in detail (skill units, elements and performance criteria) that will be used for the training materials development. The described approach is a classical one for skill set provision on the ECQA platform. In chapter three was described the qualification and certification system developed by the ECQA that shall be used for the examination and certification of the new created job role of Research-Entrepreneur at the European Level. Also, there have been debated the case of a local e-learning platform development in the field of entrepreneurship. This will better satisfied students training, for the master and the PhD. students' needs in the university, but also, employees and unemployed person's requirements for training programs in the lifelong learning system.

The presented research results were gained because of our collaboration at the European level, in the context of a Lifelong Learning Programme, Leonardo da Vinci (503021-LLP-1-2009-1-BE-LEONARDO-LMP): Certified EU Researcher – Entrepreneur, founded with support from the European Commission. Also, the presentation of this paper is connected with the dEUcert project (Dissemination of European Certification Schema ECQA, 505101-LLP-1-2009-1-AT-KA4-KA4MP). This project has been funded with support from the European Commission. This paper and communication reflects the views only of the author, and the Commission cannot be held responsible for any use which may be made of the information contained therein.

References

1. Bosman, N., Acs, Z.J., Autio, E., Codura, A, Levie, J.: GEM - Global Entrepreneurship Monitor, Executive Report, Babson College, Universidad del Desarrollo (2008)
2. Draghici, A., Draghici, G.: New business requirements in the knowledge-based society. In: Cunha, M.M., Cortes, B.C., Putnik, G.D. (eds.) Adaptive Technologies and Business Integration: Social, Managerial and Organizational Dimensions, pp. 2111–2243. Idea Group Publishing, Information Science Publishing, IRM Press, CyberTech Publishing and Idea Group Reference, USA (2006)
3. European Commission: Helping to Create an Entrepreneurial Culture – A Guide on Good Practice in Promoting Entrepreneurial Attitudes and Skills through Education (2008), http://europa.eu.int/comm/enterprise/entrepreneurship/support_measures/training_education/index.htm
4. European Commission: Directorate-General for Enterprise and Industry: Entrepreneurship in Higher Education, Especially Within Non-Business Studies. Final Report of the Expert Group (2008), http://europa.eu.int/comm/enterprise/entrepreneurship/support_measures/index.htm
5. Entrepreneurship in Europe, http://www.euractiv.com/en/innovation/entrepreneurship-europe/article-117477 (update January, 29 2010)
6. Izvercianu, M., Draghici, A.: The University Entrepreneurship Education. The case of Politehnica University of Timisoara. In: Simion, M.G., Talpasanu, I. (eds.) Proceeding of the 3rd Annual Congress of the American Romanian Academy of Arts and Sciences (ARA), pp. 238–241. Polytechnic International Press Canada, Wentworth Institute of Technology Boston (2008)
7. Messnarz, R., et al.: Assessment Based Learning Centers. In: Proceedings of the EuroSPI 2006 Conference, Joensuu, Finland (2006); Also Published in Wiley SPIP Proceeding in June (2007)
8. Messnarz, R., et al.: The EQN Guide, Graz, Austria (2008)
9. Monitor Group, Path to Prosperity – Promoting Entrepreneurship in the 21th Century. Technical Report (2009)
10. ResEUr : Certified EU Researcher – Entrepreneur. Lifelong Learning Programme, Leonardo da Vinc. Contr. no. 503021-LLP-1-2009-1-BE-LEONARDO-LMP (2009)
11. Riel, A.: EU Certificates and Knowledge Communities in Europe: An unbeatable Symbiosis. In: Keynote at EQN Founding and Dissemination Conference, Krems, Austria (2006), CD-ROM
12. Tornatzky, G., et al.: Innovation U: New University Role in Knowledge Economy. Southern Growth Policy Board, USA (2002)
13. Tracona, A.: Entrepreneurship Development – Key Issues and Challenges. Presentation at: CEEMAN Forum on Executive Education Executive Education and Entrepreneurship Development, Trieste, November 26-27 (2009), http://www.vlnmedia.net/ceeman/

Using People CMM for Dealing with Resistance on Implementing ITIL

Raul Nunes da Silva, Miguel Mira da Silva, and Nelson Gama

Instituto Superior Técnico, Lisboa.,
1, 1049-001 Lisboa, Portugal
raul.silva@ist.utl.pt

Abstract. There are reports that show that the main responsible for ITIL implementation project failures is people's resistance to change [1]. So, in order to improve ITIL adoption success rates, we have to invest in overcoming this particular problem.This work has the goal of reducingresistance rates by creating a framework that uses People CMM practices to overcome real organizational problems faced by organizations throughout their ITIL processes implementation. The first version of the framework is scheduled to be ready in July 2010 and will include the Incident Management process.

Keywords: ITIL, People, People CMM, Maturity, Resistance to Change.

1 Introduction

Importance of Information Systems (IS) on organizations is ever growing. We have witnessed the transition of IS from a business support role towards a business partner role [2]. This growing impact on organizations success lead to an also growing demand on IS management. To satisfy this demand, organizations turn themselves to the IT Service Management (ITSM) discipline.

ITSM strives to improve the alignment of IT efforts with business needs, and to manage the efficient provision of IT services with guaranteed quality [3]. Several frameworks were developed to help organizations reach their goal of better IS management. One of the most popular frameworks is ITIL – Information Technology Infrastructure Library. ITIL is a collection of the industry's good practices over the years, organized in such a way that organizations can structure themselves around the services lifecycle.

ITIL benefits are documented on its books, but nevertheless a good number of ITIL adoption projects don't reach its end. The fact is that implementing ITIL is not easy[2]. There are reports that show that the main responsible for these failures is people's resistance to change [1]. So, in order to improve ITIL adoption success rates, we have to invest in overcoming this particular problem. Some work has been done that addresses organizational problems in ITIL implementations, particularly resistance to change [4].

Laudon and Laudon[5] state that every IS has 3 dimensions: Organizations, Management and Technology. The key elements of organizations are its people, business

J.E. Quintela Varajão et al. (Eds.): CENTERIS 2010, Part II, CCIS 110, pp. 259–263, 2010.

processes, politics and culture. Management's job is to make sense out of the many situations faced by organizations, make decisions and formulate action plans to solve organizational problems. Technology can be computer software, hardware and such.

Similarly ITIL demands the balance of 3 components: people, processes and technology (see Fig. 1). Processescan improve the efficiency and effectiveness of the organization. Technology can help execute those processes by reducing time, effort and costs of executing those processes. People play a fundamental role: they execute the processes and use the technology. Metaphorically, we can see people as servers that run a given program. The processes are the code of that program. If the server doesn't understand that code, it won't run it.

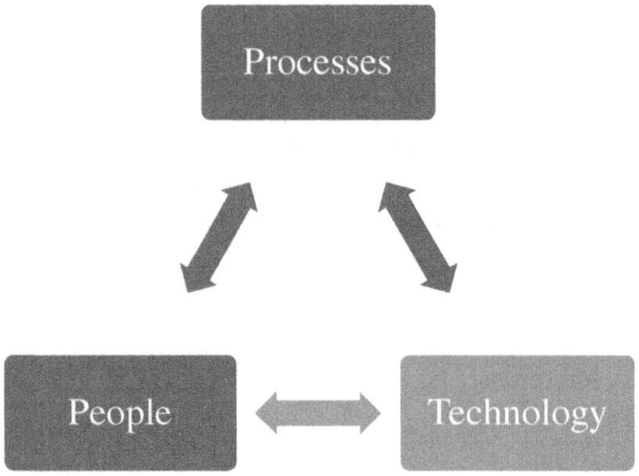

Fig. 1. Relation between People, Processes and Technology

We can have the best and most streamlined processes ever designed, but if we don't have the people with skills to execute them, they're useless, and vice-versa. Or if the two match perfectly but people are limited to using only papers and pencils, chances are that things won't be that efficient.

One of the questions lies on balancing this triangle. Technology is becoming a commodity[6]. I.e., the tools that support ITSM exist, and acquiring them or not is a matter of budget. Thus the core of the equation lies on the People–Processes alignment.

2 Problem

It's rather obvious that it's different implementing horizontal and methodical processes on distinct organizations. Each organization has a different environment, culture, and more important – people. People change from organization to organization. And the maturity of the work methods of these people also changes. Probably it's easier and faster implementing ITIL processes on an organization that already uses PMBOK, COBIT and/or VAL IT, than implementing them on a small organization of 5 people who use ad-hoc processes.

So, another question appears: how do organizations decide if they are ready or what's the best course of action on implementing ITIL? Should they implement 3 or 4 processes at the same time? Should they follow a big-bang approach? Or should they implement ITIL one process at a time? But if they do, won't they be wasting precious time and money, since it will take longer to collect the benefits?Should they be focusing their efforts on something other than ITIL?

3 People CMM Framework

People Capability Maturity Model (PCMM) is a roadmap for implementing workforce practices that continuously improve the capability of an organization's workforce. This capability is translated in the shape of practices for attracting, developing, organizing, motivating, and retaining its workforce. Thus, the People CMM establishes an integrated system of workforce practices that matures through increasing alignment with the organization's business objectives, performance, and changing needs [7].

The People CMM was first published in 1995, and has successfully guided workforce improvement programs in companies such as Boeing, Ericsson, Lockheed Martin, Novo Nordisk IT A/S, and Tata Consultancy Services[7].Although the People CMM has been designed primarily for application in knowledge intense organizations, with appropriate tailoring it can be applied in almost any organizational setting[7]. The current version (2.0) was published in July 2009.

The choice relied on PCMM because it is a tool that has a detailed description in terms of stages, practices, goals, policies and other components that make it easy to use across organizations. Plus, the fact that it's free to download facilitates the adoption of this work itself, since organizations won't have to incur costs.

4 Proposal

To solve this problem, the goal of this work is a framework that balances the maturity of the process framework and the maturity of the organization's work methods. Fig.2 illustrates an example of this relation, where in order to advance to a higher level of ITIL maturity (measured, for instance, in the number of operational ITIL processes) there is a pre-requisite that says that the work force maturity of the organization has to be at level 2. Basically, we will be able to know if the organization has the necessary work force infrastructure to successfully implement a given ITIL process. Plus, if not, it will also provide the organization with the practices that are lacking, so they know where to invest their resources if they are willing to.

The work methods and practices will be evaluated with the support of the People CMM framework (Section 3).

Although there are works being made on ITIL Maturity Models, the scope of this work only includes the Incident Management process. This choice was based on a work that concluded that ITIL implementations should start with Incident Management, since it lays the ground for other processes. With that in mind, it is also the first process that we will include in our solution.

So, for instance, let's imagine the case of an organization that wishes to implement ITIL. The first step is to assess the maturity of our work force, in terms of which PCMM practices are followed and which are not. Then, based on the results, we predict what are the practices we lack that may compromise the adoption of certain ITIL processes. This way we can not only know what are the processes who's implementation is more likely to succeed, but also what we should we be investing on in terms of work force practices.

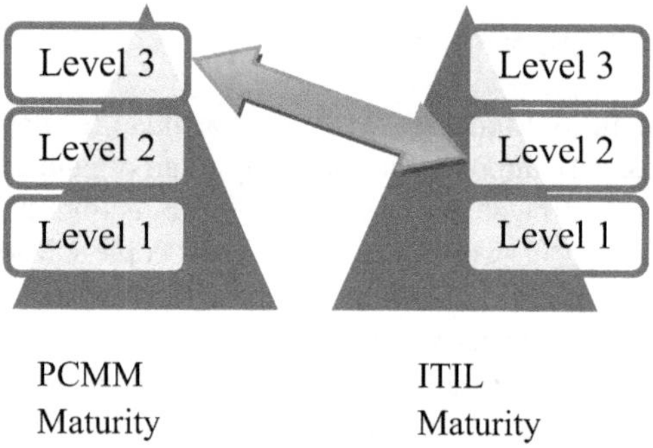

Fig. 2. The alignment between work force maturity and the process maturity

5 Preliminary Results

This work follows the Action Research methodology as described by Baskerville[8]. This methodology is used since the middle 20th century in medical and social sciences. The late 1990's witnessed a more academic use of this methodology, and especially on the IS area [8]. This methodology is based on a 5 step cycle (Fig. 3). The method produces highly relevant research results because it is grounded in practical action, aimed at solving an immediate problem while carefully informing theory [8].

As we are writing this paper (March 2010), we are on the "Action Taking" phase and applying this solution to a public organization in Portugal with 10.000 employees in total and about 200 employees on its IS Department. We are assessing which

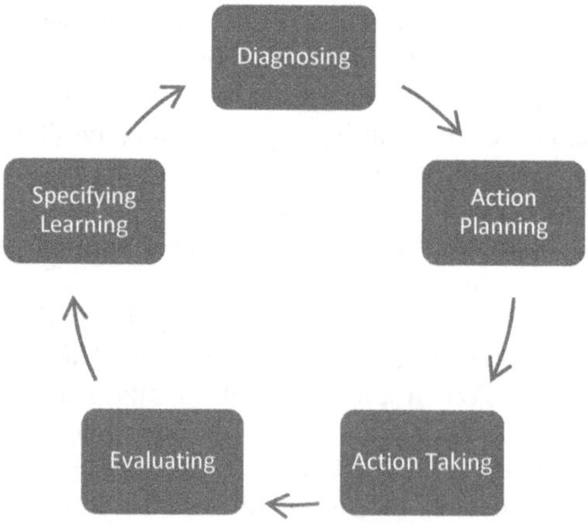

Fig. 3. The Action Research cycle [8]

PCMM practices exist in order to plan an ongoing ITIL implementation – specifically the Incident Management process. That experience is included in the "Specifying Learning" phase of the research methodology and will help developing the first version of the framework. This work is scheduled to finish in July 2010.

6 Conclusion

Thisarticle addressed the particular problem of organizational resistance on implementing ITIL, which is responsible for a large percentage of implementation projects failure. We explained the importance of people in the scope of this particular problem, and how they are a fundamental element in overcoming this situation.

We proposed a theoretical solution based on the People CMM, a maturity model that helps organizations improve their work force in terms of practices, organizational infrastructures and such. We can use these elements to create an integrated framework that establishes what is necessary in order to implement each ITIL process. This helps achieving the co-evolution of people and processes, reducing resistance and helping the organization to adapt.

This is a work in progress, already being applied to a public organization on Portugal. The results obtained by that experience will help developing the framework and the first version is scheduled to be completed in July 2010.

This iteration only includes the Incident Management process, but future work includes the subsequent mapping of key PCMM practices for each ITIL process. Also, in order to help organizations implementing ITIL, an implementation roadmap should be developed in order to provide a holistic framework that is able to guide them throughout the adoption program.

References

1. Evergreen Systems.Developing the business value of ITIL Survey results (2006)
2. Roepke, R., Agarwal, R., Ferratt, T.W.: Aligning the IT human resource with business vision: The leadership initiative at 3M. MIS Quarterly 24, 2 (2000)
3. Brenner, M.: Classifying ITIL Processes; A Taxonomy under Tool Support Aspects (2006)
4. Figueiredo, S., Mira da Silva, M.: Gestão da Mudança na Implementação ITIL. In: 4[a] Conferência Ibérica de Sistemas e Tecnologias de Informação (2009)
5. Laudon, K., Laudon, J.: Management Information Systems: Managing the Digital Firm. Pearson Education, London (2006)
6. Carr, N.: IT doesn't Matter. IEEE Engineering Management Review 32, 1 (2004)
7. Curtis, B., Hefley, W., Miller, S.: People Capability Maturity Model 2.0. Carnegie Mellon University - Software Engineering Institute (2009)
8. Baskerville, R.: Investigating information systems with action research. Communications of the AIS 2, 3es (1999)
9. Nicewicz-Modrzewska, D., Stolarsk, P.: ITIL implementation roadmap based on process governance (2008)
10. Sharifi, M., et al.: Lessons learned in ITIL implementation failure. In: International Symposium on Information Technology 2008 (2008)

Enterprise Resource Planning System in a Multinational Enterprise: Users' Attitude Post-Implementation

Tiago Almeida[1], Leonor Teixeira[1,2,3], and Carlos Ferreira[1,4]

[1] Department of Economics, Management and Industrial Engineering, University of Aveiro, Portugal
[2] Governance, Competitiveness and Public Politics (GOVCOPP), University of Aveiro, Portugal
[3] Institute of Electronics and Telematics Engineering of Aveiro (IEETA) Portugal
[4] Operational Research Centre (CIO), University of Lisbon, Lisbon, Portugal
{a31754,lteixeira,carlosf}@ua.pt

Abstract. This paper analyzes the impact of the implementation of *SAP R/3* in a Multinational Portuguese Organization (MPO), defining some Critical Success Factors (CSFs). In order to understand the motivations of end-users prior to implementation and to analyze the behavior after a change (post-implementation), a study based on a questionnaire was carried out. The sample included 67 users of *SAP R/3* that were present throughout the process. Considering the results, we can conclude that the implementation of *SAP R/3* in MPO was successful, and the respondents consider their work more productive and achieve easier access to information. The existence of a solid team to support the project was established as a major facilitator in the whole process, in opposing with the limited time and lack of training that emerged as barriers to the implementation. It was also found that the learning period assumes a high importance in the success of the implementation, once increasing the training time reduces the need for support to the end-users.

Keywords: ERP, Implementation, SAP R/3; Training, Critical Success Factors.

1 Introduction

Research literature on the Enterprise Resource Planning (ERP) systems has grown significantly in recent years, particularly concerning the identification of Critical Success Factors (CSFs) in ERP implementation [1], [2]. Due to the diversity of areas supported by the ERP, medium and large companies are acquiring this type of software in order to improve their processes through a centralized data management. Most of the ERP software also allows the redesign of business processes in order to eliminate tasks that have no value, and consequently the employees can focus on specific activities that increase productivity. However, implementing such systems requires a cultural, organizational and business processes changes that may influence the success of the implementation. Moreover, some projects are too expensive, not

J.E. Quintela Varajão et al. (Eds.): CENTERIS 2010, Part II, CCIS 110, pp. 264–273, 2010.

only financially, but also in the length of its implementation (from one to three years) involving people, technology and know-how [1], [3], [4], [5].

This paper aims to contribute to the identification of CSFs in the implementation of ERP systems through a study accomplished in a *Multinational Portuguese Organization* (MPO). The system chosen by MPO was the *SAP R/3* and the present study focus on the perception of the end-users and their behaviors when faced with the changes driven by the ERP system.

2 Implementation Process of ERPs

ERP systems are based on integrated modules which aim to collect and process data to provide reliable information to support decision making, increasing the organizational efficiency. Thus the companies can obtain a higher financial return if they adopt and use this kind of system correctly [6], [7], [8].

According to Boudreau and Robey [9] the acceptance and success of ERP systems depend on the implementation process. During this process, users can criticize the project for its costs, effort required, and gaps. Indeed there are difficult and onerous phases in the implementation process, often with a negative impact on the organizations. Davenport [10] and Banker *et al.*, 1988 cit by [11] reveal that more than half of these projects are not successful. Hong and Kim [12] presented a study with worst results, highlighting the existence of 75% of ERP projects without success. Moreover, Scott and Vessey [13] states that 90% of ERP projects are delayed.

2.1 Implementation Risks

Some ERP projects modify the organizational balance of the rights, privileges, obligations, feelings and responsibilities established along the time. Modify these elements may take time, cause disorder and need more resources to support the training [8]. There are risk factors that influence the implementation of ERP, such as the difficulty of acceptance, user's resistance, difficulties transferring the knowledge to computer systems, etc. According to [5] and [14], people not involved and without prior knowledge about the system tend to reject and to create difficulties. Thus, the training process is seen as one of the most important factors in the success of ERP implementation [15], [16], [17]. Another key-factor in the implementation of ERP is the awareness of end-users for the systems transition [9]. In this phase, the organizations should approach the transition process cautiously and with a comprehensive plan [18].

2.2 Influence of Psychosocial Factors

Nowadays, it is recognized that psychosocial factors are often critical in the implementation of an ERP. Boddy *et al.* [19] affirm that organizations sometimes introduce new systems, ignoring human factors and using inadequate control methods, causing failures.

Abdinnour-Helm *et al.* [3] state that the user's preparation in the pre-implementation phase is essential to obtain a positive attitude. These attitudes are precursors of a particular behavior pattern, and frequently positive attitudes generate positive behaviors. When a person does not adopt that attitude, tends to follow practices that will ultimately affect his/her performance in the medium and long term. People are willing to do their work if they feel they are acting in accordance with their interests and personal goals [19]. Therefore it is important to measure the motivation levels and user satisfaction, once they are evaluation mechanisms to determine the success of a system [20]. For Lander, *et al.* [21] the mechanisms of building trust between team members and other stakeholders in the project are also important factors. In turn, Jones *et al.* [22] suggest that similar cultures facilitate the exchange of knowledge during the implementation of ERP.

Whilst end-user training is predominant in early stages of the implementation process, there is an evident need of continuous training [10], [23]. Abran and Nguyenkim [24] show that the maintenance phase of user support represents 24% of the total time spent by the project team.

3 Research Methodology

The present study was based on an implementation of the *SAP R/3* system in a MPO, coming to benefit the experience of the researcher who followed all stages of this implementation project. This research attempts to understand the motivations and behavior of end-users face to the new reality impelled by the new system, and evaluate their satisfaction after a change. To this end, it was used a questionnaire to collect data, having been applied 3 months after the system start-up.

3.1 Instrument Validity and Description

The content validity of a questionnaire refers to the representativeness of item content domain. In order to validate the questionnaire used in this study, we followed a validation process in two phases. In the first phase, the questionnaire was validated using judge's method, applied to a panel composed by 5 experts, selected according to the following criteria: higher education with knowledge in information systems area and 10 years, at least, of work experience in the same area. Based on results of this phase we developed a second version of the questionnaire (pilot questionnaire). This version was applied to a group of 5 elements, i.e., end-users of *SAP R/3* and employees of the company in the study (MPO). This phase of the validation process also led to small changes in the questionnaire which came to compose the final version.

At the structural level this questionnaire was composed by 27 questions, grouped into 4 areas: socio-professional characterization, training processes in *SAP R/3*, transition process between systems, and changes in job performance. These areas aim to obtain data to: (i) characterize the sample on demographic and personal data; (ii) assess and characterize the training process in *SAP R/3*; (iii) assess the opinions of respondents regarding the duration and relevance of training; (iv) assess the procedures and conditions of respondents regarding the use of the system; (v) assess the opinions of respondents with respect to the transition process between systems and the post-implementation phase; (vi) assess and characterize the job performance of respondents in the face of change; (vii) assess the acceptance degree of the respondents on the implemented system; and, (viii) identify the positive and negative aspects in the implementation, adaptation and utilization of the *SAP R/3* system.

3.2 Data Collection

The distribution of the questionnaire was made after the request and authorization of the Department of Information Systems and Business Process (DIS&BP) of the MPO, and applied during April 2009. Ninety (90) questionnaires were delivered and sixty seven (67) were correctly answered. The filling was made individual and manuscripts and the data analysis was performed through software STATISTICA® [25].

In order to be included in the sample, the participants had to be MPO employees; to use at least one of the modules of the system *SAP R/3* and be present in the transition between systems. The sample consisted of 67 users (32 males and 35 females). Respondents were mostly aged between 20 and 39 years and 66 of them with Portuguese nationality. The great majority of participants (51) have been employed in this company for less than 3 years.

4 Results and Discussion

In order to carry out this study, we analyzed the three main stages of the implementation processes: i) training process, ii) transition between systems, iii) changes in job performance, covering the pre, during and post-implementation phases.

4.1 Training Process in *SAP R/3*

In the process of training was concluded that the majority of respondents (88%) received training on the use of *SAP R/3* in the studied company. However, only 49% had training in all the modules that they used. Several authors [15], [16], [17], [26] show that training is a key factor in the implementation process. In accordance with the percentage of users that were in the training, it is expected that this factor positively influence the implementation of the system. However, approximately half of the respondents had no training in all the modules that they used, which may arise some difficulties which could threaten the functioning of the ERP in the post-implementation.

Of all the participants, only 30% consider that the training time was sufficient. However, and in spite of 51% did not have training in all the modules that they use, most of the participants (83%) consider that the training received was in accordance with the applied modules. This relationship could be identified as a false facilitator in the implementation process, since the behavior may be biased because they have previous knowledge about the functionalities and potentialities of *SAP R/3*. This way, users can adopt practices that affect their performance in the medium or long term. Concerning the learning time is noteworthy that 15% of respondents have received training lasting less than 1 day, 36% between 1 and 3 days, 24% at 4 to 5 days and 25% more than 5 days. Several authors [15], [16], [17] refer that training is one of the most important factors in the success of an ERP implementation; however, those authors don't indicate standardized times. In this sample was verified that the training time was not uniform, presenting a considerable variability.

4.2 Transition Process Between Systems

Concerning the transition process between systems, almost all (96%) of people covered in this study understands the reason why the company has implemented the *SAP R/3*. This factor appears as a facilitator in the implementation process, since actors tend to respond positively when objectives are known [3], [19]. It was also observed that the majority (73%) of respondents did not feel prepared to use the software. This factor may be incurred as a barrier to the good practices, since the transition between systems is considered by Boudreau and Robey [9] and Al-Mashari [18] as a key factor in the implementation of ERP.

During the transition between systems, 94% of users required support, the great majority relied on co-workers (76%) and the UNIK team (62%) to overcome difficulties. Less frequent was the request for assistance to supervisors and the use of manuals. These results are consistent with the theory of Sarker and Lee [27]; they defend that communication between colleagues and a good support team constitutes an essential condition for successful implementation.

In the perspective of 42% respondents, the transition to *SAP R/3* has caused difficulties at work. The lack of time to complete tasks, the lack of training and the inefficient data transfer, emerge as unsatisfactory factors. The lack of computer resources (computer, printer, or other) does not present as a difficulty. Only 8% of respondents mentioned that there was another kind of difficulty, such as problems in data transferring from legacy systems to SAP, producing unreliable and inappropriate information.

4.3 Changes in the Work Performance

Relatively to the job performance, it was concluded that more than half of the respondents (67%) consider their work more productive using the *SAP R/3*, and with this new system the majority (75%) have easier access to information they need. According to O'Brien [28] the facilitated access to information is a fundamental characteristic of the Information Systems (IS), thus will positively influence the work performance. However, 33% of respondents do not consider their work more productive, a factor that may be related to the normal organizational restructuring that usually comes from the implementation of a new system [8]. After implementation, the great majority (84%) of respondents are aware of the specific functions in the *SAP R/3*, appearing as an advantage in efficiency of use [20]. Almost all respondents (99%) consider the system a relevant tool for the company.

Most people consider that in training and usage processes, the system met their expectations. One of the elements favorable to job performance relates to the expectations presented by the actors, which is a critical element of quality management in the project [29]. Once the expectations were appropriate, in training and usage, these characteristics emerge as a predictor of quality in the work performed.

Almost all respondents (99%) consider the system useful. This factor foresees a systematic and continuous use, contributing once again for the good performance. According to the general opinion of respondents, *SAP R/3* simplified data management (introduction and control), improved access to information and made the work more complete and functional. As disadvantages, were presented difficulties in adapting to the system, an increase of complexity and delays in completion of tasks.

Analyzing the answers to the open question, we can verify that the number of advantages presented is greater than the number of disadvantages, thus it is possible to infer that the respondents conceive the system as a positive tool for the implementation of their work. The advantages presented are corroborated by Pinto [5] and Souza [30], affirming that the use of a central database originates significant organizational challenges. However, these challenges are offset by the functional scope of the system, simplifying and improving access to all information. Also according to Pinto [5] and Boudreau and Robey [9] during the adaptation process criticism and resistance to the project can appear by the effort required and gaps, justifying, this way, the disadvantages presented by those respondents. Bresnahan and Brynjolfsson [31] affirm that it can take years for people to demonstrate a positive feeling in relation to the change, so the presented negative factors will not be a consequence of the implementation failure but part of the normal process to the systems implementation.

4.4 Association between Pairs of Variables

After the characterization of individual variables made previously, we present a bivariate analysis that intends to show the existence of a relationship between pairs of variables.

(Q_A) '*Duration of training in SAP R/3 in the MPO*' and (Q_B) '*Need for support during the transition to the SAP R/3*'.

To analyze the relationship between the issues 'Q_A' and 'Q_B', two time periods were considered in training ('<=3 days' and '>3 days'). Using Chi-square test (χ^2) confirms that the hypothesis of independence is rejected for a significance level of 5%, with the value from a *test statistic* (TS)=5,57>χ^2(1; α=0.05)=3,84 and *p-value*=0,02. The data show an association between variables, suggesting that the need for support from users decreases with the increase of the training time. The obtained values are shown in Table 1.

Table 1. Contingency table [32] resulting from crossing the answers to Q_A and Q_B

		Q_B		
		Yes	No	Total
Q_A	<3 days	38	0	38
	> 3 days	25	4	29
	Total	63	4	67

(Q_C) '*Adequacy of preparation for starting to use the SAP R/3*' and (Q_D) '*Need for support during the transition to the SAP R/3*'.

Q_C and Q_D were analyzed in order to ascertain a possible relationship between feeling prepared and the need for support at the time of transition.

The analysis of Table 2 shows that the majority of respondents (73%) did not feel prepared to start using the system, felt the need to support during the transition. Moreover, although the majority of respondents (14/18) felt prepared to use the

Table 2. Contingency table [32] resulting from crossing the answers to Q_C and Q_D

		Q_D		
		Yes	No	Total
Q_C	Yes	14	4	18
	No	49	0	49
	Total	63	4	67

system, the support was required. This may be related to the period of training that possibly did not cover the entire practical component and/or theoretical, failing to foresee all the difficulties. It can be related to the inadequate use of the system, where the data entered incorrectly originate errors in other areas. The reliability and accuracy of these data tend to be a problem in the planning of the operations [5].

The use of Chi-square test (χ^2) confirms that the assumption of independence is rejected for a significance level of 5%, with the value from a *test statistic* (TS)=11,58>χ^2 (1; α=0.05)=3,84 and *p-value*=0,0007. Thus, there is an association between the variables, suggesting that users who do not feel prepared to use SAP needed help at the time of transition.

(Q_E) *'Ease to access information with the SAP R/3'* and (Q_F) *'Perception of increased productivity at work after the implementation of SAP R/3'*.

In order to understand whether the facilitated access to information is related to the perception of work productivity of users, Q_E and Q_F were crossed.

Table 3. Contingency table [32] resulting from crossing the answers to Q_E and Q_F

		Q_F		
		Yes	No	Total
Q_E	Yes	63	3	66
	No	1	0	1
	Total	64	3	67

Table 3, shows that 76% of users who consider the simplified access to information also agreed that its performance has become more productive with the implementation of the new system. They also show that 24% of respondents think that, although having better access to information, the productivity in the tasks will not be increased.

The use of Chi-square test (χ^2) confirms that the assumption of independence is rejected for a significance level of 5%, with the value from a *test statistic* (TS)=6,98>$\chi^2_{(1;\ \alpha=0.05)}$=3,84 and *p-value*=0,0083. This result suggests an association between ease access to information with the *SAP R/3* and the perception of work productivity after its implementation, confirming the data previously presented.

5 Findings, Conclusions and Limitations

Considering our results, it can be concluded that in general the implementation of *SAP R/3* was successful. However, there are gaps that should be tackled in future implementations to optimize the results.

From the analysis of the training process, we can conclude that more than half of respondents consider their work more productive using *SAP R/3*, and most accesses more easily to the information. It was also verified that the majority of those respondents have received training in the company. These factors appear as positive points, influencing the success of the implementation.

For most respondents, the system met the expectations in the training process and usage. In the transition between systems most people understood the reason why the administration had to implement the *SAP R/3*. Since these indicators emerge as predictors of quality in the executed work is important that, in future implementations, users also have this previous knowledge.

It was also possible to verify that, when facing difficulties using the system, the great majority of respondents know who can help them, normally the support team. This team appears as an essential element in the support of implementations, the users should be aware of it to communicate effectively.

It was found that almost half of the participants had no training in all of the modules of *SAP R/3* they use, which may arise some difficulties. Thus, in future implementations the training process should include all areas covered by the end-users.

Most respondents did not consider the time training to be sufficient and did not feel prepared to use the software. However, we can verify that as training time increases, the support need in *SAP R/3* decreases. Thus, to overcome these barriers, there must be an increase in the training time in future implementations.

The majority of respondents refers that the lack of documentation to help guide the system presents itself as an obstacle. However, the DIS&BP created and made available user help guides, so it is necessary to promote the possibility and need for consultation.

Regarding the use of *SAP R/3*, approximately half of respondents consider it complex. In order to blur this negative factor, a solution is to customize the system, which facilitates its use and continuous improvements.

With the analysis of the results obtained through questionnaires and attendance the implementation of *SAP R/3*, we can conclude that end-users require ongoing support. Thus, not only the theoretical and practical aspects are important in the initial phase, but would also need the practical attendance post-implementation. In addition, it would be important to determine training time in agreement with the contents to standardize the teaching processes.

According to Cardoso (2003) cit by [33], the implementation of an integrated management system such as *SAP R/3* consumes on average 2 years. Once the implementation of the project had the duration of 6 months, is possible that more time was needed to customize the whole software, to define procedures, and at the same time to train all users.

Like any research this also presents some limitations, opening, however, new ideas and suggestions for further work to be developed in this or other areas. Given the number of individuals in the sample, approximately 30% of the population, we can consider the results as a good source of information which allows transposing the values for the remaining areas of the company in study. The time elapsed between the implementation and data collection was relatively short (3 months), which on the one hand is a limitation of the study, on the other hand is an advantage. To evaluate changes in work performance after a short time of use may be biased, once the users are still in an adaption phase to the new system.

In a future research of this nature, it would be pertinent to collect data in a later period (6 months after implementation), to increase the sample number and diversify it in other companies of the Group. It would also be pertinent to accomplish a study on the impact in the organizational structure, analyzing how it suffered modifications. Given that there were changes in procedures, employees may arise with new functions and/or new departments, or even reduce the number of human resources (organizational redesign).

The data obtained in this study appears as prevention indicators and guidelines for the success of future implementations of integrated systems, once for the managers is important to know the impact of the events in all functional areas, as well as its performance, in order to be able to react immediately to market fluctuations.

References

1. Ngai, E.W.T., Law, C.C.H., Wat, F.K.T.: Examining the critical success factors in the adoption of enterprise resource planning. Comput. Ind. 59(6), 548–564 (2008)
2. Tchokogué, A., Bareil, C., Duguay, C.R.: Key lessons from the implementation of an ERP at Pratt & Whitney Canada. International Journal of Production Economics 95(2), 151–163 (2005)
3. Abdinnour-Helm, S., Lengnick-Hall, M., Lengnick-Hall, C.: Pre-implementation attitudes and organizational readiness for implementing an enterprise resource planning system. European Journal of Operational Research 146(2), 258–273 (2003)
4. Ng, C.S.P., Gable, G.G., Chan, T.: An ERP-client benefit-oriented maintenance taxonomy. J. Syst. Softw. 64(2), 87–109 (2002)
5. Pinto, J.P., Gestão de Operações na Indústria e nos Serviços 2.ª ed, LIDEL, Lisboa (2006)
6. Beynon-Davies, P.: Information Systems. An Introduction to Informatics in Organisations. Palgrave, England (2002)
7. Chou, S.-W., Chang, Y.-C.: The implementation factors that influence the ERP (enterprise resource planning) benefits. Decision Support Systems 46(1), 149–157 (2008)
8. Laudon, K.C., Laudon, J.P.: Management Information Systems: management the digital firm, 9th edn. Pearson Education, New Jersey (2006)
9. Boudreau, M., Robey, D.: Enacting integrated information technology: A human agency perspective. Organization Science 16(1), 3–18 (2005)
10. Davenport, T.H.: Putting the enterprise into the enterprise system. Harvard Bus. Rev. 76(4), 121–131 (1998)
11. Subramanian, G., Hoffer, C.: Implementation of Enterprise Resource Planning (ERP) Systems: Issues and Challenges. Idea Group Inc, Penn State Harrisburg (2007)
12. Hong, K.-K., Kim, Y.-G.: The critical success factors for ERP implementation: an organizational fit perspective. Inf. Manage. 40(1), 25–40 (2002)
13. Scott, J.E., Vessey, I.: Managing risks in enterprise systems implementations. Commun. ACM. 45(4), 74–81 (2002)
14. Youngberg, E., Olsen, D., Hauser, K.: Determinants of professionally autonomous end user acceptance in an enterprise resource planning system environment. International Journal of Information Management 29(2), 138–144 (2009)
15. Barker, T., Frolick, M.N.: ERP implementation failure: A case study. Information Systems Management 20(4), 43–49 (2003)
16. Gallivan, M.J., Spitler, V.K., Koufaris, M.: Does Information Technology Training Really Matter? A Social Information Processing Analysis of Coworkers' Influence on IT Usage in the Workplace. J. Manage. Inf. Syst. 22(1), 153–192 (2005)
17. Robey, D., Ross, J.W., Boudreau, M.C.: Learning to implement enterprise systems: An exploratory study of the dialectics of change. Journal of Management Information Systems 19(1), 17–46 (2002)
18. Al-Mashari, M., Al-Mudimigh, A., Zairi, M.: ERP: A taxonomy of critical factors. European Journal of Operational Research 146, 352–364 (2003)

19. Boddy, D., Boonstra, A., Kennedy, G.: Managing Information Systems: An Organizational Perspective, 1st edn. Pearson Education, Edinburgh (2002)
20. Orlikowski, W.J., Barley, S.R.: Technology and institutions: what can research on information technology and research on organizations learn from each other? MIS Quarterly 25(2), 145–165 (2001)
21. Lander, M.C., et al.: Trust-building mechanisms utilized in outsourced IS development projects: a case study. Information & Management 41(4), 509–528 (2004)
22. Jones, M.C., Cline, M., Ryan, S.: Exploring knowledge sharing in ERP implementation: an organizational culture framework. Decision Support Systems 41(2), 411–434 (2006)
23. Nah, F.F.-H., Faja, S., Cata, T.: Characteristics of ERP software maintenance: a multiple case study. Journal of Software Maintenance and Evolution: Research and Practice 13(6), 399–414 (2001)
24. Abran, A., Nguyenkim, H.: Analysis of maintenance work categories through measurement. In: Conference on Software Maintenance, IEEE Computer Society Press, Los Alamitos (1991)
25. Statsoft-Inc. STATISTICA (data analysis software system), version 6 (2001), `http://www.statsoft.com`
26. Peslak, A., Subramanian, G.H., Clayton, G.: The phases of ERP software implementation and maintenance: A model for predicting preferred ERP use. Journal of Computer Information Systems 48(2), 25–33 (2006)
27. Sarker, S., Lee, A.S.: Using a case study to test the role of three key social enablers in ERP implementation. Information & Management 40(8), 813–829 (2003)
28. O'Brien, J.: Introduction to Information Systems: essentials for the internetworked e-business enterprise, 10th edn. International Edition, Irwin/McGraw-Hill (2001)
29. PMI, A Guide to the Project Management Body of Knowledge. 3ª ed. Pennsylvania- Project Management Institute, Inc. Project Management Institute (2004)
30. Souza, C.A.: Sistemas Integrados de Gestão Empresarial: estudos de caso de implementação de sistemas ERP. FEA/USP: São Paulo (2000)
31. Bresnahan, T.F., Brynjolfsson, E.: Information technology, workplace organization, and the demand for skilled labor: Firm-level evidence. Quarterly Journal of Economics 117(1), 339–376 (2002)
32. Everitt, B.S.: The Analysis of Contingency Tables. Chapman & Hall, New York (1994)
33. Júnior, R., Ferreira, L.: Avaliação de um sistema ERP-SAP R/3 como Instrumento para gestão financeira na área de contas a pagar em uma empresa de Telecomunicações. Universidade Católica de Brasília, Brasília (2006)

SME Managers' Most Important Entrepreneurship and Business Competences

Caroline Dominguez[1], João Varajão[1,2], Leonel Morgado[1,3], Irene Oliveira[1], and Fernanda Sousa[4,5]

[1] Department of Engineering, UTAD-University of Trás-os-Montes e Alto Douro, Vila Real, Portugal
{carold,jvarajao,leonelm,ioliveir}@utad.pt
[2] Centro ALGORITMI, University of Minho, Guimarães, Portugal
[3] GECAD, UTAD-University of Trás-os-Montes e Alto Douro, Vila Real, Portugal
[4] Faculdade de Engenharia, University of Porto, Portugal
fcsousa@fe.up.pt
[5] CITTA – Research Centre for Territory Transports and Environment, Porto, Portugal

Abstract. The requirements of an increasing globalized and competitive economy lead managers to search for training solutions which can rapidly bridge the gap of their lacking skills, knowledge or competences. To assert with adequate training programs, in particular for SMEs managers, a study was conducted in six European countries with the objective of identifying the most relevant competences they need to fulfill. A literature review and several interviews with business associations' executives resulted in a list of 34 competences which were organized in four categories: personal, team management, business and technical. These competencies were put at trial through a survey conducted among 154 SMEs managers who had to evaluate each proposed competence with the attribution of a relevance degree. Although we show that SME managers should be well prepared in a rich set of complementary areas to perform their job, it is clear that some of the competences are crucial for them to tackle today's challenges. This paper presents a ranking of the competences by importance as perceived by managers. These findings can help training institutions wishing to design new training programs which more in line with managers' needs.

Keywords: SME, manager, competences, skills, Europe.

1 Introduction

SME managers are confronted with an increasingly unstable, complex and changing economic context. They must know how to combine a set of key diversified competences to lead the company on the road of competitive development. They also must adapt themselves to a set of challenges that they are not always well prepared to face. Universities and professional training institutions have a key role to play in this context. Through their adequate training offer, they can be essential partners for SME managers towards the road of success. On the basis of a previously elaborated

J.E. Quintela Varajão et al. (Eds.): CENTERIS 2010, Part II, CCIS 110, pp. 274–282, 2010.

Framework of SME managers' necessary competences [1] which resulted from a study conducted in six European countries (Austria, Finland, Greece, Italy, Portugal and Romania), this article presents the outcome of an inquiry realized among managers of SMEs with the objective of identifying and characterizing the competences from the Framework that are considered most important. This should help training institutions to prioritize their educational actions towards SME managers and be more effective in their partnership towards SME's competitiveness. The first section of this paper presents the results of recent studies on this matter. The section on methodology highlights the research process used in the study. In the main section, the achieved results will be presented. Finally, the chapter ends up presenting some opportunities for future development of this work.

2 Background

Between 2002 and 2007, the number of SMEs has increased by over 2 million. Most that new firms are created in the service sector and are micro enterprises [2]. Across the member states of the European Union (EU), there are about 19.6 million small and medium-sized enterprises (SME) in the non-financial business economy, with up to 250 employees, representing 99.8% of all businesses and 67.1% of the non-financial business economy workforce [3]. To support the growth and development of existing SMEs and promote the creation of new SMEs, the European Commission (EC) adopted in June 2008 the 'Small Business Act' for Europe, reflecting the EC political will to recognize the central role of SMEs in the EU economy [4]. In spite of the important role played by such firms in the European economy, there is a lack of specific training for people heading and/or managing SMEs, and the training that is available "tends to serve either start-ups or medium sized firms" [5]. Furthermore, training for heads of SMEs should be different from training for employees: heads of SMEs "exhibit activist and pragmatist learning styles, prefer learning by doing and favour problem-centred approaches that offer flexibility" (id., p. 3).

Aiming to identify the relevant competences of SMEs' managers, it was developed a study [1, 6] in several European countries, that comprised the analysis of several works [2, 7-13] and the conduction of interviews with representatives of business associations. From that study resulted a Framework of SME's manager competences, which were organized in four categories: personal; technical non-finance; business & finance; and team management. In this context, the sense given to "competence" is the following: aptitude, ability or set of theoretical or practical knowledge necessary to achieve a certain purpose. Personal aspects are all competences related to the manager's personality that are vital in order to manage an enterprise effectively. Team management aspects are all the competences that are needed in order to create and lead a team and make full use of each team member's capacities. Technical aspects are all competences that help the manager to fulfill everyday tasks and functions in the enterprise. Finally, business & finance aspects are all competences that allow a manager to deal with the basic financial and business tasks of the enterprise. Table 1 presents the elements of each category of the Framework.

Table 1. SME managers' entrepreneurship competences Source: [1, 6]

Category	Competence
Personal	Attitude towards uncertainty and risk Innovative spirit Fulfillment of tasks and goals Self-confidence Communication skills Ability to discover new opportunities Conceptual ability
Team management	Negotiation and decision-making Time management for own work and the team's work Communication to the team of clear expectations of performance Regular supply of feedback to the team on its performance Full use of the capacities and knowledge of the team Promote mutual confidence Develop autonomy of a group Raise awareness of collective responsibility Ability to build and lead a team (leadership spirit)
Technical non finance	Ability for project management Ability to create and provide strategic/tactical/operational plans Management of human resources from an organizational perspective (allocation/attribution of tasks) Management of other resources (non-human) Awareness of corporate social responsibility Knowledge of the administrative/bureaucratic process for founding a company Knowledge of the legal requirements for business Knowledge of the most important legal forms of business ownership Process analysis and change management
Business & Finance	Knowledge of general business conditions and functions Knowledge of what to think about when deciding whether to found a business or not Knowledge of foreign trade and international trade relations Distinguish the financial issues between different company sectors (manufacturing/services) Management of the different performance functions within an enterprise Understanding of different forms of financing (self-financing, external financing) Basic sales-planning skills Knowledge of accountancy and taxes Ability to plan and control: direct costs, overhead costs, cost prices, gross and net sales price, and earnings/profits

For a detailed description of these competences please see [6].

3 Methodology

3.1 Objective

With the purpose of identifying and characterizing the most important competences and skills that European Small and Medium Enterprise (SME) entrepreneur/managers need to be able to perform her/his job, we carried out a study with the participation of SME managers.

The general methodology involved a survey that was conducted particularly to inquire which management competences/skills the participant managers are more relevant for the success of a SME, and to know among these, which they felt they needed more training.

3.2 Subjects

The survey, undertaken from July to September 2009, focused on small companies of six European countries. The subjects in this study consisted of the general managers of the companies. This particular audience was preferred because SMEs across the 27 member states of the European Union represent about 99% of all businesses [3]. Therefore, the use of this target group seemed most appropriate.

3.3 Questionnaire

A questionnaire (the survey instrument) was formulated (see Appendix A for selected portions) and sent to managers of SMEs, identified according to their gross revenue and number of employees.

The content and structure of the questionnaire was created based on a Framework of SMEs' managers competences [1]. The proposed questionnaire was pre-tested with a sample of twelve managers from SMEs of participant countries (two per country), to validate its content and readability and to improve some aspects of the questions. The necessary changes were made to the final questionnaire, which was edited in an online survey tool.

A briefing letter was subsequently sent to the participant managers regarding the scope and goals of the study, including a link to an Internet webpage which allowed the completion of the questionnaire online.

3.4 Data Representativeness

The survey was mailed to the managers of a sample group from the universe of SME European companies by gross revenue and number of employees. In order to obtain a representative sample, we chose to use a casual sample of companies from six countries: Austria, Finland, Greece, Italy, Portugal and Romania. The total answers obtained were 154.

4 Most Important Competences of an SME Manager

Respondents attributed a level of importance to each presented competence of the questionnaire. This procedure permitted to order each competence as the overall result

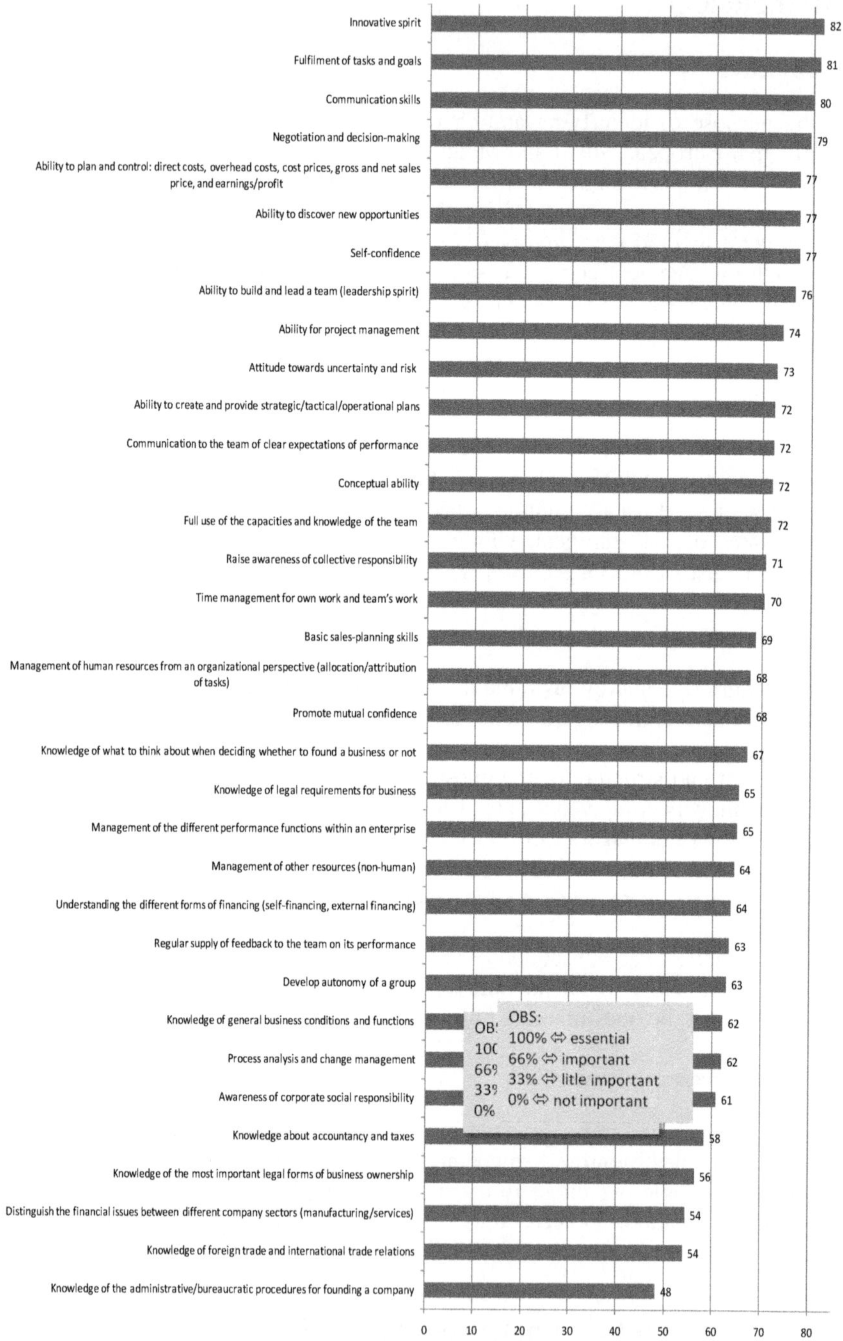

Fig. 1. Ranking of SME managers' competences

of all answers and respective graduation. The statistic analysis of the collected data allowed us to identify the competences that SMEs managers regarded as most important. As we can see in Figure 1, all 34 competences are considered relevant.

A first set of competences, that we can name as the top 4, three are related to personal characteristics of managers (innovative spirit, fulfillment of tasks and goals and communication skills) and one with team management (negotiation and decision making abilities). In a very dynamic economic context, it is understandable that managers need to be able to generate innovative responses, decide in an adequate frame of time to implement them, communicate/negotiate them to all stakeholders, implement the necessary changes and put them in practice (goals) in order to challenge competitors and seduce customers.

A second set of "less" important but still very important competences are related to business and finance (ability to plan and control costs), to personal characteristics (ability to discover new opportunities and self-confidence) and to team management (ability to build and lead a team).

We stress here particularly the importance given to the necessity of planning and controlling costs in the context of increasing market pressure due to competitiveness and the recent financial crisis.

The following competences in order of importance are of very mixed characteristics.

The competences that are on the bottom of the list, that is to say the ones considered less important among all of them, relate to technical non financial aspects and business and financial aspects, specifically concerning the foundation of company. It is interesting to underline that knowledge about foreign trade and international relations is included in this last set of less important competences. The typical low degree of internationalization of SMEs might explain this situation. Most SMEs are concerned by issues dealing with their "local", more natural economic environment.

It deserves to be noted that all of the personal characteristics are considered of great importance, with five of them being at the first seven positions of the ranking.

5 Conclusions and Future Work

Through a survey applied to 154 SME managers of six European countries and its subsequent statistic analysis, it was possible to put at trial 34 competences that were previously listed as necessary and order them by their level of importance. Although results show that all competences were classified as relevant, it is possible to identify that the first top eight relate essentially to personal and team management, although they include one business and financial one, the ability of planning and controlling costs. The competences at the bottom of the list concern the ones dealing with company's foundation and internationalization.

Subsequent work will consist in analyzing the results of a survey which had the objective of identifying the competences in which SME managers need more training and cross this information with the one that was here presented. It will be also tested these results depend on some SMEs managers' characteristics like age, experienceand activity sector. That will enable educational agents to format their training supply to meet the more pressing needs according to the specific characteristics of the SMEs managers and target groups.

References

1. Velegrakis, G., et al.: SME managers' required entrepreneurship and business competences (poster). In: CENTERIS - Conference on ENTERprise Information Systems, UTAD: Esposende, Portugal, pp. 725–726 (2009)
2. Audretsch, D., et al.: First Section of the Annual Report on EU Small and Medium-sized Enterprises. In: European Commission, Directorate General Enterprise and Industry, EIM (2009)
3. Schmiemann, M.: Enterprises by size class - overview of SMEs in the EU. In: Office for Official Publications of the European Communities: Luxembourg (2008)
4. EC, Communication from the Commission to the Council, the European Parliament, the European Economic and Social Committee and the Committee of the Regions - "Think Small First" - A "Small Business Act" for Europe, European Commission Directorate-General for Enterprise (2008)
5. NJM European, A Study and Analysis of Management Training~Techniques for the Heads of SMEs, particularly Using the Information and Communication Technologies (ICTs), Report for the Directorate-General for Enterprise of the European Commission under contract DGENT 99/C/A3/31 S12.128934 (2000)
6. Velegrakis, G., et al.: SME managers' required entrepreneurship and business competences. In: Cruz-Cunha, M.M., Varajão, J.E. (eds.) E-Business Issues Challenges and Opportunities for SMEs: Driving Competitiveness. IGI-Global (2010)
7. BCC, Annual Report on the SME sector in Romania. Bucharest Chamber of Commerce Publications, Bucharest (2008)
8. HRAKK, Description of the main contents of the Finnish entrepreneurs. HRAKK Publications, Hyvinkaa (2009)
9. Pichler, J.: SME-specific "profiles", strategic potentials and attitudes toward internationalization in the enlarged EU (2009)
10. DIDA, Description of the Italian entrepreneurs. DIDA Publications, Rome (2009)
11. Tampere, Finnish Survey on Collegiate Entrepreneurship. Tampere University of Technology (2006)
12. Klen, E., Pereira-Klen, A., Gesser, C.: Towards the sustainability of virtual organisation Management. In: Apêndice XII – artigo anexo ao questionário validação etapa (February 2009)
13. Pais, C.: As representações da Liderança Eficaz no contexto empresarial do Norte de Portugal. Dissertação de Mestrado em Psicologia Social e das Organizações (2003); Universidade Fernando Pessoa: Porto.Smith, T.F., Waterman, M.S.: Identification of Common Molecular Subsequences. J. Mol. Biol. 147, 195–197 (1981)

Appendix: Questionnaire

According to your experience, what management aspects do you consider relevant for the manager of an SME? (For each of the following aspects, please select the answer that better reflects your opinion.)

Competence	Not important	Little important	Important	Essential
Attitude towards uncertainty and risk	□	□	□	□
Innovative spirit	□	□	□	□
Fulfilment of tasks and goals	□	□	□	□
Self-confidence	□	□	□	□
Communication skills	□	□	□	□
Ability to discover new opportunities	□	□	□	□
Conceptual ability	□	□	□	□
Negotiation and decision-making	□	□	□	□
Time management for own work and the team's work	□	□	□	□
Communication to the team of very clear expectations of performance	□	□	□	□
Regular supply of feedback to the team on its performance	□	□	□	□
Full use of the capacities and knowledge of the team	□	□	□	□
Promote mutual confidence	□	□	□	□
Develop autonomy of a group	□	□	□	□
Raise awareness of collective responsibility	□	□	□	□
Ability to build and lead a team (leadership spirit)	□	□	□	□
Ability for project management	□	□	□	□
Ability to create and provide Strategic/tactical/operational plans	□	□	□	□
Management of human resources from an organizational perspective (allocation/attribution of tasks)	□	□	□	□
Management of other resources (non-human)	□	□	□	□
Awareness of corporate social responsibility	□	□	□	□
Knowledge of the administrative/bureaucratic process for founding a company	□	□	□	□
Knowledge of the legal requirements for business	□	□	□	□
Knowledge of the most important legal forms of business ownership	□	□	□	□
Process analysis and change management	□	□	□	□
Knowledge of general business conditions and functions	□	□	□	□
Knowledge of what to think about when deciding whether to found a business or not	□	□	□	□
Knowledge of foreign trade and international trade relations	□	□	□	□
Distinguish the financial issues between different company sectors (manufacturing/services)	□	□	□	□

Management of the different performance functions within an enterprise	□	□	□	□
Understanding of different forms of financing (self-financing, external financing)	□	□	□	□
Basic sales-planning skills	□	□	□	□
Knowledge of accountancy and taxes	□	□	□	□
Ability to plan and control: direct costs, overhead costs, cost prices, gross and net sales price, and earnings/profits	□	□	□	□

Adaptive Access Control Modes Enforcement in Organizations*

Sérgio Guerreiro[1], André Vasconcelos[1,2], and José Tribolet[1,2]

[1] CODE - Center for Organizational Design & Engineering, INOV, Rua Alves Redol 9, Lisbon, Portugal
[2] Department of Information Systems and Computer Science, Instituto Superior Técnico, Technical University of Lisbon, Portugal
sergio.guerreiro@ist.utl.pt, andre.vasconcelos@dei.ist.utl.pt, jose.tribolet@inesc.pt

Abstract. Granting the correct access between the agents and the artifacts is nowadays in the organizations agendas. The risk of allowing unauthorized accesses to critical information requires new solutions that are capable of dealing with a holistic perspective. Adaptive OACM refers to the capability of enforcing fine-grained access policies to business processes, services and information systems whenever facing changes, for instance, governance policies. This paper proposes an OACM ontology based in the RBAC, UUID, Rules and architectural model concepts. For exemplification purposes we instantiate the concepts of the ontology to an approval expense problem.

Keywords: ACM, RBAC, Artifacts, Organization, Workflow, Services, Informational entities.

1 Problem statement

The access control modes (ACM) that are necessary to authorize a fine-grained access to organizational artifacts bounds an organizational wide problem. Moreover, if the artifacts are located in different architectural layers of an organization, or cross organizations, then an additional effort is needed. Organizational ACM (OACM) is thus defined as the structural aspects for granting or revoking the correct access between the agents and the artifacts. Typically, the ACM strategies are applied to silos inside the organization [5][9]. For each silo, a set of well-known requirements is used, *e.g.:* applications authorization, operating systems authorization or database authorization. However those approaches are not suitable for an organization-wide perspective. With this work we seek for a complete fine-grained rastreability between the agents (either Human or machines), the artifacts, their actions and the orchestration between the actions. An application example for this endeavour is the cloud computing environment [19][20] where the access to the artifacts in the cloud must consider the interoperability between the different Persons and systems working in a integrated manner.

* This work was partially supported by the Fundação para a Ciência e a Tecnologia (SFRH / BD/ 43252 / 2008).

J.E. Quintela Varajão et al. (Eds.): CENTERIS 2010, Part II, CCIS 110, pp. 283–294, 2010.

From other point of view, the adaptability quality of an information system is broadly referenced in the foundations of Software Engineering, *e.g.*: the recommended practices for software requirements IEEE 830-1998 [17] and the software architecture [21]. The software adaptability is identified, among others, as extra-functional properties of a system that should be included in its design. The adaptability quality in Software Engineering aims in minimizing the software deterioration due to change [18]. Also in the normalized systems theory presented by Mannaert *et al.* [13] a strong focus is given to the adaptability of a system: the postulate 1 defines that *"a design pattern needs to be stable with respect to anticipated changes"*. We define the OACM adaptability quality as the capability to enforce new or modified access policies the organizational artifacts, in real time, with the minimal effort. To enforce the OACM we consider the artifacts from the following architectures: business processes, services and informational entities.

Therefore, with this paper we seek a solution to the adaptive fine-grained ACM enforcement in an organization by proposing a complete ontological model that includes adaptability concerns, in order to allow a fully configurable access authorization.

At this point its also relevant to state that the U.S. Department of Homeland Security [14] defines the following objectives that are strongly related with the ACM body of knowledge: *(i)* assigned in the strategic goal #5:*"Integrate DHS Policy, Planning, and Operations Coordination. We will strengthen and unify strategic and policy direction through improved strategic planning and assessment. We will ensure that these efforts are integrated with and informed by the Department's operations coordination and planning efforts. We will create and enhance a DHS operations coordination capability to plan for and coordinate non-routine, cross-cutting operations that require multi-Component activities"*, and *(ii)* assigned in the strategic goal #3:*"Improve Cyber Security. We will reduce our vulnerabilities to cyber system threats before they can be exploited to damage the Nation's critical infrastructures and ensure that such disruptions of cyberspace are infrequent, of minimal duration, manageable, and cause the least damage possible"*. These definitions reinforce the need to further investigate this problem, offering solutions that consider the overall complexity inside one organization.

This paper is the result of an action research methodology effort supported by an OACM ontology simulator, which is implemented in OO and relational database schema. It is exemplified with a classical approval expenses problem in an organization. This methodology allowed the experimentation of problem resolution strategies, as well as induced an iterative, detailed and coherent implementation of each ontology concept. The presented example is specifically concerned with the OACM issues rather than the architectural rastreability of the artifacts in the different layers. However, for OACM demonstration purposes of the fine-grained access control to organizational artifacts we defined a static relationship between them.

The rest of the paper is organized as follow. Section 2 presents the related work with the role based access control (RBAC) ACM and the existing efforts to apply it to organizations. Section 3 proposes an OACM conceptual meta-model and defines the main concepts. Section 4 exemplifies the OACM applied to a simplified approval expenses problem. Finally, Section 5 concludes and points to future work.

2 Related Work

2.1 Role Based Access Control

The standard NIST98 [5][9] models the concepts for symmetric role-based access control (RBAC) ACM to be used between the users, roles, permissions and constraints. It represents an evolution from the Discretionary Access Control (DAC), Mandatory Access Control (MAC) and other policies due to less provisioning effort needed [10]. The users are directly assigned to a role, each role has a set of associated permissions and changing the permissions affects the users associated with each role. Some well-known constraints are: separation of duties (SoD), conflict of interest (CoI), delegation of duties (DoD), binding of duty (BoD), history-based separation of duties (HsD) to newly identified constraints in the social networks such as the context constraints [4]. This model is applicable to organizational silos; however it is limited to only one kind of organizational artifact, at a single time. The NIST98 is broadly used in single architectural layers such as applications or databases [12], however the enforcement in WfMS is still an unsolved challenge [6]. Bertino *et al.* in [2][3] proposes the combination of static, dynamic and hybrid constraints to split the enforcement of RBAC in WfMS: the static constraints are processed offline and the dynamic constraints requires an execution engine to monitor the workflow sessions. Wolter *et al.* in [11] defines a set of workflow primitives and then experiments the concept of notations to express the associated constraints, however the concept of a transaction (rollback and commit concern) is not addressed by this proposal.

2.2 Organizational RBAC

Since there are no separation between the organizational and the system roles in the RBAC approach then it is not satisfactory to control the artifacts spread through the different architectures of an organization. This is true only in organizations where each Person has the same system and hierarchical role [10].

Park *et al.* in [8] proposes to unify ACM by separating the organizational and the system roles. The OR-SRA maps them, in real-time, using the concepts of constraints, roles, permissions, sessions and hierarchy. The OR-SRA is mapped accordingly with a predefined set of relations, requiring an extra effort of role engineering [1].

An alternative solution is proposed by Myong *et al.* in [7] under the scope of inter-enterprises business processes execution. Each enterprise has its own RBAC and the role domain of each one is passed through the communications. The authors argue that their approach *(i)* separates the application-level from the organization-level, *(ii)* achieve a fine-grained control and *(iii)* supports dynamic constraints. However, this proposal does not encompass the time and versioning concern, neither relates disparate architectural layers.

Zhixiong Zhang PhD thesis's in [15] extends the NIST98 standard with the concepts of Organization and Asset, justified by the incapacity of the model for the cross-organization ACM. The aim is to create a ROBAC between organizations that possess different assets. The roles are mapped with the assets and each asset has its own permission set, but the assets are not further detailed neither the relation between the assets. It also lacks in the assumption that the organizations have comparable roles. To enforce it uses a manifold that implements a virtual organization which refers to the involved assets. By security concerns, in the end it is deleted.

3 Proposed Solution

Fig. 1 depicts our proposed OACM concepts. The `users` are the ones that take actions in the organization, they might be either Persons or machines. The `model` is the core concept representing the architecture layers considered to the access control: *(i)* Workflow, is a set of orchestration steps, encompassing agents and actions; *(ii)* Services, are the actions performed; and *(iii)* Information entities, represents the entities that are computed by the actions. Each model is implemented by a set of `Fieldmodel` which represents the detail of each of the model. Further detail for each `Fieldmodel` can be expressed by the `Property` concept. Each `Fieldmodel` establish the `permission` required to execute it. Each `Fieldmodel` also requires the previous definition of a `role`.

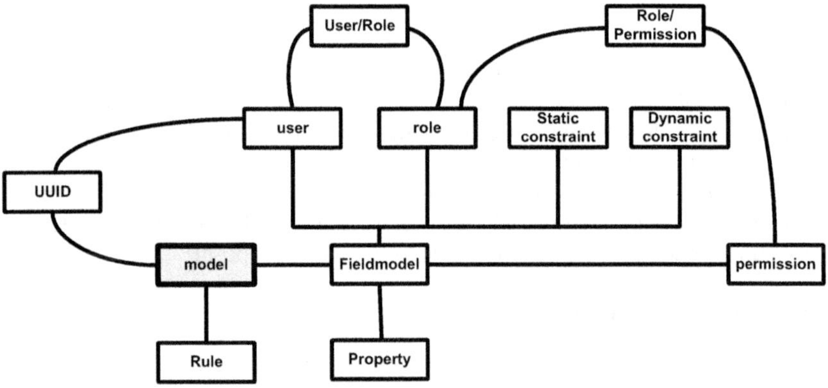

Fig. 1. OACM conceptual meta-model

Following the RBAC principles, an `user` can only execute a `Fieldmodel` if and only if *(i)* his `role` is assessed successfully by the `User/Role` mapping, *(ii)* his `role` is checked in the `Role/Permission` mapping and *(iii)* none of the `static constraint` and `dynamic constraint` are triggered. For exemplification purposes, the `static` and the `dynamic constraint` are implementing by separation of duties (SoD) policy.

Each `model` defines their set of `users` and `roles`, resulting in the creation of different identifiers for the same `user` or `role` through the 3 distinct `models`. To solve this issue, the `UUID` concept defines a transversal identification of `users` through the different `models` of the organizational.

Fig. 2 distinguishes the concepts of `model` and `session`, the first is composed by `Fieldmodel`, `roles` and `static constraint` and the second is an instantiation of the `model` by a `user` and by `dynamic constraint`. A transformation between `Role` and `User` is also required in the session.

The enforcement of the RBAC in the sessions represents the local access control, *e.g.:* each user invocation of a task within a workflow is always checked to verify if the role is correct, the permission allows and no constraint is triggered. However, a

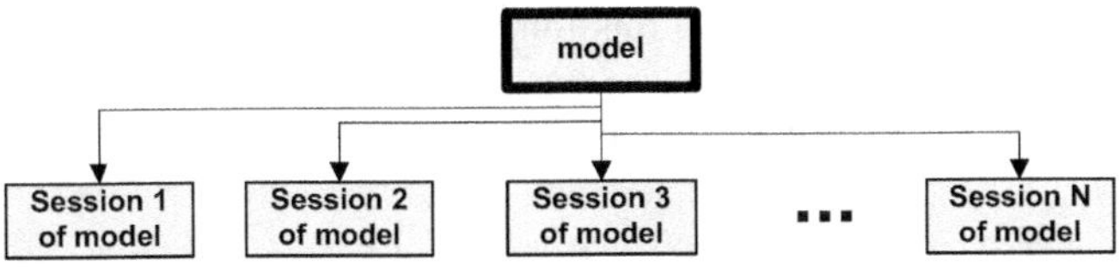

Fig. 2. Architecture of workflow, services and informational entities: `Model` and `Session`

global access control that is concerned with the relationship between the `Session` is also required, *e.g.:* the access to the workflow tasks is granted but the access to the information entities is not granted due to personal relationships of the user. To solve this issue we propose the concept of the `Rule` execution between different `Models`. The `rules` have *adhoc* definition.

Therefore, the expected results from the OACM are *(i)* the access check to the artifacts of each `model` and *(ii)* the access check between the artifacts of different `models`. The output produced corresponds to a grant or to a revoke.

3.1 Advantages of the Proposed Solution

The following advantages are identified with the proposed OACM: *(i)* not intrusive to the organizational artifacts while it establishes a virtual architecture that intercepts the execution of the sessions; *(ii)* `models` are tailor-made and with least privileges enforcement; *(iii)* `models` representation could be independent from the sessions IS architecture representation used by the organization; *(iv)* a virtual architecture only exists when needed, it is deleted in the end of the execution of the sessions, improving the security; *(v)* a virtual architecture offers an adaptability mechanism to be used by the organization and *(vi)* it is possible to refining the ACM policy in each `model`.

3.2 Primitives for the OACM Proposal

From the above concepts we summarize them as a set of definitions to be used by the OACM computational simulation. These set of definitions allow a better understanding of the related concepts as well as facilitate the development process of the simulator.

Definition 1: A `model` is a static representation of a workflow, or services, or informational entities, which are contained in an organizational environment, encompassing the `FieldModels`, the `roles` and the `staticConstraints`. The instantiation of a `model` is a `session`. A `session` includes the same information as the `model` except concerning the *(i)* `users` and their transformation process to `Roles` and the *(ii)* `dynamicConstraints`.

Definition 2: Each Person or machine, contained in and organizational environment have unique identities. The unique identities apply to the `role`, `permission`, `staticConstraint`, `dynamicConstraint` and `user`. The RBAC approach is used to enforce each identity to his `Role` and `Permission`.

Definition 3: Consider that a `model` is represented by a graph *G* composed by artifacts *A* and relationships *R*. *UR(A=user)* represents the user mapping to a role.

RP(A=permission) represents the permission mapping to the correspondingly role, and that *[]* represents the computation of a constraint. Then, the check access assessment, for one specific model, is computed by the eq. **(1)**, producing a result of *true* or *false*.

$$\begin{aligned}&\text{CheckAccess()} = \\ &G_{model}(A{=}role\ ,\ R) \cap G_{session}(A{=}UR(user)\ ,\ R)\ \cap \\ &G_{model}(A{=}RP(permission)\ ,\ R) \cap \\ &G_{model}(A{=}role[staticConstraint],R) \cap G_{session}(\ A{=}UR(user[dynamicConstraint]),R)\end{aligned} \quad (1)$$

Definition 4: The check access assessment between two different `models` is performed by *adhoc* `rules`. The rules are composed by a set of operators and predefined operations. The operators are taken from the `Model` and `session`. The structure of the *adhoc* rules is virtual and is deleted in the end of the usage.

Definition 5: The adaptability of the OACM is offered by: *(i)* the RBAC mapping, *(ii)* the `staticconstraint` and `dynamicconstraint`, *(iii)* the `uuid` mapping, *(iv)* the `fieldmodel` defined in each `model`, *(v)* the `property` defined in each `fieldmodel`, *(vi)* mapping functions such as *UR()* and *RP()* presented in definition 3 and *(vii) adhoc* `rule` definition.

Definition 6: each OACM is only valid in a limited timeframe.

4 Expenses Approval Example

A simplified expenses approval scenario is used to demonstrate the applicability of the proposed OACM. Fig. 3 summarizes the set of activities involved in the expense approval. If the employee expense's are less or equal than 500€ than the manager is able to approve from a predefined budget, however for expenses greater than 500€ a escalate procedure to the director is required. At any time, the expense requests might be rejected or cancelled. The result of enforcing the equation (1) in the models of workflow, services and information entities with a predefined access structure is a granting or a revoking to the desired access. The predefined access structure is presented in subsections 4.1 and 4.2, the models are presented in subsection 4.3, and the global enforcement in subsection 4.4.

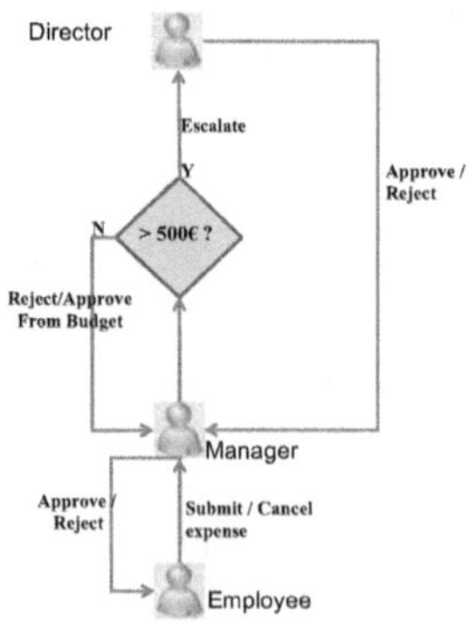

Fig. 3. Approval expense interactions including 3 Persons: employee, manager and director

4.1 Unique Identities

Regarding the definition 2, and following an approach similar to [16], Table 1 presents the universal mapping for each Person that is involved in the expense approval problem. Each Person has a different user for each model, which must be maintained separately. The UUID column allows the definition of unique identifiers to be used when designing the rules between different models.

Table 1. `UUID` - Universal access table

Person	UUID	Workflow User	Application User	Information user
António	0001	Actor1	A001	E_APP
João	0002	Actor2	J002	M_APP
Manuel	0003	Actor3	M003	D_APP

4.2 RBAC for Local Access Control

Also regarding the definition 2, each model have a specific RBAC definition, where *(i)* the workflow RBAC is defined by Table 2 and Table 3, *(ii)* the services RBAC is defined by Table 4 and Table 5 and *(iii)* the informational entities is defined by Table 6 and Table 7. Each Person has a User, with a set of related Roles for accessing each Model, and correspondingly each Role is also related with a set of Permissions for that Model. It is possible to manage (*e.g.:* add, remove or change) the Users associated with a Role and it is also possible to manage the Permissions associated with a Role.

Table 2. `UR` relationship for workflow

Person	User Workflow	Role Workflow
Antonio	Actor1	Employee
Joao	Actor2	Director
Manuel	Actor3	Manager

Table 3. `RP` relationship for workflow

Role Workflow	Task Permission
Director	Task3
Employee	Task1
Manager	Task4
Manager	Task2

Table 4. `UR` relationship for services

Person	User Service	Role Service
Antonio	A001	EmployeeService
Joao	J002	ManagerService
Manuel	M003	DirectorService

Table 5. `RP` relationship for services

Role Service	Service Permission
DirectorService	ApproveExpense()
DirectorService	RejectExpense()
DirectorService	Login()
DirectorService	Logout()
EmployeeService	ExpenseSubmission()
EmployeeService	ExpenseCancellation()
EmployeeService	Login()
EmployeeService	Logout()
ManagerService	RejectFromBudget()
ManagerService	Logout()
ManagerService	Login()
ManagerService	ExpenseEscalate()
ManagerService	ApproveFromBudget()

Table 6. UR relationship for information entities

Person	User Information Entity	Role Information Entity
Antonio	E_APP	EI_Employee
Joao	M_APP	EI_Manager
Manuel	D_APP	EI_Director

Table 7. RP relationship for information entities

Role Information Entity	Operation Permission
EI_Director	UPDATE
EI_Director	READ
EI_Director	DELETE
EI_Employee	READ
EI_Employee	CREATE
EI_Employee	DELETE
EI_Manager	DELETE
EI_Manager	CREATE
EI_Manager	UPDATE
EI_Manager	READ

4.3 Model Definition

Regarding the definition 1 for models and sessions, Table 8, Table 9 and Table 11 define the three separate models, presented in a tabular form. Firstly, Table 8 presents the sequence of tasks that are necessary to define the workflow of expenses greater than 500€, using the notation proposed in [13]. A static constraint of SoD is defined, meaning that is not allowed for the Director or Manager to approve their own expenses.

Table 8. Model definition for the approval expense workflow

Start State	End State	Task name	Role WF	Static constraint
Creation	Submitted	Task 1, Submiting	Employee	SoD
Submitted	Account available	Task 2, checking account	Manager	SoD
Account available	Approved	Task 3, approving	Director	SoD
Approved	Reimbursed	Task 4, reimbursing	Manager	SoD

Table 9. Model definition for the approval expense services

Service	Role Service	Static Constraint
ApproveExpense()	DirectorService	
Login()	DirectorService	
Logout()	DirectorService	
RejectExpense()	DirectorService	
ExpenseCancellation()	EmployeeService	
ExpenseSubmission()	EmployeeService	
Login()	EmployeeService	
Logout()	EmployeeService	
ApproveFromBudget()	ManagerService	
ExpenseEscalate()	ManagerService	
Login()	ManagerService	
Logout()	ManagerService	
RejectFromBudget()	ManagerService	

Table 10. Relation between the Services and the informational entities

service \ Information entities	Document	authorization	account	budget
Login()		R		
ExpenseSubmission()	C			
ExpenseCancellation()	RD			
Logout()		R		
Login()		R		
ApproveFrombudget()			CR	CR
RejectFromBudget()			RD	RD
ExpenseEscalate()	RU			
Logout()		R		
Login()		R		
ApproveExpense()			RU	
RejectExpense()			RD	
Logout()		R		

Table 11. Model definition for the approval expense information entities

Information entity	Operation	Role IE	Static constraint
Account	DELETE	EI_Director	
Account	READ	EI_Director	
Account	UPDATE	EI_Director	
Authorization	READ	EI_Director	
Document	READ	EI_Director	
Authorization	READ	EI_Employee	
Document	CREATE	EI_Employee	
Document	DELETE	EI_Employee	
Document	READ	EI_Employee	
Account	CREATE	EI_Manager	
Account	READ	EI_Manager	
Acount	DELETE	EI_Manager	
Authorization	READ	EI_Manager	
Budget	CREATE	EI_Manager	
Budget	DELETE	EI_Manager	
Budget	READ	EI_Manager	
Document	READ	EI_Manager	
Document	UPDATE	EI_Manager	

Secondly, Table 9 presents which services are used by each Role. The service invocation sequence is depicted in Fig. 3. None static constraint is used.

Thirdly, Table 11 specifies the information entities that are used in expense approval. Each information entity is involved in one or more operation. The informational entities that are used in each service are presented in the CRUD matrix by Table 10. None static constraint is considered.

4.4 Model Execution and Global Access Control by Rules

Regarding the definition 3, for each model from subsection 4.3, the check access assessment is performed, using the equation (1). When a row of the table is delivered then it means that the access is granted for that Fieldmodel. As expected, three different areas are identified (by thicker borders) in Table 12: the workflow, the services and information entities. The user identifies the running sessions in each area. The Persons that execute the sessions are always one of the three involved: Antonio, Joao or Manuel. Any dynamic constraint must be also considered in this step. To guarantee security when all sessions stop then this access table must be deleted.

Table 12 also presents the result of applying one rule presented by the *adhoc* equation (2) to the local check access assessment table. The result is represented by shadowed cells, it expresses the dependency between the workflow model and the informational entities layers. In this case, a session performed by Antonio in submitting the expense, automatically grants the authorization to the UPDATE account by Manuel. Therefore, the rule allow the cross model access control, which is essential to a holistic perspective of the organization.

```
CheckGlobalAccess() =
/* automatic approval for Antonio expenses*/                    (2)
   IF (Antonio submits expense in task1) THEN Manuel UPDATE Account;
```

Table 12. Execution sessions and global access control

Person	All User	All Role	workflow task	service	information entities	
Antonio	Actor1	Employee	Submiting - task1			
Manuel	Actor3	Manager	CheckingAccount-task2			
Joao	Actor2	Director	Approving - task 3			
Manuel	Actor3	Manager	Reimbursing - task 4			
Antonio	A001	EmployeeService		Login()		
Antonio	A001	EmployeeService		ExpenseSubmission()		
Antonio	A001	EmployeeService		Logout()		
Joao	J002	ManagerService		Login()		
Joao	J002	ManagerService		ApproveFromBudget()		
Joao	J002	ManagerService		ExpenseEscalate()		
Joao	J002	ManagerService		Logout()		
Manuel	M003	DirectorService		Login()		
Manuel	M003	DirectorService		ApproveExpense()		
Manuel	M003	DirectorService		Logout()		
Antonio	A001	EmployeeService		ExpenseCancellation()		
Joao	J002	ManagerService		RejectFromBudget()		
Manuel	M003	DirectorService		RejectExpense()		
Antonio	E_APP	EI_Employee			Document	CREATE
Antonio	E_APP	EI_Employee			Authorization	READ
Antonio	E_APP	EI_Employee			Document	READ
Antonio	E_APP	EI_Employee			Document	DELETE
Joao	M_APP	EI_Manager			Account	CREATE
Joao	M_APP	EI_Manager			Budget	CREATE
Joao	M_APP	EI_Manager			Account	READ
Joao	M_APP	EI_Manager			Budget	READ
Joao	M_APP	EI_Manager			Document	READ
Joao	M_APP	EI_Manager			Authorization	READ
Joao	M_APP	EI_Manager			Document	UPDATE
Joao	M_APP	EI_Manager			Acount	DELETE
Joao	M_APP	EI_Manager			Budget	DELETE
Manuel	D_APP	EI_Director			Authorization	READ
Manuel	D_APP	EI_Director			Document	READ
Manuel	D_APP	EI_Director			Account	READ
Manuel	D_APP	EI_Director			Account	UPDATE
Manuel	D_APP	EI_Director			Account	DELETE

5 Conclusions and Future Work

This paper proposes ontology for controlling the access to organizational artifacts (OACM). The ontology is exemplified with a simplified expense approval process.
As referred by the definition 5 for the general case, and particularly for this example, the adaptive OACM counterparts are: RBAC and UUID configuration, model definition and constraints and the rules definition between models. These counterparts allow an organization to control his artifacts accesses either by a local or a global perspective.

The OACM does not enclose all the security protocols needed in one organization but it is rather a structural mechanism that allows the fine-grained control access using a non-intrusive approach. Fine-grained is a continuous process of artifacts authorization running on a real-time basis. Furthermore, the enforcement result represents the OACM observability and the adaptive OACM counterpart represents the actuation. Hence, with OACM we obtain a security governance implementation capable of controlling cyber security or coordination security policies, applied to one organization.

We identify the following issues to be further researched as future work: *(i)* a comprehensive implementation of the meta-model in a real case study, the artifacts access information might be collected using interceptors and the grant/revoke operation might be implemented by remote controlling the execution of the interceptors, *(ii)* definition of a complete language set for the rules implementation and *(iii)* further develop the definition 6, integrating the time concerns in the equation (1) to achieve an history based OACM.

References

1. Atluri, V.: Panel on role engineering. In: SACMAT 2008: Proceedings of the 13th ACM Symposium on Access Control Models and Technologies, New York, NY, USA, pp. 61–62 (2008)
2. Bertino, E., Ferrari, E., Atluri, V.: The specification and enforcement of authorization constraints in workflow management systems. ACM Trans. Inf. Syst. Secur. 2(1), 65–104 (1999)
3. Bertino, E., Ferrari, E., Atluri, V.: A flexible model supporting the specification and enforcement of role-based authorization in workflow management systems. In: RBAC 1997: Proceedings of the Second ACM Workshop on Role-based Access Control, New York, NY, USA, pp. 1–12 (1997)
4. Carminati, F.E., Perego, A.: Enforcing access control in web-based social networks. ACM Trans. Inf. Syst. Secur. 13(1), 1–38 (2009)
5. Ferraiolo, D., Sandhu, R., Gavrila, S., Kuhn, R., Chandramouli, R.: Proposed nist standard for role-based access control. ACM Trans. Inf. Syst. Secur. 4(3), 224–274 (2001)
6. Hung, P., Karlapalem, K.: A secure workflow model. In: ACSW Frontiers 2003: Proceedings of the Australasian Information Security Workshop Conference on ACSW Frontiers 2003, pp. 33–41. Australian Computer Society, Inc., Darlinghurst (2003)
7. Kang, M., Park, J., Froscher, J.: Access control mechanisms for inter-organizational workflow. In: SACMAT 2001: Proceedings of the Sixth ACM Symposium on Access Control Models and Technologies, New York, NY, USA, pp. 66–74 (2001)
8. Park, J., Costello, K., Neven, T., Diosomito, J.: A composite rbac approach for large, complex organizations. In: SACMAT 2004: Proceedings of the Ninth ACM Symposium on Access Control Models and Technologies, New York, NY, USA, pp. 163–172 (2004)
9. Sandhu, R., Ferraiolo, D., Kuhn, R.: The nist model for role-based access control: Towards a unified standard. In: Proceedings of the Fifth ACM Workshop on Role-based Access Control, pp. 47–63 (2000)
10. Smith, C.: A survey to determine federal agency needs for a role-based access control security product. In: International Symposium on Software Engineering Standards, p. 222 (1997)
11. Wolter, C., Schaad, A., Meinel, C.: Task-based entailment constraints for basic workflow patterns. In: SACMAT 2008: Proceedings of the 13th ACM Symposium on Access Control Models and Technologies, New York, NY, USA, pp. 51–60 (2008)
12. Ferraiolo, D., Kuhn, R., Chandramuli, R.: Role-Based Access control, 2nd edn. Artech House, Norwood (2007)
13. Herwig, M., Verelst, J.: Normalized Systems: Re-creating Information Technology based on Laws for Software Evolvability, Koppa (2009)
14. Department of Homeland Security Strategic Plan Fiscal Years 2008–2013, Homeland Security, USA (2008), `http://www.dhs.org`

15. Zhixiong, Z.: Scalable role organization based access control and its administration, PhD Thesis (2008)
16. Slone, S.: The Open Group Identity Management Work Area, Identity Management (March 2004)
17. IEEE830:1998, IEEE recommended practice for software requirements specifications. Technical report, Software Engineering Standards Committee of the IEEE Computer Society (1998)
18. Pressman, R.: Software Engineering, A practitioner's Approach, 3rd edn. Mc Graw Hill Book Company, Europe (1992)
19. Kaufman, L.: Data Security in the World of Cloud Computing. Security & Privacy 7(4), 61–64 (2009)
20. Kandukuri, B., Paturi, V., Rakshit, A.: Cloud Security Issues. In: IEEE International Conference on Services Computing, SCC 2009, September 21-25, pp. 517–520 (2009)
21. Shaw, M., Garlan, D.: Formulations and Formalisms in Software Architecture. In: van Leeuwen, J. (ed.) Computer Science Today. LNCS, vol. 1000, Springer, Heidelberg (1995)

Organizational Knowledge: Ethics and the Importance of Trust

Gonçalo Jorge Morais da Costa*, Mary Prior, and Simon Rogerson

De Montfort University, The Gateway
Leicester, LE1 9BH, United Kingdom
goncaloj@netc.pt, mprior@dmu.ac.uk, srog@dmu.ac.uk

Abstract. The aim of this paper is to grasp the ethical dilemmas that arise into organizational knowledge and the importance of trust for diminishing these dilemmas. Therefore, it focuses three key issues: knowledge management (concept; and, schools of thought); knowledge flowing models versus ethics (mental models; the Socialization, Externalization, Combination, Internalization (SECI) model; and, Fiske's relational model); and finally, the importance of trust as a possible answer. Plus, this paper suggests that the previous models only focus knowledge as continuum process and the result of this process omits ethical and moral dilemmas (obligation to share, personal property, personal worth, autonomy, dignity, privacy, etc.). These ethical dilemmas clearly weaken a knowledge management project, and how trust is a reliable answer. The absence of empirical work should be considered a limitation of this paper; however, does not diminish the importance for this debate.

Keywords: Knowledge management; Organizational knowledge; Ethics; Organizational ethics; Trust.

1 Introduction

It is broadly recognized that society in which people live today has gradually been turned into a "global knowledge society" [1]. The knowledge society is a conception that has often appeared in the literature worldwide in recent years. The new era has also been referred by a variety of other authors: knowledge paradigm or to see the world from a knowledge perspective; knowledge economy; knowledge revolution or, knowledge capital era; knowledge era. Whatever name the "knowledge era" goes by, it is rewriting the rules of business and forcing a radical rethink of corporate values and business models of past eras, which means knowledge, is clearly a resource [2]. However, managers should realize that knowledge is bounded to people (human resources) and therefore, implicating a considerable amount of ethical and moral dilemmas through the "knowledge continuum process" (creation, retention, and sharing), which existent models of knowledge management seem to disregard.

So, knowledge is currently a key organizational resource for corporate success [3]. Plus, ethical dilemmas arise into a knowledge management project, and to recognize

* Corresponding author.

J.E. Quintela Varajão et al. (Eds.): CENTERIS 2010, Part II, CCIS 110, pp. 295–304, 2010.

these assumptions and the importance of trust is critical for managers, in order to reduce considerably the risk of losing organizational competitiveness. In conclusion, this paper discusses: the concept of knowledge management; the interaction of knowledge flow models with ethics; and, the importance of trust.

2 Knowledge Management

2.1 The Concept

During the literature review process it is possible to acknowledge several definitions regarding knowledge management, as for instance, the one of [4]: knowledge management is the acquisition and use of resources to create an environment in which information is accessible to individuals and in which individuals acquire, share and use that information to develop their own knowledge and are encouraged and enabled to apply their knowledge for the benefit of the organization. Nonetheless, [5] echoes that two myths exist concerning knowledge management technology´s features: they deliver the right information to the right person at the right time; and, they can store human intelligence and experience (utopian perspective)!

Thus, a knowledge management project embraces two different concepts: the learning organization and organizational knowledge. Learning organizations are adaptive to their external environment, continually enhance their capability to change or adapt, develop collective, as well as, individual learning, and use the learning results to achieve better results [6]. Meanwhile, the essence of organizational knowledge entails two perspectives: "knowledge as a process" that focus the issues regarding creation, use and recreation, as well as, the dynamics of such process; and, "knowledge as a product", that spotlight the way knowledge is shared, used and stored. These analytical dimensions only recognize the process or the results, not embracing the ethical dilemmas that arise in organizational knowledge. So, this assumption imposes the following questions: can we encounter ethics concerning organizational knowledge? Do managers realize that these moral dilemmas exist?

2.2 Schools of Thought

Knowledge management is a reasonably recent research field, and therefore seems to engage a lack of conceptual stabilization, recognized by the insufficient empirical research and literature. Despite this conceptual youth, several schools of thought have arisen, originating a multiplicity of uses or applications in knowledge management. From them it is possible to distinguish three perceptions considering dissimilar geographical and historical contexts, as well as traditions or cultures that propitiate a theoretical orientation. A further analysis, allow us to catalogue these orientations as "more Japanese", "more European" and, as "more American."

The first school argues that organizations are conceived as creative "entities of knowledge", and for that, pleading the idea that knowledge is a process as [7], [8] demonstrate. The second approach assumes as presupposition the attempt to measure knowledge resources, namely through some European authors [9], seeking to audit intangible resources, accountancy and publishing, through intellectual capital indicators and appropriate systems that allow its measurement and popularization. Finally, the third perspective engages technology potential as a supportive tool to organizational processes, relating them with knowledge generation and management. Information and communication technologies are considered relevant to knowledge management, because they make possible optimization regarding extracting, structuring, codifying, storage, recovering and applying individual and organizational knowledge (see for example of [10]).

3 Knowledge Flow Models vs. Ethics

3.1 Mental Models vs. Ethics

Organizational context can be characterized as a melting pot of people. People that present innate skills in different levels, which means in each step in the reasoning process the problem solver will have different "analytical speed" [11], which means that workers less faster in their mental construction (or internal representation) of the problem situation could be dependent of other workers. Another important question to be raised is: in a sharing environment can we morally oblige people to work faster than their innate skills [12]?

Another important issue to focus is the implicit truth of a propositional logic. In spite of, [13] pleads the principle of truth in a human reasoner (particularly one that is ignorant of formal logic), is more likely to construct a model of what is true in presented information rather than of what is false: so the argument can be criticized... The main law of biology is the survival of the strongest and for that, competition is intrinsically bounded to that subject. In that sense, can we automatically deduce that people are constructing mental models based on truth when they have to share it [14]? As a form of defence, people can try to modify such principle, or during the transmission process can engage a different perspective on their mental construction.

3.2 SECI Model vs. Ethics

Researchers have created several frameworks and classifications concerning the existent types of knowledge transfer. For instance, [15] identifies five knowledge transfer situations usually seen in practice: serial transfer, near transfer, far transfer, strategic transfer, and expert transfer. Adopting a different perspective based on the actors involved in the process of knowledge transfer, [16] discerns four types, namely shared work producers, shared-work practitioners, expertise seeking novices, and secondary knowledge miners.

These frameworks, however, focus primarily on concepts such as the purpose of knowledge transfer, the actor involved (knowledge consumer, knowledge intermediary, or knowledge provider), the kind of knowledge needed, and challenges in finding and selecting knowledge. Research and commentary around the issue of ethics in knowledge transfer usually does not distinguish between knowledge transfer and knowledge sharing; however, the former has an instrumental connotation while the latter has a social connotation. This research has regarded the creation of ethical environments that promote sharing [17]; utopian organizational cultures and communities of knowledge sharing [18]; the paradox of the trade-off between holding personal tacit knowledge for individual productivity versus sharing that knowledge for organizational productivity [19]; and the use of ethics and self-interest as counter determinants of knowledge sharing [20]. Thus, the ethics of knowledge transfers and conversions become extremely important due to the individual loses sole rights to knowledge. Is this a transfer of property or personal worth [21]?

As an individual's private attribute, organizational programs that aim to forcibly develop knowledge-sharing cultures could violate individual privacy rights. These violations could become central in the ongoing debate regarding human rights protection, as a responsibility of multinational companies as well as governments. Do organizations "own" their employees knowledge, or is this knowledge an "attribute" of an autonomous individual and subject to protection under human rights to privacy or security-of-person? Is the development of knowledge-sharing organizational structures the rightful exercise of organizational intellectual property rights, or is it an invasion of worker privacy? Must there be an explicit employment contract that defines these intellectual property rights in a fairly manner [21].

Knowledge exists in different forms, and different forms may involve different conflicts. The conflicts sometimes pit organizational rights to knowledge against individual rights to knowledge. Such rights arise from accepted human rights frameworks that include property rights and privacy rights [22], and therefore this conflict is framed by cultural values that are shaped by national boundaries and organizational norms.

There is a debate whether knowledge can exist beyond the individual. This question seems to rests on how we define knowledge. Some definitions of knowledge emerge from the field of expert systems, encompassing structures beyond just information to include the rules for processing information. Other definitions arise from the viewpoint of knowledge as an organizational property, similar to a knowledge base, that encompasses routines and processes that contextualize information and enable action. Still others characterize knowledge as an innately human attribute, something that resides in the living mind of a person, because the mind must identify, interpret and internalize knowledge.

From a different perspective, organizational knowledge is also a knowledge asset or the "firm-specific resources that are indispensable to create values for the firm" [7]. Given their unique characteristics, knowledge assets cannot be immediately sold or bought. This is especially valid if knowledge assets are not in an articulated form but rather in the employees' minds or as know-how [7]. Consequently, buying and selling organizational knowledge involves transferring groups of individuals with established patterns of working together. These transactions can be achieved through knowledge alliances, joint ventures, mergers and acquisitions. The potential for hostile mergers and acquisitions opens avenues for the seizure of rights to individual knowledge by organizations whose ethical posture might contravene the moral beliefs of some of these individuals.

Moreover, organizational knowledge has a limited commercial value if it is not embedded in a particular setting. For instance, managerial experience and knowledge about customers, suppliers and competitors is "trapped inside the minds of key-employees" [7] and therefore, this knowledge may be useless. This observation offers additional support to our argument that an organization has the right of property over the employees' organizational knowledge. Hence, organizations depend on employees' behaviour to create and to transfer knowledge [23].

Personal knowledge may be excluded from manageable knowledge. For example, Klynveld Peat Marwick Goerdeler (KPMG) defines intellectual property as "not just patents, trademarks, copyrights, database rights and other pure intellectual property, but other forms of articulated knowledge, such as business processes, methodologies and know how" [24]. This means that some organizations will not consider personal knowledge as intellectual property. The transfer of personal knowledge is not well understood, and is often regarded by economists and social scientists using a "cost-free" assumption. Instead, the transfer of tacit knowledge is known to be difficult without the transfer of people. In some ways, personal knowledge is regarded as more easily managed, since it can be "more readily bought and sold" by hiring and firing individuals [7], which the authors do not agree.

Thus, the transfer of personal knowledge engages ethical decisions regarding personal worth. Not surprisingly, a circumspect employee might withhold personal knowledge and avoid sharing knowledge. An employee might hold back his personal knowledge in the interest of maintaining job security [19]. This holding also arises self-interest issues, namely when organizational culture views knowledge sharing as a setting of reciprocity, or strong competition for performance among workers within the organization [20].

3.3 Fiske's Relational Model vs. Ethics

Within communal sharing relationships, knowledge is perceived as a common resource, rather than an individual property. Knowledge is not personally marked, since it belongs to the whole group. Knowledge is freely shared among people belonging to the same group or dyad, following the idea "what's mine is yours", and however some common substance is required. It is important to realize that this common substance between people can be based on different objects or different grounds for cohesion, which means a dilemma: do people of different groups' value in the same way the sense of membership [25]? Although communal sharing is frequently not the dominant structure for sharing knowledge organization-wide, there might exist some subsets within the organizational context where knowledge is being shared. Furthermore, people might share knowledge with others, since they feel connected with them based on shared ideological objectives or based on solidarity, which implies another dilemma: if "what's mine is yours" how it is possible that the model advocates that communal sharing is not the dominant structure [26]? Supposedly, if knowledge is a common resource should be longitudinal to the organization.

In authority ranking knowledge is perceived as a mean to display rank differences, whether rank is based on formal power, expertise or age. Higher a person's rank better access to knowledge [27]. A person with a higher rank, that shares knowledge with someone lower in rank demonstrates his nobility and largesse and expects to get authority or status in return. A subordinate shares knowledge because either he has to or, because he wants to gain favour with his superior. In both cases the subordinate can expect a kind of "pastoral care" in return. In this respect knowledge sharing is motivated by power differences [28]. People are less or not willing to share knowledge when it can change their balance of power negatively. "Negative" knowledge is frequently withheld by window dressing behaviour and a knowledge overload may originate from largesse and sweet-talk, which generates the following question: who people evaluate as negative knowledge (negative knowledge can be seen as gossip) [29]? There is a standard evaluation process to power balancing regarding knowledge?

Within equality matching relationships knowledge is perceived as a mean of levelling out knowledge sharing efforts. The principle behind knowledge sharing is based on the exchange of knowledge for similar knowledge. Knowledge is being shared because someone else has shared something similar before or, because one expects something similar in return. It is the desire for equality that motivates knowledge sharing. But in ethical terms how could a person identify equality [28]? Quantifying knowledge, for example, you shared two pages of knowledge? This does not seem reasonable. Or qualifying that shared knowledge, for instance, you share highly quality knowledge; but does that knowledge represent the same quality? A person could already know what is being shared. Plus, can we morally obliged a person to share something in return by sharing knowledge oneself [21]? People are less or not willing to share knowledge when nothing similar can be shared in return within a reasonable time span [27].

Into market pricing relationships knowledge is perceived as a commodity which has a value and can be traded. Knowledge is being shared because one receives a compensation for it (not being similar knowledge or status). People are motivated to share knowledge by achievement. When the perceived compensation is not high enough, people are less or not willing to share knowledge, so which means a dilemma: if knowledge is traded to whom belongs the intellectual property? And in ethical terms, what happens when people, organizations, or even countries cannot obtain such knowledge due to their budget restrictions? [30] So a "knowledge divide" is created.

4 The Importance of Trust

Trust involves risk taking; that is, both parties know that the actions of one party can materially influence the other, but both share ideas, concerns or issues truthfully notwithstanding. The sociological literature conceptualizes trust as either the property of individuals, social relationships, or the social system with disproportionate attention to behaviour based on actions at an individual level [31]. When seen as a characteristic or property of individuals, trust is a personality variable, thereby placing accent on individual characteristics like feelings, emotions, and values. A second perspective observes trust as a collective attribute that can be drawn upon to achieve organizational aims. It may therefore be applied to the institutional basics of society. The third treats trust as a valued public good facilitated and sustained by a social system.

These three dissimilar levels of trust are interrelated. On the individual level, you trust an individual to do something based on what you know of his disposition, his ability, his reputation and so forth not merely because he says he will do it. On the collective level, if you don't trust an agency or organization with which the individual is affiliated, you will not trust him to fulfil an agreement [32]. In addition, individuals consider the background, culture, and social system of another when seeking to determine whether to trust him. It is the interconnectedness that advocates how building trust on the micro-level contributes to the determinant of a more abstract form of trust on the macro-level [33].

Moreover, a considerable number of academics contend that trust is rather difficult to produce intentionally. For example, [34] suggests that as a rational account of human behaviour, trust can only be produced in informal, small, closed and homogeneous communities which are able to enforce normative sanctions. It is unclear how; precisely, to create trust within communities, especially in diverse or heterogeneous societies, or as [35] states insecurity and conformity may produce such results. Still, many researchers continue to search for conditions that may help to facilitate trust and thereby allow efforts to create it deliberately.

Trust is a social mechanism that is embodied in structures of social relations. Social structure is important not only for the formation of social capital, but also for the generation of trust itself. It allows a more rapid proliferation of obligations and expectations, imposing sanctions on defection from an obligation, and helps to generate reputation [34]. In addition to social relations, shared norms are a source of trust, as pointed out by [36] defines trust as "the expectation that arises within a community of regular, honest, and cooperative behaviour, based on commonly shared norms, on the part of other members of the community."

As explained previously knowledge can be categorized along a continuum running from the explicit to the tacit; and, the "natural" process of knowledge management in an organizational context is the dynamic transformation process, and governing the worker's need to create, capture and share knowledge. For that, managers should create a favourable atmosphere, where knowledge that is not protected through legislation is not an inhibition factor for workers. In that context another problem arises, to whom belong the intellectual property rights: to the worker that transformed tacit knowledge into explicit knowledge, to a team of workers, or to the organization that supplied the atmosphere and necessary means? A clear position by the managers will allow a clear answer.

So far, we have considered the need of trust in knowledge sharing and knowledge protection, but what can be considered as correct and wrong in knowledge change? The challenge that managers face is complex [37], because it not only depends on organizational core values, but also the ethical code of each worker. In fact, workers behaviours or attitudes (values) dynamics can be contradictory to organizational values [38] or not, assuming that organizational values socialize them in some key issues [39]. Beside the previous analysis managers own discourse also face ethics as [40] states. A stance ethical discourse entails stringent requirements for those in the organization. The primary responsibilities inherent in the organizational ontology by the discourse ethics, then, stand or fall on two assumptions:

- normative claims to be valid have cognitive meaning and can be treated like claims to truth;
- the justification of norms and commands requires that a real discourse be carried out and thus cannot occur in a strictly monological form.

The first assumption is vital, but it places a particular responsibility on every speaker. What is said must be believed by the speaker and should have a rational basis. More specifically, a claim may well warrant assessment, but the assessment should be made on rational epistemological grounds, rather than on preferences or biases. It should be noted that rationality introduced is not the reductionist plead by some economists. The reduction may frequently take the form of quantification, which is valid and necessary most of the time, but obscure at other circumstances. Most organizations have some form of hierarchical structure, which is necessary to ensure that decisions are made and directions are chosen. And, the communicative action is not easy or simple. It requires an ethical stance that recognizes that every individual entails a commitment to truth, leading to trust.

5 Conclusion

It is clear that any model configures a reality representation, meaning that errors in its conception are admissible. Beside, knowledge management is a recent research field leading to plausible critics to the existent models. So, this paper aims not to suggest that these knowledge flow models are invalid, but to reinforce the idea that is essential to evaluate the existent ethical and moral issues that occur during the process of generation, creation and use of knowledge within an organization. However, mental models entail mental fluxes, therefore the praxis for understand personal knowledge meaning that is not comparable with an organizational "stream"; the other models at some extent can be compared because both debate organizational flows, however aiming for dissimilar contexts. The first debates organizational in a traditional sense (companies), and the second as collective/societal knowledge.

Although, can trust be the "key" for diminish these ethical dilemmas? Having in consideration all the previous sections, it seems that indeed trust plays as a vital role; nonetheless, a definitive answer is extremely difficult to obtain because contexts are not easily reproduced; so, each organization represents a case study and a possible different answer, leading to a necessary analysis off organizational values, managers values and workers values within that specific organization.

Acknowledgments. The first co-author of this paper would like to distinguish the remarkable endeavour of Ms. Mary Prior and Professor Simon Rogerson regarding their support, as well as to Nuno Sotero Alves da Silva for his insightful comments and critics to the previous versions of this contribution. Finally, also to thanks ISLA Leiria for its financial assistance with reference to CENTERIS 2010.

References

1. Savage, C.: `http://www.kee-inc.com/dawn`
2. Nicolau, I.: A Gestão do Conhecimento como Instrumento para a Gestão Competitiva. Revista Economia Global & Gestão 2(10), 21–44 (2005)
3. Martion-Rios, C., Erhardt, N.L.: Organisational Knowledge Transfer Through Human Resource Management: International Diffusion of Managerial Performance Management. European Journal of International Management 2(2), 170–191 (2008)
4. Brelade, S., Harman, C.: A Practical Guide to Knowledge Management. Thorogood, S.l. (2003)
5. Malhotra, Y.: Why Knowledge Management Systems Fail? Enablers and Constraints of Knowledge Management in Human Enterprises. In: Koening, M., Srikantaiah, T. (eds.) Handbook on Knowledge, pp. 87–112. Springer, Heidelberg (2004)

6. Bennet, D., Bennet, A.: The Rise of the Knowledge Organization. In: Holsapple, C. (ed.) Handbook on Knowledge Management, pp. 5–20. Springer, New York (2004)
7. Nonaka, I., Teece, D.J.: Managing Industrial Knowledge: Creation, Transfer and Utilization. Sage Publications, London (2001)
8. Nonaka, I., Toyama, R., Byosiere, P.: A Theory of Organizational Knowledge Creation: Understanding the Dynamic Process of Creating Knowledge. In: Dierks, C., Antal, A., Child, J., Nonaka, I. (eds.) The Organizational Learning and Knowledge, pp. 491–517. Oxford University Press, New York (2003)
9. IAS 38: International Accounting Standards 38 Intangible Assets. International Financial Reporting Standards, London (2003)
10. Lampropoulos, L., Michalakos, S., Anagnostopoulos, A., Pouloudi, N.: Enabling the Exploitation of Tacit Knowledge: Open Issues and Opportunities. In: ETHICOMP 2005, paper 39. Linkoping University, Linkoping (2005)
11. Nesse, R.M., Lloyd, A.T.: The Evolution of Psychodynamic Mechanisms. In: Barkow, J., Cosmides, L., Tooby, J. (eds.) The Adapted Mind: Evolutionary Psychology and the Generation of Culture, pp. 601–626. Oxford University Press, New York (1992)
12. Goldman, A.I.: Ethics and Cognitive Science. Ethics 103, 337–360 (1993)
13. Fiske, A.P., Haslam, N., Fiske, S.T.: Confusing One Person with Another: What Errors Reveal About the Elementary Forms of Social Relations. Journal of Personality and Social Psychology 60(5), 656–674 (1991)
14. Lohman, D.F.: Reasoning Abilities. In: Sternberg, R., Davidson, J., Pretz, J. (eds.) Cognition and Intelligence: Identifying Mechanisms of the Mind, pp. 225–250. Cambridge University Press, New York (2005)
15. Dixon, N.M.: Common Knowledge: How Companies Thrive by Sharing What They Know. Harvard Business School Press, Boston (2000)
16. Markus, M.L.: Toward a Theory of Knowledge Reuse: Types of Knowledge Reuse Situations and Factors in Reuse Success. Journal of Management Information Systems 18(1), 57–93 (2001)
17. McDaniel, C.: Theoretical Issues in Organizational Ethics. In: McDaniel, C. (ed.) Organizational Ethics: Research and Ethical Challenges, pp. 17–38. Cornwall, Asghate (2004)
18. Wilson, T.D.: The Nonsense of Knowledge Management. Information Research, 8 (2002), `http://informationr.net/ir/8-1/paper144.html`
19. Costa, G.J.M., Prior, M., Rogerson, S.: Individual Ethics and Knowledge Management: Arising Conflicts. In: ETHICOMP 2010, pp. 117–129. University of Pavia, Mantua (2008)
20. Wang, C.-C.: The Influence of Ethical and Self-Interest Concerns on Knowledge Sharing Intentions Among Managers: An Empirical Study. International Journal of Management 21(3), 370–381 (2004)
21. Du Plessis, J.C., Britz, J.J.: Slave or Sibling: A Moral Reframing the Corporate Knowledge Sharing Community. Open University, Johannesburg (2007)
22. Dulipovici, A., Baskerville, R.: Conflicts Between Privacy and Property: The Discourse in Personal and Organizational Knowledge. The Journal of Strategic Information Systems 16(2), 187–213 (2007)
23. Bock, G.W., Zmud, R.W., Kim, Y.-G., Lee, J.N.: Behavioural Intention Formation in Knowledge Sharing: Examining the Roles of Extrinsic Motivators, Socialpsychological Forces, and Organizational Climate. MIS Quarterly 29(1), 87–111 (2005)
24. KPMG: Intellectual Gold- KPMG's European Intellectual Property Survey Reveals the Value Hidden in Europe's Leading Companies. KLegal, London (2002)

25. Verweij, M.: Towards a Theory of Constrained Relativism: Comparing and Combining the Work of Pierre Bordieu, Mary Douglas and Michael Thompson, and Alan Fiske. Sociological Research Online, 12 (2007), `http://ideas.repec.org/s/sro/srosro.html`
26. Gannon, M.J.: Cultural Metaphors: Their Use in Management Practice and as a Method for Understanding Cultures. In: Lonner, W.J., Dinel, D.L., Hayes, S.A., Sattler, D.N. (eds.) Online Readings in Psychology and Culture, Center for Cross-Cultural Research, Western Washington University, Bellingham (2002)
27. Bolender, J.: The Genealogy of the Moral Modules. Minds and Machines 13(2), 233–255 (2003)
28. Bolender, J.: Two Accounts of Moral Diversity: The Cognitive Science of Pluralism and Absolutism. Yeditepeḋe Felsefe 1(3), 52–110 (2004)
29. Michelson, G., Mouly, S.V.: You Didn't Hear it From Us But... Towards an Understanding of Rumour and Gossip in Organizations. Australian Journal of Management 27, 57–65 (2002)
30. Costa, G.J.M.: The Handbook of Ethical Issues and Social Dilemmas in Knowledge Management: Organizational Innovation. IGI Global, Hershey (in Press)
31. Misztal, B.A.: Trust in Modern Societies: The Search for the Bases of Social Order. Polity Press, Cambridge (1996)
32. Schoorman, F.D., Mayer, R.C., Davis, J.H.: An Integrative Model of Organizational Trust: Past, Present, and Future. Academy of Management Review 32(2), 344–354 (2007)
33. Uslaner, U.M.: The Foundations of Trust: Micro and Macro. Cambridge Journal of Economics 32(2), 289–294 (2008)
34. Coleman, J.S.: Foundations of Social Theory. Harvard University Press, Cambridge (1990)
35. Yair, G.: Insecurity, Conformity and Community: James Coleman's Latent Theoretical Model of Action. European Journal of Social Theory 11(1), 51–70 (2008)
36. Fukuyama, F.: Trust: Social Virtues and the Creation of Prosperity. Free Press, New York (1995)
37. Sackett, P.R., DeVore, C.J.: Counterproductive Behaviours at Work. In: Anderson, N., Ones, D.S., Sinangil, K.S., Viswesvaran, C. (eds.) Handbook of Industrial, Work and Organizational Psychology, pp. 145–164. Sage, London (2002)
38. Costa, G.J.M., Prior, M., Rogerson, S.: Trustworthy and Ethical Environment in Knowledge Management: A Dilemma to Solve! In: Network Ethics 2009, just presentation, Catholic University of Lisbon, Lisbon (2009)
39. Taormina, R.J.: Interrelating Leadership Behaviours, Organizational Socialization, and Organizational Culture. Leadership & Organizational Culture 29(1), 85–102 (2008)
40. Rhen, A.: Good Times, Bad Times- The Moral Discourse of Time and Management. Revista Comportamento Organizacional & Gestão 8(1), 49–59 (2002)

Trust in 'E': Users' Trust in Information Resources in the Web Environment

Alison J. Pickard, Pat Gannon-Leary, and Lynne Coventry

Northumbria University, Newcastle upon Tyne, NE1 8ST, United Kingdom

Abstract. The paper describes a Joint Information Systems Committee (JISC)-funded project, conducted by a cross-disciplinary team, examining trust in information resources in the web environment employing a literature review and online Delphi study with follow-up community consultation. A tool was developed from analysis of the literature and discussed in the consultation. Elements comprising the tool include external factors, internal factors and user's cognitive state. Each element is detailed and discussion focuses on the key issues of risk and return on investment as perceived by stakeholders.

Keywords: trust, information environment, return on investment, risk.

1 Introduction

This paper reports on a UK Joint Information Systems Committee (JISC)-funded study on users' trust in information resources in the web environment. This study involved a cross-disciplinary team from Information & Communication Management, Learning & Teaching and Psychology & Communications Technology and had three aims. Firstly, to provide an overview of the ways in which trust is either assessed or asserted in relation to the use and provision of resources in the Web environment for research and learning. Secondly, to assess what solutions might be worth further investigation and whether establishing ways to assert trust in academic information resources could assist the development of information literacy, and, thirdly, to 'help increase understanding of how perceptions of trust influence the behaviour of information users.

2 Background

As Hagar [1] states '*Little attention has been paid in information science to issues of information and trust..., particularly such questions as, What sources of information do people trust? Which information providers do people trust?*' This situation stands in marked contrast to research in the field of e-commerce, where research on trust is quite well progressed. As early as 1999 an influential report by Studio Archetype/Sapient and Cheskin Research [2] argued that in order to develop a successful e-commerce business: '*The factors that produce a sense of trustworthiness need to be identified, in their entirety. Their interactions need to be understood, and their relative importance determined*'. Since then, 10 years' of studies on trust in e-commerce (Briggs [3]) and,

J.E. Quintela Varajão et al. (Eds.): CENTERIS 2010, Part II, CCIS 110, pp. 305–314, 2010.

more recently, on trust in e-health have underlined the importance of factors such as website appearance, site usability, credibility and personalised content in helping to establish online trust (Patrick et al [4]; Sillence et al [5]).

This paper brings together the e-commerce, e-health and information trust literature to provide a broader picture of what is already known around issues of trust in the use of web resources within higher education (HE) and to create a model representative of the trust in information seeking process.

3 Methodology

The first phase of the project methodology comprised desk-based reviews of relevant literature that analysed and synthesised the outcomes of existing research and studies in the three areas of interest, i.e. how users place their trust in digital information resources in the web environment; means by which digital information providers currently engender trust in their resources; and the desirability and feasibility of certifying the authenticity and provenance of digital information resources to the end user. In doing this, a modified version of a systematic literature review was employed. Two team members were engaged in searching and together they built an Endnote ™ library based on the retrievals, sharing selection and assessment criteria and key search terms. The final Endnote™ library contained more than 400 references. The ultimate selection of references to include in the study was made on the basis of their appropriateness to the aims of the project and to a model of trust which was concurrently being developed by the team.

The second phase of the project methodology involved community consultation of the findings from phase 1 with users and providers using an on-line modified Delphi study and a round table. This was to validate and extend the findings from the literature review; to establish users' and providers' perceptions of the desirability and feasibility of certifying authenticity and provenance and, in addition, to explore the potential for developing a framework of trust that could help develop information literacy. The online modified Delphi took the form of 7 open-ended questions, responses were received from 26 respondents, of whom four were librarians, two researchers, one PhD student, seven students, six academic staff, three commercial providers, two managers (one resource manager & one research operations manager) and one student support officer. One respondent was also representing the professional association CILIP. The round table was in essence a semi-structured face-to-face meeting of the individual questionnaire respondents who, having recorded their initial individual ideas, had the opportunity to share and discuss these – facilitated by the research team – and then engage in ranking procedures to assist in the determination of priorities. The event consisted of four activities based around consultation and negation. Participants were divided between four tables, each table being engineered to accommodate a pre-defined combination of users. 20 respondents who completed the questionnaire were also able to attend the round table event and included three librarians, three members of academic staff, two researchers, two commercial providers, two managers, one PhD student and seven students. Again, one participant was representing CILIP.

4 Results

People make trust decisions regularly in respect of web-based behaviour, e.g. that they are 'talking' to the right person (e.g. their bank), that their children are not accessing pornographic sites etc. Perceived trust or credibility has a strong influence of people's willingness to engage with online activities such as shopping or banking, where sensitive information is involved. However, with education, students seem more than willing to engage with online information. This may, in part, be attributable to their perceived self-efficiency in terms of their experience with technology. They may enter higher education (HE) with experience of search engines such as Google but lack of experience in information retrieval using more scholarly databases. Their past experience with Google and similar search engines may have led to a perception that Google is trustworthy and, given that their use of Google does not involve sharing sensitive information such as financial details or personal information, they are unlikely to have had a negative experience to make them disposed to distrust.

From a review of the literature, three factors affecting trust/credibility of online information have been identified. These are external factors, internal factors and user's cognitive state. It would appear that user's cognitive state and external factors influence a user's decision as to whether or not to conduct an internal assessment of information.

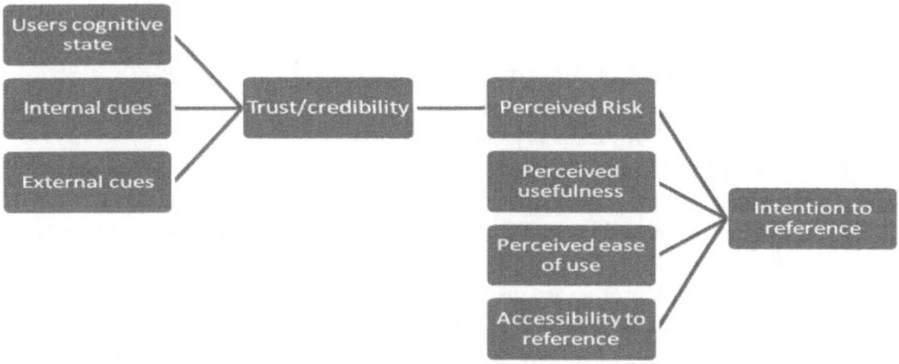

Fig. 1. Trust model

External Factors

Agarwal and Prasad [6] found external factors that impacted on user beliefs about usefulness and ease of use of information technology. These factors give external cues of credibility or trustworthiness and include the following:

- Whether or not the information must be paid for or is free – students, e.g., are unlikely to want to pay for information (OCLC [7]);
- Seals of approval such as HONcode or TRUSTe (Walsh [8]);
- Credibility rating systems controlled institutionally (that might use authority, currency, objectivity etc to rate) – if a library did this it could be seen as an extension of their collection development function (Herring [9]);

- Preapproved databases, e.g. JSTOR or ERIC (Baker [10]);
- PIC labels that certify the trustworthiness of a site (Walsh [8]);
- Digital signatures that ensure authenticity of author and information (Bradley [11]);
- Recommendations from others (peer reviews via eBay, Amazon or a peer reviewed journal, lecturers recommendation in the case of students) (Shippensburg[12]) which lends what Liu [13] terms reputed credibility;
- Rankings (Hess & Stein [14]);
- Offline credibility, i.e. sites with strong offline credibility might be assumed to have equal/commensurate amounts of credibility in their online forms; information based on a respected print source (Lubans [15]);
- Presentation of the site or the provider, e.g. site ownership is explicit (Hertzum et al [16]); and
- Ease of use of the site (Fogg [17]).

Internal factors

In additional to external cues, there are factors linked with internal cues of information's credibility/trustworthiness including the following:

- Accuracy, freedom from errors and verifiable elsewhere (Rieh [18]; Hung [19]);
- Authoritative, i.e. reputation of the source, qualifications etc (Herring [9] Hung [19]; McKnight & Kacmar [20]);
- Objectivity, i.e. fact rather than opinion (Hung [19]);
- Currency, i.e. site displays a recent date, information contained is topical, up to date (Rieh [18]; Lubans [15];Weiler [7]);
- Coverage, i.e. comprehensive, in depth (Klein [21]; Grimes & Boening [22]; Metzger et al [23]; Hung [19]; Weiler [7]);
- Presentation and format, i.e. quality of writing, structure (Rieh[18]; Hung [19]);
- Affiliations of source or site (traceable by tools such as WhoIS, traceroute, wslookup) (Rieh [18] Hung [19]);
- Source motivation, i.e. why are they publishing this information (Rieh [18]);
- Citations, i.e. by whom has reference been cited; inclusion of references (Liu [13]); and
- Type of 'object', e.g. a journal, a blog (Princeton [24]).

User's cognitive state

In addition to external and internal cues, the user's cognitive state impacts on their beliefs about credibility or trustworthiness of online information sources. McKnight and Kacmar's study [20] provided evidence that **initial** information credibility is built through three general dispositions:

- Disposition to distrust
- Trust in general technology
- Risk propensity

McKnight and Kacmar also found that, in terms of **building** information credibility important factors were:

- Trusting beliefs
- Perceived reputation
- Willingness to explore information

These are among the factors linked with cognitive state that include the following:

- Need for closure (Amichai-Hamburger et al [25]);
- Need for cognition (Verplanken et al [26]; Amichai-Hamburger et al [25]);
- Willingness to explore (McKnight & Kacmar [20]);
- Motivation or disposition to believe that may be intrinsic or extrinsic (Weiler [7] ; Lim [27]);
- Purpose (Rieh [18]; Collis & Moonen [28]);
- Prior knowledge (Rieh & Belkin [18]);
- Time available (Verplanken et al [26]; Klein [21]; Metzger et al [29]);
- Ability (Collis & Moonen [28]);
- Past experience with site (Lim [27]) which lends what Liu [13] terms earned credibility;
- Past experience with the author or their institution (Rieh [18]);
- Propensity to trust (Mayer et al [30]; McKnight & Kacmar [20]);
- Trust in technology (McKnight & Kacmar [20]);
- Risk propensity (McKnight & Kacmar [20]));
- Faith in humanity (McKnight & Kacmar [20]);
- Suspicion of humanity (McKnight & Kacmar [20]);and
- Internet anxiety (McKnight & Kacmar [20]).

All three factors – external cues, internal users and user's cognitive state interact in information seeking to lend trust in, and belief in the credibility of, the information found. There are two elements of trust involved here, firstly, trust in the methods involved in finding the information and, secondly, trust in the information retrieved. Once the information is found, the user has to make the decision as to whether or not to use it for their purpose/s. At this stage, consideration is given to the perceived risk in using the information and its perceived usefulness for the intended purpose/s, also to how easy it is to use and how accessible it is.

Perceived risk and perceived usefulness

Seleznyov [31] describes trust as ''... *a measure of willingness of a responder to satisfy an inquiry of a requestor for an action that may place all involved parties at risk of harm, and is based on an assessment of the risks and reputations associated with the parties involved in a given transaction*''. (Seleznyov 2004: 99). Several authors on the concept of trust have highlighted the fact that the presence of risk creates a need for trust (Seligman [32]) and that willingness – and freedom – to accept rather than reject that risk is a vital dimension of trust (Mayer et al [30]). Willingness indicates the voluntary nature of trust as opposed to being coerced or exploited into risk-taking. Trusting behaviour, trusting intentions or behavioural trust are also differentiated from confidence or belief in something which may not involve taking any action based on that confidence or those beliefs and, consequently, will not involve any related risk-taking. (Mayer et al [30]). Risk features in many definitions of trust (Mayer et al [30]) and, as Corritore et al [33] say, risk is particularly relevant in the online environment.

The stakeholders in the community consultation were asked to consider risks in the information environment rather than in e-health or e-commerce and to give consideration to the potential rewards or return on investment of using that information. These, participants, were told, did not have to be 'paired' although some participants pointed out that, in certain instances, the risks might be the opposite of the rewards. Table 1 below summarises their thoughts on these issues.

Table 1. Risks and rewards in the information environment

Risk	Reward
To the information provider	***To the information provider***
Cost of maintenance, quality etc – limited future if not implemented	Income generation/ funding
Poor service – loss of respect/reputation	Positive feedback from others
Negative impact on the organisation	Positive PR – credibility, status, reputation
Loss of business	Positive impact on others – sharing good practice
Litigation – slander/libel/breach of copyright/plagiarism	Integrity
Costs in time & effort as well as money	
To the information user	***To the information user***
Failure/having to repeat a year/ loss of degree/job & concomitant financial risk – paying back fees if fail	Academic achievement/recognition, e.g. high marks, high level pass, degree leading to job
Disappointment	Personal well-being, sense of achievement, impressing family, friends, tutors
Discredit – linked to professional body	Praise/prizes/kudos – being referenced by others
Chance of being 'found out' and challenged	Progression in studies & career, employability
Lack of knowledge & high uncertainty	Peer placement, 'top of the class'!
Leads to wrong decision making	Education/lifelong learning
Public embarrassment, condemnation, e.g. climate change data	Transferability
	Confidence in (search) strategy

In discussion, situated context was mentioned and the effect this has on the weighting of the risk. The higher the risk, the more effort was invested, the more intensive the searching and the greater necessity that the information be trustworthy. Participants commented how, if they used information well, then people would believe in them, i.e. they would be more credible. In the case of an academic member of staff, e.g., they hoped that such good use of information would inspire students to go away and research for themselves exhibiting similar good use of information. In the case of an information provider, the reputation of their organisation was 'on the line' and their service was unlikely to be used again by a client who was misled, given misinformation or given information that was not well presented. In both cases participants felt that there was a potential reward if they and, by inference, their organisation had high credibility in information provision since this would lead to good PR and more income (in the form of more students in the case of the academic).

Choice of information resource may be based, among other factors, on purpose and the degree of risk involved. With health information, e.g., there is a high degree of risk since it has the potential to benefit/harm a large number of people (Mayer et al 2[30]). Users seeking such information need a guarantee that websites visited meet a minimum quality standard, e.g. that information contained thereon is vouched for by suitably qualified professionals (Mayer et al 2[30]).

Under what circumstances do users feel strongly enough about the quality of information they access to deem a form of certification, such as some of those identified amongst the external cues and used on websites containing medical or health information, desirable? If they do feel strongly, and if librarians are to play a role in this, do users have similar respect for information professionals as they do for medical professionals? In terms of credibility rating systems, e.g., would users trust digital information resources more if librarians or publishers reviewed them and gave them a seal of approval?

In the community consultation workshop members believed that, if a HE library subscribed to a resource it could be trusted and if a web page was hosted on an academic site it was more trustworthy than such a page hosted on an independent site. However, they queried who would be held accountable if information provided was proved inaccurate or untrustworthy.

Technically certification is feasible but how desirable is it? It could be advantageous in terms of simplifying and reducing the complexity of information seeking in the digital environment. It could negate the need for users to visit numerous web sites prior to finding out if the content were suitable for, or accessible to, them; and presumably organizations would benefit from more standards and codes of conduct being adopted more widely with a concomitant improvement in user trust.

Members of the community consultation workshop believed that certification from commercial organizations was questionable since, e.g. it could involve 'paying the subscription and getting the badge' and wondered how such schemes were policed. They felt that information was subjective and difficult to certify and discussed whether certification could be done formally by a University or less formally through peer reviews whilst still involving the individual seeking the information in cross-checking to verify information and to build up a layer of trust and confidence.

5 Concluding Remarks

From the literature and from the consultation it would appear that there is a limit to what can be done by certification and what, ultimately, must be left for human/social judgement in relation to authenticity/integrity/provenance of information. Many certification procedures are basically about trust in identity and identity alone does not guarantee that the information provided or warranted by an organization can be trusted, since much is dependent on the policies and degree of integrity of the organization. Potential users of information provided by such organizations may still need to establish trust in the behaviour of that organization, i.e. entity-centred trust (Gil & Artz [34]) as opposed to content trust. The use of certification assists the transference process of trust building, i.e. you need to trust the ability/integrity/reputation of the information provider acting as third party that awards the certification such as a librarian, a manager of a digital repository or a publisher before you trust the content of the information provided. If such third parties work in partnership to help users to develop skills that enable them to recognize not only external cues such as certification but also internal cues about information and how it is presented this should help users make informed choices in their use of literature during and beyond their time in HE, to avoid risk and to reap the maximum return on their investment.

In addition to perceived risk and perceived usefulness, the trust model posits that ease of use and accessibility play a part in a user's decision to trust, and use, information for their purpose/s. Research [35, 36] has indicated that student users find search engines such as Google easier to than some of the federated search systems and portals provided by HE libraries. They similarly find the 'one-stop shopping' nature of Google as more accessible than the multiple approaches sometimes demanded by library portals. In consequence, they may use Google to the exclusion of library systems and may risk compromising the quality of their search results and concomitantly compromising the quality of their work and their originality of thought (Grimes & Boening [22]). If students take this surface, utilitarian approach to learning, then there is a further risk that they will fail to engage in behaviours associated with self-regulated learning and will not develop information literacy skills (Wiley & Goldman [37]) that would transfer into the work place.

The project team now wishes to take the research forward. The community consultancy indicated that the trust model is valid but this validity needs to be tested further in follow-up research with HE users.

References

1. Hagar, C.: Who Do You trust? Information Seeking During the UK Foot and Mouth Crisis. Library and Archival Services (in press)
2. Studio, Archetype/Sapient and Cheskin Research.: eCommerce Trust Study 33 (1999)
3. Briggs, P., Burford, B., De Angeli, A., Lynch, P.: Trust in Online Advice. Social Science Computer Review 20, 321–332 (2002)
4. Patrick, A., Marsh, S., Briggs, P.: Designing Systems That People Will Trust. In: Cranor, L., Garfinkel, S. (eds.) Security and Usability: Designing Secure Systems That People Can Use. O'Reilly & Associates, Sebastopol (2005)
5. Sillence, E., Briggs, P.: How Do Patients Evaluate and Make Use of Online Health Information? Social Science & Medicine 64, 1853–1862 (2007)
6. Agarwal, R., Prasad, J.: Are Individual Differences Germane To The Acceptance Of New Technology? Decision Sciences 30, 361–391 (1999)
7. Weiler, A.: Information Seeking Behaviour in Generation Y Students: Motivation, Critical Thinking and Learning Theory. Journal of Academic Librarianship 31, 46–53 (2005)
8. Walsh, P.: Content Labels, Explaine In Plain English, `http://segala.com/blog/content-labels-explained-in-plain-english/`

9. Herring, S.D.: Using the World Wide Web for Research: Are Faculty Satisfied? Journal of Academic Librarianship 27, 213–219 (2001)
10. Baker, N.: Copy But Don't Disbind. Library Journal 130 (2005)
11. Bradley, R.: Digital Authenticity and Integrity: Digital Cultural Heritage Documents as Research Resources. PORTAL 5, 165–176 (2005)
12. Shippensburg University, Ezra Lehman Memorial Library.: Internet Use Survey-Analysis. Shippensburg, PA (2000)
13. Liu, Z.: Perceptions of Credibility of Scholarly Information on the Web. Information Processing and Management 40, 1027–1038 (2004)
14. Stein, K., Hess, C.: Information Retrieval in Trust-Enhanced Document Networks. Semantics, Web and Mining 4289, 65–81 (2006)
15. Lubans, J.: Students and the Internet, `http://www.lubans.org`
16. Hertzum, M., Andersen, H.H.K., Andersen, V., Hansen, C.B.: Trust in Information Sources: Seeking Information from People, Documents, and Virtual Agents. Interacting with Computers 14, 575–599 (2002)
17. Fogg, B.J., Marshall, J., Laraki, O., Osipovich, A., Varma, C., Fang, N., Paul, J., Rangnekar, A., Shon, J., Swani, P.: Treinen.: What makes web sites credible? In: ACM CHI 2001 Conference on Human Factors in Computing Systems, pp. 61–68. ACM Press, New York (2001)
18. Rieh, S.Y., Belkin, N.J.: Understanding Judgment of Information Quality and Cognitive Authority in the WWW. In: Preston, C.M. (ed.) 61st ASIS Annual Meeting, pp. 279–289. American Society for Information Science, Silver Spring (1998)
19. Hung, T.Y.: Undergraduate Students' Evaluation Criteria When Using Web Resources for Class. Journal of Educational Media and Library Sciences 42, 1–12 (2004)
20. McKnight, D.H., Kacmar, C.: Factors of Information Credibility for an Internet Advice Site. In: Hawaii International Conference on Systems Sciences (2006)
21. Klein, B.D.: User Perceptions of Data Quality: Internet and Traditional Text Sources. Journal of Computer Information Systems 41, 9–15 (2001)
22. Grimes, D.J., Boening, C.H.: Worries with the Web: A Look at Student Use of Web Resources. College & Research Libraries 62, 11–23 (2001)
23. McKnight, D.H., Choudhury, V., Kacmar, C.: The Impact of Initial Customer Trust on Intentions to Transact with a Web Site: A Trust Building Model. Journal of Strategic Information Systems 11, 297–323 (2002)
24. Princeton Survey Research Associates International: Leap of faith: Using the Internet Despite the Dangers: Results of a National Survey of Internet Users for Consumer Reports WebWatch (2005)
25. Amichai-Hamburger, Y., Kaynar, O., Fine, A.: Effects of need for cognition on Internet use. Computers in Human Behavior 23, 880–891 (2007)
26. Verplanken, B.: Need for Cognition and External Information Search: Responses to Time Pressure During Decision-Making. Journal of Research in Personality 27, 238–252 (1993)
27. Lim, K., Park, S.Y.: An Exploratory Approach to Understanding the Purposes of Computer and Internet Use in Web 2.0 Trends. In: Proceedings of World Conference on Educational Multimedia, Hypermedia and Telecommunications, pp. 4332–4337 (2009)
28. Collis, B., Moonen, J.: Flexible Learning in a Digital World: Experiences and Expectations. Kogan Page, London (2001)
29. Metzger, M.J., Flanagin, A.J., Zwarun, L.: College Student Web Use, Perceptions of Information Credibility, and Verification Behavior. Computers & Education 41, 271–290 (2003)

30. Mayer, M.A., Karkaletsis, P., Archer, P., Ruiz, P., Stamatakis, K., Leis, A.: Quality labelling of medical web content. Health Informatics 12, 81–87 (2006)
31. Seleznyov, A., Ahmed, M.O., Hailes, S.: Co-Operation in the Digital Age: Engendering Trust in Electronic Environments. BT Technology Journal 22, 95–105 (2004)
32. Seligman, A.B.: The Problem of Trust. Princeton University Press, Princeton (1997)
33. Corritore, C.L., Kracher, B., Wiedenbeck, S.: On-line Trust: Concepts, Evolving Themes, a Model. International Journal of Human-Computer Studies 58, 737–758 (2003)
34. Gil, Y., Artz, D.: Towards Content Trust of Web Resources. Journal of Web Semantics 5, 227–239 (2007)
35. Fast, K.V., Campbell, D.G.: "I Still Like Google": University Student Perceptions of Searching Opacs and the Web. Proceedings of the American Society for Information Science and Technology 41, 138–146 (2004)
36. Breeding, M.: Technology for the Next Generation. Computers in Libraries 26, 28–30 (2006)
37. Wiley, J., Goldman, S.R., Graesser, A.C., Sanchez, C.A., Ash, I.K., Hemmerich, J.A.: Source Evaluation, Comprehension, and Learning in Internet Science Inquiry Tasks. American Educational Research Journal 46, 1060–1106 (2009)

Security Culture in Small and Medium-Size Enterprise

Luis Enrique Sánchez[1], Antonio Santos-Olmo[1], Eduardo Fernández-Medina[2], and Mario Piattini[3]

[1] Departament R&D, Sicaman Nuevas Tecnologias, Juan José Rodrigo 4, 13700 Tomelloso, Spain
{Lesanchez,Asolmo}@sicaman-nt.com
[2] Research GSyA Group, University of Castilla-La Mancha, Paseo de la Universidad 4, 13071 Ciudad Real, Spain
Eduardo.FdezMedina@uclm.es
[3] Research Alarcos Group, University of Castilla-La Mancha, Paseo de la Universidad 4, 13071 Ciudad Real, Spain
Mario.Piattini@uclm.es

Abstract. The information society depends ever-increasingly on Information Security Management Systems (ISMSs), and these systems have become vital to SMEs. However, ISMSs must be adapted to SME's specific characteristics, and they must be optimised from the point of view of the resources which are necessary to install and maintain them. Furthermore, when installing ISMSs, the majority of models have until now been centred on technical and management aspects, and the third aspect, which is institutional and is of particular relevance to SMEs, has been virtually ignored. In this paper we present the importance of the security culture for SMEs, along with our proposal to introduce this concept into SMEs in a progressive and sustainable manner. The model is currently being applied in real cases, thus leading to a constant improvement in its application.

Keywords: ISMS, Security Culture, SME.

1 Introduction

Security culture is of great importance when maintaining an ISMS in SMES, but until now the majority of models have concentrated on covering technical and management aspects, whilst aspects related to social factors have been left to one side [1]. Von Solms [2] therefore states that information security should not centre solely upon these two orientations (technical and management), but should be completed with a third orientation (institutional or security culture). The principal function of each of the aforementioned orientations would therefore be:

- *Technical orientation:* This deals with the technical direction of information security through the use of the computing system installations, such as authentication and access control services.

J.E. Quintela Varajão et al. (Eds.): CENTERIS 2010, Part II, CCIS 110, pp. 315–324, 2010.

- *Management orientation*: This came into being when the top management became involved in information security as a result of the evolution of the Internet and electronic business activities, along with tasks with which to prepare security in information, policies, procedures, and methods, and the designation of a person who would be responsible for security.
- *Institutional tendency:* This is parallel to the first and second orientations and includes the creation of a corporate security culture dealing with regulation, certification, measurement and concerns about the human aspect in information security.

The objective of institutionalization is to construct an information security culture in such a way that information security becomes a natural aspect of all the organization's employees' daily activities [2]. Information security culture is developed with the intention of controlling the improper use of information by information system users [3, 4]. In an information security culture the employees' behaviour contributes to the protection of data, information and knowledge [4], and information security becomes a natural part of these employees daily activities [5]. The potential value of an information security management culture was demonstrated by Galletta [6], who showed that between 20-50% of employees reveal information related to the company or make inappropriate use of the information system [7-9]. According to a study carried out by Ernst&Young [10], an important advance in the establishment of the security culture has taken place in recent year, but much work still remains to be done.

Many governments have made great efforts to attempt to improve the level of security in their companies. The intention of the United Kingdom's group of information security policies (DTI) [11] is, therefore, to assist businesses to effectively manage their information security and to provide a set of documents which serve as a starting point. The "OCDE guidelines for security in information systems and communication" [12] describe the need for a greater awareness and understanding of security questions and the necessity to develop a "security culture".

This paper continues in Section 2, in which the main research proposals focusing on security culture are briefly described. Section 3 provides a short introduction to our proposal for the progressive introduction of security culture in SMEs. Finally, in Section 4 we show our conclusions and future work.

2 Related Work

The majority of recent research into information security culture [13-19] stresses that a corporative culture that includes a security culture is a transcendent collective phenomenon and can be designed by an organization's own management. Nosworthy [13] puts particular emphasis on the fact that organizational culture plays an important role in information security, since it allows the organization to resist changes that occur in its system. Although the majority of research works coincide on the importance of a security culture for ISMSs [13], no clear definition of the concept of "security culture" [19], has been provided, and different points of view exist:

- Siponen [20] states that "information security awareness" is a state in which an organization's users are conscious of their mission in security, which can be divided into two categories: i) application framework (the regulation, certification and measurement of institutionalisation activities); and ii) content (human aspect).

- On the other hand [21, 22] suggest the establishment of a *training and cooperation culture* with the employees, based on a progressive adaptation of the organization's security management and the users' individual values and behaviour.
- Dhillon [23] has a wide view of the term "security culture", and defines it as the behaviour of an organisation's users which contributes to the protection of data, information and knowledge.
- Para For Chia [24] information security culture is a fundamental aspect, and this work defines a set of dimensions which are important for measuring the information security culture's efficiency: i) the growth in importance of information security; ii) long and short term equilibrium, goals, policies, procedures and continual improvement processes; iii) cooperation and collaboration; iv) attention to the objectives of auditing and fulfilment. However, this list has recently been criticised by Helokunnas [25], who particularly emphasises the human aspects of information security.
- Straub [26] maintains that in information systems it is almost always assumed that a person belongs to a single culture, and therefore proposes the theory of social identity which can be used as a basis for research into information security culture. Social identity culture suggests that each individual is influenced by a multitude of cultures.
- Dojkovski [27] put forward the idea of constructing an SME oriented ISMS, taking the security culture as its central point. This was done by analysing the state of SMEs in Australia, and the conclusion was reached that in the last fifteen years security risks in Australian SMEs has increased as a result of greater access to the Internet, but that the level of information security and awareness in SMEs has not maintained a good rhythm and continues to be low.
- Sneza [28], proposed the construction of an ISMS by taking the development of information security culture as its central point, and bearing in mind how people think and behave. This was done by basing the framework on the establishment of the security culture on qualitative aspects at the expense of quantitative aspects. The framework was defined by carrying out a study on Australian SMEs with less than 20 employees [29].
- Finally, a report presented by ABS [30] considers security culture to be a key aspect of ISMSs, and develops a general framework for information security based on eight dimensions. Chia [19] applied these eight dimensions to the areas of information security and identified the main information security factors in each dimension.

Although recent studies demonstrate SMEs' concern with regard to the difficulties involved in developing an information security culture [31], the fact is that a security culture has a series of additional problems when it is installed in SMEs. According to Dojkovski [27] and Hutchinson [32], SMEs are particularly badly affected in the search for an information security culture in comparison to large companies. There are various reasons for this:

- SMEs lack the funds, time and knowledge which are necessary to coordinate information security, or an efficient manner in which to impose an information security culture [33, 34].
- SMEs do not tend to have access to policies or procedures, and information system users' responsibilities have not been defined [35].
- SMEs are more susceptible to national influences, such as changes in legislation, than large companies [36].

As a conclusion we should highlight that various security management frameworks oriented towards the development of information security culture have been developed [2, 5, 14, 16, 22, 25, 37-39], but that these tend to be oriented towards large organisations. However, according to other research works [27, 40] the frameworks for SMEs should be based on a study of their real necessities in order to identify and develop a specific framework for them.

Experts have proposed various conceptual frameworks with which to manage information security including information security culture on the basis of initiatives regarding policy management, awareness, training and education [41, 42]. However, these frameworks may be more appropriate for medium-sized and large organisations owing to the resources which are necessary. Various frameworks with which to establish security culture have appeared in recent years and are based on: organizational culture and information security culture measurement [5, 15]; shared values [35]: information security phases, maturity levels [2]; measures related to the development of the individual, group and organisation, which allow deficiencies in security material to be discovered [14]; the socio-technological level of information security [43]; user moral and ethics-based measures [20]; informal awareness methods [22]; key concepts in organisational culture [16]; capacities of personnel [38]; organisational learning [39]; and a multifaceted focus [24]. While these frameworks are clearly valuable, they centre on fragments of the theoretic field and are not integrated into a complete common framework. What is more, they do not tackle the special requirements of SMEs.

Kuusisto [44] therefore reached the conclusion that no regulation exists which is appropriate for managing security in SMEs, and that there is principally a necessity for models which are valid and which will permit the security culture in SMEs to be increased.

3 ISC-SME: Installing Security Culture in SMEs

The main objective of this process is to establish a security culture based on the users who will have to work with the company's information system, and without which the users will be unable to access this system.

During the development of this research we have tested various methods through which to establish a security culture in SMEs. The procedure that we have finally decided to implement consists of giving employees a series of security-related tests associated with ISMS regulations, with the objective of maintaining and improving the company's security culture without high maintenance costs.

The principal idea is that the users of the information system will have to obtain a "certificate of cultural level". This certificate could be withdrawn and must be periodically renewed to guarantee that the necessary level of security culture continues to be maintained.

It has been shown that the simplicity and the short amount of time involved in carrying out this activity lead to the progressive creation of a security culture in its users. The automation of this culture avoids additional maintenance and planning costs, and ensures that the security culture remains inherent to the information system itself.

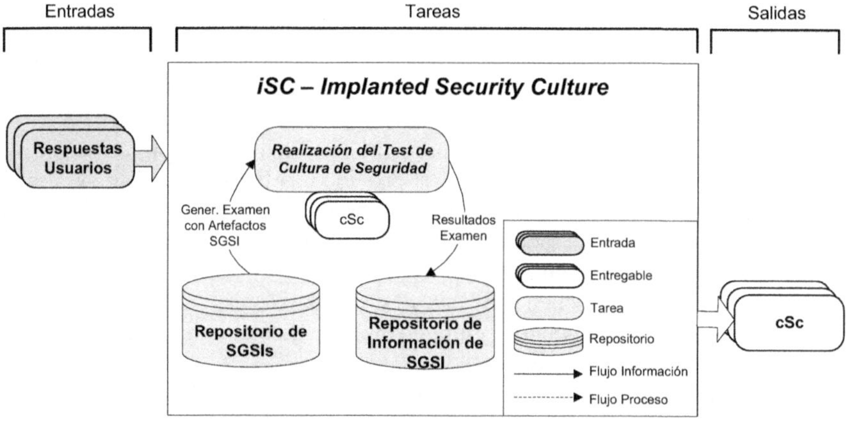

Fig 1. Schema of ISC process

En la Fig. 1 shows a detailed schema of the inputs, tasks and outputs of which this task consists:

- **Inputs:** The inputs are the users' responses to the test with regard to questions about the regulations generated by the system.
- **Tasks:** The sub-process consists of a single task concerned with the issuing of security certificates.
- **Outputs:** The outputs of this sub-process consist of the security culture certificates, all supposing that five out of a possible ten marks are obtained in the test. Otherwise the certificate will not be issued. Any users that fail the test are advised to study the security manual included in the ISMS, or to attend a security management course to increase their knowledge of this subject.

The objective of the process is to evaluate any user who wishes to access the company's information system with regard to his/her knowledge of the ISMS's regulations, in order to determine whether s/he is suitably prepared to access this system.

Limiting users' access until such a time that they are able to demonstrate that they have a basic knowledge of how they should behave with the system mitigates the risks to which the system is exposed, thus obliging users to progressively increase their security culture at a low cost.

If the user fails the test s/he must once again study the information regarding the ISMS or attend a security management course to attain the level of knowledge required to access the system.

This task consists of two different processes: i) Obtaining a security culture certificate; ii) Renewing the security culture certificate.

The first time that a user accesses the information system s/he must accept the company's security policy. This guarantees that that the user will read, albeit quickly, the company's policy (thus improving the security culture). The user must then pass an initial test consisting of 20 randomly-chosen questions related to the company's ISMS.

If the user does not correctly answer 50% or more of the questions in the test, his/her "security culture" for the company's information system will be considered to be inadequate, and s/he must continue to take the test until a mark of 5 or more is achieved. The user cannot access the company's information system until s/he has attained an appropriate level of "security culture". This guarantees that the culture will be efficiently implanted.

Once the user has passed the test, his/her mark is stored in a register, s/he is given a "security culture" certificate, and access is provided to the information system. The mark obtained in the initial test is important if the user wishes to maintain the certificate, since this mark may be modified according to the user's behaviour when carrying out other tasks in the system.

The second process of which the "carrying out the security culture test" is composed is the renewal of the security culture (SC) certificate, either because it has expired or because marks have been lost.

In order to avoid interference with the users' day-to-day work, they are notified of the certificate's expiry 1 month before the expiry date comes into effect, thus permitting them to take the appropriate tests at the moment best suited to them during that period. The system reminds users of the time remaining to renew the certificate on a daily basis. Once the expiry date is reached, if the user has not taken and passed the test, then his/her access to the system is blocked until the certificate is renewed.

Given that the time taken per resource (TpR) is one of the methodology's principal success factors (particularly in SMEs), we have estimated the time needed to install the security culture, and have reached the conclusion that the process' simplicity makes it totally acceptable for SMES (it has been estimated that 1 to 2 hours may be needed to obtain the initial certificate, consisting of approximately 90 minutes to read the security policy and understand the elements of the ISMS, and 30 minutes to take and pass the test). The investment of time will only take place initially since, although the certificate must be renewed periodically, the security policy only needs to be read and passed in the initial step. Experience obtained in the test cases carried out shows that information system users consider this to be a reasonable investment of time.

Finally, it is worth mentioning that those users who 'saved time' by not reading the security policy had to repeat the tests several times, and eventually spent as much time on this as they would have done if they had read the policy. Either of these two methods could be considered as correct since both lead to the objective of planting the initial seed of "security culture" in the users.

This simple task signifies that users never lose sight of the importance of keeping their level of security culture updated. Likewise, given that the test consists of a random selection of questions regarding the company's security regulations, the users obtain an ever-increasing and intuitive awareness of these regulations at a minimum cost.

However, certain events may lead the marks in the security culture certificate to alter: i) breaches of security regulations; and ii) loss of the security culture certificate as a result of having less than the required amount of points.

This research has led us to the conclusion that the greater the company's security culture, the greater the number of users who are reported, particularly when these reports do not imply serious sanctions against the person reported.

When a security incident is reported and the person responsible for security considers that this report is justified and therefore approves it, this not only affects the company's global security level, but also the punctuation in the security culture certificate of the user who has committed the breach of security. Each breach implies the loss of one point from the security culture certificate (cSc). These points consist of the mark initially obtained in the security culture test, less any points that have been deducted during the certificate's period of validity for breaches of the company's regulations. If the loss of points owing to security breaches causes the security culture certificate's marks to drop below 5 points, the certificate is withdrawn from the user, along with his/her access to the company's security information system, until a new security certificate is obtained.

This process serves as a preventative control to make the information system users aware of the fact that security breaches have their price. However, the measure is not excessive and users do not therefore reject it. This control does not imply a representative management cost for the company in either time or resources, but supposes an important reinforcement through which to establish a correct security culture.

In conclusion, this activity allows users to obtain a security culture certificate in a simple manner, thus facilitating their increase in knowledge of the ISMS and evaluating their level of knowledge of it.

4 Conclusions

This paper shows the importance of the security culture of ISMSs in SMEs, along with how the MSM2-SME methodology [45] has been incorporated and the advantages that its use has supposed.

This simple process fulfils the principals which, according to the OCDE [12], all ISMS instalment and maintenance methodologies should follow if they are to have a correct information security culture, thus guaranteeing the success of the ISMS in the company.

The characteristics of this process and its orientation towards SMEs have been very well received, and its integration into the MSM2-SME methodology has allowed us to increase the success rate of the maintenance of ISMSs in SMEs.

All future improvements to the security culture process will be oriented towards reducing non-fulfilment of security management by information system users, whilst always respecting the cost of resources and orientation towards the security culture.

Acknowledgments

This research is part of the following projects: BUSINESS (PET2008-0136) granted by the "Ministerio de Ciencia e Innovación" (Spain), SEGMENT (HITO-09-138) project financed by the "Consejería de Educación y Ciencia de la Junta de Comunidades de Castilla-La Mancha", SISTEMAS (PII2I09-0150-3135) project financed by the "Consejería de Educación y Ciencia de la Junta de Comunidades de Castilla-La Mancha" and MEDUSAS (IDI-20090557) project financed by the "Centro para el Desarrollo Tecnológico Industrial. Ministerio de Ciencia e Innovación" (CDTI).

References

1. Eloff, J., Eloff, M.: Information Security Management - A New Paradigm. In: Annual Research Conference of the South African Institute of Computer Scientists and Information Technologists on Enablement Through Technology, SAICSIT 2003, pp. 130–136 (2003)
2. Von Solms, B.: Information Security - The Third Wave? Computers and Security 19(7), 615–620 (2000)
3. Magklaras, G., Furnell, S.: The Insider Misuse Threat Survey: Investigating IT misuse from legitimate users. In: International Information Warfare Conference, Perth, Australia (2004)
4. Dhillon, G., Backhouse, J.: Current Directions in Information Systems Security Research: Toward Socio-Organizational Perspectives. Information Systems Journal 11(2), 127–153 (2001c)
5. Schlienger, T., Teufel, S.: Information Security Culture - From Analysis to Change. In: 3rd Annual IS South Africa Conference, Johannesburg, South Africa (2003)
6. Galletta, D.F., Polak, P.: An Empirical Investigation of Antecedents of Internet Abuse in the Workplace. In: AIS SIG-HCI Workshop, Seattle (December 2003)
7. CSI/FBI, Tenth Annual CSI/FBI Computer Crime and Security Survey. Computer Security Institute, USA (2005)
8. ISBS, Information Security Breaches Survey 2006. Department of Trade and Industry, UK (2006)
9. AusCERT, Australian Computer Crime and Security Survey. AusCERT (2005)
10. Ernst&Young, 2006 Global Information Security Survey. Ernst & Young (2006)
11. DTI. The_Empirical_Economics_of_Standards (2005), `http://www.dti.gov.uk/iese/The_Empirical_Economics_of_Standards.pdf`
12. OECD, OECD Guidelines for the Security of Information Systems and Networks: Towards a Culture of Security, O.f.E.C.-o.a.D. (OECD). Editor, Paris (2002)
13. Nosworthy, J.: Implementing Information Security in the 21st Century - Do You Have the Balancing Factors. Computers and Security 19(4), 337–347 (2000)
14. Martins, A., Eloff, J.H.P.: Information Security Culture. In: IFIP TC11 17th International Conference on Information Security (SEC 2002), Cairo, Egipt (2003)
15. Schlienger, T., Teufel, S.: Information Security Culture: The Socio-cultural Dimension in Information Security Management. In: IFIP TC11 17th International Conference on Information Security (SEC 2002), Kluwer Academic Publishers, USA (2002)
16. Zakaria, O., Gani, A.: A Conceptual Checklist of Information Security Culture. In: 2nd European Conference on Information Warfare and Security, June 30-July 1. University of Reading, UK (2003)

17. Zakaria, O., Jarupunphol, P., Gani, A.: Paradigm Mapping for Information Security Culture Approach. In: 4th Australian Conference on Information Warfare and IT Security, Adelaide, Australia (2003b)
18. Schein, E.H.: Organizational Culture and Leadership, 2nd edn. Jossey-Bass, San Francisco (1992)
19. Chia, P.A., Ruighaver, A.B., Maynard, S.B.: Understanding Organizational Security Culture. In: Proc. of PACIS 2002, Security Culture, Japan (2002b)
20. Siponen, M.T.: A conceptual foundation for organizational information security awareness. Information Management & Computer Security 8(1), 31–41 (2000)
21. Von Solms, B., Von Solms, R.: Incremental Information Security Certification. Computers & Security 20, 308–310 (2001)
22. Vroom, C., Von Solms, R.: Towards information security behavioural compliance. Computers & Security 23(3), 191–198 (2004)
23. Dhillon, G., Managing Information System Security. M.P. Ltd., Great Britain, 210 (1997)
24. Chia, P.A., Maynard, S.B., Ruighaver, A.B.: Exploring Organisational Security Culture: Developing A Comprehensive Research Model. In: IS ONE World Conference, Las Vegas, USA (2002)
25. Helokunnas, T., Kuusisto, R.: Information security culture in a value net. In: 2003 IEEE International Engineering Management Conference (IEMC 2003), Albany, New York, USA, November 2-4 (2003b)
26. Straub, D., et al.: Toward a Theory-Based Measurement of Culture. Global Information Management 10(1), 13–23 (2002)
27. Dojkovski, S., Lichtenstein, S., Warren, M.J.: Challenges in Fostering an Information Security Culture in Australian Small and Medium Sized Enterprises. In: 5th European Conference on Information Warfare and Security, Helsinki, Finland, June 1-2 (2006)
28. Sneza, D., Sharman, L., Matthew John, W.: Fostering information security culture in small and medium size enterprises: An interpretive study in australia. In: Fifteenth European Conference on Information Systems. University of St. Gallen, St. Gallen (2007)
29. ABS, 1321.0 - Small Business in Australia. Australian Bureau of Statistics (2001)
30. Detert, J., Schroeder, R., Mauriel, A.J.: A Framework For Linking Culture and Improvement Initiatives in Organisations. The Academy of Management Review 25(4), 850–863 (2000)
31. Taylor, M., Murphy, A.: SMEs and eBusiness. Small Business and Enterprise Development 11(3), 280–289 (2004)
32. Hutchinson, D., Warren, M.: e-Business Security Management for Australian Small SMEs - A Case Study. In: Proceedings of the 7th International We-B (Working for E-Business) Conference, e-Business: how far have we come? Electronic Commerce Research Unit ECRU, Australia (2006c)
33. Dimopoulos, V., et al.: Approaches to IT Security in Small and Medium Enterprises. In: 2nd Australian Information Security Management Conference, Securing the Future, Perth, Western Australia, pp. 73–82 (2004b)
34. Furnell, S.M., Gennatou, M., Dowland, P.S.: Promoting Security Awareness and Training within Small Organisations. In: 1st Australian Information Security Management Workshop. Deakin University, Geelong, Australia (2000)
35. Helokunnas, T., Iivonen, L.: Information Security Culture in Small and Medium Size Enterprises. In: e-Business Research Forum – eBRF 2003. Tampere University of Technology, Tampere (2003)

36. Warren, M.J.: Australia's Agenda for E-Security Education and Research. In: TC11/WG11.8 Third Annual World Conference on Information Security Education (WISE3). Naval Post Graduate School, Monterey (2003)
37. Von Solms, R., Von Solms, B.: From policies to culture. Computers & Security 23(4) (2004)
38. Furnell, S.M., Clarke, N.L.: Organisational Security Culture: Embedding Security Awareness, Education and Training. In: 4th World Conference on Information Security Education (WISE 2005), Moscow, URSS (2005)
39. Van Niekerk, J.C., Von Solms, R.: Establishing an Information Security Culture in Organisations: an Outcomes-based Education Approach. In: ISSA 2003: 3rd Annual IS South Africa Conference, Johannesburg, South Africa, July 9-11 (2003)
40. Hutchinson, D., Warren, M.: Australian SMES and e-Security Guides on Trusting the Internet. In: Fourth Annual Global Information Technology Management World Conference, Global Information Technology Management Association (GITMA), USA (2003)
41. Knapp, K.J., et al.: Information Security: Management's effect on culture and policy. Information Management & Computer Security 14(1), 24–36 (2006)
42. Lichtenstein, S.: Internet security policy for organisations. Unpublished thesis (PhD) (public version), ed. S.o.I.M.S. Monash University, Melbourne, Australia (2001)
43. Stanton, J.M., et al.: Analysis of end-user security behaviors. Computers & Security 24, 124–133 (2004)
44. Kuusisto, T., Ilvonen, I.: Information security culture in small and medium size enterprises. In: Frontiers of e-business Research 2003 (2003)
45. Sánchez, L.E., et al.: Managing Security and its Maturity in Small and Medium-Sized Enterprises. Journal of Universal Computer Science (J. UCS) 15(15), 3038–3058 (2009)

Towards an Enterprise System Learning Environment to improve the Competence-Building for Enterprise Systems in Higher Education

Dirk Peters[1], Liane Haak[1], and Tobias Schlömer[2]

Carl von Ossietzky Universität Oldenburg, Faculty II
[1] Department of Computing Science, Chair of Business Information Systems I / VLBA
[2] Department of Business Administration, Economics, and Law, Vocational Studies and Economic Education
Ammerländer Heerstr. 114-118, 26129 Oldenburg, Germany
{dirk.peters,liane.haak,tobias.schloemer}@uni-oldenburg.de

Abstract. Within this contribution a framework of an Enterprise System Learning Environment (ELSE) is introduced on the basis of an Adaptive Learning Cycle. This framework integrates learning into Enterprise Systems, like e.g. ERP systems, under the consideration of the underlying business processes. The idea of this approach is to track, analyze and categorize the learner's behavior during the learning process based on e.g. case studies, in order to generate more individual and adequate learning material and to measure the success or failure within the cycle. On the basis of these results the competence-building for learners like students, workers, etc. can be improved, in order to gain a higher knowledge level and a better understanding of ES in general.

Keywords: Enterprise System, Higher Education, Enterprise System Learning Environment, Adaptive Learning Cycle and Application Usage Mining.

1 Introduction

The actual situation in the field higher education is affected by universities with high drop-out rates, shoestring resources and increasing pressure of competition. Besides, they are fighting with manifold public criticism. Concurrently the change from the industry to a knowledge society enhances the relevance of universities as knowledge imparting institutions. So investments in education have a high Return on Investment. But the increasing amount of students and the enormous costs of this education bare the need to more efficiency and effectiveness in teaching. The classic lecture without the interaction with students has no cheaper alternative, because more interaction causes more effort in time and resources. Individuality and attractive learning offers could be only realized, if they compete in economic aspects. So, high-quality teaching stands in tension with economic aspects. The aim is to receive an increase in productivity of the teaching through the rise of the

J.E. Quintela Varajão et al. (Eds.): CENTERIS 2010, Part II, CCIS 110, pp. 325–334, 2010.

output (i.e. satisfaction and learning success) under concurrently reduction of the input (teaching effort).

To achieve an acquirement in factual and practical knowledge as well as in specific professional comprehensive competencies, a learning progress with interaction between the instructor and the learner is necessary. But the result is difficult to measure and depends much on the input and engagement of the learner. Both, instructor and learner have to invest in the teaching process, which makes it important to consider the input and output within the learning process. The actual conversion of the degrees to the bachelor and master system following the bologna process and the resulting demand on competence orientation entail new requirements for the higher education system. They contain a change of the objectives in academic teaching from the primary scientific education to a professional oriented competence-building. This requires new teaching and learning forms to build up competence.

Basically, academic teaching can be differentiated in three major tasks: the knowledge transfer, the knowledge application, expanding and deepening the knowledge revision. The aim should be to utilize the knowledge and to build up problem-solving competence. But the initial euphoria about the potentials of pure eLearning disappeared [1] and we need methodic foundered instruments of evaluation for specific teaching and learning situations to build up this specific competence.

This contribution introduces an approach for a new learning environment for Enterprise Systems (ES). The concept focuses on the needs of teaching and learning in higher education institutes. After this motivation, a short introduction in ES will be given in the next section, followed by essentials in the competence-building theory and the Adaptive Learning Cycle. Afterwards an overview about technical learning solution is given and explained in detail. The paper closes with the conclusions and a future outlook.

2 Enterprise Systems

Business Informatics and Business Information Systems deal with the development and application of theories, concepts, models, methods and tools for the analysis, design, and usage of information systems [2]. ES such as Enterprise Resource Planning (ERP) systems represent an automated partly system of a comprehensive operational information system in form of integrated application systems. They support nearly all operational business processes and are highly complex. Higher education institutes, like universities or universities of applied science, can not ignore the need to teach these well know application and information systems. Though, interferences and complexity of the different perspectives in computer science, business economics and the technology aspects make teaching and learning quite difficult in this field. Students need to be taught on practically approved systems to develop their own practical experience besides the theoretical lectures. Therefore ES offer the capability for future pedagogic innovation within higher education, which results from the possibilities in illustration, visualization and simulation of business and decision-making processes to students [3].

The main goal of using ES, such as e.g. ERP systems, Business Intelligence, etc., in higher education is to prepare the students for real work life and to give them practical experience in the application of these technologies. Although many studies have shown that graduates with experience with ERP systems have better chances on the job market [4], [5], [6]. Hence, it is not a question anymore, that skills and knowledge in the development and application of ES are highly recommended and a component of a modern academic education. But especially [6] has shown in his study, that the successful integration of ERP systems in the actual teaching is not that easy and requires a detailed planning. The different needs of instructor and learner have to be considered as well as the business process context within the systems to achieve a progress in learning.

3 Competence-Building and Adaptive Learning Cycle

Learning theories are scientific theories that are needed to clarify, which conditions and which reasons effect the learning processes. Teaching theories include common didactic models, but also the more technological discipline of instructional designs. All in all there are three big approaches for explaining teaching and learning: the behaviorism, the cognitivism and the constructivism. With the constructivist approach a fundamental subject-related perspective on learning and teaching entered the whole discussion since the 1980s. The constructivist approach of learning and teaching emanates from the primacy of construction. Learners are considered as self-directed and self-organized creators of knowledge [7]. With this perspective finally the learner is the centre of theory building: learners, who construct self-directed their own world and their knowledge about the world.

3.1 Competence-Building

The constructivist learning paradigm leads to shifted roles of teachers/lecturers and learners. Lecturers create learning situations together with learners. That means i.e. that learners can follow up their own action objectives, learners take the responsibility for their thinking, knowledge and acting and options to design learning environments should be offered to learners [8]. Following those suggestions for creating learning environments, learners will acquire and develop professional competence. In this context of higher education, professional competence means a constructive bundling of single competences, that people need to cope with specific job-specifications [9] and leads to a competence model – based on the previously presented learning theory.

In our understanding six competence dimensions constitute professional competence. They are related in a circular connection [9], [10], [11]. Due to that circular structure, it is not possible to promote only a single competence, professional competence can only be developed as a whole (see Figure 1). The main components of professional competence are the knowledge-competence (know-that), the creative-competence and the social-competence. The methodical-competence (know-how), the moral-ethical-competence and the abstraction-competence bring in bridging functions: they connect the three components and create the circular structure of the model.

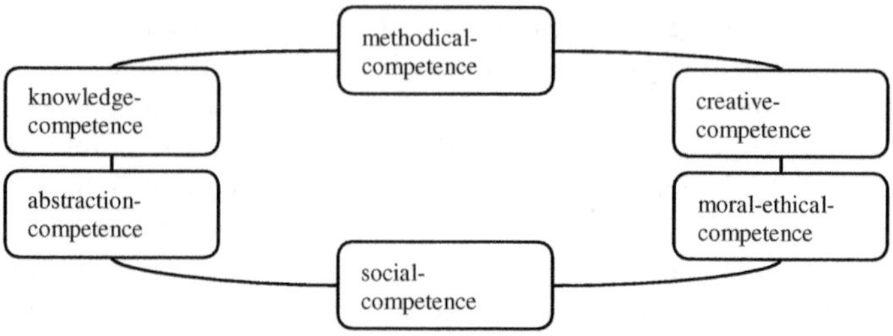

Fig. 1. Model of Professional Competence [9]

First of all, professional competence means to have knowledge-competence. It includes task-, organization-, process- and workplace-related knowledge [12]. Employees develop their individual knowledge-competence by gaining new experiences and connecting them with previous experiences. This cognitive process of construction is marked by individual percipience and experiencing [13]. Another important core competence is the creative-competence: it describes the transformation of own ideas and concepts in order to deal with job-specific tasks and issues in business [14]. An essential pre-condition for vocational creating is that employees get an appropriate scope for following up their own ideas. The social-competence represents the skills for a situation-adequate interaction with other people and is expressed in the capacity for teamwork, the ability to cooperate, professional communicative skills and also the ability to solve conflicts [15].

The methodical-competence (know-how) bridges the knowledge-competence with the creative-competence in the circular model of professional competence. Methodical-competence enables the strategically planned and task-oriented transformation of existing knowledge, behavior patterns and skills when diverse tasks and problems have to be managed [16]. Through the connection of the creative-competence with the social-competence, the moral-ethical-competence is generated: it is regularly demanded in social contexts when there is a need to solve a problem conjointly. Many companies declare code of conducts that are based on ethical values such as equity, solidarity, responsibility and fairness. Those values offer a normative orientation for employees and they help them to create convincing proposals that make sense for all involved individuals [17]. Finally, the abstraction-competence is a result of bridging social competence with knowledge-competence: firstly, it is expressed as the ability to generalize (abstract) the own knowledge and the own experience in a way that other people can understand it. For the development of professional competence adequate concepts for teaching and learning have to be offered and need to be applied to the higher education environment.

3.2 Adaptive Learning Cycle

Today's learning material does not respond to different education levels of the students and their fields of study. Some students are studying economics, some others computer science, e.g. Thus, the learning groups are often very heterogenous from different point of views and there are still problems occurring from missing background information as well as the differences in the domain knowledge of the learners. Following the constructivist learning paradigm, the focus is on the learner itself. The orientation on the individual replaces the principle of orientation on the participants, which concentrates on bringing participants into the institution of adult and continuing education. This development is resulting from the fact that traditional educational systems are not considering the learner's needs. By orienting on the learner and his behavior, the learning process has a higher degree of individualization. This results in a higher self-organization and a more independent learner.

In the following section we present our technical oriented approach to improve the learning progress in the educational area. The aim is provide a technical solution and consider the personal learning process and progress to improve learning material and teaching methods. It is a new method to give learners and teachers a feedback about the individual problems of the learning group within the material and the tasks itself to enhance the education in the field of ES in Higher Education. This learner-oriented view assumes that an improved learning environment is based on the individual and his or her specific qualification [18]. In our approach we focus on an Adaptive Learning Cycle (ALC) where exercises and tasks are adapted to the individual state of the learner (see Figure 2).

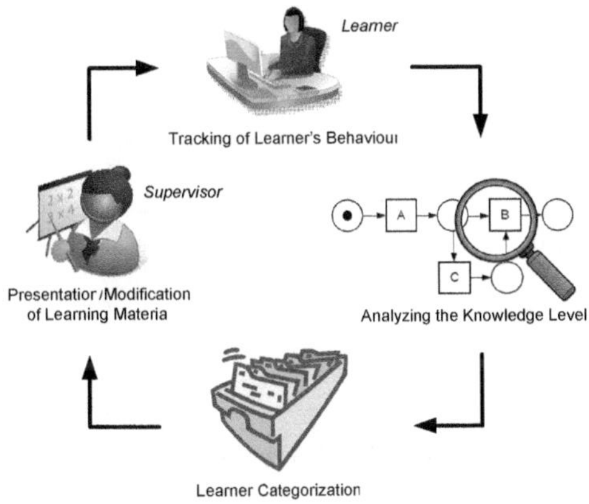

Fig. 2. Adaptive Learning Cycle [18]

The ALC is subdivided into four areas: Initially, it starts with the tracking of the learner's behavior, while he is performing a specific task or transaction in the system. On the basis of this information, it is possible to analyze the learner's behavior and derive some detailed information about the knowledge level, strengths and weaknesses or general information about the learner and his familiarity with the system. This leads to a categorization of the learner as a result of the analyzing phase. Depending on the assigned category, the learning material can be modified by an advising entity (a lecturer e.g.) and presented to the learner. The effectiveness of this new advisement can also be measured by our approach. More precisely, the success of the new modified learning material, which was presented to the learner, can be analyzed via a second run through our ALC. If applicable, a new categorization of the learner can be made. The concrete functionality will be described within the framework of the Enterprise System Learning Environment.

4 Enterprise System Learning Environment

The ESLE framework, which is shown in Figure 3, consists of different layers. After a short introduction of each part of the framework, every single layer will be described in more detail in the following subsections. The basis of the ESLE framework is the ES with the underlying business processes. In our context, this ES with the corresponding business processes is the main objective the user needs to understand. Therefore, the behavior of each user can be tracked by the tracking component of the ESLE. As described in the ALC, this tracking can be carried out during the daily work integrated into a workplace, during a training course or in a curricular environment for example.

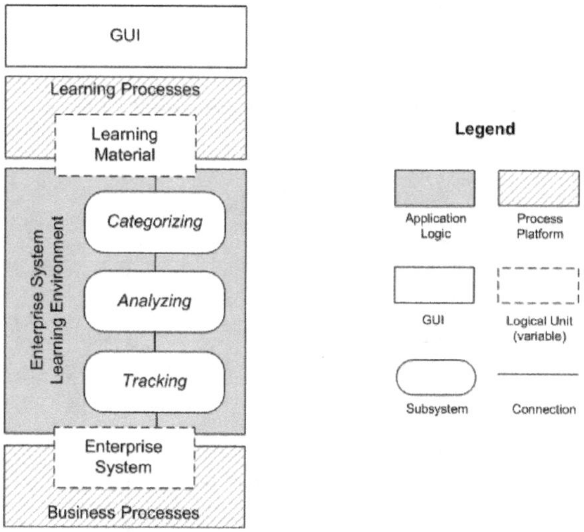

Fig. 3. ESLE Framework

In the next step, the ESLE can analyze the tracking information which was recorded before and find out specific patterns according to the knowledge level of the performing user. In this part different mining technologies, like Application Usage Mining (AUM) or Educational Data Mining (EDM), come into operation [19], [20]. These technologies are described in section 4.2. The analysis leads to a categorization, where different users can be divided into groups. This categorization can be done on the basis of variable characteristics, like knowledge level, systems familiarity or degree of target achievement, e.g. As a result of the categorization phase, the learning material for each user will be modified according to their individual state. The learning material itself has a major impact on the learning process. The learning process bears resemblance to the underlying business process.

The success of the generation of different learning materials can also be measured by the ESLE, because iterations within the learning process are tracked and analyzed as well. The visualization of the learning material and the ES itself are shown to the user via the ELSE GUI, which combines the interface of the ES with the learning material the user has to work with. The graphical user interface matches the regular user interface of the ES with the learning material which is presented to the learner. As already introduced in the first sections, the learning environment should be as much workplace-integrated as possible. Therefore the learning material can be presented directly in the ES, in order to give the learner a realtime problem solution.

4.1 Business Processes and Enterprise Systems

The main objective of our research is the improvement of the competence-building for ES in the field of higher education. ES in form of business information systems are getting more and more complex, whereby the handling those systems requires an improved knowledge of the interacting users. Furthermore, integrated ES affect different divisions of an enterprise, which also leads to a rising complexity. Most of the business processes of today's enterprises are realized within ES, like ERP systems for example. Finally, every user needs to understand the underlying business logic which is supported by the system.

In the introduced ESLE framework (see Figure 3), this business logic in form of business process is the basis for the creation of learning material. Therefore we define the business processes as the main objective in the learning process and as the domain, which needs to be understood by the learner. Within the considered ES the user, which is also the learner in our case, leaves traces in form of entries in specific log-files, which are provided by the most of the ES by default. In a SAP ERP system for example, we have a huge amount of transaction data recorded by the system during the regular use. This transaction data can be used for the generation of behavior patterns and the visualization of knowledge levels of different users within the ELSE. It builds up the interface between ES and ESLE.

4.2 Tracking, Analyzing and Categorizing in ELSE

The tracking of the learner's behavior is the initial phase of the ALC, which was introduced in section 3.2, and the first step the ESLE is performing as a subcomponent. Here, the learner is performing a specific task according to his exercise in the system. It is important that the learner acts in his working environment in order to maintain a familiar working and also learning atmosphere. Regarding the technique of tracking the learner's interaction with the system, there are a lot of possibilities existing. The already mentioned and most obvious solution is the logging of transaction data via trace-files and protocols. Most systems already deliver this possibility more or less. In a SAP ERP system for example, a huge amount of data is collected while the system is used. In so called user-trace-files detailed information (e.g. name of the performing user, transaction codes, input values, time duration, etc.) about the performed interaction between the user and the system is stored. This allows us to deduce detailed information concerning the learner's behavior. Kassem uses this technique in his Application Usage Mining (AUM)-approach [19]. In his work, he achieves an optimization of business processes on the basis of the described tracking information. Hence, his focus is on the identification of unused business processes in an enterprise system in order to optimize them.

The biggest challenge is, to find out the individual state of each learner in order to categorize these types for a most effective learner support. Therefore we have the tracking information from the previous step, which has to be analyzed in this following step. The superior aim of the analyzing phase within the ESLE is to find out meaningful information about the knowledge level of the learner. In this part we can benefit from a widespread experience in mining techniques, which will be introduced in the following more in detail.

Data Mining is the major discipline for generating information or detecting patterns in a huge amount of unstructured and raw data [21]. The use of this information is depending on the domain in which the information is needed. Data Mining is the basis of all mining technologies, but in the field of Higher Education we have to take different specific mining technologies into account. *Process Mining* is one specific area of Data Mining and aims on process knowledge in general. Therefore, Process Mining extracts data, which describes the execution of processes in order to store, transfer and reuse the process knowledge in form of models or schemas [22]. A very close related technique to Process Mining is the method of *Workflow Mining*. It is used to control, optimize, execute and monitor business processes. As an example, enterprises often run different business processes which are not really needed in practice. Via Workflow Mining these processes can be identified and displace or changed. In contrast to this, some other business processes which are used very frequently can also be identified with Workflow Mining and optimized later on [23]. All these processes can be identified from transaction data or event logs of an enterprise software system in order to generate the described effects. An approach which aims on the identification and optimization of business process in an enterprise is the already mentioned AUM-approach by Kassem.

Data, Process and Workflow Mining are not directly addressed to the field of analyzing the knowledge level of a learner. They can only help with the identification of patterns in unstructured data belonging to different application areas. Therefore, we have to take other approaches into account. One idea, which deals with educational data, is the *Educational Data Mining* (EDM). It is used to convert raw data from educational systems like interactive learning environments, computer-supported collaborative learning or administrative data from schools and universities, to meaningful information to better understand the learner. This emerging discipline is primarily used by educational software developers, learners, teachers, parents and other educational researchers [20]. For the learner categorization, as the third step in our ALC and the last subcomponent of the ESLE framework, the usage of different mining techniques is not sufficient enough. The challenge for the categorization is to integrate the intended learning target of the actual task the learner performs in the system into the applied mining technique, like EDM for example.

4.3 Learning Processes and Learning Material

The result of the categorization phase will affect the future learning material which is presented to the learner. Because of the adaptive individuality of our approach, the learning material is specific to each learner. According to the category the learner has been classified before, the following tasks are more or less difficult then the task assigned before. Especially in this phase of the ALC the advising entity, like a supervisor or teacher, can influence the assignment of tasks. For example, if the majority of learners were categorized on a very low knowledge level, the teacher has to rethink the initial situation. Furthermore, the way how the learning material is presented can be influenced by the teacher as well. The adequacy of the presented learning material or future tasks can be measured in the following analysis within the ALC of the state of the learners. If the learning material was adequate, the next categorization will provide information of a successful knowledge increase.

Learning processes are the basis for the generation of learning material. It needs to be defined, which aim a specific exercise has and if it fits into the learning process the learner is following in the moment. In section 4.1 we underlined the importance of the understanding of the underlying business processes. The business processes are linked very close to the learning processes. The similarities and differences between learning processes and business processes are part several other scientific investigations [24].

5 Conclusions and Future Work

After a short reflection of the actual situation in the field of higher education institutes, we found out that there are new needs for teaching and learning and new requirements for the higher education system at all. A professional oriented competence-building is one of the major challenges universities and universities of applied sciences are facing today. On this problem, we introduced the Adaptive Learning Cycle, which describes the concept of our idea and contains an approach how exercises and tasks are adapted to the individual state of the learner. On this basis the ELSE framework gives an overview about the different components we are using in our approach. In a next step these components need be defined in a more detailed way in order to determine concrete requirements for a reference architecture and the first prototypical implementation of this approach. Finally, the ESLE needs to be evaluated in a curriculum of a university for example, to measure the potential in comparison with other existing approaches like e.g. case studies.

References

1. Gabriel, R., Gersch, M., Weber, P., Venghaus, C.: Blended Learning Engineering: Der Einfluss von Lernort und Lernmedium auf Lernerfolg und Lernzufriedenheit - Eine evaluationsgestützte Untersuchung. In: Breitner, M. (ed.) Technologiebasiertes Lehren und Lernen, Passau (2006)
2. Kurbel, K.: Das Studium der Wirtschaftsinformatik. In: Kurbel, K., Brenner, W., Chamoni, P., Frank, U., Mertens, P., Roithmayer (eds.) Studienführer Wirtschaftsinformatik, Gabler, Wiesbaden, pp. 17–23 (2009/2010)
3. Ask, U., Juell-Skielse, G., Magnusson, J., Olsen Dag, H., Päivärinta, T.: Enterprise Systems as Vehicles of Pedagogic Innovation - Enterprise System Inclusion in Higher Education. In: Proceedings of the 5th International Conference on Enterprise Systems, Accounting and Logistics (5th ICESAL 2008), Crete Island, Greece, July 7-8 (2008)
4. Boyle, T.: Technical-Oriented Enterprise Resource Planning (ERP): Body of Knowledge for Information Systems Programs: Content and Implementation. Journal of Education for Business, 267–274 (May/June 2007)

5. Johnson, T., Lorents, A.C., Morgan, J., Ozmun, J.: A Customized ERP/SAP Model for Business Curriculum Integration. Journal of Information Systems Education 15(3), 245–253 (2004)
6. Strong, D.M., Fedorowicz, J., Sager, J., Stewart, G., Watson, E.: Teaching with Enterprise Systems. Communications of AIS 17(article 33) (2006)
7. Müller, K.R.: Berufliches Lernen und Lerntheorie. In: Kaiser, F.-J., Pätzold, G. (eds.) Wörterbuch Berufs- und Wirtschaftspädagogik, 2nd edn., Klinkhardt, Bad Heilbrunn (2006)
8. Fosnot, C.T.: Constructivism: A Psychological Theory of Learning. In: Fosnot, C.T. (ed.) Constructivism: Theory, Perspectives and Practice, pp. 8–33. Teachers College Press, New York (1996)
9. Rebmann, K., Tenfelde, W.: Betriebliches Lernen. Hampp, München (2008)
10. Rebmann, K., Tenfelde, W., Uhe, E.: Berufs- und Wirtschaftspädagogik, 3rd edn. Gabler, Wiesbaden (2005)
11. Schlömer, T.: Die Sustainability Balanced Scorecard als Lerngegenstand in der Berufsbildung für eine nachhaltige Entwicklung. In: Duensing, M., Schwithal, T., Tredop, D. (eds.) Kapital, Kompetenz, Konflikte, BIS, Oldenburg, pp. 175–193 (2008)
12. Kauffeld, S.: Weiterbildung: eine lohnende Investition in die berufliche Zukunft? In: Frey, A., Jäger, R., Renold, U. (eds.) Kompetenzmessung – Sichtweisen und Methoden zur Erfassung und Bewertung von beruflichen Kompetenzen, Landau (2003)
13. Schmidt, S.J. (ed.): Der Kopf, die Welt, die Kunst. Konstruktivismus als Theorie und Praxis, Böhlau, Wien (1992)
14. Kehl, V., Kunzendorf, M., Wolf, M.: Die berufliche Handlungskompetenz im Zeichen visualisierter Arbeitskontexte. In: Ott, B. (ed.) Eigene Kompetenzen erkennen und fördern, ChangeX-Edition, Erding, pp. 47–70 (2006)
15. Reetz, L.: Zum Zusammenhang von Schlüsselqualifikationen – Kompetenzen – Bildung. In: Tramm, T., Sembill, D., Klauser, F., John, E.G. (eds.) Professionalisierung kaufmännischer Berufsausbildung, Lang, Frankfurt am Main, pp. 32–51 (1999)
16. Jäger, P.: Der Erwerb von Kompetenzen als Konkretisierung der Schlüsselqualifikationen, Universität Passau (2001), http://www.opus-bayern.de/uni-passau/volltexte/2003/17/pdf/jaeger.pdf (24.02.2010)
17. Lempert, W.: Prinzipien der Auswahl, Entwicklung und Verwendung moralischer Dilemmata als Materialien für die berufliche und berufspädagogische Aus-und Weiterbildung, Zeitschrift für Berufs-und Wirtschaftspädagogik, 98/2002, pp. 330–353 (2002)
18. Peters, D., Haak, L., Marx Gómez, J.: Learner-oriented Approach for Enterprise Systems in Higher Education using TEL-based Concepts. In: Proceedings of the Second International Conference on Computer Supported Education (CSEDU), Valencia, Spain (2010)
19. Kassem, G.: Application Usage Mining: Grundlagen und Verfahren. Shaker, Aachen (2007)
20. Baker, R. S. J. d., Barnes, T., Beck, J. E. (eds.) Proceedings of the 1st International Conference on Educational Data Mining, Montreal, Quebec, Canada (2008)
21. Peterson, H.: Data Mining. Verfahren, Prozesse, Anwendungsarchitektur (2005)
22. Schimm, G., van der Aalst, W., ter Hofstede, A., Weske, M.: Mining most specific Workflow Models from Event-based Data. In: Proceedings of the International Conference BPM, Eindhoven, pp. 25–40 (2003)
23. Remberg, J.: Grundlagen des Process Mining. GRIN Verlag (2008)
24. Bergenthum, R., Desel, J., Harrer, A., Mauser, S.: Learnflow mining. In: DeLFI. LNI, vol. 132, pp. 269–280, GI (2008)

Investigation into the Use of Microsoft SharePoint in UK Higher Education Institutions

Julie McLeod[1], Sue Childs[1], James Lappin[2], and Gavin Siggers[3]

[1] School of Computing, Engineering and Information Sciences, Northumbria University, Pandon Building, Camden St, Newcastle upon Tyne, NE2 1XE, UK
Julie.mcleod@northumbria.ac.uk
[2] Thinking Records Ltd
http://thinkingrecords.co.uk
[3] Healdan Consulting Ltd
http://www.linkedin.com/pub/gavin-siggers/13/77b/89b

Abstract. This paper describes an investigation of the use of Microsoft SharePoint in UK higher education institutions (HEIs). The study was funded by Eduserv, and conducted by Northumbria University in 2009. It aimed to discover how SharePoint was used, the views of stakeholders and any lessons learnt. The study comprised: a literature review; a telephone survey of IT Directors/Managers in 40 HEIs; an online survey with responses from 47 HEIs; an online community consultation; three detailed case studies; a public event. The study found that most UK HEIs were using SharePoint to some extent. Aspects of the SharePoint implementations - procurement, implementation approaches, drivers, critical success factors, use in teaching and learning and research, and barriers - are described. The conclusions look to the future of SharePoint use in UK HEIs as the 2010 version of the product becomes available. The transferability of the findings to other sectors is discussed.

Keywords: SharePoint, implementation, higher education sector, United Kingdom.

1 Introduction

Interest in Microsoft SharePoint solutions is growing within UK higher education (HE) and the wider public sector. In 2009 Eduserv, under their Research Programme, funded a study into the use of SharePoint by Higher Education Institutions (HEIs). Eduserv's aims were:

- to improve HEIs' understanding about the level and nature of interest in SharePoint and whether it is justified in terms of accepted good practice
- to enhance Eduserv's understanding about the uptake and usage of SharePoint solutions in the UK HE community and influence their 2-3 year plans for service provision in line with their charitable mission.

Eduserv is a not-for-profit organization dedicated to the development and delivery of technology solutions for the public sector. The study was undertaken by Northumbria University using a team of internal and external staff.

J.E. Quintela Varajão et al. (Eds.): CENTERIS 2010, Part II, CCIS 110, pp. 335–344, 2010.

With SharePoint 2007, Microsoft launched onto the market an extremely versatile and wide ranging product that can be used for:

- hosting and managing websites, intranets and portals
- providing collaboration sites for teams and groups to share information, news, and resources
- document management
- provision of some social computing capabilities
- process improvements through the implementation of workflows
- drawing in data from other organizational systems for use within the SharePoint environment
- a development platform within which applications can be written.

Since its launch in November 2006, SharePoint 2007 has seen a growing uptake in most sectors, including HE, in the UK and internationally. The reasons for its rapid growth can be ascribed to: (i) the flexibility that it gives teams to configure their own working environment. The more corporate-centric ECM (Enterprise Content Management) and EDRM (Electronic Document and Records Management) systems have largely failed to catch on in HE and SharePoint seems to provide an alternative that is more acceptable to local teams; (ii) the selling power of Microsoft, which already enjoys good relations with many IT departments; and (iii) its integration with Microsoft Office and Outlook (particularly Office 2007).

The versatility and flexibility of SharePoint give rise to its two main weaknesses. First, SharePoint is often described as 'a jack of all trades and master of none'. Unlike many other ECM systems SharePoint is not a modular system, e.g. if an organization purchases SharePoint for its intranet it finds that it has all of the other capabilities of SharePoint available to it. As a result some organizations use SharePoint 'because we have it' rather than because it is necessarily fit for the particular purpose. Secondly, SharePoint implementations are hard to govern. 'SharePoint sprawl' (the unfettered expansion of team sites and sub-sites) is an acknowledged phenomenon, and the records management features of the product are both weak and very difficult to implement.

The opportunities for the UK HE sector stem from: (i) a large user base using one product. These opportunities include sharing of best practice, specific tools and SharePoint 'web parts'; and (ii) influence on the market place.

The threats stem from: (i) the risk of lock-in to one vendor. This is acute with SharePoint 2007, which only runs on a Microsoft stack (Windows and SQL server); and (ii) damage to existing, more specialist, systems, such as line of business systems and Virtual Learning Environments (VLEs).

2 Project Methodology

The study was undertaken by Northumbria University over the summer and autumn of 2009, using a team of internal and external staff. The study's methodology was qualitative, comprising: a literature review, a telephone survey, an online survey, an online community consultation, three detailed case studies and a public event.

An initial review of selected current literature on SharePoint in the HE sector: Because SharePoint 2007 is a relatively recent phenomenon and a proprietary product, little has been published in peer-reviewed academic literature. This was established through searches of relevant information and education databases (i.e. LISA, ERIC and the British Education Index) and a journal contents page search (via Zetoc).To ensure coverage of current information, searches were also conducted during July and August 2009 on the websites of HEIs and on the web using Google. The review was largely confined to the UK HEI sector, although some examples from overseas (US and the Netherlands) were included.

A telephone survey of a purposively selected sample of UK HEI IT Directors/Managers: 40 HEIs were interviewed between August and October 2009; this represented approximately 25% of the UK HEI population and reasonably matched the population in terms of type of HEI and geographical location.

An online survey targeted at IT Directors and SharePoint Project Managers: An online survey was made available via SurveyMonkey and advertised through listservs. It was conducted in the last two weeks of October 2009. Informed by the telephone survey, this survey obtained further information on the scale and nature of HEI SharePoint use. 51 responses were received from 47 different HEIs.

An online community consultation with a wider range of stakeholders in HEIs: A brief questionnaire was made available via the project website and advertised through a wide range of listservs: response was via email. The aim was to enable professional groups, institutions, vendors and individuals with an interest in SharePoint in the UK HE sector to express their views on its impact and on what the sector needs to do to maximize the opportunities it offers and to minimize any risks. The consultation was widely publicized and open from 21 October to 9 November 2009; seven responses were received.

Detailed case studies of the use and potential future use of SharePoint in three HEIs: Face-to-face interviews were held with small numbers of staff in different roles.

A public event: The meeting, 'Use of Microsoft SharePoint in UK Higher Education Institutions', was held in London on 25 November 2009. The presentations comprised interim findings from the project and case studies from a number of HEIs who had experience of implementing SharePoint. About 100 people attended the event.

3 Project Findings

The detailed findings from the study can be found on the project website at http://www.northumbria.ac.uk/sharepoint_study. A summary is provided here under key headings: literature review; uptake; procurement; implementation approaches; drivers; critical success factors; role in teaching and learning; role in research; barriers.

3.1 Literature Review - Sample of References Found

Because SharePoint 2007 is a relatively recent phenomenon and a proprietary product, little has been published in the peer-reviewed academic literature. The material that we found comprised information on websites and blog posts. These described how people were using, or planning to use, SharePoint or gave individuals' views on the pros and cons of SharePoint. A sample of the items found is given in the References section [1-24]. This review found that SharePoint has spread rapidly in HE and has been put to a wide variety of uses. Implementations range from team sites supporting team collaboration (the most common use), to specific functions (e.g. teaching and learning), to portals for staff and/or students to access key resources from one place

In most of these implementations SharePoint use is the decision of teams or departments. This makes an interesting contrast with the standard implementation method for ECM systems and EDRMS, where top-down decisions designate which parts of the organization will receive the system.

3.2 Uptake of SharePoint 2007 within the UK HE Sector

The study suggests that most UK HEIs are using SharePoint to some extent. In the telephone survey of 40 UK HEIs, 78% said that they were making some use of SharePoint. A further 47 UK HEIs completed an online survey and 61% said that they were making some use of SharePoint. Dominic Watts, UK HE Business Manager at Microsoft, estimated that, 80% of UK HEIs were using SharePoint in some form at the time of the study (Personal communication, 11 September 2009). However, it should be noted that this use is not always across the whole HEI but might be focused in one part of the organization or for one specific purpose, and an HEI might have one or multiple SharePoint implementations.

SharePoint's rise in use over a few years is noteworthy given the relative lack of success of other ECM systems in HE. Whereas the other big vendors of proprietary ECM systems (IBM, Oracle, Open Text, EMC etc.) all have HE customers, none of them has established any dominance in the sector. The majority of HEIs in the study were not using a proprietary ECM system before SharePoint 2007 appeared.

The uptake of SharePoint 2007 in UK HEIs could be related to several factors, e.g.:

- SharePoint is easier to procure than most of its ECM system competitors
- SharePoint 2007 is versatile
- SharePoint 2007 devolves power to teams and end-users
- SharePoint 2007 is a platform with a large ecosystem around it.

3.3 The Procurement of SharePoint by UK HEIs

Most of the HEIs surveyed had procured SharePoint licenses though their Microsoft Campus Agreement. The Microsoft Campus Agreement allows an HEI to: (i) choose which Microsoft software (both client and server software) it wishes to use; and (ii) designate how many users, devices or servers it wishes to be able to use or run that software. Microsoft prices the campus agreement according to the numbers of users/servers/devices that will use or run the chosen software. Most HEIs in the study have included the Client Access Licences (CALs) for SharePoint 2007 in their campus agreement.

This should not be taken to imply that SharePoint 2007 is free for universities. The CAL licenses staff and students to use SharePoint, but in most cases HEIs still need to pay for additional facilities and services as well as development and project costs. The complexity of SharePoint 2007 can require complex development/configuration, often requiring the use of external consultants. Nevertheless SharePoint is still perceived as being a low cost solution in comparison to other proprietary ECM systems.

3.4 Implementation Approaches

Two broad types of approach to implementing SharePoint within UK HEIs were observed in the study, which can be characterized as the organic, bottom-up approach and the corporate, top-down approach.

The organic, bottom-up approach typically comprises the provision of collaborative team sites for local work groups. A part of the organization starts using or providing SharePoint team sites and the implementation grows organically over a period of time. The main strength of the organic approach is that, because it is focused on providing sites where teams need and want them, there is generally high user acceptance and adoption. However, it can result in 'SharePoint sprawl'. The main challenge for the organic approach is the issue of scalability.

The corporate, top-down approach typically comprises the use of SharePoint as an intranet and/or a portal, though most of these projects also involve (or envisage) the provision of collaborative team sites for local work groups. Institutions taking a corporate approach choose to implement SharePoint for a specific purpose or purposes as a corporate project with dedicated corporate resources. The corporate approach starts with bigger ambitions and more resources than the organic approach. With this approach HEIs are able to begin with the infrastructure and support arrangements that they need in order to sustain the implementation on an institution-wide scale. Corporate approaches are more likely to need customization than organic approaches. The main challenge with the corporate approach is that institutions that have no prior experience with SharePoint are launching with very demanding projects. SharePoint 2007 is not an easy product to install and configure, and the learning curve is very steep.

3.5 Drivers Behind SharePoint Implementations

SharePoint is a system with a wide variety of functionality that can be put to a wide variety of different uses. The SharePoint implementations explored in this study vary widely in their scale and scope. However, it is possible to identify a relatively small list of drivers behind the implementation of SharePoint within HE: to improve services/systems/management; collaboration; the SharePoint product itself; and user demand. Improvements of services/systems/management are too many and too specific to list here but some examples are automating cross institution processes, replacing networked/shared drives or public folders, centralization, web-based services, personalization, a point solution. SharePoint is primarily seen as a collaborative tool, and collaboration can be needed across-schools/departments, with colleagues outside the institution, and for document management. SharePoint is seen as a stable, long term product providing required functionality and fitting in with an existing Microsoft environment. User demand could come from existing small scale implementations requiring scaling up to corporate-wide coverage, or from knowledge of implementations in other organizations.

3.6 Critical Success Factors for SharePoint Implementations

Critical success factors (CSFs) apply to organizations adopting a corporate approach to SharePoint implementation or to any implementation that needs to be sustainable and scalable. The main CSFs that emerged were: a clear focus; a clear relationship between SharePoint and other systems; governance arrangements; managing customizations; training and advice. SharePoint has such a wide functionality scope and can be put to so many different uses, that an organization needs to identify and focus on what aspects it wants to implement. SharePoint functionality will duplicate that of other HEI systems so SharePoint's scope and relationship to these other systems needs to be clarified. To prevent SharePoint sprawl governance arrangements need to be established, e.g. planning SharePoint's technical and information architectures; managing and controlling the provision of new collaborative team sites. Most SharePoint implementations will need customizations. These need to be identified and managed and the necessary skills obtained, possibly by the use of external consultants in the short term, but by training of in house staff for the long term. As SharePoint is a complex system, end users need training and advice to enable them to make best use of the system. This can be a challenge for organic implementations, where the HEI does not know in advance who is going to become a SharePoint user.

3.7 SharePoint and Teaching and Learning

The vast majority of UK HEIs already have a VLE, which in effect acts as a content management system for teaching and learning content. VLEs enable HEIs to provide students with access to learning materials, news and information relating to their courses. The market for VLEs in the United Kingdom is dominated by two systems: Blackboard (a commercially licensed system) and Moodle (an open source system). Microsoft would like SharePoint to be perceived and used as a VLE, but in terms of market share it is a long way behind the two leaders in the VLE market. Only two examples of HEIs deploying SharePoint as their institutional VLE were identified during the study. However, SharePoint is being used in teaching and learning, but generally for specific purposes for which the institutional VLE is not so suited. One HEI that offers custom MBA courses for external clients uses SharePoint to provide each client with a customized learning environment accessible through the client's website. Another HEI uses SharePoint when students are doing a group project or a group presentation.

3.8 SharePoint and Research

The market for systems to support the research activities of HEIs is much smaller, less homogenous and not as mature as the market for VLEs. The demands of a HEI in relation to research are many and various, the nature of research projects is much more diverse (scientific data, text, audio, performance etc) than the nature of taught courses. It is hard to conceive of research needs being satisfied by one package; indeed there is no dominant provider of research support systems within HE.

However, some of the HEIs in the study were using SharePoint to support research projects, particularly for collaboration with external partners. The largest scale attempt was found at Oxford University who are defining a template SharePoint team site for research teams to use for their research projects. Cranfield University, one of the case study HEIs, were gathering requirements for a research information system to help them assess themselves for the REF, the next UK research quality assessment exercise.

3.9 Barriers to Adopting SharePoint in Higher Education

There are various barriers to adopting SharePoint in the UK higher education sector: technical, people and organizational.

Examples of SharePoint functionality and technical features that act as barriers are: SharePoint is a complex product with a complex architecture. It is not particularly usable 'out-of-the-box' and requires complex development/configuration to reduce the product scope. SharePoint 2007 only works under the Microsoft environment causing incompatibility problems with the other systems and products used by HEIs.

Examples of organizational factors that act as barriers are: the difficulty of balancing demand for SharePoint versus control of the implementation. SharePoint sprawl can be a serious problem if the organic approach is adopted. If a centralized, controlled approach is adopted it can place enormous demands on the governance structure. The additional resources and costs for SharePoint implementation - development costs, costs of consultants, investment in staff training - can be high.

Examples of people factors that act as barriers are: the skills needed for configuring and implementing SharePoint which are often lacking in HEI IT staff so consultants with such expertise may need to be employed. SharePoint is not simple to use so end-users will need training.

Some HEIs had doubts about the feasibility of deploying SharePoint across the whole of the organization. In theory SharePoint is an information system that crosses the divide and spans both the administrative and academic functions. In practice SharePoint was found to have been stronger within the administrative functions than academic functions.

4 Conclusions

This article has presented a sector survey/view of the use of SharePoint. The aim of the survey was to discover how SharePoint was used in UK HEIs, and obtain the views of the stakeholders involved and the lessons learnt they had learnt. The study discerned two distinct types of SharePoint implementation in UK HEIs: (i) organic, bottom up implementations which started small and evolved over time without a pre-existing strategy or plan; and (ii) corporate, top down implementations setting out to achieve specific objectives. The two approaches have different advantages and challenges. The implementations observed had a relatively small list of drivers: to improve services/systems/management; collaboration; the SharePoint product itself; and user demand. A number of critical success factors for SharePoint implementations were identified: a clear focus; a clear relationship between SharePoint and other systems; governance arrangements; managing customizations; training and advice. Lessons learned were: the need to be aware of the amount of initial customisation required; the importance of using external consultants in the right way i.e. working alongside them, so that HEI staff can learn the skills; the importance of user education as there is often more than one way to do something in SharePoint.

Though the study was sector specific, many of its findings are transferrable to other sectors in the public, private and not for profit domains. There seems no reason to think that large organizations, particularly those where parts of the organization or individuals have some freedom of action to initiate bottom up implementations, would not be able to benefit from the lessons learnt in the UK HE sector. The details of specific use, particularly in the areas core to HE – teaching and learning and research – would not be so widely transferrable but could be transferrable to HE sectors in other countries.

The research was conducted in the summer and autumn of 2009. Looking ahead to 2010 and beyond the following trends in the UK HE sector can be anticipated.

Beginnings of the adoption of SharePoint 2010. SharePoint 2010 was launched in May 2010, though it may well be 2011 before it starts to have an impact in HE. SharePoint 2010 has many improvements over the 2007 version, e.g. improved workflow, enhanced business intelligence tools, 'in-place' records management, sophisticated search, more social computing functionality. However, a number of the more advanced capabilities are only found in the Enterprise version.

Slow inroads into the teaching and learning function. There is no prospect, in the near future, of SharePoint challenging the market leaders for institutional VLEs. Currently SharePoint seems to be being used at the margins of teaching and learning, filling in for areas where VLEs are weaker. It has a long way to go before it is anything more than marginal to teaching and learning.

Increase in the average size of SharePoint implementations. When the study was conducted many of the implementations examined were at an early stage. The boom in SharePoint use came in 2008 and 2009 as HEIs started to pick up on SharePoint 2007. We will see the maturation of many implementations which are currently less than one year old. This is likely to bring with it some governance challenges (for example 'SharePoint sprawl') which are not apparent when implementations are smaller. It will also increase the percentage of staff and students in HE familiar with SharePoint as a working environment.

Competition from Google Apps for the collaboration space. It seems that the most likely form of new competition in the collaboration space will be Google Apps which offers significantly less functionality, but operates on a web hosted subscription model (as well as offering a free basic version) which may appeal to HEIs that want to avoid the complexities of the configuration and management of SharePoint.

Formation of at least one UK HE SharePoint User Group. It is surprising that there is a lack of UK HE SharePoint user groups. There are two JISCmail groups (SharePoint-Scotland and YH-SharePoint) but traffic on these two lists is low. The formation of one or more active SharePoint user groups would seem to be essential given the high level of take up in the sector, the complexity of the product, the customization and configuration challenges it poses, and the range of uses to which it can be put. Such a user group, or groups, could: support the sharing of knowledge across the sector; provide the sector with a voice in relation to both Microsoft and to vendors within the ecosystem around SharePoint; enable the sector to explore the implications of Microsoft's increasing dominance within higher education, as domination of the collaboration space is added to its domination of operating systems, e-mail servers, and office software.

References

1. Bradley, B.: What is your firm's SharePoint balance?. SharePoint Magazine, July 22 (2008), http://sharepointmagazine.net/news/what-is-your-firms-sharepoint-balance
2. Fleming, R.: Moodle Web Parts for SharePoint 2007 Released, Microsoft The HE Blog, May 24 (2007), http://blogs.msdn.com/ukhe/archive/2007/05/24/moodle-web-parts-for-sharepoint-2007-released.aspx
3. Gaitten, S.: SharePoint My Sites Suck. The Bamboo Team Blog, April 16 (2009), http://community.bamboosolutions.com/blogs/bambooteamblog/archive/2009/04/16/sharepoint-my-sites-suck.aspx
4. Goings, J.: SharePoint: Not the Social Answer. Jim Goings Blog, March 31 (2008), http://www.jimgoings.com/2008/03/sharepoint-not-the-social-answer/
5. Gotta, M.: Microsoft Continues to Fill SharePoint Social Gaps. Collaborative Thinking Blog, March 31 (2008), http://mikeg.typepad.com/perceptions/2008/03/microsoft-conti.html#
6. Jeffreys, P.W., Lee, S.: University of Oxford Online Environment. WebLearn and Nexus – Which Tool for Which Activity? Version 1.5, June 29. University of Oxford, Oxford (2009), http://www.ict.ox.ac.uk/odit/projects/groupware/project/109ODIT.pdf
7. JISC, Regional Support Centre, Scotland North & East: SharePoint Forum, http://www.rsc-ne-scotland.ac.uk/forums.php#SP
8. Leuders, D.: SharePoint Sprawl. The SharePoint Records and Information Management Blog, April 28 (2009), http://sharepointrm.wordpress.com/tag/sharepoint-sprawl/
9. Liverpool John Moores University.: What is Microsoft SharePoint? July 27 (2009), http://www.ljmu.ac.uk/cis/SharePoint/index.htm
10. McNiece, I.: Kingston University: the Future's Bright with 2007 Office, OfficeRocker Blog, January 15 (2007), http://blogs.msdn.com/officerocker/archive/2007/01/15/kingston-university-the-future-s-bright-with-2007-office.aspx
11. Microsoft.: Case Studies. Northumbria University. University Moves to Head of the Class with Microsoft Full-Decision Support System. Microsoft, June 26 (2009), http://www.microsoft.com/casestudies/Case_Study_Detail.aspx?casestudyid=4000004670
12. Watts, D.: SharePoint in Education – Putting Students at the Centre of Learning, Microsoft The HE Blog, December 19 (2008), http://blogs.msdn.com/ukhe/archive/2008/12/19/sharepoint-in-education-putting-students-at-the-centre-of-learning.aspx
13. Microsoft: Microsoft Office SharePoint Server 2007. Teaching and Learning for the 21st Century. Microsoft (2008), http://cid-7eaaf78c88e9bfad.skydrive.live.com/self.aspx/Blog%20files/SharePoint%20in%20Education.pdf

14. Microsoft: Case studies. Kingston University. University Reinforces Excellence in Research with Innovative Blogs and Shared Research Sites, January 16 (2007), http://www.microsoft.com/casestudies/Case_Study_Detail.aspx?CaseStudyID=200917
15. Miller, W.: Towards Knowledge Management: EMC After the First Year. Presentation to the UCISA Electronic Document and Records Management Seminar (2009), http://www.ucisa.ac.uk/~/media/groups/cisg/events/2009/EDRMS/will_miller_ucl%20pdf.ashx
16. Olsen, J.: Why Isn't My SharePoint Environment Social? SharePoint Land Blog, August 26 (2009), http://www.sharepointjoel.com/Lists/Posts/Post.aspx?List=0cd1a63d-183c-4fc2-8320-ba5369008acb&ID=253
17. Russell, K.: Utrecht University Has Chosen for Blackboard as VLE. Keith Russell's Blog, 11 July 11 (2008), http://keithrussell.blogspot.com/2008/07/utrecht-university-has-chosen-for.html
18. Browne, T., et al.: 2008 Survey of Technology Enhanced Learning for Higher Education in the UK. UCISA (Universities and Colleges Information Systems Association) (2008), http://www.ucisa.ac.uk/publications/~/media/290DD5217DA5422C8775F246791F5523.ashx
19. UCL Information Services Division. ADS SharePoint, http://www.ucl.ac.uk/isd/staff/ads/sharepoint
20. University of Kent Information Services. Sharing with SharePoint (June 2009), http://www.kent.ac.uk/is/news/issue13/sharepoint.html
21. Norman, M., et al.: Groupware Project Definition: Scope of Project, University of Oxford, http://www.oucs.ox.ac.uk/groupware/docs/GroupwareProjectSpecificationv1pt1.pdf
22. Peterson, N.: Hub and Spoke Model of Course Design, Commentable Site of the Center for Teaching Learning and Technology, Washington State University, June 4(2008), http://wsuctlt.wordpress.com/2008/06/04/hub-and-spoke-model-of-course-design/
23. Universiteit Twente. Quickscan SharePoint: Eindrapport, February 29 (2008), http://www.utwente.nl/elo/rapporten_quickscan_sp/d_sharepoint_eindrapport_v10.pdf
24. Watts, D.: How Far has SharePoint Come in UK Higher Education? Microsoft The HE Blog, March 26 (2009), http://blogs.msdn.com/ukhe/archive/2009/03/26/how-far-has-sharepoint-come-in-uk-higher-education.aspx

Adoption of Authenticated Peer-to-Peer Academic Networks – A Case Study of a Failure

António Tavares[1] and Luís Amaral[2]

[1] Escola Superior de Tecnologia, Instituto Politécnico do Cávado e Ave, Lugar do Aldão, 4750-810 Vila Frescainha S. Martinho BCL, Portugal
ajtavares@ipca.pt

[2] Departamento de Sistemas de Informação, Universidade do Minho, Campus de Azurém, 4800 - 058 Guimarães, Portugal
amaral@dsi.uminho.pt

Abstract. The use of P2P applications in universities has been mainly focused on questions related to file sharing and copyright violation, and little attention has been given to the development of secured and authenticated P2P applications, specially conceived to academic environments. In this paper, we describe Bumerang, an authenticated campus P2P network, which despite technological quality and top level institutional commitment, didn't reach critical mass of users, failing at the individual adoption level. To understand the factors that contributed for this result, we make a retrospective analysis of the process of conception and diffusion including results from the network activity. We conclude that we must reinforce their perceived utility, deal with the security concerns with new approaches and stay away from using the P2P term.

Keywords: peer-to-peer file sharing; authenticated peer-to-peer networks in academic environments; technology adoption; UTAUT; case study.

1 Introduction

The core characteristic of the Peer-to-Peer (P2P) technology is the possibility of sharing digital resources – digital contents, processing power, bandwidth and storage – in a free and equal way, amongst the members of a community (peers) in a self-regulated way [1].

Although this technology demonstrated its potential in business and project domains with global impact [2] and maintains a high presence in the global Internet traffic [3], there are still few application domains that have exploited it on a large scale [4]. According to several authors [5, 6] the potential of P2P is not wet being met, due to technical and non-technical reasons. The excessive controversy with anonymous P2P file-sharing networks and copyright violation, maintains the research focus around technological and legal issues [7]. In the case of academic environments, despite the recognized potentialities of P2P technology and applications to share and collaborate in academy [8], the organizations imposed a lot of restrictions to the attempts of exploring P2P potentialities.

J.E. Quintela Varajão et al. (Eds.): CENTERIS 2010, Part II, CCIS 110, pp. 345–354, 2010.

In this paper, we describe our experience with Bumerang, a secure and authenticated P2P campus network. It was developed at the University of Minho, in a unique context of institutional commitment and openness to innovation, which is a rare combination when it comes to P2P. However, against our expectations, and despite the recognized technological quality, the Bumerang network did not reach critical mass of users and resources to be self sustained. It failed at the individual adoption level, hinder the development of its full potential. This result was mainly related to human factors, in the area of Technology Adoption and Diffusion [9, 10]. With the study of this failure, we expect to enrich the knowledge about the factors that contribute to the individual adoption of this kind of P2P networks.

2 Related Work

The P2P phenomenon started at the universities with Napster in 1999. Quickly, they was brought to the middle of the digital rights battlefield [11, 12], raising serious problems to the attempts of exploring P2P potentialities in academic environments. Despite the difficulties, there were a few cases of P2P networks specially conceived and configured to academic environments. However, like Bumerang, these projects had a common problem: they had difficulties in acquiring critical mass of users in order to be self sustainable and develop their full potential.

Lionshare was the most visible project in this area, with large resources and institutional support. It had facilities for authenticated P2P collaboration learning among the members of an academic community. The final results indicated that the authentication and access control features wasn't appeal to students, because their perception of P2P was that it was for sharing "any type of files" [13]. At May 2009 Lionshare was discontinued.

The SPIRE project tried to explore Lionshare in the support to informal repositories at the UK academia. Due to technical difficulties and to the believe that "it would be a fruitless effort to attempt to combine the high levels of security necessary to reassure academics and their institutions with the flexible paradigm of P2P" [14], the project team abandoned the Lionshare implementation.

vuCRN [15] was a prototype of an authenticated P2P network for legally information sharing between academics and researchers, imposing authentication and DRM mechanisms. The purpose of the research team was to use file sharing as the beginning of larger P2P network with an unlimited potential for collaboration between academics and researchers.

Finally, regarding empirical studies about individual adoption of authenticated P2P networks in academic environments, as far as we known, Lin et al [16] is the single empirical study available. The study analyzed the use of P2P network for information sharing in collaborative learning, and concluded that the adoption and use by students was low and was only positively related with subjective norm. This study reinforces the necessity for further work in this area, in order to explore the full potential of P2P in academic environments.

3 Bumerang Conception and Diffusion

Bumerang resulted from the project "P2P Knowledge Sharing" [17], which we started at the end of 2004, in response to the challenge of built a P2P platform, at the University of Minho, in order to "create and spread a culture of knowledge share between students, teachers and other staff, supported in applications of P2P technology". It´s important to note that the central challenge posed to the project, was the exploitation of the P2P technology in an academic environment. Three main goals were defined to the project:

Explore the potentialities of the technology to support communities of knowledge share, regarding formal and informal processes or relations, in the rich social and cultural environment of the academic community;

Explore the potentialities of the technology regarding the possibility of sharing and aggregating resources, with more or less institutional intermediation and control. The idea was to build a scenario where the academic technological infrastructure could be reinforced, with low costs through a larger P2P network, using resources from individuals (e.g. students) or entities (e.g. schools and departments);

Guarantee the maximum protection of the organization from the potential dangers of the use of this technology.

3.1 Potential Problems and Solutions

We wanted explore a disruptive and problematic technology minimizing the risks for the institution. Hence, the protection of the organization was the main goal of the project, and was addressed considering problems at the legal, technological and social dimensions:

Legal problems: Copyright violation and personal image violation or defamation;

Technological problems: uncontrolled usage of the computational resources and infrastructures; the guarantee of service quality; and external attacks to the network;

Social problems: internal resistances from technical and academic staff related to the negative connotation of P2P, and to the overlapping of functionalities with other services; problems with the University public image, due to the problematic and uncertain external context around P2P, at national and international levels.

To deal with legal problems, a clear legal context was defined to regulate the relation between users and institution, in order to the University defends itself in cases of legal litigations. This was achieved with the definition of the general use terms agreement, together with the guarantee of the identification of the authors of violations, using a user institutional authentication process.

The technological problems were approached through control mechanisms together with a closely relation with the Communications Services (SCOM) – unit responsible for the University network infra-structure. SCOM controlled the authentication of the users and the access to the network from the outside of the University, which was available only through a Virtual Private Network (VPN), slowing the access to the network from outside the University.

Regarding the University public image, we followed an overcautious approach, adopting a low profile and the avoidance of conflicts, in the internal and external contexts. This was achieved with a restrictive publicize strategy based essentially in the word of mouth, especially between students, and the availability of the project website restricted to the inside of the University network.

Finally, in order to deal with internal resistances about services overlapping and the lack of some resources, we delivered the growth and sustainability of the system to the participants. This way, we expected that they perceived the utility and potentials of the system and contributed with their own services and resources, adopting a bottom-up process to the growing of the system.

3.2 Bumerang Concepts and Architecture

The users participated in the Bumerang network trough communities. A community could be open to all members of the network our closed to a restricted group of members. A user could simultaneously belong to several communities in the system. Fig. 1 shows the global structure of the Bumerang P2P network, based on JXTA technology, whose members were: peers, super-peers and the Bumerang server.

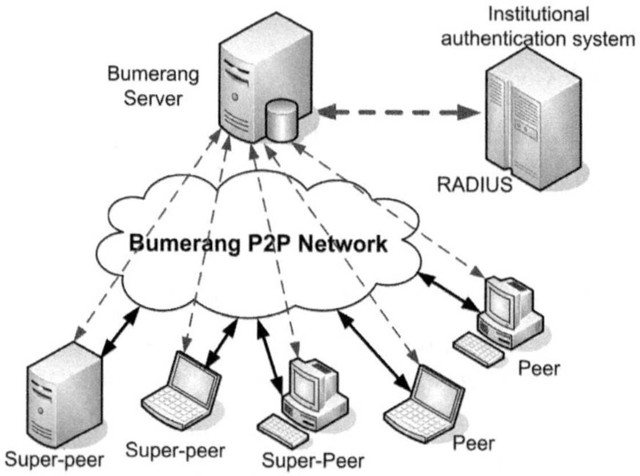

Fig. 1. The Bumerang P2P network: peers, super-peers, and Bumerang server

Bumerang peer was the application used by any peer participating in the network and had to be installed in each machine. It was built with plug-ins, allowing the development of an extensible application for each peer. Because each peer was associated to a user, who participates simultaneously in several communities, a peer could dynamically add plug-ins according to the requirements and resources of the different communities which the user belonged to.

The user disseminated links inside a community, to the local files he wants to share, using advertisements - messages that contained information about the files (metadata). These were automatically propagated to all members of the community that were online, which could download the files as long as the sharer was online. There were no restrictions to the size of the files. The user could also send instant messages to members of the communities and participate in chats. A plug-in to send files directly to another user was available at the end of the first semester of operation of the network.

Bumerang server was the central element in this network. It contained: the databases which audited the system, using the system logs; the tools for the administration and configuration of the system; and the authentication mechanism.

Super-peers were peers with more power and capabilities, used to ensure systems' scalability and performance. A peer could become a super-peer by using a special plug-in. Each community could have its own super-peers which could be fixed or mobile, permanent or temporary.

Community: The concept of community was the way by which the users participated in the Bumerang network and simultaneously was the base of the growth and sustainability of the network.

A community was composed by a set of users that shared a common interest, interacting and sharing knowledge inside it, and gradually defined its own profile, built its own identity and had its own resources. A community could create new services on their own (e.g. plug-ins), having the possibility to provide the new service to other communities or to the entire institution. This way, we expected to have a diversity of communities that translated the structure of the academic community in all dimensions – formal and informal.

Persistence: One of the major problems with P2P networks and applications is the volatility of the system, due to the instability of their peers, which are permanently connecting and disconnecting. This brings the problem of resource availability, which increased in the case of Bumerang because the majority of the peers are portable devices (laptops) connected to the wireless campus network. In Bumerang, despite the predictable system instability, we did not provide a persistence service due to internal resistances from some technical and academic staff.

4 Bumerang Results

In order to analyze the Bumerang results, we use a holistic approach, resorting to data triangulation: quantitative data about the network activity; qualitative data about the complex context of the design and implementation of Bumerang, including news and events occurred in the internal or external organizational context; and qualitative data among users and non-users (10 interviews), in order to understand their behaviors and expectations. The analysis is guided by the model of individual adoption of P2P authenticated academic networks [18], presented in section 4.2.

4.1 Network Activity

We have logs from more than two years of Bumerang activity at the University of Minho, from 23/11/2005 to 9/4/2008. These logs had inconsistencies, caused by the experimental nature of the project. We developed an application which uses consistency and consolidation heuristics, and generates a system representing the Bumerang entities (users, files and communities) and their temporal activity, summarized in Table 1. A deep analysis of this data is outside the scope of this paper.

Table 1. Static and Temporal entities

Static Entities		Temporal Entities	Time interval of consecutive...	
Users	397	Period	server activity	64
Files	3.188		*(between periods the system is off or blocked)*	
Shares	4.865	User Session	user activity in the network	2.821
Downloads	1.639	Community Session	community activity	6.291
Communities	135		*(at least one user was connected to the community)*	
Open	89	User Community Session	user activity in a community	140.296
Closed	46	File Community Session	file availability in a community	4.428

The *files* detected in the network (3.188) were classified according to Type and UseType. *Type* was based on the files extension and *UseType* was based on the use of the file, considering the categories work and entertainment. Work relates to academic work, and Entertainment includes all the other activities – we didn't consider aspects related to illegal file sharing.

The results for *UseType* are: considering number of files, 22% to work and 78% to entertainment; considering size of files, 12% to work and 88% to entertainment.

The *users* of the network were classified according to their gender, position (student, teacher, staff and undefined) and scientific area (Informatics, Engineering, Science, Medicine, Architecture, Management, Law, Social Sciences and Others). The researcher position was included in the staff position.

The results are: Gender (Male 85%, Female 8% and Undefined 7%); Position (Student 93%, Staff 6%, Teacher 1% and Undefined 1%). Regarding the distribution of users according to area and position, we have some relevant facts: 86% of students were from Informatics, Engineering or Science; from the group of non-students (29), 28% (8) were members from the staff of University Documentation Services, which included the Bumerang development team (5). These 8 members were responsible for the major activity of the network.

Temporal activity and Events: The major network activity occurred in the first 4 months, from 23 November 2005 to 28 March 2006. The first significant failure of the system (13 days) occurred during July 2006, which means it was operating 8 months almost uninterrupted, continuing operating uninterrupted until December 2006. After that, its operation had a significant breakdown, with large periods totally disconnected.

There were several events that could affect the individual adoption of the system. The events were: news in the media about P2P litigation and websites closed in Portugal; internal publicizing; and a national award that was given to the project by a Governmental Agency (UMIC) and SUN Microsystems, during November 2006. Apparently, only the last event had some effect on the network activity. The other events occurred after the initial period when the major network activity occurred.

4.2 Individual Adoption Results

The model of Individual Adoption of Academic P2P Systems [18] in Fig. 2, is an extension to UTAUT [10] with factors related to: adoption of collaborative technologies [19.20], Network Externalities, Social Exchange Theory [21] and Perceived Risk [22]. The findings for the constructs in the adoption model are described next.

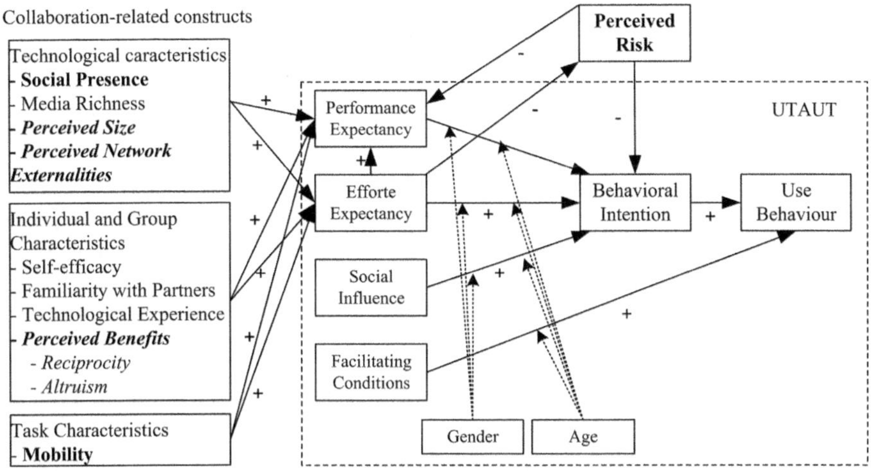

Fig. 2. Individual Adoption of P2P authenticated academic networks

Performance Expectancy: Performance expectancy relates to how well individuals believe the Bumerang helped them to perform their academic activities, and has the strongest influence on the individual intention of using the system [10]. In the interviews the distribution of very large files and the spontaneous distribution of files in a community, were considered useful.

However, the interviewed pointed the useless of the Bumerang network to the exchange of files for academic activities, considering the existing alternatives. Regarding the distribution of very large files, it was pointed that was rarely used. All the interviewed associated P2P mainly with piracy and copyright violations in anonymous P2P file sharing networks.

Based on the classification of files by *useType* and the size of files, we can validate the above results. The use of the network to support work activities gives a more precise measure of the construct Performance Expectancy. The network data indicates that the system was used mainly to exchange entertainment material. The files related to work represent 12% of the total files considering size, and 22% considering the number of files. About the exchange of large files related to work activities, only 10 files with size larger than 50 MB were exchanged. Considering the files exchanged in communities, the results indicate that from a total of 135 communities, none was used mainly to work activities.

Effort Expectancy: Effort expectancy relates to how the users found the Bumerang easy to use. All the interviewed, considered Bumerang easy to use and intuitive [10]. This is confirmed with the very few messages asking help to the support staff. The major problems were related to the authentication process and the use of VPN to access from the outside of the University.

Social Influence: Social Influence relates to the extent to which an individual perceives that it is important others think that he should use the system [10], in other words, how the use of Bumerang will affect their image or please their supervisor or co-workers. Based on logs and interviews, we have no evidences related to these construct. In academic environments, this construct is generally relevant in scenarios where the instructor plays a critical role in motivating students to use of the technology. Considering our data, we only had 6 teachers using the system for a short period of time.

Facilitating Conditions: Facilitating conditions relates to the extent to which an individual perceives the availability of organizational and technical resources to support the use of the system [10]. The majority of interviewed users consider that Bumerang had a good technical support.

The technical staff was very responsiveness to the problems reported by users. However, we must considerer two distinct periods:

- From start to December 2006 the project had permanent technical support, with small periods of inactivity occurring during weekends or holydays;
- After December 2006, the project team ended, and the permanent technical support ceased, causing a stop of 2 months, followed by other large stop periods.

When the award from UMIC and SUN Mycrosystems (see section 4.1.) was announced (during November 2006), appeared a new slight activity, interrupted by Christmas holidays. In the reopen of the academic activities (January) the network remained closed, without technical support, which promoted the final breath of the system.

Perceived Risk: Perceived Risk relates to the individual perception about losses and damages in using the system [22]. This can be measure by the identification of profiles of users and communities, according to the type of files they exchanged. We have no means to verify copyright violation, and there was no report of abuses our defamation, however, the interviewed reported lawsuits as a significant perceived risk.

Technological characteristics: *Social Presence* relates to the individual perception about capacities of the technology in transmitting the presence of the other users in the system [19]. In Bumerang, all users were visible and represented by an icon, with two stages: online or offline.

Perceived size of the system relates to the individual perception about the size of the system, regarding the number of files available and the number of active users. According to the interviews, this construct had a strong influence on the perceived usefulness of the system. "When I connected there wasn't anyone there" was pointed during an interview. The large number of small user sessions without any exchanged file reinforces this result.

Perceived Network Externalities relates to the individual perception about the influence that the size of the system has on its potential benefits [21]. The results are the same as for Perceived size.

Individual and Group characteristics: The constructs related to collaboration technology [20]: experience with a particular technology (Technology Experience); perceived self-efficacy in using the technology (Self-efficacy); and the familiarity with the communication partners (Familiarity with Partners), can be measure by the user's profiles according to area.

We have a total of 90% of users from the areas of Informatics, Engineering and Science, indicating a high level of technology experience and self-efficacy. We considered the staff in this group because they were mainly informatics.

Task characteristics: Regarding task characteristics, mobility is related to the extent the user tasks require that he must be outside the work environment [19], in this case, the University network.

The mobility in Bumerang was limited to the IP address of the University, due to security concerns. The only way to access the network from the outside of the University was by using a VPN, which slowed and difficult the use of Bumerang outside of the University. According to the interviews, this construct had a strong influence on the perceived usefulness of the system – "I couldn't work with it at home, so I couldn't rely on it to my work".

5 Conclusion

In this paper, we have presented Bumerang, a secured and authenticated P2P campus network, and described the complex process of its design and implementation, which includes technological, legal and social constraints, and the results from the network activity.

Against our expectations, the network did not reach critical mass to be self sustained, failing at the individual adoption level. The presented results indicate that the users didn't consider the system useful to their academic activities, associating P2P with sharing files related to entertainment activities. Moreover, a security mechanism like VPN, was considered a strong limitation to mobility, and consequently, to the utility of the system.

The useless of the system in the user's academic activities is according to the theoretical models of Technology Adoption and Diffusion by individuals [9, 10] is the most important factor that influences the intention of the users in using the technology.

Concluding, in order to explore the potential of authenticated P2P networks in academic environments, we must reinforce their perceived utility and deal with the security concerns with new approaches. We must also stay away from using the P2P term, which is poisoned by the anonymous file-sharing networks and copyright concerns, affecting the perceived utility. We must describe P2P in a different way, like file back-up and synchronization or cloud computing, which is been made by a new generation of P2P tools and services, like LiveMesh and Dropbox. The comparison of Bumerang results with the results obtained with these new tools, in academic scenarios, will give more insights in the individual adoption of authenticated P2P networks in academic scenarios.

References

1. Steinmetz, R., Wehrle, K.: Peer-to-peer systems and applications. Springer, Berlin (2005)
2. Anderson, D.P., Cobb, J., Korpela, E., Lebofsky, M., Werthimer, D.: SETI@home - An experiment in public-resource computing. ACM Commun. 45, 56–61 (2002)
3. Singel, R.: Peer-to-Peer Passé, Report Finds. Wired Magazine (2009)

4. Walkerdine, J., Hughes, D., Rayson, P., Simms, J., Gilleade, K., Mariani, J., Sommerville, I.: A framework for P2P application development. Computer Communications 31, 387–401 (2008)
5. Sigurdsson, H.M., Halldorsson, U.R., Hasslinger, G.: Potentials and challenges of peer-to-peer based content distribution. Telematics and Informatics 24, 348–365 (2007)
6. Hughes, J., Lang, K.R., Vragov, R.: An analytical framework for evaluating peer-to-peer business models. Electronic Commerce Research and Applications 7, 105–118 (2008)
7. Nagaraja, K., Rollins, S., Khambatti, M.: Looking beyond the Legacy of Napster and Gnutella. IEEE Distributed Systems Online 7 (2006)
8. ONU: UN Recommendation in favour of P2P in Science. In: Civil Society Science Information Working Group (2004)
9. Davis, F.D.: Perceived Usefulness, Perceived Ease Of Use, And User Acceptance Of Information Technology. Mis Quarterly 13, 319–340 (1989)
10. Venkatesh, V., Morris, M.G., Davis, G.B., Davis, F.D.: User acceptance of information technology: Toward a unified view. Mis Quarterly 27, 425–478 (2003)
11. Ennis, D., Anchan, D., Pegah, M.: The front line battle against P2P. In: Proceedings of the 32nd Annual ACM SIGUCCS Conference on User Services, pp. 101–106. ACM, Baltimore (2004)
12. Putter, J.: Copyright Infringement v. Academic Freedom on the Internet: Dealing with Infringing Use of Peer-to-Peer Technology on Campus Networks. Journal of Law and Policy 14, 419 (2006)
13. Halm, M.: LionShare: Connecting and Extending Peer-to-Peer Networks (Final Report). Pennsylvania State University (2006)
14. White, D.: LionShare in the UK: 'technical and political pros and cons' Report. In: JISC Project Secure personal institutional and inter-institutional repository environment (SPIRE) (2006), http://spire.conted.ox.ac.uk/
15. Zhang, Y.C., Shi, H., Wang, X., Zhang, J.Y.: Collaborative legal information sharing on P2P network. In: Proceedings of 2007 Ifip International Conference on Network and Parallel Computing Workshops, pp. 41–47 (2007)
16. Lin, F., Lin, S., Wang, Y.: Can Peer-to-Peer Networks Facilitate Information Sharing in Collaborative Learning? In: Proceedings of the 41st Annual Hawaii International Conference on System Sciences, p. 5 (2008)
17. Tavares, A.: Partilha de Conhecimento P2P (Report). Universidade do Minho, Braga, Portugal (2004)
18. Tavares, A.: Como usar redes P2P autenticadas em contexto académico? In: 8ª Conferência da Associação Portuguesa de Sistemas de Informação, Setubal (2008)
19. Dennis, A., Venkatesh, V., Venkatraman, R.: Adoption of Collaboration Technologies: Integrating Technology Acceptance and Collaboration Technology Research. Working paper, TR-142-1, Information Systems Department, Indiana University (2004)
20. Venkatesh, V., Dennis, A.R., Brown, S.: Predicting Collaboration Technology Use: Integrating Technology Adoption and Collaboration. Journal of Management Information Systems (forthcoming)
21. Song, J., Walden, E.: How Consumer Perceptions of Network Size and Social Interactions Influence the Intention to Adopt Peer-to-Peer Technologies. International Journal of E-Business Research (IJEBR) 3(4), 49–66 (2007)
22. Xu, H., Wang, H., Teo, H.: Predicting the Usage of P2P Sharing Software: The Role of Trust and Perceived Risk. In: Proceedings of the 38th Annual Hawaii International Conference on System Sciences (HICSS 2005), vol. 7, pp. 201–211. IEEE Press, New York (2005)

ESEIG Mobile: An m-Learning Approach in a Superior School

Ricardo Queirós[1] and Mário Pinto[2]

[1] DI-ESEIG/IPP & KMILT, Porto, Portugal
ricardo.queiros@eu.ipp.pt
[2] DI-ESEIG/IPP & KMILT, Porto, Portugal
mariopinto@eu.ipp.pt

Abstract. In recent years, mobile learning has emerged as an educational approach to decrease the limitation of learning location and adapt the teaching-learning process to all type of students. However, the large number and variety of Web-enabled devices poses challenges for Web content creators who want to automatic get the delivery context and adapt the content to mobile devices. In this paper we study several approaches to adapt the learning content to mobile phones. We present an architecture for deliver uniform m-Learning content to students in a higher School. The system development is organized in two phases: firstly enabling the educational content to mobile devices and then adapting it to all the heterogeneous mobile platforms. With this approach, Web authors will not need to create specialized pages for each kind of device, since the content is automatically transformed to adapt to any mobile device capabilities from WAP to XHTML MP-compliant devices.

Keywords: SOA, interoperability, services, e-learning.

1 Introduction

In our University we use a Learning Management System (LMS) to provide access to the learning resources and activities. In a recent survey (see section 3) we verify that a large number of students use mobile devices. They are already experienced with mobile technology, and are eager to use their devices in e-Learning scenarios. Another argument for the usage of mobile devices results from the students' profile since most of them is already employed while studying part-time. This situation decreases the chance to attend virtual events synchronously. Moreover, we also noticed that the students present different mobile devices with different characteristics that difficult the user experience regarding the access to mobile content. Based on these facts, we argue the need to automatically deliver uniform educational content on particular devices, normally referred as content adaptation.

In this paper we explore the use of open source technologies to provide a better design experience regarding mobile learning (m-Learning) content adaptation and promoting the "write once run anywhere" concept.

J.E. Quintela Varajão et al. (Eds.): CENTERIS 2010, Part II, CCIS 110, pp. 355–363, 2010.

The remainder of this paper is organized as follows: Section 2 defines context delivery and enumerates several initiatives working on this subject. In the following section we present a survey made in our School regarding mobile devices. Then, we introduce the architecture of ESEIG Mobile and the design of its internal components. Finally, we conclude with a summary of the main contributions of this work and a perspective of future research.

2 State of Art

The concept of Content Adaptation is commonly related to mobile devices. Due to the variety of types and technologies supported they require special handling through a series of content transformations, in the deliver process, made by the content provider (server) [1]. Instead of authors having to create specialised pages for each kind of device, content adaptation automatically transforms an author's content to match the device characteristics. Some examples of such features are related with their limited computational power, small screen size, constrained keyboard functionality and media content type supported. The W3C Device Independence Working Group described many of the issues [2] that authors must face in an environment in which there is an increasingly diverse set of devices used to access Web sites.

One approach is to use the common capabilities of the mobile devices and ignore the rest. Finding the Lowest Common Denominator (LCD) of the capabilities of target devices, will allow to you design a site that will work reasonably well in all devices. In order to allow content providers to share a consistent view of a default mobile experience the Best Practice WG has defined the Default Delivery Context (DDC) as a universal LCD [3]. This purpose is commonly adopt, however it limits the devices with better capabilities than LCD and decreases the use of a wider and heterogeneous mobile audience.

There are different adaptation points in the delivery of content to the device: server-side, in-network and client-side. The former needs to negotiate which version of a document should be delivered to a user in order to define the delivery context. One of the most widely used delivery context information is through the HTTP accept headers. These headers can be used to obtain the capabilities of a requesting device, such as, MIME types, character sets, preferred reply encoding and natural languages. In addition to the accept headers, the User-Agent header includes not standard information about the device and the browser being used. This lack of standardisation increases the difficult to interpret and extend this data [4].

To overcome these difficulties emerged in recent years the device profiling concept - a repository of device capabilities, where a user agent (client) can supply the profile to the content provider (server), which can then adapt the content to suit the client device capabilities. The definition of the structure of the profile data is being covered by several standards, such as [5], [6] and [7].

Recently, to overcome the UAProf issues, the W3C MWI (Mobile Web Initiative) have outlined specifications for a Device Description Repository. These specifications include a formal vocabulary of core device properties and an API [8]. The consortium also published a working draft for a new independent language specification named

W3C's DIAL (Device Independent Authoring Language). This specification is a language profile based on XHTML 2 and XForms, and uses the DISelect vocabulary to overcome the authoring for multiple delivery contexts. One known implementation is the XDIME language. Targeting e-Learning, several extensions appears in recent years to expose the LMS (e.g. Moodle) in mobile devices. One such case is the Mobile Moodle (MOMO).

In recent years others specifications arises regarding this subject. It's the case of WNG [9] and WURFL. The Wireless Abstraction Library New Generation (WNG) is a Java tag-library that supports the use of universal mark-up for wireless devices. WNG allows the developer to write a web application once and have optimized content delivered to a variety of devices.

WURFL is a repository of wireless device capabilities describing the capabilities of common wireless devices worldwide and providing an API to programmatically query the capability repository.

3 Mobile Experience Survey

An exploratory study concerning mobile devices usage was made at our Institution. The aim of this study was characterizing the mobile devices usage, namely the diversity of mobile technologies and services used by students and professors, and analyzing future expectations concerning the usage of m-Learning platforms.

3.1 Research Methodology

The survey was made using a questionnaire, sent to the Institution community, which includes almost a thousand and two hundred students, and eighty teachers. The questionnaire was sent by e-mail to all teachers, and the students were invited to answer the questionnaire through the Moodle e-Learning platform. The questionnaire was accomplished with a brief description of the study and their objectives, and it was structured in three main sections:

- Inquired profile: student or teacher;
- Services and technological characteristics: it comprises the identification of the main mobile services used and technological issues concerned with mobile devices;
- Educational mobile contents: it comprises the expectations about the usage of m-Learning platforms, the main services that they would like to use and the m-Learning constraints.

3.2 Results and Discussion

We received one hundred and fifty valid questionnaires answers. From these ones, thirty two were from teachers and one hundred and eighteen were from students. Only two students answered that they haven't mobile devices. Regarding those who have mobile devices, we analyze that the majority of them owns a mobile device with Internet connection as shown in Figure 1.

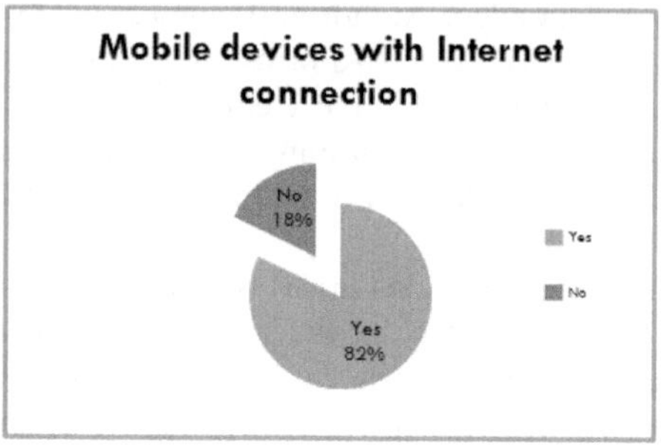

Fig. 1. Internet connectivity

In fact, according to the survey results, eighty two percent of inquired persons have mobile devices with internet connectivity; from these ones, eighty six percent use internet connectivity based on GPRS (General Packed Radio Service) or WAP (Wireless Application protocol) technology, and only twelve percent of mobile devices support WiFi (Wireless LAN) technology.

One question addressed in the survey was about the main mobile services generally used by inquired persons. Figure 2 summarizes the achieved results.

Another issue addressed in the study was the potential role and expectations about educational mobile contents and services. Figure 3 summarizes the most relevant educational mobile services, according the survey answers.

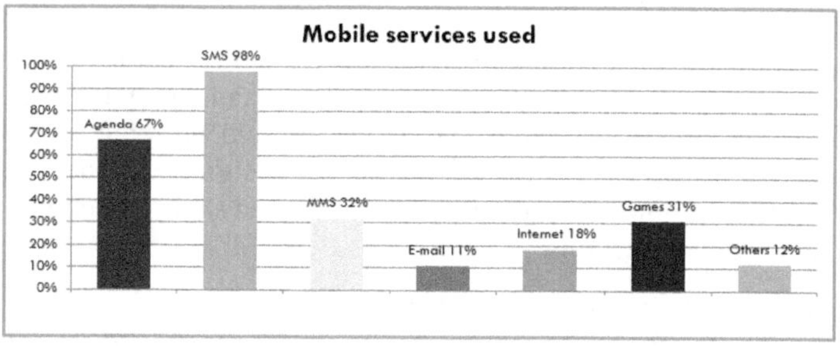

Fig. 2. Mobile services used

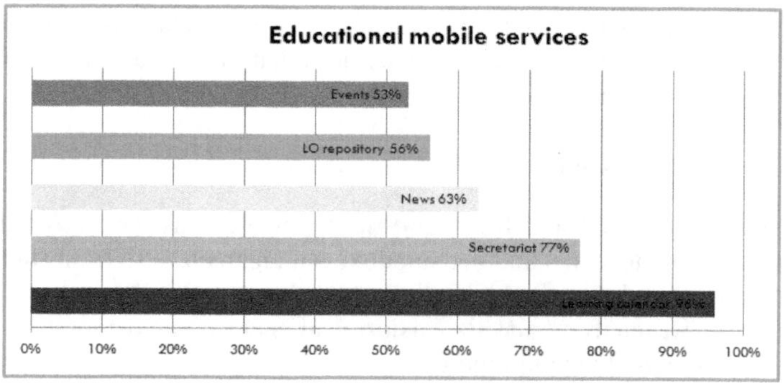

Fig. 3. Educational mobile services desired

On the other hand, Figure 4 presents the main m-Learning constraints identified through the survey. The cost of the Internet provider, the screen dimensions and resolution are some of the students' complaints regarding the use of mobile devices.

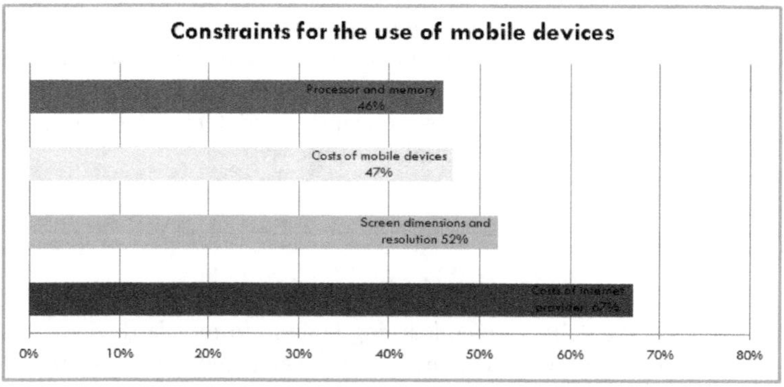

Fig. 4. Main constrains for the use of mobile devices

The survey also includes two questions to analyse the expectations about the value added that m-Learning can bring to the students learning process. These questions are based on a likert scale of five degrees [10], from nothing important (level one) to very important (level five).

One of them if about the potential role of m-Learning in the learning student's process: eighty six percent on inquired persons answered from important to very important, like shows Table 1.

Table 1. Role of m-Learning in the learning students process

Likert scale	Answers (%)
Nothing important	3%
Some significance	13%
Important	39%
Significant	34%
Very important	13%

Another question is about the potential role of m-Learning in the distribution/access to learning contents: eighty five percent answered that m-Learning could perform an important or very important role in this field as shown in Table 2.

Table 2. Role of m-Learning in the distribution/access to learning contents

Likert scale	Answers (%)
Nothing important	4%
Some significance	11%
Important	38%
Significant	42%
Very important	5%

According the survey results it is possible to present some considerations:

- Almost all students and teachers use mobile devices with internet connectivity, however these devices present different characteristics and support different technologies;
- There are a set of educational mobile contents and services, identified by inquired persons, that they would like to use in a m-Learning platform;
- A large percentage of students and teachers recognize the potential contribute of m-Learning in supporting educational contents and services, bringing added value to the learning students' process.

4 Overall Architecture

Based on the previous survey, we decided to design an open system, called ESEIG-Mobile, to uniform the delivery of e-learning content to mobile devices. The ESEIG-Mobile system comprises two components – the **Core** and the **Repository** – that can be integrated in any e-Learning system. Figure 5 shows the inclusion of these two components in a typical e-Learning system. The Core component receives HTTP requests, performs the respective transformations in the requested resource and delivers an adapted content based on the capabilities of the requester device, stored in a special repository. This repository stores information about capabilities and features of many mobile devices. The repository is based on WURFL, an XML configuration file.

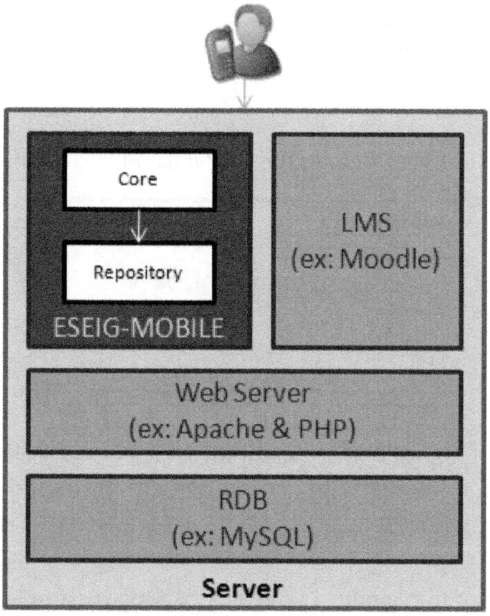

Fig. 5. Overall architecture

4.1 The ESEIG-Mobile architecture

The architecture of the ESEIG-Mobile system is described by the UML component diagram shown in Figure 6.

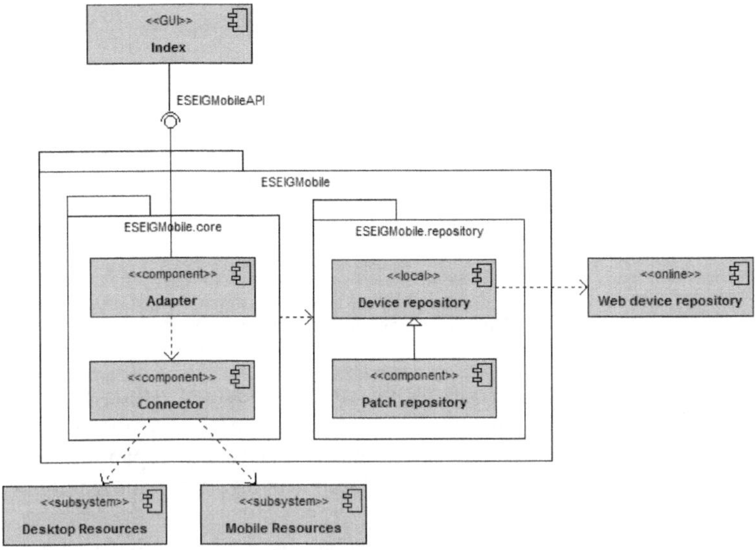

Fig. 6. Component diagram of the ESEIG-Mobile system

The component diagram includes two main packages:

- The **core** package: receives HTTP requests and adapts content based on the capabilities of the device stored in a special database formatted as an XML configuration file;
- The **repository** package: includes a repository with device capabilities and a patch to handle new updates.

The **core** package includes two main components: the Adapter and the Connector component. The former is responsible for adapt the contents requested by the client device. This adaptation will be ensured, in a near future, by the use of WNG [10]. WNG is a JSP tag library that abstracts the mark-up differences in all known wireless devices and allows the page creation similar to HTML, while delivering WML, C-HTML and XHTML Mobile Profile to the client device. Device capabilities are queried dynamically using the WURFL API. The connector component deals with the information querying and merging from the specific resources. The connector component handles the connection with web resources.

The **repository** package contains a file with a large list of device features based on WURFL. The WURFL is an open source database (XML file) of wireless device capabilities. The WURFL repository can synchronize with a public repository of the WURFL DB where the developer community can make new additions to the WURFL DB. The **Patch repository** is a small XML file called *wurfl_patch.xml* that can enrich WURFL data dynamically. This file stores modified/enhanced groups and capability lists for new or existing WURFL devices. When the WURFL is parsed, the patch file is also imported to build a modified version of the device database.

In Figure 7 we present the schema file of the WURFL repository.

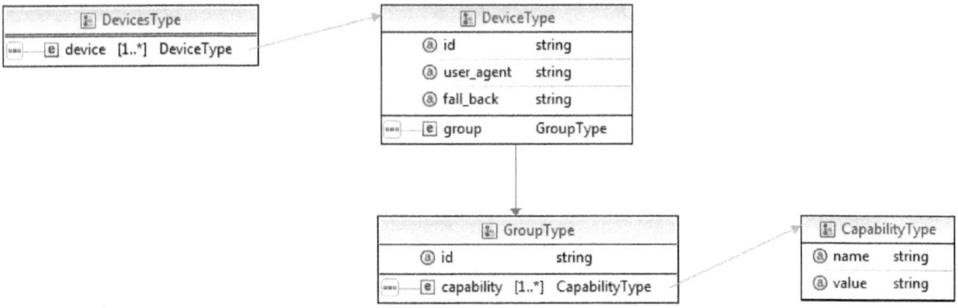

Fig. 7. The WURFL schema

The WURFL is based on the concept of family of devices. All devices are descendent of a generic device, but they may also descend of more specialized families. This mechanism, called *'fall_back'*, lets programmers derive the capabilities of a given phone by looking at the capabilities of its family, unless a certain feature is specifically different for that phone.

For instance, Nokia phones support tables because *fall_back* is defined as generic (WURFL default) as described in the following piece of code:

```
<device user_agent="Nokia" fall_back="generic"
id="nokia_generic">
 <group id="ui">
  <capability
      name="break_list_of_links_with_br_element_recommended"
      value="false" />
 </group>
</device>
```

4.2 Evaluation

In this moment ESEIG-Mobile is in early development as we are only detecting if the HTTP request is made from a mobile device. We use the WURFL API to query the repository based on the *User Agent* header of the request and present a resource suitable to the respective device capabilities. The following snippet of code demonstrates how the detection is performed and how we can query a particular device capability:

```
...
require_once('./wurfl_config.php');
require_once(WURFL_CLASS_FILE);
$userAgent = $_SERVER['HTTP_USER_AGENT'];
$wObj = new wurfl_class();
$wObj->GetDeviceCapabilitiesFromAgent($userAgent);
$max_colors = $wObj->getDeviceCapability('colors');
...
```

The result is the adaptation of a suitable web resource according with the requester device capabilities as shown in Figure 8.

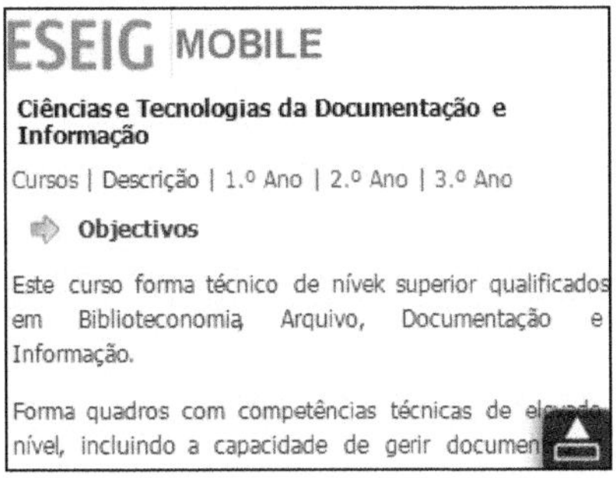

Fig. 8. An ESEIG-Mobile resource

5 Conclusion

In this paper, we presented several approaches for defining delivery context and also a survey targeted to ESEIG students and teachers that base our work. The survey demonstrated the real perspectives and expectations of students and teachers' community, in this field of educational mobile contents.

We presented also the design of an open system for the delivery of suitable e-Learning content to the mobile devices of our students. The mobile devices advent could enable a more useful proximity between students and teachers, facilitating and promoting the learning process.

Our work is in progress, but we expect some challenges in the prototype implementation process regarding, for instance, the transformation of the Web resources in the WNG format. For this task we are considering using XSLT to formally describe the transformations.

References

1. Zhang, L., Kunz, R.: 12th IEEE International Conference on Engineering Complex Computer Systems (2007)
2. Authoring Challenges for Device Independence, `http://www.w3.org/TR/acdi/`
3. Mobile Web Best Practices 1.0 (2008), `http://www.w3.org/TR/mobile-bp/#ddc`
4. Delivery Context Overview for Device Independence, `http://www.w3.org/TR/di-dco`
5. `http://www.w3.org/Mobile/CCPP/`
6. UAProf., `http://www.openmobilealliance.org/`
7. `http://wurfl.sourceforge.net/`
8. `http://www.w3.org/2005/MWI/DDWG/`
9. Passani, L.: Introducing WALL: a Library to Multiserve Applications on the Wireless Web, `http://wurfl.sourceforge.net/java/tutorial.php`
10. Jameson, S.: Likert Scales, how to (ab)use them, vol. 38, pp. 1212–1218. Blackwell Publishing, Malden (2004)

E-Learning as a Shared Service in Shared Services Centers

Agostinho Sousa Pinto

Porto Polytechnic, Porto, Portugal / University of Minho, Guimarães, Portugal
apinto@iscap.ipp.pt

Abstract. An organization is an entity of systemic nature, consisting of one or more people interacting with each other to achieve common goals, being one of its greatest challenges the attempt to follow the evolution of their environment.

Adoption of Technologies and Information Systems enables organizations to improve their information flow and, when used strategically positively differentiates, providing competitive advantages, for the dissemination and updating of organizational knowledge. This dissemination in a global world requires the adoption of distance communication procedures, e-learning.

Shared Services an organizational management model, continue to be implemented in Economic Groups and Public Administration, with the aim to provision of services appropriate to each Internal Customer or Organizational Unit, collaborative and virtual, supported by a single technology platform and enterprise architecture service-oriented. The implementation model of shared services proposed here, three-layer model, adds e-learning as a shared service.

Keywords: Shared Services, E-learning, Management and Organizational Knowledge.

1 Introduction

Organization success depends on their ability to interact with the environment, i.e., its ability to operate globally. If this new reality represents, on one hand, a constraint on their activities and even on their own survival, leading to new challenges and threats may, moreover, provide new business opportunities to avail of.

An organization is an entity capable of producing goods and services better than competition and whose goods and services and the activity itself are in the interests of third parties such as customers, employees, or to affected entities, positively and negatively, by the work on organization. [Sousa, 1990]

An organization can be identified as an open system. The open systems exchange matter, energy and information regularly with the environment and are fundamentally adaptive because, to survive, they need to adjust, continually to the changing conditions of the environment. That adaptability is a continuous process of learning and self-organizing of the open system. System is a set of elements dynamically interrelated, developing an activity or function to achieve one or more objectives or assumptions. Speaking, generally, in systemic nature, is intended to refer to the

J.E. Quintela Varajão et al. (Eds.): CENTERIS 2010, Part II, CCIS 110, pp. 364–373, 2010.

overall operation, total and integrated, in which the whole is greater [or different] than the sum of its parts. [Chiavenato, 1992]

E-learning is education just-in-time integrated with value chains of an organization. It is the individualized and detailed delivery of dynamic learning content in real time, aiding the development of knowledge communities, linking students and professional experts. [Drucker, 2000]

The underlying principle for e-learning is that the tools and knowledge necessary to perform a job are promoted by the workers, wherever they are. The focus of learning revolves around the people. This contrasts with traditional education, which usually brings together a group of people around the learning, i. e., a typical school environment.

E-learning has its origins in computer-based training [Computer-Based Training CBT], which was an attempt to automate education, relief from the instructor and enhance rates of learning appropriate to each learner.

The focus of e-learning extends and improves the CBT picture by an approach of learning that removes time barriers and distance and customizes learning to the user and business needs. [Barker, 2000] The key to success is the ability to reduce cycle time to learn and adapt the learning content to the learner and their environment.

Shared Services Centers have emerged in order to maximize effectiveness and efficiency of organizations. Shared Services concepts are based on three principles: standardization, consolidation and reengineering, in which the transaction processing and other services may be performed centrally or in different locations.

If the adoption of technology e-learning by Shared Services Centers, does not represent much difficulty, the definition of e-learning model and its acceptance by the Client Organizations, including their human resources, has setbacks that justify a planning and change strategy, only possible with a real framework of e-learning in shared services.

This article presents a simple structure, starting with the summary that presents the outline of the work. Then, in Chapter 1 is presented the introduction, that contextualizes the work, presented the motivations for the study. Next is the review of literature, where, in Chapter 2 are presented the studies on shared services and in Chapter 3 are presented the studies on e-learning. Chapter 4 is devoted to the intended contribution of this article. Finally, in Chapter 5 is presented the conclusions which indicate future work, finishing with the bibliography used.

2 Shared Services

Shared services are a collaborative approach aimed at optimizing human resources, capital and other corporate resources, focusing on a new business unit (Shared Services Center) (semi)-autonomous designed to promote efficiency, create value, reduce costs and provide excellent services to the entire Organization. According to Quinn [2000] there are four models of Shared Services, Basic Model, Marketplace, Marketplace Advanced and Enterprise Independent.

The adoption of information technology allows companies to improve with technology, their information flow and, when used strategically, serving as facilitator of organizational processes, positively differentiate organizations by providing them with competitive advantages. [Janssen & Joha, 2008]

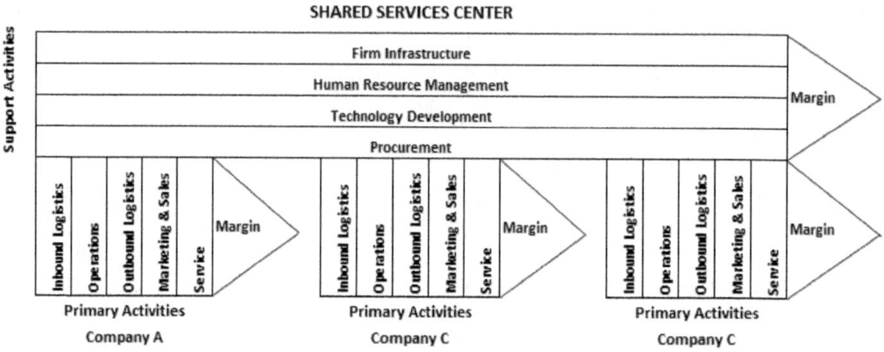

Fig. 1. Shared Services and Porter Model

The role of IT in organizations has changed significantly, evolving from administrative support to a strategic role, supporting and defining business strategies. [Henderson & Venkatraman, 1993]

The definition of strategic alignment differs among authors, depending on the focus of your quest. However, some definitions which are considered as the most significant, put the focus on the alignment between the Strategic Planning of Information Systems and Strategic Planning of the Organization. (Mendoza, 2009)

The alignment between the Strategic Planning of Information Systems and Strategic Planning of the Organization may be conclusive for the development of business competitiveness. Thus, one should seek to identify the factors that influence its implementation. These factors deserve special attention from organizational managers [Teo & Ang, 1999] to increase the effectiveness of that alignment.

The context in which the push factors of strategic alignment between the Strategic Plan for Information Systems and Strategic Business Plan, need to be clear. That is, identify the Critical Success Factors that favor the alignment between the Planning of Information Technology and the Strategic Organizational Planning. [Löbl, Bobsin, & Visentini, 2008]

The development of e-learning as a service in a Shared Services Center, is justified by the convenience to provide simultaneously a set of information, in heterogeneous environments, characterized by cultures, customs and different languages, social organizations and different time zones.

There is an economy of scale when the expansion of production capacity of one company or industry results in an increase in total production costs less than, proportionally, to the product. As a result, the average production costs fall in the long term. For a given cost function, the existence of economies of scale can be checked using the concept of elasticity of cost, which is determined by the ratio between the relative change in average production costs and the relative variation of the quantities produced [Lootty & Szapiro , 2002].

Associated with the concept of economy of scale is associated the concept of economy of scope1 or of diversification. The economies of scope are derived from the share of tangible and intangible resources in the production of multiple business units, resulting in reduction of global joint costs of production, with impacts on reducing unit costs of each product line. The economies of scope and diversification occur, as we have seen, when the production of various products by the same firm is superior to that produced by several companies, each producing a single product.

Globalization and Technology and Information Systems lead to strategic changes a fundamental aspect nowadays [Bradley, Hausman, & Richard, 1993]. In fact, globalization, technology and Information Systems have reinforced each other, since globalization calls for innovation in Information Technologies. Organizations need to coordinate their global operations through the Technology Information Systems, while the actual development in information technology has boosted the organizations to be more global in their business.

The strategy of globalization has been accompanied by a number of important changes in technology and information systems, since they have suffered not only the impacts of strong growth and diversification, but also had to be a support to the whole transformation process.

2.1 Models of Shared Services

The basic difference of shared services when compared with centralization of services is the strategy to focus on internal customer - the business units. [Quinn, Cooke & Kris, 2000]

Shared services are not in any way the centralization, as awry can be mentioned. The concept of centralized brings with it a "corporate" mentality. [Schulman, Lusk, Harmer, Dunleavy, & Schulman, 1999]. Schulman clarifies the difference between the centralized model and shared services, defining shared services as the concentration of organization resources instead of centralization of the organization's resources.

The approaches adopted to focus on internal customer involve reduced costs from economies of scale and attention to quality level required to support services.

Second [Quinn, et al., 2000] there are four models of shared services that have evolved from the basic model, resulting from the consolidation of support activities into one unit:

Basic model-It has as main characteristics the concentration of activities and transactions of support in a single location and the compulsory use of services by business units. The main objective of this model is the use of economies of scale to reduce costs and standardization.

Marketplace model - With the evolution of the basic model comes the marketplace model. The use of services by business units is not obligatory. Skilled professionals and consultants are recruited. The range of services offered is expanded in order to satisfy all the needs of business units.

Advanced marketplace model - In the evolution of the models, consolidates the marketplace advanced. With it, opens the possibility of purchasing services in both the CSP and by the business units. In this environment, only the services that prove to be competitive with the market still operating internally. The expertise gained in developing the model provides the delivery of some services with high quality and competitive costs.

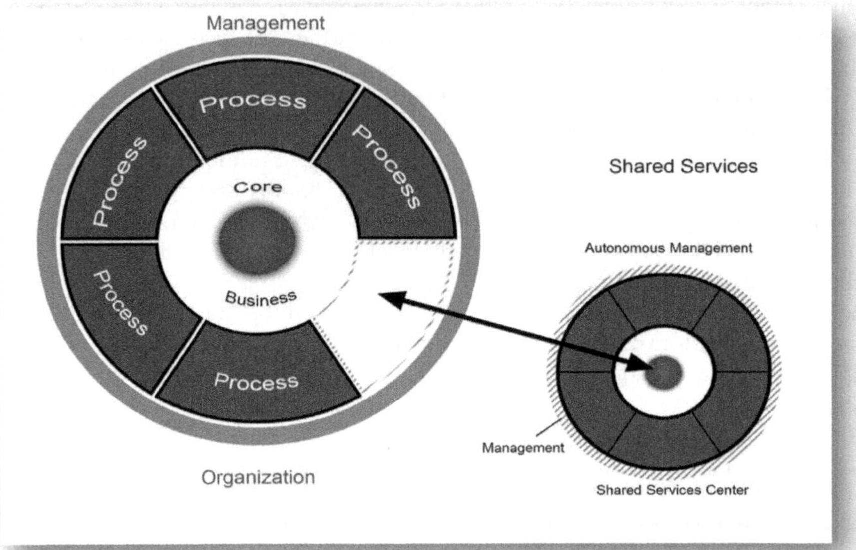

Fig. 2. Model of Shared Services

Independent Company Model - The last step in the evolution of shared services is its structure as an independent business using the skills acquired in the evolution of the organization from a basic model. Services are provided to multiple clients with the aim of the new company to generate revenue and profits for its maintenance in the market.

2.2 Enterprise Architecture

Organizations are unique and complex realities. In its characterization is usual to consider such diverse topics as the chain of custody and reporting, business processes, information required for business management, systems and information technology, among others. The representation of all those aspects in an integrated and consistent way is far more demanding than their individual representation.

The ability to change of the organization is heavily dependent on how the various aspects of the organizations cited above, are aligned and are known by the organization. In this sense, shared and understood representations by all are essential, because they allow detecting differences between the reality that it is and what should be. The enterprise architecture is reflected in the representation of organizations that, through continued practice, allows aligning its various constituent aspects in an integrated environment. Taking the convergence all aspects as its central goal, eliminating the so-called misalignments.

The concept of Enterprise Architecture has been developed and enriched over the past decades, being in genesis a work tool called as "Zachman Framework for Enterprise Architecture". The "Framework" is a semantic structure which is a form of descriptive representation of any object that crosses two aspects: the key questions - "what," "how, where," "who," when" and "why "- with the prospects of those who make these issues: the owner, the designer, the builder [Zachman, 2004].

Rarely this framework displays a consistent architecture and is part of an overall strategy for management. However, any change in operation or structure of the organization is conditioned by a reengineering effort in IT's. The restructuring of the IT architecture is the main barrier for the transformation of old enterprises and can result in frustration and expense due to IT projects that failed's becoming a great source of organizational inertia. [Nolan & Croson, 1995]

3 E-Learning

The implementation of e-learning technology or b-learning [blended learning], a combination of methods of teaching / learning classroom and distance, found a turbulent journey of adoption, experiencing moments of euphoria but also dismay.

Learning based in the Emitter is called first Wave [teacher, trainer, teaching materials of distance learning and self-study on and off line, etc..], the learning that takes place via the b-learning, defined as second vague and, finally, the one that involves all systems of teaching and learning [Distributed Technologies, Interactive Technologies and Collaborative Technologies], defined as the third wave. [Fernandes, 2005]

The application of new paradigms of distance training or combined training with a classroom component and another component at a distance using information technology and communications have not evolved according to expected. Observing the evolution of Education and Vocational Training schemes or distance leads to the conclusion that is unparalleled progress of other technical and scientific with the Teaching and Education. [Fernandes, 2005]

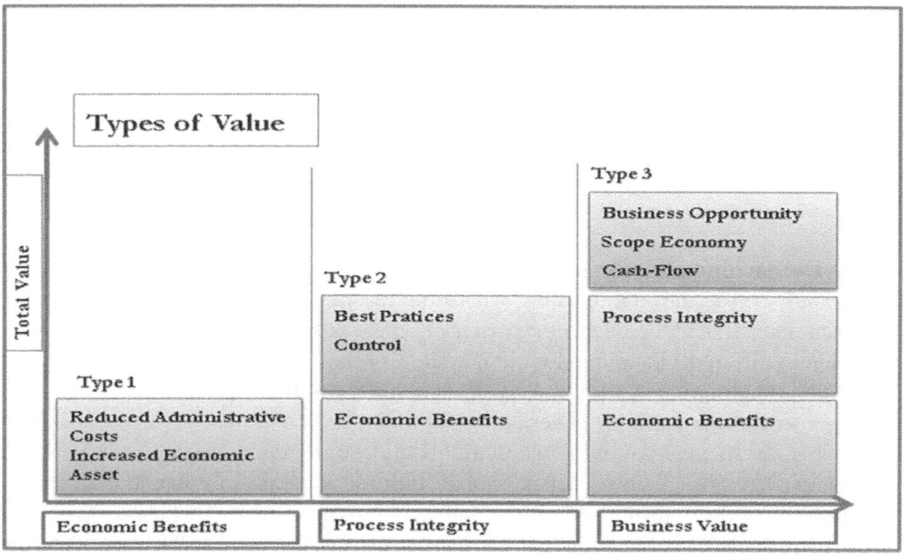

Fig. 3. Technologies for e-learning

The evolution of societies is dependent on lifelong learning, recognizing that everyone, regardless of age or social status, remain able to dominate and profit from the development of personal and professional level.

Is widespread belief that the success of this new paradigm of lifelong learning is dependent on new forms of technology to support the teaching / learning process.

3.1 Basics of e-Learning

3.1.1 Ontologies for e-Learning

Ontology is part of metaphysics that studies being in itself, its properties and methods by which it manifests. [Dictionary Online Porto Editora] In philosophy, ontology is a theory about the nature of existence, about what kinds of things exist; ontology as a discipline studies such theories. Researchers of artificial intelligence and Web used ontology as the description of a formal concept and shared, in a particular field of interest. Ontologies are specifications of the concept and corresponding vocabulary used to describe a domain [Gruber, 1993].

By defining shared theories, of common domain, ontologies help people and machines to communicate concisely, supporting the exchange of semantics and not just syntax. It is therefore important that any semantics for the Web is based on an ontology explicitly specified. Thus, consumers and producers can reach a shared understanding by exchanging ontologies that provide the vocabulary needed for discussion.

3.1.2 Semantic Web and e-Learning

The fundamental property of the architecture of the Semantic Web enabled by a set of appropriate agents, provides a powerful approach to meet the e-learning demands: efficient, just-in-time and learning task relevant. Learning material is semantically annotated, which, for a new need can be easily combined in a new way of learning. [Aroyo & Dichev, 2004]

In fact, the Semantic Web could be exploited as a very suitable platform for implementing a system of e-learning, because it provides all means of e-learning: ontology development, ontology-based annotation of learning materials, their composition in training courses and delivery of assets of learning materials through portals of e-learning. [Anderson & Whitelock, 2004]

3.1.3 E-Learning and Metadata

Compared with traditional teaching where the teacher plays the role of intermediary between the student and learning material, the learning scenario in e-learning is completely different: instructors no longer control the supply of material and students are able to combine learning material according to their preferences. Thus, the management of the learning material should be on their own. However, regardless of the time spent to create training material, this may be useless unless it can be searched and indexed easily. What becomes critical with the increase of content and types of learning. A solution to monetize the content is produced using metadata. At a more basic level, metadata can be understood as a set of tags that can be applied to any resource, regardless of who created them, what tools they used or where they are stored. Tags are, in essence, data that describes data. Tagging metadata enables organizations to describe, index and search their resources being essential to reuse them.

3.2 Technologies of Support to e-Learning

Technologies can be Distributed, Interactive and Collaborative. Distributed Technologies represent the formal and traditional pedagogy. Grounded in secular practices, such as the Distance Learning building, the e-learning from the 1st wave. About Interactive Technologies must be said that in a scientific perspective, they are also in the behavioral area, because we learn by repetition, imitation and trial/error. That is, through simulations and training it is possible to develop the acquisition of skills and capabilities. There are in these technologies a qualitative leap, which comes to move on transmission of information, pure and simple, the performance focusing on action by the student / trainee, hoping some of this initiative. The enterprise technologies, used since the e-learning of the 2nd wave, reach the fullness with the 3rd wave, by boosting the student / trainee to assimilate new concepts and accommodation, within established parameters, in perfect interaction with the group it belongs to. Here, the collaborative or cooperative is not only an asset, but also the engine of the process itself. [Fernandes, 2005]

4 Conclusion

Organizations that want to achieve and sustain competitive advantage need to improve the knowledge and skills of their workers. E-learning and knowledge management are separate disciplines but with the same objective of achieving the purpose of increasing organizational knowledge. [Mallinson & Vos, 2008]

If the goal is the adoption of e-learning by the Shared Services Centers, technology does not present any difficulty, the definition of the type of e-learning and its acceptance by the client organizations, including human resources, has setbacks that justify a planning and change in strategy, only possible with a real framework of e-learning in shared services.

The first Shared Services Centers installed, were inspired by the centralized model, which led to the implementation of the basic model, differing on self-governance, value for money and the vision of customer service, using, however, a "pricing" distribution costs incurred. In the difficulty of demonstrating the nature of costs, it add the need to invest and increase productivity on the part of managers of the centers, and thus counter the dissatisfaction of some customers forced the emergence of more open models, using a market logic. The diversity of business, the different states of technology use and the different sensitivities of managers, determine the level of service to contract, causing mismatches between what is needed and what Shared Services Center has to offer.

In this context where shared services have proven to be a good solution for many organizations and e-learning has established itself as an inescapable reality in organizations, we intend to define the framework for e-learning in shared services, taking into account all its specificity. It is necessary to define, among other things, in what context it makes sense to use e-learning, identify the positive and negative aspects of shared services that are inherited by e-learning, which recommended the technological solution and what type of e-learning to be taken in each context, what strategy to follow to promote the services, how to measure the impact of e-learning in the acceptance of shared services, until the cost of e-learning is behavioral.

The introduction of a new service with the features of e-learning for a Shared Services Centers, means knowing which is the impact of that adoption in the organizational architecture and what is the influence of the new service on existing services.

Organizations, as complex systems, interdependent, want to reach a stable state, believing it to be possible by adapting to changes in the external environment. Yet what modern science has shown, such as the theory of chaos, this balance is the exception rather than the rule. In this context the Shared Services Centers, as providers of services, need to maintain sufficient stability to ensure the level of service, but the ability to innovate and respond to different levels of service requested. E-learning is a process based on technology that allows today's update of organizational knowledge. The Shared Services Centers, defining enterprise architecture, adopting ontologies that define e-learning and rules for the Semantic Web, are able to provide a quality service to all its partners seeking for the constant stability, supported by the theories of science organization. The adoption of e-learning services and the Shared Services Centers requires a strategy and framework that becomes a value for the entire organization.

References

1. Anderson, T., Whitelock, D.: The educational semantic web: Visioning and practicing the future of education. Journal of Interactive Media in Education 1, 1–15 (2004)
2. Aroyo, L., Dicheva, D.: The new challenges for e-learning: The educational semantic web. Educational Technology & Society 7(4), 59–69 (2004)
3. Barker, P.: Designing Teaching Webs: Advantages, Problems and Pitfalls. Educational Multimedia, Hypermedia & Telecommunication, pp. 54–59 (2000)
4. Bradley, S., Hausmann, J., Richard, L.: Nolan: Globalization. Technology and Competition. In: The Fusion of Computer and Telecommunications in the 1990s, Harvard Business School Press, Boston (1993)
5. Chiavenato, I.: Gerenciando pessoas: o passo para a administração participativa. Makron Books, São Paulo (1992)
6. Drucker, P.: Além da revolução da informação. HSM Management 18, 48–55 (2000)
7. Fernandes, A.A.: Um e-Learning para o Séc. XXI – "Como implementar o on-line numa Organização". Associação para a Promoção e Desenvolvimento da Sociedade da Informação (2005)
8. Gruber, T.: A translation approach to portable ontology specifications. Knowledge acquisition 5, 199 (1993)
9. Henderson, J., Venkatraman, N.: Strategic alignment: Leveraging information technology for transforming organizations. IBM Systems Journal 32(1), 4–16 (1993)
10. Janssen, M., Joha, A.: Emerging shared service organizations and the service-oriented enterprise. International Journal 1(1), 35–49 (2008)

11. Löbler, M., Bobsin, D., Visentini, M.: Alinhamento entre o plano de negócio eo plano de tecnologia de informação das empresas: análise comparativa através dos níveis de maturidade e fatores críticos de sucesso. Journal of Information Systems and Technology Management 5(1), 37–60 (2008)
12. Lootty, M., Szapiro, M.: Economias de escala e escopo. Economia industrial: fundamentos teóricos e práticas no Brasil. Rio de Janeiro: Campus (2002)
13. Mallinson, B., Vos, L.: A Theoretical Investigation of the Synergy Between Enterprise E-Learning and Knowledge Management. Information Systems Development: Challenges in Practice, Theory, and Education 1, 483 (2008)
14. Mendoza, G.: Alignment of IT projects with business strategy: An analysis of the interrelationships between the factors affecting IS alignment at strategic, tactical and operational levels (2009)
15. Nolan, R., Croson, D.: Creative destruction: A six-stage process for transforming the organization. Harvard Business School Pr., Boston (1995)
16. Quinn, B., Cooke, R., Kris, A.: Shared services: mining for corporate gold. Financial Times Prentice Hall, Englewood Cliffs (2000)
17. Schulman, D., Lusk, J., Harmer, M., Dunleavy, J., Schulman, D.: Shared services: adding value to the business units. John Wiley & Sons, Chichester (1999)
18. Sousa, A.: Introdução à Gestão. Uma abordagem sistémica. Editorial verbo (1990)
19. Teo, T., Ang, J.: Critical success factors in the alignment of IS plans with business plans. International Journal of Information Management 19(2), 173–185 (1999)
20. Zachman, J.: Enterprise architecture and legacy systems, getting beyond the "legacy" (2004)

Mediation and Virtual Learning Environments

Irene Tomé

Faculdade de Ciências Sociais e Humanas, Universidade Nova de Lisboa
Av. de Berna, 26-C
1069-061 Lisboa, Portugal
irenetome@gmail.com

Abstract. In recent years research which has been undertaken on the teacher-student pedagogic relationship has been unanimous in stating that a learning model focused on the social interaction of the learning individuals is much more effective in their development. We can therefore say that the interactive model is of paramount importance in the teaching-learning process, taking as its central focus the mediation conducted by the teacher, by a more experienced colleague, by an adult or through educational multimedia programmes. Thus, the role of the mediator can and should be considered as an agent of change, to the extent that through this mediation the learner can bring meaning to the learning of strategies and their usefulness. How should the teacher/mediator manage this function in virtual learning environments? How can the interactions be defined? Or, furthermore, which mediation strategies can and should be implemented? This reflection concerns the tension between teacher, student, knowledge and the harmony generated by the work of pedagogic mediation

Keywords: Virtual learning environments, teaching-learning strategies, online pedagogic skills, interaction, mediation.

1 Introduction

I think that never were the issues pertaining to the teaching-learning process, the role of teachers and students, along with curriculum development and pedagogical models discussed as much as they were in the last third of the twentieth century.

Interactive Communication Systems[1] and the products which emerged from them targeted at education and vocational training were not only concerned with the organisation and structuring of knowledge, but also with motivating students within a given context. It is really important to create good environments and learning contexts that facilitate positive emotional experiences in order to maintain ongoing motivation for learning. The gradual improvement of computers and their respective programs, as well as the emergence of the Internet that has made electronic distance learning possible, have contributed to this fact. Whether in relation to the face-to-face model, or in

[1] It is considered that Interactive Communication Systems bring together two sets of systems: The technological system composed of computers, software and tele-teaching and the teaching and pedagogic system composed of content, contexts and communities of learners.

J.E. Quintela Varajão et al. (Eds.): CENTERIS 2010, Part II, CCIS 110, pp. 374–380, 2010.

relation to the traditional distance learning model, it was not that the electronic teaching-learning model brought with it an improvement in the acquisition of knowledge, but rather in that the difference lies in the new forms of interactive communication, teaching and learning made possible by the Internet, which the traditional model of distance learning did not offer.

Sometimes questions arise about whether a certain model of education is or is not better than other models. A number of studies have been carried out, the result of observations and academic research, but none of them firmly argues for the primacy of one model over others. Each model has specific objectives and audiences, the models being used in accordance with individual and organisational needs and contexts, with regard to space and time. It should be noted that teaching models which are completely electronic in nature should be excluded from models aimed at childhood and adolescence. In both cases it is considered essential to promote socialization, face-to-face interaction - essential factors for growth, development, facilitation of learning - and not place the child or adolescent alone in front of the computer, cut off from contact with others. Neither the development of the child nor the adolescent is sufficient to enable them to plan and manage a process of autonomous learning, in an open and flexible structure, with regard to time, space and activities. The willingness to learn, individual construction along with social interaction, situations involving sharing, construction, deconstruction and new constructions requires a face-to-face pedagogic model.

However, the teacher can and should make use of multimedia educational programs, the Internet and learning platforms, to provide resources, guidance for reading, or research into the nature of educational support for these age groups. Virtual learning environments promote diverse forms of teaching and learning, and provide multiple opportunities for interaction which are an effective support for the use of content (text, images, sound), as long as they are imbued with a conceptual philosophy of e-learning. Laurillard (1993) and Lim (2001) have set out a conversational model for virtual learning environments based on four processes: to enable discussion, interaction, reflection and adaptation, implemented through being based on theories of teaching and learning (I. Tomé and B. Detry, 2001: 646-647). In this way it is vital to develop virtual learning spaces, in so far as the educational domain is one of the important sectors for the development of multimedia systems, since these enable, as M. Farzad and S. Paivandi (2000: 53), have indicated, "the development of an educational society, where locations, means, times and training are multiplied".

Virtual communities or virtual learning environments have also shown themselves to be as an alternative curriculum model to face-to-face teaching-training models for the adult population seeking to acquire or update knowledge and skills. This model is intended to bridge distances and the lack of local schools or training centres, and also provide educational support for students who need this.

2 Teaching and Learning On-Line

The idea of technology still causes some unrest in the area of teaching and learning. This is due in part to the difficulties imposed on the educational system, the lack of dialogue between the parties, and the prejudices that still exist, but which are gradually being dismantled. In the twenty-first century it is no longer acceptable to have a mechanistic view of education, with passive teachers, reactive interaction, the function of which being the simple transmission of knowledge, in fulfilment of a strictly prescriptive methodology. Nowadays more and more students come to schools with different profiles, levels of knowledge and difficulties and school is not the only source of knowledge. We therefore need to establish another form of dialogue between the teacher, students and knowledge.

Given these problems it is advisable to reflect on the teaching-learning process at multiple levels, from student characteristics, their levels of knowledge, their skills, the role of the teacher and institutional initiatives, in order to implement various learning strategies and face-to-face and online pedagogic models. I believe learning to be the central concept, the core of the whole educational system, on which must be implemented new attitudes to generate new skills, whether the chosen model be face-to-face, electronic or a mixed one.

However, the form of access to information, knowledge, coupled with the fact that computers can enable an interactive environment with the user, have provided new learning environments and the provision of new educational services. In this way students and teachers can benefit from innovative learning environments by implementing various methods and using different learning strategies. The teaching and learning technologies delivered by the Internet enable the construction of interactive pedagogic platforms, which through collaborative and interactive participation strategies, form flexible educational spaces and enable online pedagogic support, bridging the isolation of the student, through the development of synchronous or asynchronous communication. The integration of video, sound, images and texts, knowledge and expertise shared on a network throughout the world enables a relational dynamic that students are developing into a new spatial and temporal reality.

But how do teachers know what to do when faced with change and the refashioning of curricula and practices? The teaching and learning models made possible through virtual learning environments are much more than that which the technologies enable, as they represent a complete change in the pedagogical model of teaching and learning. In the words of Garrison (2008: 5) "the key is" among other assumptions (...) "in fundamentally rethinking the curriculum in order to involve the student, in restructuring and replacing the form of contact of the face-to-face classroom".

To answer the question raised above, there is no need to give recipes, but at the same time reflect on teaching and curriculum strategies to be used in order to promote learning. I do think that there good or bad strategies or learning methods. There are rather methods and strategies that are useful for some students and not for so others, since everything depends on their cognitive styles, their motivation, and their difficulties. What matters is that educational actions are appropriate, and within the same subject there are diverse approaches to teaching so that students, in a dynamic process of learning, can unblock their difficulties, obtain information and relate it to the construction of knowledge. This dynamic process of learning is understood as the various activities undertaken by the student through observation, experience, interactions with the teacher and peer sharing and cooperation.

The transformation that one wishes to be seen implemented in the teaching and learning system through the use of technologies, or rather of interactive communication systems, inevitably involves a relational approach, where teachers and students act both actively and interactively, engaging in personal and group learning strategies, managing and enabling motivation and helping students to engage in reflection. Otherwise technology would become an extremely poor educational resource, since it would just be a tool to be learned and to offer access to content in an agreeable manner.

So what means be used? What means should teachers make use of to implement the teaching and learning strategies that they wish to implement? P. Vianis (2009:210) has stated that "it serves no purpose" 'giving' working strategies and methods to students, of the 'ready to go' type, if they are still a long way from reflecting on their learning process, in so far as they may not rethink, nor assimilate them". What is thus important is that the "key" is the understanding that the students have concerning the efficacy of the strategies.

However, teaching and learning online is not easy, as it requires skills and profiles along with motivation and specific strategies. The needs and motivation to learn are the conditions that can overcome the obstacles and difficulties inherent in this model of education.

If needs and motivation are considered the driving forces behind the act of learning, we cannot forget the importance of leverage which can maintain and nurture the desire to learn. Thus, it is much more important that we learn to define how to implement a learning strategy, instead of considering the learning strategies to use. With some minor variations in terminology, but with similar guidelines, all those researching the teacher-student pedagogic relationship are unanimous in stating that the model which focuses on the social inclusion of the individual who is learning will be much more effective when compared to others that could be used. We can therefore state that when the online teaching and learning model uses structured environments, based on the social constructivist theory of Vygotsky, to enable interaction between teacher and student, collaborative learning between students, it promotes reflection and an experience that other types of distance learning cannot. This interactivity, this relationship of help, underlying the process of the development of reflective competence, requires a mediating role on the part of the teacher.

We thus have here one of the key roles of teachers, in that they must know their students and try out various strategies in various contexts, so that they can see the effectiveness of each strategy, but above all so that they can understand the reason for their efficacy, given that learners do not know other strategies, except those which they use, and so how can they evaluate their relevance and efficacy relative to those which they do not make use of? Without learning mediated by the teacher or by a more senior colleague, the learner has many more difficulties in obtaining positive results. But this mediation can be also performed by stimulating learning environments, or through multimedia educational programs, in which the mediator, despite not being present, has contributed with his/herknowledge in the conceptualization and development of the means which seek to increase the capacity of the learner to make use of learning situations.

The work of mediation is a difficult line between teacher, student and knowledge. Houssaye (1993) states that it is a linked triangle, where the teacher has either a somewhat direct role, or a lesser role according to the extent of the students' needs or difficulties. This involves maintaining a very delicate balance, of managing when to know how to stay at a distance or to intervene. We may consider that the art of teaching is

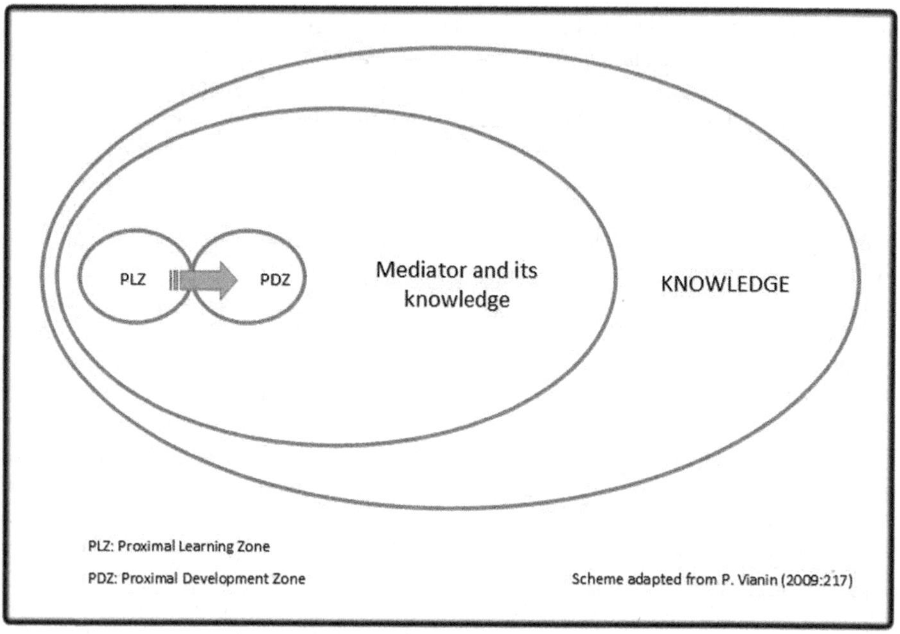

Fig. 1. Proximal Learning Zone and Proximal Development Zone

based on the combination of the existing tension between these three points: teacher, student, knowledge and the harmony established in the linking of these points.

As illustrated in Figure 1, the mediator (teacher, more experienced colleague, an adult – in the case of children - is an agent of change, in that through him/her the learner can give meaning to learning strategies and their usefulness. Constructivism centres students in the teaching-learning process, making them responsible for learning, and it is their knowledge, their cognitive development (PLZ). In this area, they build their knowledge through cognitive activities that they explore; this is the Piagetian process of assimilation-accommodation. But this is not enough as they need a mediator to help them go further, which will help to broaden horizons, to teach them to learn learning strategies (PDZ)[2]. It is this Vygotskyan socio-constructivist interaction which allows the learner to develop cognitive methods and modalities, which are determinant factors in their development. Through mediation with others, who help them make better use of knowledge, they will give utmost importance to issues related to the problems posed by the need to learn to learn - a privileged field of metacognition. For teachers, they must focus on an attitude of continuous monitoring, encouraging, suggesting, clarifying questions, so that learners will develop and acquire the notions of self-esteem, self-regulation and autonomy.

---

[2] Mediation is also very often called *scaffolding*. The concept can be understood as a teaching and learning strategy mediated by the teacher. Students will place scaffolds on their knowledge "building", gradually constructing and securing their knowledge. This methodology or strategy can and should be used by the teacher as a facilitating agent, as a bridge joining what students already know and what is needed to attain that which students still do not.

2 Final Considerations

The pedagogical potential contained in virtual learning environments and the role it is desirable that these new means take on in the actual process of change, provide dynamic and flexible teaching situations. Their use as devices mediating knowledge and as support to students is becoming widespread at all levels of education, thereby breaking with the unity of time, place and action. These platforms are the support that best supports the social constructivist theory of learning.

Of course, this change is not seen at the level of concepts and principles in educational sciences, such as knowledge, collaborative learning, self-regulated learning, motivation, cognitive development. Thus, this change is not changing the theoretical foundations of teaching and learning, but at the level of pedagogic practices. Many studies have shown that the absence of interaction, teaching and pedagogical strategies, of emotional and cognitive relationships, are reasons for lack of success in teaching models based on virtual learning environments. Palloff and Pratt (1999) consider the interactions generated between students and between teacher and students as the as key to the success of students, . For Zimmerman (2002) this will provide a boost in the motivation that students feel to learn, because the higher this behavioural state, the more easily they engage in activities designed to facilitate learning.

Thus, we can consider that the terms "interaction", "motivation" and "mediation" are keywords, among others, when we situate learning in virtual environments.

What changes in teaching and learning online is the way of looking at things, as Maragliano (2004) has stated. It changes the teacher-student relationship. It is a process that involves its own development concerning things taught; it changes the relationship with the learning resources, no longer separated from each other, but connected, or rather connectable within a network perspective; it changes the centre of the action, which is no longer just teaching and its organisation, to also and mainly be that of learning and its individual and group dynamics. Teachers and students used to the face-to-face model need to become familiar with virtual and network learning environments not because of external requirements, but because of personal requirements. The computer must first become personal, and should be a tool to use to cultivate the curiosity of each one, feeding their propensity to enter into relationships with others, playing, in a certain "living" sense, and then it can become, as happens naturally, a teaching and pedagogic resource for each one, where the attention should be centred on "how to do" and not so much on "how can we use".

In light of the argument that has developed throughout this reflection, the central issue, directly linked to educational and pedagogical practices, relates to the "How?" The answer to this question brings us to the "way of doing", i.e. how to teach and learn through a virtual learning environment. How to effectively implement pedagogical practices?, Which motivating strategies to develop?, Which communication mode to use?, Which features to choose?, How to innovate and produce content? How to establish communication and implement support methods? All this implies a choice of pedagogical procedures and competence in reconciling theories, techniques and practices. It is then for teaching, pedagogy and learning theories and not computer science, to choose which technological resources, which means of interaction and mediation to enable and serve teaching methods and strategies in order to significantly improve learning, through the mediation of teachers who will thus provide a differentiated pedagogic experience.

References

1. Cachapuz, A.: A Educação e a Formação na Sociedade da Informação. In: Sociedade da Informação na Escola, pp. 51–54. CNE, Lisboa (1998)
2. Cañas, A.: Algunas Ideas sobre la Educación y las Herramientas Computacionales Necesarias para Apoyar su Implementación. Institute for Human and Machine Cognition, University West Florida, Pensacola (1998)
3. Charlier, B., Peraya, D.: Transformation des regards sur la recherche en technologie de l'éducation. Bruxelles: Éditions De Boeck (2007)
4. Daniels, H.: Charting the Agenda: Educational Activity after Vygotsky. Routledge, Oxford (1994)
5. Depover, C., et al.: Enseigner avec les technologies. Presses de l'Université du Québec, Québec (2008)
6. Dias, P.: Desenvolvimento de objectos de aprendizagem para plataformas colaborativas. In: Barrientos, X., et al. (eds.) Actas do VII Congreso Iberoamericano de Informática Educativa, pp. 3–12. Universidad de Monterrey, Monterrey (2004)
7. Farzad, M., Paivandi, S.: Reconnaissance et validation des acquis. Anthropos, Paris (2000)
8. Garrison, D., Vaughan, N.: Blended Learning in Higher Education. Framework, Principles and Guidelines. Jossey Bass, San Francisco (2008)
9. Garrison, R., Anderson, T.: e-Learning in the 21st. Century. Routledge Falmer, London (2003)
10. Hirschsprung, N.: Apprendre et enseigner avec le multimédia. Hachette, Paris (2005), http://edutice.archives-ouvertes.fr/
11. Houssaye, J.: La pédagogie: une encyclopédie pour aujourd'hui. ESF, Paris (1993)
12. Laurillard, D.: Rethinking University Teaching: a Framework for the Effective Use of Educational Technology. Routledge, London (1993)
13. Lebrun, M.: eLearning pour enseigner et apprendre: llier pédagogie et technologie. Bruylant-Academia, Louvain-la-Neuve (2005)
14. Lim, C.: The dialogic dimensions of using a hypermedia learning package. Computers & Education 36, 133–150 (2001)
15. Maragliano, R.: Delega-se na máquina um problema que é afinal essencialmente didáctico. At the elearningeuropa.info website. Consulted, Amy 2006 (2004), http://www.elearningeuropa.info/directory/index.php?lng=pt&page=doc&doc_id=5148&doclng=8
16. Palloff, R., Pratt, K.: Building learning communities in cyberspace. Jossey-Bass Publishers, San Francisco (1999)
17. Palloff, R., Pratt, K.: O aluno virtual. S. Paulo, BR: ARTMED Editora (2004)
18. Rosenberg, M.: E-learning: Strategies for Delivering Knowledge in the Digital Age. McGraw-Hill, New York (2001)
19. Stephenson, J.: Teaching and Learning Online: New Pedagogies for New Technologies. Stylus Publishing, Sterling (2005)
20. Tomé, I., Detry, B.: As redes de aprendizagem em suporte multimédia. In: Actas da II Conferência Internacional de Tecnologias de Informação e Comunicação na Educação, 9-11/Maio. Braga (2001)
21. Vianin, P.: La motivation scolaire. Comment susciter le désir d'apprendre? Éditions de Boeck, Bruxelles (2007)
22. Vianin, P.: L'aide stratégique aux élèves en difficulté scolaire. Éditions De Boeck, Bruxelles (2009)
23. Wolfs, J-L.: Méthodes de travail et stratégies d'apprentissage. Éditions De Boeck, Louvain-la-Neuve (2001)
24. Zimmerman, B.J.: Attaining self-regulation: a social cognitive perspective. In: Boekaerts, M., Pintrich, P. (eds.) Handbook of self-regulation. Academic Press, New York (2000)

On the Substantiative Experiment Study of Proxing Assurance between OpenID and SAML: Technical Perspective for Private Information Box Project of Japanese e-Government

Masakazu Ohashi[1], Nat Sakimura[2], Tatsuki Sakushima[3], and Mayumi Hori[4]

[1] Chuo University, 742-1 Higashinakano, Hachioji-shi, Tokyo, 192-0393, Japan
ohashi@fps.chuo-u.ac.jp
[2] Nomura Research Institute, Marunouchi, Kitaguchi Building, 1-6-5 Marunouchi, Chiyoda-ku, Tokyo, 109-0005, Japan
n-sakimura@nri.co.jp
[3] Nomura Research Institute America, 1400 Fashion Island Blvd. Suite 1010, San Mateo, CA, 94404 USA
tatsuki@nri.com
[4] Hakuoh University, 1117 Daigyouji, Oyama-shi, Tochigi, 323-0041, Japan
hori@fc.hakuoh.ac.jp

Abstract. The substantiative experimental study of private information box project of Japanese e-Government proved the effectiveness of the New Authentication Extension Technology to combine different social infrastructures to create new Secure services between Public Sector and Private Sector(Citizen). Though there are still issues to cope with outside of the realm of technology including accountability of each participants and the level of the service, OpenID and SAML are key federated identity protocols. Both SAML and OpenID define mechanisms in support of expressing assurance information on protocol messages, respectively Authentication Context and the Provider Authentication Policy Extension (PAPE). In deployment scenarios that require proxying from one of the protocols to the other, it becomes necessary to map to and from the corresponding assurance mechanisms. This paper provides theoretical and experimental study on this mapping and related issues.

Keywords: OpenID, SAML, Authentication Extension, Contract Exchange, Proxing Assurance, Information Box Project.

1 Introduction

In ubiquitous network society, various internet services are being provided now. Moreover, it has come to be created innovative services in internet service fields which will be user-focused by being connected with the existing infrastructure and these diversified services suitable for the user needs. However, in the current environment, these services can not allow a useful connection to other services on original

J.E. Quintela Varajão et al. (Eds.): CENTERIS 2010, Part II, CCIS 110, pp. 381–390, 2010.

specification and different specification between public sector and private sector. With the rapid development of authentication services, the system which makes existing each service and infrastructure connect to keep providing the trusted information services are necessary. It is suitable for user's needs in the future. This issue is especially important in the recent condition of rapid increase of mobile internets because of increasing the need of e-commerce for improvement and a great concern for security. In the e-commerce market, a considerable volume of information and transactions are exchanged online(Ref.19).

2 Technical Overview of Private Information Box Project

The purpose of our study is to prove and develop a new authentication technology by sharing the Authentication Extension Technology to combine different social infrastructures to create new Secure services between OpenID and SAML among the existing infrastructures and the effectiveness of authentication technology between different organizations. Internet, user and devices are collaborate through one-stop authentication. In some cases, Authentication does not allowed a helpful connection among services with original and different specification. Our objective is to develop a new authentication transfer technology through more demonstrative experiments for the research. The authentication exchange technology enables internet service user to extend the connectivity service between public authority and private user that registers different authentication systems.

Figure 1 shows overview of Private Information Box Project. Green Arrow shows OpenID Contract eXchange. Figure 2 shows Experimental Study Sequence of OpenID CX (OpenID Get/Post Binding).

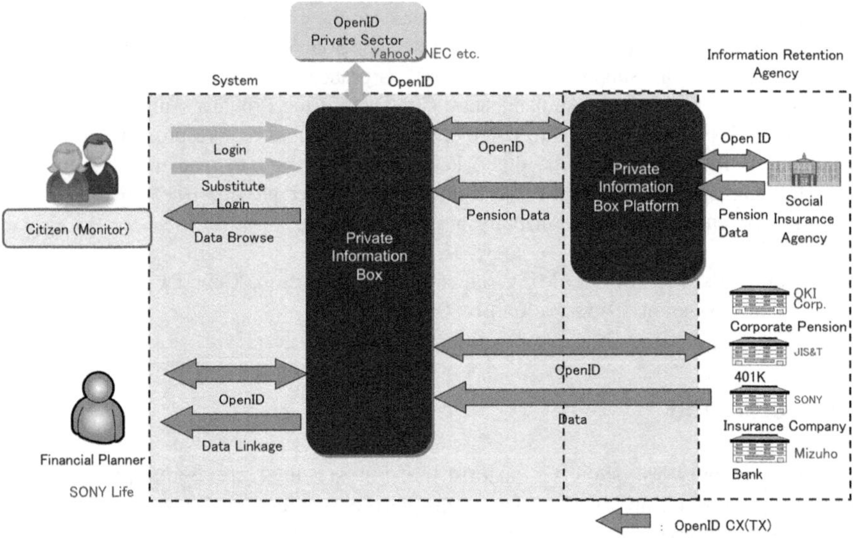

Fig. 1. Overview of Private Information Box Project(Ref.11)

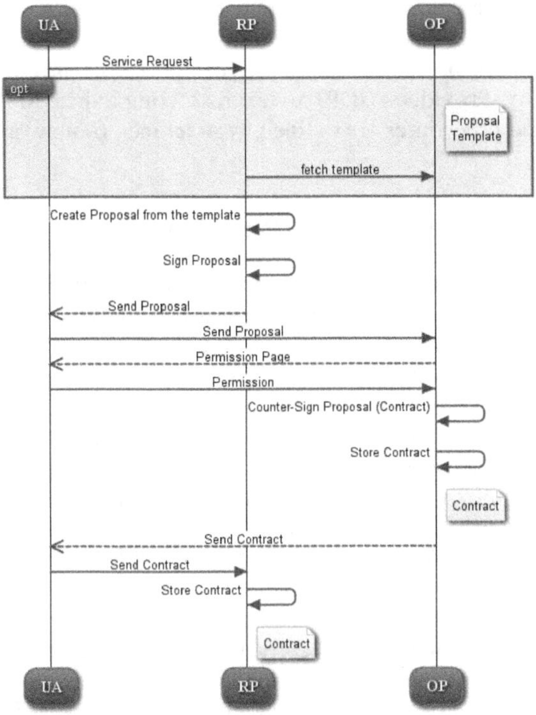

Fig. 2. Experimental Study Sequence of OpenID CX (OpenID Get/Post Binding) (Ref.11)

3 Technical Method of Proxing Assurance between OpenID and SAML

OpenID and SAML are two major federated identity protocols that have been adopted in government, education and many other industries. In many cases, either one of the protocols is employed to implement their identity federation but rarely both are used simultaneously in a interoperable manner.

When collaboration of social infrastructures among public sectors and private sectors is considered, the environment is usually heterogeneous. Many systems in government and education already have adopted SAML as their standard federated identity protocol among organizations. On the other hand, OpenID is more likely to be adopted among new comers such as Web 2.0 service providers as well as enterprises that are considering identity federation to enhance their services with better user experience. This heterogeneity will continue to support diversity in technical preferences. In this environment, how the systems which employ different federated identity protocols are interoperated each other is the key issue to be solved.

Madsen and Sakushima suggest assurance information that is conveyed in federated identity protocols can be used to inter-connect two protocols in a interoperable manner[20]. Both OpenID and SAML define such mechanisms to express assurance information on protocol messages. The assurance information is usually categorized into some levels, which are called "levels of assurance (LOA)". LOA are defined by assurance frameworks such as OMB M04-04[13] and NIST SP800-63[12] not by protocols. However, the protocols provides mechanisms to enable an Identity Providers (IDP) to express compliance to a certain LOA on which policies and procedures are defined by assurance frameworks and followed by the IDP.

3.1 OpenID Provider Authentication Policy Extension

OpenID Provider Authentication Policy Extension (PAPE) is an OpenID protocol extension which allows a Relying Party (RP) to request particular authentication policies to an OpenID provider (OP) in authenticating an end user and the OP to express whether it meets the policies in an assertion message[20].

OpenID PAPE specifies three authentication method policies which OP applies to authenticating users, Phishing-Resistant, Multi-Factor and Physical Multi-Factor. Those policies are sort of a starting point to cover the most common use cases. If those policies are not sufficient, additional policies can be defined and introduced. PAPE also support conveying LOA as more abstract policies; however a mean RP requesting a specific LOA to OP is not provided while RP is able to request three authentication method policies to OP. To remediate this issue, the US government's Federal Identity, Credential Access Management (ICAM) has developed OpenID 2.0 Profile and defines a mechanism to specify a LOA in a request message by adding the LOA policy into the authentication method policy mechanism [2]. Although lack of mechanism to express a LOA policy from RP in the current PAPE specification can be remediated, we hope that the future specification will provide a more standardized way to do so and support symmetry in request and response messages.

3.2 SAML Authentication Context

SAML Authentication Context (AC) provides mechanisms by which the SAML IDP and SP can indicate the nature of authentication so that SP is able to request IDP more information additional to the assertion itself in order to assess the degree of confidence[1]. The SAML AC specification defines a syntax for writing an XML schema which is definition of authentication context declarations in SAML.

Since SAML is a markup language based on XML, any SAML AC declarations can be added into SAML-based messages. The specification also defines a number of Authentication Context classes which are written by following the SAML AC syntax for simplifying their interpretation. There are twenty five pre-defined AC classes in the specification including Kerberos, MobileTwoFactor, Password, Public Key and so forth. Although those classes are pre-defined for convenience, some of them can be out of context because how authentication takes place depends on technologies, culture and convention adopted by people in a certain region or industry. LOA is a more universal concept can be used in any region or industry. It is also more interoperable and light-weight as a protocol. SAML has recently defined the LOA profile based on SAML AC[7]. SAML Identity Assurance Profile provides standard means for SAML IDP and SP to exchange LOA information.

3.3 Sequences of Proxying Assurance between OpenID and SAML

Madsen and Sakushima has created recommendations for the entity playing the role of protocol proxy between OpenID and SAML, differenciated by the protocol supported by the eventual consumer of the assertion, which are OpenID RP or SAML SP[10]. The recommendations are written in a way to support bi-directional; however, only either one of sequences can be employed in order to implement a proxy system.

3.3.1 Proxying OpenID Request to SAML IDP

For proxying an OpenID request to a SAML IDP, the sequence starts by an user visiting OpenID RP first with an arbitrary user agent (UA) such as a web browser. OP is the proxy which plays a role as SAML SP to SAML based-IDP. (Figure 3)

The user provide either his full OpenID URI or an OP Identifier which only specify the OP where the user is registered. In terms of privacy, initiating authentication with the OP Identifier is very useful. If the OP receives the OpenID authentication request contains a PAPE LOA policy URI that the OP is unable to satisfy, the OP can choose to proxy the request to the SAML IDP which supports it. Since the SAML LOA profile defines a metadata mechanism by which a SAML IDP can advertise the levels of assurance it supports, this mechanism can be used to choose appropriate IDPs. Obviously, the OP must maintain a mapping table of SAML IDPs coordinating with the requested LOA. Also, the OP should maintain mapping identifiers between two protocols in order to identify the user at this OP is the owner of the identifier in an assertion from the IDP. To make this mapping possbile, NameID in a assertion from SAML IDP must be persistent.

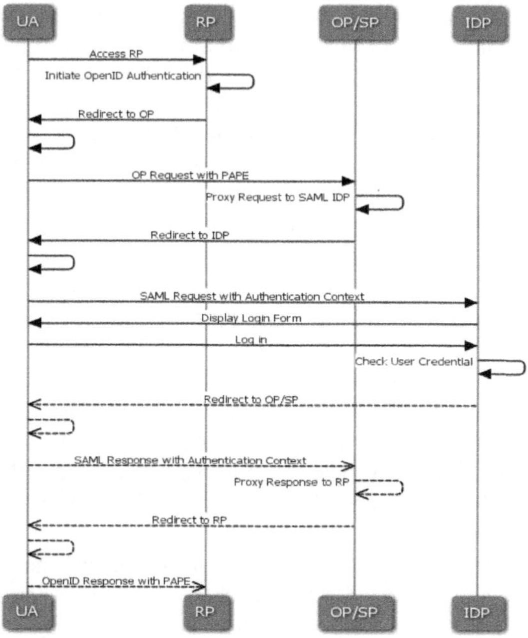

Fig. 3. The Sequence of proxying an OpenID request to SAML IDP

Once the proper SAML IDP is chosen, the OP composes a SAML Authentication Request message with the requested LOA class URI in a SAML Requested Authentication Context element and sends it to the SAML IDP.

The SAML IDP validates the request with the SAML metadata mechanism which creates trusted relationship among SAML based entities. Therefore, establishing trusted relationship in advance is required. After validating the request, the IDP displays a login form to the user and wait for user entering an id and credential. If any other authentication method policies beside a LOA policy are requested, the IDP should also apply the policies when authenticate users. When the IDP authenticates the user properly, it returns the SAML assertion which contains the LOA class URI supported by the IDP in a SAML Authentication Context element to the OP. The OP as the SAML SP validates the assertion with the same metadata mechanism. If it is legitimate, the OP converts the assertion into an OpenID positive assertion with the PAPE LOA policy URI and sends it to the RP. The RP eventually validates the positive assertion in an OpenID manner and extracts the PAPE LOA policy URI from the message. For the RP to make an entitlements decision for users, the PAPE LOA policy must meet or exceed what the RP originally requests when initiating the authentication.

3.3.2 Proxying SAML Request to OP

For proxying a SAML request to an OP, the sequence starts by an user visiting SAML SP first with an arbitrary user agent (UA) such as a web browser. IDP is the proxy which plays a role as OpenID RP to OP. (Figure 4)

In a SAML-based authentication, the SP and the IDP must have a trust relationship based on the same metadata mechanism described in 3.3.1. The SP uses the metadata to specify the IDPs to which it can send authentication requests. the SP can register more than one IDP but must establish a trust relationship with it in advance and provide an access such as a banner to that IDP on the login page. Unlike OpenID, the user does not have to provide his identifier to the SP. All he has to do to initiate authentication is to click a banner of the IDP where he is registered. When the user clicks the banner, this authentication flow is initiated. If the IDP receives from the SP the SAML authentication request contains a LOA class URI in a SAML Requested Authentication Context element, the IDP can choose to proxy the request to the OP which supports it. The IDP must maintain a mapping table of OPs coordinating with the requested LOA. The IDP as the proxy can register multiple OPs supporting the requested level and display the list of OPs so that users can choose their preferred OP. Also, the IDP should maintain mapping identifiers between two protocols in order to identify the user at this IDP is the owner of the identifier in an assertion from the OP. To make this mapping possbile, Claimed Identifier returned in a assertion from OP should be mapped to SAML's persistent NameID. Or Name ID can be generated from a specific attribute sent from the OP. What type of an identifier must be in NameID is dependent on the definition of NameID in a SAML metadata at the requested SP.

The OP extracts the PAPE LOA policy from the request message and display a login form to the user. If the OP is capable of handling multiple methods to authenticate users, the OP can suggest the user authenticate with the most qualified method based on the requested LOA. If the user is authenticated properly, the OP

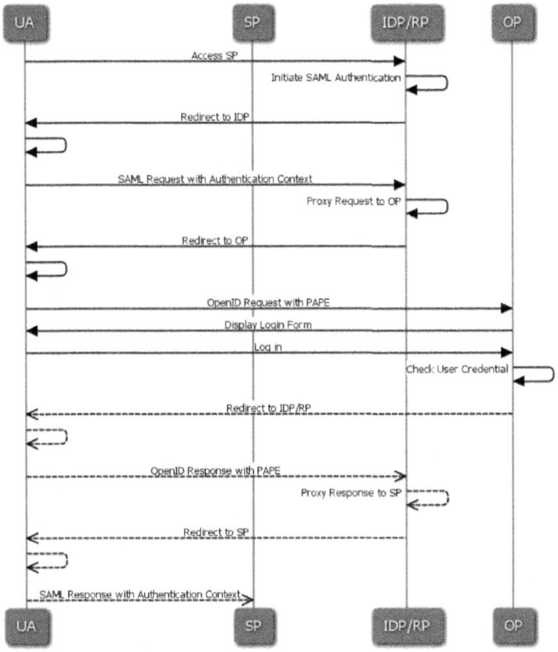

Fig. 5. The Sequence of proxying a SAML request to OP

returns the OpenID positive assertion which contains the PAPE LOA policy URI supported by this OP to the IDP. The IDP as the OpenID RP validates the assertion. If it is legitimate, the IDP converts the assertion into a SAML assertion with the LOA class URI in a SAML Authentication Context element and sends it to the SP. The SP eventually validates the assertion and extracts the LOA class URI from the message. For the SP to make an entitlements decision for users, the LOA class must meet or exceed what the SP originally requests when initiating the authentication.

4 Empirical Study of Proxing Assurance between OpenID and SAML

We examined the possibility of collaboration among government, corporations, and citizen by building an information sharing environment prior to applying proxing assurance between OpenID and SAML into the data management system which utilizes the information shared within the OpenID CX. Second, we examined the effectiveness of the authentication system and evaluated whether the external systems are capable of high-level utilization such as its proficiency of producing knowledge out of information, presenting data effectively, and storing know-how (Ohashi.edi,2003b). The following criteria were examined by the demonstration experiment utilizing the collaborative work test bed.

1) The possibility of collaboratively creating digital contents in the distributed environment. All the materials in the visual library were stored, managed, and safely exchanges in an integrated system without making duplications at organizations within in the distributed environment.

2) The potentialities of connecting different organizations through the iDC with high-speed network and of building a system with which users can exchange safely large amount of data on-line and on-time. Its effectiveness of arousing an academic curiosity for the further development of high-speed, large capacity data and information exchange and sharing.

3) The capability of the Proxing Assurance between OpenID and SAML and the OpenID CX servers to operate interactive control functions even when clients and their servers are located in an IP unreachable area.

Especially, the capability of prompting the collaborative work while protecting the data privacy by allowing users to switch the collaborative workplaces according to their object where access is controlled by each organization so that only permitted group members have the authority to share data. One-stop services is the original goal for promoting the e-Government System. As a means to realize one-stop services that integrates variety of services, portal has been reviewed and implemented from the beginning of the stage by government and with collaboration between public and private sectors. Implementing this system into the interface between public sector and clients, and implementing not on the portal (server) but on clients (users) would bring about a new way to realize one-stop services (22:Web Services Initiative,2005). There are two main advantages of citizen-centric one-stop services:1)No need of the portal systems that could be a major burden to construct 2)No need for portal to posses personal information. Building of a portal system is very difficult. From the point of authentication and organizing interfaces, it is difficult to develop a portal after each service has been developed. Additionally, it is also difficult to build a portal before any service will be developed because it means to design a gigantic system from scratch.

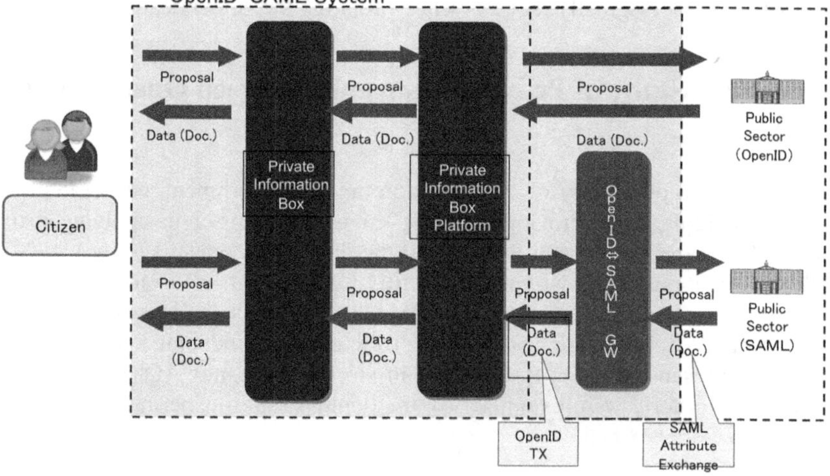

Fig. 6. Empirical Study of Proxing Assurance between OpenID and SAML(Ref.9.)

5 Conclusion

As the demand for better services increases, our study reveals important implications to many Internet services. We believe that our study that incorporates the Proxing Assurance between OpenID and SAML is truly innovative and meets the urgent need in the Ubiquitous Society. In the future, with this technology, we expect the service to expand so as to enable close relationship inside of government and private sector.

Our study proved the effectiveness of the New Authentication Extension Technology and Proxing Assurance between OpenID and SAML to combine different social infrastructures to create new Secure services between Public Sector and Private Sector(Citizen). Though there are still issues to cope with outside of the realm of technology including accountability of each participants and the level of the service, we expect this service to be soon available in the real world.

Acknowledgments. This paper is mainly based on work in the Digital Citizen Project funded by METI (Ministry of Economics, Trade and Industry) with contract with NRI(Nomura Research Institute). We would like to thank METI and the project members for their help in gathering information in preparing this paper.

References

1. Authentication Context for the OASIS Security Assertion Markup Language (SAML) V2.0 (2005), `http://docs.oasis-open.org/security/saml/v2.0/saml-authn-context-2.0-os.pdf`
2. Federal Identity, Credentialing, and Access Management, OpenID 2.0 Profile (2009), `http://www.idmanagement.gov/documents/ICAM_OpenID20Profile.pdf`
3. Hori, M., Ohashi, M.: Implementing Adaptive Collaborative Telework in Public Administration. In: Hori, M., Ohashi, M. (eds.) eAdoption and the Knowledege Economy: Issues, Applications, Case Studies, pp. 708–714. IOS Press, Amsterdam (2004a)
4. Hori, M., Ohashi, M.: Applying XML Web Services into health care management. In: Proceedings of the 38th Annual Hawaii Conference on System Science, Hawaii (2005a)
5. Hori, M., Ohashi, M.: Adaptive Collaboration:The Road Map to Leading Telework to a More Advanced and Professional Working Format. The Journal of the IPSI BgD Transaction on Advanced Research Issues in Computer and Engineering, IPSI Bgd Internet Research Society, 6–42 (2005b)
6. Hori, M., Ohashi, M.: The Municipality's Role for Building of the Regional Health & Medical Welfare Information Services System. Journal of Policy & Culture 13 (2006a)
7. Hori, M., Ohashi, M.: On the Study of Collaborative Telework in the Infosocionomics Society. Journal of Policy & Culture 13 (2006b)
8. Hori, M., Ohashi, M.: Citizen-Centric s-Healthcare Management Based on the XML Web Services. In: Cunningham, P., Cunningham, M. (eds.) Exploiting the Knowledge Economy, Issues, Applications, Case Studies, pp. 957–964. IOS press, Amsterdam (2006c)
9. Hori, M., Ohashi, M., Ssuzuki, S.: Citizen-Centric Approach and healthcare Management Base on the XML Web Serrvices. In: Proceedings of the 12th European Conference on Information Technology Evaluation, p. 241 (2005)

10. Madsen, P., Sakushima, T.: Deployment Guide for Proxying Assurance between OpenID and SAML v3, OpenID, Kantara Initiative Deployment Guideline draft (2010)
11. Ministry of Economics,Trade and Industry edited, Report of Digital Citizen Project (2010)
12. National Institute of Standards and Technology (NIST), Electronic Authentication Guideline, NIST Special Publication (SP) 800-63, Version 1.0.2 (2006), http://csrc.nist.gov/publications/nistpubs/800-63/SP800-63V1_0_2.pdf, Draft Revision 1, http://csrc.nist.gov/publications/PubsDrafts.html#SP-800-63-Rev.%201
13. Office of Management and Budget (OMB), E-Authentication Guidance for Federal Agency, OMB Memorandum 04-04, 13 (2003), http://www.whitehouse.gov/omb/memoranda/fy04/m04-04.pdf
14. Ohashi, M. (ed.): The Report of Society for the Advance Study on e-Society, The Society of the Basis for e-Community (2003a)
15. Ohashi, M. (ed.): Knowledge-Based Collaborative Work, The Report of Supplementary Budget Project of the Ministry of Post and Telecommunications (2003b)
16. Ohashi, M. (ed.): The Report of the Advanced Studies for the Social Capital of e-Society, The Society of theBasis for the e-Community (2004)
17. Ohashi, M. (ed.): XML Web Services for Next Generation & A view of Citizen Centric. Kinokuniya Co. Ltd., Japan (2005)
18. Ohashi, M., Hori, M.: The Theory of Economics for Network Societ, pp. 2–5, 106–118. Kinokuniya Co., Ltd., Japan (2005)
19. Ohashi, M., Hori, M.: Security Management Services Based on Authentication Roaming between Different Certificate Authorities. In: Proceeding of CENTRIS 2009, pp. 201–214 (2009)
20. OpenID Foundation Japan CX Working Group edited, Contract Exchange (CX) Extension Use Cases and Requirements (2009)
21. OpenID Provider Authentication Policy Extension 1.0 (2008), http://openid.net/specs/openid-provider-authentication-policy-extension-1_0.html
22. Sakimura, N., Sakushima, T., Nara, H., Blackmer, S.: Contract Exchange Extension 1.0 Draft 1, Kantara Initiative Deployment Guideline draft (2010)
23. SAML V2.0 Identity Assurance Profiles Version 1.0 Committee Draft01 (2009), http://www.oasis-open.org/committees/download.php/36496/sstc-saml-assurance-profile-cd-01.pdf
24. Web Services Initiative,Web Services Application Guideline, pp.29–31, 66 (2005)
25. Web Services Initiative, The Report of Web2.0 and Citizen Centric Technology (2007)

Automatic Extraction of ICT Competences from Unstructured Sources

Valentina Janev, Vuk Mijović, and Sanja Vraneš

The Mihajlo Pupin Institute, Volgina 15,
11060 Belgrade, Serbia
{Valentina.Janev,Vuk.Mijovic,Sanja.Vranes}@institutepupin.com

Abstract. Competence management is an important research object in the more general area of human resources management and knowledge management. This paper describes the process of enhancing the individual ICT competence models built from the self-declared knowledge of experts with information extracted automatically from documents using custom Unstructured Information Management Architecture (UIMA) text analysis components. The application aims to identify and extract main expertise areas of ICT experts from two types of documents: published documents (journal / conference papers) and unpublished documents (project documentation). In addition, CV files are used to extract computer skills of different types. The identified ICT competences are exported in such a format that can automatically populate expert profiles built in OWL format. The proposed approach extends the functionalities of existing enterprise information systems and offers possibilities for development of future Internet services.

Keywords: ICT, competences, semantic technologies, information extraction, expertise profiles.

1 Introduction

Competence management (CM) is an important research object in the more general area of human resources management and knowledge management. Two different meanings of the concept of "competence" (building blocks of competency models) within the corporate environment could be distinguished:

- Expert competences are specific, identifiable, definable, and measurable knowledge, skills, abilities and/or other deployment-related characteristics (e.g. attitude, behavior, physical ability) which a human resource may possess and which is necessary for, or material to, the performance of an activity within a specific business context. *Competence modeling* is thus a process of determining the set of competencies that are required for excellent performance in a particular role [1].
- Organizational core competencies are aggregates of capabilities, where synergy is created that has sustainable value and broad applicability for an organization [2]. Defining competency models for an organization and performing skills gap analysis which provides essential data for the undertaking of a range of

J.E. Quintela Varajão et al. (Eds.): CENTERIS 2010, Part II, CCIS 110, pp. 391–400, 2010.

training and development and performance improvement activities is known as *Competency management*.

Competency analysis within an enterprise aims at identifying the knowledge and skills on individual level required to perform the organization's business activities so that they may be developed to fit the requests of work life reality. Depending on the adopted approach to competence management, different individual competence models can be developed, e.g. job, functional, core, or leadership competency models. Core competency models identify the critical skills, knowledge, and abilities that are required for success for all individuals in a particular organization. This creates a common language and an agreed upon standard of performance among employees. Job competency models describe the behaviors, knowledge, and skills required for exceptional performance for any particular job. As a result, individuals and their managers can evaluate performance against an observable standard.

EU policy including the Bologna Process (started in 1999, see http://www.ond.vlaanderen.be/hogeronderwijs/Bologna/) and the European Research Area initiative (commenced in 2000, see http://ec.europa.eu/research/era/) underlines the importance of the transferability and comparability of competences, skills and qualifications within Europe. Therefore, this paper aims at introducing an approach that enables extraction of ICT competences from existing structured and unstructured sources and their formal representation as an OWL models.

2 Competency Management in ICT Domain

ICT field includes the following sub-disciplines: computer science, information systems, computer engineering, software engineering and information technology. The Association for Computer Machinery, the world's largest educational and scientific computing society (see http://www.acm.org/) and the IEEE Computer Society, an organizational unit of the Institute of Electrical and Electronics Engineers (see http://www.computer.org/) have taken a leading role in providing support for higher education in ICT in various ways, including the formulation of curriculum guidelines and defining competences i.e. capabilities and knowledge expected for ICT graduate. Since 1968, they provided curriculum guidance (see http://www.acm.org/education/curricula-recommendations) on computing at approximately ten-year intervals (1968, 1978, 1991, and 2001).

According to the ACM high-level categorization of Information Systems graduate exit characteristics, for example, the future ICT professionals, scientists, and engineers, should have technology knowledge in the following domains: *Application Development, Internet Systems Architecture and Development, Database Design and Administration, Systems Infrastructure and Integration,* and *IS development* (*Systems Analysis and Design, Business Process Design, Systems Implementation, IS Project Management*). *Internet Systems Architecture and Development*, for example, includes Web page development, Web architecture design and development, design and development of multi-tiered architectures and experience with Web programming languages such as Java, PHP, Pyton, HTML, RDF, etc.

Except technical knowledge ICT professionals, scientists, and engineers should be capable of analytical and critical thinking and have soft skills (*Interpersonal, Commu-*

nication, and *Team Skills*). Soft skills, sometimes known as "people skills," are personal attributes that enhance an individual's interactions, job performance and career prospects. Companies value soft skills because research suggests and experience shows that they can be just as important an indicator of job performance as hard skills.

ICT graduates should be also familiar with business fundamentals (*Business Models, Functional Business Areas, Evaluation of Business Performance*). Based on this, ICT professionals develop management skills and leading abilities. Management skills include skills for problem solving, goals setting, organizing, realization of decisions and enforcement of measures, performing control and evaluating results, costs planning, delegating and constant improvement. Leading abilities are skills for clear mediating of information, interpersonal conversation, notifying, activating energy, creating possibilities, motivational leading, conflicts solving, stimulating co-workers, mutual cooperation, positive treatment with others, and other.

In general, we can depict the skills of ICT expert/professional as is presented in Figure 1.

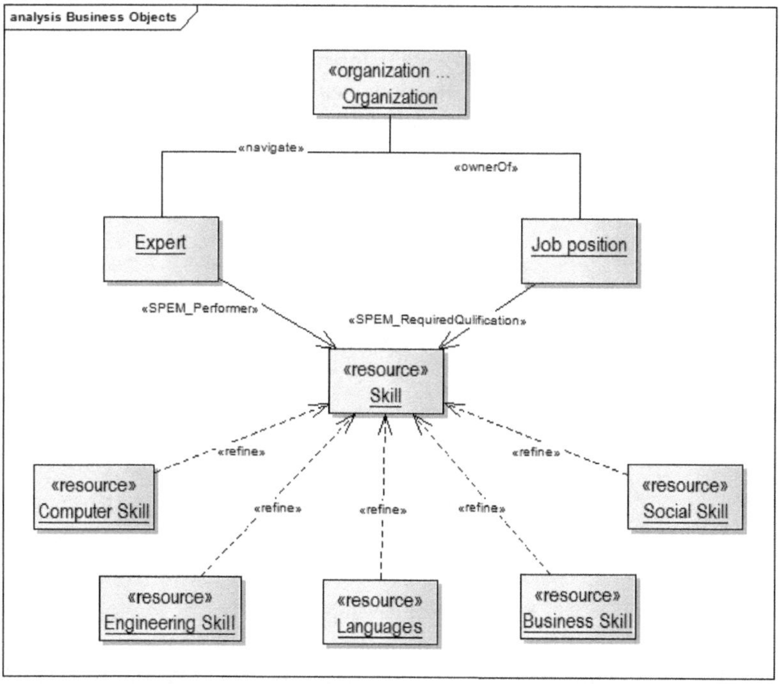

Fig. 1. UML representation of ICT Characteristics

3 Ontology-Based Approach to Competency Management

Ontology engineering is a new field in information science, which studies the methods and methodologies for building ontologies (formal representations of a set of concepts within a domain and the relationships between those concepts). Ontology engineering provides standards and structures that allow information to be described in a way that captures *what it is*, *what it means* and *what it's related to* - all in a machine-readable form. This enables machines as well as people to understand, share and reason with them at the execution time and offers new possibilities for enterprise systems to be networked in meaningful ways. Ontologies form the backbone of the Semantic Web[1].

European Union, through its chief instruments for funding research (FP5 - The Fifth, FP6 – The Sixth and FP7 – The Seventh Framework Programs), has financed several projects that focused on ontology-based competence management. As a result of these projects, several prototype systems have been developed [3], [4] and few ontologies were made publicly available [5]. The research work had also a positive impact on several European Public Employment Services [6]. Some of them have already introduced (e.g. Germany, Norway) or are at the moment working on improvements of their matching (vacancies and job seekers) processes by shifting more emphasis to competences.

Motivated by the need to express the core competences of the researchers and organizational units of the "Mihajlo Pupin" Institute (MPI) in a machine processable format by using standards and classifications that will allow interoperability of data in the EU research and business space, we adopted an ontology-based approach to expertise profiling and retrieval [7].

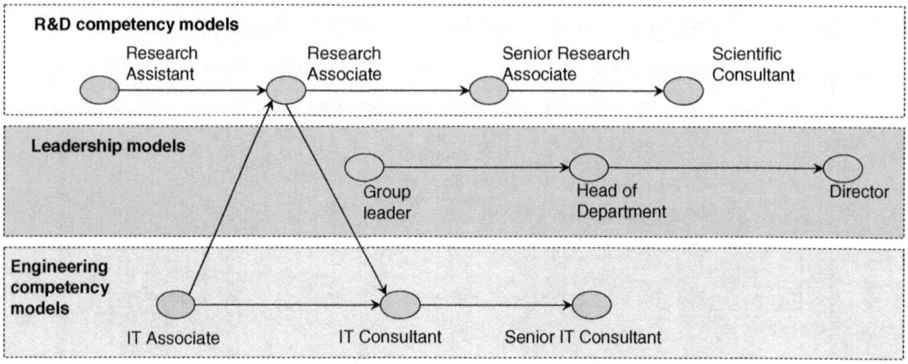

Fig. 2. Career development paths

3.1 Development of Job Competency Models at the Mihajlo Pupin Institute

Using the "Mihajlo Pupin" case study, we can in general illustrate the career development paths of the engineering staff as is presented in Figure 2. Nodes represent different employment positions, while the arcs show the possible development paths. Building a competency model means identification of the competencies employees

[1] The Semantic Web is an extension of the current web in which information is given well-defined meaning, better enabling computers and people to work in cooperation. See http://www.w3.org/2001/sw/

need to develop in order to improve performance in their current job or to prepare for other jobs via promotion or transfer. The model can also be useful in a skill gap analysis, the comparison between available and needed competencies of individuals or organizations. An individual development plan could be developed in order to eliminate the gap. Important variables to be considered during the development of a competency model are the use of skill dictionaries, or the creation of customized ones. For example, a competency model for a "Senior Research Associate" might include competencies such as analytical approach to work, excellent problem-solving skills, technical competence and experience, good organizational skills, independence and objectivity, ability to communicate, attention to detail, project-management skills, ability to distinguish between the strategically important and the trivial, negotiation.

3.2 Building Expert Profiles Models in OWL format with *TopBraid* Composer

The "Mihajlo Pupin" ontological knowledge base was designed and built using the *TopBraid Composer* an enterprise-class modelling environment for building semantic applications that are fully compliant with the W3C standards (see the TopQuadrant's Web site at http://www.topquadrant.com/). The tool provides powerful *Input facilities* (see Figure 3) that enable integration of diverse knowledge sources and services. It supports many inference engines that can run alone or in a sequence. Using the *Top-Braid Suite Export facilities* the developed models can be deployed to *TopBraid Live Server* or exported/merged/converted to RDF graphs that can be exploited with other client applications e.g. with *OntoWiki* [8].

After the ontological knowledge base was designed, the next step was to populate the ontology i.e. import data into the ontology and create instances. Manually creating of ontologies is a time consuming task. Semantic Web community has delivered many high-quality open-source tools (e.g. the D2RQ server) that can be used for automatic or semiautomatic ontology population i.e. to convert the facts trapped in the legacy systems or business documents into information understandable both for machines and people. Table 1 summarizes some types of competences that were extracted from structured (e.g the SAP HR management system) and unstructured sources.

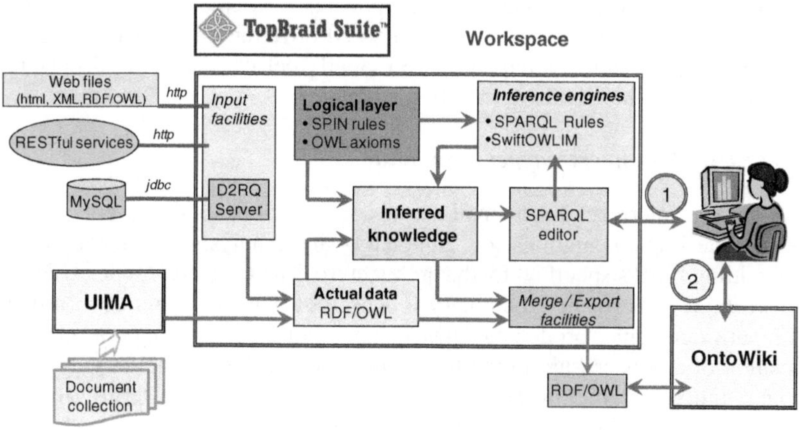

Fig. 3. The TopBraid Composer workspace

Table 1. Integrating competences from structured and unstructured sources

Sources	Type of competence	Content
Structured - SAP HRM system stores self declared competences of the experts	ICT main research field	A category from a catalog defined by Serbian Ministry of Science
	ICT subfields	unlimited list of ICT areas
	Key qualifications	Free text in Serbian language
	Key experiences - responsibilities	Free text in Serbian language
	Foreign languages	Items from a catalog of foreign languages
Unstructured - documents in .doc, .pdf, .txt, etc.	Computer skills	7 different competence types are extracted and transformed into structured format
	Project Experience	Major ICT fields of project expertise is identified and transformed into structured format
	Publications	An extensive list of topics of interest is extracted and transformed into structured format

Rest of the paper discusses the use of the Unstructured Information Management Architecture (UIMA) open source tool for building custom text analysis components for automatic extraction of experts' competences from unstructured sources.

4 Building Custom Text Analysis Components with UIMA

UIMA stands for the Unstructured Information Management Architecture (see http://incubator.apache.org/uima/) and is a component architecture and software framework implementation for the analysis of unstructured content like text, video and audio data. In 2009 OASIS (Organization for the Advancement of Structured Information Standards, http://www.oasis-open.org/) announced UIMA as standard technology for creating text-analysis components. The major goal of UIMA is to transform unstructured information to structured information so that appropriate data processing and search technologies can efficiently deliver the newly discovered content in response to the client requests or queries.

4.1 The UIMA *ConceptMapper* Annotator

UIMA defines interfaces for a small set of core components that users of the framework provide implementations for. Annotators and Analysis Engines are two of the basic building blocks specified by the architecture. The *ConceptMapper* UIMA Annotator is a high performance dictionary lookup tool that maps entries in a dictionary onto input documents, producing UIMA annotations. It also supports including the association of any necessary properties from the controlled vocabulary as part of that mapping. Individual dictionary entries could contain multiple terms (tokens), and *ConceptMapper* can be configured to allow multi-term entries to be matched against non-contiguous text. For example, using the following dictionary entry

```
<token canonical="MS.NET"
area="useProgrammingLanguage">
    <variant base="MS.NET"/>
    <variant base=".NET"/>
</token>
```

we can deduce that the expert is using language "MS.NET" if this information is found in his CV documents. Next, using the following dictionary entry

```
<token canonical="Image_Processing_Pattern_Recognition"
area="topic_interest">
    <variant base="Imaging"/>
    <variant base="Image Processing"/>
    <variant base="Pattern Recognition"/>
  </token>
```

we can deduce that the expert is interested in image processing based on different keywords found in his documents (publications and working documents).

4.2 The MPI *CompetenceAnalysis* Component

The *MPI CompetenceAnalysis* component was built upon the UIMA annotator i.e. the UIMA Sandbox. The dictionary was built using the ICT taxonomy of European Research Areas (IST ERA, http://www.kooperation-international.de/eu/themes/info/detail/data/2962/?PHPSESSID=c332). The taxonomy structures the ICT technology areas into four main categories:

C1 - Electronics, Microsystems, Nanotechnology;

C2 - Information Systems, Software and Hardware;

C3 - Media and Content, and

C4 - Communication Technology, Networks, Distributed Systems.

In addition, the dictionary contains vocabulary of computer skills that is used for extracting expert experience with *Programming languages, Operating systems,*

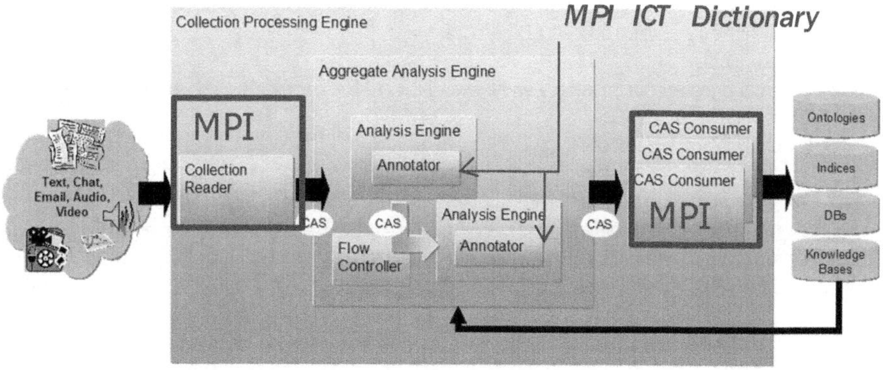

Fig. 4. High-Level UIMA Component Architecture from Source to Sink

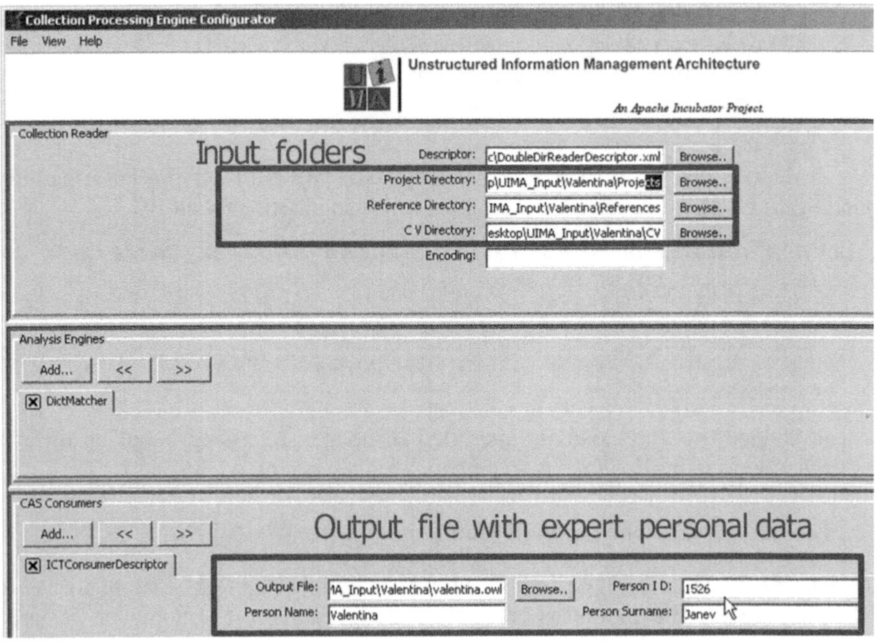

Fig. 5. The MPI *CompetenceAnalysis* component

Hardware, WEB technology, SW Solutions, Modeling environments, Development Tools, etc.

The *MPI Collection Reader* was built because the source documents are coming from different parts of an expert's computer and tokens are mapped accordingly to different concepts. The *MPI CAS Consumer* was built because we wanted to customize the processing made by *ConceptMapper* annotator and prepare the output results in an OWL format suitable for integration in existing expertise knowledge base.

Currently the *MPI CompetenceAnalysis* component assumes that the input documents belong to a single person and exports an OWL file whose content looks like:

```
<ict:Person rdf:ID="ID_1526">
<Global_ID
rdf:datatype="http://www.w3.org/2001/XMLSchema#integer"
>1526</Global_ID>
<ict:topic_interest_project
rdf:resource="http://www.institutepupin.com/ict.owl#Sem
antic_Technologies"/>
<ict:topic_interest_reference
rdf:resource="http://www.institutepupin.com/ict.owl#Ima
ging_Image_Processing_Pattern_Recognition"/>
...
<ict:useOperatingSystem
rdf:resource="http://www.institutepupin.com/skills.owl#
Windows"/>
```

```
<ict:useDBMS
rdf:resource="http://www.institutepupin.com/skills.owl#
MS_SQL_Server"/>
<ict:useSoftwareSolution
rdf:resource="http://www.institutepupin.com/skills.owl#
SAP_ERP"/>
...
</ict:Person>
```

5 Concluding Remarks

Virtually integrated organizations seek to link their individual core competencies through cost-sharing and risk-sharing agreements, so that these organizations can act as a larger, single entity. Competency management and finding expertise (either a person or/and accompanied knowledge items) in such a dynamic and often complex organizational structure, that is supported by an extended information system, is a challenging issue.

This paper discussed the process of building expert profiles in a form of ontology database by integrating competences from structured and unstructured sources. In particular, it presented the MPI *CompetenceAnalysis* component that was developed at the "Mihajlo Pupin" Institute in order to objectively identify and extract the key expertise of employees and automate the ontology population process. What has been achieved so far is automatic identification and extraction of skills from available structured and unstructured sources and semi-automatic population of the ontology database. Structured sources (SAP HCM knowledge pool) store expertise items that are based on evidences (e.g. certificates) or declared by the experts themselves at HR Department and entered in the knowledge pool by an officially assigned person. Once the expertises have been extracted from unstructured documents using the MPI *CompetenceAnalysis* component, the results have to be checked by the officially assigned person prior to integration into the ontology database. Automatic analysis has advantages compared to manual analysis because of the objectiveness of results. Our analysis has shown that manually created lists of expertise were not an exhaustive description of the person's expertise areas. Introducing standard classification of ICT expertise facilitates data integration and interoperability of expertise data within the European Research Area and beyond.

Acknowledgments. This work has been supported partly by the EU Seventh Framework Programme (HELENA - Higher Education Leading to ENgineering And scientific careers, Pr. No.: 230376) and partly by the Ministry of Science and Technological Development of the Republic of Serbia (Pr. No.: TR-13004).

References

1. Ennis, M.R.: Competency Models: A Review of the Literature and the Role of the Employment and Training Administration (ETA). U. S. Department of Labor (2008), http://www.careeronestop.org/COMPETENCYMODEL/info_documents/OPDRLiteratureReview.pdf

2. Lahti, R.K.: Identifying and integrating individual level and organizational level core competencies. Journal of Business and Psychology 14(1), 59–75 (1999)
3. Bizer, C., Heese, R., Mochol, M., Oldakowski, R., Tolksdorf, R., Eckstein, R.: The Impact of Semantic Web Technologies on Job Recruitment Processes. In: Proc. of the 7th Internationale TagungWirtschaftsinformatik 2005 (WI 2005), Bamberg, Germany, pp. 1367–1383 (2005)
4. Draganidis, F., Mentzas, G.: Competency Based Management: A Review of Systems and Approaches. Information Management and Computer Security 14(1), 51–64 (2006)
5. Schmidt, A., Kunzmann, C.: Towards a Human Resource Development Ontology for Combining Competence Management and Technology-Enhanced Workplace Learning. In: Meersman, R., Tari, Z., Herrero, P. (eds.) OTM 2006 Workshops. LNCS, vol. 4278, pp. 1078–1087. Springer, Heidelberg (2006)
6. Müller-Riedlhuber, H.: The European Dictionary of Skills and Competences (DISCO): an Example of Usage Scenarios for Ontologies. In: Paschke, A., et al. (eds.) Proc. of the 5th International Conference on Semantic Systems (I-SEMANTICS 2009), J. UCS Conference Proceedings Series, Graz, Austria, pp. 467–479 (2009)
7. Janev, V., Duduković, J., Vraneš, S.: Semantic Web Based Integration of Knowledge Resources for Expertise Finding. International Journal of Enterprise Information Systems 5(4), 53–70 (2009)
8. Auer, S.: Methods and Applications of the Social Semantic Web. In: Vraneš, S. (ed.) Semantic Web and/or Web 2.0: Competitive or Complementary? pp. 100–128. Academic mind, Belgrade (2008)

CBR Technique in Veterinary Pathological Anatomy

Paulo Tomé[1] and Helena Vala[2]

[1] School of Technology of Viseu
ptome@estv.ipv.p
[2] Agrarian School of Viseu and
Center for Studies in Education
hvala@esav.ipv.pt

Abstract. Veterinary Pathological Anatomy consists in the application of criteria based in the knowledge of the macroscopic and histological lesions to obtain a final pathological diagnosis. The aim of this specific diagnosis is, generally, to determine which disease affects the animal, in case of being alive, or what the cause of death in case it was death.

Unlike human medicine, dedicated to a single specie, the Veterinary Medicine is dedicated to different animal species, usually grouped into specialties based in affinity of species (e.g. pets - dogs and cats, ruminants, exotic species, etc). Also pathological anatomy uses exhaustive classifications of different types (e.g. infectious diseases, metabolic diseases, endocrine diseases, neoplasm's, etc.). So the urgent need to compile all available information to obtain a diagnosis, in a short period of time, which will help to save the animal life, is the constant challenge placed to the professional experts in the area concerned.

The proposal of using the Case Based-Reasoning (CBR) technique in this area aims at offer a training tool to the professional and attendants, as well as a research instrument to analyze the similarities or deviations of the diagnosed cases, to improve the veterinarian pathologist's performance and therefore achieve greater success in helping clinicians saving more animals.

Keywords: CBR technique, Veterinary Pathological Anatomy.

1 Introduction

The use of past knowledge is an important issue in Veterinary Pathological Anatomy. Usually the professionals of the domain use knowledge of the domain, such as (Organization World Health, 2008); (Scott, Jr., & Griffin, 2000); and (Jubb, Kennedy, & Palmer, 1993), and their previous experience.

The authors described the application of a CBR system that assists veterinary pathologists professionals to improve its performance in obtaining a final diagnosis. Pathological diagnosis is a supplementary diagnostic test, usually ordered by the veterinarian clinician, in order to direct treatment to administer to the sick animal, or

J.E. Quintela Varajão et al. (Eds.): CENTERIS 2010, Part II, CCIS 110, pp. 401–405, 2010.

living members of a group of animals (e.g. cattle), in which a death occurred. Thus, although the methods used are similar to those used in human medicine, the ends are quite different.

As far as we know, no system of artificial intelligence has ever been applied or implemented to diagnosis areas of the veterinary medicine. The system proposed on this paper is applied to the generation of solutions for real clinic cases submitted to pathological complementary diagnosis exams, using for this purpose 921 real cases, integrated to the specific knowledge of the professional of the area.

2 Pathological Diagnosis

Pathological diagnosis is based on the World Health Organization International Classification of Tumours of Domestic Animals and Pathology of Domestic Animals Classifications (Organization World Health, 2008). Also it considers the identification animal data, clinical history (including physical exam), macroscopic lesions and mostly histological aspects, including cellular characteristics and organizational patterns. Finally the definite diagnosis is emitted based on the specific knowledge of the professional veterinary pathologist.

On applying an intelligence model at Pathological diagnosis, the major difficulty arises from the fact that the descriptions of macro and microscopic lesions are mostly qualitative, based on the pathologist observation, which gives an inaccurate degree of subjectivity, depending on of the perception of the observer.

Generally the professionals in this area choose to register only the existence of a certain lesion in the organs/tissues that are watching and not by quantifying.

Depending on the examination of a certain kind of lesions, registered in the macroscopic exam and in the microscopic exam, the pathologist delivers its diagnosis, conducting a detailed and prolonged study on the case.

The development of a tool that would relate certain lesions present with a given diagnosis, would be an useful tool to help the pathologist, saving time and cuts and the subjectivity inherent. We also believe that this system could have many applications in research field. The tool applies CBR (Aamodt & Plaza, 1994).

3 The Reuse of Experience Pathological Anatomy and Routine Histopathological Diagnosis Domains

As already mentioned, we applied CBR in The Reuse of Experience Pathological Anatomy and routine Histopathological Diagnosis domains. In our system was implemented the four phases cycle of Aamodt and Plaza (Aamodt & Plaza, 1994). The system implements the retrieve, reuse, revise and retain phases and has a repository with cases and knowledge domain. The overall system structure is shown in Figure 1.

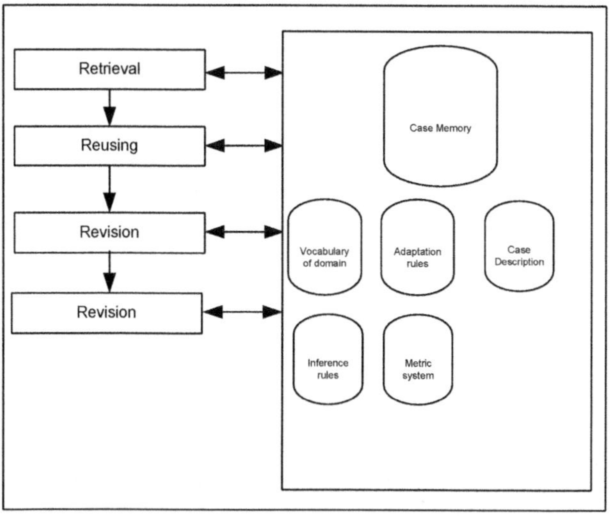

Fig. 1. Software Tool Structure

The system has two main parts: client and server. In the client part the users can insert new cases and retrieve solutions for their cases. The client part is implemented through a web browser. In the server part is implemented the CBR technique. As previously mentioned, we implemented the Aamodt and Plaza (Aamodt & Plaza, 1994) model. Bellow we explain each component of the server part of our system.

As can be seen in Figure 1, the system as components for storing data and has components for doing some of the systems tasks. The components: case memory, vocabulary of domain, adaptation rules, case description, inference rules and metric system store data while the components: retrieve, reusing, revision and retaining implements the system tasks.

It is worth to mention that the system has in the case memory two types of cases: one for Pathological Anatomy and other for Histopathological. Each case is stored as a frame (Minsky, 1974). Each case is divided according the Kolodner (Kolodner, 1993) proposal into: objective, characteristics and solution. The characteristics and the solutions are pairs of *name* x *value*.

In the domain vocabulary module are the stored the most frequent expressions used to describe cases of both domains. After the use of the system in the set of 921 cases this module stores 6197 terms.

The adaptation rules module stores information about how diagnosis can be adapted. In this module there can be stored if-then rules (Cawsey, 1998) for defining how diagnosis can be adapted based on case' characteristics.

The Inference rules module is also build of if-then rules. These rules are based on the knowledge defined in the books described in (Organization World Health, 2008).

As previously mentioned, the cases are structured through attribute x value approach. All case' characteristics are expressed in text. Usually the veterinarians describe situations, through text description, in a free way. The same happens when the veterinarians define a diagnose. Because of that, the searching of old cases is based on text analysis. So, the metric system is based on comparing similar text expressions.

As previously mentioned, the system was tested in a set of 921 real cases. These cases were previously resolved by specialists' veterinarians. Above we explain the final results of the system use. The retrieval process only considers case with a level of similarity greater than 66.6%. In the set of 921 the system found 641 with a level of similarity greater than 66.6% which it mean that 69,6% of cases could be adapted.

We also measured the level similarity between the solution proposed by veterinarians and the solution proposed by the system. The Figure 2 shows level of similarity between the solution proposed by veterinarians and the solution proposed by the system.

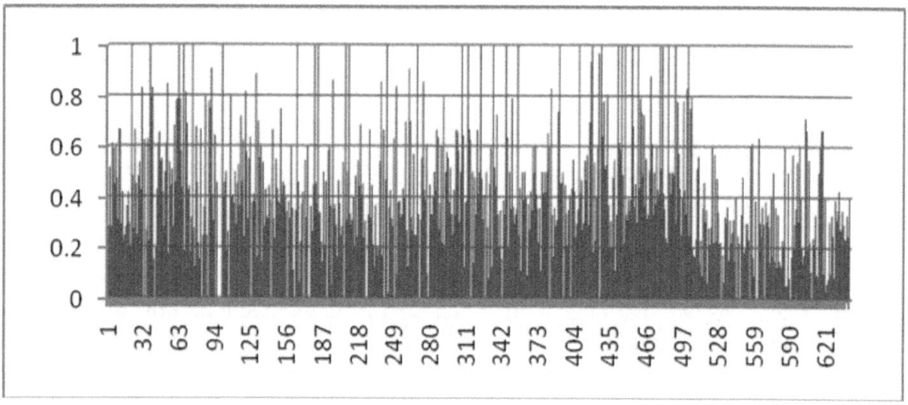

Fig. 2. Level of similarity between solutions

As shown in Table 1 the system proposed 47.1% of solution with a similarity greater than 40% of the solution proposed by the veterinarians. Only 16.8% of cases have solutions in the range 0 to 20%.

Table 1. Analysis of level of similarity between solutions

Level of solutions similarities	[0 , 0.2[	[0.2 , 0,4[	[0.4 , 0.6[	[0.6 , 0.8[	[0.8 , 1]
Number of cases	108	231	166	80	56

Conclusion

In this paper we propose a software system that can be used to assist veterinary pathologists professionals to improve its performance in obtaining a final diagnosis. The system applies CBR techniques to get past resolved situations and propose it to professional veterinaries.

The system as tested in a set of 921 real cases and the results obtained are very positive. The number of similar cases is high and the quality of proposed solutions is also high.

In a near future the authors will structure a set of standard attributes for the definition of the cases characteristics and solutions. The authors believe that if the cases were described in a standard way best results can be achieved.

References

Aamodt, A., Plaza, E.: Case-based reasoning: Foundational issues, methodological variations and systems approaches. AI-Communications 7(1), 39–52 (1994)

Cawsey, A.: The Essence of Artificial Intelligence. Prentice-Hall, Englewood Cliffs (1998)

Jubb, K.V., Kennedy, P.C., Palmer, N.: Pathology of domestic animals, vol. I, II and II. Academic Press, London (1993)

Kolodner, J.: Case-Based Reasoning. Morgan Kaufmann Publishers, San Francisco (1993)

Minsky, M.: A Framework For Representing Knowledge. Massachusetts (1974)

Organization World Health, International Classification of Tumours of Domestic Animals. vol. I, II, III, IV, V, VI, VII, VIII. Schulman FY, 2nd series (2008)

Scott, D.W., Miller Jr., W.H., Griffin, C.E.: Muller and Kirk's Small Animal Dermatology, 6th edn. Saunders (2000)

Moderated Regression: Effects of IT Infrastructure Integration and Supply Chain Process Integration on the Relationships between RFID Adoption Attributes and System Deployment Outcomes

Rebecca Angeles

Faculty of Business Administration, University of New Brunswick Fredericton
P O Box 4400, Tilley Hall # 308B
7 Macauley Lane, Fredericton, New Brunswick E3B 5A3, Canada
rangeles@unb.ca

Abstract. This empirical study investigates the ability of information technology (IT) infrastructure integration and supply chain process integration to moderate the relationships between the importance of the perceived seven adoption attributes and system deployment outcomes, operational efficiency and market knowledge creation in radio frequency identification (RFID)-enabled supply chains. The moderated regression procedure suggested by Aguinis was applied and indicated that three adoption attributes, relative advantage, results, and image turned out to be the most important attributes in these RFID systems.

Keywords: Supply chain management; radio frequency identification (RFID); technology adoption and diffusion; operational efficiency; market knowledge creation; IT infrastructure integration; supply chain process integration.

1 Introduction

Studying RFID adoption attributes will be a continuing exercise as research uncovers more issues that need to be addressed. Using the online survey method, this study focuses on the seven adoption attributes that are very likely to impact the executive decision to deploy RFID to pursue either operational efficiency or market knowledge creation or both in their supply chains. This study also investigates the influence of information technology (IT) infrastructure integration and supply chain process integration on the relationships between each of the RFID adoption attributes and the two dependent variables, operational efficiency and market knowledge creation. Moderated regression analysis is used to undertake this determination.

2 Literature Review

This study is part of larger exploration on the importance of RFID in the supply chain on account of its potential to render information visibility that will, in turn, solve a

J.E. Quintela Varajão et al. (Eds.): CENTERIS 2010, Part II, CCIS 110, pp. 406–415, 2010.

number of supply chain problems such as the "bullwhip effect" or distortion of signals down the value chain due to lack of accurate information. Previous published work on the larger study has featured the relationships between the elements that constitute IT infrastructure integration and supply chain process integration and four system deployment outcomes that are typical of a supply chain: exploitation, exploration, operational efficiency, and market knowledge creation [1,2]. In another related study, the relationships between absorptive capacity attributes or organizational routines and business processes used by firms to acquire, assimilate, transform, and exploit knowledge, and two system outcomes, operational efficiency and market knowledge creation were explored [3]. In this second study, the ability of IT infrastructure integration and supply chain process integration to moderate the relationships between the independent and dependent variables was also tested. The study presented in this paper is a piece of the aforementioned more comprehensive inquiry, that focuses on the relationship between the perceptions of study respondents of the importance of seven adoption attributes of RFID and two system outcomes, operational efficiency and market knowledge creation. More importantly once again, the ability of IT infrastructure integration and supply chain process integration to moderate these relationships was investigated.

2.1 Independent Variables: RFID Adoption Attributes

Rogers' [4, 5] review of more than 3,000 studies on diffusion of innovations has resulted in the identification of five general adoption attributes: relative advantage, compatibility, complexity, observability, and triability. Numerous attempts early on at conceptualization and empirical testing resulted in mixed and inconclusive findings, attributed mainly to the lack of a solid theoretical foundation. To improve on this situation, Moore and Benbasat [6] developed a refined instrument intended to measure individual and organizational perceptions of adopting an IT innovation. Two more attributes, image and voluntariness of use, were added to the original five constructs by Moore and Benbasat [6]. "Image" refers to "...the degree to which use of an innovation is perceived to enhance one's image or status in one's social system" [3, p. 195] and "voluntariness of use" refers to "...the degree to which the use of the innovation is perceived as being voluntary or of free will" [6, p. 195]. In this study, the Moore and Benbasat formulation was chosen over other rival frameworks such as the "technology acceptance model" (TAM) because of the former's breadth of coverage of adoption attributes. TAM, an adaptation of the Theory of Reasoned Action, puts forth that perceived usefulness and perceived ease of use determine a person's intention to use a system with intention to use mediating the relationship with another variable, actual system use [7]. These two TAM concepts are included in the Moore and Benbasat model as well. Davis et al. [7, 8] referred to the concept of "relative advantage" as "perceived usefulness" within the context of the technology acceptance model, where "perceived usefulness" is understood to mean an end users' perception of the degree to which the new technology could raise their job performance level within their organizations.

In this study, selected items from the instrument of Moore and Benbasat [6] were used and modified to reflect perceptions of representatives who may be involved in the RFID implementation for firms that intend to use RFID in their supply chains. The seven RFID adoption attributes used in this study are the following: (1) relative advantage: the superiority of the new technology over the one it is replacing; (2) compatibility: congruence of the perceptions of the new technology with the existing values, needs, and experiences of potential end users; (3) ease of use: how easy or difficult it is for end users to learn to use the new technology; (4) visibility: how evident the results of using the new technology will be to observers; (5) triability: ability to test the new technology on a pilot basis; (6) image; and (7) result demonstrability (i.e., the ability of the technology to deliver actual results).

2.2 Dependent Variables: RFID System Deployment Outcomes: Operational Efficiency and Market Knowledge Creation

In this study, the construct "operational efficiency" was measured as the mean of the following items [9]: (1) meeting agreed upon costs per unit associated with the trading partner; (2) meeting productivity standards associated with the trading partner; (3) meeting on-time delivery requirements with respect to the trading partner; (4) meeting inventory requirements (finished goods) associated with the trading partner; and (5) responding to the trading partner's other requests. On the other hand, "partner-enabled market knowledge creation" was measured as the mean of the following items: (1) better understand the needs of customers; (2) find better ways of distributing/selling the products; (3) improve service for the end customers; (4) better understand the market segments being served; (5) better understand new and emerging markets; (6) better understand intentions and capabilities of competitors; and (7) develop strategies to compete in the market, that would not have been possible otherwise [9].

2.3 Moderator Variables: IT Infrastructure Integration and Supply Chain Process Integration

IT Infrastructure Integration. IT infrastructure integration is defined as the degree to which a focal firm has established IT capabilities for the consistent and high-velocity transfer of supply chain-related information within and across its boundaries. The formative construct introduced by Patnayakuni, Rai, and Seth [10] was adopted in this study and used both conceptually and in the instrumentation as well. They define IT infrastructure integration in terms of two subconstructs, data consistency and cross-functional SCM application systems integration. The extent to which data has been commonly defined and stored in consistent form in databases linked by supply chain business processes is referred to as data consistency [10]. Data from legacy systems of supply chain trading partners need to be accessed to produce useful, integrated data, and to be able to transport this data into various datawarehouse structures. Cross-functional supply chain management applications systems integration is defined as the level of real-time communication of a hub firm's functional applications that are linked within an SCM context and their exchanges with enterprise resource planning (ERP) and other related interenterprise initiatives like customer relationship management (CRM) applications as well [9].

Supply Chain Process Integration. In this study, supply chain process integration is defined following the construct used by Malhotra et al. [9]: the degree to which a hub firm has integrated the flow of information [11], physical materials [12], and financial information [13] with its value chain trading partners. This formative construct has three subconstruct components: information flow integration, physical flow integration, and financial flow integration [14]. Information flow integration refers to the degree to which a firm exchanges operational, tactical, and strategic information with its supply chain trading partners [9]. The instrument used in this study measures the sharing of production and delivery schedules, performance metrics, demand forecasts, actual sales data, and inventory data, for information flow integration. Physical flow integration refers to the level to which the hub firm uses global optimization with its value chain partners to manage the flow and stocking of materials and finished goods, and is measured in terms of multi-echelon optimization of costs, just-in-time deliveries, joint management of inventory with suppliers and logistics partners, and distribution network configuration for optimal staging of inventory [9]. Financial flow integration is defined as the level to which a hub firm and its trading partners exchange financial resources in a manner driven by workflow events [9]. In this study, the financial flow integration items measure the automatic triggering of both accounts receivables and accounts payables [9].

3 Hypotheses to Be Tested

This study purports to test the following four hypotheses:

H1: The positive relationship between each of the RFID adoption attributes and operational efficiency will be moderated by IT infrastructure integration --- i.e., the higher the level of IT infrastructure integration, the greater the positive relationship between each of the RFID adoption attributes and operational efficiency.

H2: The positive relationship between each of the RFID adoption attributes and market knowledge creation will be moderated by IT infrastructure integration --- i.e., the higher the level of IT infrastructure integration, the greater the positive relationship between each of the RFID adoption attributes and market knowledge creation.

H3: The positive relationship between each of the RFID adoption attributes and operational efficiency will be moderated by supply chain process integration --- i.e., the higher the level of supply chain process integration, the greater the positive relationship between each of the RFID adoption attributes and operational efficiency.

H4: The positive relationship between each of the RFID adoption attributes and market knowledge creation will be moderated by supply chain process integration --- i.e., the higher the level of supply chain process integration, the greater the positive relationship between each of the RFID adoption attributes and market knowledge creation.

4 Methodology

Data for this research study were collected using an online survey questionnaire intended for a more comprehensive study of RFID that covered the following topics: 1) critical success factors for RFID implementation; 2) RFID adoption motivation --- exploitation versus exploration; 3) absorptive capacity attributes associated with RFID use; 4) RFID system outcomes --- operational efficiency versus market knowledge creation; and 5) IT infrastructure integration and supply chain process integration requirements of RFID. Only the section of the study that focuses on RFID adoption attributes and system deployment outcomes is featured in this paper. Members of the Council of Supply Chain Management Professionals (CSCMP) were contacted and invited to participate in the study. A total of 126 firms responded to the relevant section of the study. The low response rate is due to the length and depth of the questionnaire that covered an extensive range of topics.

4.1 Moderated Regression Procedure

Moderated regression analysis tests whether the relationship between two variables changes depending on the value of another variable (i.e., interaction effect) [15].

Regression analysis was conducted to test the hypotheses presented in this study. The moderated regression procedure requires testing first order effects, which in this study, will be referred to as "model 1." A model 1 simple regression tests the direct effects of a predictor variable on a dependent variable. As the independent variable, each of the RFID adoption attributes was regressed against each of the dependent variables, operational efficiency and market knowledge creation. The variance in the dependent variable on account of the independent variable is noted using the R^2 value. Then, the regression procedure testing second order effects is conducted, which will be referred to as "model 2" in this study. A model 2 regression duplicates the model 1 regression equation and adds the product term which includes the hypothesized moderator variable.

It is important to determine how large the change in R^2 should be in order to qualify as "practically significant" or one that should merit serious attention [15]. After conducting a Monte Carlo simulation, Evans [16] stipulated that "...a rough rule would be to take 1% variance explained as the criterion as to whether or not a significant interaction exists in the model...." (p. 320). Empirical and simulation results appear to indicate that a statistically significant R^2 change of about 1 percent to 2 percent demonstrates an effect size worthy of consideration. The results in this study include significant R^2 change values within the range with a maximum value of 6.9 percent and a minimum value of 1.0 percent, which indicate considerable significant moderating effects of IT infrastructure integration and supply chain process integration.

5 Findings

5.1 Moderated Regression Analysis (MRA) Findings

As a first step prior to the actual moderated regression procedure, separate multiple regression runs were conducted with all seven adoption attributes as independent variables for each of the two dependent variables, operational efficiency and market knowledge creation. There were serious multicollinearity issues with all seven independent variables in the two multiple regression models. To solve this problem, the number of independent variables was reduced until the multicollinearity issue disappeared. Only three adoption attributes made it to the final regression models: relative advantage, result demonstrability, and image. Only these three adoption attributes were, therefore, used in the MRA procedure.

The four other adoption attributes, compatibility, ease of use, visibility, and triability were not included in the MRA procedure because of the multicollinearity they introduced in the models. It is interesting to note that in testing an earlier instrument developed by Hurt and Hubbard [17], the authors arrived at the finding that triability and observability, which corresponds to visibility in this study, did not emerge as separate factors. They explained this outcome as having two possibilities: 1) perhaps, there was an instrumentation flaw that resulted in not clearly delineating the two concepts and 2) it is possible, too, that the study participants treated the two attributes as a single concept. Compatibility and ease of use appear to be somewhat related issues also. In the study, compatibility is defined as the congruence of perceptions of the new technology with existing values, needs and experiences of the end users. The familiarity of the users could naturally lead to ease of use of the new technology.

IT Infrastructure Integration Capability as Moderator Variable with Operational Efficiency as a System Outcome. More substantial results are shown here in descending order of importance based on the percent R^2 change resulting from the introduction of a product term, ITIntegrateCat1, in the multiple regression equation. This is the nominal variable that represents the mean of data consistency and cross-functional process integration, the two components of IT infrastructure integration. Tables 1 and 2 show the results of running two regression models: model 1 showing the relationships between the predictor variables and operational efficiency, without the product term and model 2, the regression results with the inclusion of the product term.

Table 1 shows the results with operational efficiency as the dependent variable and IT infrastructure integration capability as a moderator variable. IT infrastructure integration significantly moderates the relationship between the following predictor variables (i.e., RFID adoption attributes) and operational efficiency in descending order of importance: 1) image; 2) result demonstrability; and 3) relative advantage. The table column labelled "% Variance Explained by Moderator with Product Term" indicates the contribution of the product term --- which is the product of the moderator variable, in this case, IT infrastructure integration and the specific predictor variable. And so, for instance, in the case of image, for instance, the product term would be the product of image and IT infrastructure integration (i.e., Image3XIntegrate1). The next column label shows "F Value of Model 2 (degrees of freedom), which means that the F value of model 2 which includes the product term is shown along with the degrees of freedom for that regression model. The significance of the F change from model 1 to model 2 is indicated by the last column.

The relationships between the predictor variables and operational efficiency as moderated by IT infrastructure integration should be interpreted accordingly. Let's take the case of image, again, the predictor variable whose relationship with operational efficiency is significantly moderated to the greatest extent by IT infrastructure integration. About 62.4 percent of the variance in operational efficiency is explained by image and IT infrastructure integration as indicated by model 1 in Table 1. Model 2 is, then, introduced by including the product term (i.e., Image3XIntegrate1) which represents the interaction between image and IT infrastructure integration. As shown on Table 1, the addition of the product term resulted in an R^2 change of .069, $F(3,120) = 90.436$, p<.000. This result supports the presence of a moderating effect. In other words, the moderating effect of IT infrastructure integration explains 6.9 percent of the variance in the increase of operational efficiency over and above the variance explained by image and IT infrastructure integration as separate independent variables.

Table 1. MRA for Operational Efficiency with IT Infrastructure Integration as Moderator

Independent Variables: Selected RFID Adoption Attributes (N=126)					
Dependent Variable: Operational Efficiency					
Moderator: ITIntegrateCat1 (Nominal variable for product term)					
RFID Adoption Attributes	Model 1: R^2 Without Product Term	Model 2: R^2 With Product Term	% Variance Explained by Moderator with Product Term	F Value of Model 2 (degrees of freedom)	Significance of F Change
Relative Advantage	.780	.804	2.4%	166.351 (3, 122)	p<.000
Result Demonstrability	.730	.760	3.0%	126.405 (3, 120)	p<.000
Image	.624	.693	6.9%	90.436 (3, 120)	p<.000

Supply Chain Process Integration as Moderator Variable with Operational Efficiency as a System Outcome. Table 2 shows the results with operational efficiency as the dependent variable and supply chain process integration capability as the moderator variable. Supply chain process integration significantly moderates the relationship between the following predictor variables and operational efficiency in descending order of importance: (1) image; (2) result demonstrability; and (3) relative advantage.

Table 2. MRA for Operational Efficiency with Supply Chain Process Integration as Moderator

Independent Variables: Selected RFID Adoption Attributes (N=126)					
Dependent Variable: Operational Efficiency					
Moderator: SCMIntegrateCat1 (Nominal variable for product term)					
RFID Adoption Attributes	Model 1: R^2 Without Product Term	Model 2: R^2 With Product Term	% Variance Explained by Moderator with Product Term	F Value of Model 2 (degrees of freedom)	Significance of F Change
Relative Advantage	.778	.788	1.0%	151.343 (3,122)	p<.000
Result Demonstrability	.733	.751	1.8%	120.396 (3,120)	p<.000
Image	.627	.669	4.2%	80.910 (3,120)	p<.000

About 62.7 percent of the variance in operational efficiency is explained by image and supply chain process integration as indicated by model 1 in Table 2. Model 2 is, then, introduced by including the product term (i.e., Image3XIntegrate2) which represents the interaction between image and supply chain process integration. As shown

on Table 2, the addition of the product term resulted in an R^2 change of 4.2 percent, $F(3,120) = 80.910$, $p<.000$. This result supports the presence of a moderating effect. In other words, the moderating effect of supply chain process integration explains 4.2 percent of the variance in the increase of operational efficiency over and above the variance explained by image and supply chain process integration as separate independent variables.

IT Integration Capability as Moderator Variable with Market Knowledge Creation as a System Outcome. Table 3 shows the results with market knowledge creation as the dependent variable and IT infrastructure integration as the moderator variable. IT infrastructure integration significantly moderates the relationship between the following predictor variables and market knowledge in descending order of importance: (1) image; (2) result demonstrability; and (3) relative advantage.

Table 3. MRA for Market Knowledge Creation with IT Infrastructure Integration as Moderator

Independent Variables: Selected RFID Adoption Attributes (N=126)					
Dependent Variable: Market Knowledge Creation					
Moderator: ITIntegrateCat1 (Nominal variable for product term)					
RFID Adoption Attributes	Model 1: R^2 Without Product Term	Model 2: R^2 With Product Term	% Variance Explained by Moderator with Product Term	F Value of Model 2 (degrees of freedom)	Significance of F Change
Relative Advantage	.670	.697	2.7%	93.500 (3,122)	p<.000
Result Demonstrability	.680	.716	3.6%	100.982 (3,120)	p<.000
Image	.607	.660	5.3%	77.602 (3,120)	p<.000

About 60.7 percent of the variance in market knowledge creation is explained by image and IT infrastructure integration as indicated by model 1 in Table 3. Model 2 is, then, introduced by including the product term (i.e., Image3XIntegrate1) which represents the interaction between image and IT infrastructure integration. As shown on Table 3, the addition of the product term resulted in an R^2 change of .053 or 5.3 percent, $F(3, 120) = 77.602$, $p<.000$. This result supports the presence of a moderating effect. In other words, the moderating effect of IT infrastructure integration explains 5.3 percent of the variance in the increase of market knowledge creation over and above the variance explained by image and IT infrastructure integration as separate independent variables.

Supply Chain Process Integration as Moderator Variable with Market Knowledge Creation as a System Outcome. Table 4 shows the results with market knowledge creation as the dependent variable and supply chain process integration as the moderator variable. Supply chain process integration significantly moderates the relationship between the following predictor variables and market knowledge in descending order of importance: (1) image; (2) result demonstrability; and (3) relative advantage. About 63.5 percent of the variance in market knowledge creation is explained by image and supply chain process integration as indicated by model 1 in Table 4. Model 2 is, then, introduced by including the product term (i.e., Image3XIntegrate2) which represents the interaction between image and supply chain process integration. As shown on Table 4, the addition of the product term resulted in an R^2 change of .034 or 3.4 percent, F(3,120) = 80.678, p<.000. This result supports the presence of a moderating effect. In other words, the moderating effect of supply chain process integration explains 3.4 percent of the variance in the increase of market knowledge creation over and above the variance explained by image and supply chain process integration as separate independent variables.

Table 4. MRA for Market Knowledge Creation with Supply Chain Process Integration as Moderator

Independent Variables: Selected RFID Adoption Attributes (N=126)					
Dependent Variable: Market Knowledge Creation					
Moderator: SCMIntegrateCat1 (Nominal variable for product term)					
RFID Adoption Attributes	Model 1: R^2 Without Product Term	Model 2: R^2 With Product Term	% Variance Explained by Moderator with Product Term	F Value of Model 2 (degrees of freedom)	Significance of F Change
Relative Advantage	.682	.694	1.2%	92.084 (3,122)	p<.000
Result Demonstrability	.703	.716	1.3%	100.744 (3, 120)	p<.000
Image	.635	.669	3.4%	80.678 (3,120)	p<.000

5.2 Conclusion and Future Research Directions

All four proposed hypotheses were partially supported in this study. Both variables, IT infrastructure integration and supply chain process integration, moderate the relationships between selected RFID adoption attributes and the two dependent variables examined in this study, operational efficiency and market knowledge creation. Between the two moderator variables, however, IT infrastructure integration tempered a greater degree of the variance between selected RFID adoption attributes (i.e., image, result demonstrability, and relative advantage) in a fairly consistent pattern and the dependent variables, operational efficiency and market knowledge creation. Future research efforts should investigate firms that have implemented RFID in their supply chains and validate the actual impact of IT infrastructure integration and supply chain process integration.

References

1. Angeles, R.: Anticipated IT Infrastructure and Supply Chain Process Integration Capabilities for RFID and Their Associated Deployment Outcomes. Intl. J. of Info. Mgt. 3, 219–231 (2009)
2. Angeles, R.: Anticipated IT Infrastructure and Supply Chain Process Integration Capabilities for RFID and Their Associated Deployment Outcomes. In: Proceedings of the ACM iiWAS Workshops: ERPAS 2008: Business and Service Model, pp. 634–646 (2008)

3. Angeles, R.: Moderated Multiple Regression of Absorptive Capacity Attributes and Deployment Outcomes: The Importance of RFID IT Infrastructure Integration and Supply Chain Process Integration. Intl. J. of Info. Sys. and SCM 3, 25–51 (2010)
4. Fichman, R.G.: Information Technology Diffusion: A Review of Empirical Research. In: Proceedings 13th International Conference on Information Systems, Dallas, Texas, pp. 195–206 (1992)
5. Rogers, E.M.: Diffusion of Innovations. Free Press, New York (1983)
6. Moore, G.C., Benbasat, I.: Development of an Instrument to Measure the Perceptions of Adopting an Information Technology Innovation. Info. Sys. Res. 2(3), 192–222 (1991)
7. Davis, F.D.: Perceived Usefulness, Perceived Ease of Use, and User Acceptance of Information Technology. MIS Q. 13(3), 319–339 (1989)
8. Davis, F.D., Bagozzi, R.P., Warshaw, P.R.: User Acceptance of Computer Technology: A Comparison of Two Theoretical Models. Mgt. Sc. 35, 982–1003 (1989)
9. Malhotra, A., Gosain, S., El Sawy, O.A.: Absorptive Capacity Configurations in Supply Chains: Gearing for Partner-Enabled Market Knowledge Creation. MIS Q. 29(1), 145–187 (2005)
10. Patnayakuni, R., Rai, A., Seth, N.: Relational Antecedents of Information Flow Integration for Supply Chain Coordination. MIS Q. 23(1), 13–49 (2006)
11. Lee, H.L., Padmanabhan, V., Whang, S.: The Bullwhip Effect in Supply Chains. Sloan. Mgt. Rev. 38(3), 93–102 (1997)
12. Stevens, G.C.: Successful Supply Chain Management. Mgt. Dec. 28(8), 25–30 (1990)
13. Mabert, V.A., Venkatraman, M.A.: Special Research Focus on Supply Chain Linkages: Challenges for Design and Management in The 21st Century. Dec. Scs. 29(3), 537–550 (1998)
14. Mangan, J., Lalwani, C., Butcher, T.: Global Logistics and Supply Chain Management. John Wiley & Sons, Hoboken (2008)
15. Aguinis, H.: Regression Analysis for Categorical Moderators. Guilford Press, New York (2004)
16. Evans, M.G.: A Monte Carlo Study of the Effects of Correlated Method Variance in Moderated Multiple Regression Analysis. Orgl. Beh. and Human Dec. Proc. 36, 302–323 (1985)
17. Hurt, H., Hubbard, R.: The Systematic Measurement of the Perceived Characteristics Of Information Technologies: Microcomputers as Innovations. In: Proceedings of The ICA Annual Conference, Montreal, Quebec (May 1987)

Supporting the Operation of Semi-structured Work Systems

Jose Faria[1], Joao Silva[2], and Helder Marques[3]

[1] Assistant Professor, University of Porto - Faculty of Engineering
Institute for Systems and Robotics
jfaria@fe.up.pt
[2] Researcher, University of Porto - Faculty of Engineering
joao.silva@fe.up.pt
[3] Researcher, University of Porto - Faculty of Engineering
helder.marques@fe.up.pt

Abstract. A semi-structured work system (SSWS) combines business processes and activities with different specification levels, from highly structured workflow processes to loosely structured collaborative activities. In the first part of the paper, the fundamental concepts regarding business process management systems are reviewed in order to highlight their shortcomings as far as the management of SSWS is concerned. The second part of the paper discusses the requirements of information systems targeted to support effectively the activity of SSWS. The final part of the paper introduces a system that was developed accordingly to those requirements and the preliminary results of their application.

Keywords: Business process management, workflow systems, loosely structured processes, semi-structured work systems.

1 Introduction

Nowadays, business process management (BPM) is widely recognized as a main approach for organizational analysis and design. In fact, as stated in [1], business process thinking is becoming mainstream thinking. The roots for this may be found in three main strands of management: quality management (QM), workflow management systems (WFMS) and business process re-engineering (BPR), that act together to make business process concepts, approaches and tools ubiquitous elements in business management and information systems design.

QM is mainly concerned with customer satisfaction and quality assurance, i.e., the guarantee that the products and services provided to the clients are in conformance with their specification. In the context of QM, process analysis is mainly employed to identify the operations involved in the provision of a product or service, and to identify the potential causes of non-conformity at the output. Once identified, these causes are systematically eliminated through the continuous improvement of products, processes and services. WFM mainly seeks the improvement of organization efficiency through work automation, whereas BPR seeks dramatic improvements on efficiency and effectiveness through a radical redesign of business processes.

J.E. Quintela Varajão et al. (Eds.): CENTERIS 2010, Part II, CCIS 110, pp. 416–425, 2010.

The distinctive feature of the BPM approach stays on the fact that organizations are analyzed and designed as a set of interacting cross-functional processes, instead of a set of functional departments. Processes analysis is an effective way to get a global understanding of the operations of complex organization and discover its "hidden" aspects where, very often, lie the opportunities to improve. BPM also offers an integrated framework for the organizational analysis, design, control, management and improvement that eliminates (or at least shortens) the gap between business analysis and information system design.

WFMS are the primarily solution to support the execution of business processes. Initially introduced in the office environments, WFMS have evolved from document flow automation to fully support of the entire business processes life cycle [2]. Underlying the workflow approach is the idea that the formalization of business processes into prescriptive workflow models that are managed automatically by a computer system provides significant gains in productivity, faster communications throughout the entire organization, easier execution control, more expedite treatment of exceptions, and automatic performance assessment.

A typical workflow application guides users through the task at hand and provides the context for the execution of each task. In cross functional processes of large organizations, this is a fundamental advantage because users just have to know the few steps they execute and do not need to understand the process in its entirety. Particularly, newcomers will be able to execute their specific tasks without having to know the global process.

However, experience also shows that these assumptions not always hold true and that workflow systems may not be the better solution to support the execution of a business process, as it is discussed hereafter.

WFMS are based on a *mechanistic* view of the business processes. In fact, a process model is seen as a deterministic algorithm, such that the execution of the predefined sequence of steps leads to the accomplishment of the process goal. However, as remarked in [3], certain types of work do not posses such a deterministic behavior and cannot be formalized well enough to safely entrust an enterprise application.

This may happen because the business goals, the internal structure and the work methods of an organization change too quickly over time and workflow applications cannot keep that pace of change. Also, the detailed process steps and their sequencing are not known in advance and differ from instance to instance. This is typically the case when the work that needs to be done is mainly determined by the intended outcome, rather than the process itself. Typical examples are requirements analysis or request for proposal processes.

These considerations are particularly true for highly specialized knowledge based processes, such as those mentioned in [4], where the execution of each instance depends on the skills, experience, and judgment of the primary actors. In [5] these processes are denoted as *artful* processes in the sense that there is an art to their execution that would be extremely difficult, if not impossible, to codify in an enterprise application.

Another fundamental assumption of WFMS stays on the idea that here is *a single best way* of executing a process, which is codified in the process model, and that it is possible to find such optimal model through an a priori process analysis, performed before the execution of the process actually takes place. Our field experience with knowledge based processes also contradicts this idea. In fact, we see that the previous knowledge about a process is often incomplete and that it is not possible to determine, a priori, the optimal process model. Instead, the model *emerges* a posteriori from the continued observation of the process instances, an observation that reveals hidden aspects and highlight best practices that are not perceived in advance.

2 Business Processes Supporting Systems

As discussed above, when a business process consists on a pre-defined sequence of steps whose alternative paths and exceptions are known in advance, the most effective solution to support its execution will be a WFMS (figure 1.a). In a typical workflow application, task creation and assignment is managed automatically by the computer system, as well as all the interactions between the people involved in the process are mediated by the computer system. Also the structure of the content of the process, namely documents that are produced during its execution is also predefined. Therefore, workflow solutions fit well with business processes having a high number of instances and whose execution can be strictly specified. In these circumstances, the implementation of a workflow system will certainly boost productivity.

Specialized knowledge based processes require a different approach. These processes involve a lot collaboration and intensive interaction between the people involved. The detailed work content is often decided *on the fly* depending on the situated evaluation of the process by the people involved. Process steps do not have *crisp* boundaries in terms of responsibility and starting and ending points. Everyone involved should be aware of the process global state, not only on the specific tasks assigned to them as in WFMS.

WFMS lack the degree of flexibility required to effectively support loosely structured processes and this hampers their widespread use as business processes supporting systems. In recent years, there have been many attempts to introduce more flexibility into workflow systems (see, for example, [6], [7] and [8]).

Case management systems (CMS) are flexible computer systems that are often employed to support the execution of such loosely structured processes. A typical CMS offers a number of shared resources such as a task manager; a shared repository for documents; ad hoc communication tools, e.g., instant messaging, blogs, and news; along with several other tools and utilities, e.g., agenda and wiki.

Yet highly flexible, CMS also present important drawbacks regarding the support of business processes. In a CMS, tasks, documents and notifications are explicitly (and manually) created by the users without having to comply to a pre-defined structure (figure 1.b). If this improves flexibility, it also reduces efficiency because it is much more prone to errors, and hampers the controllability of the processes.

Also the reuse of the knowledge generated within each process instance becomes much more difficult. In fact, the lack of a pre-defined content structure makes more difficult to browse through the processes' content and automatically gather relevant information from different process instances, which is a fundamental requirement in the context of knowledge based processes.

In our view, WFMS and CMS do not offer an effective solution to support semi-structured work systems containing loosely structured processes. Instead of trying to introduce more flexibility in WFMS or more structure in CMS, we advocate that a new synthesis of methods and tools should be looked for and give rise to a new class of business process supporting systems specifically targeted to semi-structured work systems. The central ideas underlying these systems will be discussed below and the interested reader may found additional information on this topic in [9], [10] and [11].

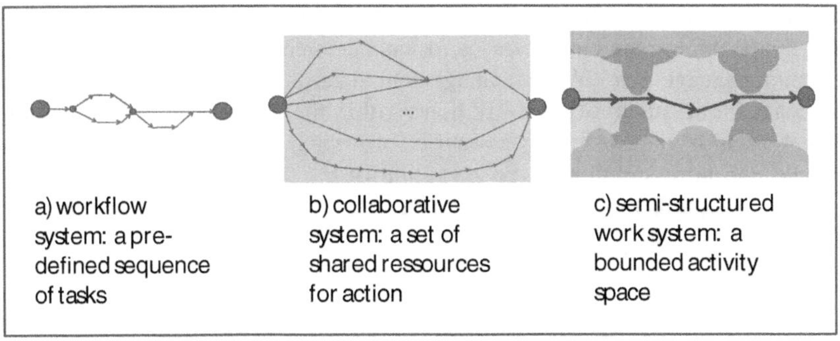

Fig. 1. Work supporting systems

In a loosely structured process, the work is governed by a set of rules of different nature from organizational policies, to operational procedures and mandatory constraints [12]. Figure 1.c illustrates how work is managed in a loosely structured process. The execution of the process is bounded by a set of constraints imposed by the organization. Some of them are mandatory (hard constraints), whereas other are recommendations corresponding to best practices (soft constraints). In this context, the process model is not intended to prescribe the detailed execution of the process, as in WFMS, but should be seen as a reference model that provides guidance to the actors involved in the process.

From the observation of the activity, work patterns are likely to emerge [13]. A pattern may include structure (process steps), user roles and contents describing the operational procedures and methods. Patterns are a way of sharing best practices and progressively promote work standardization. This way, a semi-structured work system could be seen as an intermediate stage in a progressive evolution, from a unstructured system to a mature one where, ideally, all the processes will be fully defined and standardized.

However, more work specification does not always mean higher organizational maturity. In fact, some processes and activities are not prone to a fully standardization and should remain semi-structured, e.g., new product development, engineering projects, processes involving inquiries and investigations, etc.

Several other reasons may justify the adoption of a semi-structured approach. Examples are (i) the number of instances of the process is small and does not justify the development of a dedicated workflow application, (ii) the goals and the operational methods change too quickly overt time and (iii) there are multiple exceptions in the execution of the process ("the exception is the rule") and so it will not be feasible to create a full model of the process.

3 Semi-Structured Work Supporting Systems

We see a business supporting system as a tool for structured collaboration, i.e., the supporting system organizes and structures the collaboration accordingly to the model of the process, but it does not control the execution of the work as a WFMS would do. In order to be effective, the supporting system should offer a set of tools and features belonging to three main categories: work management, information management and interaction management. Work management regards the planning, control, log and performance assessment of the work done within the work system. Information management regards the storing, versioning, browsing and searching of the contents produced and accessed during the execution of the processes' instances. Interaction management regards the communication between the actors involved in the execution of the processes.

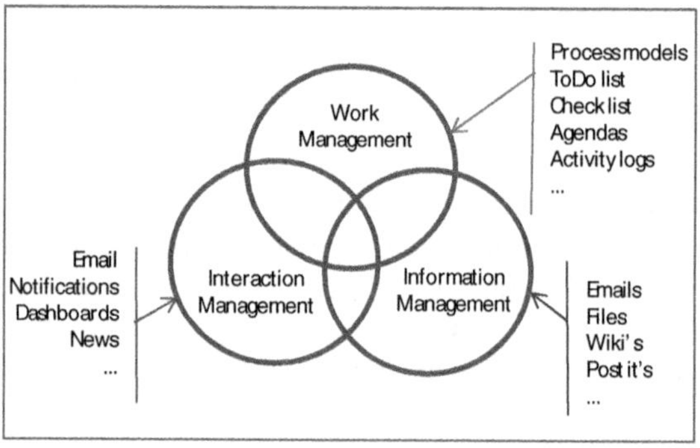

Fig. 2. Main functionalities of SSWS supporting systems

A full discussion of the features relating these three groups of functionalities is out of the scope of this paper. Hereafter, we will just present a brief discussion of the main requirements for the SSWS supporting systems.

Work management tools: As stressed before, a SSWS contains processes with different specifications levels and the same process model may lead to very different control strategies. If the model has a prescriptive nature, then the processes may be managed by a workflow system where the major user interface is the task list automatically managed by the computer system. If, however, the model just provides guidance and does not strictly prescribe the steps of the process, an interface based on a check list is a more effective control approach, because it provides control without imposing a strict ordering upon the process tasks. On the other hand, it transfers part of the control of the process from the computer system to the users.

A combination of these two approaches may also be considered. Some tasks may be automatically created by the computer systems depending on the status of the process, whereas others may be managed manually. Some dependencies between the steps of the process may be specified so that some tasks on the check list are activated or deactivated depending on the process state. An effective supporting system for a

SSWS should offer task management tools able to support processes presenting different levels of specification.

Information management tools: Loosely structured processes are typically knowledge intensive processes, where knowledge is simultaneously an input and an output of the process. A piece of knowledge produced in a given process step, e.g., a document such as a proposal, a contract or a requirements specification, will certainly be accessed in later steps of the process. However, it is very likely that the artifacts and knowledge produced within a process instance be also re-used outside its boundaries.

During the execution of a process instance, it is very important to provide easy access to the documents produced by the process. However, those documents often have a value *per se* and so, once the processes are finished, it should be possible to browse, re-arrange and recombine the documents associated to different instances of the process. In order to allow this kind of flexibility, documents and contents should not be attached directly to the processes' instances, as it often happens in WFMS. Instead, there should be independent hierarchies for process instances and documents. This way, it will be possible to provide easy access to the relevant documents during process execution and, at the same time, offer knowledge browsing and management from the outside of the process.

Very often, the set of instances of a given process share a number of reference documents, such as, procedures and work instructions, internal and external regulations, etc. Also, it often happens that a particular set of instances share a number of common documents. For example, the minutes of a management meeting or an email message may contain information relevant to several instances.

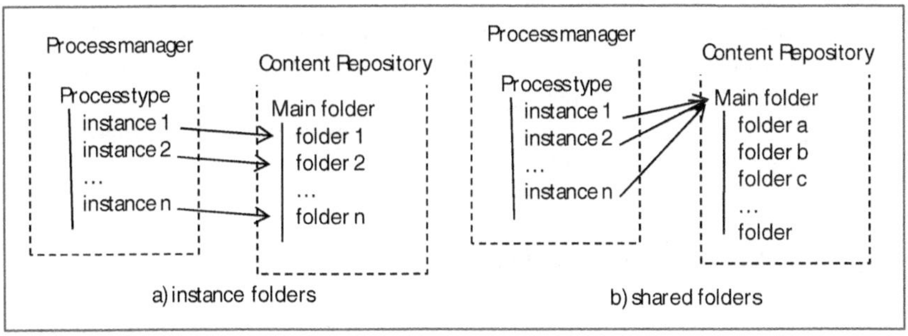

Fig. 3. Association modes between process instances and document repository

A SSWS supporting system should be flexible enough to accommodate different associations between the process instances and the folders of document repository. Two association modes are represented in figure 3. In figure 3.a, there is a folder for each process instance, which is created automatically each time a new process instance is created. When the process is invoked at the user interface, the system will provided direct access to the corresponding documents. In figure 3.b, there is a single association to a common top folder shared by all the instances to the process type, and the subfolders are explicitly created by the users. They may decide to create a subfolder (i) for a particular instance, (ii) for common documents or (iii) for a particular subset of instances that share their documents. In this implementation, when a process instance is invoked, the user interface will point to the top folder and it is up to the users to browse from the top folder and find the particular content they need.

Interaction management tools: Interaction management is the third functional dimension of SSWS supporting systems. Here, we distinguish between low and high level interaction tools. Low level tools offer basic communication services such as email, instant messaging and notifications. High level interactions include structured communications tools such as debates, blogs and wikis.

In this paper, just low level interaction tools will be considered. They mostly deal with the sending and publishing of messages that help users keep aware of the current status of the processes in which they are involved, particularly on the tasks assigned to them. In a typically WFMS notifications are, for the most part, generated and sent automatically by the computer system. This may lead to an overload of messages with little or no value at all to the users. In a SSWS, a higher flexibility is needed so that actors may decide on the content of the messages as well as on when, to whom, and how messages should be sent.

In order to analyze the interactions that take place within a work system the following framework may be considered:

- The *events* that should be notified, e.g., task assignment and completion, new document upload, document or schedule update, etc.
- The *channels* that will be used to convey the information, e.g., email, notification list or dashboard panel.
- The *target* of the information, i.e., the people to which the information is relevant, e.g., a specific actor, the people involve on a particular process instance, those involved in similar instances, etc.
- The *content* of the message, which may be created automatically, edited by the user or a combination of both. In this case, the computer system creates a base message that can be edited by the user before it is sent.
- The *dispatch* method of the messages, which may be performed automatically by the computer system, or confirmed by the user.

4 Supporting System Prototype

A first prototype of a SSWS supporting system was developed accordingly to the ideas discussed above. It is currently being used at the Technical and Maintenance Department of a large service organization where it supports a large range of processes and activities from equipment maintenance to project management.

Some of the processes are highly structured, whereas others are much loosely defined: preventive maintenance is a typical example for highly structured processes, whereas equipment deployment and preventive maintenance are examples for loosely structured processes. It may also happen that, within the same process, some stages are highly specified whereas others are loosely defined. For example, the management of a complex project involving the acquisition of equipments and services from external suppliers, contains rather prescriptive stages regarding contracting and payment, where the work instructions are fully specified. On the contrary, the stages concerning the physical provision of the service have a much lower specification level. Here, managers have much more room to plan and conduct the work accordingly to the characteristics and goals of each specific process instance.

As each system user has to manage both prescriptive and non prescriptive processes, the supporting information system should be able to support multiple processes with different specification levels, a kind of flexibility that conventional business processes management systems do not offer.

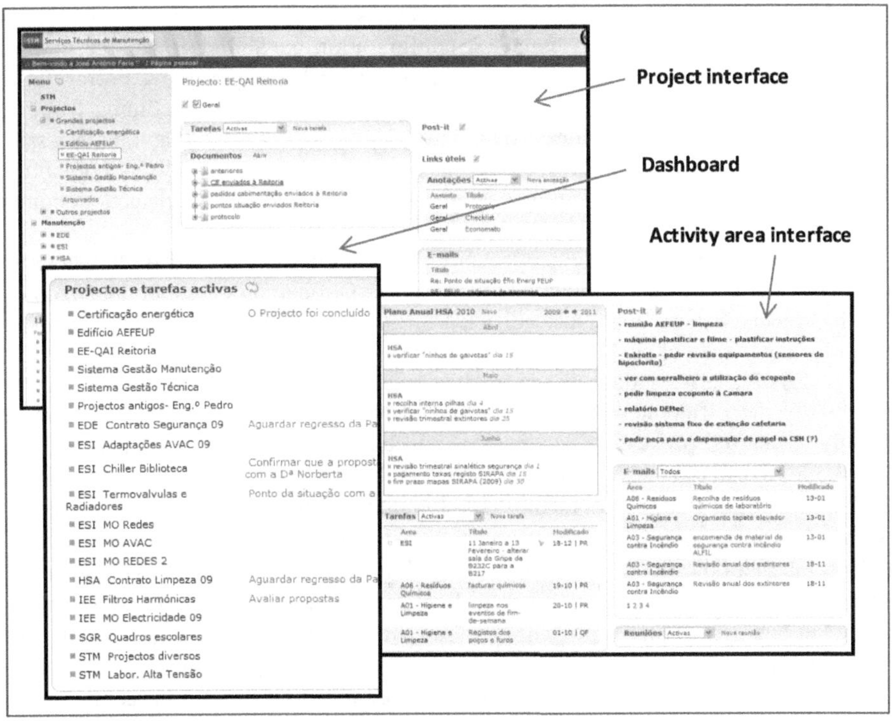

Fig. 4. SSWS supporting system prototype

Figure 4 shows three snapshots of the user interface. The system offers several interfaces conceived for each particular activity type, e.g., project management, maintenance management, technical management and expenditures management. Each interface gathers all the contents relevant to the execution of a particular process or activity, e.g., document folders, meeting minutes, task list, notes and emails. Information maintained in databases may also be combined in the same user interfaces with other types of content. The system includes dashboards where information from different processes is gathered in order to provide a monitoring of the ongoing activities. Also, several automatic and semi-automatic interaction mechanisms were implemented to ensure that concerned users are notified about process status and content updates.

5 Conclusions

As it was discussed in the paper, we are looking for a new synthesis of concepts and tools having in mind the operational support of SSWS. Many of those concepts and tools may be found in existing systems. From workflow systems, we retained the idea of a process model that frames the work to be done, the automatic management of that work (task creation and assignment, sending of notifications, logging of events, performance assessment) and the provision to each user of a suitable context to perform its tasks. As in collaborative systems, we offer a set of general purpose tools that are available to users, as well as extended configuration capabilities in order to adapt system interfaces to the specific requirements of each process type. From content management systems, we hold the idea of aggregation of contents coming from different sources (e.g., file folders, data bases and email tools) that are accessible through the same browsing tools, as well as user interfaces adapted to individual user profiles. Finally, from document management systems, we took the ideas of document classification, searching and versioning.

A first prototype was developed according to the ideas discussed in the paper and is currently in use. It offers integrated work, information and interaction management, and has received very positive feedback from the users. However there is plenty of room for new research and development regarding the analysis, design and support of SSWS. Firstly, new modelling and analysis methods are needed in order to capture effectively the different types of rules and constraints that govern the execution of loosely structured processes. Secondly, it will be necessary to develop process managers able to execute those models and manage the associated contents.

Another topic that needs further development is the integrated development of people and processes. The execution of knowledge based processes with intensive human interactions should not ignore the individual persons, with their idiosyncratic characteristics, who actually perform it. Process models may be stable at an abstract level, but key execution details will certainly differ from instance to instance depending on the individuals or the small-teams that actually perform them.

Our field observations often show that the formalization of a business process and the implementation of a corresponding support system not only change the operational procedures but also causes fundamental changes on people beliefs and behaviors. These changes often "open the door" to new developments at the process model or the support system that were unfeasible in a first moment. This is an idea very close to that of the *learning organization* introduced in [14]. Learning is associated with changes in the work methods and operational procedures, but also with deeper changes on people mental models, behaviors and beliefs. In other words, if processes are changed and improved by people, the introduction of new a work process will change the mind of the people involved in its execution. These changes will, in turn, offer the conditions to introduce new improvements on the process.

The main objective of our research activity is the development of a unified approach for the analysis, design and management of work systems containing processes with different degrees of specification, together with a set of modelling, analysis and management tools. Such approach will allow learning organizations to move seamlessly their work systems along the specification axis and embrace such virtuous cycle towards higher organizational maturity levels.

References

1. Sharp, A., McDermott, P.: Workflow modelling: tools for process improvement and application development. Artech House, Boston (2001)
2. van der Aalst, W.: Business Process Management Demystified: A Tutorial on Models, Systems and Standards for Workflow Management. In: Desel, J., Reisig, W., Rozenberg, G. (eds.) ACPN 2003. LNCS, vol. 3098, pp. 1–65. Springer, Heidelberg (2004)
3. Alter, S.: Service system fundamentals: Work system, value chain, and life cycle. IBM Systems Journal 47(1) (2008)
4. Bider, I.: State-Oriented Business Process Modeling: Principles, Theory and Practice, PhD Thesis, Royal Institute of Technology and Stockholm University, Sweden (2004)
5. Hill, C., Yates, R., Jones, C., Kogan, S.L.: Beyond predictable workflows: Enhancing productivity in artful business processes. IBM Systems Journal 45(4) (2006)
6. Mangan, P., Sadiq, S.: A constraint specification approach to building flexible workflows. Journal of Research and Practice in Information Technology 35(1), 21–39 (2003)
7. van der Aalst, W., Adams, M., Ter Hofstede, A., Pesic, M., Schonenberg, H.: Flexibility as a service. In: Chen, L., Liu, C., Liu, Q., Deng, K. (eds.) DASFAA 2009. LNCS, vol. 5667, pp. 319–333. Springer, Heidelberg (2009)
8. Kammer, P., Bolcer, G., Taylor, R., Hitomi, A., Bergman, M.: Techniques for supporting dynamic and adaptive workflow. Computer Supported Cooperative Work: An International Journal 9(3), 269–292 (2000)
9. Jørgensen, H.D.: Interaction as a Framework for Flexible Workflow Modelling. In: ACM GROUP 2001, Colorado, USA, September 30-October (2001)
10. Dustdar, S.: Caramba—A Process-Aware Collaboration System Supporting Ad hoc and Collaborative Processes in Virtual Teams. Distributed and Parallel Databases 15, 45–66 (2004)
11. Andersson, B., Bider, I., Perjons, E.: Business Process Support as a Basis for Computerized Knowledge Management. In: Althoff, K.-D., Dengel, A.R., Bergmann, R., Nick, M., Roth-Berghofer, T.R. (eds.) WM 2005. LNCS (LNAI), vol. 3782, pp. 542–553. Springer, Heidelberg (2005)
12. Pesic, M., Schonenberg, H., Van Der Aalst, W.: DECLARE: Full Support for Loosely-Structured Processes. In: 11th IEEE International Enterprise Distributed Object Computing Conference (2007)
13. Moody, P., Gruen, D., Muller, M., Tang, J., Moran, T.: Business activity patterns: A new model for collaborative business applications. IBM Systems Journal 45(4) (2006)
14. Senge, P.: The fifth Discipline: the art and practice of the learning organisation. Random House, UK (2007)

Ontology: An Analysis of the Literature

Joselice Ferreira Lima[1,2],
Cléia M. Gomes Amaral[3], and Luís Fernando R. Molinaro[1]

[1] University of Brasilia (UnB) Campus Darcy Ribeiro, Brasília – Brazil 70910-900
[2] Federal Institute of Technology North of Minas Gerais (IFTNMG)
[3] Pontifical Catholic University of Minas Gerais (PUC Minas)
Joselice.f.lima@gmail.com, cleiamga@hotmail.com,
Molinaro@nmi.unb.br

Abstract. This work features a literature review about the ontology. From a study of literature are identified the types, methodologies, tools and languages used in the development of ontological tools. The result is an overview of the literature with definitions about ontologies in the area of computational systems, and the perception of researchers about the problems concerning the activity of creating and use of ontological tools. It is noticed that applications involving ontologies are significantly to academic conceptual and to create prototypes .

Keywords: ontology, concepts, literature review.

1 Introduction

The consulted literature consists of journal articles most cited in the area of ontologies and computer system in the period from 1990 to 2009, mostly in English. These studies show that the ontology have a crucial role in mapping the information, reason why it is studied by several research areas. The ontology is a subject that is growing in academic activity to improve the principles to show the modeling of domain in the specifical area and using these models to boost the functioning of information systems.

In [3] the authors claim about the relationship between science and ontology, focusing on the vision domain of knowledge: "While the role of science is to explain the nature, the role of ontology would describe, organize and systematize the knowledge gained by scientific discoveries".

In [23] the authors argue that a computer scientist, to build complex information systems and conceptual models need to examine the environments in which they will operate in arrangement of the data and knowledge they will return. In order to be understandable and reusable, these models must combine with formal semantics precision and cognitive transparency and effectiveness, since it incorporates more sophisticated and heterogeneous modeling paradigms. The ontology is presented as an emerging resource that has enormous potential to improve the information understanding and absorption for their organization and management [9,10].

In [16] it defines ontology as a specification of a conceptualization: a description of concepts and relationships that exist in a domain of interest.

J.E. Quintela Varajão et al. (Eds.): CENTERIS 2010, Part II, CCIS 110, pp. 426–435, 2010.

The aim of this paper is to provide a review of the literature on ontology involving concepts, application, types and life cycle, particularly addressing the most cited in computation and systems of information because there are a scarcity in the literature of standardized definitions and specifical terms. Thus, this research is classified as exploratory, as its purpose is to clarify the concepts and ideas, and provides an overview of this issue in the context of computing.

The paper is structured in 3 sections: firstly the introduction, which presents the research context. The second section presents the understanding of most cited authors on the subject, describes the ontology development methodologies, the tools and languages, showing the life cycle of an ontology. Finally the third section concludes with remarks on the literature.

2 Understanding the Concept of Ontology

The term ontology comes from the Greek ontos (being) and logos (word). Although the study of being have their roots in studies of Aristotle and Plato, the use of the term ontology to describe this branch of philosophy is much more recent, having been introduced between the seventeenth and eighteenth centuries by German philosophers. According to [37] The term was coined in 1613 by Rudolf Goclenius.

In [17] states that "An ontology is an explicit specification of a conceptualization. In computing, ontology is a technical term that denotes an artifact that is designed for one purpose, which can be used to allow the modeling of knowledge about some domain, real or imaginary. In his article Ontology (2009), [21] made a further clarification of his definition, making the essential points of this new definition of ontology the objects, concepts and other entities that are supposed to exist in some area of interest. It is the relationships between them. Analysing, an ontology defines (specifies) the concepts, relationships and other distinctions that are relevant for modeling a domain. The specification takes the form of vocabulary and of representational definitions (classes, relations, and so on), which provide meaning to formal vocabulary limitations on its consistent use.

In [31] the subject ontology is the study of categories of things that exist or may exist in some domain. Basically, an ontology consists of concepts and their relations, their definitions, properties and constraints that are described in the form of axioms.

Different definitions provide different views on the same reality. In [8] it comments that some of the perceived problems in the literature on ontology of information systems are merely terminological. The development of a specifical ontology requires defining a set of concepts and their relationships. Some authors provide definitions depending on the process and the construction, regardless of its use in applications. Although there is no consensus on the concept of ontology, several studies have been conducted [8,17,18, 21,22, 23, 24, 31,32] in terms of definition concept systems, covering its definition, application and development methodologies, tools, mapping, reuse and others elements . Thus, [8] comments that ontologists in the area of information systems are influenced by the experience of working in semantic networks, which formal structure imposes a division of all entities (or whatever is represented) in two main categories: concepts, represented by points, relationships between concepts represented by links. From there a third category was introduced, when it became clear that not only the concepts have to be represented, but also the properties of concepts, once concepts, also known as classes, are used in a broad sense. They can be abstract or concrete, elementary or composite, real or imaginary. Finally, a concept can be anything about which something is said, and therefore could also be a description of a task, function, action, strategy.

2.1.1 Types of Ontologies

The reason of differences in definitions can be based on the nature (types or classifications) derived from the forms of their applications. Next examples of the types of ontologies in the literature are presented. In [35] on the degree of formality- they are freely expressed in natural language. In [26] on the application - written in one language and then converted for use in various systems, reusing it. In [14] on the degree of genericity – it defines the primitive of representation - as frames, axioms, and other attributes - declaratively. There has been several projects highlighting the types of ontologies.

2.1.2 Nature of Ontologies

There are several proposed classification of the term ontology. The most often cited in literature, according to [5, 15] will be presented in a simplified manner, namely: Knowledge representation - captures the primitive representation of knowledge formalized in paradigms of knowledge representation [36]; General Ontology (common) - includes vocabulary related to things, events, time, space, causality, function behavior, etc.; [27] Metaontologies - also called "generic ontologies" or Core Ontologies [36], which are reusable in multiple domains; Domain ontologies - are reusable in a given area [27, 36]. Provides a vocabulary of concepts in a domain and their relationships on the activities that occur in this area and on the theories and principles governing that domain elements; Ontology of tasks - provides a systematized vocabulary of terms used to solve problems associated with tasks that may or may not be the same domain [36]; Tasks domain Ontologies - are reusable task ontologies in a specific area, but not in various fields; Ontologies application - contains the necessary knowledge for modeling a particular domain [27]. There are others whose cases are not presented.

2.1.3 Ontological Components

Ontologies are built in any area. It is necessary to identify all the elements that surround it, as well as its structure and fitness for the domain area.

In [5] it is reported that ontologies provide a common vocabulary of an area and define, with different levels of formality, the meaning of terms and relations among them. It is considered that the ontologies knowledge uses five types of components: classes - are usually organized into taxonomies. Sometimes, the notion of ontology is diluted in the sense that taxonomies are considered complete ontologies. Relationships - represent a kind of interaction among domain concepts. They are generally used in rules or formulas to infer knowledge in the ontology. They represent a kind of interaction among the concepts in the field. (N: n); functions - represent a special case of relations that constitute a special case of relations (n-1); axioms - are used to model sentences that are always true. Can be included in an ontology for several purposes, such as defining the meaning of ontology components, the values of attributes and arguments of relations; instances - are used to represent specific elements. They describe the instances of one concept. Instances are used to represent the elements of the domain. There are others which cases were not mentioned for it depends on the design of the ontology.

2.1.4 Levels of Ontologies

Some of the best known high-level ontologies:

Sowa - includes categories from various sources. The highest concept is considered the universal type and the lowest level is absurd type. The subtypes of universal type are primitive concepts that combined, generate new concepts [31]. GUARINO and Welry - divided into two categories: universal and particular. The particular ones are considered abstract concepts. The universal ones are abstract concepts that can be instantiated in individuals. The authors claim they can prove that each property can be instantiated in at least one of these levels of hierarchy [25]. IEEE (SUO) - A Standard Upper Ontology (SUO) is the higher standard (upper) ontology merging sponsored by IEEE. It is a standard that specifies an upper ontology to support computer applications such as data interoperability, search and information retrieval and natural language processing [33].

2.2 Ontologies Development

Ontology engineers argue that the techniques for developing ontologies have been developed in various fields of knowledge. In the following sections, we present a brief review of literature on methodologies, tools and languages for building ontologies.

2.2.1 Criteria for the Development of Domain Ontology

The intention here is to present briefly some design criteria and a set of principles that prove it useful in the development of ontologies. [2, 17, 18] argue that it should have clarity and objectivity - the ontology should provide the meaning of terms defined by purpose and provide definitions and documentation of natural languages; completeness - a definition expressed in terms of preference over a partial definition; coherence - allows inferences that are consistent with definitions; extensibility - means that new terms, general or specialized, should be included in the ontology such that it is not necessary to review the current definitions; ontological commitment - refers to the agreement to use the shared vocabulary in a coherent and consistent way; ontological distinction in principle - means that classes in an ontology should be separated. Diversification of hierarchies to increase the power supplied by a system of multiple inheritance. Modularity - to minimize coupling between modules; minimization of the semantic distance between similar concepts - means that similar concepts are grouped and represented using the same primitive; standardization of names - when it is possible.

2.2.2 Methodologies

In [30] apud Fernandez, Gomez Perez and Corcho (2004) argue that "the methodology and method are distinct concepts, as a methodology refers to knowledge about methods, ie, determining" how "and" when "a given activity may be performed. Thus, a methodology is composed of methods that have their own techniques. " They are used for development, integration, evaluation, which there are others and the examples will not be displayed.

In [5] some methodologies for the development of ontologies are proposed, such as Ring and Uschold [35] presents general steps for building an ontology, identifying the purpose, the concepts and relationships between concepts. The terms used refer to that concept. Then, the ontology must be documented and evaluated. Grüninger and Fox [16] - introduce a formal method that identifies usage scenarios of ontology. It uses natural language to determine the scope of ontology. Data are extracted about the concepts, properties, relations and axioms, which are formally defined in PROLOG. In Fernández-López [12] an ontology is built on another ontology by re-engineering. The construction uses the domain knowledge. The main activities are: specification, conceptualization, formalization, implementation and maintenance, called Methontology. The methodology for ontologies integration provides the integration of different methodologies, eg, FCA-Merge: Use of natural language processing and formal review of concepts you want to integrate, resulting in a set of concepts. The valuation methodologies utilize Ontology philosophical principles to assess errors in the development of ontology. In [15] it evaluates errors in the construction of ontology from the domain structure in taxonomy and knowledge bases. Takes into account the work done from the evaluation of ontologies and the criteria used.

In [3] they comment that there are several methodological proposals for organizing the structure of terminological ontologies and their relationships, but related to the "methods used to survey your domain terminology and delimitation of its scope, especially considering the reuse of ontologies" there is a lack in the literature.

2.2.3 Tools for Ontologies Development

The tools for ontologies development provide significant gains. They may assist in the development of ontologies, and the examples do not cover an exhaustive review of the literature, namely: Ontolingua - provides the construction of ontologies shared among groups. Allows access to a library of ontologies, language translators and an editor to create and navigate the ontology [11]; OntoEdit - is a graphical environment for editing ontologies, which allows viewing, navigation, encoding and modification of ontologies. The conceptual model is stored using a standard ontology that can be mapped in different representation languages; Protege - is an interactive environment for designing ontologies, open code, which provides a graphical interface for editing ontologies and an architecture for creating knowledge-based tools [28]; WebODE - Environment for ontological engineering that supports most of the activities of ontology development. Integration with other systems is possible, importing and exporting ontology markup languages [2].

In [3] it explains that the software for the development of ontologies have "features that enable the 'understanding' of the users' needs, since they propose the interpretation of search needs, adding also the answer to it."

2.2.4 Ontologies Development Languages

Traditional languages are recognized in literature for its representation of ontologies, as Ontolanguage. The standards considered for Web languages are, among others: OIL (OntologyInference Layer), DAML + OIL (DARPA Agent Markup Language), RDF (s), XOL (Ontology Exchange Language) and OWL (Ontology Web Language) [7, 15] . The definition of language depends on the project in development.

The methodologies applied to ontologies development present distinct life cycles, although the acquisition and formalization phases always appear in all cycles. Thus, the acquisition builds up a conceptual model, and the formalization a formal model [4].

2.3 Approach about the Life Cycle of An Ontology

In [3] it is developed the proposal to represent the cycle of an ontology through diagrams using the technique of a concept map. Figure 1 shows the state of the art of research on creation of ontologies [9] and on their mapping and maintenance [10] proposed by the authors. In this paper, the authors took care to explain the procedures adopted. However you cannot display the four processes through conceptual map, but how representativeness is presented in Figure 1 - general issues about ontology through the concept map.

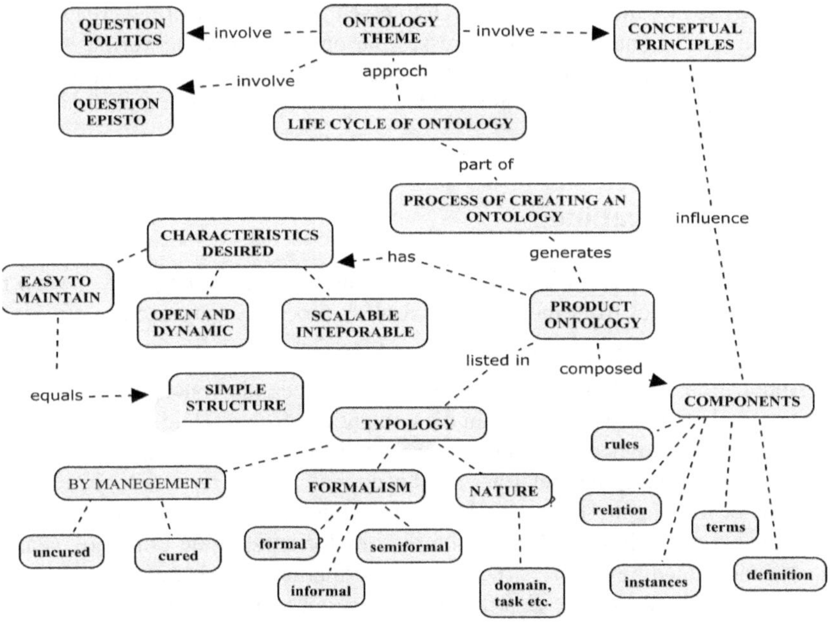

Fig. 1. General Issues Related to ontologies [3] modify

The [3] teaches that for an optimized use of an ontology, it must have requested features: it must be opened, dynamic, easy to maintain, climbable, interoperable and it must have a simple, clear and modular structure. An ontology presents as its components: definitions, terms, instancies, relationships and rules. It is worth saying that a few ontologies use rules. As for the instancies, they refer to the individual objects in that domain. In this article will not be presented in detail maps that were developed in [3] due to the short space for description on the Process of Creation, Maintenance Process and Procedure of Using an Ontology. However the process of creating an ontology involves the lifting subprocess and the choice of the creation forms and design principles [3, 9, 10]. As a result, an ontology is generated. Regarding methods of creation, one can choose the methods of reasoning: inductive, deductive and analytic-synthetic. The choice involves epistemological issues. The literature shows that works propose principles for the conception or design of ontologies. Among the authors who have studied these issues are [22, 34, 35, 29]. As for the process of maintaining an ontology, it involves versioning subprocesses and evaluation, and other mechanisms for reuse of ontologies, the latter two being used by the process of creating ontologies [3, 9, 10].

The versioning involves the management related to the acquisition, modification and deletion of concepts. The process of Using an Ontology involves the integration of systems and databases in order to match data and services and resources description and recovery for different purposes [3, 9, 10]. The use of ontologies typically involves the use of software agents, which should be able to use the ontology applied to describe the services, resources or data to be integrated.

In [3] the use of concept maps allowed to reveal an overview of the creation, maintenance and use of ontologies. It addresses the ontology and the various categories that unfold on the various aspects of theoretical and practical, highlighting the relationships between them. The vision provided by the map is a major contribution to the literature on the subject.

3 Final Considerations

In the literature reviewed, the term ontology is used as much the point of view conceptual as the product from the ontological work process, being used in a variety of projects in different research areas:

a) Applications involving ontologies vary from academic conceptual prototypes to enterprise applications. Researchers in the computing systems state that the ontologies used to represent knowledge in specific areas [13, 35] show the importance of using well-established conceptual relations to the consistency of terminological structure and for the development of taxonomy that should compose the structure of the ontology [21]. The researches emphasize, the reasons for creating an ontology: sharing a common understanding of the structure of information among people in a domain; allow the reuse of knowledge in a domain; analyzing and management of the knowledge in the domain of certain area.

b) The literature does not show the existence of an ontology definition standard. In the process of modeling a knowledge domain there are various possibilities to develop an ontology in order that they should reflect specific processes of the organizations, which complicates the view on the existence of a development of the standard model. This variability feature of methods that can infer difficulty in creating of ontologies as organization tools and information use in an organization, should also be seen as a favorable feature, since the lack of standard models can lead the development of more suitable tools to the reality of organizations. Therefore, there is not any result, as a product, but a tool for understanding organizational knowledge closer to the reality of the institution.

c) Another point to note is that the literature reveals the not being of a unified concept for their own understanding of ontology, which is designed both as a concept, a term, a tool, a process or method by several authors analyzed.

d) It is perceived that the development of an ontology requires a process of continuous interaction of different areas of knowledge, but it is possible a distinction of roles when the focus on the application of ontology is given. It follows that it must bear in mind that an ontology is a model of a domain, real or imaginary, and the domain of concepts in the ontology reflect this reality that is being modeled or understood.

Acknowledgments

This work was supported by the Faculty of Technology, University of Brasília (UnB), Coordination of Personnel Improvement of Higher Education (CAPES).

References

1. Almeida, M.B., Bax, M.P.: An overview about ontologies: survey about definitions, types, applications, evaluation and building methods. Ci. Inf., Brasília 32(3), 7–20 (2003)
2. Arpirez, J.C., et al.: Web Ode: A Scalable Workbench For Ontological Engineering. In: International Conference On Knowledge Capture Proceedings Of The International Conference On Knowledge, Victoria, British Columbia, Canada (2001)
3. Campos, M.L.A., Marcondes, C.H., Lira, L., Costa, L.C., Campos, L.M., Malheiros, L.R.: Ontologies: representing the research in the area through conceptual maps, VIII ENANCIB –28, Salvador, Brazil (October 31, 2007)
4. Cantele, R.C., Adamatti, D.F., Ferreira, M.A.G., Sichman, J.S.: Reengineering and Ontologies: Analysis and Application, `http://www.lti.pcs.usp.br/Pergamus/pubs/Cantele-etal04-WWS.pdf`
5. Corcho, O., Fernández-López, M., Gómez Pérez, A.: Foudations Ontology. Technical Roadmap v1.0 (2001)
6. Corcho, O., Fernández-López, M., Gomez-Pérez, A.: Ontoweb, technical roadmap V 1.0 (2001), `http://babage.dia.fi.upm.es/ontoweb/wp1/OntoRoadMap/documents/D11_v1_0.pdf`
7. Corcho, O., López, M.F., Gómez-Pérez, A.: Methodologies, tools and languages for building ontologies. Where is theis meeting point? Data & Knowledge Engineering 46, 41–64 (2003)
8. Corcho, O., Gomez-Perez, A.: A Roadmap to Ontology Specification Languages. In: Dieng, R., Corby, O. (eds.) Knowledge Engineering and Knowledge Management. Methods, Models and Tools, pp. 80–96. Springer, Berlin (2000)
9. Ding, Y., Foo, S.: Ontology research and development. Part 2 - a review of ontology generation. Journal of Information Science 28(5), 375–388 (2002)
10. Ding, Y., Foo, S.: Ontology research and development. Part 1 - a review of ontology mapping and evolving. Journal of Information Science 28(2), 123–136 (2002)
11. Farquhar, A., Fikes, R., Rice, J.: The ontolingua server. In: USA: A Tool for Collaborative Ontology Construction, pp. 707–727. Academic Press, Duluth (1997)

12. Fernández-López, M., Gómez-Pérez, A., Pazos-Sierra, A., Pazos-Sierra, J.: Building a Chemical Ontology Using Methontology and the Ontology Design Environment. IEEE Intelligent Systems & their Applications, 37–46 (January/February 1999)
13. Fernández, M., Gómez-Pérez, A., Juristo, N.: Methontology: From Ontological Art Towards Ontological Engineering. In: Symposium on Ontological Engineering of AAAI, Stanford, California (1997)
14. Gómez-Pérez, A., Rojas, Benjamins, V.R.: Overview of knowledge sharing and reuse components: ontologies and problem-solving methods. In: Proceedings of the Workshop on Ontologies and Problem-Solving Methods, Stockholm, Sweden (1999)
15. Gómez-Pérez, A., Corcho, O.: Ontology Languages For The Semantic Web. IEEE Intelligent Systems 17(1), 54–60 (2002)
16. Grüninger, M., Fox, M.S.: Methodology For The Design And Evaluation of Ontologies. Toronto, Canada: Technical Report. University of Toronto (1995)
17. Gruber, T.R.: A Translation Approach To Portable Ontology Specifications. Knowledge Acquisition 5 (1993)
18. Gruber, T.R.: Toward Principles of the Design of Ontologies Used for Knowledge Sharing. International Journa of Human Computer Studies 43, 907–928 (1995)
19. Gruber, T.: Ontology. In: Liu, L., Tamer Özsu, M. (eds.) The Encyclopedia of Database Systems. Springer, Heidelberg (2009), `http://Tomgruber.Org/Writing/Ontology-Definition-`
20. Gruber, T.: What Is An Ontology (1996), `http://Www-Ksl.Stanford.Edu/Kst/What-Is-An-Ontology.Html`
21. Guarino, N., Giaretta, P.: Ontologies And Knowledge Bases. Towards A Terminological Clarification. In: Toward Very Large Knowledge Bases, pp. 25–32. Ios Press, Amsterdam (1995)
22. Guarino, N. (ed.): Formal Ontology In Information Systems. Ios Press, Amsterdam (1998)
23. Guarino, N.M., Mark, A.: Applied Ontology: Focusing on content. IOS Press and the authors (2005)
24. Guarino, N.: The Ontological Level: Revisiting 30 Years Of Knowledge Representation. In: Borgida, A.T., Chaudhri, V.K., Giorgini, P., Yu, E.S. (eds.) Conceptual Modeling: Foundations and Applications. LNCS, vol. 5600, pp. 52–67. Springer, Heidelberg (2009)
25. Guarino, N., Welty, C.: A Formal Ontology Of Properties. In: Dieng, R., Corby, O. (eds.) EKAW 2000. LNCS (LNAI), vol. 1937, pp. 97–112. Springer, Heidelberg (2000)
26. Jasper, R., Uschold, M.: A Framework For Understanding And Classifying Ontology Applications. In: Ijcai 1999, Ontology Workshop, Stockholm (S. N., S.L.) (1999)
27. Mizoguchi, R., Vanwelkenhuysen, J., Ikeda, M.: Task Ontology For Reuse Of Problem Solving Knowledge. In: Proceedings Of Ecai 1994 Towards Very Large Knowledge Bases, 1994, pp. 46–59. Ios Press, Amsterdam (1995)
28. Noy, N.F., Musen, M.A.: Prompt: Algorithm And Tool For Automated Ontology Merging And Alignment. In: National Conference On Artificial Intelligence, Austin, Tx, vol. 12, 17, pp. 450–455 (S. N., S. L.) (2000)
29. Reich, J.R.: Ontological Design Patterns for the Integration of Molecular Biological Information. In: Proceedings of Gcb 1999 Conference on Bioinformatics, Hannover, Germany, pp. 156–166 (1999)
30. Silva, D.L., Souza, R.R., Almeida, M.B.: Ontologies and controlled vocabularies: comparison of methodologies for construction. Ci. Inf., Brasília 37(3), 60–75 (2008)
31. Sowa, J.F.: Building Sharing And Merging Ontologies (2001), `http://Users.Bestweb.Net/~Sowa/Ontology/Ontoshar.Htm`

32. Sowa, J.F.: Ontology, Metadata, And Semiotics (2000), http://Www.Jfsowa.Com/Ontology/Ontometa.Htm
33. Suo, W.G.: Standard Upper Ontology Working Group, Standard Upper Ontology, http://Suo.Ieee.Org/
34. Uschold, M., King, M., Moralee, S., Zorgios, Y.: The Enterprise Ontology? In: Uschold, M., Tate, A. (eds.) The Knowledge; Engineering Review. Special Issue On Putting Ontologies To Use, vol. 13 (1998), Also Available From Aiai As Aiai-Tr-195
35. Usckold, M., Gruninger, M.: Ontologies: Principies, Methods An Applications. Knowledge Engineering Review 11(2) (1996)
36. Van, H.G., Schreiber, A.T., Wielinga, B.J.: Using Explicit Ontologies in Kbs Development. International Journal of Human-Computer Studies 46(2-3), 183–192 (1997)
37. Welty, C., Guarino, N.: Supporting ontological analysis of taxonomic relationships. Data & Knowledge Engineering 39(1) (October 2001)

Developing Dynamic Reports Using Rich Internet Applications

Luís Matias

Departamento de Engenharia Informática, Faculdade de Engenharia, Universidade do Porto
Rua Dr. Roberto Frias, s/n 4200-465 Porto – Portugal
LIAAD-INESC Porto L.A. Rua de Ceuta, 118, 6º; 4050-190 Porto - Portugal
luis.matias@fe.up.pt

Abstract. In the business world, there are several software tools to generate reports automatically. We can do it with software like Crystal Reports and we can use different options to configure the reports. However, we observed that it is not flexible in several points like the structure of the data base or the changing of report's parameters after its generation. To solve this problem, we propose the using of RIA – Rich Internet Applications in order to build dynamic reports. These dynamic reports will allow us to change the report's contents and parameters after its first generation. With this, it will be possible to ask for different data in runtime, with no need for generating new reports. To implement this solution using RIAs, we tested and compared two different technologies: Microsoft Silverlight and Adobe Flash. We expected that the Silverlight should be more reliable than Flash in this context because it was integrated in the .NET framework. After our experiments, we concluded that the dynamic reports can be generated using RIAs. For that solution, we stated that Silverlight was better than Flash because it's easier to use and to develop with.

Keywords: Dynamic, Reports, Crystal, RIA, Flash, Silverlight.

1 Introduction

In the business world, over the last years, we witnessed the creation of several tools destined to support the automatic generation of reports from different sources and data types. These reports usually have rigid models that are independent from its data source if it has a previously defined structure.

One of the more capable and reliable software tool to do this type of interaction is Crystal Reports [1]. However, this type of applications has, due to its nature, high level restrictions to the information retrieval process based in the generated reports. It is possible to resume big data set in small lines, like annual invoices. In the opposite way, it is not allowed to do the inverse and see what lines fulfill that sum or change, in a runtime environment, the timeline that we want to report and analyze.

To fulfill this type of requests, it was proposed to develop prototypes of a new type of reports: dynamic reports. The dynamic reports are reports that are automatically generated and that allow analysis and changing with no need to do a new generation of it. We will be able to do it in runtime. To solve this problem, we used RIA's – Rich

J.E. Quintela Varajão et al. (Eds.): CENTERIS 2010, Part II, CCIS 110, pp. 436–445, 2010.

Internet Applications. In this context, we tested and compared the two dominant technologies that implement RIA's nowadays: the Microsoft Silverlight and the Adobe Flash [10], in a way to understand which one of these technologies would be the best solution to our problem. We hope to conclude that it is possible to develop applications to support automatic generation of dynamic reports with the two chosen technologies, especially with Microsoft Silverlight.

This paper is structured as follows: Section no.2, titled "Automatic Report's Generation", states a general perspective about this problem. Section 3 has the title "Dynamic Reports with RIA's" and it states, in a general way, the RIA's basic characteristics and the main requirements to build a prototype created with this type of technology, based in Management Control. The Management Control basic functions and characteristics are also mentioned. In the section 4, the results obtained by the developing of the two prototypes are lightly described, considering the requirements previously defined. Section 5, titled "Comparative Study between RIA's technologies", exhaustively describes the results obtained through the analysis of the developing and the using of the prototypes. The sixth section of this paper presents a small discussion about the results obtained in the previous section. Finally, the section 7, "Conclusions", presents the main conclusions of the work.

2 Automatic Report's Generation

The automatic generated reports are commonly used since the early 90s, with the reports associated to the starters' software-based database management system for non-professional use: the Office and the Lotus Suite [2, 3]. However, it only became a standard feature when the Crystal Reports was introduced in the market. The Crystal Reports is a Business Intelligence application. This type of applications is commonly used in the collection, integration, analysis and presentation of information to support the decision. Originally developed for Business Objects, this application is used to develop and generate reports with several types of data sources. A large number of applications use OEM (Original Equipment Manufacturer) versions of Crystal Reports as its own tool of reporting generation.

The reports generated using Crystal Reports allow multi-applications and multi-database. They can also be used in the conception of those applications. However, the flexibility ends here: the Crystal Reports needs the data structure to be exactly the same as the first data base used to generate it. Despite the fact that we can configure the reports with different data sources, the report can never be changed after its generation. If you consider that the time needed to generate is as big as the data source, this must be considered as a serious problem to solve when we want to, for instance, compare reports related to different timelines.

3 Dynamic Reports with RIA

The dynamic reports are reports that can be changed after its generation, like a dynamic query with some parameters (i.e. the beginning and the end date of a period). These reports are generated from a data set and they can be manipulated after its generation to demonstrate different perspectives. They must be portable and easily accessed, like an web portal, to be used in different situations. These characteristics present one clear requirement: we need to implement a web application to implement a dynamic report as it is described above.

However, it is not the best solution to use a traditional web application. As it is stated by Christodoulou Stygaras in [14], these applications present several problems with the processes, the configuration and the data. This last one is particularly important, because they do not support interactive explorations of the data, compelling the user to navigate the hypertext to see the desired data [15].

The traditional web applications were extended in several directions to improve interactivity and ease of use. The RIA followed one of these directions. It is the mix between the interactive and the multimedia user interface functionality of the Desktop applications and between the portability offered by the Web tools, allowing to build Rich applications with data and also with multimedia contents, like dynamic charts and media clips. Next, it is explained how the RIA can be a solution to implement Dynamic Reports and how we will use it.

3.1 RIA as a Solution

The problem that we have is RIA related. There are several technologies available to implement a RIA. In this case, we compared two different technologies that were able to develop the same type of applications to use in this context.

The RIAs are web applications that are usually executed under browser's plug-ins. We described, in some bullet points, the main characteristics of RIAs:

- They support the graphical render and the inclusion of media clips – video and audio;
- They are easily installed because they are executed in a plug-in that adapts itself to the technological reality it finds (browser, operative system, etc.). This characteristic allows it to maintain the user experience with every platform used to execute it. The maintenance of these applications is simple because their plug-ins are automatically updated;
- They appear as more secure applications because they are usually pre-compiled and they sometimes use the sandbox's concept to the platform they are executed over. This will limit their access to the client.
- They have a better performance because they shrink the existing latency, comparing to the traditional web applications that need to constantly connect themselves to the server to allow it to process the data.

In order to develop an application to automatically generate dynamic reports, we chose to develop a prototype focused on Management Control.

3.2 Management Control Requirements

The Management Control is the discipline that studies the impact of the Strategic Management on the organizations based in metrics that evaluate their performance [5]. Using tangible values to measure intangible characteristics of the organization, like its branding or its CRM (client relationship management), it is possible to evaluate the current and future impact of a strategy on the operational results. We can easily verify, for instance, if the organization profit has grown like the expected and if the budget defined to certain activities is enough to achieve the defined goals.

We found some methodologies in the market which implement a more efficient Management Control over the organizations. One of the most important is the Balanced ScoreCard [4, 13]. With this, it is simple to justify our choice - because it is highly suitable to our software market: the top managers need - usually as support to their decision processes – of large amounts of data.
An example of a map needed by the Management Control, in its financial perspective, is the balance sheet's temporary map [17].

3.3 Prototype Requirements

After the analysis of the RIAs characteristics and of the Management Control requirements, we defined the following list of requirements to the prototypes [7]:

- To develop one or more Management Control maps in a application with dynamic contents and dynamic configurations, in runtime environment using RIAs;
- To develop mechanisms to obtain, in runtime, different perspectives of the maps;
- Strong visual components and highly intuitive and appellative aspect.
- To allow the automatic generation of bar charts or other chart types;
- To allow the generation of several maps simultaneously using different configurations using the automatic generation of charts;

These requirements were used to develop two prototypes of applications to automatically generate dynamic reports to support the Management Control. One of the prototypes was developed using Microsoft Silverlight and other with the Adobe Flash. The results are presented in the following section.

4 Results of the Developed Prototypes

Two prototypes of the desired application were created: one using Silverlight, other using Flash, as it is stated in the following sections.

4.1 Flash Prototype

This prototype was easily developed, using the Adobe Software Development Kit for Flash. It is, similarly to the other prototype, connected to a database running locally in a Microsoft SQL Server using a web service. It was not too hard to develop some animations or a user friendly interface, but it was really hard to find a way to generate charts in runtime. It is really hard to develop your own Flash controls and you can't use anything from the OS. So, the last two defined requirements were not accomplished.

4.2 Silverlight Prototype

Like the previous one, the prototype was easily developed. It is possible to change some parameters of the map, as shown in the Figure 1.

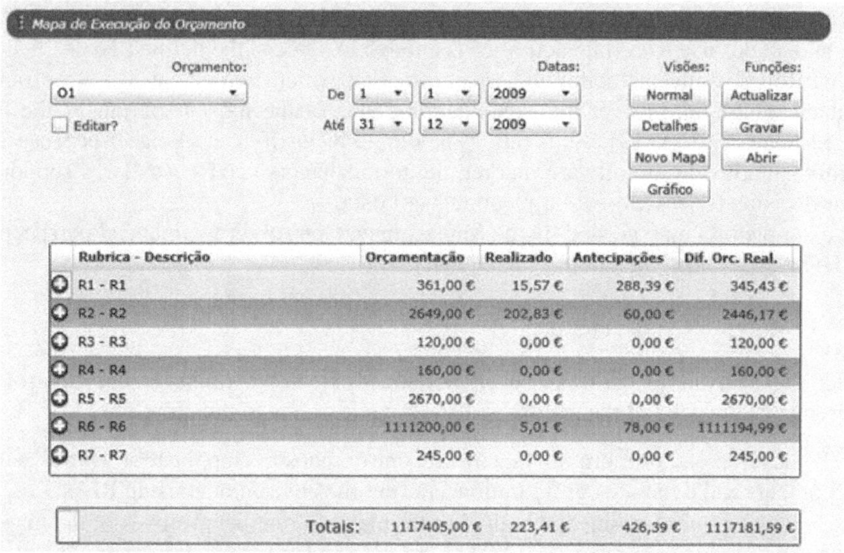

Fig. 1. Screenshot of the Silverlight prototype

Using the Silverlight Toolkit, it is possible to include chart components that are easily fed using LINQ – Language Integrated Query [16]. You can see the buttons on the left to navigate through the lines used in the represented sums, you can change the budget used to feed the map or the dates used to generate it. You are able to create a new map and you can save it in a file using Silverlight Isolated Storage, as you will be able to see in the further sections. Both prototypes can be accessed by a browser.

4.3 Prototype Development Results

The prototypes and the maps above prove that there are many things to improve from the old Crystal Reports maps. These prototypes are more flexible, more portable and more user-friendly than the older ones. Like that, they fill the gap found in Crystal Reports transforming the Dynamic Reports into a reality. Now, we need to know which of the technologies is best to continue this work on Dynamic Reports.

5 Comparative Study between RIA's Technologies

In the previous sections, the basic characteristics of a RIA and the prototypes developed using two different RIA technologies were explained. Considering these characteristics and the context we want to use them, we defined the following metrics to measure and compare the RIA's technologies:

User Experience – this metric pretends to measure the capacities of the technologies to develop a good user experience like the interactivity's levels, the graphic render, the quality of the media clips and the global performance;

Security, Communication and Client's Access - this metric pretends to measure the security level of the technology and how can we access and change the data in the Client and to communicate with other applications;

Installation and Execution – these metric measures defines the prerequisites needed to install and execute an application of this kind and which are the requirements of the client's application;

Maintenance and Reliability – we measure the effort to maintain this applications working as the reliability proportioned by the technology;

Developing Easiness – it is defined if it is – or if it is not – easy to develop applications with this technology;

These metrics were used to measure and compare the RIA's technologies: Silverlight and Flash, like you can verify in the following lines. A ranking from zero to five stars (☆) was defined for each one of the metrics to support a tangible evaluation of the technologies.

5.1 Adobe Flash

Using the previous section and the RIA's market analysis done in [7], the following analysis to Adobe Flash was concluded:

User Experience ☆☆☆☆ The Adobe Flash allowed a good user experience because it has several possibilities to include different rendered animations and audio/video streaming. It has a large amount of possibilities to support the interaction and a high level of styling. The Flash assures the quality of the reproduction independently from the client's monitor resolution (vector-based).

Security, Communication and Client's Access ☆☆☆ In order to communicate, Flash didn't demonstrate any functionality to allow the connection to Database Management Systems. However, it can use MSMQ – Microsoft Message Queuing [18] to communicate with other local applications. Due to its communication limitations, Flash is really secured to execute a presentation of this type. Flash is in the market from many years till now and, with that, it developed a real trustful relationship with their users: programmers and consumers.

Installation and Execution ☆☆☆☆☆ Flash supports the majority of existing operative systems and browsers like Windows 9x, Linux, Opera, IE, Mozilla Firefox, MacOS, Safari, etc... It can be executed in a browser's plug-in or in an isolated player as a standalone application. The applications developed using Flash are short-sized and the plug-in startup is really fast.

Maintenance and Reliability ☆☆☆☆ Flash's reliability is high due to its long years of existence. The Flash's plug-in is easily maintained because it is automatically updated. The generation of standalone applications requires a new compilation of all components every time the presentation is changed.

Developing Easiness ☆☆ It is not simple to develop in Flash. It only supports one programming language: the Action Script. This language requires a high learning curve because it is not a standard programming language and it is not used in other applications besides those who are developed with Flash. Therefore, the source code can't be used again in other context. It is not possible to use any OS (operative system) controls and the animations are built using the frames that are shown. Flash only uses the matrical transformations to animate its presentations - we must somehow assure that the client will maintain the application's frame rate. If this doesn't happen, our animation can last for 1 or for 5 seconds (!), for instance. Flash's developing environment was designed merely to develop Flash applications and it requires a long time to learn. This developing environment is graphical and, due to that fact, it is more suitable to use for designers than for programmers.

5.2 Microsoft Silverlight

Now, using the previous section and the RIA's market analysis done in [7], the following analysis to Microsoft Silverlight was concluded:

User Experience ☆☆☆☆☆ The Silverlight has a set of capabilities similar to Flash. Rendered animations, streaming of audio and video, etc...

However, it's global performance it greater than Flash's. The compilation of its applications is made using CLR - Common Language Runtime [11]. Every language that uses this type of environment is managed code's languages: languages that are compiled first in a virtual machine, then, executed by the CPU.

On the other hand, Silverlight presents a technology that distinguishes itself from other technologies: the Deep Zoom. The Deep Zoom allows us to randomly zoom in large images with an enormous performance [10]. The Silverlight possesses one more unique characteristic: graphic acceleration supported by hardware, with the technology Direct3D.

Security, Communication and Client's Access ☆☆☆ Like Flash, Silverlight hasn't got any functionality to allow the direct connection to Database management systems. However, it is not allowed to access the client file system. The simplest way to turn over this problem is to use a web service.. As far as security is concerned, we can define Silverlight like a pretty secure platform. This fact occurs because Silverlight is executed in a sandbox. A sandbox typically restricts the access to the platform's native API, controlling the resources that the application can and cannot use like the disk space and the memory space, the access to system's information, the read of input devices, etc... To minimize those effects, the Silverlight uses the Isolated Storage [9]. One of the Silverlight's biggest limitations is its need to communicate asynchronously [8].

Installation and Execution ☆☆☆ The Silverlight is also executed in a browser's plug-in but it does not support many standard platforms like the Linux operative system or the Opera browser. It does not support any execution outside of a browser like a standalone application. Like Flash, the plug-in startup is fast but their files have a bigger size. As we observed, they are, in average, 10 times bigger as they don't compress any of its source files. Beside the fact that it needs several source code files to its execution, it's dependencies are not built-in in the application.

Maintenance and Reliability ☆☆☆☆ Like Flash, the plug-in has an easy maintenance because it is automatically updated. Despite its short time in the market, Silverlight uses technologies largely used to build business oriented applications (.NET,C#,VB .NET, CLR, etc.). Consequently, the programmers state a high reliability to Silverlight.

Silverlight has different source files and because of that the files that are responsible for the communications protocols, data queries, design, etc. are easily identified. With that, it's easy to create new applications and functionalities using tested and existing source code (C# code, for instance).

Developing Easiness ☆☆☆☆ Silverlight mainly uses technologies from .NET framework in its applications like CSharp, VB, WPF, WCF, ASP.NET and LINQ. These languages are commercially used to develop applications with all type of business plans. Therefore, its source code can be used over and over again.

The used IDE (Integrated Development Environment) is also well known – Visual Studio – and the most programmers have a great familiarity with its use. Silverlight has the Expression Blend as IDE too. This tool allows us to edit our applications design and it is pointed to the designers themselves. The creation of Silverlight's animations is, again, very easy: it is possible to define time-based animations. We can merely define the first and the last state and the render software generates the remaining states throughout the time. The Silverlight use the Windows Presentation Foundation framework as platform to use several Windows's controls without any integration efforts.

However, this technology has negative points too. The projects debugging is simple because it is possible to edit just a small component of the project without compiling it all. But we need to consider the slow startup of the application because it needs an ASP.NET server to be running, located locally or abroad.

6 Discussion

Using the described work, the prototypes and the analysis previously done, we present in Table 1 a summary of the whole study.

Table 1. Comparative study between Flash and Silverlight

	Adobe Flash	MS Silverlight
User Experience	☆☆☆☆	☆☆☆☆☆
Security, Communication and Client's Access	☆☆☆	☆☆☆
Installation and Execution	☆☆☆☆☆	☆☆☆
Maintenance and Reliability	☆☆☆☆	☆☆☆☆
Developing Easiness	☆☆	☆☆☆☆

As we can see through the table analysis, in 25 possible points, the technologies could not achieve grades above 80%. The Silverlight had one point more than Flash. This is relevant but, in our opinion, is far from being decisive. In a technological perspective, the Flash's market share is high and this makes Flash the best option. However, observing the unique characteristics of both technologies, we can say that Silverlight has bigger potential to grow comparing with Flash and it will become a really serious competitor in a short time. The Flash is a tested and commercial format with great portability e adaptability to different platforms and its executables are short sized. These characteristics should maintain it as market leader in the near future.

However, in a market with a constant expansion as the RIA's one, there are characteristics that will define how will the software applications be in the future – the use of those applications in mobile devices. In this aspect, the Flash will have more constraints to move on with the natural market's evolution. In our opinion, those characteristics are 3D Hardware graphic acceleration; Time-based animations; Programming languages easy to understand and usable in different contexts.

Observing these characteristics, we can say that Silverlight presents itself in the front line to succeed Flash in the RIA's market. If Flash does not evolve itself in this way, it could become obsolete in a medium term period.

In the specific context of developing a tool to automatically generate dynamic reports, both technologies prove to be sufficient to accomplish it. However, the Silverlight presents a better performance due to its developing easiness and user experience, allowing building complex applications to automatically generate dynamic reports, in a richer and faster way.

7 Conclusions

Nowadays, the reports can no longer be represented by blank and white paper reports, strictly static in the way they represent information and hard to search and to extract relevant information.

The automatic generation of dynamic reports is, in our opinion, the future of this kind of information representation. The developing of this kind of tools using RIA is possible and highly profitable in the products' quality and programming perspective.

Comparing the technologies used to implement these solutions, the Microsoft Silverlight demonstrated to be the best solution for, essentially, two reasons: on one hand, its user experience that transforms the views and the editions of the reports in simple and pleasant operations. On the other hand, the developing easiness allowed by the using of the .Net framework is high because the Silverlight uses technologies belonging to that framework, well known and largely used in the whole world like CSharp.

As future work, we will develop a multi-database architecture that will allow us to develop, in a medium term future, a commercial product to automatically generate the dynamic reports supporting one, or more, platforms.

References

1. Peck, G.: Crystal Reports 2008: The Complete Reference. McGraw-Hill Professional, New York (2008)
2. IBM. liveSite - Website Content Management Software (2009), `http://www.lotusmuseum.com/` (obtained in January 1, 2010)
3. Microsoft. The Microsoft Office Fluent user interface overview (2009), `http://office.microsoft.com/en-us/products/HA101679411033.aspx` (obtained in January 1, 2010)

4. Kaplan, R.S., Norton, D.P.: The Balanced Scorecard. Harvard Business School Press, Boston (1996)
5. Rodrigues, J. A.: Controlo de Gestão e Performance (2007), http://www.indeg.org/cursos/mestradosexecutivos/contabilidade/controlo/ (obtained in February 16, 2009)
6. Ezell, J.: Silverlight vs. Flash: The Developer Story (2008), http://weblogs.asp.net/jezell/archive/2007/05/03/silverlight-vs-flash-the-developer-story.aspx (obtained in February 19, 2009)
7. Moritz, F.: Rich Internet Applications (RIA) (January 2009), http://www.flomedia.de/diploma/documents/DiplomaThesisFlorianMoritz.pdf (obtained in January 5, 2009)
8. Microsoft. Data Points: Service Driven Apps. With Silverlight 2 and WCF, http://msdn.microsoft.com/en-us/magazine/cc794260.aspx (obtained February 17, 2009)
9. Microsoft. Isolated Storage (2009), http://msdn.microsoft.com/en-us/library/3ak841syVS.80.aspx (obtained in February 17, 2009)
10. Microsoft. Deep Zoom (2009), http://msdn.microsoft.com/en-us/library/cc645050VS.95.aspx (Obtained in February 17, 2009)
11. Microsoft. Common Language Runtime Overview, http://msdn.microsoft.com/en-us/library/ddk909chvs.71.aspx
12. Microsoft. Microsoft Message Queuing (2008), http://www.microsoft.com/windowsserver2003/technologies/msmq/default.mspx (obtained in February 16, 2009)
13. Kaplan, R.S., Norton, D.P.: The Execution Premium - Linking Strategy to Operations for Competitive Advantage. Harvard Business School Press, Boston (2008)
14. Christodoulou, S.P., Styliaras, G.D., Papatheodorou, T.S.: Evaluation of Hypermedia Application Development and Management Systems. In: 9th ACM conference on Hypertext and Hypermedia, pp. 1–10. ACM Press, Pittsburgh (1998)
15. Preciado, J.C., Linaje, M., Sanchez, F., Comai, S.: Necessity of methodologies to model Rich Internet Applications. In: WSE - Proceedings of the Seventh IEEE International Symposium on Web Site Evolution, pp. 7–13. IEEE Computer Society, Washinton (2005)
16. Microsoft. Swiss MSDN Team Blog : Silverlight 2 Beta 1 + WCF + LINQ to SQL (March 2008), http://blogs.msdn.com/swiss_dpe_team/archive/2008/03/17/silverlight-2-beta1-wcf-linq-to-sql-a-powerfull-combination.aspx (obtained in January 5, 2009)
17. Horwitz, S.: The Sensory Order and Organizational Learning. In: Koppl, R., Horwitz, S. (eds.) The Social Science of Hayek's the Sensory Order. Advances in Austrian Economics, vol. 13. Emerald Business (2008)

Smart Web Services: Systems' Integration Using Policy-Driven Automatic Configuration

João C.C. Leitão and Miguel L. Pardal

Instituto Superior Técnico, Technical University of Lisbon
Av. Rovisco Pais, 1
1049-001 Lisboa, Portugal
{joaoleitao,miguel.pardal}@ist.utl.pt

Abstract. Web Services (WS) are an important tool for the integration of enterprise applications. With a growing set of WS related standards (WS-*), the technology has become increasingly more complicated to configure and manage, even more so when the Quality of Service (QoS) requirements of the system are changing. This paper presents the results of a study conducted on the ability of the major Web Services implementations to adapt to changing QoS attributes. Their shortcomings are then used as motivation for SmartSTEP, a proposal for a more advanced policy-driven automatic configuration solution.

Keywords: Web Services, Quality of Service, Information Systems Integration, Policy, Automatic Configuration, Java, STEP Framework.

1 Introduction

Enterprise applications have demanding requirements: many users, large volumes of data, ever-changing business rules, and multiple systems' integration interfaces to connect to other applications [1]. The fundamental challenge is *change* so there is great value in techniques that enable information systems to quickly adapt to changes in requirements.

Web Services (WS) [2] and Service-Oriented Architectures (SOA) [3] are a technology and architecture, respectively, which propose *services* as the building block for flexible information systems. WS technology is defined by multiple IETF, W3C, and OASIS standards.

A Web Service is defined as a network access endpoint to resources: data and business functions [2]. Although this endpoint can be accessed in many different ways, the most common is SOAP[1] [4], an extensible XML-based protocol for exchanging information in distributed environments.

[1] Although SOAP was initially defined as Simple Object Access Protocol, the 1.2 version of the standard dropped this definition and simply refers to itself as SOAP.

J.E. Quintela Varajão et al. (Eds.): CENTERIS 2010, Part II, CCIS 110, pp. 446–454, 2010.

The two major Web Services implementations are Windows Communication Foundation (WCF) [5] and Metro [6]. There are also open-source implementations, such as Apache Axis2 [7].

Recently, these projects have been focusing on the support of WS related standards (WS-*). These were created to extend the Web Services functionalities and capabilities and include standards like WS-Security [8].

Another important WS-* standard is WS-Policy [9], a framework for expressing policies that refer to capabilities, requirements or other characteristics of an entity.

This paper presents the results of an extensive analysis conducted on the Quality of Service (QoS) features of WCF, Metro and Axis2, with special interest in their configuration and limitations. To overcome the identified limitations, a proposal for a new approach and a real world use scenario of its capabilities are also described.

2 Service-Oriented Ideas

Erl [3] presents the eight principles of SOA: services share a formal contract, abstract underlying logic and are loosely coupled, autonomous, composable, reusable, stateless and discoverable.

In Web Services the formal contract is defined using an XML-based language known as WSDL (Web Services Description Language) [10]. This contract presents all the information that describes a service in a standard *machine-readable* format. The data types and message structures are described as XSD (XML schema definitions), which can be used by code generation tools to create appropriate representations in any supported programming language. This is called a *contract-first* approach, whereas the development of the service's implementation followed by the automatic generation of the WSDL is known as a *code-first* approach [11].

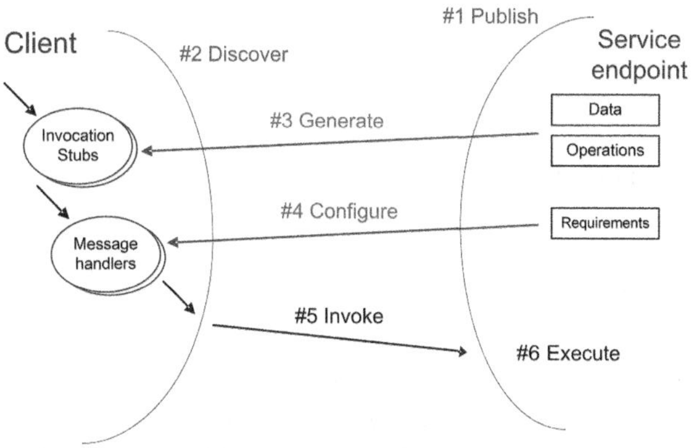

Fig. 1. Web Service binding process [12]

Regardless of the chosen approach, the WSDL and other metadata must always be published: as an accessible resource (URL), a service endpoint as defined by WS-MetadataExchange [13] or using a service metadata repository, like UDDI [14]. This is represented in Figure 1 as step #1 in the Web Service binding process.

Using these mechanisms the clients can retrieve the contract (step #2) and create the necessary code – *stubs* – to convert their data into the format specified by the service (step #3).

Services often have other QoS requirements that need to be met, like security or reliability. These requirements can be stated as policies, which can be used in step #4 to configure *message handlers*, components responsible for executing the required operations to meet the non-functional requirements. Examples include: message ciphering, security token validation, and transactional support.

After the successful configuration, the service can be invoked (step #5) and executed (step #6).

3 Web Services Implementations

This section presents how the major WS implementations support WS-* standards and describes their configuration mechanisms. The section ends with a comparison table to summarize their configuration features.

3.1 WCF

WCF [5] is part of Microsoft's .Net Framework since version 3.0 (2006). It bundles several communication technologies, from .Net Remoting to Web Services, supporting several WS-* standards.

In WCF, the entire configuration is done in the *Web.config* file. Using a .Net specific XML-based syntax, one can define the features to use as well as any necessary parameters.

The code-first development is based on this configuration file and code annotations. Visual Studio[2] provides wizards that can be used to create or edit configurations. In a contract-first approach the configurations can be automatically created by code generation tools. Most code generation tools available can interpret policies defined in the WSDL as long as these are already supported by WCF's supported WS-* standards [15].

To extend the platform, one must extend or even override system classes [16]. This extensibility goes as far as creating elements to use in configuration files or defining a new WSDL generator to include custom policies.

3.2 Metro

Metro is Sun Microsystems' Java-based [17] Web Services stack. Version 2.0 was released on November, 2009. The Web Services Interoperability Technology (WSIT) package is built on top of the JAX-WS 2.2 (Java API for XML Web Services) [6] core engine and implements the WS-* standards [18].

Metro's configuration is based on WSDL and *sun-jaxws.xml* configuration file that defines mappings between the contract and the service implementation.

---

[2] Product home page: http://www.microsoft.com/visualstudio/

The code-first approach is based on two sources: annotations on service implementation classes and a *wsit-*.xml* configuration file. This file is a simplified WSDL and defines the policies to apply to each supported element (messages, operations, endpoints).

In a contract-first approach, the entire configuration is based on the WSDL and its policies. Some of the platform's specific configuration is also policy-based, using system configuration policies. Metro's code generation tools only support system pre-defined policies, as required by the implemented standards.

Custom policies are ignored in compilation, but prevent the Web Service from being correctly deployed, as they are not recognized by the platform on initialization. In version 2.0 of Metro, custom policies are entirely unsupported.

Any additional behavior should be implemented using JAX-WS Handlers [6] or using the *DeclarativeTubelineAssembler* [19] feature. Another way of achieving similar results is by manipulating Metro's source code to attach a custom module.

One of the new features in Metro 2.0 is *dynamic reconfiguration*, which enables the remote management of a Web Service's policies at runtime. This feature is based on JMX (Java Management Extensions) [20], a Java technology that enables management and monitoring of applications, by dynamically loading and instantiating classes.

3.3 Axis2

Apache Axis2 follows a different approach from the other platforms. It contains the core functionality for Web Services, but the main WS-* standards are available as independent modules [21]. These modules can then be attached to the Axis2 core and used in applications as necessary.

The modules announce the policies they can handle, so that any defined policy can be handled by the proper module. This enables the creation of custom modules to handle any additional behaviors and respective policies. Additional application behaviors can be implemented in a custom *MessageReceiver*, a class that defines how messages should be handled.

Axis2 configuration is based on the *services.xml* file. In a code first approach, this configuration file should define the policies and their targets. In a contract-first development, the code generation tools provided by Axis2 are used to create the configuration file.

The Web Services hosting in Axis2 is also different from any other platform, as it is a Web Application itself. The very Web Services it supports are deployed as modules, which are simple JAR packages. These packages often use the AAR (Axis Archive) file extension, but do not differ from the normal JAR structure.

This is the base for another important feature of Axis2: *Hot Deployment*. Axis2 supports the deployment and initialization of services without having to restart the main Web Application. The attachment of new modules requires redeployment, but their association with the running applications can be made without restarting them.

3.4 Discussion

The following table summarizes the main features of the studied platforms.

Table 1. Features of existing Web Services implementations

Area	Feature	WCF	Metro	Axis2
Policies	WS-Policy	Yes	Yes	Yes
	Custom policies	Yes (1)	No	Yes
	Server-side policy alternatives	No	No	No
Configuration	WSDL-based configuration	No	Yes	Yes (2)
	Runtime policy configuration	No	Yes	Yes
	Automatic reconfiguration (3)	No	No	No
Extensibility	Extensible platform	Yes	Yes	Yes
	Modular platform	No	No	Yes
	Message handler extensibility	Yes (1)	Yes	Yes
	Message handler hot deployment	No	No	Yes (4)

(1). Requires WCF extensions
(2). WSDL and custom configurations
(3). Without user intervention
(4). If available in Axis2 Web Application

Figure 2 proposes a *dynamic binding spectrum* based on the moment where non-functional requirements can be changed, leading to the reconfiguration of message handlers.

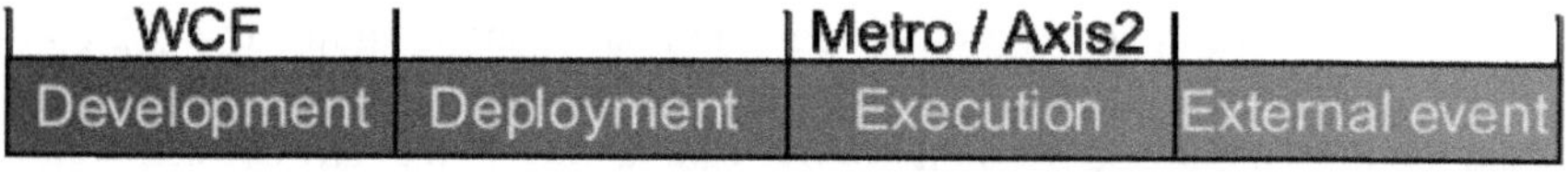

Fig. 2. Dynamic binding spectrum

Development and *Deployment* are the implementation and loading phases of the application, respectively. The *Execution* phase includes any action made on the system by some part of the system itself (management interfaces are considered as part of the system so this feature is considered to be in this phase). Anything that acts on the system but is not initiated by it is considered as an *External event* (e.g. incoming message). A system with the ability to reconfigure itself as a reaction to this type of event is normally referred to as a self-adaptive system [22].

WCF is the easiest platform to develop secure and reliable services without great knowledge of WSDL or WS-Policy languages, mainly due to the IDE support. The main disadvantage lies in the lack of runtime configuration support.

Metro and Axis2 both support runtime configuration of policies through management interfaces, which is why they are placed in the execution phase of the spectrum.

Metro has many other features which make it one of the best equipped Java Web Services platforms in use. Other than the unsupported policy extensibility, there aren't many weaknesses. This and other features are planned for upcoming releases. The most important downside of Metro is that it requires some knowledge of WSDL and WS-Policy languages, even in code-first development.

Axis2 is clearly a platform with extensibility and customization in mind, as it can support virtually any feature. Although there are modules supporting the main WS-* standards, there are still many without a public stable implementation. The implementation of a module from scratch is a very complex procedure.

4 SmartSTEP

STEP Framework [23] is an academic open-source multi-layer Java enterprise application framework, with support for Web Applications (Servlet/JSP) and Web Services. Its main design goals are *simplicity* and *extensibility*. The framework's source code is intended to be small and simple enough to allow any developer to read it and understand it thoroughly, as part of a learning process.

SmartSTEP aims to support user-free automatic reconfiguration of QoS capabilities, thus achieving the last phase of the dynamic spectrum: reconfiguration based on an external event (see Figure 2). The proposed feature list is composed by all the features on Table 1, including those unsupported by all studied platforms, namely server-side policies, automatic reconfiguration and handler hot deployment.

4.1 Proposal

In the current version of the STEP framework, message handlers are supported using an *extension engine* [23]. This engine is conceptually similar to the JAX-WS Handlers, but it integrates with other STEP layers, namely the business logic layer (services). The engine executes several extensions sequentially, where each extension manipulates the message that results from the execution of the previous extensions. The execution ends when all required extensions where executed or an error is detected. Currently these extensions are configured using static property files, which prevent runtime modification of the extension sequence or even deployment of new extensions.

This proposal requires a more dynamic approach, so the extensions will be packaged as independent JAR files, following the modular approach used by Axis2. Each JAR will have a specific configuration file to identify a class responsible for the *auto-installation* of the extension.

The extension JAR's should then be placed in a directory that will be periodically checked for new files. Once a new JAR is detected, it will be loaded and the specified installation class will be invoked. This new approach enables the *runtime deployment* of extensions, which can then be used in different applications.

The extension execution sequence should also be dynamic, enabling the usage of a different sequence for different messages. This can be achieved through *factories*, classes that create an extension sequence given a message context. Basic factories should be implemented as part of the framework. The implementation of custom factories should also be supported, thus covering any special configuration scenario. This feature makes *automatic reconfiguration* possible, as it can create a new extension sequence for each sent or received message.

Policies can be supported by mapping a *policy namespace* to an extension. This association should be done using configuration files, which can be *updated and reloaded in runtime*, without any code manipulation.

When policy alternatives are defined in the server contract, any received message should indicate the alternative used by the client in the outbound processing, so the server can use the correct inbound extension sequence. This indication should be a *header* in the SOAP message, taking advantage of the policy attachments specification [24]. The definition of *server-side policy alternatives* can be a useful feature when a server needs to support multiple configuration scenarios.

5 Use Scenario

To demonstrate the usefulness of policy-driven automatic configuration as proposed for SmartSTEP, a real world use scenario was picked: insurance sales.

Many insurance salesmen spend much of their time outside the office, where the prospective clients are. In order to perform their tasks, they need to communicate with the office's main system, which must be prepared to deal with requests that originate inside or outside the corporate network. We will assume that requests from the inside use a different security scheme than the ones from the outside (Figure 3).

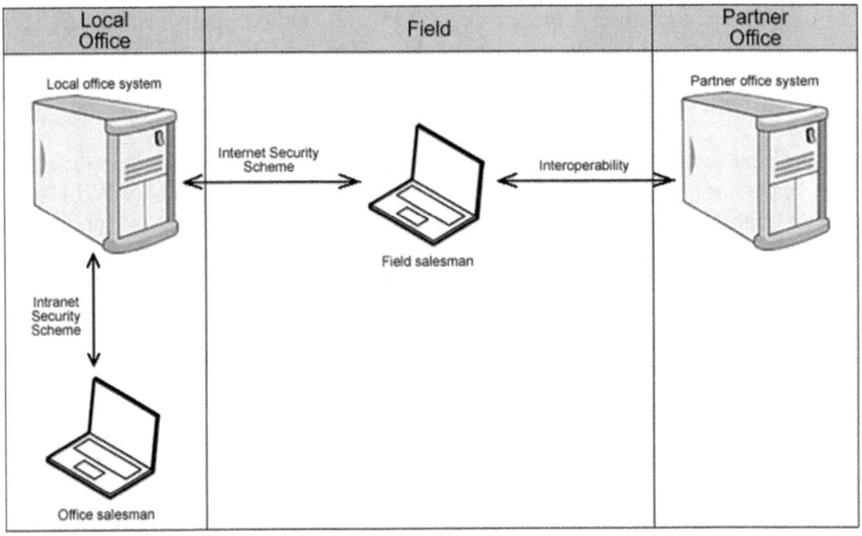

Fig. 3. Real world scenario

This situation would require that the office system provided two or more connection points, each with different configurations, creating a significant administrative burden. With server-side policy alternatives, one could define multiple configuration scenarios for one connection point, which would be properly activated whenever a new request was received.

The choice is then made by the client application, which would be prepared to activate the necessary measures according to some environmental parameter. This is possible with automatic reconfiguration and the ability to customize the configuration process to consider the environment.

This customization applies not only to security, but to other requirements. For instance, an application running on a PDA does not have the same available resources as a laptop. These limitations could be considered to create other configuration profiles.

Another important requirement is interoperability (as seen in Figure 3). A salesman might need to retrieve information about a client from a business partner, which might require an unsupported feature. By installing a new extension, the new feature could be ready to use in minutes, without the need for professional technical assistance.

In other platforms, this simple scenario would require multiple applications or extensive configurations, and any update would require professional technicians. With SmartSTEP, applications would be flexible and powerful enough to infer all configurations and *adapt*.

6 Conclusion

Our study of the most popular WS implementations shows that even though they support many WS-* standards and configuration options, they are not as dynamic and extensible as one could wish for. WCF is completely static from the configuration point of view. Metro and Axis2 are more dynamic, but some of their mechanisms are hard to extend or even to work with.

SmartSTEP tries to incorporate the best ideas from the studied implementations into STEP, maintaining its main characteristics: simplicity and extensibility. All proposed features were extensively researched and are considered feasible given the time and complexity constraints.

6.1 Future Work

The next step in the SmartSTEP project is the implementation of the proposed features and their evaluation using the use scenario and performance metrics.

These features open new doors for STEP, making possible to implement new independent modules to support virtually any WS-* standard and possibly publish them in an on-line STEP extension repository, shared by the whole development community, creating new learning opportunities. This would not only be an interesting work from the extensibility point of view, but it can also help in achieving interoperability with other WS platforms.

Acknowledgments

The authors acknowledge the STEP designers and community for their contributions to the framework's source code.

Miguel L. Pardal is supported by a PhD fellowship from the Portuguese Foundation for Science and Technology FCT (SFRH/BD/45289/2008).

References

1. Hohpe, G., Woolf, B.: Enterprise Integration Patterns: Designing, Building, and Deploying Messaging Solutions. Addison-Wesley Professional (2003)
2. Alonso, G., Casati, F., Kuno, H., Machiraju, V.: Web Services - Concepts, Architectures and Applications. Springer, Heidelberg (2004)
3. Erl, T.: Service-Oriented Architecture (SOA): Concepts, Technology, and Design. Prentice-Hall, Englewood Cliffs (2005)

4. Gudgin, M., Hadley, M., Mendelsohn, N., Moreau, J.-J., Nielsen, H.F., Karmarkar, A., et al.: SOAP Version 1.2 Part 1: Messaging Framework, 2nd edn. (2007), http://www.w3.org/TR/soap12-part1/
5. Lowy, J.: Programming WCF Services, 2nd edn. O'Reilly Media, Sebastopol (2008)
6. Kalin, M.: Java Web Services: Up and Running. O'Reilly Media, Sebastopol (2009)
7. Tong, K.K.: Developing Web Services with Apache Axis2. TipTec Development (2008)
8. Nadalin, A., Kaler, C., Monzillo, R., Hallam-Baker, P.: Web Services Security: SOAP Message Security 1.1 (2006), http://docs.oasis-open.org/wss/v1.1/wss-v1.1-spec-errata-os-SOAPMessageSecurity.pdf
9. Vedamuthu, A., Orchard, D., Hirsch, F., Hondo, M., Yendluri, P., Boubez, T., et al.: Web Services Policy 1.5 - Framework (2007), http://www.w3.org/TR/ws-policy/
10. Chinnici, R., Moreau, J.-J., Ryman, A., Weerawarana, S.: Web Services Description Language (WSDL) Version 2.0 Part 1: Core Language (2007), http://www.w3.org/TR/wsdl20/
11. Sosnoski, D.: Code First Web Services Reconsidered (2007), http://www.infoq.com/articles/sosnoski-code-first
12. Pardal, M.: Segurança de aplicações empresariais em arquitecturas de serviços (2006)
13. Davis, D., Malhotra, A., Warr, K., Chou, W.: Web Services Metadata Exchange (WS-MetadataExchange) (2009), http://www.w3.org/TR/ws-metadata-exchange/
14. Bellwood, T., Capell, S., Clement, L., Colgrave, J., Dovey, M.J., Feygin, D., et al.: UDDI Version 3.0.2 (2004), http://www.oasis-open.org/committees/uddi-spec/doc/spec/v3/uddi-v3.0.2-20041019.htm
15. Web Services Protocols Supported by System-Provided Interoperability Bindings, http://msdn.microsoft.com/en-us/library/ms730294.aspx
16. Skonnard, A.: Extending WCF with Custom Behaviors (2007), http://msdn.microsoft.com/en-us/magazine/cc163302.aspx
17. Arnold, K., Gosling, J., Holmes, D.: Java(TM) Programming Language, 4th edn. Prentice Hall, Englewood Cliffs (2005)
18. Metro Specifications, https://metro.dev.java.net/guide/Metro_Specifications.html
19. Declarative Tubeline Assembler One Pager, http://wikis.glassfish.org/metro/Wiki.jsp?page=DeclarativeTubelineAssemblerOnePager
20. Kreger, H., Harold, W., Williamson, L.: Java(TM) and JMX: Building Manageable Systems. Addison-Wesley Professional (2003)
21. Apache Axis2 Modules, http://ws.apache.org/axis2/modules/index.html
22. Heuvel, W.-J.v., Weigand, H., Hiel, M.: Configurable adapters: the substrate of self-adaptive web services. In: ICEC 2007: Proceedings of the ninth international conference on Electronic commerce, pp. 127–134. ACM, Minneapolis (2007)
23. Pardal, M., Fernandes, S.M., Martins, J., Pardal, J.P.: Customizing Web Services with Extensions in the STEP framework. International Journal of Web Services Practices 3(1-2), 1–11 (2008)
24. Vedamuthu, A., Orchard, D., Hirsch, F., Hondo, M., Yendluri, P., Boubez, T., et al.: Web Services Policy 1.5 - Attachment (2007), http://www.w3.org/TR/ws-policy-attach/

Web4Desktop, a Framework for Improving the Usability of Web Applications

Bogdan Carstoiu and Dorin Carstoiu

"Politehnica" University of Bucharest, Spl. Independentei 313, Bucharest Romania
bcarstoiu@gmail.com, dorin.carstoiu@yahoo.com

Abstract. The cloud computing model leads to the increased penetration of the web applications in the office environment. Designed in many cases to replace traditional desktop software, web applications still lack many of the valuable features present on the desktop that increase usability and productivity. Due to the highly isolated design of the browser, it is currently impossible for web applications to communicate with desktop environment, which usually means sending messages or receiving event notifications. This is often required in order to let the person using the application know about the important events happening in the minimized browser window. By contrast traditional applications can take the control of the desktop at any time. The paper introduces the Web4Desktop framework, a browser/client based architecture designed to overcome these limitations by proving a secure infrastructure that allows web applications to communicate with any desktop software implementing the Web4Desktop API. The framework can be utilized to add desktop integration to existing web applications, a step that requires only minimal changes in the web application's code and greatly improve the user experience because these applications will start to behave more like desktop software.

Keywords: Cloud computing, Java Script, web security, web usability, browser plug-in, business and office software, web applications.

1 Introduction

The cloud computing introduces a commodity model that can be associated with the traditional utilities: gas, electricity, telephony and water. In this model users access computing resources when they need them according to their requirements and without any delivery location limits. When looking at the cloud, we can do it from two different perspectives [7].

The first is the infrastructure cloud, usually implemented using interconnected VM and offering provisioning capabilities for end-users who run their own software in the deployed infrastructure. Amazon was the first company that popularized the infrastructure cloud.

The second is the software platform cloud that gives users access to ready to use, easily deployable, infinitely scalable applications. Usually, these applications are delivered using the standard web browser, due to the unmatched level of abstraction

J.E. Quintela Varajão et al. (Eds.): CENTERIS 2010, Part II, CCIS 110, pp. 455–464, 2010.

offered. Some examples are Salesforce.com and Google Apps. When looking at the two cloud models, we notice that the complexity and the challenges are much bigger with the software platform as it involves paradigm shifts. Software vendors have already started migrating traditional software applications to the cloud, the most notorious example being Microsoft who will introduce a web based, pay per use alternative to the popular Office suite.

2 Common Issues with Web Applications

The software platform cloud changes the way how software applications are designed, written and deployed. The delivery model that allows anyone to access the software remotely without requiring special clients, the flexibility and the cross platform compatibility are the undisputed advantages that favor web applications in the cloud race. When comparing the web applications to the desktop software, many issues rise on the user experience. From this perspective, there are a few important disadvantages of the web applications the industry is still looking for solutions:

Poor Visual Capabilities. In the past years, much progress was made in order to deliver better visual effects in the browser screen. The possibilities are limited with the HTML language and RIA frameworks like Flash or Silverlight are still far from simulating a real desktop experience. Future HTML standards like HTML5 will not solve this limitation, meaning that not all applications can be migrated to the browser in the next years [6]. The visual capabilities are however sufficient to implement productivity and business applications.

JavaScript Cannot Do Everything. JavaScript is the main engine available for programmers to render dynamic websites [3]. Although technically RIA frameworks might offer better possibilities, Silverlight and Flash involve more than HTML and are controlled by powerful corporations [4]. JavaScript is constantly evolving and ended doing much more than it was originally supposed to do, but its capabilities are still limited. As JavaScript (JS) runs on the client side, the browser can handle a lot of expensive processing. Unfortunately, JS engines built in browsers have slightly different behavior and performance, meaning that AJAX applications can experience cross platform compatibility issues.

Polling Is Inefficient. When the AJAX idea occurred, it used the technologies available. The technology behind involved periodically polling HTTP resource for changes and updating the interface objects based on these changes. While this model might work fine in small deployments, for cloud applications designed to serve millions of users resources are poorly spent. In order to provide a prompt user interface, web applications poll resources as frequent as each second, in most cases to discover that nothing happened. The server side application has to process the request and answer to it, leading to inefficient bandwidth and resources usage. Various notification/callback like models that are supposed to solve this issue were released by several organizations and are expected to replace polling in the next years [5],[10],[11].

Too Much Network Connectivity Required. Traditionally, web applications can be used only when the client is online, able to connect to the server, even though HTTP does not require persistent connections. This is a major inconvenience for these applications when the Internet connection is not available. The industry is trying various solutions in order to enable an offline mode, one of them being Google Gears [8]. Additionally, the speed of many web applications highly depends on the Internet connection speed, rather than on the local computer speed, as it happens with desktop software.

Poor Desktop Interaction. Normal desktop applications can interact with any other software running on the same system, or even more, they can access the operating system resources. From the software developer and end-user perspective, this translates into unlimited possibilities. The web application is running highly isolated in the browser; the free communication with the desktop is undesired and very limited. In fact, the only way for a desktop application to communicate with the desktop is through a security breach.

3 Related Work

Several approaches to solve this problem have been made by using specialized desktop clients that communicate directly with the web application, usually using REST methods [9]. Successful cloud based applications like Salesforce.com have such desktop clients that are designed to improve user productivity or to integrate the software with desktop applications like Microsoft Outlook. No specific developments designed to make the web application feel like desktop software were found.

The advantage of using a HTTP enabled desktop client, shipped as an add-on to the web application and installed in the operating system is that it's relatively easy to implement. It also improves the user experience, but only in a lower degree due to its limitations.

The desktop client cannot synchronize with the web application. The desktop client must query the REST resources in order to get information about the web application status, but the information retrieved is usually delayed due to the polling mechanisms.

The desktop client does not have any information about the user navigation in the web application. It cannot know how the user is navigating in the web application interface, unless this state is saved in a shared database.

This technique puts an additional load on the database layer. Both the application and the desktop client must save new information in the database in order to communicate, or they must use other methods for sharing information, like host based queues.

Polling is used by both the desktop client and the web application. The desktop client can signal the web application by saving information in the database, which is polled periodically by the web part. The same happens when the web wants to send a message to the desktop client. The polling architecture creates much overhead and the responsiveness is still bad.

Additionally, because there is no connection to the browser experience the desktop client has to authenticate to the REST resource, which eventually means that it must save some credentials on the local machine.

Even if the above limitations are tolerated, the desktop client still does not know where the web application is running, which means that it is not able to point the user to the browser window with a mouse click or to perform specific actions inside the interface.

The polling issue can be avoided with a connection based, client/server design involving the local desktop client and a specialized server running on the application side. From the system architecture perspective this approach is even more complicated as it introduces new components on the server side, expensive connections between the client and the server that have to be maintained, and firewall rules management on the user machine.

4 Architecture of the Web/Desktop Integration Framework

4.1 Requirements of the Web/Desktop Interaction

The paper introduces a framework that makes the web application / desktop communication possible in a secure way, dramatically increasing the user experience and allowing web developers to access the desktop. Most web applications require at a particular moment to notify the desktop about an event, to query a desktop resource or to receive commands from the desktop. This happens especially with productivity and business applications because they are parts of intensive and/or complex workflows [1]. When a web application is running, it is doing this in a browser window or tab, making it difficult for users to switch between opened applications, as all browser windows look more or less identical. When users want to focus on a running web application, it is relatively easy to do it when only a browser window is opened, but becomes more difficult when several browser windows are opened. Browser tabs complicate the issue even more, because they introduce a new level of navigation inside the browser window.

Some web applications have to notify the user about events, for example a calendar component in a collaboration application wants to let the user know that a meeting is scheduled in 15 minutes. In order to do this, the application will raise a browser pop-up window that can be noticed by the user only if he focuses on the application browser window. To overcome this limitation, the application can currently play an alert sound, but this is not enough.

Collaboration applications often require presence information, transmitted between people in the same group. While there are some JavaScript solutions for determining whether the user is Idle or not, the most reliable way would be to detect Idle using the OS exposed methods. Accessing such information from the browser is not possible with current technologies.

Web instant messaging is embedded in many web applications, but there are several usability issues with these components, because there is no information on the desktop about the messages received in the browser while the user has no focus on it. Native desktop applications do this by dispatching messages to the operating system notification area, which allows the user to see the received messages.

4.2 Architecture of the Web/Desktop Integration Framework

One of the challenges when developing the framework was to make it generic enough, but still not to affect the security of the system. Because conceptually the framework features a bi-directional gateway between the web application and the desktop, most of the concerns when designing the system surrounded the gateway. On a high level, the framework was designed to answer to the following requirements:

Easy installation and setup for users – the application must interact with the desktop using a plug-in installed in the browser. On the desktop level each web application must come with its own client designed to work with that specific web application only.

Desktop accessibility for web developers – the browser plug-in provides a consistent interface to the web application developers, accessible using JavaScript. The interface must be generic enough to be used by all web applications.

Lightweight code, no complexity – The browser plug-in should not add overhead to the browser and must expose a light, easy to implement interface. Complexity must be hidden from the browser.

The web application is not trusted – the framework does not trust web developers to secure their own code, it assumes that mistakes happen and enforce security at a higher level. Encryption is used to build a trust model.

Customized client – In order to provide accessibility and functionality on the desktop level, each web application will come with its own desktop client that communicates with the browser plug-in.

Control to the user – it must be simple for end-users to control which web applications "talk" to the desktop; usually it is enough to close the desktop part of the application, but it is also possible to un-trust the application from using the framework.

The design is layered in order to limit the impact of security issues, to simplify management and to speed-up the development on multiple platforms. The browser module is separated in four layers (fig 1):

Web Security Interface (WSI) – the security interface intercepts all calls from the web application and checks for their security. It handles the web application's registration to the system, the trust management and JS request validation. At this level, all the requests that are not properly authenticated are filtered.

Developer Interface (DI) – it implements parsers for the JavaScript functions registered by the plug-in and available to web developers. When a call is received from the desktop it executes the proper JS handler in the web application. On this layer the transition between JS calls and internal API calls and vice-versa is made.

Internal broker (IB) – The internal broker manages the communication between the desktop client and the web application. It dispatches messages to the desktop clients registered, manages communication flows, receives messages from the desktop after they were authenticated and validated and forwards them to the Developer Interface where they are going to be converted in JS calls.

Desktop Security Interface (DSI) - the security interface intercepts all calls from the desktop application to the broker and checks for their security. It handles desktop application's registration, trust management and API call security validations.

The desktop side (client application) uses an API written in C++, which can be ported to any other programming language. There are no specific constrains on this level, developers can access anything on the operating system level.

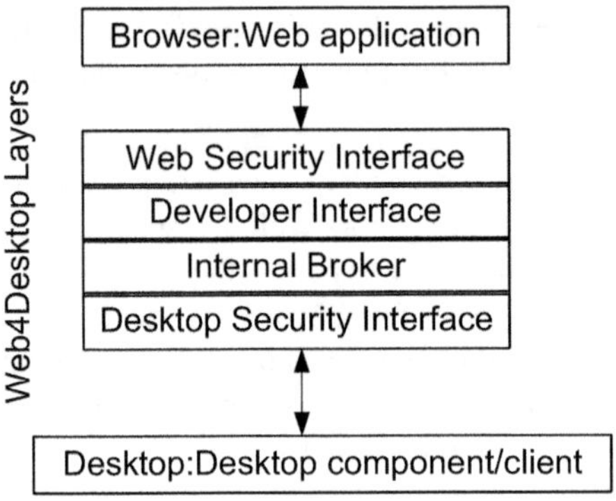

Fig. 1. Overview of Web4Desktop Layers

4.3 Functions

1. Registration of the web application to Web4Desktop. In order to detect the presence of the Web4Desktop browser plug-in, the web application will call the JavaScript function:

`ApplicationRegister($AppName)` where:

`$AppName` – the name of the web application or an identifier. This is usually hardcoded in the desktop client code, because the desktop client is designed to work with $AppName only.

If the ApplicationRegister is not present, then the plug-in is not available and the web application can offer to the end-user the possibility to download and install it. If the $AppName was forbidden in the plug-in configuration, an error code is served. This is the only case when the ApplicationRegister immediately rejects the registration, because normally the browser plug-in does not care about $AppName at the initial registration. The trust management model requires the web application to authenticate to the browser plug-in before being able to send any message. Each person using the web application will have stored in its database at the server level a connection key that is usually auto-generated, called $UserKey. When the plug-in receives the ApplicationRegister request, it replies to the web application with a pseudo random 32byte string, called $SessionKey. The web application computes in JS a confirm hash using this string:

`$ConfirmHash = SHA1($SessionKey+SHA1($UserKey))` and calls:
`ApplicationRegisterConfirm($AppName,$ConfirmHash)`

If the plug-in can find the $AppName in the local database, because it was previously registered, it will verify the $ConfirmHash with the stored information. If the $AppName was not previously registered, it will prompt the user in the browser to add the $UserKey, which will be hashed and stored in the local database. Due to usability issues it's recommended for the web application to design a special section that handles the one time registration of the application to the plug-in. The plug-in must receive the ApplicationRegisterConfirm no more than 5 seconds after it served the ApplicationRegister answer, otherwise the Web Security Interface will reject the function call. When the $ConfirmHash matches the value computed internally, the application is considered registered and the plug-in will accept hashed signed messages from that browser window. It should be noticed that the web application always trusts the browser plug-in, but this is normal for the web, all applications trust the browser.

2. Sending messages to desktop client using Web4Desktop. All messages sent must be trusted by the Web Security Interface. A message is trusted if it is properly signed by the registered application and if the call is made from the same browser window where the application registered originally. The web application can send messages to the desktop client by the following JavaScript function:

```
ApplicationMessage($AppName,$MessageBody,$ContextID,
    $Object,$MicroTime,$SecurityKey)
```

$MessageBody – the JSON message that will be passed to the desktop client. This can contain commands for the desktop application, messages to be displayed etc. The API does not impose any limitations on this level; *$ContextID* – a context which is known by the desktop client and allows it to filter the messages received; *$Object* – when object is not NULL, it's a callback to an interface object. This means that a message dispatched to the desktop client can be related to this $Object, allowing developers to create special effects like click on message to trigger anything in the web application interface; *$MicroTime* – this is the micro-time when the message was generated. It is helpful for the desktop client to discard old messages or to record the message generation time precisely, because the receiving time can be different; *$SecurityKey* – the security key is obtained from applying the following hash:

```
SHA1($MessageBody + $MicroTime + $SessionKey +
    SHA1($UserKey))
```

The Web Security Interface will discard messages with wrong $SecurityKey, or messages with a $MicroTime older than five seconds.

3. Checking for the presence of the desktop client. The web application can also inquire about the presence of the desktop client, by executing:

```
DesktopPing($AppName,$MicroTime,$SecurityKey)
```

The Desktop client will reply with a JSON package that contains the version of the application and the uptime. The format of the message is standardized and is available in the desktop client library. This way the application is able to know whether the desktop application is running and listening for its messages. From the usability point of view, this means that the web application can show a message to the user telling him to start the desktop client. *$SecurityKey* is obtained by hashing *$MicroTime, $SessionKey and SHA1($UserKey).*

4. Restricting desktop client to listen only to messages on some contexts. The web application can tell the desktop client to which contexts to listen during the active session. By default, the desktop client will listen to all contexts.

```
RegisterContext ($AppName,$ContextList,$MicroTime,
    $SecurityKey)
```

$ContextList – a JSON formatted list of contexts
$SecurityKey – the security key is obtained from applying the following hash:

```
SHA1($ContextList + $MicroTime + $SessionKey +
    SHA1($UserKey))
```

5. *Closing the web application current session.* This is necessary when the web application is closed. By default, the session expires in 3600 seconds.

```
ApplicationClose ($AppName,$MicroTime,$SecurityKey)
```

$SecurityKey – the security key is obtained from applying the following hash:

```
SHA1($MicroTime + $SessionKey + SHA1($UserKey))
```

4.4 Desktop Client Component

Once the desktop client component is started, it will try to contact the browser plug-in to signal its existence. Usually, the desktop component is preconfigured with the *$UserKey* on installation and this can also be changed later. It depends on the implementation, but in most cases it makes sense to have user profiles on the desktop client, especially when the client is installed in a multi user environment. Due to obvious security reasons, we require the desktop client to trust the Browser plug-in when it receives messages from the web application and the Browser plug-in to trust the desktop client. It should be noted that it is much more sensitive for the desktop to correctly identify the source than it is for the browser plug-in. When the desktop client starts, it executes the following API function:

```
DesktopRegister($AppName)
```

If the browser plug-in knows about this *$AppName*, the Desktop Security Interface will answer to the API call with a hash and a session key:

```
SHA1($AppName+SHA1($UserKey)),$DesktopSessionKey
```

$DesktopSessionKey is a random 32byte string. If the authentication is successful on the Desktop side, the desktop client will reply with:

```
DesktopRegisterConfirm($ConfirmHash) where:
$ConfirmHash=SHA1($DesktopSessionKey+SHA1($UserKey))
```

This way, the Desktop Security Interface can verify that the Desktop client shares the secret as well.

Dispatching messages to Desktop. All messages received from the web application with ApplicationMessage JS call are converted by the Developer Interface to an API call. This call is dispatched by the Broker Interface to the desktop client:

```
DesktopMessage("MessageBody","ContextID,"Object",
    "MicroTime","SecurityKey") where:
$SecurityKey=SHA1($MicroTime+$DesktopSessionKey+
    SHA1($UserKey))
```

This happens with the other messages as well. The architecture allows having more than a single desktop application listening to the browser plug-in.

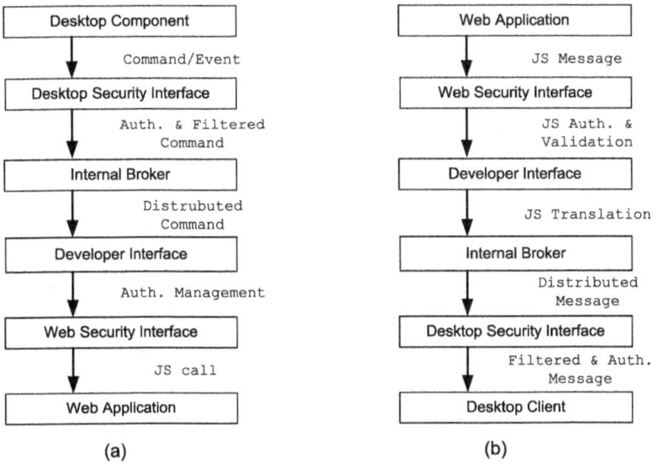

Fig. 2. Command or event going from the desktop client to web (a) and message from web application to desktop client (b)

Dispatching Commands to the Web Application. The web application will register callback functions in order to permit the Desktop application to execute commands directly in the interface (2). This happens with replies to messages, when the user clicks on a message, or with other functions that are not strictly related to the messages received. For example, the Desktop client might feature a menu that allows the user to jump to a particular section of the web application. In this case, the Desktop client will change the focus on the window/tab where the web application is running and will execute the JS function. This is dispatched using:

`DesktopToWeb($Object,$MicroTime,$SecurityKey)` where

$Object – the callback that is eventually processed by the callback routines registered on the web application

$SecurityKey – the security key is obtained from applying the following hash:

```
SHA1($Object + $MicroTime + $DesktopSessionKey +
    SHA1($UserKey))
```

Desktop clients should also take advantage of the fact that the client knows where the web application is running and when the icon in the notification area is clicked, the browser window can open, simulating a desktop application.

5 Conclusions

The web application integration in the desktop environment can dramatically improve usability and productivity for most applications targeted to business users. While the unavailability of this functionality might not be a factor to stop the management decision to replace traditional software with web applications, it certainly helps decision makers accelerate the process. It is hard to measure the economical impact of the lower productivity, missed meetings and messages that might occur with a web application; therefore it is important for web software vendors to address these issues early.

The Web4Desktop framework proposes a different approach to the integration, by creating an environment where web applications can decide when and how to communicate with the desktop. The desktop client that is shipped as an add-on to the web application can be as simple as a tray application. The framework does not require important changes in the AJAX web application; to notify the desktop client it is only necessary to execute a JS function exposed by the browser plug-in, whenever this is necessary, according to the utilization scenarios. In order to allow the desktop client to trigger actions in the web interface it is necessary to create a handler in the web application for all functions called from the desktop client.

By using a browser centric approach, the synchronization with the browser is perfect, the possibilities are limited only by the developers of the application and the transition to the web application is simplified for the end-users.

References

1. Carstoiu, B., Carstoiu, D.: High Performance Eventually Consistent Distributed Database Zatara. In: 6th International Conference on Networked Computing INC 2010 (accepted 2010)
2. Daswani, N., Kern, C., Kasevan, A.: Fundations of Security; What Every Programmer Need to Know. Springer, Heidelberg (2007)
3. Flangan, D.: JavaScript: The Definitive Guide, 5th edn. O'Reilly Media, Sebastopol (2006)
4. Microsoft Silverlight Home page, http://www.silverlight.net/getstarted/
5. HTML5. W3C Working Draft (March 4, 2010), http://www.w3.org/TR/html5/
6. Harold, E.R.: New elements in HTML 5, http://www.ibm.com/developerworks/library/x-html5/?ca=dgr-lnxw01NewHTML
7. Amerheim, D., et al.: Cloud Computing Use Case White Paper (2009)
8. Google Gears, http://gears.google.com/
9. Castello, R.L.: Building Web Services the REST Way, http://www.xfront.com/REST-Web-Services.html
10. Dojo toolkit, http://dojotoolkit.org
11. Web sockets, http://www.w3.org/TR/websockets

Author Index

GPSR Compliance

The European Union's (EU) General Product Safety Regulation (GPSR) is a set of rules that requires consumer products to be safe and our obligations to ensure this.

If you have any concerns about our products, you can contact us on ProductSafety@springernature.com

In case Publisher is established outside the EU, the EU authorized representative is:

Springer Nature Customer Service Center GmbH
Europaplatz 3
69115 Heidelberg, Germany

Batch number: 10844619

Printed by Printforce, the Netherlands